The Economics
of Public Finance

THE

ECONOMICS

OF

PUBLIC FINANCE

Third Edition

by Philip E. Taylor

Professor of Economics, The University of Connecticut

New York   THE MACMILLAN COMPANY

To Margaret Bronson Taylor

Preface

A new edition of a textbook is expected to bring its facts as nearly up to date as possible, within the limitations imposed by lags in availability of data and lead-times required in the writing and publishing process. Beyond this, a revision permits the orientation of the text to reflect shifts in relative importance of fiscal problems and changes in the economic and political context in which these problems appear. Further, advances in thought with respect to public finance constantly provide opportunities for the treatment of new material and the more effective treatment of older material, to enrich the content of the course. And finally, a revised edition can make use of the enlargement and standardization of theoretical concepts which other courses are able to provide for the student.

This revision attempts to make use of all of the above opportunities. Within the limits of feasibility, the facts are current. The policy discussions are oriented toward conditions of moderate instability, in which the society is as concerned to avoid inflation as to avoid underemployment. It is recognized that the economic and political world has brought the objective of economic growth almost to a par with the objective of stability. In dealing with these matters it is assumed that the student is familiar with at least the bare outlines of national income theory, and that the theoretical base for discussions of stability and growth policies can be taken for granted, with only slight review. The era of big government has sharpened once again the age-old issue of resource allocation between the private and public sectors of the economy, while recent literature makes possible more precise analysis of the issue. A new chapter on the budget as an allocative instrument has been added in this edition. Probably the most startling recent developments in the field of public finance are to be found in the area of state and local governments, and a new chapter dealing with their critical problems is virtually required. Another major revision analyzes the possibilities of strengthening the federal personal income tax, permitting it to assume the major role demanded of it in the future. While these are the larger changes to be found, lesser alterations appear frequently, to keep in step with contemporary public finance. As in previous editions, however, the dual goals of informing the reader as to facts while orienting the study toward analysis of problems, are pursued.

Much guidance has been received through comments gathered by the publisher's representatives from both users and nonusers of previous editions. While they are unnamed here, they will, it is hoped, realize that their judgments are highly respected if not always followed. I have profited greatly from the thoughtful suggestions offered by Professors Ruby Morris and Katherine Finney of Connecticut College. Present and former associates at the University of Connecticut have patiently borne my impositions upon them, and have made useful suggestions on a variety of topics. Though I have kept no log of these corridor conversations, I am keenly aware of my debt to Melvin Lurie, Rudolf Rhomberg, Joel Dirlam, Emanuel Melichar, and Dorothy Goodwin. Miss Goodwin has, in addition, applied her special competence in this field to the reading and criticism of large sections of the manuscript. While I offer my thanks to all of these, they are absolved from responsibility for what has finally appeared.

Philip E. Taylor

Storrs, Connecticut

Contents

Chapter 1
**INTRODUCTION: PUBLIC FINANCE IN ITS ECONOMIC AND
POLITICAL SETTING**   1

THE NATURE OF THE STUDY OF PUBLIC FINANCE, 1: Public Finance, 3;
The Questions of Public Finance, 3; Method, 5. GOVERNMENT FI-
NANCE AND BUSINESS FINANCE, 5. GOVERNMENT STRUCTURE IN THE
UNITED STATES, 7: Powers of Federal and State Governments, 8. THE
FEDERAL TAXING POWER, 12. RECOMMENDED READINGS, 14.

Chapter 2
FISCAL ADMINISTRATION   15

THE BUDGET, 15: Preparation of the Budget, 17; Legislation of the
Budget: Appropriations, 18; Revenue Measures, 19; The Federal "Legis-
lative Budget," 19. PROBLEMS OF THE BUDGET, 22: Measurement of
Administrative Efficiency, 22; Difficulties with Budget Projections, 23;
Control of Annual Expenditures, 25; General vs. Specific Appropria-
tions, 29; Allotment of Appropriated Funds, 30; Dedication of Revenues
to Special Funds, 30. WHEN IS A BUDGET BALANCED? 33: Balance an
Accounting Concept, 33; Definitions of Basic Concepts, 34. MULTIPLE
BUDGETS, 36: Ordinary and Emergency Budgets, 36; Ordinary and
Capital Budgets, 37. OTHER AGENCIES OF FISCAL ADMINISTRATION, 38:
The Treasury, 38; The Comptroller, 39; The Banks, 40.

Appendix to Chapter 2
**ALTERNATIVE MEASUREMENTS OF FISCAL OPERATIONS:
THE CONVENTIONAL BUDGET, THE CASH BUDGET, AND
THE NATIONAL INCOME ACCOUNTS**   41

The "Conventional Budget," 41; The "Cash Budget," 42; Governmental
Receipts and Expenditures in the National Income Accounts, 46.
RECOMMENDED READINGS, 47.

Chapter 3
PUBLIC EXPENDITURES: TRENDS AND THEIR SIGNIFICANCE   48

EXPENDITURE TRENDS, 48. INTENSIVE EXPANSION OF GOVERNMENTAL FUNCTIONS, 53: Defense Expenditures, 54; Highways, 55; Education, 57; Urbanization, 60. EXTENSIVE EXPANSION OF GOVERNMENTAL FUNCTIONS, 62: Depression-Born Functions, 62; Relief Programs, 65. ATTITUDES TOWARD INCREASING PUBLIC EXPENDITURES, 68. CONTROL OF PUBLIC EXPENDITURES, 71: Tax Rate Limitation, 72; Debt Limitation, 73; Pay-As-You-Go, 75. GRANTS-IN-AID, 77. PUBLIC EXPENDITURES AND ECONOMIC CONDITIONS, 80. RECOMMENDED READINGS, 82.

Chapter 4
FISCAL POLICY AND THE LEVEL OF ECONOMIC ACTIVITY   84

MEASUREMENT OF AGGREGATE ECONOMIC ACTIVITY, 84. DETERMINANTS OF THE RATE OF ECONOMIC ACTIVITY, 85: Behavior of Private Consumption Expenditures, 89; Behavior of Private Investment, 91. INCOME-INDUCING EFFECTS OF FISCAL POLICY, 96: Income-Inducing Effects of Government Expenditure, 97; Income-Inducing Effects of Combined Taxing and Spending, 99; Income-Creating Effects of a Balanced Budget, 101; Effect of an Unbalanced Budget upon Income, 103. CONCLUSION, 109. RECOMMENDED READINGS, 110.

Chapter 5
GOVERNMENT EXPENDITURE AND ECONOMIC INSTABILITY   111

ECONOMIC "STAGNATION," 116. COMPENSATORY SPENDING IN THE CYCLE, 117: Case I: Anticipations Falling, 118; Case II: Anticipations Rising, 120. CONDITIONS OF BUSINESS CONFIDENCE, 121. COMPENSATORY SPENDING IN A STAGNANT ECONOMY, 125. COMPENSATORY POLICY SINCE WORLD WAR II, 126. RECOMMENDED READINGS, 130.

Chapter 6
FISCAL PROGRAMS TO PROMOTE STABILITY   132

POLICIES TO STIMULATE AGGREGATE DEMAND AND EMPLOYMENT, 133: Expenditure Programs, 133; Tax Reduction, 139. POLICIES TO LIMIT AGGREGATE DEMAND, 142: Expenditure Reduction, 143; Tax Increases, 144. EXPENDITURE VARIATIONS VS. TAX VARIATIONS, 148. AUTOMATIC COMPENSATORY MEASURES, 151. RECOMMENDED READINGS, 156.

Chapter 7
ALLOCATION OF RESOURCES BETWEEN THE PUBLIC AND PRIVATE SECTORS OF THE ECONOMY 157

The Nature of Public Goods and Services, 161. The "Budget Principle," 166. Public Expenditures and Economic Growth, 168. Are Budgetary Objectives Consistent with Each Other? 172. Recommended Readings, 176.

Chapter 8
PUBLIC DEBT: ITS NATURE AND ITS MANAGEMENT 178

Gross Debt and Net Debt, 178. The Trend of Government Debt, 182: Federal, 182; State and Local, 184. Composition of the Federal Debt, 185: Interest-Bearing and Non-Interest-Bearing Debt, 186; Public and Special Issues, 190; Maturities, 191. Retirement of Debt, 193: Refunding, 193; Conversion, 194; The Sinking Fund, 196. Contingent Liabilities of the Federal Government, 197. State and Local Debt, 199: Default, 202. Problems of Debt Management, 202. Recommended Readings, 206.

Chapter 9
PUBLIC DEBT AND THE MONEY SUPPLY 207

Monetization of the Public Debt: Currency Expansion, 209. Monetization of the Public Debt: Credit Expansion, 210: Mechanics of Credit Expansion, 211; Supply and Use of Member Bank Reserve Funds, 213; Credit Expansion in World War I, 217; Credit Expansion in World War II, 219; Credit Expansion Following World War II and the Treasury-Federal Reserve Controversy, 223; Public Debt Monetization; Summary, 227. Recommended Readings, 229.

Chapter 10
THE BURDEN OF DEBT 230

The Obverse of Debt: Credit, 230. The Benefits of Public Debt, 232. The Burden of the Debt as Related to Its Principal, 234. The Burden of Interest Payments, 236. Minimizing the Debt Burden, 238: Borrowing vs. Taxation for Debt Service, 238; Dispersion of Debt Ownership, 239; National Income and Debt Burden, 240; Reduction of Debt Burden by Manipulation, 241. Borrowing and the Cost of War, 241: Postponement of War Costs, 242; Distribution of War Costs, 242. Conclusions Concerning Public Debt Burdens, 245. Recommended Readings, 247.

Chapter 11
PUBLIC REVENUES: GRANTS, GIFTS, AND ADMINISTRATIVE
REVENUES   248

> CLASSIFICATION OF REVENUE RECEIPTS, 248: *1*. Grants and Gifts, 249;
> *2*. Administrative Revenues, 250; *3*. Commercial Revenues, 251; *4*.
> Taxes, 252. GRANTS AND GIFTS, 254. ADMINISTRATIVE REVENUES,
> 255: Fees, Licenses, and Permits, 257; Fines and Forfeitures, 258;
> Escheats, 259; Special Assessments, 259. CONCLUSIONS WITH RESPECT
> TO ADMINISTRATIVE REVENUES, 261. RECOMMENDED READINGS, 263.

Chapter 12
COMMERCIAL REVENUES: GOVERNMENT BUSINESS
ENTERPRISES   264

> NATURE OF COMMERCIAL REVENUES, 264. REASONS FOR GOVERNMENT
> OPERATION OF COMMERCIAL ENTERPRISES, 265: Ineffectiveness of Regu-
> lation in the Public Interest, 265; Unwillingness of Private Capital to
> Assume Risk, 267; Sales of Government Surplus Goods, 269. BUSINESS
> ENTERPRISES OF THE FEDERAL GOVERNMENT, 271. BUSINESS ENTER-
> PRISES OF STATE GOVERNMENTS, 274. BUSINESS ENTERPRISES OF LOCAL
> GOVERNMENTS, 275. DETERMINATION OF PUBLIC PRICES, 277. REC-
> OMMENDED READINGS, 280.

Chapter 13
TAXES: ALLOCATION OF TAX BURDENS   282

> REVENUE IMPORTANCE OF TAXES, 283. OBJECTIVES OF TAXATION, 284.
> ALLOCATION OF TAX BURDENS, 287: Two Fundamental Considerations,
> 287; Possible Bases of Tax-Burden Allocation, 288; Cost and Benefit,
> 290; Ability to Pay, 292; Sacrifices and the Rate of Taxation, 293; The
> Case for Progressive Taxation, 296. DISTRIBUTION OF BURDEN IN
> SUMPTUARY TAXATION, 301. SUMMARY, 302. RECOMMENDED READ-
> INGS, 303.

Chapter 14
TAX INCIDENCE AND OTHER EFFECTS   305

> THE MEANING OF "INCIDENCE," 305. THE CONDITIONS OF TAX SHIFT-
> ING, 306: The Role of Price in Tax Shifting, 306; Forward and Backward
> Shifting, 307. GENERAL ANALYSIS OF TAX SHIFTING AND INCIDENCE,
> 312: I. Taxes Imposed on Net Income, 312; II. Taxes Imposed on
> Property Ownership, 317; III. Taxes on the Production or Sale of Goods,
> 318. OTHER INFLUENCES UPON TAX SHIFTING, 324. OTHER EFFECTS
> OF TAXES, 326: Effects Created in the Process of Shifting, 327; Effects
> Resulting from Incidence, 327. CONCLUDING OBSERVATIONS ON SHIFT-
> ING AND INCIDENCE, 328. RECOMMENDED READINGS, 329.

Chapter 15

PROPERTY TAXATION 331

STEPS IN ADMINISTRATION OF THE PROPERTY TAX, 332: Assessment, 332; Equalization, 338; Apportionment, 340; Collection, 341. THEORY OF THE GENERAL PROPERTY TAX, 341: Ability, Benefit, and the Incidence of Property Taxes, 343; Theory of Taxation of Intangibles, 344. CLASSIFIED PROPERTY TAXES, 346. TAXATION OF THE "UNEARNED INCREMENT" FROM LAND, 349. COUNTER-CYCLE USE OF PROPERTY TAXES, 351. THE PROPERTY TAX: CONCLUSION, 352. RECOMMENDED READINGS, 354.

Chapter 16

PERSONAL INCOME TAXATION 356

REVENUE IMPORTANCE OF PERSONAL INCOME TAXES, 356. EARLY HISTORY OF FEDERAL PERSONAL INCOME TAXATION, 358: The Civil War Income Tax, 358; The Income Tax of 1894, 359; The Corporation Tax of 1909 and the Sixteenth Amendment, 360. OUTLINE OF FEDERAL INCOME TAX COMPUTATION, 361: *1.* Adjusted Gross Income, 362; *2.* Deductions from Adjusted Gross Income, 362; *3.* Taxable Income, 364; *4.* Application of Tax Rates, 364; *5.* Credits Against the Tax, 369. COVERAGE OF THE FEDERAL PERSONAL INCOME TAX, 370. COLLECTION AT THE SOURCE, 372. STATE PERSONAL INCOME TAXES, 379. RECOMMENDED READINGS, 382.

Chapter 17

THE NATURE OF NET INCOME FOR TAX PURPOSES 384

WHAT IS AN INDIVIDUAL INCOME? 387. THE INCOME PERIOD FOR TAX PURPOSES, 388. EXCLUSION OF CAPITAL ITEMS FROM INCOME, 391. CAPITAL GAINS AND LOSSES, 394: Nature of Capital Gains and Losses, 394; Survey of Federal Treatment of Capital Gains and Losses, 396; Are Capital Gains Income?, 400; Common Objections to Capital Gains Taxation, 401. IMPROVEMENT IN TAXATION OF CAPITAL GAINS AND LOSSES, 406. RECOMMENDED READINGS, 408.

Chapter 18

TAXATION OF PERSONAL INCOME FROM BUSINESS CORPORATIONS 409

THE FEDERAL CORPORATION NET INCOME TAX, 409. RELATION OF PERSONAL TO CORPORATE INCOME TAXATION, 411: The History of Integration and Dis-Integration, 414; Possible Methods of Eliminating Both Double Taxation and the Undistributed Earnings Loophole, 420. RECOMMENDED READINGS, 426.

Chapter 19
STRENGTHENING THE PERSONAL INCOME TAX   427

INCOME TAX CHANGES TO PROMOTE UNIFORMITY AND EQUITY, 429: *1*. Exclusions from Adjusted Gross Income, 429; *2*. Deductions, 431; *3*. Exemptions, 434; *4*. Tax Credits, 435. THE EFFECT OF PROPOSED CHANGES UPON THE TAX BASE, 435. TAX RATES, 437. COUNTER-CYCLE ADJUSTMENTS IN THE PERSONAL INCOME TAX, 444. RECOMMENDED READINGS, 446.

Chapter 20
TAXES ON SALES   447

TYPES OF TAXES ON SALES, 447: Customs Duties, 447; Taxes on the Production, Sale, or Use of Particular Goods, 448; Turnover Taxes, 451; Retail Sales Taxes, 452. EXTENT OF EXCISE AND SALES TAXATION, 453: The Federal Government, 453; State Governments, 455; Local Governments, 459. SHIFTING OF TAXES ON SALES, 460: Limitations upon Forward Shifting, 461; Legal Aids to Shifting, 463. THE CASE FOR THE SALES TAX, 464: *1*. Stability of Revenues, 465; *2*. Cost of Collection, 466; *3*. Regressiveness of Sales Taxes, 467; *4*. Sumptuary Possibilities, 468; *5*. Immediate Revenues, 468; *6*. Tax-Consciousness, 469. COMPENSATORY POSSIBILITIES IN THE SALES TAX, 469: Unintended Economic Effects, 469; Commodity Taxes as Intentional Compensatory Instruments, 471. RECOMMENDED READINGS, 475.

Chapter 21
DEATH AND GIFT TAXES   476

THEORIES OF DEATH TAXATION, 477: *1*. Benefit, 477; *2*. State Partnership, 477; *3*. The Back-Tax Theory, 478; *4*. Ability to Pay, 478; *5*. Redistribution of Wealth, 482. INCIDENCE OF DEATH TAXES, 485. RECENT HISTORY OF DEATH TAXATION, 486: The Federal Credit for State Death Taxes Paid, 487. REVENUE PRODUCTIVITY OF DEATH TAXES, 490. GIFT TAXES, 492. INTEGRATION OF DEATH AND GIFT TAXES, 494. THE PROBLEM OF SITUS IN STATE DEATH TAXATION, 495 COMPENSATORY USE OF DEATH TAXES, 497. RECOMMENDED READINGS, 497.

Chapter 22
BUSINESS TAXES   499

THE NATURE OF BUSINESS TAXES, 499: The National Tax Association's "Model Tax Systems," 499; More Recent Theories of the Business Tax, 501. TYPES OF STATE BUSINESS TAXES, 504: Business Taxes on Net Income, 505; "Business" Taxes on Gross Income, 505; Capital Stock Taxes, 506; Taxation of Special Types of Business, 507; Productivity of

State Business Taxes, 507.   FEDERAL BUSINESS TAXES, 508: The Federal Corporation Income Tax, 508; The Federal Excess Profits Tax, 510; Evaluation of Excess Profits Tax Experience in World War II, 516; The Excess Profits Tax of 1950, 517.   INCIDENCE OF BUSINESS TAXES, 519.   INCIDENCE AND THE RATIONALE OF BUSINESS TAXATION, 521. RECOMMENDED READINGS, 523.

Chapter 23
TAXES ON EMPLOYMENT AND MISCELLANEOUS TAXES   524

TAXES ON EMPLOYMENT, 524: The Old Age and Survivors' Insurance Taxes, 524; Unemployment Compensation Taxes, 526; Incidence of Social Security Taxes on Employment, 528; Social Security Taxes in the Revenue System, 534.   COUNTER-CYCLE SOCIAL SECURITY TAXATION, 535.   POLL AND CAPITATION TAXES, 537.   THE UNJUST ENRICHMENT TAX, 539.   RECOMMENDED READINGS, 542.

Chapter 24
STATE AND LOCAL FINANCE IN THE NATIONAL ECONOMY 543

STATE AND LOCAL GOVERNMENTAL RELATIONSHIPS, 545.   FISCAL PROBLEMS OF LOCAL GOVERNMENTS, 546: Promotion of Efficiency, 546; Lowering of Service Standards, 549; Increasing Revenues, 552.   FISCAL PROBLEMS OF STATE GOVERNMENTS, 556: Expensive Functions of State Governments, 556.   POSSIBLE SOLUTIONS TO THE STATE-LOCAL FISCAL "CRISIS," 558: Solutions Available to State and Local Governments, 562.   STATE-LOCAL FINANCE AND ECONOMIC STABILITY, 577.   RECOMMENDED READINGS, 582.

INDEX   585

SOURCES OF GENERAL FACTUAL INFORMATION
USEFUL TO STUDENTS OF PUBLIC FINANCE

Statistics of Government Income, Expenditure, Debt:

FEDERAL:

Budget of the United States Government, Washington, Government Printing Office, Annual.

Detailed statistics on budget and trust fund receipts and expenditures. Figures for the last completed fiscal year, the current year, and the year following. The Special Analyses select and reclassify to show various implications of budget plans.

Annual Report of the Secretary of the Treasury, Washington, Government Printing Office.

A primary source of statistical and other information on federal finance. In some general categories (receipts, expenditures, gross debt), time series go back to 1790. Publication is usually delayed about two years.

Treasury Bulletin, Washington, Government Printing Office, Monthly.

Current budget receipts and expenditures, cash receipts and payments, and special emphasis on debt operations.

Daily Statement of the United States Treasury and *Monthly Statement of the Receipts and Expenditures of the United States Government,* Washington, Government Printing Office.

The most up-to-date publication of statistics on receipts, expenditures, and public debt.

STATE AND LOCAL:

U.S. Bureau of the Census, *Compendium of State Government Finances,* Washington, Government Printing Office, Annual.

Statistics of receipts, expenditures, debt, cash balances, by states and aggregated. Prior to 1942 this publication was entitled *Financial Statistics of States.*

U.S. Bureau of the Census, *Compendium of City Government Finances,* Washington, Government Printing Office, Annual.

Statistics of receipts, expenditures, debt, cash balances, by city and aggregated. Prior to 1942 this publication was entitled *Financial Statistics of Cities.*

Up to 1931 statistics were published for cities over 30,000 population; between 1932 and 1941 from cities over 100,000 population; and since 1941 from cities over 25,000 population.

U.S. Bureau of the Census, *Summary of Government Finances,* Washington, Bureau of the Census, Annual.

Contains summary fiscal statistics for federal, state, and local governments. Its particular virtue is that it contains data for small local governments, including municipalities under 25,000 population, and special districts.

Other Economic Statistics:

Survey of Current Business, Washington, Government Printing Office, Monthly.

Statistics of National product and income, and a variety of detailed business indexes and statistics, many from other sources than the Department of Commerce.

Federal Reserve Bulletin, Washington, Board of Governors of the Federal Reserve System, Monthly.

Original source of money, banking, and finance statistics. Republishes some federal fiscal statistics.

Monthly Labor Review, Washington, Government Printing Office, Monthly.

Publishes statistics of prices, employment, wages, and labor conditions, as originated by the Bureau of Labor Statistics.

Tax Systems:

FEDERAL:

United States Statutes at Large, Washington, Government Printing Office, Annual.

The official publication of federal laws. The statutes appear in chronological order of their signature into law. A picture of the federal tax structure can be had, therefore, only by piecing together the legislation over a period of years.

United States Code, Washington, Government Printing Office, 1958.

In this publication the statutes are grouped together by subject titles. Thus, the internal revenue statutes are combined into an Internal Revenue Code. Amendments are incorporated into laws, and a picture of legislation in effect at the time of publication is available. The 1958 Code is the sixth edition.

Tax Services (Looseleaf).

These are expensive and highly detailed services, primarily for use of the tax practitioner. The Prentice-Hall *Federal Taxes* and/or Commerce Clearing House *Standard Federal Tax Service* may be found in many libraries.

Tax "Courses".

Both Prentice-Hall and Commerce Clearing House publish an annual volume describing the provisions of the federal tax laws. There is descriptive text of the provisions, and some problems. The titles are, *Federal Tax Course* and *Federal Tax Guide,* respectively.

State:

State Tax Guide, Chicago, Commerce Clearing House, Looseleaf.

This up-to-date publication presents tax systems by states and also tables indicating the states employing particular taxes. Rates and major provisions of the tax laws are given.

Tax Systems, Chicago, Commerce Clearing House, 1952.

Prior to the ninth edition (1942) this publication was entitled *Tax Systems of the World.* Under that title it was prepared by the Tax Research Foundation, and was done in considerably more detail and with more concern for fine distinctions than has been the case since. Publication was apparently discontinued with the 1952 edition.

(A list of recommended readings pertinent to the subject discussed will be found at the end of each text chapter.)

The Economics
of Public Finance

CHAPTER 1

Introduction:
Public Finance in its Economic
and Political Setting

THE NATURE OF THE STUDY OF PUBLIC FINANCE

Quite probably the most significant development in the American economy during recent decades has been the rise of government to a position of impressive influence upon nearly all economic activity. This fact is, in a general way, well known, and yet a few comparative figures may help to demonstrate the order of magnitude of current governmental operations. In the year 1958, taxes and fees paid to federal, state, and local governments in the United States amounted to $115 billion. This amount is almost exactly equal to the amounts spent by the population for the consumption of food, clothing and accessories, and tobacco in that year.[1] Governments contributed almost 13 per cent of the national income in the United States in 1958. This contribution was greater than that of retail trade, of services, or of finance and real estate, and was almost half as large as that of all manufacturing.[2] Nearly eight million people worked as civilians for governments in 1958, and they represented about one-eighth of the civilian labor force in that year. Only slightly more persons were employed in retail trade, and less than a million more were employed in all durable goods manufacture.[3] About two-fifths of all debt in the United States in 1958 was debt of governments; government debt was larger than either corporate debt or private noncorporate debt, but about one-third smaller than the two combined.[4]

[1] *Survey of Current Business*, July, 1959, pp. 17, 21.
[2] *Ibid.*, p. 13. The contribution of governments to national income is the value of the service of government employees.
[3] *Monthly Labor Review*, October, 1959, pp. 1156–60.
[4] *Survey of Current Business*, May, 1959, p. 12. Total debt was $901.8 billion, and private debt $534 billion, of which $294 billion was corporate.

A nation living under the threat of war will inevitably undertake heavy expenditures. The claim may thus be made that the level of fiscal operations in recent years has been abnormally high, and that generalizations based upon recent experience are unwarranted. However, through the decade of the nineteen-thirties, expenditures of all governments in the United States averaged just under one-fifth of gross national product[5] of the American economy; during the first (war) half of the decade of the nineteen-forties, governmental expenditures rose to an annual average of over one-third of gross national expenditure, and during the second (quasi-peace) half of that decade the proportion fell to one-fourth. Given the state of international politics and the scale of demands placed upon government by its citizens, one would be rash indeed to predict that in the foreseeable future government expenditures will fall significantly below one-fourth of gross national product.

The channeling of so significant a share of the income stream through government cannot but have effects of great magnitude upon the whole economy. The impact of taxation and governmental spending upon the amount and distribution of real income is such as to deserve much better than the customary economy of hard thinking and the frequent repetition of dogma with respect to public finance. Government is very big business; its financial operations are so significant to economic well-being as to merit the maximum of penetrating analysis and understanding.

The ultimate goal of the study of public finance is to develop proper fiscal policy. This implies that the purpose of the study is to determine what *should* be done in the fiscal field, and what should be done evidently involves careful evaluation of the effects of what is being done as well as projection of new and sometimes daring plans for the future. "Fiscal policy" embraces matters of policy at various levels, ranging from matters of local concern, such as the desirability of erecting a new grammar school, to matters of broad national policy such as the proper sphere of governmental fiscal activity in relation to the operation of the economy as a whole.

There is much to recommend postponement of definition of a field of study until that study is completed.[6] The bare bones of definition take on muscular and organic significance as the study progresses, and only at the

---

[5] Gross national expenditure (gross national product) is the sum of personal consumption expenditures, gross expenditures for investment goods in the private economy, net foreign investment, and government purchases of goods and services.

[6] Professor Jacob Viner is reported to have defined economics as "what economists do." (K. E. Boulding, *Economic Analysis*, New York, Harper, 1941, p. 3.) Such circumlocution may call forth condemnation from the logician, but not from the teacher who has experienced the futility of defining a field to which the student is just being introduced.

end do the implications of the definition have real meaning. Nevertheless an obligation arises at the outset to make some observations designed to give the reader some preliminary "feel" of his whereabouts.

Public Finance

Public finance deals with the finances of the public as an organized group under the institution of government. It thus deals only with the finances of *government*. The *finances* of government include the raising and disbursement of government funds. Public finance is concerned with the operation of the *fisc*, or public treasury. Hence, to the degree that it is a science, it is the *fiscal* science; its policies are *fiscal* policies, its problems are *fiscal* problems.

Public finance is not concerned with the direct regulatory functions of government over the private economy. It is not concerned with such matters as the regulation of railroads and public utilities, monopolies, banks, and security markets, except as administration of these programs involves expenditure of public funds or as taxes may be used for purposes of regulation. Government affects the private economy in very many ways, but public finance is concerned only with the raising and disbursement of funds by government. However, as we shall see in later chapters, the raising and disbursement of government funds may themselves have a significant effect upon the level at which the economy operates.

The raising and disbursement of government funds by no means constitute a narrow field of problems. Determination of appropriate measures for raising funds implies an understanding of the flow of production from and income through the private economy, and therefore of the way the whole economy works. Determination of an appropriate expenditure program implies insight into such vast fields as the effects of public spendings upon the income stream of the whole economy, the relative social utilities of governmental services and private spendings, and the impact of change in government's expenditures upon the structure and philosophy of government. The field is thus both broad and deep; the solution of fiscal problems requires coordination of the efforts of many specialists.

The Questions of Public Finance. Who these specialists are and what they do are indicated by the kinds of questions asked of public finance. Some of the questions asked are of the Who? What? Where? Why? type and are answerable only by cause and effect analysis. Such questions therefore call for application of the scientific method and require scientific answers. Other questions are of the Should? Ought? May? type and require value judgments. Some of the specialists are thus necessarily scientists and some are artists. Remember that we are concerned in public finance with the determination of appropriate fiscal policies, which under democratic government must be not only right, but also feasible; not only capable of improving fiscal or economic conditions, but also capable of adoption.

Listed below are some (but not all) of the questions asked of public finance.

1. What are the effects of a fiscal proposal or practice upon:
    national production and income?
    the national standard of living?
    distribution of wealth and income?
    the financial markets?
    particular localities?
    particular lines of business?
    particular economic groups?
2. What are the effects of the proposal or practice upon:
    the rights of citizens?
    the structure and form of government?
    international relations?
3. Is adoption of the proposal possible?
4. How do we:
    procure the necessary personnel?
    procure the materials?
    get the job done efficiently?

The various parts of question 1 are answerable by the economist, since they involve knowledge of the structure of the economy and the forces which make it operate as it does. Question 2 can be answered by the political scientist, with assistance from the political philosopher, who is inclined toward the more esoteric aspects of government, and the lawyer, who is the practitioner in rules and regulations.

Question 3 requires an answer from the politician, whose function the London *Economist* has described as follows:

. . . there are men who have politics in their blood, just as artists are born to paint, and who will devote their lives to practice of their art even if they have to starve to do so. But the professional politician is not merely inevitable, he is necessary. He is the practitioner of the art of the possible, without whom almost everything is impossible. He is the man who gets things done, and his reward, his meat and drink, is power. From him cabinets draw their strength and parties their cohesion.[7]

Question 4 must be answered by the administrator, whose art lies in organization, in getting the right people for the right jobs, in programming

[7] "What Kind of M. P.'s?" *The Economist,* Vol. CL, No. 5343, January 19, 1946, p. 85.

the work, in putting on the right amount of pressure in the right places at the right times. His art is constantly directed toward his goal of efficiency.

These are the specialists whose particular abilities and accomplishments are required if proper answers are to be given to the questions asked of public finance. Many of the questions listed above can be answered by specialists independently of one another. But the final questions, "Do we want it?" "Can we afford it?" can usually be answered only by integration of the results of specialized investigation and opinion.

This book is primarily concerned with the economic aspects of public finance. From time to time political limitations upon change are cited, and practical possibilities are briefly considered. On the whole, however, conclusions are drawn from the viewpoint of the economist. In many branches of public finance the questions are so essentially economic that his viewpoint should be considered supreme. In other branches, where his view does not carry supreme authority, conclusions are stated as first approximations, to be qualified or amended by other specialists.

Method. Two approaches to the economics of public finance are necessary, the institutional and the analytical. A description of the governmental and economic institutions through which public finance operates is basic to the study. Administration of appropriate fiscal policy is accomplished by and within the framework of this governmental structure and through various economic institutions. Not only do existing legislation and existing governmental and economic organization represent useful starting points for critical study, but recognition of inherent resistance to change in the institutions (whether desirable or not) is conducive to a healthy point of view with respect to the types of fiscal policy which may be feasible.

The analytical approach applies the techniques of economic analysis to the materials of public finance. The techniques of economic analysis are essentially those techniques which relate causes and their effects, isolating and evaluating the various forces which operate together to make the economy behave as it does—or should. We shall therefore draw heavily upon economic "theory." It is hoped that readers will have gained some previous acquaintance with economic analysis or theory, although the theoretical aspects of the problems discussed in this book do not presuppose a high degree of competence along this line.

Government Finance and Business Finance

What similarities and what differences are to be found in government fiscal operations as compared to monetary operations of private business? It has sometimes been said that government and business are fundamentally dissimilar in that government adjusts its tax income to its desired scale of expenditures, whereas business must adjust its expenditure to its income. While there is an aspect of coercion in government's taxing power which is not available to ordinary business, the distinction mentioned is hardly real. Both government and business (and consumers) resort to borrowing when current revenues are inadequate to accomplish what they wish to do. Income for business is not necessarily a more fixed quantity than for government. Businesses often increase income by first increasing expenditure, and loans fill the gap. Government borrows in anticipation of tax receipts, and borrows to spend to increase national income, from which flows increased tax receipts. On the other hand, considerations of the adequacy of tax revenues and ability to manage debt inevitably condition the scale of expenditures which government undertakes.

There are differences, however, between government and business with respect to their financial operations. Business determines the advisability of expenditure almost exclusively in terms of its capacity to produce revenue *for the business*. Government, on the other hand, spends to promote general welfare, where no direct revenue is anticipated. Even though government may spend to support the economy and to promote business prosperity, the increment to national income thus generated does not accrue to government unless government chooses to tax it away from individuals. Government is in a position to finance improvements of a general nature and activities for which financial return is uncertain or long delayed. The objectives and motives of government in making expenditures are thus different from those of private business.

Another difference between government and private business lies in the different degrees of their coercive authority. By and large, where popular government is practiced, government policy is determined more democratically than is business policy. But once determined, tax measures are coercive, since the alternatives of not earning taxable income, not buying taxed goods, not accumulating an estate prior to death, or not owning property leave little opportunity for reasonable choice. The only way to avoid a general sales tax is not to buy. It should be noted, however, that to the extent business is monopolized, eliminating choice among qualities and prices of useful articles, an effective coercion is present. Benjamin Franklin's assertion that the only human certainties are death and taxes testifies to the coerciveness of fiscal power. It obviously follows that coercive power implies great responsibility in the formulation of fiscal policy; such power is ultimately justified only by its fruitfulness for the general good.

While it is true that government's potential income has much broader limits than does the income of any single private business, that government may take a longer and larger view with respect to the desirability of an expenditure, that it can ignore the absence of direct money return, and that its rules are more coercive than those of business, government and business do operate in the same economy. Government takes taxes out of the general income stream, it spends its funds into the general income stream, it borrows funds from the same sources as does private business, it employs private concerns to produce for it, and fiscal policy stands or falls by its effects upon the private economy. A much healthier approach to fiscal policy results from consideration of government as an element in the economy than is to be had from assuming government to be a peculiar excrescence upon it.

Governmental Structure in the United States

A basic fact, having many implications for public finance in the United States, is the multiplicity of governmental units. An American citizen is affected by the expenditure programs and the revenue-raising programs of several layers of government. For he is not only a citizen of the United States, but he cannot be an American citizen without being subject also to government by a state and a local subdivision of the state.[8] Government therefore means federal, state, and local government. In the category of "local government" we include county, township, and municipal government, and for purposes of administration or finance the municipality may be subdivided further into "special districts"—school districts, fire districts, sewer districts, and so forth—created to carry on functions and improvements of a local nature. The multiplicity of local governmental units has reached astounding proportions in some areas. The Bureau of the Census found that in 1957 there were 102,353 governmental units in the United States having sufficient autonomy to justify their being called independent governments. The total was distributed as follows:[9]

Federal	1
States	48
Counties	3,047
Townships	17,214
Municipalities	17,167
School Districts	50,463
Other Special Districts	14,423

By states, the number of governmental units varies principally with the

[8] Unless, of course, he has residence in the District of Columbia, which is governed by a local subdivision of the federal government.

[9] U. S. Department of Commerce, Bureau of the Census, *Governments in the United States, 1957*. This report shows a heartening reduction by 52,763 of governmental units in the United States since 1942, due to extensive reorganization of school districts.

degree of local autonomy granted to boards administering local school districts. Nebraska, which maintains autonomous school districts, had 6,659 governmental units, while Rhode Island, which does not, had 91. The piling up of governments makes for complexity in establishment of intergovernmental relationships, overlapping of administrative jurisdictions, division of authority, and inability of the average citizen to exercise his responsibility intelligently.

The student of public finance will do well to understand, at least in broad outline, the relation of one type of government to another in the United States. An understanding of this relationship will serve (1) to establish principles pointing to the types of functions to be performed at different governmental levels, and (2) to remind the student that fiscal idealism may run afoul of political fact.

Powers of Federal and State Governments.[10] In a democratic society ultimate authority rests with the citizen; "governments derive their just powers from the consent of the governed." Although "sovereignty" in democracy resides in the people, in the sense that the people represent the ultimate authority, it is possible to speak of a *sovereign* government—a government which has supreme governmental authority and is not subject to the control or authority of another government. A sovereign government is free to determine its own action (within the limits of authority granted to it by its citizens), although *it* may choose to limit those actions by contract or by law.[11]

In the United States, a citizen lives under two *sovereign* governments, federal and state. The areas in which each government is sovereign are either defined or implied by the Constitution of the United States. Local governments—county, township, city or village, and special districts—are not sovereign in any sense. They are political subdivisions of the state, created by the state or under state authority, and exercising powers granted to them by the state. Since local governments do what they do under authorization from the state government (authorization being granted both by the local government's charter and by the statute laws of the state), questions of conflict of authority arise only between federal and state governments.

[10] The student of government will recognize that this section represents but a bare summary of the general subject. The only defense which can be made of the ruthless elimination of detail and qualification is lack of space and the relative insignificance to this type of study of detail and qualification.

[11] For example, when government borrows it sells securities (contracts) which bind it to certain financial promises to repay principal and to pay interest; or it may limit the amount of its borrowing by law establishing a limit to gross debt.

The supreme law of the land—the Constitution of the United States—defines, partially by implication, the areas of supremacy of federal and state governments. After reserving some rights and powers to the people by denying them to both federal and state governments, the Constitution enumerates the powers of the federal government and reserves the remainder to the states. Rights reserved to the people include the basic protection of citizens against suspension of the habeas corpus privilege; ex post facto legislation; irresponsible charges of treason; abridgment of the freedom of religion, speech, assembly, and the press; unreasonable search and seizure; deprivation of life, liberty, or property without due process of law; inadequate opportunity or representation before the courts; denial of the right to vote on account of race, color, or previous condition of servitude. The above list is not complete, but does indicate the areas in which citizens are legally immune from interference by any level of government.

The powers of the federal government are in part specifically granted to it and in part granted by prohibition of their use by the states. The "enumerated" powers of the federal government which are significant to the study of public finance are:

1. To lay and collect taxes uniformly throughout the United States, to pay the debts and provide for the common defense and general welfare of the United States.

2. To regulate commerce with foreign nations and among the several states.

3. To coin and regulate the value of money.

4. To establish post offices and post roads.

5. To raise, support, and regulate an army and navy.

6. To adjudicate controversies between states.

The states are expressly prohibited from practices interfering with or impairing the performance of these functions by the federal government.

Article X in amendment of the Constitution states: "The powers not delegated to the United States by the Constitution, nor prohibited by it to the states, are reserved to the States respectively, or to the people." Thus we may say that, among the powers not reserved to the people, the federal government has authority over those matters which affect foreign relations and foreign commerce, interstate commerce, the respect of states for the actions of other states and the rights of citizens of other states, and the establishment of uniform coinage, weights, measures, and postal systems. The remaining powers belong to the states and are limited to authority over intrastate affairs so long as exercise of that authority does not encroach upon the federal interstate or international domain.[12] The boundary line at which federal authority ends and state authority begins is not a clear nor fixed line. The boundary at any given time is drawn by interpretations of the courts in specific cases. The tendency through the last half-century has been to expand the bounds of federal authority by an increasingly more liberal interpretation of the term "interstate commerce."

This dualism in American government creates problems which are important to the study of public finance. The burden of taxation upon the individual citizen is the sum of federal, state, and local taxes. There is little that can be done, except on the volition of federal or state government, to eliminate discriminatory double taxation of American citizens who reside within a given state. There is little that can be done, except voluntarily by states, to provide uniformity among themselves in tax methods or tax burdens. It is impossible by direct legal methods to enforce integration of federal and state tax systems. It is impossible by direct legal methods to force state and local governments to coordinate their tax and expenditure policies with those of the federal government for the purpose of counteracting the movements of the business cycle. The absence of power to enforce uniformity may, of course, have its desirable aspects. Superior authority may not always be accompanied by superior wisdom; the absence of supreme centralized authority can obviate the possibility of general application of unwise policy.

However inadequate the legal authority of the federal government may be in imposing its financial will or wisdom upon the states, the tremendous financial resources provided by its taxing and borrowing power have served it well as a substitute therefor. The instrument of grants-in-aid has enormously extended the practical power of the federal government over the states. By the offer of federal money (with strings attached) for the construction of highways within the states, the federal government has in effect dictated[13] the creation of highway departments in state governments, the appropriation of state money for the construction and maintenance of

---

[12] In the *Houston, East and West Texas Railway* vs. *United States* case (1914), the Supreme Court stated: "Wherever the interstate and intrastate transactions of carriers are so related that the government of the one involves the control of the other, it is Congress, and not the State, that is entitled to prescribe the final and dominant rule, for otherwise Congress would be denied the exercise of its constitutional authority and the State, and not the Nation, would be supreme within the national field." 234 U. S. 351–352.

[13] Although, as Professor Bittermann states, the methods of the Bureau of Public Roads have been more persuasive than coercive and dictatorial. (Henry J. Bittermann, *State and Federal Grants-in-Aid*, New York, Mentzer, Bush & Co., 1938, p. 282.)

particular roads and highways, the location and type of road construction, and the earmarking of certain state revenues for highway construction. Under the Social Security Act of 1935, grants-in-aid were successfully utilized to encourage the states to appropriate money for uniform programs of unemployment compensation, old-age assistance, child health and welfare, general public health, vocational rehabilitation, and aid to the blind.[14] Obviously the federal government had no legal authority under the Constitution by which it could force the states to undertake such projects according to federal standards. But the offer of "dollar-for-dollar" in federal money was too attractive for the states to ignore, and they voluntarily fell into line. Few would deny that to date the result has been good, both in getting desirable things done and in improving the quality of state administration of highways and of many welfare activities.

It is obvious that the federal government, by offering to pay a part of the cost of a new or expanded activity, can lure the states into activities they might not otherwise undertake. It is less obvious that federal fiscal power can influence the character of state tax systems. The classic instance of this is the manner in which the states have been brought into line with respect to death taxation. Prior to 1924 the states pursued independent and varied policies with respect to the taxation of estates at death. Some even advertised themselves as good states in which to die, because they had no such taxes. But when the federal government raised its death tax rates, and permitted a credit against the federal tax of state death taxes paid, the death-tax-free state not only lost its former attractiveness, but unless it enacted a state tax equal to the federal credit it sacrificed revenue which could be had without additional burden upon the taxpayer. The result of federal death tax policy which began in 1924 and continues to the present has been to bring the states into line in both the type of tax imposed and the severity of rates. This is a perfectly legal use of the federal taxing power, although its effect is quite evidently that of introducing a high degree of elasticity into the constitutional concept of federal and state governments, each supreme in its own area.

The reader will see an element of practical conflict between the federal government's responsibility to promote the general welfare and the denial of federal authority to compel uniformity of policy within the states. For matters of taxation and of governmental functions do affect welfare, and lack of uniformity in state policy makes for unevenness in welfare standards among the states. The instruments of grants-in-aid and tax credits make

[14] *Cf.* Bittermann, *op. cit.*, Ch. XII.

the decision of the states to fall in line an easy one, though in matters of extreme importance to a state the possibility of independent choice of policy is still open and legally protected.

The Federal Taxing Power

Bills for raising revenue must conform to the constitutional limitations upon the taxing power. These limitations are:[15]

1. "Congress shall have power to lay and collect taxes, duties, imposts and excises, to pay the debts and provide for the common defense and general welfare of the United States; . . ."[16] This grant of authority is extremely broad. "General welfare" has been interpreted so liberally by the Court as to include the welfare of relatively small special classes. Nevertheless, the welfare objective, liberally interpreted, may not be used by Congress to accomplish objectives denied to it by the Constitution. Thus in the AAA case (1935) the Court held that with respect to the constitutionality of a tax on the processors of agricultural products for the purpose of paying benefits to farmers who reduced acreage, "We are not now required to ascertain the scope of the phrase 'general welfare of the United States' or to determine whether an appropriation in aid of agriculture falls within it. Wholly apart from that question, another principle embedded in our Constitution prohibits the enforcement of the Agricultural Adjustment Act. The act invades the reserved rights of the states. . . . The tax, the appropriation of the funds raised, and the direction for their disbursement, are but parts of the plan. They are but means to an unconstitutional end."[17]

2. ". . . all duties, imposts, and excises shall be uniform throughout the United States."[18] This applies, of course, only to *federal* revenue measures. It does not mean that the amounts collected from the various states by a given indirect tax must be equal; but simply that individuals and concerns, in whatever state they are located, are subject to tax rates uniformly established on taxable things uniformly defined. For example, a federal unemployment compensation tax is imposed on employers of four or more employees who are employed by them at least twenty days per year, each day being in a different week. The rate of tax is uniform for all employers,

---

[15] *Cf.* F. A. Ogg and O. P. Ray, *Introduction to American Government*, 6th Ed., New York, Appleton-Century, 1938, pp. 466–9.

[16] Article I, Section 8.

[17] *U. S. vs. Butler*, Jan. 6, 1936. Quotation from *House Document* No. 386, 73rd Cong., 2nd Session, p. 9.

[18] Article I, Section 8.

in whatever state they may be situated, and the amount of tax paid is the rate times the wages of employees. Thus the amounts of tax paid by employers vary with the number of employees and the amount of wages paid to the employee. So long as the definition of employers subject to the tax, the tax rate, and the tax base are uniform throughout the United States, the constitutional requirement of uniformity is satisfied.

3. "No tax or duty shall be laid on articles exported from any state."[19]

4. The final constitutional limitation, "No capitation or other direct tax shall be laid, unless in proportion to the census . . ." is no longer significant. The only "direct" tax now used by the federal government is the income tax, which is permitted under the Sixteenth Amendment: "Congress shall have power to lay and collect taxes on incomes, from whatever source derived, without apportionment among the several States, and without regard to any census or enumeration."[20] The limitation would thus be effective only if the federal government wished to levy a direct tax on property. If there were a federal poll tax, it would presumably be levied according to the census, and thus would be legal. The automobile use tax (1942–1945) was not a direct tax on property (an automobile), but an excise on the *use* of that property. Thus use and not ownership of an automobile was the basis of the tax, and being an "indirect" tax it was not subject to the constitutional limitation here considered. (Since it was uniformly applied, this tax met the uniformity requirement for indirect taxes in (2) above.)

There appears to be a fairly widespread notion that it is illegal to utilize the taxing power for other than revenue purposes—that taxation for purposes of regulation is not permitted. Such is not the case. So long as the tax is within the limitations listed above and so long as the regulatory function contemplated is not denied by the Constitution, Congress may use the indirect method of accomplishing regulation by taxation as well as the direct method of establishing rules of conduct. Fortunately for fiscal policy, no legal provision requires that tax measures be used for revenue purposes only. In 1865, Congress imposed a 10 per cent tax on the circulation of state bank notes. The effect, as well as the intention, of Congress was to tax state bank notes out of existence. It could have been done by direct legislation prohibiting their circulation, but Congress chose rather to use the tax method. In approving this method the Court said in part: "Having . . ., in the exercise of undisputed constitutional powers, under-

---

[19] Article I, Section 9.
[20] Effective February 25, 1913.

taken to provide a currency for the whole country, it cannot be questioned that Congress may, constitutionally, secure the benefit of it to the people by appropriate legislation. To . . . [this] end, Congress may restrain, by suitable enactments, the circulation as money of any notes not issued under its own authority."[21]

RECOMMENDED READINGS

General:

Colm, Gerhard, "Why Public Finance?", *National Tax Journal,* September, 1948; reprinted as Chapter 1 in *Essays in Public Finance and Fiscal Policy,* N.Y., Oxford, 1955.

    A first-rate and relatively simple analytical discussion of the nature of public finance, the reasons for recognizing it as a special area of economic study, and the appropriate methods of approach to its study.

Seligman, E.R.A., "Public Finance," *Encyclopaedia of the Social Sciences,* N.Y., Macmillan, 1934.

    A useful treatment of the scope of public finance, with considerable historical detail. Does not discuss the more recent broadening of the field to include the general economic consequences of stabilization policy.

Taxing power:

Shultz, William J., and Harriss, C. Lowell, *American Public Finance,* Sixth Edition, 1954, N.Y., Prentice-Hall, Chapter 7.

    A recommended detailed discussion of this field. The material may be found in other editions of the book.

[21] *Veazie Bank* vs. *Fenno,* 8 Wall. 549 (1869).

CHAPTER 2

Fiscal Administration

THE BUDGET

The budget is the master financial plan of a government. It brings together estimates of anticipated revenues and proposed expenditures for the budget period, and from these estimates the activities to be undertaken and the means of their financing can be inferred. Only in the budget can a unified view of the scope and character of governmental activity be seen, and only here can the financial direction which government is planning to take be discerned. Ideally, the budget is a statement of careful estimates and honest intentions. In practice it is too often less than this. Ideally also, the budget document permits the average citizen to see fiscal policy in integrated form; in practice the picture is often excessively complex even for the legislator whose business it is to legislate budgetary plans.

The "executive budget," prepared by the chief executive (with the aid of the budget department or bureau) and presented to the legislative branch of government for translation into legislation, is the preferred type of budget and is more commonly used by the larger governmental units. The alternative is a "legislative budget," prepared by or for a committee of the legislative branch for adoption by that branch. Three arguments favor the executive budget: (1) the chief executive will be held largely accountable by the public for the results of fiscal operations during the fiscal period, whether or not he is in the main responsible, and is therefore entitled to present *his* budget; (2) one of the admitted functions of the chief executive in governments in the United States is that of recommending general governmental policy—charting the governmental course—for implementation or revision by the law-making branch; and (3) the largest share of expenditures will almost certainly be spent by agencies of the executive department of government. As will be seen, presentation by the executive of the budget plan in no way encroaches upon the proper sphere of the legislature, since

15

its proposals are made effective only by translation into law by the legislature.

The Budget and Accounting Act of 1921[1] established the present federal budget system. It imposed upon the President the duty of transmitting the budget to Congress early in each regular session. It created a Bureau of the Budget, first placed in the Treasury Department and in 1939 transferred to the Executive Office of the President,[2] to prepare the budget for the chief executive. The Budget Act defines the required contents of the budget in some detail, the more important of which are:

1. The President's estimates of the expenditures and appropriations necessary in his judgment for the ensuing fiscal year, except that estimates for the legislative branch of the government and the Supreme Court shall be transmitted to him and he shall include them in the budget without revision.

2. The President's estimates of receipts during the ensuing fiscal year, under

      a. revenue laws existing at the time the budget is transmitted, and

      b. revenue proposals, if any, contained in the budget.

3. The expenditures and receipts of the last completed fiscal year.

4. The President's estimates of the expenditures and receipts during the fiscal year in progress.

5. The amounts of appropriations, including balances of appropriations from prior fiscal years, available for expenditure during the fiscal year in progress.

6. Balanced statements of the actual or estimated condition of the treasury at the end of the last completed fiscal year, the fiscal year in progress, and at the end of the ensuing fiscal year if the financial proposals contained in the budget are adopted.

7. All essential facts regarding the indebtedness of the government.

8. Such other financial statements and data as in his opinion are necessary or desirable in order to make known in all practicable detail the financial condition of the government.

9. If for the ensuing fiscal year estimated receipts plus any prior surplus are less than the estimated expenditures, the President shall recommend in the budget new taxes, loans, or other appropriate action to make up the deficiency.

10. If the aggregate of such receipts and such surpluses is greater than

---

[1] Sixty-seventh Congress, 1st Session, Chapter 18. Approved June 10, 1921.

[2] By Reorganization Plan I, pursuant to the Reorganization Act of 1939.

estimated expenditures, he shall make such recommendations as in his opinion the public interests require.

The scope of the budget's contents is indicated by the requirements listed above. It is designed to show the financial results of fiscal policy for the last completed fiscal year, the probable results for the current year not completed (since the budget is presented in January and the fiscal year ends June 30), and the President's recommendations concerning receipts and expenditures for the next fiscal year. While the federal budget document makes expenditure proposals in great detail, it customarily gives far less careful attention to revenue measures, leaving such matters for separate legislative consideration. In recommending a fairly detailed schedule of expenditures it in effect recommends a desired scale of governmental activities. So far as the President wishes to change the scale of governmental activities—to add or subtract functions—his general policies are reflected in the budget and advocated in the budget message. The budget is thus the focal point of fiscal policy.

Preparation of the Budget

Preparation of the federal budget for the fiscal year beginning July 1 normally begins in late spring of the previous year. In May and June the general contours of the budget are being formulated, based upon current forecasts. At this time the budget process is immeasurably assisted if the chief executive can lay down general policy guidelines indicating the general magnitudes of planned expenditures and expected revenues, in what major fields increases or decreases are desired, and what the revenue prospects suggest as to general tax policy. By the end of June each major agency should be advised as to its allowed expenditure ceiling, within which it plans the distribution of its expenditures. Examiners from the Bureau of the Budget, each a specialist in the activities of one or more agencies, assist the agencies in preparation of their budgets. Beginning about September, hearings are held at which the agencies present their proposals to the examiners who, in turn, make recommendations concerning agency budgets to the Director of the Budget. In the Director's review, in October and November, agency budgets are aligned as far as possible with the executive program and policy. The final stage is concluded, hopefully, by December 15, when the President reviews the budget and makes a final decision as to each proposal. Very frequently a careful examination of agency proposals proves the ceilings to have been too restrictive, and in the last stages of preparation the general contours of the budget must be altered to accommodate the realities of the situation. Up to late 1957, for example, the White House and the Bureau of the Budget were talking of a total expenditure figure of $70 billion for fiscal 1959. This would have been $2 billion less than was then estimated for fiscal 1958, in spite of successful orbiting of Soviet satellites and a developing recession. The figure actually put into the budget some two months later was not $70 billion, but $73.9 billion. By the beginning of fiscal 1959 (on July 1, 1958) expenditures for fiscal 1959 were being estimated at $78–$80 billion.

If the President's budget contains recommendations for new revenue legislation, these recommendations will have come to him from the Treasury or other advisers, members of Congress, or the public. By late in December the budget is "locked up" and sent to the printer, and about the middle of January it is presented through the budget message to the Congress.

Legislation of the Budget

Appropriations. Upon receipt of the President's budget by Congress, the expenditure proposals are sent to the Appropriations Committees of the Senate and House. There the budget requests for the various agencies are distributed among subcommittees for careful study. The subcommittees may conduct hearings, calling representatives of interested agencies to justify their requests. Eventually the appropriation bills are "reported out" of committee and are debated and voted on by the legislative bodies. When passed by both houses, frequently with differences ironed out in Conference Committee, they are sent to the President for signature, after which they become law. The time elapsing between presentation of the budget to Congress and signature of appropriation bills by the President depends upon the time required to get the bills through Congress. Since the budget is presented to the Congress in January and the appropriations are made for the fiscal year which begins July 1, the appropriations job is expected to be done in a period of just over five months. The result is that there is nearly always a rush to legislate appropriations in the last few hours before termination of the fiscal year, and not infrequently important agencies begin the new fiscal year without knowing how much money they will be allotted in the appropriation act.[3]

[3] Prior to passage of the Legislative Reorganization Act of 1946, the various appropriation bills originated in a dozen or so different committees in each legislative house. This Act created a single Appropriations Committee in each house, in the hope that centralization of responsibility would bring about both greater efficiency in legislative action and more sensible allocation of funds among the many functions of government. In practice, the change appears to have made little difference one way or the other. Subcommittees of the Appropriations Committee study and recommend individual appropriation bills, and the various subcommittees appear to operate about as independently of one another as did the various independent committees prior to 1946. The Appropriations Committee itself is so large that its deliberations are more like debates of the whole legislative house than deliberations of a working committee.

There is no formal acceptance or rejection by Congress of the President's budget as a whole. The degree of acceptance is indicated by comparison of the revenue and appropriation bills passed with the amounts recommended in the President's budget. In England the budget is presented by the Chancellor of the Exchequer, representing the Prime Minister's government. If an issue is made of the budget, the government stands or falls on the formal acceptance or rejection of the budget by the House of Commons.

Revenue Measures. The Constitution requires[4] that all bills for raising revenue originate in the House of Representatives, the principle being that measures of such importance to the welfare of citizens should be required to pass first that legislative body which is the largest and most representative of the people before it can proceed on its way toward becoming law. A revenue bill is first reported to the House of Representatives by its Committee on Ways and Means. If voted by the House, the bill goes to the Senate, where Finance Committee hearings may be conducted. A bill is then reported out to the Senate and is debated and possibly revised on the Senate floor. The Senate bill, possibly quite different from that passed by the House, is then put in shape by the Conference Committee, composed of members of both houses, for passage by both the Senate and the House of Representatives before it can be sent to the President for signature.

In our discussion of the course of the budget from preliminary estimates to final appropriations and revenue measures, we have perhaps overemphasized the formal aspects of budgeting. This has been done to counteract the too-common assumption that the sum of expenditures or revenues results in purely haphazard fashion from individual and unrelated acts of Congress. This is not the case. On the other hand, in the process of making appropriations there are many informal pressures brought to bear. Established governmental agencies recognize that effective working relations with the legislative branch pay off in appropriations. Specific requests for information from legislators are given early and devoted attention, cultivation of legislative leaders by executive agencies is part of their job, and favorable treatment of persons or groups with whom the agency has dealings will normally line up these groups in support of adequate appropriations. In this respect the new and unsophisticated agency may suffer because it has not learned how to win friends and influence legislators.

The Federal "Legislative Budget." The Legislative Reorganization Act of 1946 introduced into the federal fiscal picture a curious creature officially called a "legislative budget." It was not a true budget, for it prescribed only

[4] Article I, Section 7.

"the maximum amount to be appropriated for in such year," without recommendation of the component parts of the total. The Act required that by February 15 of each year (less than a month after the President's presentation of his budget to the Congress) a joint committee of the legislative houses was to set an over-all ceiling of expenditures for the year, and individual agency appropriations were to be fitted into this total.

It is to be noted that this "legislative budget" was not substituted for the traditional executive budget practice but was in addition to it, the ceiling to be determined after "giving due consideration to the budget recommendations of the President." The plan originated out of the perennial feeling of frustration by the Congress, the sum of whose individual appropriations seemed nearly always to be higher than individual members had hoped it would be. It was apparently believed that if appropriation activities could begin with establishment of an over-all ceiling, it would be easier for legislators to exercise self-control in their action on individual appropriation bills.[5]

Two weaknesses of the plan doomed it to complete failure. The first, and more significant, weakness was that it attempted the impossible in requiring the establishment of a total before there could be any real knowledge of the components of that total. Representatives of both political parties admitted on the first attempt to administer the plan that the ceiling could be only an "intelligent guess," and that they were being asked to "pick a figure out of the air." The second, and somewhat related, weakness was that the plan was politically embarrassing. An intrepid Congress which boldly established an expenditure ceiling which would be popular in an atmosphere permeated with the persistent desire for governmental economy would almost inevitably find at the end of the session that it had failed to respect its own ceiling. And if its ceiling were realistic the political opposition would be afforded an opportunity to charge wasteful intent. It was to be expected, therefore, that the majority party in the Congress would normally be hesitant to bind itself to any total figure picked "out of the air."[6]

[5] A proposed Senate amendment to the Reorganization Act would have "solved" the problem of fitting individual appropriations into the approved figure by keeping a cumulative total of legislated appropriations and ringing a gong when the ceiling had been reached. (*Cf.* John D. Morris, "New Budgeting System Undergoes First Test," *The New York Times*, March 2, 1947.) Presumably at that moment all appropriation activity would cease.

[6] This is less true, however, when the legislature is controlled by one political party and the Presidency by another, as was the case in 1947 when the "legislative budget" plan became effective. On that occasion the Congress used the budget ceiling as an instrument for producing the greatest possible political embarrassment to the President, promising to establish a ceiling far below the total recommended in the executive budget.

These weaknesses of the "legislative budget" ceiling plan caused its early abandonment. The first year, the two houses of Congress failed to agree on any figure and gave up any attempt to compromise their differences over a total which was by its very nature essentially meaningless. Subsequently an attempt was made to move the date for establishment of the ceiling late enough in the session to permit the determination of a realistic figure. But postponement of the date until appropriations were made clearly negated the purpose of the plan, for its purpose was to maintain a restraining hand on the Congress while appropriations were being legislated. More recently the plan has fallen into disuse by common consent.

The abortive federal "legislative budget" experience represents another in a long line of failures of "gadgets" designed to bolster or replace careful and intelligent legislative action on expenditures.[7]

The essence of expenditure budgeting is that the total of appropriations is derived as a sum of individual appropriations proper for the performance of desired functions. If the individual appropriations are reasonable, the total will be reasonable. But the federal "legislative budget" idea begins with a round-sum legislated total which "looks about right" and proceeds to force individual appropriations into that total. The committees which did preliminary work on establishment of the ceiling in 1947 claimed it to be but an "over-all objective" which imposed no strict compulsion upon the Congress. It appears that at best the plan would represent only a waste of Congressional time and effort; at worst it could place the budget in a strait jacket which vitiates the budgetary purpose of directing the expenditure of public funds toward realization of a maximum of national welfare. Since the Congress determines appropriations in any case, with the President's budget as a guide, it is difficult to see any real advantage in the "legislative budget" complication.

Problems of the Budget

The earlier pages of this chapter have shown the procedures in creation of the executive budget, and in its transformation into fiscal legislation by

[7] The House Committee on Appropriations in 1951 abandoned the "one package" system of appropriations it had adopted the year before. It had long been felt in some quarters that control over expenditures was weakened by the separate consideration of a dozen or so individual appropriation bills, and that combining all appropriations into one single "package" would somehow produce savings. In the one year of trial, savings had not made themselves apparent to a majority of the Committee. Further, no agency's appropriation could be legislated until the amounts for all agencies were determined. This not only kept all spending agencies on tenterhooks through a major part of the session, but the Senate was unhappy to have the huge package dumped in its lap late in the session.

the legislative branch of government. The budget system is set up to provide a maximum of thoughtful and purposeful control of receipt and expenditure operations. It presumes competence on the part of both governmental branches concerned with it. But the budget system, containing
flexibility and wide latitude for the exercise of competent judgment in fiscal
policy, allows equally wide latitude for the exercise of bias and incompe-
tence. If the principle of democracy in government is sound, then the concept of the budget as an instrument of democratic fiscal planning is sound.
It does not follow, however, that any particular budget practice is immune
from criticism, or that one type of budget practice is not superior to another.
In the following paragraphs, the more persistent problems relating to the
budget and some practices which are destructive of good budgeting are
briefly considered.

Measurement of Administrative Efficiency. There is little room for
disagreement on the proposition that whatever government does it should
do efficiently. This generally means that governmental functions should be
performed as cheaply as the standard of performance required will allow.
It does not mean that the amount paid to a direct-relief recipient must
exactly equal that amount which wards off starvation. But it does mean
that administratively the maximum possible amount of an appropriation for
relief should reach those whom it is intended to benefit, and the minimum
possible amount should be dissipated in administration or waste. Or, if
government is embarking upon a program of extraordinarily heavy spending in order to inject purchasing power into the economy, the funds should
be directed so as to have maximum impact. In this case efficiency would
imply that the maximum possible amount of the money used should find
its way to those points of impact, and not be wastefully lost en route.

Granted the objective of efficiency, how can the budgetary authorities or
the legislative authorities measure administrative efficiency? When governmental activities are as highly specialized and technical as they now are,
how can the President, the Budget Bureau, or the Congress measure the
degree of efficiency in administration of the various activities? In general,
the administrator of the activity, who presumably knows his activity better
than anyone else, is in the best strategic position to bring about efficiency.
And for the same reasons his position is most strategic for measuring efficiency, although his judgment may well be conditioned by the fact that
his agency is largely his creation and therefore he either cannot or will not
see its inefficiencies. If each administrator were to be given the final judgment on the efficiency and the requirements of his agency, the budget would
be constructed on the unamended original estimates of the spending de-

partments. This would in fact amount to complete renunciation of their responsibilities by the budgeting authorities.

Clearly it is imperative that the budget department or bureau be provided with competent and specialized personnel who become intimately acquainted with the operation of particular agencies. For instance, the budget department of a state government should have at least one budget examiner who is an expert in highway engineering and the administration of the highway department. He then becomes a specialist in the operations of that department without being a member of it. He can thus be an impartial and competent judge of efficiency in the expenditure of highway funds; he can recommend, through his chief, specific allocation of appropriations which will bring about desired changes in the department's expenditures. He must possess two qualifications for his job: intimate knowledge of the agency whose budget requirements he is to examine, and cordial independence of the chief of that agency. Such a competent and specialized examiner or officer is required for each of the larger spending agencies; it is both infeasible and less important that those agencies whose expenditures are small be examined to the same degree.

But it is equally important that the legislative branch of the government exercise competent judgment as to the degree of administrative efficiency. Such competence must reside in the appropriations committees or subcommittees. At the federal level the subcommittees on appropriations devote considerable energies to the judgment of administrative efficiency. Agency heads are constantly called upon in hearings to justify agency organization and practice, and legislators take particular pains to point out inefficiencies in administration. The power to withhold funds from agencies or from projects regarded as inefficient places the legislative branch in a peculiarly strategic position to force improvement. And it is customary for key members of appropriations subcommittees to become highly specialized in the operations of the agencies over whose appropriations they wield a great deal of power.

Difficulties with Budget Projections. By its very nature, a budget represents estimates of receipts and recommended payments during a future period. In the case of the federal government, the estimates appearing in the budget document which is presented in January are prepared shortly before its presentation, but apply to a period which will end some eighteen months later. Since the revenues of the federal government are derived largely from taxes on net personal and corporate income, and since net income is subject to quite marked change over rather short periods, revenue estimates are likely to prove incorrect by fairly wide margins. The same is true of expenditure estimates, though a major factor in expenditure variation from budget projections is Congressional action to spend more or less than recommended.

The figures given below indicate the variation in realized budget receipts, budget expenditures, and surplus or deficit, from the original estimates presented in the budget document for the particular fiscal year. Differences are measured in billions of dollars, negative $(-)$ figures representing lesser receipts or expenditures and lower surplus or higher deficit.

	1954	1955	1956	1957	1958	1959[8]
Budget receipts	— 4.0	—2.3	8.1	4.7	—4.5	— 7.4
Budget expenditures	—10.8	—1.0	3.9	3.6	.1	5.3
Surplus or deficit	5.8	—1.3	4.2	1.2	—4.6	—11.8

In general, it is evident that predictions of receipts have missed the mark by a greater margin than predictions of expenditures. This is due very largely to unrealized forecasts of business conditions, though to a much lesser extent it is due to errors in the projected effects of tax changes upon receipts in 1954 and 1955.

It would be easy to attribute variations in expenditures from budget predictions entirely to actions of the Congress in departing from executive budget recommendations. While this is a factor in the variation, it must be noted that some budget expenditures are open-ended, in the sense that Congressional policy has been established to make expenditures as recipients qualify to receive payments under existing legislation. Examples of this are agricultural price support programs, under which the government guarantees to purchase (actually, in the first instance, to make loans on) any part of a crop offered; and public assistance grants to the states, where the federal contribution depends upon the amounts of state expenditure. In the fiscal year 1959 it appears that about half of the difference between expenditures as estimated in January and as estimated in September, 1958, was due to inaccurate projections of expenditures under open-ended programs.

One could hardly object to changes occurring as a result of changed conditions; in fact, a rigid system would be clearly undesirable. But if the budget is to serve as an instrument of fiscal planning, it is obvious that incorrect projections make for unrealistic planning, and any improvements which could make projections more accurate would strengthen the budget as a planning instrument. Specific suggestions for improvement are difficult

[8]For the fiscal year 1959, the comparison is with midyear estimates rather than with final results.

to come by. It seems administratively impossible to bring the budget presentation closer in time to the period which it covers, because of the time required by the Congress in appropriation activity. But too often the budget figures are constructed for political effect—to reflect fiscal ideals rather than fiscal realities. If a balanced budget is the fiscal ideal, it is apparently safer politically to project a balanced budget and have things turn out differently than to seem to announce in the budget document a planned deficit.

Control of Annual Expenditures. Appropriation acts do not appropriate actual expenditures to be made during a particular year. Rather, what is appropriated is the authority to obligate funds for specified purposes during the period. The agency receiving the appropriation can then commit these funds and the Treasury will make payments when due. Most agencies operate from year to year on funds currently authorized by the legislative branch, i.e., it is expected that expenditures will equal appropriations during the year.[9] In some important cases, however, an agency is permitted to commit funds appropriated in one year over a period of years. This is done when an agency is carrying out programs of a continuing nature, contracting now for delivery at some future date as yet not definitely known. The agency must have obligational authority to cover the cost of contracts or agreements before they may be made, but payment will occur in some future fiscal year. Obligational authority will thus be provided in a given year sufficient to permit the agency to meet current expenditures and also to contract for future delivery of goods and services.

The federal budget document for 1958, for example, estimated actual payments during the year to be made from authorizations as follows:

From current authorizations	$40.4 billion
From permanent authorizations	7.6 ”
From appropriations to liquidate contract authorizations	.1 ”
From revolving and management funds	−.5 ”
From balances of prior authorizations	24.2 ”
Net budget expenditures	$71.8 billion

It will be noted that only about 55 per cent of budget expenditures during the fiscal year 1958 were expected to be made from ordinary appropriations provided in that year, i.e., "current authorizations." The "permanent authorizations" are appropriations automatically made in amounts required to cover certain expenditures over which the legislature

---

[9] Commitments to make payments may not exceed the amounts of obligational authority provided in the appropriation acts, though actual expenditures (payments by Treasury checks) will lag somewhat behind commitments. Thus, payments may be made in a particular year from appropriations—and commitments—made in a previous year.

has no choice; in fiscal 1958 almost all of the $7.6 billion of such authorizations was for interest on the public debt. "Appropriations to liquidate contract authorizations" represent a continuing need to carry out arrangements made in the past under a system no longer followed to any significant degree. In past years the Congress has granted agencies the authority to contract for future payment, with the understanding that when payment on these contracts comes due, current appropriations will be made in these amounts. "Revolving and management funds" have been set up for a number of agencies, with an original provision of funds from which advances can be made, and with the expectation that repayments will be made subsequently. In 1958 it was expected that repayments would exceed advances by about a half-billion dollars.

The important item in the table for our present purposes is expenditures "from balances of prior authorizations," i.e., appropriations of previous years, mainly for defense and foreign aid. The amount of such expenditures is seen to have represented about a third of total budget expenditures for the year. This situation reflects the need to undertake long-range programs, without knowing specifically at what times particular payments will be required.

At the same time, the Congress naturally feels that its control over expenditures in any particular period is limited when an agency has a backlog of obligational authority against which it can draw at will. Expenditures may rise during a period when legislative policy favors a reduction, because the agency is not heavily dependent upon current authorizations for its current expenditures. One recent proposal has been to terminate all appropriated authorizations at the end of each year, eliminating any carry-over. This would mean that the Congress would review yearly the status of all programs stretching over a period longer than a year, and appropriate for each year the amounts deemed necessary to continue the programs. This would be tantamount to appropriating annual expenditures rather than obligational authority, and would permit somewhat closer control over expenditures than is at present possible. On the other hand, the agencies involved feel that their freedom to project long-range programs would be severely restricted. This is of course true, in the sense that the legislative body could terminate a program before completion if it chose. Whether this closer year-by-year scrutiny of programs is desirable from an operational point of view would depend upon the wisdom of the Congress in making its annual appropriations.

General vs. Specific Appropriations. Reasonable compromise should be maintained in appropriation acts between general appropriations which allow freedom of the agency to allocate funds to specific projects, and appropriations which are so specific as to prevent adjustment to changing conditions. The principal argument for general appropriations runs in terms of the more advantageous position of the administrator than that of Congress for determining proper allocations of funds. The argument for specific appropriations calls attention to the fact that general appropriations inevitably grant a degree of legislative power to the administrator, and when carried to excess, largely vitiate the principles of budgeting. The proper type of appropriation lies somewhere between the two extremes, and conditions will determine whether it lies nearer the one or the other. However, normally the act should be at least specific enough to detail lump sums for salaries, travel, printing, supplies, equipment, and such general categories.

Much enthusiasm has appeared in recent years for a revision of the form in which the budget document is presented, to make of it what is known as a "performance budget." The items in such a budget would represent functions to be performed or activities to be undertaken by the agency in question, broken down in sufficient detail to be meaningful to the legislative branch and to the general public. There is a strong tendency to draw up budgets in the form and under the categories of past years; gradually this practice tends to combine activities in such a way and under such a title as to make the purpose of the proposed expenditure obscure. On the other hand, proposed expenditures for particular functions tend to become scattered through miscellaneous titles, which militates against intelligent direction of expenditures by the appropriating bodies.

Adoption of the practice of performance budgeting would not involve revolutionary change in present methods. By recasting the form of the budget document it would simply make more evident the purpose for which an appropriation is asked. Within such a classification by function, there would still be room for subclassification into such categories as personal services, materials and supplies, and capital outlays whenever such subclassification would encourage the intelligent allocation of funds.[10]

In time of war, appropriations for the military branches of government are made very general. A large part of such appropriations is to be spent approximately one year following the enactment of the appropriation law, and no Congress can possibly predict with much accuracy the directions which the war will take. The general staff may find one weapon wholly

[10] The case for a performance budget at the federal level was briefly stated and examples of the types of revision which would be involved were presented by the "Hoover Commission" in 1949. See *Budgeting and Accounting*, a Report to the Congress by the Commission on Organization of the Executive Branch of the Government, February, 1949, pp. 7–13 and Annex I.

unusable, because of change in location of the battlefield or the development of counterweapons by the enemy, while an entirely new weapon may promise such success as to warrant heavy production. In addition, for reasons of security, highly specific appropriations in public documents may be unwise. It would clearly have been unwise for Congress to have spelled out in specific detail the purposes for which funds were granted for missile development in recent years.

On the other hand, the specific appropriation has often been used by the legislative branch as a tool to limit the power of the chief executive or an executive agency. If agency regulations are believed to usurp legislative authority or to misinterpret the intent of Congress, specifications in that agency's appropriation act may bring it into line. Congressional fear of, lack of confidence in, or lack of cordiality toward the executive branch will be likely to lead Congress to spell out in greater detail the uses to which appropriated funds may or may not be put.[11]

Inadequate Veto Power. When both houses have passed a legislative act by at least simple majorities, the act is sent to the President for approval. If he approves, the act becomes law. If he exercises his veto power, the act is sent back to Congress, and may become law only when passed by two-thirds vote of both houses.[12] The President, however, may approve or veto only the whole act; he may not approve some sections and veto others. If an appropriation act contains undesirable provisions, he must weigh the undesirability of legalizing these provisions against the desirability of making the appropriation effective. If he vetoes the whole bill, Congress may pass it over his veto, and at the very least the appropriation bill is delayed. If he accepts the bill, he takes the bitter with the sweet. Particularly unfortunate is the "rider," a provision in a bill, usually unrelated to the bill itself and incapable of passage on its own merits, which hopes to

---

[11] Note, for instance, the following provisions of the Office of Price Administration Appropriation Act for the fiscal year 1945:

". . . No part of this appropriation shall be directly or indirectly used for the payment of the salary or expenses of any person who directs the formulation of any price policy, maximum price or ceiling . . . unless . . . such persons shall be qualified by experience in business, industry, or commerce . . ." (This provision was directed against "professors" in OPA.)

". . . none of the funds appropriated in this Act shall be used to pay the salary or expenses of any person fixing maximum prices for different kinds, classes or types of processed fruits and vegetables which are described in terms of specifications or standards, unless such specifications or standards were, prior to such order, in general use." (Directed against grade labeling.)
U. S. *Stat.*, 78th Congress, 2nd Session, Chapter 304, June 28, 1944, p. 601.

[12] Ignoring the pocket veto, in which case the President takes no action within ten days and Congress adjourns prior to the expiration of this period. In this case the bill is dead and remains so unless initiated anew at a later session.

"ride" through the Congress and the executive on the back of needed legislation.

Whatever the verdict on other grounds, presidential power to veto sections of bills while accepting other sections would help to improve the effectiveness of the budget. (The Constitution of the Confederate States of America, though in other respects almost identical with the Constitution of the United States, gave to the President the power of item veto.) This would strengthen the President's hand in seeing his budget through to fruition in legislation, and would seemingly not materially reduce legislative authority. Sections of bills vetoed by the chief executive could still be made law by passage over his veto. Thus Congress would still possess power to override objections by the President, but only when Congress is so sure of its desires that it passes the bill by a two-thirds vote in full view of the President's stated objections.

Supplementary or Deficiency Appropriations. A supplementary or deficiency appropriation is made subsequent to passage of a general appropriation for an agency. It is designed to provide funds for projects or activities for which inadequate funds to support a desired level of performance had been voted. When the budgeting agency effectively controls the commitment of funds by the agency—through quarterly or other allotments of appropriated funds—the request for a supplementary appropriation will usually meet with sympathetic Congressional action, provided the program continues to be acceptable. The supplementary appropriation practice can, however, be abused when an agency has simply programmed its expenditures improperly and can practice "sandbagging," by threatening to cut its expenditures in areas where the cuts will be most telling and unpopular, unless adequate appropriations are forthcoming.

There are other occasions in which unforeseen contingencies arise, requiring a higher rate of expenditure than had been planned. In such cases it is of the essence of good budgetary procedure that interim analysis, evaluation, and choice be substituted for strait-jacketed expenditure schedules. For this reason, in spite of opportunities for abuse, the deficiency appropriation is an essential feature of good financial operation.

In state governments, with biennial legislative sessions, appropriations are made for two-year periods. In such cases need for intersession provision of funds may frequently occur. But the principle is the same. Until executives and legislatures become omniscient, there will be a place for the deficiency appropriation. Since state legislatures are usually in session only for a short period during the biennium provided for in the budget, deficiencies and emergencies are normally provided for by one of two methods:

(1) allowing the governor or budget officer to approve emergency expenditures in excess of appropriations while the legislature is not in session, and (2) appropriation of a lump sum contingent fund to be administered by the governor and/or a commission of financial officers.

It is evident that, although provision for emergency appropriations is a necessary part of the budget system, loose and irresponsible use of them can threaten that system. If deficiency funds are appropriated to bail out agencies which have simply failed to live within their budgets for no reason other than prodigality or mismanagement, the budget has failed in its function. A loose, openhanded system of providing for deficiencies may well do more harm than good.

Allotment of Appropriated Funds. Most budget systems, federal and state, provide for quarterly, monthly, or other allotments of appropriated funds to the spending agencies. The primary reason is to maintain operations at a fairly stable, or appropriately seasonal, level throughout the budgeted period. It guards against expenditure at so rapid a rate at the beginning of the period as to stop activity of the agency toward the end or to bring the agency in for a deficiency appropriation. On the other hand, it discourages excessive, fear-inspired frugality during the early months of the period, followed by possibly wasteful expenditure at the end.

Allotments are generally administered by the budget department. Obviously, the schedule of allotments to the agency during the budgeted period should be tailored to the normal needs of the agency. A highway appropriation should not be alloted in equal monthly installments in latitudes where construction and repair of highways can be carried on during only a portion of the year; allotments should follow the seasonal curve of activity.

Dedication of Revenues to Special Funds. Probably the worst danger to good budget practice in state governments is the dedication of particular revenues to particular funds, from which particular activities are financed. By this system, income is channeled into any number of separate accounts, large and small, with little opportunity for transfer between accounts. The state treasury is thus not a single treasury, into which receipts are covered and from which payments are made according to a budgetary schedule of planned distribution. It is a miscellaneous group of more or less independent treasuries.

At the center is the general fund, which must support the general functions of government, largely support emergency expenditures, and stand ready to make up deficits in other funds. Next is the highway fund, supported by gasoline taxes, motor vehicle registration fees, operators' license fees, and miscellaneous receipts from automobile dealers' and repairers' fees. The highway fund supports the construction and maintenance of highways, possibly the state police, and the various motor vehicle regulatory activities.

Trailing off from the two largest funds mentioned above may be fifty or sixty special funds of various sizes, some so small that the activities they support may spend less than a thousand dollars per year. The larger of these funds will probably be dedicated to the financing of welfare activities, such as old-age assistance, and of state universities and colleges. The smaller may administer the examination of barbers, of hairdressers and cosmeticians, or of embalmers.

The system of financing by funds to which particular revenues are dedicated has grown up through pressure from two directions: from the federal government in connection with grants-in-aid, and from particular classes of tax- and fee-payers. In connection with its grants for highway construction, matched by the states, the federal government has exerted strong pressure upon the states to dedicate gasoline tax revenues to highway construction and maintenance. There appear, however, to be possibilities of changing this arrangement if the states really wanted to do something about it, although they would place themselves under severe opposition from automobile tax- and fee-payers.

Public campaigns, with signs, stickers, speakers, and literature against "diversion" of gasoline taxes and automobile fees from highway to general use, have been common throughout the country. They are inspired by business groups—automotive trades groups, gasoline dealers, automobile associations, etc.—which stand to gain from more and better highways, and their arguments make enough sense to gain the support of a large majority of citizens. As matters stand, the term "diversion" implies governmental stealing from motorists, and not, as it should, the appropriation of one of the states' richest sources of revenue for the particular benefit of the motorist class.[13] In one state the governor proposed in his budget message that several of the state boards examining the qualifications of potential entrants into various professions be merged, that examinations be set and judged by professional men but that administration be centered in one commissioner. The suggestion was quickly defeated, largely under the leadership of the state medical society, which publicly decried "political" interference in the determination of qualifications of doctors. Basically, the issue was

[13] It should be mentioned, however, that in many cases gasoline taxes and fees imposed upon motorists were originally legislated on the promise that their revenues would be used for highway purposes. In such cases the cry of "diversion" has a reasonable basis.

whether professional fees should be covered into the general fund and administered under the budget system.

The segregation and earmarking of special receipts for special purposes has the effect of removing from budget practice its real reason for being—the intelligent control of expenditures. In the case of agencies financed by earmarked receipts, appropriation is a mere formality; the agency has allocated to it the amounts which the earmarked revenues are expected to bring in. Transfer of money from one fund to another ("diversion") is normally very difficult. The general fund, which probably covers from one-third to one-half of the states' expenditures and which alone is subject to effective budget control, may be called upon to make up deficits in special funds, but seldom benefits by transfers of surpluses from these special funds. Some consequences of this system have been evident in many states since World War II. With the phenomenal growth in school population, public school facilities nearly everywhere have become grossly inadequate. In most states, state aid to local education must be provided out of the general funds, which have been so limited as to permit educational grants on a very inadequate scale. On the other hand, highway construction and maintenance have proceeded on a grand scale, comparatively speaking, because their dedicated revenues have greatly increased. This divergence of scales of public living with respect to public education and highways in recent years can hardly be explained in terms of the public's rational choice. It is largely the result of the abandonment of budgetary control of expenditures by creation of special funds with earmarked revenues—letting the size of particular tax revenues determine the scale of expenditures.

Financing by special funds leaves the legislature and the public pretty much in the dark as to the results of a particular year's fiscal activity. Has the government operated at a surplus or a deficit? One answer to this question can be had by determining the algebraic sum of surpluses and deficits of all funds. But once determined, what does it mean, when a surplus in one fund cannot be transferred to another? The tendency has been to measure surplus or deficit only with respect to the general fund, and to try to balance the receipts and expenditures of that fund. But this means that intelligent control applies to only a fraction of the state's fiscal operations.[14]

The nature of the solution to the problem is clear, though its obstacles

[14] The federal government has so far wisely avoided the compartmentation of its revenues, except in the cases of certain trust funds, the most important of which are social security tax receipts. One can only hope that this wisdom will persist, though a recent suggestion that royalties from federal off-shore oil resources be allocated to public education would constitute a serious break in the dike. The danger is, of course, that because the object of proposed expenditure is a popular one, the method of its provision will escape careful scrutiny.

in public opinion are equally clear. Everyone is in favor of effective budgeting in the abstract, and yet few favor abolition of a practice which makes
really effective budgeting impossible. Not all special funds could be eliminated. For special reasons the sinking fund—for retirement of debt—should
be segregated. Legal restrictions require that certain trust funds be segregated. And special functions such as old-age insurance and unemployment
compensation as now in force must be segregated from general functions
when collections are in the nature of premium payments to a dedicated
reserve fund. All other receipts should go to the general fund, and all other
payments be made from it. Only then can budget unity be approached.

The logical extension of dedication of gasoline taxes for highway construction, doctors' fees for the benefit of the medical profession, and hairdressers' fees for the benefit of hairdressers is the dedication of tobacco
taxes for the particular benefit of smokers, liquor taxes for the particular
benefit of drinkers, and property taxes for improvements to property. In
the final stages of such dedication, relief payments must cease because the
indigent cannot pay their way; the legislature, the courts, and the executive,
if they are to continue to exist at all, must produce services for a price. The
budget department can be dismissed, since "earmarking" has relieved it of
any duties.

When Is a Budget Balanced?

Balance An Accounting Concept. Much public discussion has centered
around "balancing the budget," but much disagreement is found—in full
view of the figures—as to whether a particular budget is balanced. The
"balance" of the budget is an accounting concept and requires some elemental understanding of the purpose and basic characteristics of government accounts.

The prime function of government accounts is to demonstrate to those
responsible for fiscal policy, and to the public, the results of past fiscal operations. Estimates for the future should be presented under the same accounting and reporting classifications. This implies that financial statements be
presented in an understandable form, and that the budgeting and accounting agencies exercise care that items are properly classified. Proper classification involves consistent recognition of the objective of accounting and
reporting—portrayal of the condition of the finances resulting from fiscal
operations.

A balance sheet approach, showing assets and liabilities of government,
is useless for this purpose. The principal liabilities of government would be
its oustanding debt, representing legal claims of others against the treasury.
The assets of government would certainly include its cash on hand, but

beyond this, assets have relatively little meaning. A value could be assigned to public buildings and government-owned equipment, but these "assets" do not exist for earning income and are not real assets in the customary sense of the term. They exist for government consumption, and can obviously not be used as offsets against debt liabilities to demonstrate the condition of the treasury. There may be those who would list the taxpaying capacity of the citizens as an asset of government. The valuation of this "asset" would be arbitrary and meaningless for any useful purpose in accounting. Since government is essentially a service agency and not a producing business, the balance sheet can produce no useful information.

But it is important to know the relation of income to outgo during a given period. This relation will show whether fiscal policy has resulted in surplus or deficit; it will indicate the direction in which the treasury is moving. This is the kind of fact which is needed in the charting of future fiscal policy.

Definitions of Basic Concepts. The condition of the treasury is improved when net receipts exceed net expenditures over a period of time. The basic categories of income and expenditure may be defined as follows:

1. *Revenue receipts are receipts which increase the usable funds of the treasury without increasing its debt obligations; or which reduce its debt obligations without reducing its usable funds.* They improve the net condition of the treasury.

2. *Cost payments are payments which reduce the usable funds of the treasury without reducing its debt obligations.* They worsen the net condition of the treasury.

3. *Non-revenue receipts are receipts which increase the usable funds of the treasury, but increase correspondingly the debt obligations.* They are receipts which have no net effect upon the condition of the treasury.

4. *Non-cost payments are payments which reduce the usable funds of the treasury, but reduce correspondingly the debt obligations.* They are payments which have no net effect upon the condition of the treasury.

Most items of revenue receipts are covered in the first clause of definition (1) above. The second clause of the definition is included for completeness to take care of taxes which are paid to the treasury by turning in treasury securities.[15] Revenue receipts include practically all receipts except

---

[15] Treasury Tax Series Notes were first sold in 1941. They were acceptable by the Treasury in payment of income, gift, and death taxes, accomplishing two purposes: (1) they provided securities in which taxpayers could invest funds accumulated for tax payments at interest, and (2) they made funds available to the Treasury prior to tax date. Cf. *Annual Report of the Secretary of the Treasury*, 1943, p. 55. Government bonds have regularly been acceptable in payment of federal death taxes.

those borrowed through the sale of treasury securities, and amounts which come into the treasury for special trust funds—such as retirement and insurance funds—and must be immediately transferred to those funds. The exceptions mentioned in the previous sentence are non-revenue receipts.

Cost payments include practically all payments except those used for retirement of debt and transfers to special trust funds such as those mentioned in the paragraph immediately above. It is to be noted that interest paid on the public debt is a cost payment, while payments of the principal of the public debt are non-cost payments. This follows from the definitions.

Receipts are classified as revenue or non-revenue solely on the basis of their effect upon the treasury's net condition. Those which increase treasury funds without equally increasing obligations are revenue receipts; the others are non-revenue receipts. Likewise, payments are classed as cost or non-cost solely on the basis of their effect upon the treasury's net condition. Those which reduce treasury funds without equally reducing obligations are cost payments; the others are non-cost payments. The source of funds received or paid is not to be considered; only the effect on the treasury's condition is significant. Thus, funds raised from income taxes (revenue receipts) may be used for debt repayment (non-cost payments), while borrowed funds (non-revenue receipts) may be used for purchase of office supplies (cost payments).

If the concepts above are properly understood, the question "When is a budget balanced?" can be correctly answered by the following propositions:

A budget is balanced if during the budget period revenue receipts are exactly equal to cost payments.

If revenue receipts for the budget period are greater than cost payments, the difference is budget surplus.

If revenue receipts for the budget period are less than cost payments, the difference is budget deficit.

Two general types of non-revenue receipts have been mentioned: receipts from borrowing and receipts for the account of special trust funds. From a common sense point of view the latter cannot enter into determination of surplus, deficit, or budget balance because the treasury never had real title to them and they therefore did not increase the usable funds of the treasury. The former were necessary *because of* a budget deficit, and thus do not enter into determination of that deficit. Similarly, two general types of non-cost payments have been mentioned: repayment of debt and transfers to special trust funds. The latter cannot enter into determination of surplus or deficit because their transfer cannot worsen the condition of a treasury which never had real title to them. They were from the start dedicated to trust funds and thus were never usable funds. Net repayment of debt[16] becomes possible *because of* a treasury surplus; it cannot enter into determination of surplus or deficit.

It should be quite apparent that nothing is to be learned with respect to budget balance by comparing total receipts (revenue plus non-revenue receipts) with total payments (cost plus non-cost payments). Except for minor time adjustments, such a comparison would always show the budget in balance, no matter how large the true surplus or deficit. And to the extent that any non-revenue receipts or non-cost payments are allowed to creep into surplus or deficit determination, the picture of surplus or deficit will be distorted and incorrect.

Multiple Budgets

The function of the budget is to make fiscal control and planning possible. This being the case, the more comprehensive the budget, the more it brings into one unified picture past fiscal performance and future fiscal plans, the better it will perform its function of control. From time to time suggestions have been made recommending that more than one budget be prepared, presenting in each the facts and recommendations concerning the financing of specialized functions. Two of these are described and considered briefly below.

Ordinary and Emergency Budgets. In periods of war, depression, and similar emergencies when the pattern of receipts and expenditures is inevitably greatly altered, it has been recommended that two budgets be prepared. The ordinary budget would present the budget for functions which are relatively permanent and are therefore "ordinary" functions. The emergency budget would present data for functions of an emergency character and therefore presumably of short duration.

In 1933 the federal government of the United States began the practice of segregating in its budget summaries the "general" and "emergency" expenditures.[17] The administration was charged with "trickery" in such segregation so as to hide the extent of "wasteful" expenditures. The "trickery"

---

[16] If, as is not uncommon, a treasury is required by law to retire some debt each year, particular debt securities may be retired in years when a deficit is incurred. The same thing occurs when debt matures in a year of deficit and thus must be replaced by new borrowing. In these cases the treasury borrows new funds to pay off old loans, and to the extent this is done there is no "net repayment of debt." It uses non-revenue receipts to make non-cost payments.

[17] See J. W. Sundelson, *Budgetary Methods in National and State Governments* (Special Report of the New York State Tax Commission, No. 14, Albany, 1938) for excellent material on extraordinary and crisis budgets. (Chapters 13 and 14.)

supposedly lay in the transfer of certain expenditures of long standing into the emergency category. Whatever the truth, and Sundelson appears to absolve the government of any intent to deceive,[18] this separation of items into separate categories did not create two budgets and was thus not a true example of multiple budgeting. It was a separation within the budget summaries and financial reports of the "ordinary" and "emergency" expenditures, for whatever value such separation might have in understanding fiscal policy. All expenditures were budgeted as usual, and all were handled in the single comprehensive budget.

It is impossible to see any real advantage to double—or multiple—budgeting in emergencies. Whatever advantages there are in the segregation of usual and unusual expenditures can be accomplished as well by summarizing the items in a single, comprehensive budget in such a way as to point out the unusual character of certain expenditures. The disadvantages are several. Multiple budgets of this type may result in applying the normal drives for efficiency, which the budget is supposed to implement, only to the ordinary budget. They create an atmosphere of suspicion of the motives of the budgeting authority which is likely to give rise to intra-governmental ill will and waste of time and effort. Furthermore, multiple budgets tend to obscure the true results of fiscal operations by scattering the results among several documents. The Agent General for Reparations described the German multiple budget system in 1927 as follows:

The budgets are presented in a manner that makes it quite impossible, even for well-informed readers, to follow them without exhaustive study and analysis. The budget as a whole contains many transfers from one budget to another; all of which tend to create confusion and to complicate the accounting.[19]

Ordinary and Capital Budgets. It has often been recommended that governments set up, in addition to ordinary operating budgets of current receipts and expenditures, capital budgets. The capital budget would include capital expenditures for important items of public construction and for publicly owned commercial enterprises. It will be noted, however, that, strictly speaking, a public building is more in the nature of a durable consumers' good than a capital item.

The general theory of segregating activities in the nature of public construction in a separate budget runs in terms of the nonrecurring nature of such expenditures. Being extraordinary expenditures, normally financed by borrowing, it is regarded as unfair that they should be allowed to produce

---

[18] *Ibid.*, pp. 180 *ff*.

[19] Quoted in Hugh Dalton and others, *Unbalanced Budgets, A Study of the Financial Crises in Fifteen Countries,* London, Routledge, 1934, p. 23.

a deficit in the general budget. Inherent in this view is the feeling that the thing that counts is whether the ordinary budget is balanced. If the ordinary budget is balanced, borrowing to finance public works becomes somehow easier to take. This view exalts the significance of a "balanced budget" and ignores the simple fact that the budget is the fiscal plan. If, therefore, public works expenditures are desirable, they should be planned through the general budget, even though a general budget deficit is thereby created. It is difficult to see how anything of real value is to be gained by the segregation of "capital" items into separate budgets. There is the usual danger, however, that segregation will divert attention from these extraordinary expenditures, and that those concerned with general fiscal planning (including the public) will be lulled into a comfortable somnolence by the calming fact of a balanced "ordinary" budget.

The same conclusions can be drawn with respect to creation of special capital budgets for government-owned commercial enterprises, such as light and water systems. There is, of course, reason for separate accounting within the agency itself, to show the detailed relations of receipts and expenditures, and the results of operation with respect to general policy as to whether the enterprise shall operate at cost, at a surplus, or at a deficit. Its revenues are, however, public revenues and its expenditures public expenditures. And provided the items are properly identifiable in the general budget, the receipts and expenditures of public enterprises should be subject to the same type and degree of planning as are any other receipts and payments.

Other Agencies of Fiscal Administration

The budget being the central planning and control instrument in fiscal administration, it is proper that it be given major attention in a study of fiscal agencies. There are, however, other agencies participating in fiscal operations, though their participation is more at the routine administrative level and less at the general policy-determining level.

The Treasury. The functions of the Treasury Department are primarily those of receiving, paying, accounting for, and safekeeping government funds. In governments at lower levels the functions of a treasury hardly extend beyond these essentially mechanical and bookkeeping functions. But in major governments such as the federal government of the United States, the Treasury is required to engage in extensive research, policy-proposing, and policy-determining functions. The Treasury is the major advisory agency to the President in matters of taxation policy, and the Secretary of the Treasury, along with the Director of the Bureau of the Budget and the Chairman of the Council of Economic Advisers, carries great authority in advising on matters of general fiscal policy.

The tax-collecting function requires a large administrative structure, not only to take in and account for revenues, but also to design administrative regulations interpreting the law, to promote compliance with the law and regulations, and to adjudicate disagreements at the administrative level. The borrowing of funds in the market—to replace securities maturing even when net new borrowing is unnecessary—requires an expert knowledge and a fine feeling for the operation of the monetary and capital markets. Only thus can large borrowing take place most favorably for the government and with a minimum of dislocation to the economy or to whatever monetary policy is being pursued.

Payments by the United States Treasury are made according to the following routine: Appropriations having been made by Congress, the Treasury notifies the spending agency of the amount of its appropriation. The agency then submits a schedule of allotments of this appropriation through the year to the Bureau of the Budget. When approved, the agency may incur obligations for a given period only to the extent of its allotment for that period. These obligations, before payment, must be approved by the Comptroller General (see below). When so approved, payment can be made by a Treasury disbursing officer, by drawing checks against the government's balance in Federal Reserve Banks.

The Comptroller. In the previous paragraph it was stated that payment must be approved by the comptroller before a check can be drawn. The principal function of the comptroller is to make certain that the expenditure conforms to the purpose for which the appropriation was made. He thus has a quasi-judicial function of interpreting the intent of appropriation acts. Because of this judicial element in his function the Comptroller General of the United States is appointed by the President for a term of fifteen years, making him, once appointed, independent of the chief executive. In state governments the officer performing the comptroller's functions is usually elected for a term equal in length to that of the governor.

Since the comptroller is presumably independent of the executive departments, his office usually performs the function of accounting control among the various agencies, maintains the basic government accounts, and audits the accounts of financial officers and agencies. In our federal government the General Accounting Office is under the administrative authority of the Comptroller General.

The Banks.[20] Although the banks are not government agencies, they perform necessary functions for the Treasury. The Federal Reserve Banks hold the active deposits of the Treasury.[21] They therefore receive moneys collected by the Treasury and pay checks drawn by the Treasury. In connection with the public debt, the Federal Reserve Banks receive applications from banks, dealers, and others, for new issues of government securities, and allot securities among these buyers according to Treasury instructions. The proceeds of sales are credited to the Treasury's deposit accounts. In addition the Reserve Banks redeem government securities, pay coupon interest, and perform other similar services. It should be realized, of course, that the Federal Reserve Banks perform these functions to a considerable extent through the member banks. The contacts which the Federal Reserve Banks have with the money markets make them valuable advisers of the Treasury in determination of the terms of issue of government securities.

[20] See Federal Reserve Board, *The Federal Reserve System, Its Purposes and Functions,* Washington, 1939, pp. 35–36.

[21] Prior to World War II the Federal Reserve Banks maintained the major part of Treasury deposit accounts. During the war the proceeds of major bond drives were maintained temporarily on deposit in commercial banks, and since the war the Treasury has continued to hold substantial deposits resulting from bond sales and tax collections in commercial banks. The Treasury draws checks, however, only against its deposits with the Federal Reserve Banks, and its balance in those banks is maintained by rather frequent transfer of deposits to them from the commercial banks. Treasury deposits with commercial banks are further discussed *infra.,* Chapter 8.

Alternative Measurements of Fiscal Operations: the Conventional Budget, the Cash Budget, and the National Income Accounts

In the text of this chapter we have used the term "budget" as if it were a single, standard, clearly defined set of accounts of the receipts and expenditures of government. The fact is, however, that since receipts, expenditures, and surplus figures may be utilized for different kinds of analyses, there exists some variety in the presentation of fiscal facts. One might be interested simply in comparing receipts or expenditures or surplus in any year, as they are conventionally set up in the budget document, with the same classifications in other years. Or one might be concerned with a more inclusive magnitude of financial transactions of the Treasury and other government agencies with the nongovernmental public. Or, finally, one may be interested in the size of employment and business activity generated directly by governmental demand. Measures to reflect all of these are now in rather wide use, and the purpose of this appendix is to point out some of the technical distinctions among them and to suggest the uses to which each may be put.

I. THE "CONVENTIONAL BUDGET"

The "conventional" or "administrative" budget of the United States is the one with which our chapter has dealt. Usually when the term "budget" is used, it is to this conventional budget that reference is made. It is the subject of the annual budget message of the President, and its estimates of receipts, authorizations, and expenditures are itemized and classified in great detail. But while the conventional budget contains the bulk of receipts of the government and payments by and through the government, the list is a conventional one, developed through long practice and amended only infrequently as the Congress changes the method of financing a given activity.

The conventional method of financing programs is to levy taxes which are paid into the general fund of the Treasury, and to make payments out of this general fund. The conventional budget thus represents a set of accounts established within the framework of those programs which are financed in this conventional manner. These accounts exclude receipts and payments managed through trust funds, to which certain receipts are earmarked for special purposes and thus are not regarded as general funds of the Treasury, and from which payments are made for these specified purposes. But though these are governmental receipts and payments, they are not technically "budget" receipts and payments, simply because they are not handled through the conventional budget. Obviously, the comparability of budget figures over a period of years is adversely affected when the Congress creates a trust fund to handle receipts and expenditures which had formerly been handled in the conventional manner through the budget. A significant recent case of this occurred in 1956, when Congress created the Highway Trust Fund, to receive certain excise taxes and make grants to states for highway construction which had formerly been items in the conventional budget.

The central criticisms of the conventional budget are therefore that its accounts are incomplete as a reflection of total financial activity of the government and its agencies, and that the (fairly infrequent) exclusion or inclusion of items makes year-to-year comparisons inaccurate.

II. THE "CASH BUDGET"

The "cash budget," more precisely named "Cash Receipts From and Payments to the Public,"[22] is designed to rectify the major omissions of the conventional budget. The intention is twofold: to combine budget and trust fund receipts and payments into a single statement, and to adjust these receipts and payments to a basis reflecting true cash transactions between the government and the public. Thus, for any fiscal year, the statement of receipts from and payments to the public provides a more accurate picture of the role of the federal government in the flow of funds in the economy; it portrays more accurately than the conventional budget

[22] These schedules are published annually by the Bureau of the Budget as a special analysis in the budget document, and monthly by the Treasury Department in the *Treasury Bulletin*.

figures can the drawing of funds from the economy and the payment of funds into the economy.[23]

The chart below shows the comparative behavior of conventional and cash budget surplus and deficit for the years 1953–1959. It is evident from

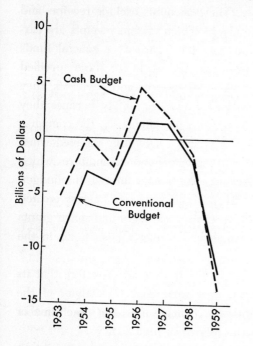

Comparison of conventional and cash-budget surplus and deficit, 1953-1959.

the chart that, during the period covered, items included in the cash budget but excluded from the conventional budget have almost always made for larger cash surpluses than conventional budget surpluses, and smaller cash deficits than conventional budget deficits. In general, the reason for this is that trust funds in the aggregate have produced surpluses. It is more important to note that the spread between cash and conventional surplus or deficit is a variable one, explainable only by careful investigation of the components involved.

To observe the major technical differences between the conventional and the cash budgets, let us look at the figures for the fiscal years 1953–1959,

[23] A still more complete picture could be given by using gross instead of net figures in the cash budget. For example the cash budget (like the conventional budget) includes a net rather than a gross figure for postal operations. When postal expenditures exceed receipts, the net difference is listed as an expenditure; in the opposite case a negative net expenditure is entered, both in the conventional and cash budgets. There are other items included also on a net basis only. The schedules thus do not give a uniformly gross picture of receipts and payments. The reason for this is that users of the cash budget figures are normally interested in cash surplus or deficit in any case.

which underlie the chart above. Recalling that we are interested in a
statement which will as nearly as possible indicate federal cash receipts

FEDERAL RECEIPTS FROM AND PAYMENTS TO THE PUBLIC, 1953–1959[a]
(Fiscal years, in $ billions)

	1953	1954	1955	1956	1957	1958	1959
Receipts							
Conventional budget receipts	64.8	64.7	60.4	68.2	71.0	69.1	68.3
Trust fund receipts	8.9	9.2	9.5	11.7	14.4	16.6	17.1
Less: Intragovernmental transactions	2.2	2.1	2.1	2.7	3.2	3.7	3.7
Receipts from exercise of monetary authority	.6	.7	.3	.2	*	.1	*
TOTAL RECEIPTS	71.5	71.6	67.8	77.1	82.1	87.3	81.7
Payments							
Conventional budget expenditures	74.3	67.8	64.6	66.5	69.4	71.9	80.7
Trust fund expenditures	5.3	7.2	8.5	9.4	13.0	16.4	18.6
Government-sponsored enterprise expenditures (net)	–.1	–.4	.1	.3	*	.3	1.3
Less: Intragovernmental transactions	2.2	2.1	2.1	2.7	3.2	3.7	3.7
Accrued interest and other non-cash expenditures	.5	.6	.6	.9	–.8	.5	2.1
TOTAL PAYMENTS	76.8	71.9	70.5	72.6	80.0	83.3	94.1
Excess of cash receipts (+) or payments (−)	–5.3	–.2	–2.7	4.5	2.1	–1.5	–13.1

[a] From budget documents.
* Less than $50 million.

from and payments to the public during a specified period of time (in this
case the fiscal year July 1 through the following June 30), we begin with
conventional budget receipts and expenditures as reported, each constituting
the largest item in the cash receipts or payments category. There must be
additions to the conventional budget figures, to give a more complete
accounting of cash flows, and certain adjustments to the conventional figures must be made to convert them to a pure cash basis. We may consider
these under three headings, and the discussion will refer back to the table
frequently.

1. Additional items to be included in the accounts. Two classes of
governmental receipts and payments are added to those presented in the
conventional budget. The first is the trust funds, of which the various "social
security" funds and the Highway Trust Fund are the largest. In addition,
there are the receipts and payments of "government-sponsored enterprises,"
such as the Federal Deposit Insurance Corporation and the Federal Home
Loan Banks, whose net payments only are entered in the payments category. (If the aggregate of these enterprises shows net receipts, the net
amount is entered as a negative payment.)

2. Elimination of intragovernmental transactions. There are many transactions between and within government accounts which obviously do not
involve the public either as payor or payee. For example, the Treasury pays
interest to the Unemployment Trust Fund on Treasury securities held by
that Fund. The amounts of these transactions are deducted both from cash
receipts and cash payments to the public. It should be evident that intra-
governmental receipts and intragovernmental payments must be equal.

3. Adjustments to a cash basis. It is the practice in the budget to include
seigniorage profit—the difference between the commodity value and the
monetary value of gold and silver—as a budget receipt, and to include
interest accrued but not paid on Savings Bonds and Treasury Bills as budget expenditures. The former is not a cash receipt from the public, nor is
the latter a cash payment to the public. Therefore, "receipts from exercise
of monetary authority" are deducted from reported budget receipts and
"accrued interest" is deducted from payments.

Included in "other non-cash expenditures" deducted from payments are
several elusive items for which adjustments must be made in order to
arrive at a pure cash figure. At times the government has made payments
in securities rather than in cash, as in the case of the United States subscription to the capital of the International Monetary Fund and the issuance of
Armed Forces Leave Bonds after World War II. These are counted as
budget expenditures when issued, but are not cash expenditures. On the
other hand, when these securities are redeemed for cash—as in the case
of the redemption of International Monetary Fund Notes in 1957—there is
a cash payment not accounted for in budget expenditures, and the payment
is entered as a negative non-cash payment, or an addition to other payments. Finally, there is some time lag between the issuance of Treasury
checks and their clearance. If clearing accounts for checks and interest
coupons outstanding are higher at the end of this year than at the end of
last year, it shows that actual cash payments are not as great during the
year as budget and other expenditure accounts indicate. To adjust expenditures to a genuine cash basis, therefore, any increase in clearing accounts
must be deducted from recorded expenditures, and any reduction in clearing accounts added to recorded expenditures.

The "excess of cash receipts from or payments to the public" is in many
respects a more meaningful figure than that of conventional budget surplus
or deficit. It reflects the difference during a period of time between total
withdrawals of cash from the public and total replacements of cash to the
public. It thus forms a basis for analysis of the economic effects of govern-

ment's financial operations which conventional budget surplus and deficit cannot do as well. It also forms a basis for analysis of the factors affecting the true cash position of the Treasury.

III. GOVERNMENT RECEIPTS AND EXPENDITURES IN THE NATIONAL INCOME ACCOUNTS

In addition to the usual fiscal reports of the Treasury and the Bureau of the Budget, governmental receipts and expenditures appear in the national income accounts. Here the concern is for measurement of the effects of governmental action upon the demand for goods and services in the economy, and this concern imposes certain modifications upon the usual budgetary or cash data.

In the gross national product statistics, "Government Purchases of Goods and Services" represent only direct purchases by governments and their agencies for currently produced goods and services. Thus, while federal budget expenditures in the fiscal year 1957 were $69.4 billion, and cash payments to the public were $80 billion, federal government purchases of goods and services in the GNP accounts for the same period were $49.3 billion. The difference is accounted for principally upon two grounds. The first is that budget or cash expenditures for land and assets not produced during the particular year are eliminated from the GNP accounts. The second, and more important, difference is that a fairly large fraction of budget or cash expenditures is broadly in the nature of transfer payments rather than direct purchases of goods and services. In cases such as the making of grants or loans to state governments, interest payments to holders of the public debt, loans to farmers by the Commodity Credit Corporation, purchase of mortgages by the housing agencies, and benefit payments to veterans or to beneficiaries of Social Security, the federal government is not the direct purchaser of goods and services but rather a transferor of funds to others.

On the receipts side there are somewhat similar differences. Federal receipts in the budget or cash accounts will include some receipts in the form of transfer payments, such as interest or profits on investments and loans, and some receipts from the sale of property not currently produced. The national income accounts exclude such receipts. Also, the national income accounts measure government tax receipts on the basis of accrued tax liabilities rather than on the basis of cash collections. In general, then, the national income accounts differ from budget and cash accounts in that the first intend to measure the direct demand by government for currently produced goods and services, and allocations from current national income to government, primarily through accrued taxes.[24]

RECOMMENDED READINGS

The budget:

The Budget of the United States, Annual, Washington, Government Printing Office.

The Budget Message will give some feel for the fiscal policies underlying a particular budget, and will summarize the intentions of the administration. A perusal of the summary tables section gives a notion of the variety of federal activities involved. The special analyses give helpful interpretations and regroupings.

Hansen, A. H., *Fiscal Policy and Business Cycles,* N.Y., Norton, 1941, Chapter 10.

Probably the best available short treatment of the subject. Discusses the literature on budget theory and multiple budgets, and introduces the generally recent approach to budget theory.

Smithies, Arthur, *The Budgetary Process in the United States,* N.Y., McGraw-Hill, 1955, Chapters 1 and 2.

The chapters cited provide a general discussion of budget purposes and procedures, and constitute a minimal use of this large and important study. The reader can profitably read much more extensively, particularly in Parts Two and Three.

Sundelson, J. W., "Aspects of Budgetary Procedure," in Groves, H. M., *Viewpoints on Public Finance,* N.Y., Holt, 1947, pp. 661–68.

A short discussion of comprehensiveness of the budget.

Fiscal management:

Bartelt, E. F., *Accounting Procedures of the United States Government,* Chicago, Public Administration Service, 1940.

Much detail concerning the mechanics of handling governmental funds. Chapters to be used should be selected in terms of the subject or agency of interest.

Smead, E. L., "Operations of the Reserve Banks," in *Banking Studies,* Washington, Board of Governors of the Federal Reserve System, 1941, pp. 260–65.

Discussion of fiscal agency, custodianship, and depository functions of the Reserve Banks for the Treasury. Most textbooks on money and banking will contain sections dealing with the relations between the banks and the Treasury.

---

[24] A table showing reconciliation of federal receipts and expenditures in the national income accounts with federal cash receipts and payments to the public and conventional budget receipts and expenditures is presented in Appendix Table F-54 of the 1958 *Economic Report of the President.* Perusal of this table is recommended for those who wish a more precise demonstration of differences.

CHAPTER 3

Public Expenditures:
Trends and Their Significance

EXPENDITURE TRENDS

Adolph Wagner, a German economist of the latter part of the nineteenth century, presented his famous "law of the increase of state activities" in these terms:[1]

Comprehensive comparisons of different countries and different times show that, among progressive peoples, with which alone we are concerned, an increase regularly takes place in the activity of both the central and the local governments. This increase is both extensive and intensive: the central and local governments constantly undertake new functions, while they perform both old and new functions more efficiently and completely. In this way the economic needs of the people, to an increasing extent and in a more satisfactory fashion, are satisfied by the central and local governments.

The statistics of expenditures throughout modern times demonstrate such persistent increase as to justify Wagner's statement of this fact as a "law." Nitti,[2] after careful study of expenditures in various countries as far back as acceptable statistics exist, concluded that centralized and decentralized governments, warlike and peaceful nations, large and small nations, show essentially similar tendencies toward marked increase, particularly during the nineteenth century. Had Nitti been able to include the first

[1] *Grundlegung der politischen Oekonomie*, Bk. VI, Chapter 3 (3rd ed., 1893), quoted in translation in C. J. Bullock, *Selected Readings in Public Finance*, 3rd ed., New York, Ginn, 1924, p. 32.

[2] F. S. Nitti, *Principi di scienza delle finanze*, 1903, pp. 64–100. Translated by C. J. Bullock and included in *ibid.*, p. 32 ff.

48

half of the twentieth century in his study, he could have shown not only a continuation but an acceleration of expenditure growth.

The figures in Table 1 show something of the growth of federal, state, and local expenditures in the United States for selected years since 1913.

TABLE 1

EXPENDITURES OF FEDERAL, STATE, AND LOCAL GOVERNMENTS, U. S., SELECTED
YEARS 1902–1958
(*in millions of dollars*)

Year	Federal[a]	State[b]	Local[b]	Total
1902	485	177	823	1,485
1913	724	372	1,670	1,766
1922	3,373	1,217	3,866	8,456
1927	2,974	1,818	5,215	10,007
1932	4,659	2,498	4,989	12,146
1936	8,493	2,550	3,775	14,818
1940	9,062	3,659	4,482	17,203
1944	95,059	3,528	4,327	102,914
1948	33,069	7,750	7,997	51,816
1952	65,408	11,213	12,163	88,784
1954	67,772	12,904	14,660	95,336
1956	66,540	15,292	17,493	99,325
1958	71,936	19,095	21,287	112,328

[a] Federal figures are net budget expenditures, taken from *Annual Report of the Secretary of the Treasury*, 1956, and from U. S. Treasury, *Final Report of the Receipts and Expenditures of the United States Government for the Fiscal Year 1958*. Grants to other governments are included; trust fund expenditures and debt retirements are excluded.

[b] State and local expenditures are taken from U. S. Department of Commerce, Bureau of the Census, *Historical Statistics on State and Local Government Finances, 1902–1953*, and from *Summary of Governmental Finances, 1954, 1956*, and *1958*. For each level of government, two types of deductions are made from total expenditures: expenditures of liquor stores, utilities, and insurance trusts; and receipts from other levels of government. The first are deducted as self-liquidating business-type expenditures. The second deduction allocates the expenditure to the level of government providing the funds rather than to the level of government making the ultimate disbursement.

It may be argued that the period covered in Table 1 is a period of abnormal government expenditure, that in the space of fifty-six years it includes World War I, the period of protracted depression of the thirties, World War II, and the marked inflation of the postwar years. That it is a period of emergencies of one sort and another may be granted; the assumption that these conditions were abnormal is not so easily granted. It is devoutly to be hoped that war will prove to have been an abnormal characteristic of the first half of the twentieth century. But war does not directly affect the expenditures of state and local governments, which have demonstrated the common upward trend during this period. And the governmental activities which appeared during the period 1929–1936 only accelerated a trend previously evident. These new activities have become so generally accepted as proper in the governmental sphere that it is quite unrealistic to expect significant reduction in the future.

Table 1 shows that federal expenditures have been most responsive to war and threats of war. During the period covered by the table, peaks of federal expenditure were reached in 1919 ($18.5 billion) and in 1945 ($98.4 billion). In 1928 they had fallen back to the post-World-War-I low of $3 billion, but expenditures were still over four times as high as they had been in 1916, on the eve of our entry into the war. The post-World-War-II low level of expenditures was in 1948 ($33 billion), a figure just under four times that in 1939. The cold war had brought federal budget expenditures up to $71.9 billion in the fiscal year 1958.

Part of the explanation of the fact that expenditures do not fall to their prewar level with the return of peace lies in the permanent price inflation that accompanies war. Another factor is the interest cost on the public debt, which in our experience has always risen very markedly during war periods. One should note also the inevitable provision of benefits for war veterans and their dependents, arising both from the generosity of an appreciative public and the effectiveness of the veterans' lobbies. But in addition there is the more complex fact of a more elaborate scale of governmental activities emerging from the war. Economic maladjustments caused by the war may justify heavy expenditures for the readjustment of agricultural production or for aid to other nations. Wartime changes in military techniques will almost surely mean continued high military expenditures in spite of substantial disarmament. And the easy spending of the war period (both public and private) will probably bring on a new crop of programs for social and economic betterment. It is thus quite unrealistic to expect that the level of expenditure will not be permanently jacked up by war.

Another fact observable in Table 1 is the marked increase in state and local expenditures during the period. Again, a part of this is attributable to increase in the price level. But aside from this factor, the state and local governments are not significantly affected by war. The increase of expenditures of such governments is accounted for largely by an increase in the standard of governmental living—the provision by governments for "the . . . needs of the people, to an increasing extent and in a more satisfactory fashion . . .," to use Wagner's words. Extension of the scope of government, as we shall see below, is one of the marked tendencies of modern times.

A clearer picture of the field of governmental activities can be gained if Table 1 is presented in real per capita terms, to correct for both price level changes and population growth. Also, the extent to which increases in the scope of government services take place at the expense of former or potential services of the private economy can be roughly shown by relating government expenditures to gross national product. Such a relationship would indicate in a general way whether expansion of governmental functions has kept pace with the increase in the national living standard. These three adjustments of figures in Table 1 are presented in Table 2.[3]

TABLE 2

EXPENDITURES OF ALL GOVERNMENTS IN THE UNITED STATES IN CURRENT AND CONSTANT DOLLARS; PER CAPITA EXPENDITURES; AND TOTAL EXPENDITURES IN CURRENT DOLLARS AS PER CENT OF GROSS NATIONAL PRODUCT

Year	1[a] Total Expenditures, Millions of Current Dollars	2[b] Total Expenditures, Millions of Constant Dollars	3[c] Per Capita Expenditures in Constant Dollars	4[d] Expenditures As Per Cent of Gross National Product
1902	1,485	3,877	48.85	
1913	2,766	6,093	63.13	
1922	8,456	13,467	122.57	12.4
1927	10,007	16,140	136.55	11.2
1932	12,146	23,266	186.32	20.8
1936	14,818	25,398	198.34	17.9
1940	17,203	29,623	224.47	17.9
1944	102,914	135,503	981.32	50.7
1948	51,816	47,923	326.83	21.1
1952	88,784	73,316	466.89	26.3
1954	95,336	76,978	473.95	26.5
1956	99,325	73,587	437.77	24.8
1958	112,328	77,090	442.88	25.0

[a] From Table 1.

[b] Total expenditures, 1902–1927, deflated by B.L.S. index of wholesale prices (1947–1949 = 100). From 1932 on the relevant implicit price deflators of the Department of Commerce (1947 = 100) were applied separately to federal and to state and local expenditures, and the adjusted figures combined to form the total.

[c] Total expenditures in Column 2 divided by population estimates as of July 1.

[d] Expenditures of Column 1 calculated as per cent of gross national product. Quarterly figures were used to determine GNP on a fiscal year basis, to correspond with fiscal year expenditures figures, from 1940 on. Prior to 1940, in the absence of quarterly GNP figures, calendar figures were used. After 1927, Department of Commerce GNP figures were used. GNP for 1922 and 1927 from Simon Kuznets, *National Product Since 1869*, National Bureau of Economic Research, 1946, p. 51. Comparable GNP figures before 1922 are not available.

[3] The reasons why the relation of government expenditures to the size of national income can at best be only a very rough measure of the governmental standard of living relative to the private standard of living will be clearly apparent after studying Chapters 4 and 5. For the present we may say that to the extent government expenditure *creates* national income the relation has a significance not of concern to us in this chapter. Thus, if an increase of 100 per cent in government spending causes an increase of 5 per cent in the national income, the ratios do have an important special significance. In this chapter, however, we are primarily concerned not with the causal aspects of government spending but with the reflection by them of the public's judgment of the direct benefits in utilities to be derived from governmental services.

Column 2 of Table 2 translates total government expenditures for the selected years into constant dollars. Thus, in 1913, governments would have spent for the same scale of activities $6,093 million instead of $2,766 million if they had been required to pay prices equal to those existing in 1947–1949. This translation of expenditures into "real" terms portrays an upward trend both more moderate and more nearly regular than that shown in the unadjusted expenditure statistics. It is well to keep in mind the significance of changes in the value of money when present expenditure levels are compared with those of earlier periods.

Column 3 of Table 2, in addition to eliminating the effects of price change as discussed in the paragraph above, eliminates the direct influence of population increase upon expenditures. A marked increase of real per capita expenditures is demonstrated even in the "normal" decade of the twenties. Reference back to Table 1 will show that this increase was accounted for by all levels of government. The rate of population growth between 1930 and 1940 was less than half that of the previous decade. Thus, adjustment to a per capita basis accentuates the greatly increased real expenditures of the thirties. When figures of total expenditures are adjusted both for price change and for population change, the post-World-War-II figures are rather surprisingly small. Per capita real expenditures, though they show some increase since the war, have increased considerably less markedly than the average reader might expect.

Calculation of the relation between government expenditures and gross national product will show something of the growing significance in the whole economy of government financial operations. In addition it gives a rough indication of the rate of increase in the standard of governmental living in relation to the rate of increase of the general living standard. In this sense it measures the change in the scale of government service with respect to change in the public's potential general scale of want satisfaction. Column 4 of Table 2 shows a small decrease in the per cent of government expenditures to GNP between 1922 and 1927; this ratio is almost doubled in 1932, followed by a slight decline in World War II. The moderate decrease in ratio between 1932 and 1940 indicates that national income was rising slightly more rapidly than were dollar expenditures. The very high proportion of GNP going to government in 1944 is but a demonstration of an inevitable situation in wartime. In that year half of the gross national product represented government purchase of goods and services. After World War II, as we observe in the column 4 figures for 1948, the relation of governmental expenditures to GNP settled down to just slightly over the prewar figure. The phenomenal increase in GNP during the decade of the forties permitted a remarkable increase in governmental expenditures without a significant rise in the proportion of expenditures to national income. One must be cautious in generalizing or in drawing hasty conclusions from the figures in column 4. National income relates to the nation as a whole and expenditures are those of government as a whole. The figures do not relate the income of particular individuals or groups to government expenditures on or services to the same individuals or groups. Nor is the income of individuals or groups related to taxes paid by or governmental borrowing from those individuals or groups. Conclusions with respect to specific benefit or specific cost to economic classes are therefore unwarranted from column 4.

Refinements of raw figures of total expenditures point to the following conclusions:

1. When figures of expenditure are adjusted for changes in the price level, real expenditures during the decade of the nineteen-twenties reveal a less marked increase over the pre-World-War-I years, while real increase during the decade of the nineteen-thirties is greater than is apparent from the raw figures.

2. Per capita real expenditures have moved in the same direction as have total real expenditures, the growth of population having been insufficient to adjust real expenditures downward during any period of significant duration.

3. The share of the GNP represented by government expenditures has shown upward tendencies through the period, even under peaceful conditions, while in war the share of income devoted to governmental purposes is gigantic.

The scale of governmental performance has expanded—as Wagner remarks—both intensively and extensively. Government has carried on certain functions throughout modern times, while new functions—out of choice or necessity—are added from time to time. The former, however, increase in coverage and quality to keep pace with the requirements of a society whose institutions change and whose standards rise. We shall discuss separately the intensive and the extensive expansion of functions.

Intensive Expansion of Governmental Functions

Three governmental responsibilities of long standing are: provision of military protection against aggression, construction and maintenance of roads and highways, and provision of public education. These three functions to an outstanding degree account for the increase of public expenditures over a period of time. Although defense, highways, and education in their modern forms are so different from the same functions a century ago as to make them scarcely recognizable as the same functions, they are government's response to the demands for better performance of traditional functions.

Defense Expenditures. The cost of defense—all of those costs related to war—has increased phenomenally through history. It includes not only outlays for men, materials, and maintenance during and between wars, but also pensions and contributions to veterans, and interest on that part of the public debt contracted for war purposes. It should embrace also those non-military expenditures involved in control of and assistance to the civilian economy in wartime.

The progress of the military arts and sciences has been so rapid that the machines of war have become extremely expensive to purchase and the rate of obsolescence extremely high. Acceptance of the obligation by government to care for men and their families injured by war, and to provide benefits in the form of bonuses, education, and rehabilitation, has enormously increased the government costs attributable to war.

Few would deny that the maintenance of an adequate defense of the nation against aggression is a primary function of government. As indicated by the preamble to the Constitution, one reason for establishing a federal government was to "provide for the common defense." But "defense" in the modern sense recognizes the necessity of carrying even a defensive war beyond our own boundaries—meeting the enemy as far as possible from our own shores. Thus an adequate defense system implies very large, mobile military forces with great striking power and well-equipped advance bases. An indication of the growing costliness of war in money spent is given in Table 3 below.

TABLE 3

Cost of Principal American Wars
(in millions of dollars)

Revolution (1775–1783)[a]	$ 113.6
War of 1812 (1812–1815)[b]	99.8
Civil War (1861–1879)[c]	6,190.0
Spanish-American War (1898–1901)[d]	275.0
World War I (31 months ended October 31, 1919)[e]	32,830.0
World War II (1940–1946)[f]	345,885.0

[a] From Shultz and Caine, *Financial Development of the United States*, N. Y. Prentice-Hall, 1937, pp. 46, 47.

[b] From D. R. Dewey, *Financial History of the United States*, 12th edition, N. Y.,

Longmans, 1934, p. 141. Figure includes War, Navy, and those interest payments in excess of expenditures for interest in 1812.

ᶜ Dewey, *op. cit.*, p. 329.

ᵈ Dewey, *op. cit.*, p. 467. Includes only the excess of War and Navy expenditures, 1898–1901, over those of 1894–1897.

ᵉ *Annual Report of the Secretary of the Treasury, 1919,* p. 26.

ᶠ *Ibid.*, 1946, p. 400. An approximate figure representing total "War Activities" expenditures, veterans' expenditures annually in excess of those in 1940, and interest payments annually in excess of those in 1940.

The figures presented above do not include expenditures for military preparation between wars. Nor do they, except to a degree in the Civil War figures, include postwar expenditures which are in the nature of "aftermath of war" items. Notable among these postwar payments are mustering-out payments, bonus payments, and pensions. This has been a large and growing item as the nation has moved from one war to the next. "All-out" war has greatly increased the number of military personnel to whom such payments are made, and the trend has been toward more and more ample payments of these types, at both federal and state levels. Table 3 shows expenditures for World War I through October, 1919, to have been approximately 33 billion dollars. The estimated total of expenditures on World War I after payment of adjusted service compensation and other "aftermath" expenditures is 45 billion dollars.[4]

The National Industrial Conference Board calculates that between 1789 and 1920, 78.9 per cent of total federal expenditures were made for war.[5] It is evident, therefore, that elimination of war offers by far the greatest possibilities for reducing federal expenditures. Curiously enough, the hardheaded "economy minded" legislators have attacked "bureaucracy" and the size of the civilian payroll of government, but have been very little concerned with programs for the promotion of peace. It is the "idealists" who have worked for peace against the tradition that war expenditure is inevitable.

Highways. Since World War I the development of the automobile has both demanded and benefited from the advance in mileage and quality of highways. The development of superhighways and systems of through highways has been most spectacular, though improvement of rural roads, construction of cut-off highways to avoid residential and business areas, and elimination of grade crossings are important aspects of road development. Greater physical impact upon highways by vehicles of increased weight and speed has required heavier construction of new roads, and more frequent

[4] See Alfred G. Buehler, *Public Finance*, New York, McGraw-Hill, 1936, p. 53.

[5] National Industrial Conference Board, *Tax Burdens and Public Expenditures*, New York, 1925, p. 4.

repair or abandonment of old and inadequate surfaces. Multiplication in numbers of vehicles using the highways, requiring wider surfaces, has added to the cost of construction.

The highway function is performed by state and local governments with considerable assistance from the federal government. In 1919 total expenditures of state and local governments for highway purposes amounted to 390 million dollars.[6] By 1921 they had increased to approximately one billion dollars, and in 1930 to 1.9 billion dollars. In 1937, with state and local treasuries severely strained, the expenditure remained at approximately the 1930 level (1.8 billion dollars).[7] The tasks of highway and road construction and maintenance have led to large grants from the federal to the state governments, and from state to local governments. The federal government has made its grants to states under conditions which require certain standards of construction and maintenance. Pressure from the federal government has consistently supported the policy of dedicating motor vehicle revenues to highway expenditure. Federal grants until 1930 had required that they be matched dollar for dollar by state funds. In 1930, since states were having difficulty in qualifying for federal highway grants because of inability to match available federal funds, the federal government began advancing funds to states chargeable against future grants, with which the states could match current federal grants. If the policy had been carried out as planned, highway work would have been drastically curtailed in later years when the states would have been required to meet all highway expenses from their own funds. In 1934, therefore, Congress released the states from the necessity of paying back these advances, and the effect was to create outright gifts from the federal government unmatched by the states.[8] This was entirely in line with the federal policy of public works for depression relief and business recovery during the thirties.

The World War II period greatly reduced expenditures on highways, both because of reduced need during the rationing period and because of the unavailability of materials and labor for construction. The states thus emerged from the war with a backlog of needed highway construction and repair, and large highway fund surpluses accumulated during the war. However, these highway fund surpluses were quickly eaten away by the urgency of the need for highway modernization and by the rapid rise in highway construction and maintenance costs. By the end of the decade

[6] Henry J. Bittermann, *State and Federal Grants-in-aid*, New York, Mentzer, Bush, 1938, p. 98.

[7] Alvin H. Hansen, *Fiscal Policy & Business Cycles*, New York, Norton, 1941, p. 123.

[8] Bittermann, *op. cit.*, p. 99.

of the forties the states and local governments were again scraping for additional revenues to meet highway expenditures. The highway funds normally are nonetheless among those most richly supported, owing to fairly generous federal grants and to the dedication of motor vehicle revenues to highway purposes.

Highway expenditures for selected years since World War II are shown in Table 4. In the table, expenditures are allocated to a particular level of government which makes the actual expenditure—i.e., highway grants to a government at another level are counted as direct expenditure of the latter.

TABLE 4

DIRECT EXPENDITURES OF GOVERNMENTS FOR HIGHWAYS,
1946, 1950, 1956, 1958*

(fiscal years, in $ millions)

	1946	1950	1956	1958
Federal	21	59	82	135
State	613	3,803	4,367	5,507
Local	1,059	2,058	2,586	3,187
TOTAL	1,693	5,920	7,035	8,829

* From Bureau of the Census, *Statistical Abstract of the United States*, 1951, *Historical Statistics on State and Local Government Finances, 1902–1953*, and *Summary of Governmental Finances in 1956* and *in 1958*.

Federal participation in highway construction was greatly expanded under the Highway Act of 1956. By this act a new national system of highways was established—the Interstate and Defense Highways—in whose construction the older pattern of equal matching of federal grants by the states was abandoned and the federal share of construction costs was raised to 90 per cent. The federal aid program under this act is to be handled through a special Highway Trust Fund, into which taxes on motor fuels, tires, and heavy vehicles will be channeled and from which highway grants to the states will be made. The plan contemplates the addition of some 2,300 miles of major connected highways to the interstate system, at a cost of some $28 billion over a thirteen-year period, while continuing the older program of substantial grants to the states on a fifty-fifty basis for other highways. While some part of the expenditures under the new program would have been made by the states in any case, the Act of 1956 promises substantial increases in highway outlays over what otherwise would have occurred. It seems probable that highway expenditures by all governments will exceed the $10 billion mark by 1960.

Education. Public education at the primary and secondary level has been, in practice, a function of local government, while higher public education has been essentially a state function. However, great disparities in financial resources among local governments have required insistence upon consolidation of schools and standardization of the quality of public education performed by those governments. Improvement and standardization have occurred largely through state control, and have given rise to large educational grants from the states to their local governments. The inadequate productivity of the property tax (the local government revenue mainstay) has necessitated state aid, and in some states substitution of other taxes for the property tax has led to the institution of state taxes shared with local governments.[9]

TABLE 5

DIRECT STATE AND LOCAL EXPENDITURES FOR EDUCATION, SELECTED YEARS[*]

| | State | | Local | |
Year	$ Million	% of Total State Expenditures	$ Million	% of Total Local Expenditures
1913	55	18.5	522	21.6
1927	218	15.0	2,017	31.7
1938	347	16.9	2,144	30.8
1948	1,081	13.7	4,298	32.9
1952	1,494	13.8	6,824	34.0
1956	2,138	17.3	11,082	45.4
1957	2,459	17.8	12,042	45.2
1958	2,873	18.4	12,909	43.8

[*] From Bureau of the Census, *Historical Statistics on State and Local Finances, 1902–1953, Summary of Governmental Finances in 1957,* and . . . *in 1958.* It should be emphasized that the expenditure is assigned to the level of government making the educational payment, not necessarily to the level of government furnishing the funds. For example, in 1956, local governments spent $3.5 billion granted to them by state governments. If assignment were made by governments providing the funds, the amounts and shares of state governments would be substantially increased in recent years, and those of local governments decreased.

While remarkable increase in direct expenditures over the period is shown for both levels of government, several observations are in order

[9] Federal aid to public education should not be completely ignored, for it is of growing importance. In the original federal cession of land to the states fairly large blocks were earmarked for schools. Subsequently, grants of land and money were made for the creation of "land grant colleges." In addition funds have been given by the federal government under various acts for the promotion of agricultural and mechanical education. During the thirties substantial amounts were spent by the National Youth Administration to help pay school and college expenses of needy students, and these NYA payments were quite generally made for performance of work for schools. In the post-World-War-II period federal payments to war veterans to support them in school, college, and job training are enormous, and of benefit to schools as well as to veterans. The postwar predicament of public education, due to rising costs and inadequate personnel, promises to result in federal programs providing substantial direct aid to local education.

which are not clearly evident in the table. Only direct expenditures are shown in the above figures; the local educational costs borne by the states through grants to local governments appear in the expenditures of the latter, though the amounts of these grants have been substantial and growing, reaching $4.5 billion in 1958. Great public interest in schools has been consistently evident, for obvious reasons, and educational lobbies have been among the most vigorous in states and cities. At the same time, the federal government has persistently avoided major participation in the educational function, limiting itself to special programs such as agricultural education, education payments under the "GI Bill," grants to local schools in areas feeling heavy impact of federal activities, and loans and grants for college housing, research, and the like.

In the early and middle nineteen-thirties there was an actual decline in education expenditures by state and local governments. There are several explanations for this: (1) The sad state of the finances, particularly of local governments, brought about rather naturally a significant decrease in expenditures on the very large item of education. (2) Federal funds were not made available for education, except work relief funds for construction of school buildings, and the states and localities were forced to depend upon their own inadequate revenue resources. (3) Educational expenditures are normally made from general revenues. In contrast to highway funds, with large and stable earmarked revenues, school expenditures came from those general funds which during the thirties were required to meet many extraordinary expenditures without being able to tap new revenue sources. (4) The depression philosophy of balancing the "ordinary" budget while the "emergency" budget was allowed to go far out of balance is probably a factor in the situation here discussed. School expenditures are a part of the long-run, ordinary expenditures. As revenues fell and need for emergency expenditures arose, the tendency was generally to pare ordinary expenditures to meet falling revenues and to borrow only for emergencies. Important as the emergency functions were, it is evident that the equally important educational function was not given equal treatment.

As a further observation, attention is called to the startling increase in state expenditures for education since World War II. The three conditions which have created this situation have been so widely experienced throughout the nation that they need be only mentioned here. The first is the rise in prices and salaries since 1945. The second is the accumulated deficit in school buildings and facilities, which were hardly adequate before the war and of which shortages of materials prevented normal additions and replacements during the war. The third is the enormous increase in the birth rate during the war years, which not only increased the size of school population, but significantly changed its composition. The number of persons 5–17 years of age increased by almost a million between 1946 and 1950.

The impact of this increase fell at first entirely upon the elementary schools, for high-school population during this period continued to fall, reflecting the low birth rates of the thirties. By the late nineteen-fifties, however, these children had reached high-school age, requiring rapid expansion of facilities there while pressure upon the capacity of the elementary schools continued to increase. Population shifts produced differential impacts upon different localities, though few localities escaped the need for expanded facilities. Continuance of high birth rates since the war suggests for the foreseeable future a continuance of expansion in educational outlays.

Urbanization. A general cause of expenditure increase which possesses aspects of both intensive and extensive expansion of functions is the concentration of population in urban centers. Urbanization has increased per capita expenditures of local (and other) governments for the administration of traditional functions as these functions are related to a more concentrated population. For example, it becomes impossible with population concentration to continue performance of police, street, or public education functions on the simple scale. If the police function is to be performed acceptably, a highly specialized and expanded department is required. The function of public education becomes specialized, with technical schools, experimental schools, and the like. Relatively more and better streets are required, traffic control becomes imperative, repair is likely to be more frequent.

The conditions of urban life impose additional requirements upon government. Where people are crowded together, new functions must be undertaken. Considerations of public health and welfare force themselves upon local government. Inspection of food and the conditions of its distribution, investigation and programs for the promotion of public health, construction and maintenance of hospitals, clinical services to the underprivileged, playgrounds and organized recreation, and adult education are examples of public response to the needs of urban living.

It is possible to show by statistics the effect of urbanization upon per capita local expenditures, as will be seen in Table 6 below.

TABLE 6

PER CAPITA GENERAL EXPENDITURES OF CITIES OF VARIOUS SIZE, 1956*

Population Group	Number of Cities	Per Capita General Expenditures
1,000,000 or more	5	$148.21
500,000–1,000,000	13	122.69
250,000–500,000	23	96.74
100,000–250,000	65	96.53
50,000–100,000	126	89.16
25,000–50,000	649	84.70
Under 25,000	16,297	45.98

* From U. S. Bureau of the Census, *Compendium of City Government Finances in 1956*. Some caution should be exercised in attributing particular significance to the low level of per capita expenditure of the under–25,000 group of cities. The figures are subject to some sampling error, but more important, local functions—particularly education—are more likely in the case of these municipalities to be carried on by separate and more or less autonomous special districts.

A word of caution is in order lest the cynical temptation be indulged to ascribe to "graft," "corruption," and "inefficiency" the increase in per capita expenditures as local governments progress in size. The real explanation doubtless runs in terms of more elaborate performance of "primary" functions and the necessity for provision of a wider range of services. There are many services which the larger municipality can perform for the citizen, and in the absence of performance by government the citizen would be required to perform them himself, probably less satisfactorily and at greater cost. Without doubt public water supply, sewage systems, public libraries, public health services, and the like not only accomplish their objectives better, but at less social cost than would alternative individual attempts at self-sufficiency. There is undoubtedly greater opportunity for corruption and inefficiency as government becomes less personal and involves the handling of larger amounts of funds. On the other hand, these very characteristics of larger local governments make feasible the employment of experts in government. They also justify and recommend the institution of standards and programs for the selection of civil servants. Those scandals involving corruption in municipal government which make the news have generally occurred in the larger municipalities. The total funds involved, however, though in some cases large, are generally small in relation to total expenditures. In the matter of efficiency, it would be difficult to demonstrate that waste is proportionately less in small than in large municipalities.

Extensive Expansion of Governmental Functions

The rising standard of living in the public economy has more than kept pace with the increase in gross national product, as indicated in column 4 of Table 2. Governments at all levels tend to do more and more for their citizens. Since the citizens have requested—or at least acquiesced in—performance of these added functions and generally higher standards of performance, we may judge that the scale of wants for public goods and services has increased more rapidly than the scale of wants for privately produced goods and services. To take a simple case, those who pay gasoline taxes are in effect choosing highways in preference to other goods which they might buy in the market place with the same money. The choice is, of course, not entirely a clear and precise choice between highways and chewing gum. But neither are the alternatives in the choices which consumers constantly make in the allocation of their incomes among various goods clearly presented to them. Buyers' choices constantly involve selection among alternatives which are complex. The payer of a gasoline tax buys highways along with his gasoline, the buyer of a house buys fire protection through his property taxes, the buyer of theft insurance may be forced by standardized policies to buy incidental coverage which he does not particularly desire, or the buyer of a ticket to a good movie pays also for a "co-feature." Purchases are commonly "tied in" with one another, partly because of the complementary nature of goods. Thus, even though choices may not be simple, the majority of the public have accepted the growing scale of governmental activities, and in so doing they have exercised essentially the same talents for judgment which they regularly exercise in the market place.

Depression-Born Functions. The decade of the nineteen-thirties was the period of major additions to the list of accepted functions of government. The severe and prolonged economic depression was the catalytic agent in this marked expansion, both by demonstrating the need for government intervention and by bringing liberal governments into power at federal, state, and local levels. New responsibilities were accepted in these three principal areas:

> Encouragements to industry, agriculture, and labor
> Extensions of controls over the economy
> Promotion of public welfare

Very general encouragements to particular segments of the economy had been begun prior to the decade of the thirties by establishment of the Departments of Commerce, Agriculture, and Labor. Informational services of a statistical or technical nature had long been performed. Aside from such general services, the developmental function had been largely confined to the questionable policies of tariff protection and, in the case of agriculture, export subsidies and grants of land and money to agricultural colleges.

Examples of the encouragement measures adopted during the thirties abound in each of the fields of industry, agriculture, and labor. The National Industrial Recovery Act granted to industry authority to engage in essentially monopolistic practices to "save the market," in return for industry promises to increase wages and employment. The easing of credit by the banking system was hoped to be effective in easing panic conditions in the capital markets. Reconstruction Finance Corporation loans to banks, insurance companies, railroads, and other industrial concerns were designed to loosen the deflationary grip on business. The public works programs significantly aided the construction industries, as did the various housing programs. The various agricultural acts to ease the farm credit situation, to improve prices by organized crop reduction, and to reduce soil erosion were designed to mitigate or cure short- or long-run difficulties. In the field of labor, the National Labor Relations Act had as its purpose the promotion and strengthening of collective bargaining. Government employment services, unemployment compensation, and old-age and survivor annuities were instituted for the particular benefit of labor, with indirect benefit to industry.

The regulatory or control functions of government prior to the depression in the early thirties were largely noneconomic. The police and justice functions centered around the protection of broad and basic social rights. In the economic sphere government regulation embraced the fields of railroad and public utility rates and practices, pure food and drug administration, food inspection, and relatively ineffectual attempts to prevent and destroy monopolies. During the depression the regulatory function expanded greatly. In fact the expansion entered so many fields and proceeded so rapidly that questions were raised in the minds of many whether government depression policy aimed at recovery or reform. The power of employers in their dealings with labor was greatly curbed, new issues of corporate securities became strictly regulated, steps were taken to remove the commercial banks to a respectable distance from the security markets, interstate motor vehicle transportation rates were brought under Interstate Commerce Commission control, regulation of common carriers by water engaged in foreign commerce was established, the Federal Communications Commission was given authority to regulate interstate and foreign commerce in communications by wire and radio, and federal regulation was instituted over electric utilities engaged in interstate commerce.[10]

In general the extension of the regulatory function proceeded from a broad definition of exploitation. Wherever economic power was utilized contrary to the public interest or detrimental to the welfare of classes or groups, government was constrained to enter the field to establish rules of conduct. The record is not entirely consistent, but during the period of economic upheaval government developed a vigorous economic conscience.

Regulatory functions are relatively inexpensive functions. They may involve large expansion of administrative personnel, but do not involve large outlays on materials or grants of money. It may be noted in passing that a not inconsiderable portion of the cost of regulation is borne by the concern being regulated.[11] The promotional or developmental functions normally require greater outlays in the form of loans, benefit payments, and purchases. In the third field of recent expansion—promotion of public welfare —money grants or public works are almost inevitable, and these functions are therefore normally highly expensive in terms of the number of persons directly assisted.

The field of public welfare embraces provision for groups or classes who are considered underprivileged in some respect. This condition may be due to a normally low income level, to inadequate education or training, to temporary unemployment, or to termination of earning power due to age, physical injury or handicap, or inadequate prior provision for economic independence. Prior to 1933 the welfare function had been performed almost entirely by state and local governments. Their activities had traditionally included provision of recreational facilities, workmen's compensation plans, and relief for a few indigent aged persons in "old folks' homes." When unemployment became critical in 1931, state and local governments made unprecedentedly large payments for direct relief of the unemployed. But the marked increase in relief expenditures during the early thirties, coupled with a severe decline in state and local revenues, so seriously threatened the financial stability of local governments in particular that a large portion of these expenditures was taken over by the federal government, either by

[10] Price control, rationing, priorities, and allocation represent the most thoroughgoing economic controls of all. They must not be ignored, although they are "war-born" and not "depression-born" controls such as are being discussed in this section.

[11] These costs to the concern fall into two categories: (1) the administrative costs of legal services, accounting and reporting, and general compliance, and (2) the additional costs which may result from accomplishment of the regulatory objective, such as reduction of profits resulting from public utility rate regulation.

the establishment of direct federal programs or by federal grants to assist the states in the performance of functions. However, federal welfare activities went far beyond the provision of temporary relief, and many long-range social security projects were instituted. Some of the permanent welfare programs, such as old-age annuities and unemployment compensation, are supported by "premium" payments during the employed period. Others, in the nature of assistance grants, place the beneficiaries in the position of being in effect wards of the state, and their benefits are paid out of funds raised by general taxation.

The principal social welfare programs which arose during the thirties fall into two general classes: (1) those temporary relief projects designed to meet the minimum requirements of unemployed and needy persons until jobs became available in the private economy, and (2) those long-range programs of the Social Security Act of 1935, in which government-administered insurance plans or outright assistance grants to special groups were established.

Relief Programs. Payments under those welfare programs which were designed to provide relief to needy persons and families, sometimes as outright grants and sometimes as wages from public employment, are listed in Table 7 below for the years 1933-1939.

TABLE 7

Relief Payments and Earnings of Persons Employed Under Federal Work Programs (Excluding Social Security) 1933–1939*

(in thousands)

Type of Program	Total Payments
General Relief (1933–39)	$6,382,259
Farm Security Administration (Subsistence) (1935–39)	100,437
Civilian Conservation Corps (1933–39)	1,733,528
National Youth Administration (1935–39)	253,834
Works Projects Administration (1935–39)	6,332,222
Other Federal Work & Construction Projects (1933–39)	3,021,219

* Source: Social Security Board, *Trends in Public Assistance, 1933–1939,* Washington, 1940, p. 3.

The figures represent payments by all governments participating; they include state and local as well as federal expenditures. All figures exclude payments for administration, materials, and equipment.

The item, "General Relief," in Table 7 represents contributions by government to the needy under various programs at various governmental levels. These payments were in general made to individuals according to need, and thus were direct relief payments as distinguished from work relief payments. The same is true of subsistence payments certified by the Farm Security Administration. All other items in the table are in the nature of work relief projects, in which payment to recipients was based upon wage rates and hours of work roughly adjusted to need. The last item, "Other Federal Work and Construction Projects," is largely the activities of the Public Works Administration, which undertook projects of public construction distinguishable from the work relief projects of WPA.

Under the various titles of the Social Security Act of 1935, the following long-range welfare programs were instituted:

> Old-age and survivors' annuities
> Unemployment compensation
> Old-age assistance
> Aid to dependent children
> Aid to the blind

The first two of these are supported by special taxes. The old-age and survivors' annuity program is administered by the federal government and benefits are paid from reserves built up by taxes collected from employers and employees. Unemployment compensation is administered by the states, and benefits are paid from reserves created by taxes on employers. The last three are public assistance programs, which are administered by the states with funds furnished by the states and the federal government. In each of these programs the federal government contributes approximately one-half of the administrative costs. Maximum monthly benefit payments toward which the federal government contributes are $50 per recipient in old-age assistance, $50 per recipient in aid to the blind, and in aid to dependent children $27 for the first child and $18 each for additional children in the same family. The proportion of federal contribution within each of these maxima is slightly over 50 per cent (75 per cent to a minimum figure and 50 per cent beyond).

Table 8 below indicates the amounts of benefits paid out under the five social security programs listed above. It should be noted that old-age and survivors' insurance and unemployment compensation did not begin on a nation-wide basis until the fiscal year 1936–1937. Although benefits to the indigent aged, dependent children, and the blind had been paid by some state and local governments prior to passage of the Social Security Act, this Act greatly increased those payments and made application of the programs nation-wide.

TABLE 8

BENEFIT PAYMENTS UNDER FEDERAL-STATE PROGRAMS FOR OLD-AGE INSURANCE;
UNEMPLOYMENT COMPENSATION; OLD-AGE ASSISTANCE; AID TO
DEPENDENT CHILDREN AND THE BLIND: 1936–1956*

Type of Program	Cumulative Benefits Paid $ millions
Old-Age and Survivors' Insurance (Federal)	25,396
Unemployment Compensation (Federal-State)	17,198
Old-Age Assistance (Federal-State)	20,265
Aid to Dependent Children (Federal-State)	6,674
Aid to the Blind (Federal-State)	823

* From *Statistical Supplement* to the *Social Security Bulletin*, 1956.

Benefit payments under the Old-Age and Survivors' Insurance Program have shown very rapid increases since 1950, when the accumulated benefit outlays were only about $5 billion. The program as a whole is organized on an actuarial basis, with earmarked taxes on workers and their employers in the earlier years not only paying for current benefits but building up a reserve fund. The increasing proportion of the population over 65 years of age as average life expectancy increases, and a continuation of the past trend toward liberalization of benefits, promise a substantial increase in the volume of OASI benefits in years to come.

Unemployment compensation payments will, of course, vary with employment conditions. Old-age assistance has been regarded from the beginning as a stop-gap provision. With the passage of time, as the old-age and survivors' insurance program provides more adequate coverage, workers reaching retirement age will be able to receive regular payments from that fund, and old-age assistance should then be applicable only to those who do not qualify under the insurance scheme. Even so, the number of persons qualifying to date has shown some increase. Aid to the blind and to dependent children should remain reasonably constant over a period of time unless benefits are increased, except as other provisions of the Social Security Act make for fewer dependent children.

The depression relief and social security activities of government, which are the most striking developments in recent decades, do not tell the whole story of welfare activities of governments. As early as 1929, approximately 10 per cent of state expenditures and 4.5 per cent of local expenditures were made for charities, hospitals, and correction. Since that time substantially expanded programs in home relief of the indigent, provision of health and hospital services, and rising standards of sanitation and recreation have been adopted by state and local governments. Federal assistance in these programs cannot be ignored, while the various titles of the Social Security

Act have tended to systematize welfare activities and involve the federal government in their financing.

Attitudes toward Increasing Public Expenditures

The facts of the increase in public expenditures are startling, and to many they are genuinely disturbing. Probably the most common bases for anxiety are the following:

1. A general feeling that public expenditures are by nature wasteful of the product of society.

2. A concern by the minority party lest the party in power perpetuate itself by the distribution of treasury largess.

3. A concern lest the expansion of government result in encroachments upon personal liberty and the field of private enterprise.

In reference to the first, the anxiety stems from (a) acceptance as a fact that government is by nature administratively wasteful and inefficient, and (b) belief that no matter how efficiently administered, government functions are by nature non-income-producing and thus a "burden" upon society.

Little need be said about waste and inefficiency. Without doubt the system of checks and balances which permeates government results in layers of authority which imply "red tape." This is true in any large organization—social, religious, business, or governmental. The ability to act quickly without reference to other authority is an attribute of dictatorial organization, and "red tape" is an inevitable characteristic of complex administrative organization and accountability in the administrative process.[12]

The notion that government is a "dead weight" upon the economy arises out of the traditional view that government is not "productive." Its functions are generally in the nature of performance of services which produce utilities for society but no direct money income to government. Because government expenditures do not directly produce their own income they are commonly thought to represent only a drain upon the income of the economy. However, government expenditures for highways undoubtedly produce at least their equivalent in income to the community in the improvement of transportation and the expansion of the automotive industries. And the income

---

[12] The term "bureaucracy" correctly refers to the system of administration according to rules, and "red tape" in greater or less degree is one of its characteristics. Popularly, however, "bureaucracy" has come to imply in everyday usage inefficiency, graft, and the promotion of excessively large organization, either to make jobs or to exalt the position of the chief of the bureau. An important analysis of this subject is *Bureaucracy and Trusteeship in Large Corporations*, Temporary National Economic Committee, Monograph 11, Washington, 1940.

produced by public education is even less direct, though doubtless real. The generation of national income by virtually all government expenditure is discussed in the following chapter.

The political aspects of the increase in public expenditures are of course subject to the interpretation which the individual chooses to place upon them. The political "outs" commonly insist that expenditures are made with the primary purpose of buying votes. Patronage is without question regularly practiced in government at all levels. Rewarding the politically faithful has its advantages in promoting party coherence, and at the same time places men of similar points of view in the various levels of the governmental hierarchy, thus promoting a minimum of wrangling in the administrative process. The open-handed spending policies of the "New Deal" were subject to heated criticism on the grounds that the primary objective of spending was to assure election. On the other hand, a balanced view will recognize that an administration maintains itself in power by pursuit of policies which the public approves. If the desired policy involves heavy spending, the reasonable view would emphasize the vote-getting power of public acceptance of the policy rather than the use of the public treasury as a political slush fund which overcomes opposition to policy with pecuniary payment.

At the same time, the provision by government of "social capital" has been a very considerable boon to development in the private sector of the economy. The provision of adequate highways and airports, a system of effective public education, the defense against aggression from outside, assistance in the maintenance of world markets, systematic conservation of natural resources, efficient development of power resources, development of atomic power, activities in the area of public health, promotion of research through large governmental outlays, and a variety of other public works have been strategic elements in the growth of the private economy.

Extension of the field of government has restricted the freedom of action of some individuals. Regulatory functions by their very nature are destructive of some individual freedoms. Most such regulation, however, has been intended to restrict the freedom to exploit, creating greater freedom of action or of choice to those formerly exploited. Limitation of the freedom of employers in dealing with their employees has greatly increased the freedom of action of organized employees. The scales may have been tipped too far in the opposite direction, but this does not necessarily condemn the exercise of control. Use of the taxing power itself limits individual choice as to the use of income, the purchase of certain goods, the establishment of residence, or the type of investment to be made. So long as general welfare—of which individual freedom is an important ingredient—is promoted, government is performing its clearly stated duty.

Expansion of government has often been characterized as a movement in the direction of socialism. Whether or not this is technically true depends upon one's definition of the term. Government obviously tends to "socialize" in the sense of subordinating individual to group welfare. An element of socialization of income inevitably occurs when progressive taxes pay for social welfare services, since the high-income groups contribute heavily to financing services whose major direct benefit accrues to low-income groups. A considerable socialization of profits from the "profit system" has occurred through personal and corporate income taxes and death taxes. Encroachment upon the traditional business field of capitalism has, however, been relatively slight in terms of social ownership of the means of production. The extensive public works program of the thirties accomplished a great deal of construction, but almost exclusively in fields noncompetitive with private enterprise. TVA and some of the emergency lending agencies which were created during depression and war possess aspects of obvious competition with private industry. However, in view of the tremendous expansion of government in that period the noncompetitive extent of public projects is remarkable.

"Socialism" refers primarily to social ownership of the means of production, as contrasted with private ownership. Government has thus progressed far toward controlled capitalism, but only in a very minor degree toward "socialism." In fact, government policies suggest quite clearly the objective of strengthening capitalism. Reduction in inequality of incomes has long been indicated as a reform to strengthen capitalism. The relief and welfare functions of government are inevitable, both to repair the ravages of the business cycle and to promote a higher standard of social living. Public works projects and lending functions during the depression were instituted to cushion the effects of the worst feature of free capitalism—its recurrent tendency to break down. "Pump-priming"—the injection of public expenditures to fill a void left by deficient private expenditures in recession—has as its goal the prevention of serious breakdown. Anti-monopoly regulation hopes to protect the private economy from disintegrating forces within itself. On the whole, therefore, with the expansion of government activities the objective of strengthening capitalism has been far more evident than the intent to socialize the economy.

Closely related to the fear that expansion of government will interfere with personal freedom is the dread of an increasing public debt. This fear expresses itself in terms of (1) the shock to orthodox attitudes created by policies which involve periodic and severe increases in debt, and (2) the recognition that debt creates both a current carrying charge in the form of interest and the probable future retirement of the principal, which promise additional taxes beginning now and continuing into the future. The problems of debt constitute a large study in themselves, and are therefore postponed for consideration in a later chapter.

Prejudice, dogma, and unbalance appear on both sides of the argument concerning the increase of public expenditure. Democracy is called upon to justify its existence in terms of efficiency and sensible policy. Bigness has many inherent propensities toward inefficiency, cumbersomeness, and favoritism which it is the function of idealism, reason, and organization to combat. Our discussion of budget control in Chapter 2 constantly emphasized the need for machinery through which conscious direction of fiscal policy toward desired ends is encouraged in the greatest possible degree.

Control of Public Expenditures

In the last analysis, real control of expenditures can be accomplished only by effective budgeting. For "control" does not necessarily mean "reduction." It means that expenditures are justified in terms of the whole welfare of society and in terms of the financial means at the disposal of government. "Control" implies that expenditures are "economic," by which we mean that resources not unlimited in quantity are devoted to their most productive uses, public and private. Economy in government thus means that budgetary decisions direct limited resources into government use only to the extent that such use is more productive of satisfactions or national income when administered by government than by the private economy. It means further that resources to be used by government be allocated among various public functions in such a way as to provide the greatest return measured against objectives.

The philosophy of control practiced by the federal government is essentially that of placing ultimate reliance upon the budget; that is, upon the common sense of the current incumbents of the legislative and executive departments. The President and the Congress are not seriously bound by constitutional or statutory strait jackets within which financial operations take place. But at the state and local levels governments are frequently restricted by formal controls. These are imposed upon local governments by the states, while at the state level they are imposed either by constitutions or by the self-discipline of statute law. Several formal controls of expenditure have been recommended, and some have been practiced. These formal controls have generally been instituted as substitutes for, and in the absence of, adequate budget procedure. Those most widely used are tax rate limits, debt limits, and "pay-as-you-go" requirements.

Tax Rate Limitation. This is a scheme for limiting expenditures by limiting revenues by limiting tax rates. It has been applied widely by the states to their county and municipal governments, and from time to time state governments have had tax rate limitation imposed upon them by their constitutions. Tax rate limits have applied almost exclusively to the property tax. This is not surprising in view of the fact that the property tax has consistently been the principal revenue measure of state and local governments.[13]

Two forms of tax rate limitation have been rather widely applied to local governments. The first, and more direct, is to establish a specific maximum property tax rate, such as 2 or 3 per cent of property valuation.[14] The second limits property tax revenues in any year to a given per cent of the previous year's property tax collections. This is not strictly tax *rate* limitation, for assessed valuations may be changed. But limitation of property tax revenues to, say, 105 per cent of those of the previous year is not uncommon, and such a procedure is likely to be in fact a limitation upon property tax rates.[15] Whatever system of limitation is employed, provision is commonly made for exceeding the limit in real emergencies. The constitutions or statute laws imposing limits generally provide that these limits may be exceeded by permission of the state tax commission or by large majority vote of the electors. It is possible to exceed the limit, but not easy.

Tax rate limitation is, however, a somewhat loose-jointed instrument for limitation of expenditures. To attempt to limit total expenditures by limiting property tax rates leaves important loopholes. The property taxes assessed are determined by multiplying the assessed value of property by the tax rate. Both the assessed value and the rate are potential variables. If the tax

[13] Many states have imposed rate limits of one sort or another on poll taxes, dog taxes, and various licenses. They are excluded from this discussion because restrictions upon such minor revenue instruments are obviously not designed to control general expenditures.

[14] This type of over-all tax rate limitation, applying to state as well as local governments, was employed in nine states in 1943. Cf. G. M. Morris, *Tax Limitation Laws,* Chicago, American Municipal Association, 1943, for a good general presentation of the case against tax limitation.

[15] It will be recognized that when, as in the case of a few states, an upper limit to over-all *expenditures* of a local government is established, a *de facto* property tax rate limit is established. For the importance of property taxes in the local government revenue picture, the local tradition of budget balance, and the slowness with which assessments are revised, combine to make the property tax rate the principal dependent variable with total expenditure.

rate is fixed by limitation, property taxes can be increased by increasing assessed valuations. Furthermore, other revenue measures may be utilized to supplement property taxes, and thus allow increase in expenditures. Finally, unless there is also a debt limit imposed, local governments whose tax revenues are limited may increase their expenditures by resort to borrowing. In smaller villages the tax rate limit works much better in limiting total expenditures than in larger cities. Small local governments are, in fact, dependent almost exclusively upon the property tax for revenue. Other sources either do not exist or cannot be made elastic. In the small towns property assessments tend to be frozen over long periods, making for great difficulty in increasing assessments. And finally, debt limits commonly are imposed along with tax rate limits.

In general, little support can be given to the practice of tax rate limitation. At best it is a poor substitute for good budgeting, implying that local governments cannot properly manage the scale of their activities. If it is effective in restricting expenditures, it imposes limitations upon those localities which choose to tax themselves more heavily in order to provide a quality of service above the usual standard. And when, as has been the case in many localities in recent years, the demands of education vastly increase expenditure outlays, one of three choices is open when tax rate limits are restrictive. The added expenditure may be covered by borrowing, if the debt limit permits. Assessed valuations of property may be raised, though this may be inconvenient, costly, or unnecessary. Or the level of expenditures must be held below that to which the community aspires. Clearly it is reasonable that communities be permitted to exercise their own options as to the scale of activity and the method of financing.

Debt Limitation. This plan is designed to restrict current expenditures of governments to a limited amount in excess of current revenue collections by establishing the maximum amount of debt which may be incurred. All states impose debt limits upon some or all of their local governments; in most of the states these debt limits appear in their constitutions, and are therefore highly resistant to change. Likewise, most state governments are limited in the amount of their borrowing by their constitutions, or by statute. The federal government operates under a statutory debt limit imposed by and subject to change by Congress.

Debt limits for local governments are most commonly stated as percentages of property valuation, though in a few cases the limits are related to annual revenue receipts. Debt limits of state governments are most frequently stated as amounts in dollars, though some relate to property valuation within the state and others depend upon recent revenues. The federal debt limit is stated as a fixed number of dollars.[16]

Most state and local debt limits exclude debt contracted for purposes which are expected to be self-liquidating, such as municipal light, water, and sewerage plants, toll highway and bridge facilities, and other similar improvements. There are scattered cases in which borrowing for other purposes is done outside the debt limit, some of the purposes being relief, street improvements, some local government buildings, and debt incurred to refund maturing debt.

No doubt the imposition of debt limits upon local governments serves to force them either to limit expenditures or to tax for current expenditures. Past defaults on local bond issues justify such action by the states, and are particularly necessary in the case of smaller municipal governments. There are, however, elements of elasticity in this system of expenditure control. When debt limits are related to assessed valuation of property, the debt limit can be increased in absolute amount by assessing property at higher figures. Exclusion of certain types of debt from such control provides an element of desirable elasticity. Considered by itself, a debt limit cannot control those expenditures met by increased taxation; this is the major escape from debt limitation.

As in the case of tax rate limitation, debt limitation falls far short of serving as an adequate substitute for budget control. It operates only on total expenditure, without regard for the relative importance of different functions financed within the debt limit, and it may well check necessary emergency functions. Local debt limits in many sections of the United States have seriously handicapped the effective functioning of local governments in recent years, particularly in connection with school construction requirements. The *Economic Report of the President* has for a number of years suggested to the states that their debt limit practices be re-examined in the light of current capital expenditure requirements. In some cases the pinch of debt limits has had the intended effect of holding down outlays; in others

---

[16] In April, 1945, the federal debt limit reached $300 billion. Since that time the following changes have occurred by legislative action:

Date	Amount of Debt Limit	"Permanent" (P) or Temporary (T)
6/26/1946	$275 billion	P
8/28/1954	281 billion	T
7/1/1956	278 billion	T
7/1/1957	275 billion	P
2/26/1958	280 billion	T
9/2/1958	288 billion	T
7/1/1959	295 billion	T
7/1/1960	285 billion	P

it has stimulated the search for new sources of local revenue. In still others the pressure of debt limits has encouraged curious practices for avoiding the restrictions, such as creating "authorities" to float self-liquidating bonds to build schools which are then leased to local governments on an annual-rental basis. There is little doubt that debt limits have been one of several factors tending to increase state aid to local education.

The federal debt limit is fixed by Congress and can be changed at any time by Congress. If it performs any service at all, therefore, that service is to urge caution from time to time in the planning of expenditure programs. Experience suggests, however, that the federal debt limit has served little purpose in limiting expenditures; its primary effect has been to obstruct orderly and sensible financial management. For whatever reasons, the executive agencies have been slow to request of the Congress necessary increases in the limit. They have preferred to wait for miracles to remove a temporary pinch, while in the meantime engaging in a variety of costly and otherwise questionable stop-gap practices in anticipation of improved revenues in the future. In 1954, free gold resources of the Treasury were utilized to meet current bills, and private funds were substituted for public funds by selling an interest in crop loans to private purchasers in the market. Again in 1957, when the debt limit was too low to accommodate necessary expenditures, these and similar maneuvers were again contemplated. On this occasion apparently none were used, but the postponement of an inevitable rise in the debt limit was accomplished by slowing down the rate of payment on established programs. It would be difficult to estimate the waste incurred in accommodating to a debt ceiling which is too low for sensible governmental operation, but it may be presumed that the cost is considerable.

On the whole, our experience indicates that debt limits for sovereign governments tend to do more harm than good. This is especially true where respectable budget practices are pursued. A rigid debt ceiling implies either that emergencies like the decline in revenues resulting from recession and the rise in defense outlays generated by the successful orbiting of satellites will not occur, or that there is already enough slack in the budget to permit cutting in some areas in order to take care of emergencies in others. Neither is a safe assumption. If the debt ceiling is tightly fitted and executive requests to have it relaxed are regarded as carrying a political onus, financial administration is unduly burdened. On the other hand, if there is ample room to maneuver under the ceiling, it can hardly be fulfilling the function which its supporters intend it to perform.

Pay-As-You-Go. This policy means simply the prohibition of borrowing. It forces upon the fiscal authority the requirement of limiting current expenditures to current receipts. Even though as a long-run policy, particularly for local governments, pay-as-you-go may be wise, it is not wise to impose the policy by general legislation. If a pay-as-you-go policy is wise in a given period, that policy should be determined upon by fiscal authorities and reflected in the budget. To impose such a policy by legislation is to abandon good budgetary practice in emergencies.

There are times when governments, like individuals and businesses, should go into debt. Borrowing is an essential part of financial management. An individual without funds who held to a pay-as-you-go policy in the face of a need for emergency surgery could get only cold comfort from the "wisdom" or orthodoxy of his policy. Historically, a large proportion of business expansion has been financed by borrowing. It is good business probably far more often than bad. For the same reasons, governments cannot afford to cripple their schools in order to meet relief obligations. And from the point of view of individual projects, pay-as-you-go is often expensive. One state government, when it decided to build a new state house, planned to do the job by the "sound" financial method of paying for the construction out of current revenues. It is reported that because of inadequate year-to-year budget surpluses the construction dragged on for a period more than twice as long as would have been possible under a bond issue. The final total cost was over twice the planned cost—the cost which would have been paid if construction had been financed by borrowing. The loss of several years' occupancy of the building and the money expense of several million dollars more than was necessary represent a high price to pay for fiscal "virtue."

Fortunately, though pay-as-you-go still remains the ideal of fiscal policy at least for most state and local governments, there are very few modern attempts to enforce it by law. The constitution of North Carolina prohibits the state and the local governments from increasing their debts in any one year by an amount greater than two-thirds of the amount by which the debt was reduced during the previous year.[17] Therefore, unless the state ran a surplus in any year, it could not borrow at all the following year. The course of the debt can therefore never be upward. It must either remain constant or decrease. This is pay-as-you-go with a vengeance, crystallizing the policy in constitutional enactment. A few states impose pay-as-you-go on the general fund by prohibiting debts for ordinary purposes. The probable effect

[17] Article V, Section 4. The exceptions are: "To fund or refund a valid existing debt; to borrow in anticipation of the collection of taxes due and payable within the fiscal year to an amount not exceeding fifty per centum of such taxes; to supply a casual deficit; to suppress riots or insurrections, or to repel invasions."

of this policy is either to declare unusual expenditures "extraordinary" or to starve ordinary functions of government to support unusual expenditures elsewhere. And it will be noted that any time a government reaches an unchanging debt limit, it must thereafter follow a pay-as-you-go policy, except in those lines in which borrowing is exempt from debt limitation.

The general conclusion with respect to "formal" controls of expenditure is that such controls may be more or less useful where potentially good budgeting is impracticable, but where good budgeting is possible they not only add very little but may work real harm. However, good budgeting is possible in almost all circumstances; formal controls are called forth by fiscal irresponsibility or by failure to respect the importance of governmental functions.

Grants-in-Aid

Grants-in-aid are contributions from governments at one level to governments at a different level. They are made from funds to which the grantor has title, and therefore do not include distribution of revenues collected by one government for another.[18] Federal grants to states and local governments are always made for specified purposes, though state governments make some unspecified grants to localities.

One or both of two major causes generally account for the existence of grants.[19] (1) The resources of governments at a lower level are inadequate to provide desired services at uniformly high standards, and thus require financial assistance from governments with greater resources. (2) Certain functions are regarded by government at a higher level to be necessary, but that government either cannot for constitutional reasons or should not for administrative reasons perform the function itself. Thus a nation-wide depression relief program should be uniform throughout the nation, but probably should be administered locally.

Grants by states to local governments have generally bulked larger in the whole transfer picture and are of longer standing than federal grants. This follows naturally from the fact that local governments are created by

[18] Taxes collected by state governments and shared by local governments have become common in recent years. These are not, however, grants-in-aid, since amounts distributed to local governments cannot be considered at any time to have been state funds.

[19] This excludes minor "uphill" transfers from government at a lower level to government at a higher level. Local governments transfer funds to states as payment on loans extended to them by the state, payments to state pension funds for local employees, transfers to states of relief funds later disbursed in state-local relief, and local advances to states for construction of state-local highways. States have made payments to the federal government on former public works loans. None of these is in the nature of a grant. See U. S. Bureau of Census, *Financing Federal, State, & Local Governments: 1941*, 1942, pp. 55–56.

and are agencies of the states. The purposes for which state aid was granted to local governments in 1958 were as follows:[20]

Education	$4,452.5 million
Highways	1,166.7 million
Public Welfare[a]	1,094.3 million
Health and Hospitals	303.0 million
Housing and Community Redevelopment	21.4 million
Purposes Unspecified	687.2 million
Other and Unallocated	220.2 million
TOTAL	$7,943.4 million

[a] Includes principally old-age assistance and aid to dependent children.

The public welfare grants to local governments are mainly for purposes for which the states themselves receive federal grant funds. These include old-age assistance and aid to dependent children, the blind, and the disabled. The other types of grants in the list, although they have steadily increased in size, are of longer standing. Of particular note are the state contributions to local education. The rationale of such grants is to be found in the need for state-wide standards of public education, which standards could not or would not be met by local governments operating independently. Poverty or niggardliness of local governments could thus create areas in which a primary function of the state is inadequately performed.

Federal grants in 1957 were as indicated in Table 9 below.

TABLE 9

FEDERAL GRANTS TO STATE AND LOCAL GOVERNMENTS, 1957*
(in millions of dollars)

Public Assistance	1,556
Highways	955
Agriculture	382
Unemployment Compensation and Employment Service	319
Education	302
Public Health, Sanitation, and Hospital Construction	134
Housing and Community Development	118
Maternal and Child Welfare	38
Vocational Rehabilitation	34
Natural Resources	27
Airports	21
District of Columbia	20
Veterans' Services and Benefits	8
Other	49
TOTAL	3,943

* *The Budget of the United States Government for the Fiscal Year Ending June 30, 1959, Special Analysis G.*

The public assistance grants are essentially matching grants, requiring approximately equal expenditure from state funds. They originated in the

[20] *Compendium of State Government Finances in 1958, p. 25.*

Social Security Act, and are made for old-age assistance and aid to dependent children, the blind, and the disabled. Highway grants were first provided in the Act of 1917 to assist the states in the construction of national highway systems and to improve rural roads. For several decades they were matching grants, but by the Act of 1946 the federal government undertook to encourage the development of an integrated national network of defense highways by granting to the states 90 per cent of the construction costs of designated arterial routes. The program was barely begun by 1957, but in the following decade is planned to reach such proportions as to involve, in combination with the old 50-50 program, annual grants for highway construction of nearly $3 billion. The federal grants for education are of a specialized nature. A large part of the total educational grants is made for construction and operation of schools in areas where federal governmental activity imposes an unusual burden upon the communities. Other than these, educational grants are made principally for higher education and for research, although there are persistent pressures to extract much more substantial federal contributions for local education. The major item in grants for agriculture is payments under the school lunch program, which is listed by the Bureau of the Budget under this heading but might as well be included under education. Aside from this, agricultural grants are made for the operation of the agricultural extension program and agricultural experiment stations. Other major items in Table 9 are reasonably self-explanatory.

The institution of grants-in-aid has accomplished the very useful governmental purpose of administering certain functions at the logical lower and more intimate level by the use of funds of the more centralized governments with more ample revenue resources and borrowing power. Some of these functions could not constitutionally be performed by the federal government, but the offer of federal funds with performance requirements has accomplished desired results. On the other hand, there are potential dangers to the grantee government. It is difficult to refuse an offer of two dollars for one, and grantee governments may find themselves purchasing services at the bargain counter beyond their means. Further, there is dual budgetary consideration of such expenditures; the budget of the grantor may consider the function worth 50 per cent of its total cost, and that of the grantee may do the same. It does not necessarily follow, however, that the function is worth its total cost to the taxpayers. There is the additional fact that, if the grantor government were to withdraw, the grantee would be forced either to bear the whole cost or—a bitter choice—drop the function.

Public Expenditures and Economic Conditions

In this chapter we have discussed the trend of public expenditures, the more important functions which give rise to those expenditures, and expenditure control. This is the traditional approach to the subject of public expenditures, and discusses materials which are essential to an understanding of what government does with its money. It is, nevertheless, an incomplete view of the economic aspects of public expenditure. It is important to add, since it is so frequently overlooked, that most government services are basic in nature; their benefits reach out into all branches of economic life. Consider for a moment the magnitude of the dollars and cents benefits to the business community and to individuals of such services as protection, highway construction, education, informational services, and provision for financial security. How productive would the economy be without these services? How could the capital accumulation necessary for technological advance in a private property economy have taken place without the protection of private property? How much lower would current levels of national production and distribution be if highway transportation did not exist in substantially the present form? How could we possibly measure the contribution of public education to production "know-how" and the transmission of information? How much has agricultural production been increased and costs reduced by dissemination of information concerning agricultural production techniques? And in the modern economy, are the economic benefits of security not virtually immeasurable? The underlying quality of typical government services justifies the conclusion that in dollars and cents benefits the costs of government are returned to the economy many times over, that the major part of peacetime government expenditures are highly productive by the very nature of the functions performed.

The narrow and traditional view of the effects of public expenditures confines itself to consideration of the social value of direct consumer services performed by government. As we have seen in the paragraph above, a major part of these services makes a basic contribution to the productive efficiency of the economy. But the broader and newer view raises questions of the economic significance of expenditure *as expenditure*.

Disregarding for the moment the usefulness of the service for which payment is made, what does the act of expenditure itself do to the flow of incomes in the economy? Educational expenditures do provide education, but how do the purchase of books, the payment of teachers' salaries, and the construction of school buildings affect the general level of economic activity, the level of employment, and the distribution of income? As book publishers, schoolteachers, and building labor and contractors receive payment from government, what do they do with their income and what difference does it make?

Clearly, in the economy incomes are passed from hand to hand; the income of A is spent and becomes income to B. The income of the grocer depends upon the expenditure by his customers of their income for groceries; employment in the publishing trade depends upon (public and private) purchases of books; total demand for construction labor and materials depends upon combined public and private building programs. Recognition of the income-inducing potentialities of spending—public as well as private— are clearly evident in attempts of local Chambers of Commerce to attract new industries, army camps, and various public works projects to their localities. It is such matters as these which the narrow view of expenditures ignores,[21] and which are so important to the general level of economic welfare as to require careful analysis.

[21] The narrow traditional view here described is not a straw man artificially set up as a target. Nearly all important writers on public finance from Adam Smith (1776) up to the present generation have limited their view of fiscal operations to simply an appropriation of private income to public use for performance of consumer services. No attempt was made to follow out that expenditure as income to its recipients. Thus, taxation was a simple subtraction from national income, and there was little if any awareness of the income-producing aspects of expenditure.

Adam Smith (*Wealth of Nations,* Modern Library Edition, 1937) believed that government expenditures were payments for "unproductive labour" (pp. 877–78), and "as smaller or greater proportion [of the 'annual produce' or national income] is in any one year employed in maintaining unproductive hands, the more in the one case and the less in the other will remain for the productive, and the next year's produce will be greater or smaller accordingly; the whole annual produce . . . being the effect of productive labour" (p. 315). We are not interested here in the controversy over Smith's distinction between productive and unproductive labor. The point is that Smith concludes that government expenditure cannot increase national product; whether or not it reduces national product depends upon whether that part of the previous year's income taken in taxes would have been spent by private persons for productive labor.

The same emphasis upon taxes as a withdrawal of funds from the private income stream and ignorance of the income-inducing effects of pouring these funds back into the stream is evidenced by Ricardo, J. S. Mill, Bastable, and H. C. Adams. This narrow view in Adams' *Science of Finance* (1906) is implied in the following: "The starting point is the fund of wealth at the disposal of the nation; the objective point is the highest development of both individual and national life; the problem is to so balance the assignment of expenditures between the various forms of consumption that the life of the people shall be nourished and the organs of the nation developed, at the point where nourishment and development are most needed" (p. 29).

Professor H. L. Lutz (reprinted, by permission, from *Public Finance,* 3rd edition, New York, Appleton-Century, 1936) reflects the same view when he says: "The test of the productivity of expenditure for public education would be the success of the educational effort in development of intelligent citizens . . . ," or, ". . . if relief expenditure prevents distress without destroying self-respect, and the instinct of self-support, it is productive" (p. 164), or, "In some degree public expenditure may add directly to the aggregate of wealth produced. Well-run government commercial enterprises, reforestation and reclamation projects, and other forms of state business are the most obvious illus-

RECOMMENDED READINGS

General:

Due, John F., "Government Expenditures and Their Significance for the Economy," in Poole, K. E. (Ed.), *Fiscal Policies and the American Economy,* N.Y., Prentice-Hall, 1951, Chapter 5.

    A general discussion at a reasonably elementary level of many economic implications of the growth of governmental expenditures.

Fabricant, Solomon, *The Trend of Government Activity in the United States Since 1900,* N.Y., National Bureau of Economic Research, 1952.

    An excellent recent study which possesses the double virtue of effective analysis and readability. Its 153 pages can be read profitably; if less time is available, Chapters 1, 2, 3, 4, 6, 7 fit most effectively into the approach of this text chapter.

Kendrick, M. Slade, *A Century and a Half of Federal Expenditures,* Occasional Paper 48, N.Y., National Bureau of Economic Research, 1955.

    A short (54-page) interpretive study with a long-range view.

Maxwell, J. A., *The Fiscal Impact of Federalism in the United States,* Cambridge, Harvard, 1946, Part I.

    The various chapters in Part I deal with various functions upon which major expenditures have been and are made. The approach is both historical and analytical.

Grants-in-aid:

Bittermann, H. J., *State and Federal Grants-in-Aid,* N.Y., Mentzer, Bush, 1937.

    The most comprehensive treatment of the general subject. Chapters 1, 2, 31 are general chapters; the remaining chapters discuss the use of grants-in-aid for specific purposes and at different governmental levels.

Blough, R., "Federal and State Grants-in-Aid," in Groves, H. M., *Viewpoints on Public Finance,* N.Y., Holt, 1947, pp. 600–608.

    Good, short discussion, with special reference to the use of grants for equalization purposes.

---

trations. Even the expenditure on ordinary services may result in the accumulation of certain assets, such as public buildings, which are a useful addition to the aggregate of community wealth" (p. 167). From Professor Lutz's point of view, production of a play by a WPA theater group could not be productive. Yet the actors, who are taken from the relief rolls, spend their wages for bread, which creates employment and income in retail stores, bakeries, and mills, and produces income to the wheat farmer. Is the purchase of bread by an actor for Paramount Pictures significantly different in its effect upon national income through the same channels?

    On the other hand, an early and refreshing recognition of the general economic effects of public expenditure is to be found in Daniel Raymond's *Thoughts on Political Economy,* 1820. Raymond was an American lawyer who wrote his *Thoughts* to "please myself" and because "I have read musty law books till I was tired." His thoughts are fresh and stimulating, though they appear to have gained very little if any following. For our present purpose, the following quotation is selected to suggest the broader view here discussed: "The body politic like the natural body is liable to fall into a state of comparative lethargy and torpor. It then becomes necessary to arouse its dormant energies, by administering stimulants. The expenditure of public money, in public works, will often produce this effect" (p. 294).

Maxwell, J. A., *Federal Grants and the Business Cycle*, N.Y., National Bureau of Economic Research, 1952.

An excellent summary of the history of federal grants and a highly intelligent analysis of their potential usefulness both in making standards of performance of functions among the states more uniform, and in economic stabilization.

CHAPTER 4

Fiscal Policy
and the Level of Economic Activity

In the foregoing chapter we noted major trends over a considerable period of time in the expenditures of federal, state, and local governments. These trends reflect decisions as to the allocation of economic resources between public and private uses, and also decisions as to the types of services preferred within the public sector of the economy. The longer-term trends are largely dominated by the behavior of defense expenditures of the federal government, and therefore reflect the state of international relations. But in addition, an impressive rise is discernible in types of governmental activity related to economic growth, such as highway construction, public education, and resource development. Expenditure trends thus demonstrate efforts toward the continuing social goals of national security, personal security, and economic growth.

But there is another major goal—economic stability—with shorter-term implications, which does not specifically appear in expenditure trends. It is the purpose of this chapter to analyze the possible impact of fiscal action upon the degree of stability in the economy.

Measurement of Aggregate Economic Activity

Any analysis of economic stability or instability (or of economic growth) requires first the development of a system for measuring economic performance. Instability is a quantitative concept, involving degrees and rates of departure from some norm. The two kinds of aggregate economic instability of major strategic importance are instability of output (or of income or employment) and instability of prices. These are the major variables, therefore, for which measurements must be provided. Index numbers of prices have been in use for a long time.

84

Measures of aggregate output (income) have been more recently developed, but are now standard data in the analysis of performance of the economy.[1] The gross national product measures for a period of time the aggregate market value of goods and services produced in the economy. Various other measures are derived from the GNP, such as net national product, national income, personal income, and disposable personal income, each representing a degree of refinement in concept appropriate to particular economic questions.

A measure of the output of the economy is, however, also a measure of the expenditure for output, since aggregate output can be measured only in money terms. And both are also measures of income, since they are two sides of the same productive process. Thus, output or product, expenditures for output or product, and income are used interchangeably to refer to the same sets of statistics. All are identical measures of the volume of activity of the economy. Another variable, employment, is commonly used interchangeably with those mentioned above; while reflection will show that it does not necessarily vary identically with the others, its variation tends to be in the same direction over short periods.

Determinants of the Rate of Economic Activity

Most readers of this chapter will have developed some familiarity in other course work with the widely accepted analysis of the determination of the level of income and employment. Expenditure (demand) calls forth output in a market economy. There are three major classes of expenditure for current output: (1) purchases of consumption goods and services by persons; (2) purchases of investment goods and services by businesses, with the intent to use them for further production or for sale; and (3) purchases by governments of the goods and services which they may choose to procure. These three categories of expenditure combined constitute aggregate expenditures in the economy for current production, and the goods and services purchased represent aggregate current output.[2] There are, of course, financial acts and transactions excluded from the purview of

---

[1] The national product and national income figures for the United States are published regularly by the Department of Commerce in the monthly *Survey of Current Business*. More detailed figures are published annually in the July issue of the *Survey*, while the occasional publication of a *National Income Supplement* to the *Survey* not only provides textual discussion of concepts and methods, but usually revises the series back to 1929.

[2] There is some forcing in the categories, in the interest of simplification. Foreign investment is included in the second category, though some of the goods and services involved are of the consumption type; and some durable consumer goods, e.g., residential housing, are also included in the official statistics with investment.

the analysis. Transfers of funds such as gifts, charitable payments, insurance premiums and benefits, taxes, deposits and withdrawals from bank accounts, and stock and bond transactions do not constitute direct purchases of goods and services. The purchase of used goods is likewise excluded, as such purchases do not involve current production.

In the aggregate, the economic process is a circuit flow of expenditures for product, creating equivalent incomes to participants in production, which may be then re-spent for further product. If the rate of aggregate spending is constant over a course of time, the rate of production or economic activity for a given period will be stable.[3] An increase in the rate of aggregate spending will increase total activity for the period, while a decrease in aggregate spending will have the opposite effect.

Instability in production or employment results from instability in aggregate spending of the economy. The norm from which departures occur is, by general usage, "full employment." This is a level of production which implies the utilization of the full potentialities of the productive system, both labor and capital, within the context of the current state of technology.[4] The full employment objective grows out of the realization that productive capacity that is not used represents goods not produced and therefore lost to society. It is further recognized that involuntary unemployment hurts individuals, and often hurts most those who are least responsible for its occurrence. Aggregate spending in excess of productive capacity produces price inflation, with its redistribution of real incomes and the probability of economic distortions which may generate recession or depression.

Since the cause of instability in economic activity is instability in spending, it becomes necessary to analyze the factors influencing the major categories of expenditure—consumption, private investment, and government. The behavior of the GNP and its major expenditure components since 1929 is shown in Figure 1 below.

[3] This assumes that both spending and production are measured either in money terms or in real terms, or that prices do not change.

[4] "Full" employment in practice takes account of the fact that in a dynamic economy some labor will at any time be in the process of changing jobs and that some capital resources will be in possession of firms in decline or liquidation. Full employment thus means the absence of *involuntary* unemployment. In practice, the economy would be considered as operating at full employment with 2–3 per cent of the labor force unemployed. The "current state of technology" implies a standard work week for the times. The fact that workers are working a 40-hour week when it would be physically possible for them to work 60 hours implies nothing with respect to the fullness of employment.

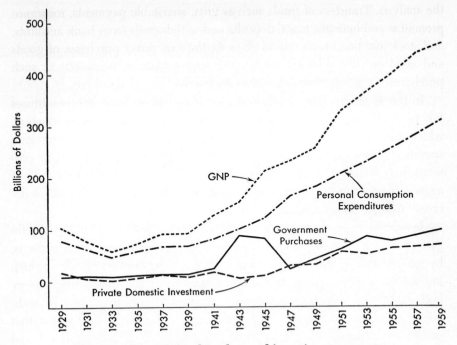

Figure 1. Gross National Product and its major components,
1929-1959.*

* From Department of Commerce, *National Income*, 1954; *Survey of Current Business*, July, 1958; and *Economic Indicators*, April, 1960. Net foreign investment is excluded as being too small to show usefully on the chart.

Without at the moment raising questions of cause and effect, the decline in business activity during the depression of the thirties was accompanied by nearly equal declines in consumption and private investment, these reductions being only very partially offset by increases in governmental purchases of goods and services. During World War II the major factor in marked rise in the GNP was the expenditures of the federal government, both private investment and consumption having been artificially restricted. In the immediate postwar years a remarkable resurgence of consumption expenditures, accompanied by a rise in private investment, more than offset the rapid decline in government purchases, and the GNP continued to climb. The 1950's are dominated by the behavior of consumption, though a general strengthening of private investment and the expansion of government expenditures in response to the Korean troubles, the intensification of the cold war, and education and highway needs, supported the upward push of consumption upon the GNP.[5]

The variations briefly referred to in the last paragraph may be more clearly demonstrated by Figure 2, which shows consumption, private investment, and government expenditures as percentages of the GNP. It should be emphasized that the proportions shown in Figure 2 are proportions of

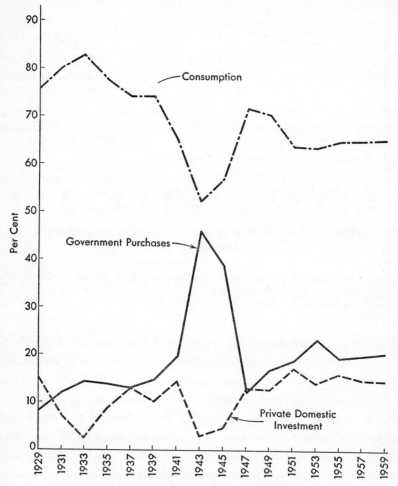

Figure 2. Consumption, private domestic investment, and government purchases as per cent of GNP.*

* Computed from figures referred to in the footnote to Figure 1. Again, the net foreign investment is ignored.

[5] The careful observer will note that since the chart is based upon two-year periods, the recessions of 1948–1949 and 1953–1954 are only vaguely evident.

a generally rising gross national product, and that the changes charted are changes in the importance of the components relative to each other.

Behavior of Private Consumption Expenditures. Figure 1 portrays the well-known fact that consumption expenditures normally represent by far the largest single component of aggregate expenditures. Barring artificial restraints upon consumption, as in World War II, and barring abnormal declines in private investment, as in the depression of the 1930's, consumption expenditures in the vicinity of two-thirds of the GNP appear normal. For the year 1957, consumption expenditures were 64.7 per cent of the GNP. This is the *average propensity to consume* in that year, i.e., the proportion of the average dollar of GNP devoted to consumption. The points on the consumption expenditures line in Figure 2 are *average propensities* to consume in those years.[6] The concept of average propensity to consume can serve, when related to the GNP, as a measure of the extent to which aggregate economic activity is directed toward serving the immediate wants of consumers. In low-productivity economies one would expect to find this average propensity higher than in rapidly developing economies, where a larger share of current production can be devoted to private or governmental investment in productive facilities and services.

For most analytical and policy purposes, however, use of the *marginal propensity to consume* is more appropriate than use of the average propensity. The reason for this is that income changes are likely to be marginal—i.e., a little more or a little less. An additional expenditure by government is typically a small addition to total income, and a change in tax rates is likely to bring a small change in before-tax income left to individuals and businesses. The marginal propensity to consume (with respect to the GNP) is the ratio of the change in consumption to the change in the gross national product. It refers to the change in consumption spending which would result from a change in the GNP.[7] Under usual conditions of con-

---

[6] Propensity to consume can be expressed as the ratio of consumption to any of the national income measures. While the APC with respect to the GNP was 64.7/100 in 1957, the APC with respect to personal income in that year was 284.4/347.9, or 81.9/100. The average propensity to consume out of disposable personal income was 284.4/305.1, or 93.3/100.

[7] The *consumption function* may be shown as a curve whose points indicate the amounts of consumption expenditure which would occur at various levels of the GNP (or other income measure) at any given time. Thus it is an average propensity to consume curve. The slope of this curve between two points is the marginal propensity to consume; i.e., the marginal propensity to consume is the fraction:

$$\frac{\text{increment to consumption}}{\text{increment to income.}}$$

If we could be assured that the consumption function had remained stable while the level of income changed, we could measure the marginal propensity to consume in

sumer motivation, if incomes rise it is expected that consumption expenditures will rise more slowly. That is, as incomes rise, other things being equal, savings rise more than proportionately with income. The same tendency is demonstrated by the fact that among higher incomes the propensity to consume is lower (and the propensity to save higher) than among lower incomes. This implies that over a course of time a redistribution of income downward—from the higher to the lower income groups—would increase both the average and the marginal propensities to consume. A change in the pattern of income distribution would change the position and/or slope of the consumption function.

Since consumption expenditures represent the major part of aggregate expenditures in the GNP, we would expect a major element in the economic effect of fiscal policies to be their effect upon private consumption. In this case, the concept implied is that of the "multiplier," which would indicate the effect over a period of time upon consumption of a government expenditure or of a change in tax rates. K (the multiplier) is equal to

$$\frac{1}{1 \text{ minus the marginal propensity to consume.}[8]}$$

To illustrate the multiplier effect by examples, suppose, first, that there is an injection by government of $100 of new and additional expenditure into the income stream. What will be the effect over a course of time of this injection? It depends, of course, on the propensity to re-spend realized income in the private economy, and we are now pursuing the re-spending only through consumption channels. Let us assume that two-thirds of addi-

---

terms of actual increments to consumption and income over a period of time. But in practice it would be difficult to be assured that the function had not shifted upward or downward; we might, in such a case, be measuring the increment to consumption from a point on one consumption function to a point on another function. Thus, at annual rates, from the second to the third quarter of 1958, the GNP rose by $10 billion and consumption expenditure by $4 billion. The marginal propensity to consume was 4/10 if the consumption function is assumed to have remained stable, but this was a period of recovery from recession and it is not entirely safe to assume that the function was not shifting.

[8] This is a specialized application of the formula for the sum of an infinite series: $S=A/(1-r)$, where A is the first term in the series and r is the ratio of any term in the series to its immediate predecessor. If a new and additional governmental expenditure is injected, the total effect upon national income through consumption re-expenditure can be expressed as $\Delta Y=k\times\Delta G$, where ΔY is the resulting increment to national income, k is the multiplier, and ΔG is the increment to government expenditure which started the process. Thus

$$\Delta Y = \frac{1}{1-\Delta C/\Delta Y} : \Delta G \text{ or } \frac{\Delta G}{1-\Delta C/\Delta Y}$$

tional income will be re-spent for consumption. Starting with the governmental injection of $100, the effect over a period of time will be:

$$\$100 + \$66.67 + \$44.44 + \$29.63 + \ldots = \$300$$

The multiplier is seen to be 3, meaning that the aggregate GNP created over a period of time as a result of the governmental injection is three times the injection.

In the practice of fiscal policy, however, we are far more interested in the short period effects of a policy action than in its total effect over an infinite period of time. We can see that when the marginal propensity to consume is 0.67 (and the multiplier 3), just over two-thirds of the total income created over an infinite period of time would have been created in the first three waves of expenditure in the series. And if the marginal propensity to consume were 0.5 (and the multiplier 2), 87.5 per cent of the total effect would occur in the first three periods. Thus, the multiplier effect through re-spending for consumption has important practical implications, even though we may be interested in the shorter period.

The multiplier effect is a matter of considerable importance in the determination of appropriate fiscal policy. When expenditure programs are under consideration, it can make a difference, so far as the generation of employment or of inflation is concerned, into what areas of the economy the expenditures are injected. An increase in government demand in an industrial segment of the economy already fully employed will have quite different results than an increase in a segment where there are idle resources. And government transfer payments to persons with a high propensity to consume (as in the case, say, of unemployment benefits) will have higher multiplier effects than payments to persons whose marginal propensity to consume is lower (e.g., interest payments to high-income persons). The same considerations will apply in tax policy. Tax relief, which leaves a larger proportion of their gross incomes in the hands of the relieved taxpayers, will be more effective in generating employment in the consumption goods fields if it is directed toward those taxpayers whose marginal propensity to consume is higher.

Behavior of Private Investment. Relative to consumption spending, business spending for investment purposes has shown a high degree of short-period volatility. This volatility is demonstrated in Figure 3, which shows percentage changes in consumption, private domestic investment, and GNP from one quarter-year to the next during the three recessions of 1948–1949, 1953–1954, and 1957–1958. Periods of recession and recovery are taken because they show degrees of instability in major components of expenditure in times when the economy as a whole is unstable. It will be

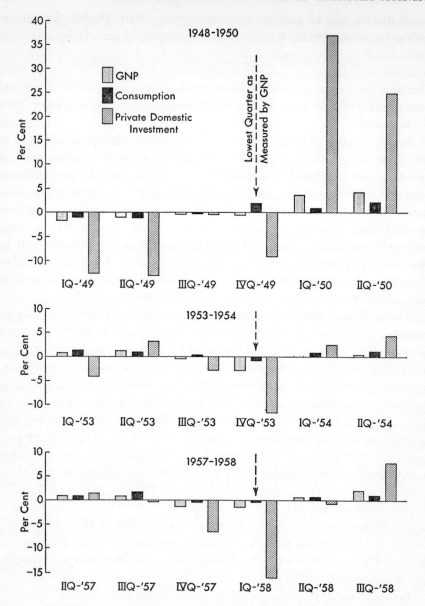

Figure 3. Quarter-to-quarter percentage changes in GNP, consumption, and private domestic investment in three recent
recessions.*

* Computed from Department of Commerce figures, using seasonally adjusted
quarterly totals at annual rates.

noted that the use of percentage changes, rather than absolute changes in billions of dollars, tends to dramatize the degree of variability in investment, for investment expenditures are much smaller in volume than consumption expenditures. But however portrayed, the fact is that in most conditions of instability in the private economy the component of private investment is considerably more unstable than that of consumption.[9]

Reasons for the relative volatility of private investment are not difficult to identify. One part of investment will be "autonomous," in response to influences other than the anticipated levels of consumption. Reasons for autonomous investment would include inventions in the capital goods area, realized or anticipated changes in the cost of materials or labor, improvements in products involving retooling, anticipated changes in the price level or in the prices of particular goods, and the need to modernize in order to maintain a competitive position. The other part of investment will be "induced," as a response to changes in the prospective rate of consumption. An anticipated or actual rise in the rate of consumption—due either to an increase in personal income or to an upward shift of the consumption function—will cause an early increase in investment in inventories and in the facilities needed to satisfy the increased consumption. On the other hand, a prospective or actual drop in consumption will cause investment plans to be withdrawn and even the replacement of depreciated capital instruments will be slowed down. We are here dealing with the "principle of acceleration," which observes that a rather small change in realized or prospective sales will be accompanied by a more than proportionate change in expenditure for productive equipment and inventories. The rate of investment in the economy at any time, including both autonomous and induced investment, will depend upon a variety of influences. In the aggregate, they amount to the prospect for profitable employment of the capital instrument. Whether autonomous or induced, investment is "lumpy," as shown in Figure 3, and this lumpiness is a major factor in economic instability.

The amount of investment in an economy may be related to its GNP (or other measure of national income) as the propensity to invest. This propensity may be measured as an average or marginally, like the propensity to consume. If the propensity to invest is equal to the propensity

[9] In a very important paper, "Federal Spending and the Stability of the Postwar Economy," Bert G. Hickman has demonstrated that since World War II, government expenditures have been even less stable than private investment. (Joint Economic Committee, *Federal Expenditure Policy for Economic Growth and Stability—Papers Submitted by Panelists Appearing Before the Subcommittee on Fiscal Policy*, Washington, 1957, pp. 357–81.) In this section, however, we are interested in the behavior of the private sectors of the economy.

to save, when both are considered in terms of the same income measure, the level of income is in equilibrium. In the circuit flow of income-realization and income-spending there are no forces at work either to increase or decrease the income level.[10] The consumption and savings plans of individuals and business firms and their investment plans are being realized. If the rate of investment is greater or less than the rate of saving, income will be rising or falling. An excess of investment over saving will normally be financed by the creation of money by the banking system; an excess of saving over investment will involve hoarding in the usual sense, or more likely the net repayment of bank loans and the destruction of money in the form of demand deposits in the banking system.

A rise in the equilibrium level at which the economy operates (excluding government for the present) will result from a rise in the rate of consumption and/or the rate of investment. If the change originates with consumption expenditures, an upward shift of the consumption function is indicated, for larger consumption expenditure out of given income is implied. Such a shift is not normally to be expected in a short period of time, though it could occur in response to the removal of artificial restrictions upon consumption during or after a war. Notable changes in the liberality of consumer credit, or mass agreement on the prospect of a rise in the price level, could also create a higher or lower consumption function. More commonly, consumption will contribute to a change in income through the marginal propensity to consume and the multiplier. In this case an original expenditure is multiplied through successive steps of re-expenditure for consumption, and the size of consumption expenditure in each step will depend upon the marginal propensity. The normal expectation is that with the usual consumption function the marginal propensity to consume decreases as income increases and vice versa. Thus, income increases (with a stable consumption function) must occur against a rising marginal propensity to save, requiring relatively rising investment offsets to these savings. Income decreases, by the same token, meet resistance from a rising marginal propensity to consume. The slope of the consumption function thus helps to establish obstacles to extreme instability of income.

A somewhat parallel analysis of the role of investment in income changes is possible. Independent or autonomous changes in the rate of investment set the multiplier process in motion, the effect being determined

---

[10] The reader will, it is hoped, understand that in this treatment of income determinants, the role of government is excluded and we are discussing the behavior of the private economy exclusively. Alternately, however, if taxes are included in savings, and government purchases of goods and services are included in investment, the governmental sector can be assumed in the treatment.

by the size of the investment injection and the muliplier. But as the multi-plier process raises consumption (and income), further increase in invest-ment may be induced through the accelerator. And therefore the total effect of an independent change in investment or in consumption begins a series of subsequent spendings in both consumption and investment which to-gether determine the aggregate effect over a period of time on the level of income. Professor Hansen has referred to this as the "leverage effect," in-volving both the multiplier and the acceleration principle.[11] The "leverage coefficient" is

$$\frac{1}{1 - (\Delta C/\Delta Y + \Delta I/\Delta Y)},$$

applying to successive waves of both consumption and investment the principle of the sum of an infinite series. For example, if the marginal propensity to consume were 75/100, and the marginal propensity to invest were 20/100, and an autonomous investment of 100 were injected into the economy, the aggregate effect upon income by rounds of re-expenditure would be as follows:

	Induced Consumption Expenditure	Autonomous and Induced Investment Expenditure	Increment to Income in This Round of Expenditure	Cumulative Increment to Income
First round		100	100	100
Second round	75	20	95	195
Third round	71.25[a]	19[b]	90.25	285.25
Fourth round	67.69	18.05	85.74	370.99
	.	.	.	.
	.	.	.	.
	.	.	.	.
At infinity	0	0	0	2000
TOTAL	1500	500	2000	

[a] The amount of consumption expenditure in the third round (71.25) is 75 per cent of the (95) increment to income in the second round. This is made up of 75 per cent of consumption in the second round (75) plus 75 per cent of investment in the second round (20). Thus, the amount of consumption spending in any round is derived from both the consumption and the investment expenditure of the previous round. All figures in the table are rounded to the second decimal point.

[b] The amount of investment expenditure in the third round (19) is 20 per cent of the increment to income in the second round (95). This is made up of 20 per cent of (75) consumption in the second round plus 20 per cent of (20) investment in the sec-ond round. The amount of investment spending in any round is derived by applying the marginal propensity to invest (.20) to both the consumption and the investment expen-diture of the previous round.

The example above assumes that the propensities (to consume and to invest) remain constant throughout the infinite period. This assumption is

[11] Alvin H. Hansen, *Fiscal Policy and Business Cycles*, New York, Norton, 1941, pp. 64–65.

made, not to imply that the propensities will necessarily remain stable in real life, but to make possible the simple determination of quantitative answers. Changes in either of the propensities will change the total income effect. But the important thing to note is that an expenditure, whether of a consumption, investment, or government character, is continued through a series of waves of re-expenditure in the private economy affecting both consumption and investment. The waves of consumption expenditure are not the whole story; the income effect occurs through both consumption and investment.[12]

The general outline so far in this chapter of the major factors determining the level of economic activity is intended to lay the foundation for a consideration of the possible effects of fiscal policies upon the stability and growth of the private economy. The analysis so far has run in terms of the behavior of individuals and business concerns in the private sector of the economy. We have referred only occasionally to the behavior of the public sector—government—so far. This is appropriate because in a free enterprise economy the effectiveness of government fiscal policy depends upon the reaction to that policy in the private sector. In the United States economy, goods are not governmentally produced. They are purchased from the private sector, and their purchase creates incomes in the private sector. Likewise, the receipts of government are exactions from private incomes, and the major economic effects of these exactions are to be found in the subsequent behavior of taxpayers in the private sector.

Income-Inducing Effects of Fiscal Policy

Government expenditures fall into two broad categories: Direct purchases of goods and services, and transfer payments. In the former category are purchases of newly produced commodities (armaments, automobiles, typewriters, etc.) and payment of salaries to government employees. In the estimates for the fiscal year 1960, direct purchases of goods and services by the federal government were expected to represent some $54 billion out of total budget expenditure of $77 billion. The remainder are transfer payments, including welfare payments, grants to other governments, interest on the public debt, governmental loans, purchases of land, and the like. In all such cases the actual purchase of currently produced goods and services can be made only by the recipient of the transfer payment.

The immediate recipients of governmental payments for goods and services are principally business concerns and government employees. If

[12] Unless, of course, one of the marginal propensities is zero.

these employees are, on the average, reasonably well-paid, we may assume a relatively low propensity to re-spend receipts. This would be particularly true under conditions of slack in the economy, when savings are flowing only fractionally into current investment.

Transfer payments, insofar as they are characterized by social security retirement benefits, unemployment benefits, grants for public assistance functions of a welfare character, GI educational benefits, progress payments to states for highway construction, and purchases of mortgages when residential construction is held up for lack of mortgage funds, suggests a high propensity for re-spending. This high propensity would be partly balanced by a relatively low propensity to re-spend interest payments on the public debt, which accrue to a saving group. In general, the average dollar of transfer payments has a somewhat higher leverage upon the economy than the average dollar spent for currently produced goods and services.

Income-Inducing Effects of Government Expenditure. Let us ignore for the present the influence upon aggregate spending in the economy of the revenue-raising aspect of fiscal action, and concentrate upon the expenditure aspect alone. We are interested in seeing how, if at all, funds available to government can have a different effect upon the circuit flow spendings than funds in the hands of the public. There are two respects in which government funds can make a difference.

First, the funds in the hands of government may be more completely spent in the first round than funds in private hands. Suppose $100 of funds to be in possession of government, and $100 in possession of the public. Suppose also that there is recession in the economy, and the combined marginal propensities to re-spend (for consumption and investment) in the private sector are .9.[13] We can then expect that the funds in private hands will produce over a period of time through successive re-spending:

$$(I) \quad \$90 + 81 + 72.9 + 65.61 + \ldots = \$900$$

To take a short-period look, we find the income generated to be $243.90 in the first three periods. But if we assume, reasonably, that the whole $100 will be spent by government, the governmentally induced series (the series being subject to the private marginal propensity of .9 after the governmental expenditure is first made) is as follows:

$$(II) \quad \$100 + 90 + 81 + 72.9 + \ldots = \$1,000$$

[13] This means that the $100 of private funds is in the particular hands which the system of income distribution determines, and their marginal propensities are .9.

The income generated in the first three periods in this case is $271. There is no magic in the difference; it results from the fact that in the governmental series there is no leakage in the first wave of expenditure, because government's propensity to re-spend is higher than that in the private sector. Looked at in a slightly different way, $100 of funds in the hands of government will have the same income-inducing effects in time as $111.10 in the private sector, given the assumptions in our example. Clearly, however, if the private marginal propensity to re-spend were 1.0, as it could be in a business boom, the difference demonstrated in the example above would not exist.

The second possible advantage in governmental spending lies in the (presumed) ability of government to select high income-generating channels into which its spending will go. Thus, while the $100 in the hands of the public is subject to a propensity to re-spend of .9, it may be that by *selecting* particular segments of the spending public with abnormally high propensities, the government can be sure that the first round of re-spending will be more than .9, perhaps .95. Government has a propensity to spend of 1.0; the spending comes into the hands of selected persons whose propensity to re-spend is .95; thereafter it gets into the economy where the propensity is .9. Under these conditions the governmental series would be:

$$\text{(III)} \quad \$100 + 95 + 85.5 + 76.95 + \ldots = \$1,050$$

and the income generated in the first three periods is $275.50. This might well represent a case where governmental funds are paid to the unemployed, whose marginal propensity to consume is very high. While the "unit multiplier" applies to the governmental expenditure in both cases, in the second case the income generated is higher because government has selected as recipients of its payments persons with a potentially high re-spending propensity whose propensity is not now effective in the private sector because of the lack of spendable income. It follows, of course, that if government payments were to go to a group with a propensity to spend lower than that marginally effective in the economy, the income-inducing effects would be reduced. Thus, if governmental payments were to go to government bondholders, and their marginal propensity to re-spend were .8, the series would become (other assumptions continued):

$$\text{(IV)} \quad \$100 + 80 + 72 + 64.8 + \ldots = \$900,$$

with the income created in the first three periods being $252.

We may conclude that, taken by themselves and independent of taxation and other revenue effects of fiscal policies, government expenditures can have a peculiarly strong leverage effect upon the level of national income attained. This is possible in situations where the extent of expenditure of funds by government and by those who are recipients of governmental payments is greater than the propensity to spend by the private economy in general. These conditions are not necessarily present at any given time. The general private propensities may be so high in boom periods as to be at least as high as the propensities of government and of the original recipients of its payments.

Income-Inducing Effects of Combined Taxing and Spending. We can now broaden our prospective to take into account both sides of the fiscal process—the receipt of revenues as well as the making of expenditures. In the analysis above we began by assuming the funds to be in possession of government. However, the process of getting the funds into government's possession will also have economic effects—of a character more or less offsetting those resulting from the spending. We assume that the funds are procured from the public by taxation, though it makes no difference to the general content of the analysis whether they are received through taxes, fees, fines, prices, interest rates, gifts, or whatever. When taxes are paid to government, the taxpayer's income available for consumption or investment is reduced, and a series of re-expenditures in the private sector which would have resulted from the availability of this income will not be realized. The net effect of government's taxing and spending upon the national income will be the difference between the income-inducing effects of government spending and the income-reducing effects from the drawing off of spendable income from the private sector.

The possible effects can be shown by examples similar in many respects to those utilized in analyzing the effects of expenditures alone on the preceding pages. On page 97, expenditure series (I) assumed a private marginal propensity to spend from an income of .9. Funds of $100 in the hands of private individuals and businesses were seen to generate income over a period of time to the extent of $900. If government were to take away the $100 from these individuals and businesses, the loss in income privately generated would amount to $900. But the $100 of tax receipts in the hands of government would, if spent on persons with the same propensities to respend income as the taxpaying group, generate income of $1,000, as shown by series (II) on page 97. This is the situation where the double-barreled fiscal action of taxing and spending has no redistributive effects upon income in the society. That is, funds are not taxed from one income group and paid to another; the recipients of governmental payments have the same propensities as the taxpayers. Even in this case, however, it is seen that the income-generating effects are greater through fiscal action than they would have been otherwise. The difference of $100 in income induced is the result of government's completely spending its tax receipt of $100, while if the $100 were left in private hands only $90 would have been spent in the first round. This avoidance of a leakage of $10, when multiplied by the coefficient of leverage,[14] gives the difference of $100.

But the process of taxing and spending can have redistributive effects, which will further influence the income-generating consequences of fiscal policy. We saw in series (III) on page 98 that if government were to select the recipients of its expenditure so as to put funds in the hands of persons with potentially higher propensities to spend, the income effects would be magnified. Series (I) (page 97) shows the income which would be generated from $100 in private hands, and therefore the amount of income lost to the economy when $100 in taxes is taken from persons with a combined marginal propensity to spend of .9. The amount of this loss is $900 in the course of time. Series III (page 98) demonstrated the creation of income resulting from government spending when it took pains to make its payments to persons with relatively high propensity to spend. This is $1,050. The difference of $150 is the national income gain resulting from the fiscal action.

But there is still a further possibility of net gain if the taxes are selectively taken from taxpayers with relatively low propensities to re-spend. This is carrying the redistribution effect a step further than in the paragraph above. Payments are made to persons with high propensities, while taxes are taken from persons with low propensities. If the propensity to re-spend for a selected group of potential taxpayers is only .8 while the general propensity is .9, and the $100 in taxes is taken from them, the loss in income over a period of time to the economy is:

$$\text{(V)} \quad \$80 + 72 + 64.8 + 58.32 + \ldots = \$800,$$

while if the expenditures are made to persons with the potentially high propensity of .95 (as in series [III]) the income generated through the spending of these taxes by government is $1,050. Here the difference is very considerable, and redistributive fiscal policy is seen to have a high leverage effect.

---

[14] See p. 95. We assume in our examples a combined marginal propensity to spend for consumption and investment of .9.

$$\Delta C/\Delta Y + \Delta I/\Delta Y = .9.$$

Since the leverage coefficient is $\dfrac{1}{1 - \Delta C/\Delta Y + \Delta I/\Delta Y}$, it is $1/(1-.9)$ or 10.

Income-Creating Effects of a Balanced Budget. It has rather generally been assumed that a balanced governmental budget—with receipts and expenditures equal—is neutral in its effect upon the level of employment and income or upon the price level. This notion is based upon the conclusion that under a balanced budget[15] the income generation resulting from government expenditure is exactly offset by the loss of income which would have been generated by the expenditures of taxpayers if they had not been taxed.[16] But this is not usually the case. In fact, a balanced budget would be neutral in its income effect only in a special set of circumstances. Our examples in the preceding paragraphs are, as a matter of fact, examples assuming a balanced budget. For in each example, the amount of original expenditure by government was exactly equal to the taxes taken from the public. The conclusion to which one is forced is that even if there is no redistributive effect in fiscal action, i.e., if the governmental payments are made to the same persons from whom the taxes are taken, a balanced budget tends to have a somewhat expansive effect upon the economy. Under given conditions a larger balanced budget has a stronger expansive effect than a smaller balanced budget. This expansiveness occurs because the expenditure by government is not subject to the leakage occurring in private expenditure when the marginal propensity to spend is less than 1. The general conclusion would need to be qualified if the private marginal propensity were 1 or more than 1. This implies that a balanced budget (dollar-for-dollar) is more expansive in effect when the economy is in recession and the propensity to invest is low than in a period of inflation when the combined marginal propensities to consume and invest may be equal to 1.

The generalizations in the paragraph above related to a condition where the taxing-spending process resulted in no redistribution of spendable funds in the hands of the public. Even so, an expansive tendency was noted, though this tendency is greater when private propensities to spend are low than when they are high. But it is probable that the taxing-spending process would accomplish some degree of redistribution in the economy. If governmental revenues are raised preponderantly by progressive taxes, taking a larger proportion from high incomes than from low, while the expenditure pattern is regressive, expenditures being made in the first instance relatively

[15] In this section we are assuming the "cash budget" rather than the "conventional budget," as the former is a more inclusive account of fiscal action and is on a cash receipts and payments basis. (See Appendix to Chapter 2 for an elaboration of the differences.)

[16] This reasoning leads to the rather interesting conclusion that so long as the budget is balanced, it makes no difference to the level of employment or to the level of prices how large the budget is. Thus a large balanced budget would be just as neutral as a small balanced budget.

heavily to lower income groups, a downward redistribution of disposable income would result. At the other extreme, a system of regressive taxes and progressive payments would accomplish upward redistribution of disposable income. And since we can assume that, among other things, the leverage coefficient is influenced by the pattern of income distribution, fiscal activity which changes the income distribution in the economy will affect the level of income creation.

To be more specific, let us take a case where the tax-expenditure process creates a more equal distribution of disposable income than would have occurred without the process. It is presumed that the propensity to re-spend at the lower income levels is somewhat greater than that at the higher income levels. If $100 in taxes is taken from taxpayers whose marginal propensity to re-spend is .8, while the marginal propensity to re-spend for the society as a whole is .9, the negative effect upon the level of income of the taxation is: $80 + 72 + 64.8 + 58.32 + . . . = $800. But the $100 of revenue in the hands of government generates the following positive effect upon income: $100 + 90 + 81 + 72.9 + . . . = $1,000. The difference ($200) is a substantial contribution to current economic activity. It is on these grounds that there is likely to be agitation for the taxation of "hoards" to provide the funds for government expenditure in depression. If the expenditures can in the first instance be made to a selected group of persons with a marginal propensity of .95, the expenditure series becomes: $100 + 95 + 85.5 + 76.95 + . . . = $1,050, and the difference (+ $250) is still greater.

The opposite case would involve an upward redistribution of disposable income through the taxing-spending process, creating a more unequal pattern of distribution. Suppose that $100 of taxes are taken from selected persons whose marginal propensity is .95, the marginal propensity being .9 for the society as a whole. In this case the negative effect of the tax payment upon aggregate income, through private expenditures foregone, is: $95 + 85.5 + 76.95 + . . . = $950.[17] If the expenditures in the first round go to persons with a marginal propensity of .8, and thereafter go into the economy with a marginal propensity of .9, the expenditure series becomes: $100 + 80 + 72 + 64.8 + . . . = $900. Here there is a net loss of income through the substitution of the governmental channel for the private channel of expenditure.

In summary, under a balanced budget—or a balanced increase in the budget—although the taxes taken from the income stream are exactly equal to the government expenditures put into the income stream, the effect is

---

[17] Keeping in mind that the first-round spending sacrificed is subject to a .95 marginal propensity, while thereafter it is subject to a .9 marginal propensity.

usually to strengthen the level of income in the economy. This is true even when the taxing-spending process does not disturb the pattern of distribution of disposable income in the economy. When the effect of the taxing and spending is to redistribute what would otherwise be disposable income from the higher income groups to lower income groups, the upward push upon aggregate income is accentuated. And the greater the degree of downward redistribution (assuming that the lower the income the greater the propensity to spend), the stronger the leverage effect upon income. Although it would be possible through the taxing-spending process to redistribute disposable income upward sufficiently to have a contractive influence upon the level of income, this is not presumed to be a common situation when government revenues are levied to a large extent from progressive taxes on personal income, from taxes on corporation net income, and from excises upon items in the comfort and luxury categories, and when government expenditures go largely for wages and salaries and for transfer payments. That a balanced budget is neutral in effect upon the level of income produced cannot be assumed as typical. The more typical expectation is that the taxing-spending process tends to raise in some degree the level of aggregate spending and income.

Effect of An Unbalanced Budget upon Income. The analysis just concluded was based upon the assumption of a balanced cash budget, where the tax and other withdrawals from private receipts are just equal to the amounts of governmental payments. We turn now to a consideration of the effects when governmental receipts and payments are unequal—when there is deficit or surplus.

The Case of a Deficit. When payments exceed receipts, government is putting into the stream of national income larger amounts than it is withdrawing. The difference between the two—the deficit—represents the net expenditure of government, whose influence upon national income over a period of time is this net expenditure multiplied by the coefficient of leverage. Employing the same method of illustration used in the balanced budget example, if the marginal propensity to spend is the same for those who pay the taxes as for those who receive the government payments (assumed to be .9 in this illustration), and if receipts are $100 while payments are $110, we get the following results:

Negative income effect of tax receipts:
$$-(\$90 + 81 + 72.9\ldots) = -\$900$$
Positive income effect of expenditure:
$$\$110 + 99 + 89.1 + 80.2 + \ldots = \$1,100$$
Net income creation $+\$200$

The net income creation of $200 with a deficit of $10 compares with net income creation of $100 (see p. 97) under the same assumptions when the budget is balanced. The difference ($100) is the additional expenditure under the unbalanced budget case ($10) multiplied by the coefficient of leverage (10 when the marginal propensity is .9).

As a generalization we may conclude that a deficit always has a more expansive (or less contractive[18]) effect upon aggregate demand than a balanced budget of essentially the same size. This is true whether the fiscal process leaves marginal propensities unchanged, or whether a redistribution of disposable receipts occurs, provided our comparison of the balanced and unbalanced budget results uses the same propensities.

Perhaps some mention should be made of the possibility that the very fact of the deficit may have some effect upon the propensities. There is the possibility that the private sector is in the grip of a fiscal orthodoxy which looks with fear and disfavor upon "deficit financing." If violation of this orthodoxy were to result in a decline in the marginal propensity to invest, the combined propensities applicable to the expenditure series might fall, and the expansive effect would be reduced. During the great depression, when the United States had its first experience with deficit financing as a conscious instrument of income generation, there was considerable concern that such unorthodox fiscal practice might adversely affect the private propensity to invest and thus fail to produce the desired effect upon the level of employment. In the intervening period, however, the amazing expansive effect of deficit spending in World War II, the "peacetime" growth since that war of heavy dependence by major industries upon government purchases of goods and services, and the development of a more sophisticated view of the role of government in promoting stability, have all but eliminated this qualification of the generalization. The orthodoxy of annually balanced budgets continues to be widely held in the abstract. But the objective of vigorous aggregate demand—whether its components are private or governmental—has become far stronger than the orthodox rule.

The Case of a Surplus. A cash surplus occurs when governmental receipts exceed payments. This means that the tax (and other) withdrawals from the private sector are greater than the governmental expenditure. This would imply that, under given propensities, a surplus would reduce aggregate demand below what it would have been under a balanced budget. Employing the assumption of a .9 marginal propensity to spend in the economy, if tax receipts were $100 while payments were $90—producing

[18] We have seen that a balanced budget may have a contractive effect if significant upward redistribution of disposable receipts occurs as a result of the taxing-spending process.

a surplus of $10—the effect over a course of time upon national income would be:

Negative income effect of tax receipts:
$$-(\$90 + 81 + 72.9 + \ldots) = -\$900$$
Positive income effect of expenditure:
$$\$90 + 81 + 72.9 + \ldots = \$900$$

Net income effect $ 0

The zero or neutral effect upon aggregate demand in this case of a surplus of $10 contrasts with an increase in aggregate demand of $200 under conditions of deficit expenditure of $10 with the same level of tax rate (p. 103). It contrasts also with the $100 increase in aggregate demand when a balanced budget is assumed (p. 97).

However, in the example above we have left the surplus of $10 hanging in mid-air. What happens to it? One possibility is, of course, that the cash balance of the treasury is simply permitted to rise by $10. This might be referred to as hoarding the surplus, not permitting the funds to return to the income stream. It is hardly likely that in a democratic society such a decision would long be permitted. A second possibility is that the prospect of a surplus would lead to a relaxation of expenditure controls or to a tax cut. Either of these cases would move us in the direction of the results expected from a balanced budget.

The third, and most likely, possibility is that the surplus would be used for debt retirement. In this case the surplus does find its way back into the income stream. If the recipients of debt repayments have the same marginal propensity to spend their receipts as the economy in general, the income effect will be the same as if there were a balanced budget. But these recipients may well have a propensity to spend lower than that for the economy as a whole, for bondholders are likely to have relatively high incomes and high propensities to save. In this case the use of the surplus for debt retirement accomplishes some upward redistribution of disposable receipts in the economy. Assuming the general marginal propensity to spend to be .9, while that of debt holders is .7, the effect of using surplus to retire debt would be:

Negative income effect of $100 tax receipts: $-(\$90 + 81 + 72.9 + \ldots) = -\$900$
Positive income effect of $90 budget expenditures: $\$90 + 81 + 72.9 + \ldots = \$900$
" " " " $10 debt retirement: $\$7 + 6.3 + \ldots = 70$

     $970

Net income effect $70

This compares with a net income effect of zero from a surplus of $10 in the same size budget when the surplus is hoarded (p. 105), and of $100 in a balanced budget of the same size (p. 97).

The results of the above analysis of the effect upon the national income of balanced and unbalanced budgets may be demonstrated graphically by the use of traditional diagrams of income analysis. In Figure 4 the effect of a balanced budget is shown, using numerical magnitudes somewhat dif-

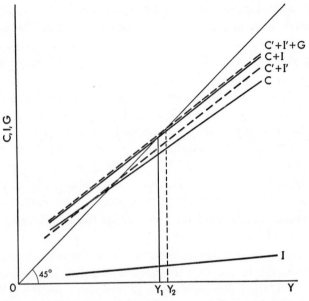

Figure 4. The effect upon income of a balanced budget.

ferent from those in the numerical examples in order to make the diagrams readable. The consumption function (C) shows amounts of consumption expenditure which would occur at various levels of GNP (Y). It has a slope of 2/3, implying a marginal propensity to consume throughout of that magnitude. The investment function (I) has a slope of 1/12, and reflects both autonomous and induced investment. Thus, the sum of the marginal propensities to consume and to invest is 3/4. Since these propensities are applied consistently to both the tax and expenditure sides of the picture, our diagram employs the assumption that the taxing-spending process accomplishes no redistribution: i.e., it refers to the situation discussed on page 99.

If there were no fiscal activity—if there were no government in the picture—the equilibrium level of national income would be OY_1. But when we consider the effects of government fiscal operations, two sorts of changes occur. The first is the income-reducing effect of a tax deduction from private spendable funds. The taxes reduce C and/or I, and the $C + I$ function drops to the position $C' + I'$. The amount by which the function falls is not the amount of taxes, but the amount of immediate expenditure which would have been made by the payers of the taxes. That is, the function falls by the marginal propensity to spend (assumed to be .75 in the diagram) times the amount of taxes. The balance of the tax money is simply transferred from savings.

The second effect is that created by the governmental expenditure for goods and services. In this balanced budget case, G—government purchases of goods and services—is equal to the whole of tax receipts, and is added to $C' + I'$ to give aggregate expenditure in the economy at various levels of Y, as shown by the function $C' + I' + G$. The net result of the two changes is a new equilibrium level of income at Y_2. The increase in income resulting from the taxing-spending operation is the excess expenditure of $C' + I' + G$ over $C + I$ times the leverage coefficient. In the diagram, since the marginal propensity to spend is 3/4, the leverage coefficient is 4, and the increase in income is four times the original net increment to expenditure ($C' + I' + G$ minus $C + I$).

Figure 5 demonstrates diagramatically the case of a budget surplus

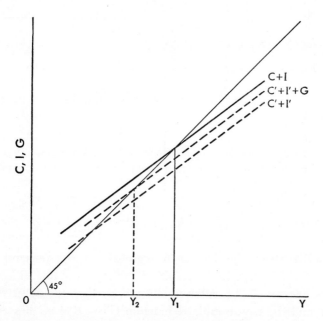

Figure 5. The effect upon income of a budget surplus.

sufficiently large to accomplish a reduction in aggregate demand (C' + I' + G). We begin with a private expenditure function ($C + I$) as in the previous diagram, which would create, in the absence of any fiscal action, an equilibrium level of income of OY_1. When government is introduced, the imposition of taxes reduces the $C + I$ function to the position $C' + I'$. The amount by which the function falls is the marginal propensity to spend for consumption and investment (.75) times the tax receipts. But government expenditure, G, is substantially less than the amount of taxes taken, and less than the amount by which the tax imposition forced a reduction in $C + I$. The new equilibrium is at OY_2, which is the leverage coefficient (4) times the net amount by which aggregate demand falls ($C + I$ minus $C' + I' + G$). The result is a level of GNP (OY_2) lower than that which would have occurred without fiscal action (OY_1). This diagram does not show any effects from re-spending the budget surplus.

Finally, the case of a budget deficit is demonstrated in Figure 6. In this

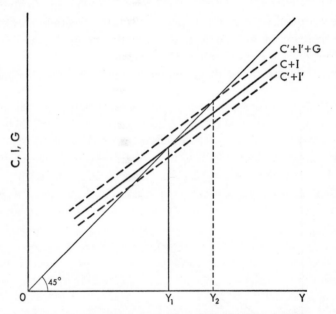

Figure 6. The effect upon income of a budget deficit.

case, $C' + I'$ portrays the decline in aggregate private demand for consumption and investment goods resulting from the tax imposition. But in this case the impact of G is substantially greater than the negative impact of taxation, and the new combined function $C' + I' + G$ lies above the original $C + I$. The equilibrium level of income increases from OY to OY_2, and this increase is the leverage coefficient (4) times the difference between $C' + I' + G$ and $C + I$. Just as our simplified case of the surplus above assumed that the surplus did not find its way back into the income stream, so in this case we make the simplifying assumption that the deficit is financed by newly created money in the banking system and not drawn from the spendable resources of individuals and businesses. Thus, the deficit is financed in such a way as not to affect private consumption and investment out of current income.

Conclusion

We have presented in this chapter the analytical basis for conclusions as to the effects of fiscal action upon the level of activity at which the economy operates. There is a constant temptation to assume that this analysis is relevant only to the case where fiscal policy is to be consciously used to stabilize the economy at a desired level. But the analysis is equally relevant for the economic effects of fiscal action which may be dictated by other than stability objectives. Thus, while the analysis offers guidelines for appropriate fiscal policy to correct excessive or insufficient aggregate demand, it also provides a basis for judging the effects upon the economy of, say, a change in the level of armament expenditures under a threat of war.

Whether fiscal action will be expansive, contractive, or neutral depends upon a variety of circumstances. Fundamentally, any net influence upon income depends upon the over-all effect of fiscal practice upon aggregate demand for goods and services. Part of this over-all effect is the direct result of government demand for goods and services through the expenditure side of the budget. The other part is the indirect effect of fiscal action upon private expenditures for goods and services. In this latter the principal influence is the tax subtraction from private spendable incomes, but impact may also be made upon private spending by the influence of government spending programs upon the profit expectations of businessmen, the price expectations of consumers, and the state of general psychology in the business environment.

This, however, only identifies the kinds of influences which governmental fiscal action may have upon the private economy. If we wish to quantify the impact of fiscal policy—to determine *how much* impact these influences may have—it is necessary to consider propensities. And though the propensities frequently cannot be quantified in any very exact sense, it is usually possible to conclude that one policy will have more or less effect than another.

RECOMMENDED READINGS

Hansen, Alvin H., *Fiscal Policy and Business Cycles*, N.Y., Norton, 1941.

This is the classic study relating fiscal policy to business cycle theory. Chapters 2 and 6 are especially useful for the purposes of this text chapter, but others could well be selected to serve more specialized interests.

Samuelson, Paul A., "Fiscal Policy and Income Determination," *Quarterly Journal of Economics*, 1942, pp. 575–605.

A highly recommended article on the general subject of fiscal policy and stability, somewhat oriented to underemployment, and giving attention to major policy issues of the time.

Wallich, Henry C., "Income-Generating Effects of a Balanced Budget," *Quarterly Journal of Economics*, 1944, pp. 78–91.

A pioneering article on the expansive influence of a balanced budget. A technically more advanced discussion of an aspect of the theory discussed in this text chapter.

CHAPTER 5

Government Expenditure and Economic Instability

One of our society's goals is that of stable economic growth. Instability implies departure from full employment at stable price levels. When labor and capital resources are idle, the society loses goods and services for which productive capacity is available, and this loss is not simply a postponement but a permanent loss.[1] In addition, unemployment represents a wholly accidental redistribution of income among persons that is likely to be most serious among persons who can afford it least. It thus represents an inhumane and antisocial occurrence that justifies the use of corrective policy wherever feasible.

Inflation, meaning a rise in a number of individual prices significant enough to cause the general index to rise, has somewhat similar social effects. While inflation may encourage a boom in employment and business activity, not all prices can rise together and a wholly fortuitous and unplanned redistribution of real incomes in the society results. Inflation may cause contortions in the economy by overdeveloping those lines in which current and temporary monetary demand permits price rises, while squeezing those lines temporarily less fortunate. Price instability complicates business planning, encourages wasteful expansion in some instances, and may well create structural disproportions in the economy which can be corrected only by recession.[2] Clearly, the realization of the social goal of stability

---

[1] Senator O'Mahoney, in testimony before a subcommittee of the Senate Committee on Banking and Currency (*U. S. Senate, S. 380,* 79th Congress, 1st Session, July 30, 1945), quoted figures from the Bureau of the Census showing that the deficiency in national income below the full employment level between 1929 and 1940 represented a loss of production amounting to $355 billion.

[2] The recession and unemployment of 1957–1958, for example, can hardly be explained without reference to the investment boom of 1956–1957.

means specifically the successful counteraction of a tendency toward unemployment or inflation.

In Chapter 3 it was seen that the scale of modern governmental activity makes government in the aggregate a potent element in the income-expenditure situation at any given time. Fiscal policy is therefore a relevant factor in economic stability or instability, and government can hardly escape responsibility for ordering its affairs so as to avoid contributing to instability. But the responsibility goes much further than this. In an essentially private enterprise economy, the governmental sector is the only one capable of centralized control. That is, the government sector is directed; the private sector is not. Thus, governmental policy should avoid *initiating* instability in the private sector; it can also be used to offset instability arising within the private sector.

Chapter 4 showed what kinds of fiscal action in general can be expected to strengthen or to weaken aggregate demand, and thus create the proper aggregate conditions for stability. But it should be obvious that policy will lack appropriate direction unless something is understood of the nature of the forces creating instability at a given time.

THE BUSINESS CYCLE

Business cycles are recurrent fluctuations of business activity observable in statistics of output, income, and employment. The cycle moves from prosperity to depression and back again, not in a uniform span of time, nor with a uniform degree of intensity. The detailed causes of the business cycle are undoubtedly many and varied, and there are many "theories" which attempt to explain it. These theories differ both as to kinds of causes and as to emphasis upon particular influences.

We shall not attempt to study carefully the areas of agreement and disagreement among particular cycle theories. For our purposes it is adequate to study causes and effects at a level somewhat below the surface and somewhat above the detailed depths of particular analyses. It is useful to begin with the recognition that general increase or decrease of production and employment is the aggregate result of conscious choices—it does not just happen. In an economy where direction of the productive process is in the hands of enterprisers who are producing for more or less remote markets, the choice to increase or decrease will be determined by enterprisers' expectations as to the prospects for adequate return. These prospects are largely dependent upon estimates as to the nature of future demand for products. Rising demand, under typical conditions of "sticky" costs, promises both larger profit margins and larger volume of sales, while falling demand produces the opposite consequences.

If profit expectations are rising, the urge to expand output to take advantage of improving markets results in increased employment of all types of productive agents—labor, capital, and natural resources. If profit expectations are falling, there is an urge to contract the quantities of productive agents employed. If, as is unlikely over more than a very short period, profit expectations are constant, the tendency is simply to replace goods used up—inventories or equipment.

The desire to expand, contract, or simply to replace has different and important consequences at different productive levels. The producers' goods industries produce for markets in which their sales are (1) for replacement of capital goods constantly wearing out, and (2) for net increase in productive capacity. The demand for their products is a "derived" demand, and whether it is great or small depends upon the anticipations of other producers, most of whom are producing for consumer markets. Decisions to expand output result in demand for more producers' goods; decisions to contract mean disappearance of demand for producers' goods for plant expansion and a decline in demand for replacement goods. Decisions to maintain production at a given level mean demand for producers' goods only for replacement. Thus a decision by a producer close to the consumer market to expand or contract, even by a small amount, has accentuated effects upon the demand for producers' goods. If industry has been expanding, the decision to cease expansion is a _contraction_ in demand for capital goods. This fact of magnification of derived demand is referred to by economists as the "principle of acceleration." It accounts for the business cycle phenomenon of much more violent fluctuation of business activity in the producers' goods industries than in the consumers' goods industries.

The business cycle contains self-generating forces which tend to terminate the phase of prosperity or of depression. In a period of recovery or prosperity, anticipations[3] are rising. Markets are expanding, and production expands by the employment of factors of production left idle during depression. The prices of goods tend to rise more rapidly than do costs of production, and profit margins are rising. Rising profit margins and expanding markets further improve the anticipations of producers. Increased employment and wages, the accumulated demand for goods which consumers

---

[3] "Anticipations" is here used in the sense in which it is used by James W. Angell in his _Investment and Business Cycles,_ New York, McGraw-Hill, 1941 (p. 15). It is a collective concept, indicating the combined influences upon the degree of optimism concerning the economic future, current need for liquid funds, tradition, and education and skill. It refers to the anticipations of both producers and consumers.

could not afford during depression, and the prospect of rising prices combine to increase demand for consumption goods.

Why does this not go on indefinitely? There are several possible reasons, operating in varying combinations and degrees in different cycles. As the economy expands, costs of production must at some point increase at a rate which at least stabilizes profit margins, and may narrow them. When the factors of production approach full employment the prices of those factors rise comparatively rapidly. This may dampen anticipations so as to lead enterprisers to stop expansion of productive capacity, which is the equivalent of a reduction of demand for producers' goods. Or the crisis may come when the banking system has extended itself to the limit in financing expansion of production or consumption. When further expansion is difficult or impossible, or if consumption is not rising rapidly enough to justify the investment boom, contraction in demand for producers' goods occurs.

Anticipations may cease to rise or may fall because of production bottlenecks in the expansion process, by government action of a restrictive sort, by fear induced by financial failures or defaults, or by occurrences in the international markets. These may be termed external influences, as distinguished from the self-generating internal influences mentioned in the previous paragraph.

Whatever the cause or combination of causes, expansion slows down, with contractive effects on some segments of the economy. Falling anticipations in these segments produce unemployment, retirement of debt, hoarding, and a general battening-down against the weather which has cumulative and epidemic effects upon the economy. This is recession and may turn into depression.

Deflation feeds upon itself, because demand declines in some areas are transmitted to other areas. If prices do not fall, unemployment must take up the slack; if they do fall, costs of production will probably fall less rapidly at first, causing narrowing of profit margins or widening of loss margins. At some point in the decline, adjustments will have occurred which arrest falling anticipations. Unemployment and competition for jobs may so reduce labor costs as to arrest the trend toward further unemployment. Idle funds and excess bank reserves may markedly lower the cost of loans and the standards required of borrowers. Inventories may have reached a low point where their replacement requires a pick-up in production. If the decline continues long enough, depreciation and obsolescence may so reduce productive capital equipment as to require replacement on a significant scale, creating respectable new demand for the products of capital goods

industries. Government relief and public works policies may check the
decline in consumption or actually increase it. Or other aspects of monetary
policy or recovery programs may produce the desired results. Whether the
causes are internal or external, there will somewhere be a lower turning
point, at which point anticipations begin to rise.

Since World War II the pace of population increase, the almost explosive
rate of technological change, the avid pursuit of higher levels of living, and
governmental policies designed to promote full employment have tended to
create a situation in which recessions terminate before serious depression
occurs. Thus, the downturns since the war—in 1948–1949, 1953–1954, and
1957–1958—have been essentially inventory recessions. The prosperity phase
terminates when businesses awaken to the fact that their rate of expansion
is not justified by the rate of consumption increase. The first reaction is to
work off inventories which, if increased at their previous rates, would involve heavy carrying costs. As orders decline, unemployment is created, but
this movement will be checked before a serious cumulative downward
movement develops. The relative stability of consumption—its failure to
rise rapidly enough to justify continuance of the investment boom—now
becomes a boon, in that it provides a high floor under the decline, making
it possible to work off inventories without undue stress.

While since World War II a variety of factors has contributed to avoidance of serious cumulative depression, these same factors have created an
almost persistent threat of inflation. Monetary demand has been adequate
to permit price increases both when cost increases have narrowed profit
margins and when they have not. For this reason monetary and fiscal
policies have frequently been designed to limit monetary demand. On the
whole, the consensus seems to indicate that monetary and fiscal policies
have worked more successfully since World War II in preventing depression
than in preventing inflation. While this may be the case, the period has in
some respects been an unusual one, preventing a fair test. The underlying
strength of economic expansion since World War II has tended over the
period as a whole to make the forces for inflation stronger than the forces
for contraction.

Also, the cold war and the population increases have imposed such
heavy expenditure demands upon the budget as to limit the flexibility
necessary for maximum effectiveness in stabilizing the economy. Finally,
the social assessment of unemployment as a more serious malady than inflation, and some experiences with price increases occurring concurrently
with unemployment, have further restricted the use of policies against
inflation.

Economic "Stagnation"

Toward the end of the depression decade of the 1930's, the protracted depression and the continuance of a large volume of unemployment while other indexes showed substantial recovery caused some students to believe that our economy had reached a stage where economic stagnation, accompanied by continuing unemployment, had replaced full employment as the economic norm. The concept of stagnation implies potentially high levels of national income where the propensity to consume is low, the propensity to save is high, and the inducement to invest is not strong enough to absorb the savings which the society would wish to make at high income levels. The equilibrium level of income is thus rather persistently below that of full employment, and the rate of economic growth is extremely low.

The concept of stagnation runs in terms of limited opportunities for new investment. In an old country, without new land to be settled or brought into production, without new natural resources to be exploited, and with a relatively stable population, one type of opportunity for expansion of new investment disappears. The frontiers on which the economy may advance become intensive and not extensive. During the nineteenth century the exploitation of new lands and resources, and production for a rapidly increasing population, resulted in an expansion of markets which produced a consistent shortage of capital for production. Under such circumstances there was no long-run danger of an excess of saving over opportunities for investment. Rather, the exploitation of markets and resources required investment beyond the capacity of the American economy to save, and expansion was financed to a considerable degree by borrowing from abroad.

In an economy with stable population, lacking possibilities for extensive expansion, opportunities for new investment must be found in the advance in technology, the substitution of new processes for old, the development of new products, and in general the raising of the standard of living. So long as there are large areas of human wants unsatisfied by economic goods, and so long as production by more efficient methods is possible, the intensive frontier exists.

It is, however, not a satisfactory answer to call attention simply to unsatisfied wants and inefficient production methods. Unless enterprisers are willing to undertake production of new goods or of more old goods, and to adopt new methods of production, the opportunities for new investment do not in fact exist. And the situation is complicated by the fact that an old economy may well be a high-income economy, in which propensity to save is high. Under such conditions opportunities for new investment must be extensive and rising, unless increased savings are to be hoarded and thus deflate the income stream below the level necessary for full production.

Monopolistic practices, such as restriction of entrance of new firms into the market by control of patented processes or by other means, high price policies, and purchase and sterilization by hoarding of revolutionary techniques of production, are destructive of expansion opportunities on the intensive margin. In the same category are monopolistic practices of labor in stretching work, requiring the employment of stand-by laborers, and resisting the introduction of new products and processes. These practices are destructive of the only frontier remaining after disappearance of the extensive frontier, and thus promote the characteristics of "maturity" stagnation.

A stagnant economy would be subject to cyclical fluctuations. However, at the peak of the prosperity phase, equilibrium might be attained at less than full employment because of the high propensity to hoard, and periods of prosperity would be comparatively short and infrequent. Net return on invested savings, after deducting for risks and the cost of investment, would be inadequate to offset the liquidity preference of savers. In such an economy depression is likely to carry the curve of business activity to lower levels and to keep it there for longer periods of time.

Maturity stagnation is at least a potential malady capable of seriously affecting high-income economies. From the point of view of government expenditure policy, underemployment diagnosed as resulting from economic maturity would be expected to react to investment injections by government in a manner essentially similar to the reaction expected from the same treatment in a period of cyclical depression. In the former case the treatment would be prolonged and result in more or less constant increases in public debt, unrelieved by significant periods of treasury surplus and debt retirement.

Compensatory Spending in the Cycle

Compensatory government spending means government spending so as to compensate for inadequacies in private spending. If the economy is below full employment, government expenditures will be increased enough to restore full employment. On the other hand, if the situation is inflationary, compensatory spending requires a reduction of government expenditure to reduce aggregate demand. The earlier discussion of the leverage process indicated that the major effects of an expenditure (and of a reduction of expenditure) occur in the early stages. Thus, if the propensities in the private economy are weak, higher levels of government expenditure will need to be continued in order to continue gaining these first effects. If private propensities are strong, the expenditure reduction must be continued for the duration of the strong propensities.

"Pump-priming" is a special case of compensation, involving a "one-shot" injection of government expenditure into the income stream, in the hope that this will so strengthen private demand as to restore and maintain full employment. Pump-priming involves a rather unrealistic view of cyclical instability, carrying an implication that underemployment is only an erratic and accidental departure from a natural equilibrium at full employment. The problem of compensatory policy is to alter tendencies toward equilibrium at less than full employment or at inflated price levels, and to establish equilibrium at full employment. Pump-priming cannot often be expected to do the job.

Compensatory spending thus implies substitution of public for the inadequacy of private spending in order to promote a desired level of income. When such a policy is pursued during recession and depression it involves heavy government expenditure; during recovery a tapering-off of compensatory expenditures is indicated, and in prosperity or boom, when the rate of private spending is rapidly rising or dangerously high, government net expenditure should become negative, i. e., show an excess of taxation over expenditure. Compensatory taxation will be discussed in later chapters; in the following sections we discuss compensatory spending in greater detail under two sets of assumed circumstances: (1) anticipations falling and (2) anticipations rising.

Case I: Anticipations Falling. It will be recalled that "anticipations" include both the anticipations of producers and of consumers. It thus is a composite of forces tending toward expansion (rising anticipations) or contraction (falling anticipations) of private expenditures for consumption and investment.

In the recession and depression phases of the cycle the propensity to hoard is rising. Producers are cutting costs to feasible limits in terms of current demand; they are using income to retire debt, maintaining minimum inventories, and not replacing depreciating equipment. They are placing themselves in a relatively liquid position. Consumers are reducing consumption toward minimal limits, paying off debts when possible, and saving in highly liquid form (hoards) to prepare for the possibility of reduced current income and employment. It will be noted that the propensity to hoard among producers and consumers results both in the retirement of loans (new money) and the building up of liquid bank balances (hoards). The hoarding largely occurs through inability of the banks to find loan outlets for these funds.

Under such circumstances, the objective of compensatory spending is to pump into the expenditure stream in any income period enough government funds to offset the income which is privately removed from the circuit flow in that period. It follows that government expenditures must thus occur in increasing volume from period to period as long as the propensity to hoard is rising. For under falling anticipations, private expenditure *and government compensatory expenditures* are subject to increasing propensity to hoard. The leverage effects of both private and public expenditures are low and falling. Compensatory expenditures should thus be injected into the income stream in such a way as to minimize leakages into hoards and to maximize the multiplier effects. Several characteristics of such compensatory spending are indicated below.

1. When national income is declining, government revenues will fall under given tax rates. Compensatory expenditures represent a net addition to total government expenditures, and a deficit will be created. The counteraction of falling anticipations requires both rising spending and falling revenues. To some it has appeared attractive to procure the funds for compensatory expenditure by taxation of hoards. In this way hoards would be transferred through government to persons with high propensity to consume, thus accomplishing a higher degree of re-spending of income than would otherwise occur. But hoards serve two useful purposes when anticipations are low. They frequently represent a planned response to the desire for liquid savings, and if taxed away would be at least partially replaced by new hoards. Furthermore, they help to hold interest rates down, creating an atmosphere in the capital markets in which some borrowing can take place even when profit anticipations are low. Thus a program of compensatory expenditure accompanied by attempts to keep the budget currently in balance is almost certain to be accompanied by a further net decrease in private expenditure, vitiating the effects of the public spending. The program must consequently be financed by borrowing.

2. Borrowing to finance a compensatory expenditure program would in most cases have less negative effect upon private propensity to spend if funds were procured out of "new money" created by the banks rather than from individual savings. The "new money" loans extended by the banks to government should be created out of new member bank reserves made available by the central bank. This would obviate any tightening of bank credit (increase in bank loan interest or higher requirements for borrowers) to potential private borrowers for consumption or investment. It may be objected

that if government were to borrow from private savers only on a voluntary basis, such borrowing would not compete with private expenditure. However, when anticipations are low and falling, interest rates must be low if private borrowing is to occur. Under high liquidity preferences, borrowing by government from private savers would be likely to skim off precisely those funds which would be available to private borrowers at lowest interest, or at least reduce the excess of potential loanable funds which maintain constant downward pressure on interest rates.

3. In the interest of accomplishing maximum income results from a given expenditure, compensatory funds should be so spent as to be subject to the least possible channeling into hoards. This principle would certainly justify first expenditure upon projects (relief or other) which put government-spent funds into the hands of those who because of unemployment or low income would quickly re-spend their new income on consumption. This increase is transmitted to investment for replacement or expansion of productive capacity. On the other hand, key improvements such as highway construction, irrigation, and water power projects may reduce costs enough to make a whole new range of investments possible. Present knowledge of the relative leverage effects of expenditure on alternative objects is highly inadequate for planning purposes; the principle, however, is clear: the original injection should take place under conditions conducive to the greatest amount of re-spending of these funds. Some further consideration of this problem will be found in the following chapter, although the reader is warned not to expect simple and categorical answers.

Case II: Anticipations Rising. When anticipations are rising, the propensity to hoard is likely to be falling, the multiplier can be expected to increase, and the result will be acceleration of opportunities for private investment. Under these conditions government will control its spending with a view to orderly expansion of the private economy toward full employment.

In the first stages of recovery, compensatory spending will remain fairly high. Too rapid withdrawal of government support of the income stream might well create premature recession. The atmosphere should be conducive to the continual rise of anticipations. Efforts to balance the budget should not be pressed strongly at this stage, either through major decrease of expenditure or increase in taxes.

As recovery progresses on a firm foundation, government injections into the income stream should be progressively reduced. Just as in the downswing these successive injections increase, so in the upswing they decrease, although the point at which net expenditure will end (the budget being balanced) will depend upon the rapidity of the recovery of private spending in relation to the amount of unemployment remaining. While in the downswing the successive injections increased because of increase in the propensity to hoard, in recovery they may be allowed to decrease because of rising propensity to spend. Thus in recovery the gap between current employment and full employment would eventually be filled by private expenditure; government may speed the closing of the gap by further expenditure.

In the later stages of prosperity—as full employment is approached—government will have retired completely from compensatory *spending*. The level of government expenditures will be determined by the current cost of performing necessary governmental functions. The level of taxation will have increased, both from natural causes arising out of increase in national income and from increased tax rates designed to produce current surpluses and debt retirement. As full employment is approached, confidence is vigorous, and takes increased taxes in its stride. At this stage surplus is used to retire a part of the debt incurred by the previous deficit spending policy.

Tax increases will apply the brakes to too-rapid "boom" expansion and tend toward stabilization of the rate of expansion. This occurs in any income period by reducing the disposable income of spenders and thus reducing effective demand in the private sector. And to the extent that tax receipts are used to retire debt in the hands of private individuals, these funds tend to be redistributed to those with relatively lower propensity to consume. If the rate of increase in consumption is stabilized, the acceleration effects upon the producers' goods industries tend to be reduced.

Failure of government to cut expenditures as full employment is approached would contribute to the appearance of bottlenecks in the expansion process. As the factors of production become relatively scarce it is improper that government continue to compete for them with the private economy. To the degree that it does compete it contributes to the development of bottlenecks, and helps to bid up the prices of those factors. Government itself may thus bring about inflation and eventually a crisis in anticipations.

Fiscal policy during a period of rising anticipations is thus conditioned by (1) the remoteness of full employment and (2) the degree to which anticipations currently depend upon deficit spending. In the early stages of recovery both considerations indicate continuation of deficit spending. In the later stages deficit spending gives way to surplus taxation, the objectives being to apply the brakes to the boom and to prevent excessive price increases while contributing little to the standard of material welfare.

Conditions of Business Confidence

The success of depression fiscal policy is so dependent upon the behavior of anticipations in terms of "confidence" as to require some observations concerning its culture. "Confidence" is difficult to measure; it is even more difficult to assay. It is in essence personal, yet subject to a remarkable amount of transmission from person to person. It is "catching," and thus subject to generation or degeneration through salesmanship or propaganda. And it is by no means always founded upon reason. It is fostered by orthodoxy and weakened by innovation which transgresses the boundaries of orthodoxy. Because it is so defiant of analysis, we are at the mercy not only of the genuine article, but also of unreasonable facsimiles of it.

Confidence has its most critical influences upon counter-cycle fiscal policy during the period of deficit spending. It is then that what appears to be an eminently promising program may, by running afoul of confidence, either produce indifferent results or results distinctly undesirable. Since the alternative to government activity to induce recovery is waiting out the recession or depression, it is important to study those factors and techniques which show promise of making expenditure policy successful.

Undoubtedly, experience with a policy helps to allay fears of its consequences, particularly if that experience has been successful. But even if it has not been markedly successful, the ability of hindsight to point out weaknesses in former techniques will help to foster support on the next attempt. The American experience in the thirties has probably gone a long way toward allaying fears of deficit spending in considerable volume during depression. Public psychology relative to relief expenditure is similar to that relative to war—it is an obligation to be stoically assumed, whatever its expense. That expense is one of the costs of maintaining an economy subject to intermittent unemployment. Expenditures for relief are compensatory expenditures, and are injected into the declining income stream under circumstances favorable to the objective of offsetting and possibly reversing that decline. Popular acceptance of relief spending is at least to a limited degree tantamount to acceptance of deficit spending. If deficit spending for relief or unemployment has become orthodox, public psychology has gone a long way toward acceptance of government as an auxiliary motor in the economy.

The sheer weight of economic literature explaining the role of government spending in depression is probably a second factor in promoting confidence in such a policy. Such an extensive area of agreement among specialists, not only as to the practical obligation of government, but as to the real possibilities of success, should have conditioned public confidence. The spending experience of 1933–1938 did not have the benefit of articulate theoretical support such as is likely to exist in any future depression.

There is no doubt that studies of the deficit spending experiences of 1933–1938 have pointed to conclusions which in the future will allow government to embark upon such a policy much better prepared to avoid earlier mistakes in the treatment of the confidence factor. It is to be expected that (1) the policy will not be accompanied by tax increases in an attempt to attain budget balance; (2) Federal Reserve policy will be directed toward the creation of new excess reserves for the member banks, from which government will borrow;[4] (3) the policy will be accompanied by the minimum of necessary punitive acts against business, either regulatory or competitive; (4) a real attempt will be made to sell the policy to the public as a program of economic engineering, by (a) stressing its recovery as distinguished from its relief aspects, (b) marshaling the impressive body of theoretical and statistical evidence favoring the policy, (c) guaranteeing expenditures in amounts and for the duration required to bring about recovery, and (d) utilizing a calendar of public works previously determined upon and accenting those projects capable of meeting long-run public need.

Some interest attaches to the experience of the United States with deficit spending during the period 1933–1938. Studies of that experience[5] indicate that public spending was reasonably successful as a compensatory device, that it prevented national income from falling as far as it otherwise would have fallen. Particularly in 1934–1936, when deficit expenditures were relatively high, public spending was largely responsible for marked net increase in national income. Furthermore, the abrupt reduction in expenditures in 1937 is regarded as largely responsible for the precipitous recession which occurred in that year and lasted into 1938.

As a pump-priming device, however, public expenditure in the thirties must be regarded as almost wholly unsuccessful. Anticipations did not rise, as indicated by the fact that propensity to hoard appears to have remained constant or to have increased during the period. Such private investment as did occur appears largely to have been made simply to provide productive capacity for current consumption needs, and did not represent investment for expanding future output.

Must we, therefore, conclude that there are no pump-priming potentialities in public spending? Generalization from the one experience with something approaching a pump-priming project is extremely dangerous. To say that pump-priming is always doomed to failure because it failed in 1933–

---

[4] This will be accomplished principally by open market purchases of securities by the Federal Reserve Banks. These purchases may be from member banks or from individuals and businesses. The Federal Reserve funds paid out—whether to banks or others—find their way into the member banks. As these new funds are deposited by member banks with Federal Reserve Banks, new legal reserves are created. Reduction of reserve requirements is another possibility.

[5] See James W. Angell, *Investment and Business Cycles*, New York, McGraw-Hill, 1941, pp. 221–34, and Sherwood M. Fine, *Public Spending and Postwar Economic Policy*, New York, Columbia, 1944, Chapter 6.

1938 policy is comparable to the generalization: "All Indians always walk in single file; at least the only Indian I ever saw did."

Certain characteristics of the 1933–1938 policy may be specifically criticized as militating against its possible success. First, it was half-hearted. Expenditures were not large enough in 1933–1934 even as modest compensatory expenditures. All through the period deficit expenditures were made primarily with a view to relief, and only secondarily was the hope expressed that as a by-product the economy might be strengthened. Deficit expenditures were usually accompanied by protestations that attempts should be made to balance the budget in each next fiscal year. This is hardly conducive to a rise in private anticipations; what is required is the pledge that the auxiliary motor of government will provide support as long as required and in the amounts required. Second, the constant dread of a series of unbalanced budgets and the desire to redress inequalities in income led to relatively high income and commodity taxation. The reverse type of compensatory tax policy was indicated.

Third, the spending program was haphazard. The very newness of the policy of deficit spending meant that no program of public projects was ready to be undertaken. There was a great deal of fumbling for recovery tools. Attempts to force re-employment at higher wages under NRA were hardly calculated to raise employers' anticipations, even under the artificially generated enthusiasm for recovery reflected in parades. And government's *quid pro quo* to business for pledges to hire more men at higher wages was codes of "fair competition," which in practice meant (and still does mean) the antithesis of competition. The consequence was price rigidity, which is an arch-enemy of adjustment in the business cycle. The gold policy and the scuttling of the World Economic Conference in 1933 rightly or wrongly suggested the probability of monetary and trade manipulation, the nature and results of which could not be forecast. Social Security, inaugurating a new concept of labor welfare and a new crop of taxes, was not generative of confidence in the breasts of business enterprisers. Contributing similarly to the decline of producer anticipations was the National Labor Relations Act, long overdue but ill-timed for success of a pump-priming project.

This is not to criticize the reform measures *per se* taken during the thirties. The timing was unfortunate from the point of view of counter-cycle fiscal policy. It can be convincingly argued that the reforms were long overdue. For our purposes, however, the important point is that many major reforms are now integrated into the economy, and additional major reforms should be adopted during the phase of fuller employment, and not allowed to collide with counter-cycle spending policy when anticipations are low.

Compensatory Spending in a Stagnant Economy

The consequences of stagnation, which were described early in this chapter, are an economy whose periods of prosperity may stop short of full employment and whose periods of depression will be longer and deeper than those of an expanding economy.

Counter-cycle fiscal programs discussed earlier in this chapter are generally applicable to both "mature" and expanding economies for identical reasons. The exception is that deficit spending even at the top of the cycle may be necessary in order to promote full employment in a naturally stagnant economy. Thus, under conditions of stagnation, the prospect would be for persistent government deficits and constant additions, though by varying increments, to national debt.

The difficulty, as in the case of cyclical reduction in income, would be in the inadequacy of investment from savings. The solution—if, indeed, there were any—would be along one or both of the following lines: (1) channeling of the excess of savings over investment into consumption, or (2) increasing the attractiveness of investment. Both of these aim at reduction of hoarding. And as before, each may be thwarted by a decline in confidence which, taken by itself, reduces anticipations.

Contemplation of the prospect of continued annual deficits might well have accentuated adverse influences upon anticipations. On the other hand, if reasonably considered, such a policy of government investment in national product is economic—and identical with similar private investment—so long as the carrying charges on the debt incurred are less than the income generated.

It is necessary, however, to keep in mind that the leverage effects of public spending in an economy incapable of reaching full employment under its own power would be relatively low. Therefore, the effects of a given increment of public expenditure would be short-lived, while service costs on the debt incurred would probably continue beyond the effectiveness of the expenditure. As compensatory spending continued, it would be necessary to generate net increases in national income toward full employment or to maintain a full-employment level of income against the mounting frictions caused by debt increase. The questions of the burdensomeness of a public debt, and the nature of the limits of the size of possible debt, will be discussed in a later chapter. For the present it is well to keep in mind that an internally held public debt is not "burdenless," as some have claimed, even though its practicable limit has been shown to be far beyond that predicted by the "orthodox" view.

The long-run possibilities of attaining and remaining at a level of full employment in a "mature" economy are thus discouraging, if deficit spending by government is considered alone. Extra-fiscal measures appear to be the only ones promising long-run salvation from stagnation. For if the extensive margins of expansion are gone, the intensive margins still possess almost unlimited potentialities for expansion. And the obstacles to expansion on the intensive margin are restrictive policies of "saving the market," where pioneering is blocked because "possession is nine points of the law."

Compensatory Policy Since World War II

Much of the previous discussion is oriented toward conditions of severe depression, and is characteristic of thinking during the nineteen-thirties and early nineteen-forties. It led in 1946, under the cloud of fear that termination of war expenditures might well produce a serious business setback in the early postwar period, to the passage of the Employment Act of 1946. The Act charged the federal government with responsibility to "promote maximum employment, production, and purchasing power," and both legislative and executive machinery were set up to work toward a goal of stability at full employment. Fiscal policy has consistently been a major interest of those to whom particular responsibility has been assigned for the maintenance of full employment.

In nearly all circles the role of fiscal action in promoting stability or instability is recognized, even though economic stabilization may not be given the highest priority in budget decisions. While compensatory policy sometimes carries an opportunist flavor, the economic facts of life are basically accepted. For example, although in the 1958 recession conservatives frequently opposed stepped-up compensatory expenditures, in 1959 they demonstrated great unanimity of opinion favoring elimination of the deficit as the central anti-inflation weapon.[6] And when policy has appeared to be inconsistent with stability requirements, it has often not been a question of acceptance of the principles but rather a failure to assess the business prospects accurately or the assignment of higher priority to considerations other than stability.

Fiscal policy in the recession of 1949–1950 turned out to be appropriate more by luck than by intelligent design. In the face of rapidly rising prices

[6] In 1959 the liberals, who are normally more enthusiastic for compensatory fiscal policy, opposed expenditure reductions on the grounds that extra-stabilization requirements were more demanding. Fearing that the drive for expenditure reduction might affect national security adversely, they generally favored rising military and foreign aid expenditures, and would compensate for them by tax increases and/or restrictive monetary policy. Some felt, however, that the inflationary dangers were overestimated, and that a high rate of economic growth demanded expansionist fiscal and monetary policies.

in 1947 and 1948 the Congress three times passed a tax reduction bill. All three times it was vetoed by the President, but on the third occasion (1948) his veto was overridden. Federal cash payments to the public had fallen from $95.2 billion in fiscal 1945 to $36.5 billion in 1948, while in the same period cash receipts from the public had fallen only from $50.2 billion to $45.4 billion. Thus, in fiscal 1947 and 1948, while consumer prices were rising 12 and 7 percentage points respectively, a cash surplus with respect to the public of $6.6 billion and $8.9 billion was being produced. This fiscal record was entirely appropriate to the times, the cash surplus undoubtedly exerting a significant anti-inflationary force. In the context, therefore, the tax reduction bill (which was estimated to involve about $5 billion of revenues on a full year basis) was hardly sensible. By coincidence, however, it became fully effective in the fiscal year 1949, concurrently with a minor decline in prices and a decline in the GNP. At the same time, the inauguration of the Marshall foreign aid plan and an increase in budgetary outlays for defense reduced the cash surplus from $8.9 billion in fiscal 1948 to $1 billion in fiscal 1949, and to − $2.2 billion in fiscal 1950. By the first calendar quarter of 1950 the GNP was on the rise after four recession quarters, and the recession had ended. While only the bare outlines of developments are here presented, it is evident that fiscal policy became appropriate for the period less because policy was properly tailored to economic conditions than because conditions adjusted themselves to policy.

As war conditions and inflationary forces returned in the period 1950–1952, not only was business booming, but tax rate increases were inaugurated. An appropriate cash surplus of $7.6 billion was created in fiscal 1951, partly because defense expenditures lagged behind their planned rate. When these expenditures doubled (from $22 billion to $44 billion) between 1951 and 1952, rising taxes were able to produce a balanced cash budget in the latter year. Though fortune and a rise in personal savings in the economy helped, the stability record was good during this period. Consumer prices rose only two percentage points in 1952 over 1951 in spite of the large defense build-up.

Policy with respect to the recession of 1953–1954 again reflects a combination of planning and luck. The attempt to stabilize and largely liquidate the Korean troubles in 1953 was accompanied by violent slashes in budget expenditures. These were reduced by $10 billion between fiscal 1953 and 1955, entirely accounted for by reductions in defense outlays. The effect of the announcement of this program helped to create weakness in the economy, and recession set in during the last half of the calendar year 1953 and lasted until the last quarter of 1954. On the other hand, accompanying the reduction in expenditures was a reduction in taxes, which moderated the economic effects of the expenditure cut. The Korean excess profits tax was allowed to terminate at the end of 1953, and some excise rates fell at the same time. A reduction of approximately 10 per cent in individual income tax rates was made effective. The full effect of these tax changes and those reductions legislated in the Internal Revenue Code of 1954 was not felt until the fiscal year 1955, by which time budget revenues had fallen by $4.4 billion below the 1953 level. In addition, the recession substantially increased trust fund expenditures, which are not included in budget expenditures. The upshot of all these actions and of recession reductions in the income tax base was a series of cash deficits of $5.3, $.2, and $7.2 billion in fiscal 1953, 1954, and 1955, respectively. The aggregate results operated in the proper direction for a recession period, although it must be seen that the budget expenditure reductions of 1954 and 1955 required a host of offsetting actions in the interest of stability, including expansionist monetary policy.

The recession of 1957–1958 occurred in a set of conditions somewhat different from those affecting the recessions of 1949 and 1954. That in 1949 was related to the completion of reconversion after the war and the disappearance of the war-created waiting lists for durable consumer goods. The 1954 recession was to some extent related to termination of the Korean build-up and the decision for major budgetary cuts. In 1957 the situation was an almost pure classic example of the adjustments following an investment boom, although throughout 1957 there was half-hearted talk of minor budget expenditure reduction. This last recession was therefore a more normal and less complicated set of conditions for the determination of anti-recession fiscal policy.[7] When recession was recognized in the last quarter of 1957, proposals for a reversal of expenditure policy were heard, partially in reaction to the successful placing of Sputnik I into space by the U.S.S.R. The first half of calendar 1958 (the last half of fiscal 1958), when the recession reached its lowest point, produced budget expenditures slightly smaller than had been estimated at the beginning of this period. The economy thus received no actual additional support from budget expenditures during this critical period, though the expectation of higher expenditures in the following fiscal year undoubtedly had some favorable announcement effect upon business expectations. As the recession deepened during the first quarter of 1958, some agitation for an immediate tax cut was heard, but it was not

[7] The secular reactions in the automobile and appliance markets and in housing construction were, in some sense, contributory and abnormal.

seriously contemplated by either the Congress or the Executive. One must conclude that whatever fiscal assistance was felt during this period resulted not from discretionary action either in the tax or expenditure field, but rather from automatic stabilizing elements incorporated into long-range policies. Most notable was the system of progressive taxes based upon net income. As incomes fell in the recession, personal income taxes for fiscal 1958 fell about $1 billion below the previous year and $2.5 billion below the official estimate made when the year was half over. Corporation income tax revenues fell $1.1 billion below the previous year's collections. Thus, although budget expenditures during fiscal 1958 were actually below their mid-year estimate, budget revenues automatically fell enough to turn what had been anticipated as a deficit of $.4 billion into an actual deficit of $2.8 billion. Outside the budget proper, cash payments into the economy through trust funds also played some part. Receipts and payments of the unemployment compensation trust fund swung from a surplus of $.3 billion in fiscal 1957 to a deficit of $1.2 billion in 1958—a swing of $1.5 billion. A swing in the same direction of $.7 billion occurred in the Old Age and Survivors' Trust Fund.

The absence of discretionary action to combat the recession during the first half of 1958 can be attributed to a variety of factors.

Throughout the period of mounting unemployment and a declining index of industrial production, consumer prices continued to edge upward. This was not "according to the book," and led to some indecision in policy-making circles as to whether the enemy was unemployment or inflation. Indeed, some felt that unemployment would be a reasonable price to pay for conditions which might, if continued longer, break the persistent upward movement of prices which had worried the economy since 1955. To others the behavior of prices in the recession seemed to indicate an underlying strength in the economy which justified optimism that the recession would soon be cured without governmental assistance. Furthermore, the postwar history had been one of short and minor recessions; the tendency had developed to look beyond the recession to the subsequent boom. If the recession was to be a short one, almost any expenditure program might become effective only after recovery was under way, and contribute to boom and inflation. Finally, during the early months of 1958 it became increasingly evident that expenditures would rise markedly and receipts fall in the fiscal year 1959, which was to begin in the middle of the calendar year 1958. Budget receipts for fiscal 1959, which had been estimated in the budget document issued in January, 1958, at $74.4 billion, were actually $68.3 billion. Budget expenditures were projected at $73.9 billion but turned out to be $6.8 billion higher. And whereas a budget surplus of just under a half-billion dollars had been predicted, a deficit of $12.4 billion was realized. The revenue reductions represented the delayed action of the effect of recession upon the tax base. The major areas in which expenditures exceeded first estimates were in agriculture, unemployment compensation extension, foreign aid, housing, and aviation. These developments, though not fully realized until later, were clearly in the wind during the period of business downswing, and undoubtedly affected business expectations favorably.

This sketchy review of fiscal policy in the postwar period would appear to permit some generalizations concerning the present state of opinion relative to the use of fiscal policy for stabilization purposes. The objective of stabilization is forced to share the stage with other economic and political objectives. The long-run objective of holding a checkrein on government—and particularly central government—in economic affairs has wide appeal, and tends to limit the possible scope of fiscal policy, particularly in periods when instability is thought to be temporary and relatively mild. The feeling that fiscal policy tends to be too much a one-way street—that it is politically much easier to run a deficit in bad times than a surplus in good times—leads to a good deal of conservatism in its use. The inability to predict with accuracy the future course of the economy often creates confusion as to what type of policy is indicated, and in this state of frustration it is often thought safer to stand pat.

But with all these practical limitations upon the ability to use stabilizing fiscal policy, one fact stands out. It is the wide acceptance of the fact that fiscal action can and does affect the level at which the economy operates. Even when there is difference of opinion as to which policy should be pursued, the rationale tends to run in terms of the effect of the policy upon aggregate demand. Two developments would seem to account for this. The first is the growth in sheer weight of fiscal operations in the economy as government has grown. The second is the development during a single generation of a widely acceptable and widely applicable body of theory with respect to the factors which affect and determine the level of economic activity.

RECOMMENDED READINGS

Hickman, Bert G., "Federal Spending and the Stability of the Postwar Economy," in Joint Economic Committee, *Federal Expenditure Policy for Economic Growth and Stability (Papers Submitted by Panelists before the Subcommittee on Fiscal Policy)*, Washington, 1957, pp. 357–81.
    Interprets postwar federal fiscal policy, showing that expenditures have

been a highly unstable factor in aggregate demand, partly because they pre-dominantly serve a defense rather than a stability objective.

Hansen, Alvin H., *Fiscal Policy and Business Cycles*, N.Y., Norton, 1941, Chapter 12.

Deals with general compensatory spending and with the special case of pump-priming.

Musgrave, Richard A., "Fiscal Policy, Stability, and Full Employment," in *Public Finance and Full Employment*, Washington, Board of Governors of the Federal Reserve System, Postwar Economic Studies, No. 3, 1945.

Discussion of the general principles of attaining full employment, with special reference to budgetary alternatives.

CHAPTER 6

Fiscal Programs to Promote Stability

Three classes of fiscal instruments are available for use in promoting stability in an essentially private economy: the scale of public expenditures, the scale of tax and other revenues, and the forms of governmental borrowing. Much of our analysis to this point has emphasized expenditures. Variation in the aggregate of public expenditures creates like changes in aggregate demand for goods and services. This occurs directly with respect to the purchase by government of current output, and the major part of budgetary expenditures at all governmental levels are seen to be of this sort. The remainder of (cash) budgetary expenditures are transfer payments, which very frequently generate private purchases.

The use of instruments for the raising of public revenues also influences aggregate demand for currently produced goods and services. When the aggregate tax "take" is varied, by more or less intensive or extensive application, disposable income in the short run varies in the opposite direction. A heavier tax imposition—other things being equal—reduces disposable income and therefore demand by taxpayers for goods and services, and vice versa. The revenue instruments are thus a kit of stabilizing tools distinct from the expenditure instruments.

Government borrowing and debt repayment do not in themselves constitute stabilizing instruments separate from those of taxation and expenditure. Borrowing is, and debt repayment may be, a consequence of the extent to which taxation and spending instruments are being utilized. However, the forms which borrowing may take, and the sources of funds being tapped, can be manipulated independently in order to influence aggregate demand. Likewise, the decision to repay or not to repay debt out of current surplus, and the selection of those debt-holders to be repaid, offer opportunities for the modification of economic conditions independently of the use of tax and expenditure policy.

Public debt and its management furnish the subject matter of Chapters 8, 9, and 10; we shall therefore pass over this class of stabilization instruments for the present and concentrate on the other two. The general principles of expenditure variation and its effect upon aggregate demand have been analyzed in previous chapters. With respect to this class of stabilizing instruments, therefore, we shall emphasize here the choice of objects of expenditure promising particularly strategic influence in various conditions of instability, and the planning necessary to make expenditure policy most effective. And while detailed consideration of particular features of particular tax instruments would hardly be possible at this stage of our study—prior to the description of forms of taxes and their economic effects—some useful generalizations can be made with respect to tax policy and stability.

Policies to Stimulate Aggregate Demand and Employment

When aggregate demand is insufficient to call forth an acceptable level of employment and production, a policy of increased government expenditure, of tax reduction, or both, is indicated. How heavily the policy is applied will depend, of course, upon the severity of the present or prospective deficiency. But even if we assume no political or other doctrinaire obstacles to an effective economic response to an economic problem, a realistic view requires that we expect at the onset of recession that there will be considerable confusion and disagreement even among experts as to the probable magnitude of the prospective decline. Those whose interpretation of the projections leads them to expect the worst will advocate heroic measures. The optimists' recommendations will range from modest proposals for tax or expenditure variations to proposals to wait until the signs are clearer. It is rather unlikely, therefore, that policy actions can anticipate recession; it will be fortunate if the time taken for debate does not so delay action as to require that it be more massive than would otherwise be necessary.

Expenditure Programs. Planning is essential to the successful employment of expenditure programs to strengthen aggregate demand. These programs cannot be improvised on a moment's notice, for they will then be unlikely to accomplish the stabilization objective while incidentally serving the objective of providing inherently useful social capital. The planning of projects implies that prior decisions will have been made at several levels. Preparation of plans involves a range of estimates as to the leverage effects of alternative projects under varying combinations of forces causing the business decline. Projects designed for a general or usual decline may not be particularly useful if a recession is peculiarly intense in particular industries. The geographical incidence of unemployment may well be an important datum in policy selection. The inherent long-run usefulness of projects is a relevant consideration; school buildings may be preferable to swimming pools. In the same category are questions of the impact of payments upon the self-respect of recipients, the avoidance of entrance into fields properly left to private enterprise, and the promotion of effective business competition. Beyond these higher-level decisions, planning must of course meet certain operational requirements—blueprints are needed for projects, and administrative organization must be provided.

Some general guidelines for the formulation and selection of compensatory spending projects in recession can be formulated. In the first place, it is useful to have the spending take hold as quickly as possible. The sooner expenditures actually enter the income stream, the more effective they can be in preventing downward pressures upon the economy from accumulating and reinforcing one another. The expenditure has not only a real income-generating effect, but it may well have a favorable announcement effect upon business anticipations. Quick action, therefore, may contain the decline within reasonable limits and permit normal recovery forces to become effective at an earlier date.

Insofar as the objective is to have a quick spending impact, it is unlikely that large projects will be undertaken first in the business decline. Large projects, no matter how well planned in advance, involve rather long "lead-times." That is, the time span between the decision to go ahead with the project and the actual payment of money is relatively long. Even though blueprints and specifications have been prepared previously, considerable time will be lost in the receiving of bids, the awarding of contracts, the organization of work by contractors and subcontractors, and the actual performance of enough work to justify progress payments. A variety of small projects must therefore be available. Most promising of all, for this purpose, may be the opportunity to enlarge the scale of programs already in force.

There are many governmental programs which are "open-ended," in the sense that the amount of expenditure depends upon the number of persons or projects able to qualify. Unemployment compensation is an almost perfect example of this. The administrative organization is in being, and increased aggregate payments are automatically made as larger numbers of unemployed persons qualify. In addition, however, if weekly benefits were increased for the duration of the emergency, and if benefit payments were continued beyond the normal time limit, even more substantial outlays would result quickly. Other public assistance programs could be treated in the same way. Furthermore, there are many governmental grant programs which are limited at any given time by the amount of the appropriation available. An increase in available funds would in most cases permit projects to go forward which are already planned but have been frozen for lack of financial support. Also, the ordinary operating agencies of government will at any time be able to revive quickly a myriad of small projects and activities which can be carried out by existing staff but which have had to be shelved because the budget had not provided for them.

What about large public works projects? Their main disadvantage is that they are spread over a fairly long period of time. Even though there may have been advance planning and the delay in beginning them is minimal, they require rather long construction periods. Thus, if the period of under-employment is short, the major spending impact of these programs may be delayed until after the upturn has started, when the major objective should be to moderate aggregate demand to reduce inflationary tendencies. At the onset of recession, it is difficult to forecast its probable severity or duration, and therefore difficult to determine the suitability of large projects. Many will be undertaken for other than the stabilization reason—the need for the project itself. Thus, a major federal highway program such as that begun in 1956, major highway replacement by a state, or additions to educational facilities by a local government—all these will usually be undertaken with-out reference to the business cycle. It would be convenient if, once begun, such projects could be speeded up when recession occurs, and slowed down in the opposite situation. Some possibilities along this line exist, but they are not very impressive. On the whole, however, to the extent that a major project can be divided into a series of parts, it will be more useful for anti-recession purposes under the short recession conditions which have generally obtained since World War II.

The principal objective of recession spending will be to influence the GNP and employment favorably. This means that government demand is to fill some part of the gap left by the deficiency of private demand. To be most effective, the expenditure should be first directed toward (1) those segments of the economy in which there are idle resources, and (2) those segments in which the propensity to re-spend is relatively high. It may well be that though there is general recession, certain segments of the economy continue strong. In early 1958, for example, heavy construction was boom-ing in spite of recession, and this was partly because of the federal highway program. To have accelerated state highway construction programs as the anti-recession measure would have been quite unwise. The increased mone-tary demand would have contributed more to rising construction prices than to rising employment. On the other hand, light residential construction had been more or less in the doldrums for some time, and the use of govern-mental funds to loosen the mortgage money market could have had sub-stantial favorable effect upon employment in that segment.

If the areas of the economy with abnormally high propensities to re-spend are to be cultivated, it is probable that those areas with high pro-pensity to consume will be most rewarding. This means that expenditure of funds first to those whose consumption spending is limited by low or falling income will produce the most dependable results. Relief payments to the unemployable and compensation payment to the unemployed can almost guarantee very high consumption re-spending. To be sure, such expenditure does not leave a train of physical facilities useful to the society in the future, but it does contribute to a healthy society in the humanitarian sense and, above all, creates demand for production. Where feasible, there is good reason to base such payments on services performed or benefits earned, for the self-respect of the recipient may be involved. But in general, the objec-tive is to get funds spent for currently produced goods and services (or to draw down inventories so new production will be forthcoming), and ex-penditures of both the relief and personal benefit type and for public works can accomplish this.

The major program for systematic payment of benefits to unemployed workers is the federal-state unemployment compensation program, pro-vided under the Social Security Act of 1935 and the various state laws. Under the program, benefits are paid during unemployment in amounts and for periods of time determined by state laws. Payroll taxes are imposed upon employers to provide the funds, at rates of taxation determined by the states. Funds are accumulated during high employment periods in the in-dividual states' unemployment reserve funds, which are maintained by the federal Treasury. As money is needed to pay benefits, the states draw upon the federal Treasury from their reserves. However, the federal government imposes a tax of $3/10$ of 1 per cent on payrolls for its own budget, to defray the administrative costs of the system, though any excess of this tax over administrative costs is returned to state reserve funds.

The effect of the unemployment compensation program upon govern-mental cash expenditures is shown below. The states deposit their unem-ployment tax receipts in the unemployment trust fund, and withdraw from this fund to pay benefits to the unemployed. The figures are deposits into and withdrawals from the fund during the fiscal years 1956–1959.[1] The fiscal

	1956 ($ million)	1957 ($ million)	1958 ($ million)	1959 ($ million)
Deposits by States	1,330	1,542	1,501	1,701
Withdrawal by States	1,287	1,511	2,926	2,797
Excess of Withdrawals	−43	−31	1,425	1,096

[1] From the federal *Budget*, 1958, 1959, 1960, 1961.

years 1956 and 1957 were years of business prosperity. Recession set in shortly after the beginning of the fiscal year 1958 and heavy unemployment continued into 1959, though many indices showed substantial upturn in the latter year. The most noteworthy fact shown by the table is the major increase ($1.4 billion) in withdrawals for benefit payments in the fiscal year 1958. It is clear that the program produces automatically substantial changes in cash expenditures in the direction required for economic stabilization purposes.

Two weaknesses of the unemployment compensation system as an antirecession expenditure measure have shown themselves in recent years. The first is that as wage and salary levels have risen the amount of weekly benefit has not kept pace. Practice among the states varies, but the Economic Reports of the President have frequently deplored the fact that a general standard of weekly benefits equal to half of weekly wages has not been attained. Benefits should not be so high as to make unemployment preferable to wage-earning, and they should not be so high as to permit significant amounts of personal savings from benefits. But the 50 per cent principle surely avoids these dangers, and if benefits fall markedly below 50 per cent, serious cuts in consumption in periods of unemployment may result.

The second weakness of the system as an anti-recession instrument is the tendency for unemployed workers to exhaust benefits in periods of protracted unemployment. The more liberal states permit the drawing of benefits for twenty-six weeks, after which time the worker must requalify for benefits by a period of employment. When benefits are exhausted, he must live on savings, borrow, or go on relief. Widespread exhaustion therefore can have serious consequences for the level of aggregate consumption. This is why in the recession of 1958, with an alarming rate of exhaustions, several states extended the benefit period on a temporary basis and the federal government provided loans to the states to finance these extensions. It was feared that widespread exhaustion of benefits could, by permitting a collapse of consumption, create the downward spiral which might turn recession into depression.[2]

The fact is that the unemployment compensation system was established to handle seasonal unemployment and unemployment related to the movement of workers from one job to another. It was not intended to provide for the unemployed in business setbacks—they were to be taken care of by

---

[2] It was also a technique for throwing a relief burden resulting from exhausted compensation benefits on the federal and state governments. Relief is usually a local government function; local budgets, depending upon the property tax, were already under great strain from education (and other) costs, and could not sustain rapidly increasing relief burdens.

relief programs of one sort or another. This fact is indicated by the provision for adjustment of the individual employer's payroll tax rate to his own employment performance ("experience rating"), by the establishment of a limited benefit period, and by relating the amount of weekly benefit to the wage rather than to need. Nevertheless, the unemployment compensation system has had its most dramatic application to recession unemployment, and this has led to strong support for the lengthening of the benefit period.

Little headway has been made in centralizing public works planning at any level of government in the United States. This is almost inevitable, unless a conscious attempt to integrate such plans is made either through the budget agency or one especially created for this purpose. The reason is that public works projects usually arise in connection with governmental services, and their planning is incidental to the performance of those activities. At the federal level, public works are either directly purchased, or loans or grants are given to other governments and nongovernmental institutions for particular purposes. Major planning of projects falls to the Bureau of Public Roads in the Department of Commerce, the Corps of Engineers of the Army, the military services, the Department of Agriculture, the Atomic Energy Commission, and the Department of Health, Education, and Welfare—all of which are usually responsible for major public works outlays. The list of projects for any budget year is a very long one, and involves most operating agencies.[3] These agencies are not encouraged to preplan projects on the basis of possible stabilization needs, and no agency exists for coordination with this end in view.

At the state level there are usually fewer agencies involved with public works, but coordination of planning is hardly any better. Major construction is normally carried out by the highway department, and education has recently involved a considerable amount of such activity. There may be a "public works department," but if so its function is usually an engineering one, connected with the overseeing of construction or maintenance. In neither case does it coordinate plans in a useful way for stabilization purposes. It would be unrealistic to assume that local governments would plan for this purpose, for these governments feel no responsibility for timing capital projects to stabilize employment. Substantially, the whole contribution of local governments to compensatory spending in the cycle is limited to relief activities.

If the problem is one of sustained economic stagnation, the planning role is relatively unimportant, for timing is a much less troublesome factor. But if

---

[3] See, for example, "Special Analysis D," *Budget of the United States, 1961,* for a list of federal investment expenditures.

public works are to be used to counter cyclical instability, it makes a great difference whether the project is tailored to the magnitude and direction of the decline, whether its impact will be felt in the right economic sectors and geographic locations, whether portions of larger projects can be speeded up, and whether the project is ready to go on short notice. This requires an economic type of planning which not only includes but extends far beyond the usual engineering plans as well as the usual budgetary decisions concerning the efficient use of resources. Without such planning, public works can play only a minor role in the downswing, and particular emphasis will have to be placed upon transfer payments to individuals and purchases of personal services.

Tax Reduction. The general purpose of tax reduction in a prospective or actual economic decline is to leave with persons or business enterprises funds which they may spend in whatever direction they are inclined. In some sense, then, government is less able to direct the expenditure into particular channels when it reduces taxes than when it increases its own spending. On the other hand, the choice of taxes to be reduced, and the particular changes that are made within broad tax instruments, can accomplish a certain amount of selection of the channels into which spending might go.

Immediacy of impact of the action is again important, particularly if the recession is a minor one or if action is delayed beyond the onset of the recession. Fortunately, this is not often a serious problem. The federal personal income tax is paid by taxpayers on pay days, or quarterly by the self-employed. The effect of a rate reduction will thus be felt soon in the form of more take-home pay. The major part of the corporation tax is also paid quarterly. In both cases the impact can be made even more immediate if the rate changes are made retroactive. Sales and excise taxes, which predominate in state revenue systems, can also be made to affect the price of goods almost immediately. The property tax of the local governments is, on the other hand, badly suited to compensatory use. It is assessed and paid usually once per year. But as was indicated above, the local governments are not likely to manage their fiscal affairs counter-cyclically in any case.

The efficiency with which a tax rate reduction will promote spending also depends on the impact of the rate change on the ultimate taxpayer. Downward revision of personal income tax rates will produce the full effect of the reduction in the form of an increase in realized disposable income. There is no loss of impact upon the taxpayer, for no one else can absorb a portion of reduction along the way. This is not necessarily the case where excises are concerned. If the tax on gasoline, cigarettes, or radios is reduced, there is no guarantee that the price will fall by the amount of the tax. In a recession, profits will almost certainly be falling, and the seller will be tempted, when the tax is buried in the quoted price, to pocket a portion of the tax reduction as an addition to his net income. The extent to which this is done will depend upon many factors which largely fall under the head of competitive conditions in the market. And if, as is presumed to be the case, the tax reduction is acknowledged to be a temporary expedient, the seller may well hesitate to lower the purchase price because of the necessity for raising it again when the tax is later increased. If the tax reduction does not result in lowered prices, no increase in sales can be expected, but this does not necessarily mean that the reduction has no impact, for an improvement in the profit position may encourage more expenditure by those who participate in profits. We will deal with this matter more fully below. The buyer would probably benefit directly from reduction of a sales tax, if the tax is not quoted in the selling price.[4] But the question here is whether the reduction in the tax rate actually is effective in encouraging buying. For expensive items there would be recognized tax savings, and buying might well be encouraged. But for small items, where the amount of the tax is not impressive on a single purchase, it seems probable that the tax reduction would be largely ignored and that there would be little effect. If, as is generally assumed, separately paid sales taxes do not seriously enter into decisions to buy or not to buy, a reduction in this kind of tax would have very minor ability to increase purchasing. In any case, it seems probable that an income tax reduction would be more effective than an excise tax reduction because, dollar for dollar, the impact of an increase in disposable income is probably stronger than the impact of a price reduction.

A major issue is whether to concentrate on stimulating consumption or investment to check the decline. If it is desired to increase disposable income in order to encourage consumption, the tax reduction will be concentrated in those areas where the propensity to consume is relatively high. Emphasis will be placed on reduction of income taxes at the lower income levels, or on reduction or elimination of excises on goods of widespread consumption and fairly elastic demand. On the other hand, if the objective is to improve the disposable income position of those whose propensities to save and invest are normally relatively high, the major policy actions indicated are reduction of corporate and other business taxes and personal income taxes on the upper-middle and high income groups.

If some sort of tax reduction is planned, one can be sure that both of these positions will be forcefully presented. Each taxpayer will be convinced

---

[4] This assumes that the basic price of the article is not raised to absorb the difference in the tax. Such action is not likely, however, in a short recession.

that the form of tax reduction best for him will be best for the economy. Questions of long-run equity will be largely irrelevant, though they will undoubtedly be presented. The real issue is, which type of policy will most effectively check the current decline. The policy to be chosen will be that which utilizes the higher existing propensity to spend, for it is unlikely that temporary tax reductions will strengthen either propensity.

The strategically preferable policy is usually that which increases the disposable income of those with a relatively high propensity to consume. The recession will be characterized, at least in its early stages, by a severe decline in investment in inventories. Sellers find themselves with goods on hand in excess of the quantities desired, and their first actions will be to cut off further purchases for inventory. This is the major characteristic of the initial decline in investment. No relief from this can be expected simply by reducing taxes on investors; relief can come only by a driving down of excessive inventory, and this can be accomplished only by sales from inventory. Strengthening consumption purchasing by tax reduction will first have a favorable effect upon consumer goods inventories, and this effect will be successively passed on to producer inventories. Let us illustrate this by an example. Assume a recession similar to the three brief dips since World War II. Sellers of household appliances find their inventories excessive in terms of their ability to move goods. They reduce their orders from appliance manufacturers, who then find their inventories of materials excessive. The manufacturers, in turn, reduce orders for steel and other component materials. Steel mills then find their inventories too high. All along the line inventory investment is reduced, and this is a reduction in aggregate demand because other elements of demand have not increased to offset this reduction. This is recession, with attendant unemployment. What good will it do to reduce taxes on investors in inventory? Substantially none, for the problem is not the availability of income to spend for inventory, but rather the unwisdom of spending as long as inventories are excessive. The solution to the problem is to wear down inventories, and this can be accomplished only if consumer purchase of appliances strengthens. If demand for appliances picks up, retail inventories will be drawn down to the point where orders are placed with manufacturers, and when their inventories are satisfactorily adjusted, they will order more steel. The key to the solution of the inventory recession is thus to increase consumer taking, rather than to make investment funds more easily available.

As the recession goes beyond inventories, and affects investment in plant and equipment, the same reasoning applies. Producers' equipment will not be purchased, no matter how available disposable income of producers, unless the equipment can be profitably employed. An increased demand for final goods is the sole basis for expansion of productive capacity. The chain of improvements which begins with the strengthening of consumer demand will eventually affect demand for producers' equipment favorably, for as orders for output increase, orders for the means of producing output will increase. It seems clear, therefore, that the tax reduction should first be directed toward increasing the disposable income of potential consumers. If successful, the decline in investment will be checked, with effects first upon inventory investment and then upon plant and equipment investment. And if the tax reduction is accompanied by an easing of monetary policy, funds will be quite adequately available to finance the recovery in investment.

In summary, when business decline is in prospect or is occurring, appropriate fiscal policies will be directed toward strengthening demand in the aggregate. All other considerations will temporarily become secondary to that of stabilization, and opportunities will be sought to fill the demand gaps causing the recession. It will usually be relatively unprofitable to attempt to strengthen directly the investment components of aggregate demand, even though these appear to be the principal trouble-makers. As we have seen, tax reduction on investors will increase their disposable income beyond what it would have been without the tax reduction. This may make them less unhappy in a recession, but it will normally be quite ineffective in strengthening private investment expenditure. Thus, tax reduction will be used to strengthen investment indirectly, by first strengthening consumption. Compensatory *expenditure* policy can be directed toward investment types of spending, by channeling funds into military hardware, highways, and public works. When the spending takes hold, it will be at least as effective when directed toward investment as toward consumption. But the difficulty is that the time required for expenditure to take hold is longer when directed toward such projects than when the funds purchase personal services or are used for personal benefit payments.

Policies to Limit Aggregate Demand

The period since World War II has been more often one of excessive than of inadequate aggregate demand. Thus, the problems of fiscal policy have been more persistently those of countering inflation than recession. When it is desired to reduce or to limit the rate of growth of aggregate demand, two avenues are open to policy in the fiscal field. The first is to limit that segment of aggregate demand for which governments themselves are directly responsible—government purchases of goods and services. The second is to limit the private segments of aggregate demand—consumption and investment. The first requires reduction or prevention of increases in governmental expenditures. The second implies principally the use of revenue measures to control the amount of private disposable income available for expenditure. However, a limitation of the amounts of government transfer payments (expenditures) to individuals and businesses can also affect private sectors of demand.

Expenditure Reduction. Whether or not expenditures are being used in a truly counter-cyclical manner will determine to a large extent whether they can be cut back when inflation threatens. If, in recession, outlays have been intentionally expanded, projects and programs will have been undertaken which are marginal in their usefulness for non-stabilization purposes. These can be cut back in a situation of full employment, either by stretching out their completion or by refusing to initiate new ones. If outlays have not been expanded in recession, it will be extremely difficult to find government purchases of goods and services which can be terminated or reduced, for the scale of outlays will have been determined by social need for the structures and services which are being purchased. This latter is largely the situation in which governments now find themselves. The major expenditures of all governments have rather grudgingly responded to increased needs; although some of them have shown remarkable increase, they are still regarded as barely adequate. State and local expenditures for education, highways, and the extension of water and sanitary facilities in growing suburban areas, and federal expenditures for defense, interest, agricultural price supports, and veterans' benefits, now compose the major share of governmental outlays. Increases in these categories have occurred against rather strong budgetary resistance that has kept the programs relatively free of "fat." And the outlays for these major functions have increased so significantly as to make budgetary resistance to outlays in other areas very rigid. Under these circumstances there is little slack to take up in budgets when expenditure reductions are desired for stability reasons. So far as direct governmental purchases of goods and services are concerned, therefore, one part of anti-cyclical policy cannot work effectively without the other—expenditures cannot be reduced in inflation unless they are increased in recession. This means that the expenditure-planning function must go beyond the readying of projects for recession and the conditioning of the public for their implementation. The planning function implies also conditioning the public for the termination or slowing down of projects in prosperity. The latter may be almost as difficult as the former.

Some items among government transfer payments are more amenable to counter-cyclical fluctuation than direct purchases of goods and services.

If standards for qualification remain the same, outlays for relief and unemployment compensation will decline when employment is high. Also, when jobs are plentiful, people who have reached sixty-five often delay qualification for benefits, because income from this source will usually be smaller than regular job income. Subsidies for support of agricultural prices may or may not fall as business booms, for agricultural prices seem to depend more heavily upon weather conditions and acreage planted in the short run than upon the level of income in the economy generally. At the other extreme, transfer payments for interest on the public debt will probably be perverse in their behavior, for business booms will probably be accompanied by higher interest rates. On the whole, however, transfer payments will probably fall in prosperity if the basis for payment in various programs remains fixed. The effect will be especially marked if qualifications are liberalized in recession and tightened in prosperity.

The tightening of money flows in prosperity requires the setting of priorities for termination of marginal payments. Those with the highest multiplier effects should be cut off first. To some extent this is likely to occur automatically, for the transfer payments reduced or terminated would have gone to persons with rather high propensity to consume. On the other hand, private investment expenditure may well be the emphatically booming element in demand, and to cut back on expenditures for investment-type goods may be especially rewarding. Highway construction in particular offers possibilities for postponement, to weaken the impact of demand upon the construction industry. Transfer of demand from production to research, to the extent feasible, would also seem to be helpful. But as a general rule, reversal of whatever policies were adopted to increase expenditures in recession will be indicated in boom periods.

Tax Increases. Fiscal policies to counter inflationary forces in boom periods will in practice require particular emphasis on the revenue side of the cash budget. The reason for this is the resistance to giving up services and capital structures when business improves, i.e., the resistance to expenditure reductions. This is not to say that tax increases will be accepted with any real enthusiasm. But if feasible expenditure reductions are very limited, the only remaining instrument for stabilization is tax increases.

Some tax increases will be found to have been built into the tax structure, and these will react in the right direction automatically. Progressive income taxes, for instance, will apply higher marginal rates as individual incomes rise into higher brackets. This will be especially effective in the lower and middle income classes, where the brackets to which the progressive rates apply are smaller and a moderate change in income makes higher rates effective. It will also be true of payroll taxes, where the rise in employment, the longer work week, and increases in wage rates expand the tax base. It will even be somewhat true of excises and sales taxes, because as incomes rise, larger expenditures for certain taxed items may be expected.

The *automatic* tax increases result from the inclination of the bases of particular tax measures to rise, and these increases occur without changes in tax rates. But there are possibilities for *discretionary* anti-inflation tax actions as well. These may take the form of changes in tax rates, redefinition of the bases of particular taxes to increase tax liability, or inauguration of entirely new tax measures. All of these require legislation, and are thus not automatic.

If discretionary tax increases are to be employed, the tax measures used may make some difference. Except in unusual cases, an inflationary boom is not likely to result from an explosive rise in consumption. A boom is far more probably the result of a major rise in private investment spending or in government spending. Three attacks are possible. A rise in the corporate income tax will curb investment incentives by making investment less profitable in terms of after-tax income. A rise in the upper-bracket personal income tax rates may also serve. But the most effective cure may lie in taxes which curb consumption. The boom in investment normally rests upon the assumption that the output of increased productive capacity and sales from increased inventories will be justified by a rise in the taking of final goods. If the taking of final goods is slowed down by the impact of higher taxes upon buyers, the basis for the investment boom may be weakened. Thus, tax increases whose major impact is upon consumption may be successful in limiting an investment boom.

Anti-inflation tax policy should rather obviously be guided by the results of analysis of the nature of inflation. The standard case is that in which monetary demand, supported by high incomes and possible net additions to the money supply, is excessive in terms of current output of goods. Though the demand pressure may not be equal in all markets, excessive demand in one or a few broad markets can bid up the prices of these goods and in so doing also bid up the prices of common ingredients of production, thus spilling over into higher costs of production in lines not experiencing heavy demand. Thus, price rises may start in one segment of the economy and spread to others. While in the latter markets the inflation may seem to be a cost-push phenomenon, it is the result of a demand-pull in markets for the former types of goods. Heavier taxation is a feasible method of controlling prices caused by the pressure of excessive demand.

This kind of inflation can be favorably influenced by heavier taxation either upon income or upon expenditure for goods and services. Income or sales and excise taxes can be employed. It is sometimes argued that to impose higher taxes upon commodities as an anti-inflation measure is self-defeating, in that the taxes themselves will be added to and thus raise prices. While it is in general true that taxes on commodities increase the selling prices of those commodities, it does not follow that the anti-inflationary objective is thereby defeated. For the tax-induced price rise is simply a technique for removing spendable income from the economy; the higher prices paid for these goods reduce the income left for expenditure on other products, and the over-all effect may be substantially the same as if income had been drained off before purchasing occurred.[5] In fact, an advantage which higher taxes of the sales or excise variety may have over higher income taxes is that the latter may fall largely on savings while the former necessarily fall on expenditure. Thus, the sales tax may penetrate to the heart of the problem of excessive demand.

The choice between higher taxes on sales and higher taxes on income involves other considerations. In the first place, if the advantage of the sales tax in striking directly at expenditure is to be fully realized, it should fall as far as possible on final purchases of goods. The objective is to drain off the disposable income which is financing excessive demand, without increasing costs of production. When the excise falls upon items which enter into the production of other items, a cost spiral is generated, the tax is pyramided by the application of the mark-up to the tax, and prices of final products rise by more than the tax. The amount of price rise necessary to drain off a given amount of purchasing power is thus greater than would be necessary if the excise were so imposed as to be incorporated only in a final price. This suggests that excises on manufactures are less efficient per dollar than excises on retail sales. It suggests also that excises upon final buyers of producers' goods, business machines, freight shipments, and telephone and telegraph services are less efficient than excises upon jewelry, luggage, and gasoline.

We have seen that an advantage of sales and excise taxes over income taxes for anti-inflation purposes is that the former fall on actual expenditure while the latter may be paid out of reduced private savings. If the latter occurs, consumption expenditure is untouched and consumption demand is not discouraged. But if the income tax increase were concentrated in those income brackets where the propensity to consume is high

---

[5] However, if the tax raises the price enough to reduce expenditures (including tax) on these commodities below what was previously spent, monetary demand may increase for other products.

and the propensity to save low, the impact of income taxes would be similar to that of sales taxes. Income taxes of this sort might be better anti-inflationary devices than sales taxes because sales taxes do normally enter into costs of production and therefore contribute to inflation while ostensibly countering it.

Inflation that appears to manifest itself first in rising factor prices instead of rising final product prices is sometimes called cost-push inflation. Rising factor prices are rising costs to producers. They cut into profit margins and give rise to product price increases. This assumes, of course, that buyers will pay the higher prices resulting, and therefore that demand is adequate to accommodate the higher prices. But it may be true that if costs do not increase, sellers will be satisfied with present prices and not press for the highest net income that the demand affords. It is, therefore, relevant to ask whether a particular tax measure under consideration will push costs up. Excises and sales taxes enter into the calculation of the Consumer Price Index, which is the standard cost-of-living figure upon which escalator wage clauses are based in some industries. A rise in these taxes (other things being equal) thus raises the price index and raises basic wage rates. This tends to reduce sellers' margins unless prices are increased, and therefore introduces an upward pressure upon prices. In other cases the relationship is less formal, but an increase in the Consumer Price Index would tend to justify demands for higher wages as a matter of right. Higher taxes on net income are far less likely to result in wage increases. These taxes are not included in the accepted price index, and workers are inclined not to regard them as a cost-of-living factor. Therefore, income taxes, while they may have less effect per dollar in reducing consumer demand—because they may be paid out of savings and not press seriously upon expenditure— do not possess the cost-increasing and price-increasing potential which partially affects the efficiency of sales taxes when used for anti-inflation purposes.

Finally, the incentive effects of the tax increase may be worth considering. Since the inflationary situation which justifies the tax increase is one resulting from excess of monetary demand over physical output at a given level of prices, any action which reduces output will have a perverse effect upon the anti-inflation policy. It may well be that to raise taxes on income will have a greater disincentive effect than to raise taxes on sales. The usual reasoning is that to take away a larger percentage of one's income makes the expenditure of effort in earning that income less worthwhile, and thus discourages productive effort. A higher tax on purchases is presumed to have less disincentive effect—it discourages purchasing but not the earning of income. So little is known of incentives that broad generalizations are unsafe, but the above reasoning would appear more applicable to the long run than to the short run. If the tax change is temporary, and is so understood, it seems unlikely that there is much practical possibility of reducing productive effort as income tax rates rise. Would absenteeism be encouraged? Would executives take longer vacations? Would production schedules be slowed down? Would less overtime work be accepted?

In practice, the ease and speed with which tax changes could be instituted would largely control the selection of instruments. Given the withholding system in income taxation, this form of tax seems to lend itself more easily to short-run manipulation of rates than others. A change in sales or excise tax rates is in fact something of an event in federal and state practice. Adjustment in income tax rates may be easier to accomplish politically. Furthermore, the consequences of particular rate changes can be more precisely foretold in the case of the income tax, and the range of variations in possible results is greater in practice. Also, at the federal level, where counter-cyclical use of taxes is most likely to be practiced, the predominant importance of the personal and corporate income taxes leaves much more room for maneuver and for choice than the excises. These factors therefore suggest that first attention will be given to the income taxes in any plan for anti-inflation taxation.

Expenditure Variations vs. Tax Variations

A practical issue which will always arise in connection with stabilization policy is whether emphasis should be placed upon expenditure policy or upon tax policy. Strong tendencies toward unemployment or inflation will probably require both, with additional help from monetary policy. But if the prospect is for mild recession or mild inflation—and any departure from full employment at stable prices is likely to begin mildly—there is at least some question as to which type of compensatory policy should be adopted *first*.

When the problem is one of combating a decline in employment, there is little doubt that, *dollar for dollar,* an expenditure increase is more effective than a tax reduction. This can be demonstrated by the procedure used in Chapter 4. We assume that private marginal propensities to spend are .9, and the leverage coefficient is therefore 10. Taking the two actions independently, the income created over a period of time by an additional dollar expended by government is

$$\$1 + .90 + .81 + .729 + \ldots = \$10,$$

while tax relief of $1 permits the private sector to create income of $9, as follows:

$$\$.90 + .81 + .729 + \ldots = \$9.$$

In terms of efficiency per dollar of budgetary changes, therefore, the expenditure increase is preferable.

When the problem is one of combating inflation, we may assume that private propensities are high. Let us assume the combined propensities to be .99. A reduction of government expenditure by $1 would, taken by itself, have the following effect upon income over a period of time:

$$-(\$1 + .99 + .9801 + .9703 + \ldots) = -\$100,$$

while taking $1 from the taxpayer would reduce the spending stream in due course by:

$$-(\$.99 + .9801 + .9703 + \ldots) = -\$99.$$

Again, the expenditure change is more efficient.

But while, dollar for dollar, we can conclude that under most conditions expenditure variation is more effective than tax rate variation, this difference is only one of several relevant factors in policy choice. A second factor is the ability to push the policy through the legislative process. Expenditures are highly resistant to reduction, but give in readily to proposals for increase. And tax rate reductions may be easier than rate increases, for reasons unrelated to stability objectives. If these observations apply to a given situation, proper anti-recession policies will be easier to legislate quickly than proper anti-inflation policies. But as between the two kinds of measures in any given business condition, tax rates seem more resistant to change than expenditures. The public seems to regard a legislated change in tax rates as more permanent, and taxpayers feel entitled to count on continuation of a rate schedule for a period long enough to permit them to adjust to it. This is less true of aggregate expenditures, which are the result of a multitude of pressures focused upon the budget process. Some tradition therefore exists in favor of relatively infrequent changes in tax rates.

A very important aspect of the choice between tax and expenditure actions is the speed with which the policy can be made effective once the decision is made to use it. It is effective only when demand for currently produced goods and services is actually influenced. Expenditure programs are subject to long "lead-times," i.e., a policy once legislated must have its organization set up, its specifications completed, and its contracts let before a significant impact can be felt. The importance of lead-times in federal public works construction can be seen in the estimates of expenditures for such construction included in the budget estimates for the fiscal year 1960.[6] To be sure, the figures here do not reflect a forced-draft program; in fact, they may reflect, in some instances, an intentional slowing down of public works to promote budget balance in 1960. But getting public works under way is a slow process. This is a major drawback, especially when the prospect is for a short period of unemployment. For not only does the program have little immediate impact; the major impact is likely to be felt after recovery is substantially complete, at which time stabilization may call for anti-inflation rather than anti-recession measures.

In contrast to expenditure programs, tax reduction can be made highly effective in a short time. The major elements in the federal tax system are personal and corporation income taxes. Approximately two-thirds of personal income tax collections are withheld from individuals' pay, and withholding occurs on pay days. Reduction or increase in rates in the withholding schedule are thus effective as immediately as the next pay day after the effective date of the change. The remaining third of personal income taxes, and most of the corporation income taxes, are collected quarterly on the basis of declared estimates for the year. Declarations can be amended on any quarterly payment date during the year. Thus, if tax rates are lowered, the estimated tax for the year is lowered, and the quarterly payment reduced. Though not so immediate in actual effect upon disposable income as a change in withholding rates, a reduction in rates on estimated tax has a relatively short lead-time. And if a larger impact is desired immediately, a retroactive effective date for rate reduction can be made. In this case, current withholding rates can be reduced to compensate for excessive withholding to date, and declarations amended to offset excessive quarterly payments to date. The immediate impact is more than proportional to the rate reduction.

In general, therefore, when the prospect is for short periods of unemployment or inflationary boom, a strong preference for first use of tax measures is recognized. Though dollar for dollar an expenditure change is more effective *when its impact is felt,* the impact of a tax reduction can be realized much more quickly in the usual case. If the departure from full

---

[6] From the *Budget of the United States Government for . . . 1960;* Special Analysis F, Table 3, p. 971.

	Cumulative to June 30, 1959	1960 Estimate	Required to Complete	Total Federal Cost
Continuing Work ($ million)	7,391	1,647	6,706	15,743
New Projects ($ million)	2	124	366	492

employment at stable prices turns out to be protracted, both policies will be required.

Automatic Compensatory Measures

If revenue and expenditure changes are intended to be used for stabilization purposes, a general and continuing policy question is whether flexibility should be permanently built into the fiscal structure or changes legislated *ad hoc* as unstable conditions arise. Flexibility involves a permanent structure of fiscal institutions—using both receipts and expenditures —which will react automatically in the right direction to counter the instability. Discretionary policy implies the weighing of probabilities for change at any given time and instituting changes designed to alter the probabilities toward stability.

The principal automatic fiscal stabilizers in the economy of the United States are:

Progressive net income taxes
Payroll taxes
Sales and excise taxes on "luxury" goods
Unemployment compensation benefits
Old Age and Survivors' Insurance benefits
Relief payments.

Among tax measures, the federal personal income tax is the most significant. This is partly because of the fact that this tax is so broadly based that changes in the GNP affect the revenues in relatively large dollar amounts. For example, the recovery in the fiscal year 1959 produced personal income tax net revenues two billion dollars larger than the same tax in the recession fiscal year of 1958. The progressive feature of this tax measure makes it a particularly useful compensatory instrument. As incomes rise, the marginal portions fall into higher tax rate brackets, and the tax obligation tends to rise at a more rapid rate than income. As incomes fall, tax payments fall more rapidly. The fact that the rates are more progressive in the middle incomes than in other sections of the income distribution pattern means that the progressive effect is widely felt where the bulk of personal incomes are. The federal tax on corporation net income is a far less effective automatic compensatory instrument than the personal tax for two reasons: the rates are in practice hardly progressive at all, and there is substantial lag in payment of the tax.

To the extent that sales and excise taxes are imposed upon those commodities whose purchase rises and falls with the GNP, these tax measures provide desired automatic flexibility. But these taxes lack the progressive character of personal income taxes, and their effect is less marked. And tax measures of this sort do not consistently fall upon goods whose purchase fluctuates with the cycle. Thus, while there may be proper automatic flexibility in excises, the degree of flexibility is typically less than that of other measures.

Payroll taxes also offer some modest automatic counter-cyclical possibilities. Since they are based upon payrolls and not incomes, the base of the tax fluctuates with income and employment. But there are limitations upon their usefulness. These taxes are imposed at a fixed rate, whatever the size of the base. The OASI tax is imposed only upon the first $4,800 of income, and the unemployment compensation tax upon the first $3,000 of wages. Fluctuations in income or payrolls above these minima thus have no effect upon the tax base or upon the amount of tax paid. Furthermore, the merit rating schemes of most states provide for considerable perverse lag in unemployment tax rate changes. While it would be helpful if the tax *rate* on payrolls were to fall in recession and rise in prosperity, the opposite frequently occurs. This results when the payroll tax rate is geared to the size of the unemployment reserve balance. In prosperous times, when payrolls are high and benefit payments low, the reserve account shows an increase and the tax rate falls. In periods of unemployment, when payrolls are low and benefit payments high, the reserve falls, and the tax rate in many states rises. This could, of course, be corrected, but to the extent that it is not, the tax effect is perverse in the cycle.

It should probably be noted that if prices (including prices of the factors of production) were more sensitive to the business cycle, the automatic stabilizing effect of tax measures in general would be greater. If wage and salary rates rose and fell quickly in the cycle, the income tax base would be more flexible, as would the base of the payroll taxes; and those excise and sales taxes whose base is the price of the product would also be more flexible. This is not necessarily to argue for greater price flexibility, but to observe that greater flexibility in prices would produce greater flexibility in revenues.

The automatic fiscal stabilizers which operate on the expenditure side of the budget principally involve transfer payments. Such programs are "open-ended," in the sense that criteria are established to qualify for the payments and the total amount paid is determined by the number of payees qualifying. The major social security programs are of this type. The most sensitive of these is unemployment compensation.. The table on page 154 shows benefit payments to have increased by almost half between the third and the fourth quarters of 1957 and to have almost tripled by the third quarter of 1958. While aggregate wage and salary payments in the economy fell by $5.5 billion between the third quarter of 1957 and the second quarter of

1958, unemployment compensation benefits increased by $2.5 billion to absorb almost half of the wage and salary decline. In addition, these benefits are untaxed by the federal personal income tax.

The Old Age and Survivors' Insurance system is an automatic stabilizer to a rather limited extent, compared with unemployment compensation. The plan permits persons sixty-five years of age (women at sixty-two) to retire and receive monthly benefits. While qualification for benefits is related to age rather than to employment condition, experience has shown that persons who may retire choose to do so in larger numbers in periods of heavy unemployment. Presumably, however, there is less movement back into the labor force when employment conditions improve, though this is possible. The use of this program as a substitute for employment is indicated in the table on page 154, particularly in the second quarter of 1958, when unemployment reached its maximum. The failure of total benefits to decline thereafter as employment rose reflects the fact that this is essentially a "one-way" stabilizing program.

Relief payments are normally made to persons who qualify by meeting the test of need. In general, those who qualify are persons who are unable to qualify for benefits under the social security programs described above. Hence there will be less fluctuation in the number of persons qualifying because of a change in the employment picture than in the case of, say, unemployment compensation. Another factor which acts to limit fluctuation in aggregate relief payments is the tendency of state and local governments to operate under rather tight welfare budgets. This means that these budgets tend to be under some strain even under good employment conditions, and there is little slack to permit increase when unemployment rises.

There are three kinds of advantages inherent in automatic or built-in compensatory measures. The first is that they act quickly. A measure of this type is fundamentally tied to a central variable in the economy which reflects changes in business activity. Taxes based upon net income, payrolls, or possibly retail sales can be expected to produce revenues which fluctuate in the same direction as the GNP and employment. Expenditure programs which gear aggregate government payments to the amount of unemployment will also fluctuate in the proper direction with changes in business conditions. Programs based upon price movements are far less dependable, but may show some of the proper kind of flexibility. When the tax or the expenditure is closely tied to a central variable, the impact of the policy may be felt even before the statistics demonstrating the need appear.

The second advantage of built-in stabilizers is that they do not become involved on each occasion with the political process. This is more than a matter of delay in recognizing trends and in making legislative or administrative decisions. It avoids human error in the projection of trends and the interpretation of current statistics. It also avoids the intrusion of non-economic considerations in policy determination. Action is automatically taken on the basis of economic factors alone, and "political" considerations are not given an opportunity to affect the results.

The third advantage of automatic stabilizers is an extension of the second, but important enough to be described separately. A weakness of fiscal policy in practice has been its irreversibility. Stability considerations become diluted by the addition of other considerations, and policy is slow to change when business conditions change. High expenditures and low taxes instituted in recession may become ends in themselves, and when the opposite business conditions obtain it is difficult to reverse policy. The same may be true of policies undertaken to combat inflation. The higher taxes and lower expenditures produce a budget surplus, which is regarded as a "good thing" because it permits debt reduction, and authorities may be loath to reverse these policies when weakness in the economy appears.

While there is much to be said for building as many automatic elements as possible into fiscal institutions, it is very unlikely that these measures alone will be adequate in all instability situations. Taken altogether, they will not be massive enough in their impact to deal with violent changes. They can do the job rather well in minor fluctuations. In major fluctuations they go to work quickly and therefore gain time for the legislative or administrative installation of discretionary policy. The major function of the automatic stabilizers in recession is to maintain consumption and thus to prevent the investment decline from initating a downward spiral. Since consumption is closely related to disposable personal income, the objective is to stabilize the latter in the face of fluctuation in the GNP. This effect can be shown by figures for the 1958 recession. In the table below the figures are presented quarterly from the third calendar quarter of 1957 to the same quarter of 1958. They are seasonally adjusted at annual rates (in $ billion).[7]

| | 1957 | | 1958 | | |
	III Qtr.	IV Qtr.	I Qtr.	II Qtr.	III Qtr.
Gross National Product	447.8	442.3	431.0	434.5	444.0
OASI benefits	7.5	7.8	7.9	8.6	8.7
Unemployment compensation benefits	1.7	2.4	3.1	4.2	4.8
Federal tax and nontax payments	37.6	37.4	36.2	36.3	37.1
Disposable Personal Income	311.5	309.9	310.3	312.9	320.4
Personal Consumption Expenditures	288.2	288.1	287.3	290.9	294.4

[7] Survey of Current Business, July, 1959, p. 15.

The table shows how much more widely the GNP fluctuates than disposable personal income and personal consumption. Some of the factors responsible for the stability of the latter two items are indicated by the indented items in the table. Old Age and Survivors' Insurance benefits rose persistently while the GNP was falling. Unemployment compensation benefits showed marked counter-cycle movement, as did federal tax payments. The stability of consumption was not wholly due to fiscal measures, but it is clear that considerable support was given by them.[8] This is the kind of result to be expected from built-in stabilizers.

In summary, the automatic stabilizers of real strategic importance are the federal progressive personal income tax and the federal-state unemployment compensation system. The latter could be made a more useful stabilizing program if the perverse fluctuation in its payroll taxes were eliminated, the amounts of weekly benefit in most states were increased, and the duration of benefits were extended. Other elements in the existing fiscal system which possess automatic stabilizing features, but to a lesser degree, are some excise taxes, some components of general sales taxes, the Old Age and Survivors' Insurance program, and the various programs for local relief. We have ignored in this discussion various governmental subsidy programs, because in general the amounts of payment under them are not tied to a central variable in the business cycle. For example, agricultural price supports would be significant stabilizers if agricultural prices moved with the business cycle. Their movement is, however, quite erratic with respect to business activity, and the amounts of subsidy vary perversely with cyclical requirements about as often as they move favorably.

Taken altogether, the automatic stabilizers clearly have a substantial stabilizing influence. They are not, however, massive enough to justify the assignment to them of the whole responsibility for fiscal stabilizing action. Their principal function is to gain time by resisting the inherent tendencies in the economy. If these tendencies are weak, the automatic stabilizers may largely do the job alone, but it is usually unsafe to depend upon them to this extent. The executive and legislative agencies of government must be in a constant state of preparedness to use the instruments of discretionary changes in revenues and expenditures if the whole arsenal of fiscal policy is to be effectively utilized for stabilization.

[8] Some undetermined part of the increased unemployment compensation benefits resulted from special federal legislation providing loans to states to extend the benefit period. This is probably not a major factor, however, as few states took advantage of it. But something less than the whole of the increased benefit payments was the result of an *automatic* measure.

RECOMMENDED READINGS

Clark, J. M., *Economics of Planning Public Works*, Washington, National Planning
Board, 1935.

The standard work on the subject. Can be very profitably read in its
entirety. Especially recommended, if time does not permit reading the whole,
are Chapters 1, 2, 3, 4, 6, 9, 10, 16.

Colm, Gerhard, "Guides and Procedures for Determining Federal Expenditure
Programs," in Joint Economic Committee, *Federal Expenditure Policy for
Economic Growth and Stability (Papers Submitted by Panelists before the
Subcommittee on Fiscal Policy)*, Washington, 1957, pp. 433–43.

Insights into the failure of budgetary procedures to serve economic goals,
and suggestions for improvement.

Hagen, Everett E., "Federal Taxation and Economic Stabilization," in Joint Com-
mittee on Economic Report, *Federal Tax Policy for Economic Growth and
Stability (Papers Submitted by Panelists before the Subcommittee on Tax
Policy)*, Washington, 1955, pp. 58–69.

A survey of stabilizing taxation, suggesting a hybrid between automatic
and discretionary flexibility, "formula flexibility," in which tax rates change
with changes in economic activity according to a predetermined plan.

Hansen, Alvin H., *Economic Policy and Full Employment*, N.Y., McGraw-Hill,
1947, Part Three.

This is an enlightening description of governmental programs to promote
full employment in England, Canada, Australia, Sweden, and the United States.

Harris, S. E., *Economic Planning*, N.Y., Knopf, 1949, Chapters 1, 4, 9.

The chapters selected are introductory to the subject (1) and deal with
recent federal experience in the United States (4, 9). The materials are
pertinent and realistic in orientation. Other chapters deal with planning
experience in other countries.

CHAPTER 7

Allocation of Resources Between the Public and Private Sectors of the Economy

The last three chapters have discussed the effects of fiscal actions upon the rate of production or income creation in the economy. We have seen that the growth in volume of fiscal activity has brought taxation and public expenditure to levels where they inevitably affect the GNP for good or for ill, and that by intelligent direction fiscal policy can offset tendencies toward instability in the private sectors of the economy. We turn in this chapter to a much older problem of public finance. It is the determination of the "proper" or optimum share of aggregate economic resources to be devoted to public use.

The central purpose of a tax system is to appropriate a portion of private incomes for public use. Government denies to the individual the free allocation of some part of his income, and these incomes appropriated from the private stream are applied to collective purposes. Their application to these purposes means that resources which could have been applied to private and individual use are allocated to collective use. The over-all inadequacy of resources completely to satisfy every want requires that allocation decisions be made. Thus, when a citizen complains that his taxes are too high, he means fundamentally that he is denied to too great an extent the command over resources which would satisfy his individual wants. He is complaining of the allocation decisions that are being made. This is one of the oldest and knottiest problems of public finance; indeed, it is one of the oldest and knottiest problems of societies organized upon the philosophy of individualism. It is the problem of the proper role of government.

. . . Our expenditures will never be—our money, our Federal money—will never be spent so intelligently and in so useful fashion for the economy as will the

157

expenditures that would be made by the private citizen, the taxpayer, if he hadn't had so much of it funneled off into the Federal Government.[1]

There are two major reasons why the Federal budget continues to rise even though it is already at record levels. First, a number of Federal budget programs are misdirected—we are trying to solve problems by spending more money, rather than by eliminating the causes that created them. Second, the Federal Government is doing things that the private economy or that State and local governments can do more efficiently.[2]

The above two quotations may be regarded as reflecting a fairly widely held public view that institutional arrangements permit the public sector to claim too large a share of our resources. The sense of the Eisenhower statement is that the purposes for which government spends are always inferior (in some sense) to the purposes for which private individuals would spend the same funds. And though the Wilde statement raises a variety of issues (and ignores the overwhelming significance of military defense in the rise of federal expenditures), its general implication is also that private claims upon resources are consistently superior in validity to public claims. Any study of the growth of public expenditures should face this issue of the wisdom of the choices in the allocation of resources.[3] The literature on this subject is not extensive, nor does the subject lend itself to highly precise analysis.

Table 10 presents as annual averages during five-year periods the value of governmental purchases of goods and services, expressed in constant dollars, and the proportions which these purchases are to the total gross national product. By converting the figures in the first column to constant

TABLE 10

FEDERAL, STATE, AND LOCAL GOVERNMENT PURCHASES OF GOODS AND SERVICES:
ANNUAL AVERAGES FOR FIVE-YEAR PERIODS, 1930–1959

Period	Purchases of Goods and Services (in billions of dollars at 1954 prices)	Per Cent of Gross National Product
1930–1934	21.1	14.8
1935–1939	27.0	15.4
1940–1944	93.8	35.5
1945–1949	60.3	20.6
1950–1954	69.1	19.8
1955–1959	76.0	18.7

[1] Dwight D. Eisenhower, in a reply to a question at the National Press Club, Washington, January 14, 1959. Transcript of news conference reported in the New York Times, January 15, 1959.

[2] Frazer B. Wilde, "Federal Expenditures in Modern America": Joint Economic Committee, Federal Expenditure Policy for Economic Growth and Stability: Papers Submitted by Panelists Appearing before the Subcommittee on Fiscal Policy, November 5, 1957, p. 158.

[3] Even if we ignore the abnormal periods of war, there has been a persistent tendency for governmental expenditures to rise. There has been, however, a less consistent tendency for the proportion of total resources allocated to government to rise.

dollars the effects of price changes are eliminated. The use of average figures for five-year periods moderates the effects of very short-term fluctuations while permitting generalizations concerning longer-term tendencies.

It will be noted that since World War II a higher plane of government purchases has been established, but except for the war years themselves, the proportion of government purchases in the GNP has remained relatively constant. In terms of the allocation of resources in the economy, a larger amount but stable share of rising GNP has been devoted to public uses. Figure 7 plots the proportions allocated to the three major components of

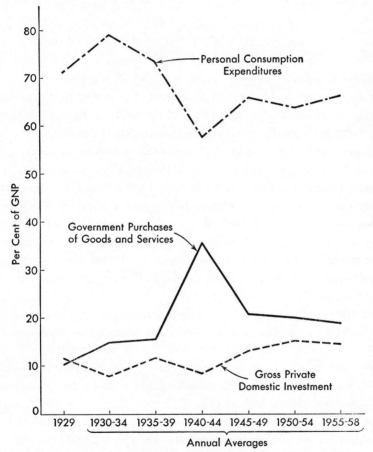

Figure 7. Major components of GNP: per cent of total GNP in
1954 prices, 1929-1959

the GNP. (The totals will vary slightly from 100 per cent in any period because the quantitatively unimportant net foreign investment has been omitted.) If in the postwar period a somewhat larger share of economic activity has been allocated to government use, at whose expense has this occurred? Not, it is evident, at the expense of domestic investment (plant and equipment, housing, inventories, and depreciation), for the postwar proportion for these purposes has risen, and is even somewhat higher than in the post-World-War-I year of 1929.[4] The implication is that the larger proportion of resources allocated for governmental use has not reduced the economic growth potential contained in private investment.

The larger share of resources devoted to governmental purposes has apparently been achieved at the expense of the share going into personal consumption, as is indicated on the chart. This does not mean, of course, that the amount of consumption expenditure has fallen, for it was $128 billion in 1929, averaged $153 billion during the war, and was $270 billion in 1955–1959, all in 1954 dollars. And it is not possible to conclude that consumption expenditure would have been higher if government purchases of goods and services had been lower. Consumption expenditure would almost certainly have been a larger *proportion* of the total, but the total itself would surely have been smaller without the governmental purchases. Further, in a high per-capita-consumption economy such as that of the United States, many of the functions performed by state and local governments provide services of a consumption character. Public education, libraries, recreation and parks, and hospitals of various types provide services which in their absence would become a part of personal consumption. In the postwar period it is the purchases of goods and services by local governments— whose purchases are largely of the types mentioned above—which have gradually risen as a percentage of the GNP. The federal share has slightly declined.

But our major purpose here is to demonstrate that an allocation problem exists and that some effective machinery for allocation is economically desirable. Resources for both private and public use are in the aggregate limited, and their efficient use requires that these resources be distributed so as to maximize their usefulness and minimize waste. In a private enterprise economy with a high degree of competition, resources tend to be allocated by "dollar votes" of individuals and groups. We believe that when individuals are reasonably intelligent and are given a wide enough variety of choices they will allocate their incomes—between spending and saving and between spending for this commodity or that—so as to maximize their

---

[4] It will be noted that while the points on the chart are generally annual averages for five-year periods, the 1929 points are for a single year. The reason for this is that 1929 is the first year for which modern and comparable GNP figures are available.

satisfactions from income. In matters of personal preference it is presumed that the individual person is the best judge of what will satisfy him. But when it comes to allocating private incomes between private and public uses a new element is introduced. Preferences in the public sector, with minor exceptions, cannot be expressed through the machinery of the market place, but must be expressed through political institutions. The allocation problem in the aggregate requires decision through the use of two sets of institutions. In the market place, under favorable conditions, the wants to be satisfied are essentially individual. In government the wants to be satisfied are frequently social in character, providing environmental benefits which are subject to marginal utility analysis only in a highly sophisticated way. The rest of this chapter is devoted to the nature of social wants and to the machinery for determining their scale and in making financial provision for them. The analysis necessarily has a strong political flavor, since we are concerned with the use of resources for the benefit of the body politic.

The Nature of Public Goods and Services

In the private sector of the economy, goods tend to be produced and distributed according to the "market principle." Under favorable circumstances of competition, consumer sovereignty holds sway, and producers, guided by the prospects of better profits in those lines where individual demands are more intense, find their profit goals best realized when they devote resources to production of the goods capable of satisfying the more pressing private and individual wants. In the market there is little problem in getting people to express their buying preferences; the problem is more likely to be that of offering wide enough choices to permit the registering of these preferences with a satisfactory degree of precision. But on the whole, when competition works effectively and when there is reasonable knowledge of alternatives, we have confidence that the market accomplishes an efficient or economic allocation of resources.

But not all wants of individuals in a society can be satisfied through the operation of the market. If this were simply because the wants were too meager to justify production for them, we should say that the market is properly performing its function by ignoring wants so low in the hierarchy. The problem is of a different sort. The wants may be intense and widespread, but institutional factors may prevent their expression. In the market place, I will not be able to get goods to satisfy my wants unless I offer to purchase at the market price. Thus the market is capable of ignoring me unless I cast my vote in favor of the product. But in the case of very many of the most important social wants, I cannot be excluded. Take, for example, national defense. The service performed (and the want satisfied) is widespread, and if it is effective for some it is effective for all the citizens. Because as a citizen I cannot be excluded from the benefits of defense no matter what I offer to pay, the importance of the want to me is not determinable under the market principle.

Suppose that at a baseball game two sets of appeals are made by passing among the crowd. One group is selling soft drinks. The other appeals for contributions for the purchase by government of an intercontinental ballistic missile. Which is likely to experience the greater effective demand? One would feel safe in expecting collections for the missile to fall well below those for the soda. But should we conclude that wants for soft drinks are really superior to those for defense? One would trust that this is not the case, but that as an instrument for the expression of preferences between these two goods the market is faulty. And the basic reason is that in the case of the soda one goes without unless he pays up, while in the case of the missile one feels that if he does not contribute others will—in one way or another—and the degree of satisfaction of his own want for defense will not be affected by the size of his contribution.

A similar situation obtains in the cases of other public wants in which the benefits may not be so wholly or so widely dispersed. Public education is a case in point. While the specific beneficiaries are those who attend school, there is substantial benefit to the whole society from widespread education. A system of exclusively private schools operating on a tuition basis would doubtless provide good schooling for those whose parents believe the specific benefits justify the price. But a system of selective education in a democratic political system would leave a large share of the population less competent to exercise the voting privilege, less aware of the amenities of social existence, less well qualified to exercise "dollar votes" in the market place, less capable of running the economic machine, and less mobile as members of the society. Everyone would suffer as a consequence. Wherever there are third party benefits involved, which are widely participated in irrespective of individual contribution, the market principle will not provide appropriate allocation of resources. In addition to education, many other public wants of this character are recognizable: those for adequate health standards, including sewage disposal, the control of air and stream pollution, and disease prevention; the postal system; highways; recreation; housing; social security; the prevention and punishment of crimes and misdemeanors; and research activities in general. Since in such major areas as these the market cannot call forth a dependable ordering of public with private wants, the market principle must be abandoned in favor of some other.

But the paragraphs above do not exhaust the situations in which the market fails to provide adequately for public wants and needs. We have suggested major areas in which, even if the wants for services are recognized by individuals, the market system does not call forth an accurate registration of those wants. There are, however, additional areas in which (1) the profit system of allocation cannot be counted upon to satisfy these wants in the proper order even if they are known, and (2) the lack of public knowledge prevents the proper ordering of wants.

The normal operation of the profit system is such as to emphasize in some areas short-term profits at the expense of long-term profits. For example, when the profit system is working well in other respects, conservation of resources is likely to be slighted in favor of short-term exploitation. It is sometimes easier for the society as a whole to postpone the use of resources than for the individual entrepreneur to postpone profit. But conservation implies not only the postponement of the use of resources in some instances; it implies that costs—often substantial—must be incurred for replacement or protection of resources being exploited currently. Thus, the replacement of mineral resources through exploration may require subsidy. And while private enterprise can effectively develop hydroelectric power resources, or even provide water for irrigation purposes, auxiliary conservation services such as flood and erosion control and reforestation will usually require either government provision or government subsidy.

Another area of failure of the profit system even under the best of private enterprise conditions is in serving the social goal of economic stability. The proper individual enterprise reaction to a prospective decline in demand is normally to reduce investment in plant and inventory, which accentuates the decline. The proper reaction to prospective boom conditions is to expand operations ahead of the boom. These natural actions accentuate instability in the economy. If stability is socially regarded as a "good thing," some limitation of the freedom of the market is called for to modify these reactions through guarantees, subsidies, or offsetting actions by government.

The market principle is also widely believed to be inadequate to control the allocation of resources economically or rationally where knowledge is lacking to permit rational decision. This situation may lead to "incorrect" decisions by either producers or consumers. Producers must to a degree anticipate demand; they must bet on success. If the odds seem to be against them, they will usually not undertake the activity, while if the odds are more·

favorable, more will be willing to take the gamble. If the probabilities are incorrectly assessed, the odds will be improperly formed, and the venture may appear to be more risky than the facts, if known, would warrant. There are examples of this to be seen in the generation and distribution of electricity. Less than 10 per cent of the rural areas of the United States were provided with electricity before 1935. Through a system of government loans (and subsidies) beginning in 1936, it has been demonstrated that rural electrification is feasible on a private basis. Electrification has since been extended so that it is available to nearly 100 per cent of farmers, through both private and public auspices. The point here is that the feasibility of handling this problem through the market principle has had to be demonstrated by an agency capable of taking the risk of experimentation. Lack of knowledge of the facts with respect to demand and cost had obstructed progress; the provision of knowledge has essentially solved the problem.

A second example is in the field of promotional rates for electricity. Prior to experimentation with low rates—principally through public power—the industry had assumed the market demand for electricity to be highly inelastic. That is, lower prices would induce only a very slight increase in kilowatt hours used, and gross receipts would fall. The facts show the assumptions to have been in error, and for most classes of users the demand has been shown to be much more elastic than expected by the private companies. Lower rates have been demonstrated to be good business policy.[5] There are other comparable areas where realization of profits may be long delayed and thus severely discounted, and where profits are realized by others than the innovators, so that the improvement of knowledge is retarded unless there is assistance from government. Examples of this are to be seen in demonstrations of the long-run profitability of fundamental research for the economy, and the long-run economic advantages of slum clearance and urban renewal. In such cases, without governmental intervention, the satisfaction of certain wants of rather high order would be delayed until after the satisfaction of wants lower in the hierarchy, if, indeed, they were to be satisfied at all.

Our final area of interest is that in which individual consumption decisions are inferior because of inadequate knowledge, and the market principle results in the allocation of resources to other than the "best" uses.

---

[5] These examples in the field of electric power may show largely the consequences of monopoly in the electric power field, and not a fair sample of the operation of the market principle. However, legal monopolies in public utilities are a fact of our system, and are not regarded as undesirable in an enterprise economy. Whether they have been laggard because of inadequate knowledge or because of inadequate competition would not seem material to this analysis.

The consumer may act entirely rationally within the limits of his knowledge, but better knowledge would cause him to rearrange preferences and cast his dollar votes differently.

This is, however, an area where a society devoted to individualism will be cautious in overriding individual preferences. In such matters as prohibition of free traffic in drugs, prohibition of the sale of alcoholic liquors to minors, requirement that poisons be clearly labeled, and compelling school attendance up to a given age, the problem is not difficult. But the line which separates the use of governmental authority for the welfare of the people and its use to exalt different aims of the state or of a ruling group over those of the people is not a clear one. Lord Acton's observation that "power corrupts . . ." may be taken as a reflection of the sort of danger involved in permitting the substitution of governmental decision for private preference to be carried too far.

The complexities of modern living make it difficult for the average person to know enough to act intelligently in his own interest. Governmental leadership in making material facts known, and governmental coercion in forcing actions which the individual might not otherwise request, therefore have a place in the process of allocating resources. The substitution of sanitary sewers for individual arrangements for sewage disposal; the encouragement if not enforcement of building codes, zoning laws, and traffic regulations; foreign aid and the undertaking of such improvements as the St. Lawrence Seaway as contributions to economic growth; and determination of the proper extent of nuclear tests—these are all examples in which governmental leadership (decision) is essential. Not all such activities involve very significant governmental claims upon resources, though some obviously do.

It seems clear that a society which relies essentially upon the market principle for distribution of resources will experience the need for a different principle of allocation in a variety of areas. These areas are those in which the market cannot call forth dependable indications of individual preferences, either because individuals will not reveal their preferences or because knowledge on the part of producers or consumers is inadequate to permit the optimum ordering of allocation to satisfy real wants. Much of economic analysis assumes the problem away. It assumes that individuals both can and will register their preferences accurately and intelligently; the problem then becomes one of simple integration of public with private wants in a model in which it is necessary only to equate marginal satisfactions as between the two. But we have seen that the market cannot call forth a measurable ordering of public wants with private wants. This means that it is impossible to conceive of aggregating individual demand schedules for public goods (expressed as quantities demanded at a range of prices), as is possible in the case of most private goods. Equating price-quantity relationships at the margin between two aggregate schedules is thus not a realistic way of thinking about allocation of resources between the private and public sectors. And as Professor Galbraith points out, advertising and emulation operate so intensively in the private sector as to cause an inherent tendency for public services to lag.[6]

The "Budget Principle"

The essence of the budget principle is the use of coercion upon individuals in the allocation of economic resources. While under the market principle the person with unusual tastes may expect to satisfy them by demanding unusual goods and services, under the budget principle minority interests are likely to be largely ignored. The majority rules. If one dislikes larger tail fins on his automobile, he may be able to buy a model with less obtrusive fins. But if a person opposes public schools or big armaments he will find it difficult to indulge his preferences. Coercion cannot be escaped, though a person with minority tastes can in some cases move to a more congenial community where the majority shares his tastes and he enjoys the privilege of coercing others to his preferences.

Since the budget principle operates by central decision, its effectiveness in accomplishing respectable allocation of resources requires both a feeling for majority preferences and the insight and imagination to propose potentially useful undertakings. Our look at budget practice in Chapter 2 implied that a sensitivity to public need and to the extent of available resources is at the heart of good budgeting. But how can the machinery of government be made to work through the budget process to provide optimum allocation of resources and minimum waste?[7]

We have seen that the market fails to call forth a dependable ordering of wants for social goods. The budget must therefore be depended upon to perform this necessary function. The old town meeting system of local government permits the direct registry of votes for and against particular patterns of resource allocation. If alternatives are offered in sufficient variety and detail and if the alternatives are clearly understood, the town meeting can be depended upon to provide a highly precise ordering of public with private wants. But most governmental units—even at the local level—have

---

[6] John K. Galbraith, *The Affluent Society,* Boston, Houghton Mifflin, 1958, pp. 260–61.

[7] A helpful discussion of methods to maximize the economic effectiveness of the budget principle may be found in Howard R. Bowen, *Toward Social Economy,* Rinehart and Company, 1948, Chapter 18.

outgrown the feasibility of having each citizen represent himself in the legislative branch of the government.

The problem of effective representation arises immediately when it becomes necessary for one person to decide for another. If representatives are fairly numerous there is reason to believe that minority preferences will at least be heard in the legislative process, and that majority preferences will be strongly enough represented to predominate. It follows that in the process of election, the candidates' position on issues of importance should be made known to the electorate with sufficient precision to permit the voter to register his scale of preferences. When the candidate is an expert in obfuscation, or at being all things to all men, and when the conservatives pose as liberals and the liberals as conservatives, the voter is unable to determine how best his scale of values can be represented. And while the two-party system tends to reduce the voter's range of choice to two candidates, most students of politics believe that party responsibility is thereby enhanced, and a more responsible attempt at satisfaction of public wants is probable.

The Wilde quotation on page 158 calls attention to the dangers to efficient use of resources in wrong-headed policy, and it is evident from the context that he has agricultural policy in mind. It may be, of course, that subsidies promote inefficiency. But almost all government expenditure involves some element of direct or indirect subsidy. Children in schools, or truckers on highways may receive services at less than imputed cost. Those who oppose a program, either rationally or in ignorance, are nevertheless required to provide financial support so long as the program is in operation. Under the budget principle majority evaluation predominates. The solution to the problem of inefficiency in allocation under the budget principle is not to throw out this instrument of allocation, but to make it sensitive to rationality. And while many would instinctively agree with the principle expressed by Mr. Eisenhower, it is patently absurd when carried to its logical extreme. Officials who enter upon public service determined to reduce the allocation of resources to public use ("cut expenditures"), are often unable to do so when confronted with the realities of the situation. This occurs at all levels of government. And it occurs far less for reasons usually ascribed—that public officials quickly become "bureaucrats" and lose their enthusiasm for economy, or that their plans are hobbled by a bureaucratic band of agency underlings—than because a close look at the situation convinces responsible officials of the continuing utility of existing programs and the persistent need for the inauguration of new functions.

The policy-maker who is irrevocably committed to the assumption that public expenditures are always too high is in most cases a candidate for a severe case of frustration. For the combined operation of the market and budget principles appears to have worked with considerable effectiveness in accomplishing—with some lags, to be sure—a reasonably satisfactory allocation of resources between private and public use. Even so, there appears to be a growing body of belief that if there is a major fault in the system, it is its bias toward private use of resources, particularly in the luxury consumption areas. Professor Galbraith makes the point dramatically:

The family which takes its mauve and cerise, air-conditioned, power-steered, power-braked automobile out for a tour passes through cities that are badly paved, made hideous by litter, blighted buildings, billboards, and posts for wires that should long since have been put underground. They pass on into a countryside that has been rendered largely invisible by commercial art. (The goods which the latter advertise have an absolute priority in our value system. Such aesthetic considerations as a view of the countryside accordingly come second. On such matters we are consistent.) They picnic on exquisitely packaged food from a portable icebox by a polluted stream and go on to spend the night at a park which is a menace to public health and morals. Just before dozing off on an air mattress, beneath a nylon tent, amid the stench of decaying refuse, they may reflect vaguely on the curious unevenness of their blessings.[8]

Public Expenditures and Economic Growth

Since World War II economic growth has assumed the status of an established and important social goal. Growth is usually defined as a rise in real output or income per capita, though it is recognized that as a social goal it embraces more than the numerical quantities of goods; real growth will involve as well some consideration of the human and social qualities of the goods and of the availability of leisure. These latter factors are not effectively measured in statistics of production and national income.

The shift during and after the war in advanced economies from a declining to an increasing rate of population growth impressed these societies with the need to increase productive activity in order to maintain levels of living for larger numbers of people. Technically, such an increase would be termed "expansion" as distinguished from "growth." But the tradition in these economies had been one of improved levels of living ("growth"), and to maintain this record of improvement per capita for a larger population implied sustained increases in production larger than in the prewar periods. In the traditionally backward economies two different kinds of developments brought the issue of economic growth to the fore. In some of these countries, notably the U.S.S.R. and China, remarkable rates of economic

[8] John K. Galbraith, *The Affluent Society,* Boston, Houghton Mifflin, copyright 1958, page 253. Quoted by permission.

growth were coupled with political determination to assume a dominant and unsettling role in world affairs. To these countries, internal growth has been of overriding importance, both for its own sake and as an industrial base for military power. Other underdeveloped countries have made economic growth a basic social objective, but have been unsuccessful in moving off dead center. The drive for economic growth is thus world-wide, not only for its own sake—the improvement of the economic welfare of people— but also because this drive has taken on a competitive character owing to the rise of new and dynamic systems troubling the waters of international politics.

The reader may at first be somewhat surprised to meet the problem of economic growth in a chapter devoted to the allocation of economic resources. But reflection will show that growth is a special aspect of the allocation problem. Traditionally, the allocation problem has been one of the proper distribution of utilities to be derived from private and public goods and services. The growth problem, however, involves principally the allocation between consumption and investment use of resources. When the proper distribution is determined in these terms, the further issue of performance through the private or the public sector arises. Thus, growth is centrally a matter of resource allocation.

While much of the literature on economic growth seems to make it depend exclusively upon expansion of productive capacity and to make expansion of productive capacity depend exclusively upon the construction of buildings and the installation of machinery, the conditions of growth are extremely complex. The strategic importance of particular factors will vary among economies at a given time, and in a given economy at different times. Clearly, however, in an economy at full employment, growth can be attained only by an expansion of the capacity to produce. But the inducement to expand productive capacity will, if sustained, require an expanding will to consume or an expanding demand for goods and services for government. If the demand is present, expansion of productive capacity will involve some or all of the following: expanded natural resources of the right types, an expanded labor force of the right skills and abilities, and expanded plant and equipment. The degree of expansion obtainable will be determined by the "rightness" of all these factors in terms of the general environment in which productive activity takes place.

There are many facets of the problem of production expansion in which the role of government is crucial. The range of decisions which must be made by government will, of course, be more extensive in those economies where by tradition the sphere of government is large and the sphere of private enterprise small. But even in private enterprise economies like that of the United States, the role of government in economic growth is impressive. The availability of natural resources will depend to a considerable extent upon past and present conservation policy. The development of major power and irrigation resources, flood control, erosion control, and the like have involved government heavily both in direct investment and in promotional policies designed to prod private enterprise and to provide technical assistance. Research leading to the substitution of plentiful for scarce resources in the creation of products, and in the improvement of productivity in agriculture, continues to be, in varying degree, a function of government. What is designated by some as "creeping socialism" may be nothing more than assistance in the creation of robust capitalism.

So far as labor resources are concerned, the size of population at any given time is essentially not subject to governmental influence. But the health and vigor of workers are affected by research and facilities for the prevention and treatment of illness and accident, research in matters of diet and consumer protection, and facilities for recreation. In all of these, governments have played a significant role, and in none is it likely that this role will or should be curtailed. Probably most important of all in the development of labor resources is education and libraries, where government provision has been and continues to be predominant. The role of education goes far beyond the specialized training for technical skills. Its functions are to develop ability to decide rationally; to formulate, communicate, and understand ideas; and to use accumulated knowledge for progress. It is a peculiarly strategic element in progress, for it not only lays the foundation for technical advance on the part of innovators but equips the general public for the acceptance of and adjustment to these innovations.

In the area of provision of the capital instruments for increased capacity to produce, governments will provide significant assistance even in economies in which the principal responsibility rests upon private initiative. The coercive powers of governments may be required to provide a reasonable rate of saving with which investment may be made. This function is usually more important in an economy whose productivity is low in relation to consumption requirements, where consumption is forcibly reduced in order to provide a current fund of savings. But from time to time it may be desirable for government even in an advanced economy to force savings through taxation or to generate new money through centrally controlled banking policy. The research function is a central one in development—particularly in those countries so far advanced that they cannot copy the technologies of others—and is peculiarly dependent upon government support. For expenditure for research is risky expenditure; it does not promise useful results in each undertaking, and many of its useful results are realizable only over relatively long periods of time, and then often by others than those who make the research expenditure. This is, of course, particularly true of basic research, as distinguished from applied research and from development.

The United States Bureau of the Budget estimates that in the fiscal year 1960, federal expenditures identifiable as research and product-development expenditures total about $5.5 billion, exclusive of that part of military procurement expenditures (estimated at $2 billion) which are reimbursements for research and development by those firms producing defense items.[9] This total breaks down into $1.3 billion for research—of which about $.5 billion is for basic research—and $4.2 billion for product development. The Bureau estimates that the federal government provides the funds for about half of all such research and development carried on in the United States. The major part of such funds go for development rather than research, and a large proportion is directed toward national security purposes. Other federal agencies making major research outlays are the Department of Agriculture, the Department of Health, Education, and Welfare, and the National Science Foundation. State governments spend some, but unknown, amounts for research, principally through state universities and colleges. On the whole, it is evident that governments carry a large share of research and development expenditures in the United States economy. That is, resources are allocated to research and development at least as heavily through the budget as through the market.

In the area of technological research and development, while a larger share of the direct expense is borne by government, the major share of the research is done by private concerns. But direct expenditure for research and development is by no means the whole story of dynamic innovation. Again the educational function, if properly performed, undergirds the whole process of scientific innovation.

We have very briefly outlined the areas of major contribution of government to the growth of productive capacity, under the heading of provision of adequate natural resources, appropriate labor supply, and necessary capital facilities. The treatment should not, however, end here. For economic growth takes place in an environment conducive to growth, and this involves a stable political society, a dependable system of individual rights and duties, an intelligent and ambitious population with proper incentives for growth, an effectively operating competitive system in essentially free mar-

[9] *The Budget of the United States Government for the Fiscal Year Ending June 30, 1960.* Special Analysis H.

kets, and a reasonable degree of economic stability over a period of time. All of these requirements heavily involve government; in fact, they are to a large extent responsibilities which a society tends to assign specifically to government.

Are Budgetary Objectives Consistent with Each Other?

As our analysis of public expenditures reaches its conclusion, it may be well to re-examine the principal goals of expenditure and to inquire into the feasibility of serving these goals consistently. The traditional objective of public expenditure has been to protect and to complement the standard of living for the society. Thus, a major undertaking of central governments has historically been that of preventing interference or invasion from outside the society. National security in recent decades has accounted for the principal share of central government expenditure. Its counterpart is provision of internal security—the protection of the rights of individual citizens against invasion by other individual citizens. In this latter the governments of states and their subdivisions participate along with the central government. But the traditional function of protection is only a part of the general function of promoting the "good life" of citizens. Adam Smith, in delineating the proper functions of government in a system of "natural liberty," alludes to those of defense against invasion and the administration of justice, and adds a third:

. . . The duty of erecting and maintaining certain public works and certain public institutions, which it can never be for the interest of any individual, or small number of individuals, to erect and maintain; because the profit could never repay the expense to any individual or small number of individuals, though it may frequently do much more than repay it to a great society.[10]

Thus, while the particular instruments for creating the good life are the institutions of economic and political freedom, these instruments will need to be complemented by the active performance of services by government. The area of these complementary services has consistently expanded as the standard of private living has risen. For example, the revolutionary integration of the automobile into the standard of living has made necessary an elaborate system of public highways. Increased leisure time, arising from increased productivity in the economy, has demanded public recreation facilities, libraries, and a host of other complementary services. And the very prosperity of most sectors of the economy so contrasts with need and squalor in other sectors as to demand programs for redistribution of welfare.

Historically, then, the functions of government have been those of protecting, maintaining, supplementing, and appropriately distributing the

---

[10] Adam Smith, *The Wealth of Nations,* 1776, Modern Library Edition, p. 651.

outpourings of the horn of plenty, which are essentially the product of free institutions. These functions may be described as falling under the general heading of the allocation of resources. Some portion of these resources is to be transferred from private to public use, in order to perpetuate the good life. More recently, as we have seen, a new emphasis has grown up within this general goal of maintenance of the good life. It is the emphasis upon economic growth, or persistent improvement in the good life. But the growth objective simply introduces a new dimension in the allocative function. If Smith were writing today of the wealth of nations, he would undoubtedly include promotion of economic growth among those public institutions which more than repay their cost to a great society.

The historically orthodox view with respect to financing transfers of resources from the private to the public sector of the economy is that the expenditures for resources should be matched by equal exactions of funds (taxes) from the public during the accounting period. Thus, since the accounting period is traditionally a year, the budget should be balanced year by year. In the real sense, the resources taken by government are equal to resources given by the public, and the "resources budget" is therefore necessarily balanced. Why not, then, balance the money budget, so that money taken from the public for the purchase of resources is equal to money paid to the public for those resources. The rule has the virtue of simplicity, and if the society must always be on guard against the coercive power inherent in the budget principle, the rule provides its own checks and balances through public resistance to tax increases.

The principle of annual budget balance has often been breached with equanimity in times of national emergency such as war. The necessity for real transfer of resources for war purposes has been recognized, but the inertia in tax rates has led to compromise with the principle of budget balance, and financial deficits have regularly occurred. And with the advent of the new objective of economic growth, there has been widespread acceptance of a deficit for this purpose. The states have regularly gone into debt for highway construction. Local governments have pressed against their debt limits to provide school facilities. Debt for water and sewerage systems has skyrocketed in recent years. Thus new emergencies, such as the automotive revolution, explosive population increase, and major geographical shifts in population, have joined the emergency of war as justifying unbalanced budgets. Public borrowing to sustain or encourage economic growth has found a long-standing parallel justification in the practice of borrowing by business for expansion purposes. But though the exceptions to the rule seem to have become more common, the rule remains pretty well intact that the allocative functions of government should normally take place within the limits of an annually balanced budget.

In more recent years the objective of promoting economic stability through the budget has gained status alongside the allocative objective. This has occurred partly because budgets have grown large in performing the allocative function, and their sheer weight in the composition of aggregate demand requires that budget policy be determined with economic stability in mind. We are thus forced to make stability a goal of policy whether we like it or not. But beyond this, recognition of the ability of fiscal policy to offset instability in the private sector has tended to make it a positive instrument for the good life. When unemployment occurs, a loss of potentially useful goods and services occurs. Unchecked inflation not only gives rise to erratic and capricious redistribution of welfare, but may also create distortions leading to unemployment. Recession is an enemy of growth, because each setback represents a deficit in output which must be made up before the economy can move to higher ground.[11]

While the allocation function of the budget continues to pay at least lip service to the desirability of annual balance, the stabilizing function is very badly served by annual balance. In fact, the very essence of a stabilizing budget is its flexibility and its intentional departure from balance. When forces in the private sector of the economy are moving toward equilibrium with underemployment, the maintenance of budget balance will not work to offset these tendencies. To cut expenditures or raise tax rates for purposes of maintaining budget balance when the tax base shrinks would only accentuate the decline. And when inflationary forces are at work and the tax base expands, to lower tax rates or to increase expenditures will only pour oil on the inflationary flames. To borrow a phrase from the Federal Reserve, fiscal policy must "lean against the wind" when the stabilization objective is to be served.

Decisions under the budget principle must sometimes weigh conflicting objectives, often of approximately equal priority. These conflicts are quite apart from those which may arise out of differences of opinion as to the appropriate long-term role of government or differences in view as to the probable course of the business cycle. In the extreme case of war there is general agreement that government's claim on resources should be greatly

[11] In the third quarter of 1957, the GNP at 1958 prices was $453.3 billion (annual rate). It dropped in the first quarter of 1958 to $429 billion, and did not recover to the previous figure until the last quarter of 1958. For the year 1957, the GNP was $451.1 billion; for 1958, $437.7 billion. At a 3 per cent annual rate of growth the 1958 figure would have been $464.6 billion. The recession thus created a GNP deficit of $27 billion in goods and services below the line of 3 per cent growth.

increased. But if this policy is continued beyond the level of full employment in the face of strong consumer demand, inflationary pressures will be created. Even in a more normal boom period, when employment is full, incomes high, and private levels of living high, there will normally occur a demand for a higher level of complementary government services because is it felt that they can be afforded. Thus, while the allocative function would increase government demand, the stabilization function would probably require not only resistance to the increase, but an offsetting action to counter the strength of private demand. Conflicts of this sort between the objectives of more public goods and more stability in the economy occur frequently.[12]

Another area of conflict has been given extensive discussion in recent years. Is the objective of maximum long-term economic growth consistent with the objective of stability? One section of opinion holds that a moderate degree of price level inflation is essential to a high rate of economic growth. The support for this view follows two lines. First, the prospect for moderate price increases encourages optimism with respect to profit possibilities, and entrepreneurs are encouraged to take advantage of this promise by expanding plant and equipment, and adopting new technology. The result is growth in the capacity to produce. Also, rising prices permit a somewhat more relaxed attitude toward rising wages, and in this relaxed attitude labor is made happy and work stoppages—which in themselves set back growth—are held to a minimum. Thus, the theory goes, the expansion of productive capacity exceeds the rate of price increase, and rising real wages and real profits occur. The rise of real wages underwrites rising consumption. The rise of real profits both justifies the investment expansion and provides internal investment funds to finance its continuance. On the other hand, this view holds that rigid stabilization policy, if effective under conditions in which money wages are gradually rising, eventually tends to reduce profit margins and thus hold back the inducement to expansion and improvement in capital investment, and a less-than-maximum rate of growth is realized.

Opposed to this view, the rigid stabilizationists raise two objections. The first is that the prospect of stable prices is most conducive to rational business planning, and the uncertainties that accompany the prospect of price change encourage many entrepreneurs to play it safe and not undertake programs of expansion. Thus, the prospect of price changes is destructive

---

[12] It may be observed that the kinds of conflicts observed above could be at least largely resolved through operation on the tax side of the budget. Thus, if expenditure increase is desired in inflation, it can be had without discarding stabilization policy if tax rates are raised sufficiently. This is difficult to accomplish in practice. For there is more inertia in tax rates than in budget expenditures, and the effects upon the economy of major and abrupt changes in tax rates may be serious.

of optimism because of the risk involved. Second, the rigid stabilizationists point rather convincingly to the danger that moderate inflation—especially when supported by government policy—will not remain moderate. There are reasons why the expectation of price rises makes this expectation come true, and buying to beat the price rise or to be in shape to profit from it may well aggravate the price rise.

To return to the argument for moderate inflation as an essential condition for optimum growth, its supporters point to a variety of institutional factors in the United States economy which militate against rigid anti-inflationary policy. Big labor, with a bias toward persistently rising money wages; big business, with low break-even points and equipped with power to get higher prices by limiting output; and big government, with its persistent need for large defense deliveries at negotiated prices—all these combine to limit the effectiveness of stabilization policy. For under such circumstances anti-inflationary monetary and fiscal policies, if applied with real spirit, may well be more successful in causing unemployment than in preventing price rises. Thus, an effort to prevent inflation may actually result in a setback in GNP when the objective is an increase in GNP.

It is easy, however, to overdramatize apparent conflict between the social objectives of stability and growth. There would be unanimity in the espousal of a single goal of stable growth. The argument is over the degree of compromise necessary between policies designed to promote stability and policies designed to encourage growth. Too vigorous application of stabilization policies in situations tending toward inflation may adversely affect growth. It should be noted, however, that no such conflict exists in situations of underemployment. Here the policy designed to generate full production is entirely consistent with policies conducive of optimum growth.

RECOMMENDED READINGS

Bowen, Howard R., *Toward Social Economy*, N.Y., Rinehart, 1949, Part IV.
 The eleven chapters of this Part analyze the nature of social economy and the relevant pricing process. The whole Part stands as a unit, but the reader may wish to select particular chapters.
Colm, Gerhard, "The Theory of Public Expenditures," *The Annals*, January, 1936, and reprinted in Colm, *Essays in Public Finance and Fiscal Policy*, N.Y., Oxford, 1955, as Chapter 2.
 An early, but far-seeing excursion into the issue of dependence upon the market for allocation of resources to the public sector.
Musgrave, Richard A., "Principles of Budget Determination," and Heller, Walter W., "Economics and the Applied Theory of Public Expenditures," in Joint Economic Committee, *Federal Expenditure Policy for Economic Growth and*

Stability (Papers Submitted by Panelists before the Subcommittee on Fiscal Policy), Washington, 1957, pp. 108–15 and 98–107, respectively.

These two papers are based upon Musgrave's analysis of the necessity for abandonment of the market principle in allocation of resources to the public sector. Implications of this fact are pursued. The material can be found in greater detail and at a higher level in Musgrave, *The Theory of Public Finance,* N.Y., McGraw-Hill, 1959.

Wilde, Frazar B., "Federal Expenditures in Modern America," in Joint Economic Committee (see under Musgrave and Heller above, pp. 153–61.

A readable presentation of the widespread popular view that the budget principle is providing too high a level of federal expenditures.

CHAPTER 8

Public Debt:
its Nature and its Management

Government debt arises out of borrowing by the Treasury from banks, business organizations, and individuals. The debt is in the form of promises by the Treasury to pay to the holders of these promises a principal sum and in most instances interest on that principal. Borrowing by the Treasury takes place when current revenue receipts (see Chapter 2) are inadequate to maintain a Treasury cash balance large enough to meet current cost payments[1] and to retire maturing debt. Borrowing is resorted to in order to provide funds for financing a current budget deficit. Such current deficit borrowing results in a net addition to public debt. In recent fiscal years, however, a major part of federal government borrowing has been to refund already existing debt as it matures. For when a Treasury obligation matures (its principal being due) the Treasury must either pay the principal sum out of current budget surplus (excess of revenue receipts over cost payments) or borrow new funds to retire old debt. The federal government debt showed a net increase in every fiscal year between 1930 and 1946, and between 1946 and 1959 the year-end public debt declined on only five occasions. Thus, throughout this period the retirement of maturing obligations has had to be accomplished fairly generally by new borrowing. Debt operations involving replacement do not, of course, result in a net increase in public debt outstanding.

Gross Debt and Net Debt

The Treasury's *gross debt* includes the principal sum of all Treasury debt obligations outstanding. Debt obligations are those represented by

[1] Interest on the public debt is, of course, a cost payment.

178

"securities"; i.e., actual contractual promises to pay. At any moment the Treasury may owe accrued but unpaid salaries of government employees; if government workers are paid every two weeks, at any time between pay days salaries will have accrued but will be unpaid. Such accrued current expenses are not a part of gross debt. Because of the mechanics of payment there may be outstanding at any moment considerable amounts of claims against the government for materials purchased, or damages awarded. These are also accrued current expenses and do not enter into the total of gross debt, although debt may necessarily be later incurred to meet these expenses. Interest on gross debt is treated somewhat differently from other accrued expenses. At any moment of time, interest will have accrued on the debt, whether or not it is immediately payable. In reporting gross debt the Treasury includes accrued interest in some cases and excludes it in others. Two examples of inclusion of accrued interest in gross debt are statistically important. Series E savings bonds accumulate interest during their life and add this interest (compounded) to the principal. A Series E bond purchased for $18.75 matures in just under eight years, at which time government pays the holder $25.00. The difference between $18.75 and $25.00 is compound interest at 3.75 per cent for 7¾ years. During the life of the bond, however, it may be redeemed for $18.75 plus accrued interest (modified by a redemption schedule designed to encourage holding the bond until maturity). At any time, therefore, before maturity the Treasury stands ready to pay the principal plus a stated amount of interest, and in reporting the gross amount of such bonds outstanding at any given moment the Treasury states their current amount including accumulated interest. A second example is that of Treasury Bills, ninety-day obligations sold on a "discount" basis. The purchaser pays the Treasury an amount which is less than the matured value of the Bill, this discount representing interest for the period until maturity. In reporting the gross amount of such securities outstanding at any moment, the final or matured value is reported; thus gross debt in this case also includes interest. In cases of this sort it is important to recognize that the reported figures of gross debt depart somewhat from our definition, though the degree of technical error in the reported statistics is not large.

The determination of net debt involves subtraction from gross debt of funds in hand, which may or may not be dedicated to debt retirement. Sinking funds are assets set aside for the specific purpose of retiring debt, and are usually created through appropriation by the legislative branch. Sinking funds have fallen into general disuse by governments in the United States. The federal government technically maintains a sinking fund account—it amounted to $12 billion at the end of the fiscal year 1959—but this consists of an authorization to use these funds for debt retirement if they are available, and is not a true cash or asset balance. States and local governments have largely substituted "serial" securities for sinking funds. These are issues which provide for retirement each year of a fraction of the issue instead of lump sum repayment at the end of a longer period. This system makes the accumulation of a reserve fund unnecessary. The fraction maturing is retired by appropriation (or by refunding) as it comes due.

A second deduction from gross debt is the amount of the Treasury balance—either in cash or in bank deposits. The Treasury balance represents liquid assets which may or may not be used for debt retirement. If borrowing is undertaken to build up the cash balance, the *net* debtor position of the Treasury is actually unchanged, since the addition to gross debt is equal to the increase in Treasury liquid assets. Operation of the Treasury at a surplus will result in an increase in the Treasury balance until it is used for debt retirement. The Treasury balance can thus increase from two (and only two) sources: new borrowing and a current excess of receipts over payments. In either case the balance should be deducted from gross debt outstanding to give a correct picture of the actual (net) debt position of the Treasury.

Net debt is thus the gross debt minus the sum of the sinking fund and the Treasury balance. The net debtor position of the United States Treasury as of June 30, 1959, is calculated as follows (in millions):[2]

Gross Debt	$275,466
Treasury Balance	5,119
Sinking Fund (No actual resources)	
Net Debt	$270,347

The *net* debtor position of the Treasury is of significance for certain purposes. It is obviously more realistic than gross debt. For instance, retirement of debt by reduction in the Treasury balance, such as took place during 1946, markedly decreased gross debt even though the Treasury was currently operating at a deficit. In such a case net debt, remaining virtually unchanged, is a far better measure of debt condition than is gross debt. Nevertheless, net debt may be misleading unless correctly interpreted. An increase in gross debt may create no immediate increase in net debt, since the proceeds of borrowing increase the Treasury balance. Over a longer period the use of the Treasury balance to meet current expenses will increase net debt to correspond to the increase in gross debt.

[2] *Daily Statement of the United States Treasury,* June 30, 1959.

Gross public debt receipts and expenditures for the fiscal year 1959 were as follows (in millions):[3]

Public Debt Receipts (New Issues)	$199,885
Public Debt Expenditures (Retirements)	191,522
Excess of Receipts	$ 8,363

The excess of public debt receipts over expenditures represents an increase during the year in the nation's gross debt. Public debt receipts represent the proceeds of sales of government securities during the year. Public debt expenditures represent payments for retirement of securities during the year. It is evident from the figures above that less than the whole of proceeds of Treasury security sales was used to pay off holders of matured or called securities.

The excess of public debt receipts ($8,363 million) shown above represents the increase in gross debt during the year 1959. In that year, the budget deficit was financed both by an increase in gross debt and by a reduction in the Treasury balance. The figures for 1959 are as follows (in millions):[4]

Budget Deficit	$12,540
Decrease in Treasury Balance	4,399
Increase in Gross Debt	$ 8,141

Summarizing the factors responsible for change in *net debt,* we find them to be:

1. Budget surplus or deficit. Budget deficit inevitably increases gross debt unless the deficit is met by a reduction in the cash balance; the excess of cost payments over revenue receipts usually requires resort to new borrowing. Budget surplus may be used to reduce debt; on the other hand, it may increase the cash balance without reducing gross debt.

2. Increase or decrease in the Treasury balance. An increase in the balance will be accompanied by an increase in gross debt unless the increase in balance is provided by a budget surplus. A decrease in the cash balance will reduce gross debt to the extent that funds are used for debt retirement and not to cover a budget deficit.

3. Decrease in the sinking fund balance. Since the sinking fund is dedicated to debt retirement, a reduction in the sinking fund balance, *without*

[3] *Daily Treasury Statement,* June 30, 1959, pp. 3, 4.

[4] From *Monthly Statement of Receipts and Expenditures of the United States Government,* June 30, 1959, p. 1. There is a discrepancy between the increase in gross debt shown here and that shown as the excess of public debt receipts over expenditures in the previous exhibit, of $221 million. This is partly accounted for by the fact that some of the figures shown here are tentative, and partly because of technicalities in the treatment of special funds.

offsetting new borrowing for current expenses or to increase the cash balance, represents reduction in gross debt.

It follows from our previous discussion that change in *net debt* can occur only on account of budget surplus or deficit. Increase or decrease in gross debt resulting in increase or decrease of the Treasury balance leaves net debt unchanged. Decrease in gross debt by expenditure from the sinking fund likewise leaves net debt unchanged.

The Trend of Government Debt

Federal. The trend of the federal government debt is shown in Table 11. Gross debt figures reflect the general trend of federal expenditures. The effect of war upon the gross debt is evident: a 38-fold increase between 1860 and 1870; a 21-fold increase between 1910 and 1920; a 6-fold increase between 1940 and 1946. Marked price increase is inherent in all three periods of war increase; nevertheless the war debt, being fixed in terms of dollars, continues at the wartime level even though prices later fall. Percentage increases of course tell only a part of the story. The 6-fold increase during the period 1940–1946 represents a dollar increase in gross debt ninety-five times as great as does the 38-fold increase during the period 1860–1870 and ten times as great as the 21-fold increase between 1910 and 1920.

The period 1870–1910 shows reduction of debt from the Civil War level and relative stability throughout the period. The decade following 1920 demonstrates consistent debt reduction at a rate averaging about $1 billion per year. This was due very largely to a relatively high level of economic activity and the high productivity during the postwar period of the tax system introduced during the war. The budget surpluses of the twenties cannot be said to have resulted from conscious determination to tax heavily for purposes of debt reduction; rather the surpluses accumulated in spite of persistent tax rate reduction. Preliminary attention is invited, in terms of the experience of the twenties, to the extreme importance of a high level of business activity and national income, both in facilitating debt retirement and in moderating the burden of high debt. The study in Chapter 3 of the new crop of governmental functions introduced during the depression decade of the thirties explains the new debt increase which began in 1931 and continued until 1940. Debt increase greatly accelerated during World War II, for obvious reasons.

An $11.5 billion reduction in gross debt occurred between 1946 and 1947 and was accomplished by the use of an abnormally large Treasury balance to retire debt. Just after termination of hostilities the Victory Loan had produced large amounts of cash funds for the Treasury. The cutback in military expenditures was more drastic than expected, while current tax revenues remained high, making possible the use of the Treasury balance for debt retirement. This remarkable reduction in gross debt, however, was not paralleled by reduction in net debt. To the extent that gross debt reduction was accomplished by use of the cash balance, net debt remained unchanged.

The gross debt, which stood at $252 billion at the end of 1948, remained relatively stable until 1953–1955, when it rose first as a result of major expenditures increase and later because of major tax cuts in the recession.

TABLE 11

U. S. FEDERAL DEBT, SELECTED YEARS, 1860–1959*
(in current dollars)

End of Fiscal Year	Gross Debt ($ billion)	Per Capita Gross Debt (dollars)	Gross Debt as Per Cent of Gross National Product
1860	.065	2.06	1.8
1870	2.4	61.06	36.2
1880	2.1	41.60	28.3
1890	1.1	17.80	9.3
1900	1.3	16.60	6.9
1910	1.1	12.41	3.7
1920	24.3	228.23	28.0
1930	16.2	131.51	17.8
1935	38.7	255.55	39.6
1940	43.0	325.23	40.6
1945	258.7	1,848.60	121.2
1950	257.4	1,696.68	90.3
1951	255.2	1,653.42	77.5
1952	259.1	1,650.06	74.6
1953	266.1	1,666.74	72.9
1954	271.3	1,670.14	74.8
1955	274.4	1,660.15	69.1
1956	272.8	1,622.64	65.1
1957	270.6	1,588.96	61.5
1958	276.4	1,587.92	63.4
1959	284.7	1,610.09	

* Gross debt and per capita gross debt figures, 1860–1956, taken from *Annual Report of the Secretary of the Treasury,* 1956, Table 16. 1957–1959 debt figures taken from *Daily Treasury Statement* as of June 30, and combined with census population estimates as of June 30.

GNP figures are taken from the following sources: 1860–1910 from W. I. King, *Wealth and Income of the People of the United States,* N.Y., Macmillan, 1915, p. 129; 1920 and 1925 from Mary S. Painter, "Estimates of Gross National Product," 1919–1928, in *Federal Reserve Bulletin,* September, 1945, p. 873; 1930 through 1951 from *National Income Supplement to the Survey of Current Business,* 1954, and for subsequent years from subsequent July issues of the *Survey.* GNP figures are for calendar years, the end of the fiscal year falling at the mid-point of the calendar year. Admittedly the figures of the GNP are not exactly comparable and therefore do not provide an entirely consistent series. King defines his "national income" as "the total product of the efforts of the citizens" (p. 124), which appears to be a close approximation to the gross national product. Painter's estimates use the pre-1947 Department of Commerce definition of the gross national product.

The next jump was in 1958–1959, when defense expansion and a recession cut in revenues caused the debt to attain its all-time peak of nearly $285 billion.

Per capita gross debt shows essentially the same increase as does total gross debt, though the over-all increase is moderated by the growth of population. Total gross debt increased approximately 4,000 times between 1860 and 1946; during the same period per capita debt increased by less than one-fourth that amount. The effect of population growth upon the per capita debt is most marked between 1870 and 1910. During this period population increased roughly two and one-half times.

The column in Table 11 which relates gross debt to gross national product demonstrates a further noteworthy modification of the raw figures of gross debt increase. Here the over-all increase between 1860 and 1946 is seventy-seven times. The remarkable increases in productivity and the price level following World War II account for the marked decline in the ratio of gross debt to gross national product during that period. Conclusions as to the significance of the gross debt-gross product ratio are discouraged at this point in our study, since there is great danger of overemphasizing the importance of the capital sum of that debt. Nevertheless it should be said that from almost any point of view the gross debt-gross product ratio is a more important datum for economic investigation of debt problems than is either total gross debt or per capita debt.

State and Local. Table 12 gives figures for selected years of state and local government gross debt. The table does not compute per capita debt or gross debt as a percentage of gross national product, as was done in

TABLE 12

STATE AND LOCAL GROSS DEBT, SELECTED YEARS, 1902–1958*

End of Fiscal Year	State Debt ($ million)	Local Debt ($ million)
1902	230	1,877
1913	379	4,035
1922	1,131	8,976
1927	1,971	12,910
1932	2,832	16,373
1936	3,413	16,061
1940	3,590	16,693
1944	2,776	14,703
1948	3,676	14,980
1950	5,285	18,830
1952	6,874	23,226
1954	9,600	29,332
1956	12,890	36,271
1958	15,394	42,656

* 1902–1952 figures from Bureau of the Census, *Historical Statistics in State and Local Government Finances, 1902–1953*, Tables 2 and 3; the remainder from *ibid.*, *Summary of Governmental Finances in 1956*, and *1958*.

Table 11 for federal debt. The reason is that such averages are meaningless on a nation-wide basis when the governmental units included vary so widely.

The statistics of state and local debt increase are not as striking as are those of the federal government presented in Table 11, until the nineteen-fifties. Nevertheless the patterns are comparable, with two exceptions: the decade of the twenties, during which state and local debt rose rapidly while federal debt was gradually pared down, and the World War II period, during which state and local governments reduced debt while the federal debt skyrocketed. The latter exception requires no explanation, since state and local revenues rose with war business activity and construction outlays could not be made.

The former exception requires investigation into the causes of the rise of state and local debt during the twenties, while federal debt was being reduced. Unfortunately, complete statistics of the type desired are not available. However, of all divisions of local government, the larger share of debt outstanding is that of cities over 30,000 population, for which statistics are available. In 1930 such cities had outstanding a combined gross debt of 9¾ billion dollars.[5] Four classes of functions made up almost 80 per cent of this gross debt. They are:

Water Supply Systems	30.0%
Schools	17.5%
All Other Public Service Enterprises	15.5%
Roadways	15.1%
TOTAL	78.1%

The state governments combined had a gross debt of $2,350 million in 1930. Of this total, 56 per cent was incurred for highway purposes, with no other purpose accounting for over 10 per cent.[6] The $1,317 million of highway debt was higher than the total of all state debt in 1922, as indicated in Table 12. During the decade of the twenties, while federal debt was being reduced by a high level of taxation and a relatively constant level of expenditures, state and local governments were making heavy expenditures of the capital outlay type which normally are financed through bond issues.

Composition of The Federal Debt

The securities making up the federal government debt may be classified three ways. The first classification distinguishes interest-bearing from non-interest-bearing debt. The second distinguishes securities available for purchase by the public from those special issues which can be held only by specified owners. The third distinguishes securities from one another on

---

[5] *Financial Statistics of Cities*, 1930, p. 520.
[6] *Statistical Abstract of the United States*, 1932, p. 211.

the basis of maturities—i.e., the time elapsing between the date of issue and the date on which the principal is payable.

TABLE 13

COMPOSITION OF THE FEDERAL DEBT, JUNE 30, 1959*

Class and Type of Security	Maturities (from issue date)	Interest Rates (%)	Outstanding ($ millions)
I. Interest-Bearing Debt			
A. Public Issues			
1. Bonds			
Treasury Bonds	6–40 yrs.	2⅛–4	84,803
Savings Bonds	7 yrs. 9 mo.–12 yrs.	2.5–3.75	50,503
Other Bonds	12–50 yrs.	3–3	8,597
Total Bonds			143,904
2. Notes	13 mo.–5 yrs.	1½–4	27,314
3. Certificates of Indebtedness	11½–12 mo.	1⅝–4	33,843
4. Treasury Bills	91–340 days	2.722–3.835	32,017
Total Public Issues			237,078
B. Special Issues	On demand after 1 yr.	1.5–4.0	44,756
Total Interest-Bearing Debt			281,833
II. Non-Interest-Bearing Debt			
A. Matured Debt, Interest Ceased	Matured	——	476
B. Savings and Thrift Stamps	On demand	0	54
C. Excess Profits Tax Refund Bonds	On demand	0	1
D. International Monetary Fund Notes	On demand	0	1,979
E. Currency			362
Total Non-Interest-Bearing Debt			2,873
TOTAL GROSS DEBT			284,706

* Adapted from tables showing "Summary of Public Debt and Guaranteed Obligations," and "Statement of the Public Debt," in *Daily Treasury Statement,* June 30, 1959, pp. 5–9.

Table 13 presents the composition of the federal debt existing June 30, 1959, combining all three types of classification mentioned above. We shall discuss the separate classifications individually by reference to the table.

Interest-Bearing and Non-Interest-Bearing Debt. The non-interest-bearing items of the debt are seen to be quantitatively unimportant. They are composed of five classes, as indicated in Table 13. When securities mature or are called for payment prior to maturity,[7] interest ceases. At any

---

[7] Most bonds are "callable," providing an option to the borrower to repay principal at any time after a stated date and prior to stated maturity.

time some called or matured securities may remain outstanding, owing to loss or destruction, or ignorance or inertia of the holder. The fact that matured securities have not been redeemed does not excuse government from its obligation to repay the principal of these securities, and their principal remains a part of the gross debt. Thrift stamps were sold during World War I, and Savings Stamps have been sold during and since World War II, to those who wish to save in amounts too small to permit purchase of bonds. The expectation is that these stamps will be accumulated by the purchaser until they can be exchanged for a bond. The stamps, however, bear no interest. The Excess Profits Tax Refund Bonds arose out of a provision in the World War II excess profits tax which permitted a corporation to take a 10 per cent credit against its tax in non-interest-bearing bonds redeemable after cessation of hostilities.[8] The International Monetary Fund Notes represent the quota subscription of the United States to the assets of the Fund. These notes are non-negotiable, pay no interest, and are payable on demand. The "Currency" item is the Treasury's legal obligation to redeem currency; it is made up principally of obligations—now largely inactive—to redeem national bank notes and "greenbacks."

Individual items in the category of interest-bearing debt vary in the amount of interest paid and in the method of paying interest. The spread of interest rates for particular types of securities shown in Table 13 represents only the upper and lower limits, and therefore does not indicate the preponderant rates on each class of security outstanding.

The Treasury's computed average interest rate on each of several security classes for selected recent years is shown in Table 14.

TABLE 14

COMPUTED ANNUAL INTEREST CHARGE BY SECURITY CLASSES,
SELECTED YEARS, 1942–1959 (AS OF JUNE 30)*

	1942 (%)	1951 (%)	1959 (%)
Savings Bonds	2.787	2.742	2.961
Marketable Treasury Bonds	2.680	2.327	2.619
" Treasury Notes	1.092	1.399	3.304
" Certificates	.564	1.875	2.842
" Treasury Bills	.360	1.569	3.317

* From *Annual Report of the Secretary of the Treasury,* 1951, p. 814, and *Daily Treasury Statement,* June 30, 1959, p. 5.

It will be noted that in 1942 and 1951, lower interest rates are identified with shorter maturities, while the reverse is roughly true in 1959. This requires some explanation. The average interest rate for any class of securities

[8] The Tax Adjustment Act of 1945 eliminated the basis for issue of these bonds.

is a function of three variable factors. The first factor is the age of the securities outstanding. In general, the period from the early nineteen-thirties to the mid-nineteen-fifties was a period of low interest rates, while interest rates of all kinds rose to markedly higher levels in the last half of the decade of the fifties. A considerable portion of marketable Treasury bonds was issued during low interest periods, and the average will not reflect changed interest rate levels as quickly as that of shorter-term securities which will have been issued largely or entirely in the higher interest period.

The second factor is the market's evaluation of the future course of interest rates. If interest rates in general are low, as they were in 1942, there is greater chance that they will rise than that they will fall. Thus, the bond buyer, who ties up his funds for a long period at fixed interest, will insist on a higher interest rate in order to capitalize the possibility of rising interest rates during the life of the bond.[9] The bill buyer, who is tying up his money for only ninety days, will not be concerned with the longer-term interest rate prospects. Thus, he will accept a rate reflecting the current low level of interest. Conversely, if interest rates are regarded as high, and there is real possibility of decline during the life of the investment, the buyer of a long-term security may be willing to accept a lower rate than that currently charged for short-term money, reflecting the estimate of interest rate decline over a period of time.

The third variable is a whole complex of factors which may be referred to as the technical condition of money and capital markets at the time of

---

[9] If he sells his marketable bond as interest rates begin to rise, he will have to sell at a capital discount, and there is no avoiding loss from rising interest rates.

The formula for present value of an investment with definite or expected maturity is: $P = A_n/(1+r)^n$, where P is present value or price one can afford to pay, A is the future payment or repayment expected, n is the number of years hence the payment or repayment is expected, and r is the rate of return the potential buyer expects to receive on investment of his funds. If I am willing to invest in Treasury Bonds at 2 per cent, I will pay par for a 2 per cent bond. This bond pays 2 per cent on the par value per year and returns the principal sum (par value) on maturity. Suppose it is a twenty-year 2 per cent bond, par value $100, issued today. The present or capital value represents a series of future payments, *viz.* $2 per year interest for twenty years and $100 principal to be repaid at the end of twenty years. Substituting in the formula we get:

$$P = \frac{\$2}{1.02} + \frac{\$2}{(1.02)^2} + \frac{\$2}{(1.02)^3} + \ldots + \frac{\$102}{(1.02)^{20}} = \$100.$$

Now let us suppose that, after holding the bond for ten years, the market rate at which equally safe investments can be made rises to 3 per cent. If I could turn my bond into $100 cash I could reinvest at 3 per cent, but I can sell it only at a discount, since potential buyers can invest at 3 per cent. The amount which a potential buyer could afford to pay for my ten-year-old 2 per cent bond would be:

$$P = \frac{\$2}{1.03} + \frac{\$2}{(1.03)^2} + \frac{\$2}{(1.03)^3} + \ldots + \frac{\$102}{(1.03)^{10}} = \$91.47.$$

issuance of the security. The scarcity or plenty of funds available for lending at various maturities will, aside from the factors discussed above, affect the interest rate. Supply and demand conditions determine plenty or scarcity. Central bank monetary policy, by affecting free bank reserves, can influence the availability of short-term funds. The savings behavior of the public can affect the supply of both long- and short-term funds. And demands upon funds can make for differential interest rates, depending upon the term of the loan. For example, a plant and equipment boom, requiring long-term funds, can create relative scarcity in the long-term capital market, and if government wishes to borrow on long-term it will need to compete for scarce funds by paying relatively high interest rates. Thus, the average rates of interest on different classes of securities will reflect to some extent the temporary conditions in the money and capital markets at the time particular securities were issued.

Any inclination to explain different rates of interest on different classes of government securities solely on "rational" grounds, i.e., on grounds of present and expected future yields, should be resisted. For there are many technical, institutional factors present in the market for these securities. Certain types of financial institutions with large amounts of investable funds may be eligible to purchase certain classes of securities while they are ineligible to purchase certain others. The great demands which they make for the classes for which they are eligible may be reflected in lower interest rates on those securities. Another factor may be the policy of the central bank. The extremely low rates on the shortest-term securities during World War II reflected Federal Reserve pegging in those markets; when the pegs were removed after the war, a significant rise in average interest rates on short-term issues is shown in Table 14. Several of these practical factors combined to make the average interest rates on notes out of line, i.e., lower than shorter-term rates, in 1951. Many of the issues of Treasury bonds were bank-restricted—not available to commercial banks—and bank funds seeking longer-term government securities for investment tended to be directed toward investment in Treasury Notes. At the same time, several recent issues of Notes have carried maturities only slightly over one year, encouraging their purchase with short-term funds. In general, the rates which various securities carry reflect the Treasury's estimate of the rates which will be acceptable to investors. Unusual situations will arise to create patterns of rates which are explainable only in terms of particular conditions in the investment markets, and generalizations are dangerous.

The comparatively low interest rates on all classes of government debt are attributable principally to the safety of those investments. The nation's great resources which stand behind the taxing power, combined with a record of government financial integrity, make government securities the safest of investments.

There are two methods of paying interest. The first is the coupon system, by which the holder of the security presents coupons to a bank on stipulated interest dates and receives his interest. Most bonds, notes, and certificates pay interest by this method, payment being made semi-annually. The second is the discount system, by which the redemption value of the security includes the accumulated interest. When the security is redeemed at maturity (or before), the redemption value combines principal and interest. Such securities are sold on a "discount basis," the buyer paying a price to the Treasury which deducts the interest through the life of the security. This method of interest payment is typical of Savings Bonds and Treasury Bills. In the case of Savings Bonds the Treasury establishes the interest (discount) rate payable by establishing the sale price, maturity date, and matured value. The small Series E Savings Bond, for instance, issues for $18.75, and at the end of 7¾ years pays the holder $25. The relation between selling price and matured value establishes the interest (discount) rate at 3¾ per cent compounded. When Bills are to be sold, the Treasury invites bids on a competitive basis. These bids are prices offered per hundred dollars par value of Bills. In this case it is evident that, since the relation between the bid price and the par value establishes the rate of discount (interest), the buyer determines the rate and not the Treasury, though the Treasury retains the right to accept or reject bids. The great advantage of this method to the Treasury is that it is assured of obtaining funds at the lowest available interest rates.[10]

Public and Special Issues. Public issues of federal securities are available for general purchase by individuals, businesses, and banks. There may be limitations upon their purchase, such as the establishment of maximum quantities of Savings Bonds purchasable in any one year. The special issues are securities issued by the Treasury for investment of government trust funds or to make deferred payment to particular classes of persons. Examples of the former are special issues of bonds, notes, and certificates for investment of reserves of the National Service Life Insurance Fund, the Old Age and Survivors' Insurance Fund, the Railroad Retirement Fund, the Civil Service Retirement Fund, and the Unemployment Trust Fund.

---

[10] It should not be assumed that the spread in bid prices is wide. Bills are sold principally to banks, which represent a highly organized market. For example, the highest bid accepted for Bills issued June 14, 1951, was $99.632 per $100 par value; the lowest was $99.628. (*Annual Report of the Secretary of the Treasury, 1951,* p. 169.) The price of Bills was pegged during the recent war and into 1947 by the readiness of the Federal Reserve Banks to buy or sell Bills at ⅜ of 1 per cent discount.

An example of the latter is the special issue of adjusted service compensation securities in 1936 to make bonus payments to World War I veterans; the veterans were paid in securities which could be redeemed at any time, but which accumulated interest until their maturity in 1946. A more recent example is the payment of terminal leave to World War II enlisted men by the issue to them of interest-bearing bonds in 1947.

Two significant situations are inherent in the special issues. The first is that special issues in every case represent either investment of reserve funds or the payment of soldiers' bonus. In the case of the former the interest rate is determined by actuarial requirements under the retirement or other plan; the Treasury is committed to provide these amounts to the various funds, whether or not they are called interest. On such issues, therefore, the consideration paramount in setting the interest rate was the solvency of the plan and not the normal desire to obtain funds as cheaply as possible. In the case of the latter the high rate of interest was set to encourage veterans to hold their securities to maturity rather than to take immediate cash.

The second—and related—situation is that the special issues represent Treasury liabilities which in most cases are assets of other federal governmental agencies. Unless arrangements are radically changed, the Treasury must always have outstanding enough debt to accommodate the investment of special trust funds. At the end of fiscal 1959 such funds totaled about $44 billion. By no means all of such funds can be expected to continue their increase, but the Old Age and Survivors' Fund may grow well beyond its present $17 billion, depending upon how thoroughly the original reserve plan is altered. Although at present considerable debt reduction can occur before government reserve plans are embarrassed by the lack of investment outlets for their funds, it is worthy of note that embarrassment is conceivable.[11]

Maturities. Four types of securities, more or less differentiated by their maturities, are listed among the public issues in Table 13. They are, in order of usual length of time to maturity, bonds, notes, certificates of indebtedness, and bills. This variety of maturities is designed to make it possible for the Treasury to appeal to almost any sector of the money and capital markets, utilizing favorable borrowing rates and designing an appropriate maturity schedule for the public debt as a whole.

The maturity dates of bonds vary widely between six and fifty years,

[11] To carry the situation further, the Treasury Department estimated that on March 31, 1959, bank investments in government debt totaled $96 billion, insurance companies held $12 billion, and other corporations and associations held $38 billion (*Federal Reserve Bulletin*, June, 1959, p. 622). These three classes of investors held $146 billion of government debt. It is clear, therefore, that private business concerns have become heavily dependent upon government debt as an outlet for investment funds.

though little useful information can be had simply by observing these outside limits. Of a total of $144 billion of bonds outstanding in the public
debt at the end of fiscal 1959, over half (55 per cent) had been originally
issued with maturities of ten years or less, one-eighth (13 per cent) between
ten and twenty years, and about one-third (32 per cent) over twenty years.
It must be understood that the figures refer to the period to maturity *from
the time of issue,* and not from June 30, 1959. The ten-years-and-under
group is heavily weighted with Savings Bonds, over one-half being of this
type.[12]

The bonds issued by the federal government represent its long-term
borrowing. After bonds, Treasury Notes have the next longest maturity
period. Those in the public debt as of the end of fiscal 1959 ranged in
maturity from just over one year to five years. Half of the individual issues
carried five-year maturities, though this group included generally smaller
issues and represented matured value of only about one-fifth of notes outstanding. Certificates of indebtedness in the public debt at the end of 1959
all had maturity dates approximately one year after issue. Treasury Bills
represented the extremely short-term borrowing of the federal government.
Until recently the Bill had had a standardized maturity of ninety-one days.
But in the debt outstanding as of June 30, 1959, there were one issue of
eleven-months' Bills, one of nine and one-half months, and two of nine
months (these were tax anticipation series, with maturities scheduled to
fall on corporation tax dates). Of the many remaining issues of Bills, half
were of 182 days' maturity and the remainder ninety-one days. The recent
lengthening of maturities among Bills has represented an attempt to fill
the gap between the traditional ninety-one day issue and the shortest certi-
ficate maturities. However, that portion of the public debt represented by
Treasury Bills must be "rolled over" (replaced) from two to four times in
a year.

The timing of maturities on a debt as large and as complex as that of
the federal government is no small task. The magnitude of operations in
replacing matured debt may be indicated by the amount of borrowing required in the fiscal year 1958. This was a year of small budget deficit ($2.8

[12] These calculations are based upon data presented in the *Daily Treasury Statement,*
June 30, 1959, pp. 6–8, where a complete listing of individual securities in the public
debt is presented. Maturities are calculated from the date of issue to the date on which
the principal is payable. Some Treasury bonds outstanding provide a call date three to
five years prior to maturity. Thus, for instance, the "3¼s of 1978–1983," issued in 1953,
pay coupon interest of 3¼ per cent, are callable in 1978 at the option of the Treasury
and payable in 1983. The callable feature permits retirement or replacement before maturity at par, thus permitting some degree of freedom by the borrower in debt management. The call feature has not appeared in any bond issue since 1953.

billion), and thus the borrowing during the year was essentially for replacing maturing debt and not for net increase in the debt. The amounts of borrowing through public issues during the year were:[13]

Bills	$ 94.0	billion
Certificates	32.0	"
Notes	7.1	"
Treasury Bonds	16.9	"
Savings Bonds	4.7	"
Total public issues	$154.7	billion

The sum of these transactions during a year represents a turnover equal to about 68 per cent of public issues outstanding at the end of 1958, and about 56 per cent of total interest-bearing debt. If maturities were arranged so as to rely less heavily on bills and more heavily on longer-term securities, the annual demands of the debt upon the money market would be reduced in any given period. The figures above, when related to the amount of securities outstanding in each category at the end of the year, give the following rates of annual turnover:[14]

	Issued during Year	Outstanding, End of Yr.	Average Turnover/Yr.
Bills	$94.0 billion	$22.4 billion	4.2
Certificates	32.0	32.9	.97
Notes	7.1	20.4	.35
Treasury Bonds	16.9	90.9	.19
Savings Bonds	4.7	52.0	.09

In view of these observations, it is not surprising that the Treasury (and monetary managers and the general public) should desire favorable conditions in the markets for its securities.

Retirement of Debt

In this section we shall be concerned with the retirement of particular issues, as well as with net reduction of the debt. It is, of course, true that if particular issues are retired and not replaced net reduction in debt occurs. But debt management in modern times has involved much more replacement of maturing debt than net retirement.

Refunding. A debt is *funded* when the Treasury borrows by sale of its securities to pay "floating" obligations, such as for services or materials. Miscellaneous obligations are thus retired by creating a new group of creditors holding a single type of security. In the technical sense there is no such

[13] Computed from *Daily Treasury Statement, end of month issues,* July, 1957–June, 1958.

[14] Figures on issues outstanding from *Daily Treasury Statement,* June 30, 1958. It would be somewhat more accurate to use in the second column figures of average amounts outstanding during the year. For our purposes, the figures used seem satisfactory.

thing as a "floating debt" of the federal government, and therefore funding does not occur at the federal level. Local governments have not infrequently paid salaries or purchased materials in "warrants," which are a form of floating debt later funded into longer-term securities or retired out of current revenues. *Refunding* is the process of replacing maturing securities with new. Securities may be redeemed because they are due or by exercising the right to "call" prior to maturity. In the latter case government exercises its option to take advantage of better current interest rates or to rearrange the maturities of outstanding debt. Most refunding operations, however, are undertaken because of the necessity of meeting maturity requirements.

Some short-term borrowing is undertaken in anticipation of tax collections or long-term borrowing. When Bills are sold in anticipation of tax receipts, it is presumed that these Bills will be retired and not replaced. However, if the rate of spending is high in relation to taxes, tax collections may be largely used up in retiring the Bills, making necessary further short-term borrowing after tax date in anticipation of later collections. When short-term borrowing occurs in anticipation of long-term borrowing, it serves the necessary purpose of making funds immediately available to the Treasury. The various war loan campaigns to sell bonds to the general public actually performed the immediate function of raising funds largely to pay off maturing Bills held by the banks. In addition, they served the highly useful purpose of transferring a larger part of the public debt to the general public.[15]

Conversion. Conversion is a special type of refunding, undertaken prior to maturity of existing loans, to gain some particular advantage to the Treasury. It could be undertaken to promote transfer of debt from banks to individuals and institutional investors, to adjust maturities of outstanding debt to a more easily manageable pattern,[16] or to reduce interest charges.

This device was used on a large scale by the British Government in 1932.[17] The purpose was to reduce interest charges on the postwar debt, and the result was to reduce the annual interest rate on slightly more than

[15] This is useful to (1) generate widespread participation in the financial aspects of the war or emergency effort, and to (2) reduce the inflationary pressure upon prices inherent in accumulated idle funds of individuals.

[16] A proposal was reported in the *New York Times,* April 8, 1946, to convert part of the United States federal debt into perpetual debt with no stated maturity date. Such a proposal emphasizes the advantages of such securities to institutional investors and to the Treasury, which would then be under no compulsions of the calendar to repay or refund. Debt retirement under such a plan would occur either by exercising the option to call the bonds for redemption or to purchase them in the open market.

[17] The story is admirably told in a series of articles and notes in *The Economist* during 1932, particularly in the Notes "War Loan" (July 2, 1932, p. 10) and "The Full Tale of Conversion" (November 5, 1932).

one-third of the debt from just under 5 per cent to less than 3½ per cent. This constituted an annual saving in interest charges of roughly £30 million. The problem was to call the existing loans and replace them with securities at lower interest rates. The lower rate securities had to be placed on the market to sink or swim on their own merits. In view of the fact that the Treasury accounts were in questionable balance and the plan was undertaken as a measure of relief to government, there was real danger that the market would not purchase the reconversion loan at low rates of interest. It was partly a question of sturdiness of the investment market against very large new financing, and partly a question of confidence in the government.

The war loans to be converted were called as of December 1, 1932. Holders of called bonds were invited to "continue" after that date in bonds of lower interest. No maturity date was established on the new bonds, though they could be called at any time after 1952. Holders who notified the government by July 31, 1932, of their desire to accept conversion bonds in exchange on December 1 were paid a cash bonus of £1 per £100 of called bonds. Those who wished cash for their called bonds were required to so notify the government by September 30; the remainder were deemed to have accepted conversion.

The Economist wrote: "Considering that, four months ago, the Government's credit was on a 4 per cent basis, at best; that sterling has undergone since mid-summer a serious depreciation; that fully 4 per cent is still obtainable on high grade bonds abroad; and that the budget is balanced precariously enough, even if we pay no more on War Debt account to the United States—the Treasury is entitled to praise for its boldness, adroitness, and success.[18] Successful as the program was, certain features of the circumstances which contributed to its success must be mentioned. It was undertaken on patriotic grounds, and was thus not successful purely on grounds of investor self-interest. The bonus payment for prompt choice to "continue" in low-rate bonds undoubtedly helped. Probably one-third of the converted debt was held by government departments, banks, and insurance companies, upon whom considerable special pressure could be put to lead the conversion parade. Probably most effective in the success of the loan was the current trade stagnation, which had created large amounts of savings looking for investment outlets. Thus, the 3½ per cent yield on conversion securities probably measured quite accurately the supply price of funds available for investment in government debt.

The British conversion problem in 1932 was a special one, owing to its timing, its magnitude, and the conditions under which it took place. When

[18] November 5, 1932, p. 824.

investment funds are readily available at low interest, conversion of a moderate portion of the debt into securities bearing lower interest can be relatively simple. Such has actually been the case in the United States. By refunding at maturity or conversion prior to maturity, the high interest bonds of the World War I (and immediate postwar) period still outstanding at the end of 1930 had by 1945 been exchanged for lower interest bonds.[19] Between 1930 and 1945 there was no year without a budget deficit, indicating that no net retirement of debt could have occurred; issues retired must, therefore, have been replaced. In these refunding and conversion operations the large supplies of otherwise idle investment funds contributed greatly to success.

The Sinking Fund. A sinking fund is a fund for retirement (repayment) of funded debt. The creation of a special fund for this purpose has had theoretical justification in the belief that government should impose upon itself requirements for orderly debt retirement. The income of the sinking fund must, of course, be provided out of general governmental revenues— i.e., regular appropriations and/or dedication of certain Treasury revenues to the sinking fund.

A federal sinking fund was first established in 1792, largely through the efforts of Alexander Hamilton. With the revision of 1795, certain revenues (principally those from sale of public lands) were dedicated to the fund. Hamilton was ridiculed for trying to retire debt without money when he proposed that the sinking fund be invested in government securities. It is clearly evident that Hamilton's intention was to have Congress impose upon itself an obligation to retire debt through the fund at the maximum possible rate, and that interest could as well be paid to the sinking fund as to nongovernmental creditors. Nevertheless, a government dedicated to economy and to the use of Treasury surplus for debt retirement could accomplish equally large debt retirements under most conditions.

The federal sinking fund now in operation calls for annual appropriations from the general fund, measured by a percentage of the amounts of debt contracted for certain purposes,[20] plus the interest which would have been

[19] With one exception: the 4¼ per cent bonds of 1947–1952, issued in 1922.

[20] (a) Under the Victory Liberty Loan Act of 1919, 2½ per cent of the aggregate amounts of Liberty Bonds and Victory Notes outstanding on July 1, 1920, less an amount equal to the par amount of any obligation of foreign governments held by the United States on July 1, 1920.

(b) Under the Emergency Relief and Construction Act of 1932, 2½ per cent of the aggregate amount of expenditures from appropriations made or authorized under the Act.

(c) Under the National Industrial Recovery Act, 2½ per cent of the aggregate amount of expenditures from appropriations made or authorized under the Act. The appropriation under these provisions for 1951 amounted to about $⅜ billion.

(*Annual Report of the Secretary of the Treasury*, 1951, p. 800.)

payable during the year on unmatured bonds and notes purchased or redeemed during the year or previous years. The latter provision embodies Hamilton's cumulative sinking fund feature. It is to be noted, however, that the appropriations to the sinking fund are simply authorizations to use these amounts of funds for debt retirement purposes. The authorizations will not be spent unless surplus funds are available, and this decision is at the discretion of the Treasury.

The use of a sinking fund by the federal government has little to recommend it. As currently used by the federal government it is well-nigh meaningless. Experience has clearly demonstrated that effective sinking fund provisions for orderly debt retirement are not necessary to create confidence of investors in federal issues. The more effective the sinking fund is in binding government to a significant amount of regular debt retirement, the more effective is the barrier to the administration of changing fiscal policy. Surplus revenues constitute the sole source of funds for net retirement of debt; wise refunding and conversion operations offer the most desirable tools for managing interest rates and maturities.

Contingent Liabilities of the Federal Government

The Treasury has contingent liability—an obligation to make good in case of default by a primary debtor—in connection with its guarantee of the obligations of certain semi-public and public corporations. The simplest and most obvious case is that of Federal Reserve Notes, which are note issues of the Federal Rerserve Banks redeemable at the Treasury or at any Federal Reserve Bank. Since these notes are a prior lien on the assets of the Federal Reserve Banks the degree of practical liability of the Treasury is so slight as hardly to deserve mention.

During the 1930's several government corporations were created to administer government policies with respect to extending credit to various segments of the economy. The largest of these were (are) the Commodity Credit Corporation, the Federal Farm Mortgage Corporation, the Federal Housing Administration, the Federal Public Housing Authority, the Home Owners' Loan Corporation, and the Reconstruction Finance Corporation with its many subsidiaries.[21] Most such corporations were created to perform lending functions, which required the raising of loan funds. Two alternatives presented themselves: provision of the funds by the Treasury out of the proceeds of its own borrowing, or direct borrowing by the agen-

[21] An excellent study of the financial relation between the Treasury and government corporation is: H. Walter Hargreaves, "The Guaranteed Security in Federal Finance," *Journal of Political Economy,* Vol. 50, August, 1942. This section leans heavily on Professor Hargreaves' findings.

cies from the capital market, the securities to be guaranteed by the Treasury. Until 1941 the latter alternative was adopted. This alternative, which was used exclusively until 1941, was first applied to the RFC when it was set up in 1932, prior to the New Deal. The arguments advanced for this course were: (1) A corporation independent of the Treasury could be a business institution immune from bureaucracy, and the Treasury would not be enticed into the banking field; (2) if such a corporation could be set up with its own borrowed funds the federal budget would not be unbalanced thereby, and this would strengthen government's ability to stand firm against miscellaneous inflationist groups; (3) the corporation's debts would be self-liquidating, and thus would not be a burden upon taxpayers. It was recognized from the beginning, however, that Treasury guarantee of principal and interest on the corporation's securities was essential. Otherwise it was highly doubtful that funds could be borrowed on favorable terms by a new corporation formed expressly to rush in where established financial institutions feared to tread.

The RFC pattern was applied to other corporations as they were organized. Before long, however, Congress violated the independence of these corporations by requiring specific loans, and violated the self-liquidating character of the loans by requiring certain agencies to pay governmental subsidies and providing for Treasury replacement of the resulting impairment of their capital.[22] By 1941 the independence and the self-liquidating aspects of many of these corporations had been seriously qualified, and funds for such corporations were henceforth to be provided by the Treasury. This method is still used. The advantages of this system are several. The needs of the agencies are coordinated with those of the Treasury; the Treasury can borrow more cheaply than can the agencies; a measure of centralized Treasury control is established, coordinating financial policies of these corporations with fiscal policy.

By the end of fiscal 1951 the amount of Treasury-guaranteed debt of governmental corporations had been reduced from a high of $6¼ billion to slightly over $29 million. However, owing largely to the change in policy in 1941, there was outstanding at the end of 1951 approximately $9 billion of Treasury debt incurred to raise funds for these corporations. Although the latter is a direct and not a contingent obligation of the Treasury, it is still largely self-liquidating. Other things being equal, the burden of debt incurred to provide capital funds for corporations carrying on a lending business is identical, whether the funds are borrowed by the corporation

---

[22] Hargreaves, *op. cit.*, pp. 564–65. The replacement by the Treasury of the capital impairment of the Commodity Credit Corporation caused by price support payments is a recent example of this.

and guaranteed by the Treasury or borrowed directly by the Treasury and lent to the corporation. If the corporation is self-liquidating, both principal and interest of either type of borrowing represent no burden upon the taxpayers.

State and Local Debt

There are important similarities between state and local debt on the one hand and federal debt on the other. Much of the previous discussion will apply in principle to state and local borrowing. The ability of states and localities to borrow depends upon the confidence of investors in the borrowing government. Confidence will be based upon the previous record of the borrowing government, the adequacy of prospective tax yields in relation to debt outstanding, and the purposes for which borrowing is done. Ability to borrow on reasonable terms is also based upon the condition of capital markets—the general availability of funds. The money markets in which state and local governments borrow are much more local in character —particularly in the case of smaller jurisdictions—and this may make for disadvantage in borrowing. On the other hand, the exemption from federal income taxation afforded state and local securities is a distinct boon, helping to offset disadvantages in borrowing to which these smaller governments are subject. Any discussion of state and local debt should emphasize strongly at the beginning the wide variation in borrowing power among these governments.

Table 15 shows the course of state and local debt since 1902. State and

TABLE 15

STATE AND LOCAL DEBT, SELECTED YEARS, 1902–1957[*]

Fiscal Year	States			Local Governments			Total State and Local Debt ($ billion)
	Long-term Debt ($ billion)	Short-term Debt ($ billion)	Total Debt ($ billion)	Long-term Debt ($ billion)	Short-term Debt ($ billion)	Total Debt ($ billion)	
1902	.2	[a]	.2	1.8	.1	1.9	2.1
1913	.4	[a]	.4	3.8	.2	4.0	4.4
1922	1.1	[a]	1.1	8.4	.6	9.0	10.1
1927	1.9	.1	2.0	12.5	.4	12.9	14.9
1932	2.6	.2	2.8	15.3	1.1	16.4	19.2
1936	3.2	.2	3.4	16.1		16.1	19.5
1940	3.3	.3	3.6	15.8	.9	16.7	20.3
1944	2.8		2.8	14.1	.6	14.7	17.5
1948	3.6	.1	3.7	14.4	.6	15.0	18.7
1952	6.5	.2	6.9	22.1	1.1	23.2	30.1
1954	9.3	.3	9.6	29.3	1.8	27.6	37.2
1958	15.1	.3	15.4	40.3	2.3	42.7	58.1

[a] Less than $50 million.
[*] From Bureau of the Census, *Historical Statistics on State and Local Government Finances, 1902–1953*, pp. 20, 22; *Summary of Governmental Finances in 1954*, p. 33; *Summary of Governmental Finances in 1958*, p. 18.

local debt was reduced during the war by high tax yields, combined with restrictions on construction and capital expenditures. After 1950 it began to rise rapidly, as financing needs for schools, highways, water and sewer extensions, and urban renewal mushroomed. State debt has grown at a faster rate than local debt since about 1950. It aggregated about one-tenth of the combined total in early years and rose to about one-fourth at the end of the period. The rapid expansion of highway construction and increased participation in local capital expenditure, notably schools and roads, accounted for most of this shift.

Short-term borrowing has played a very minor role in state and local finances. This is in marked contrast to the importance of short-term borrowing in federal finances. By definition in the table, long-term debt is that which has a maturity date over one year from the date of issue. Most short-term borrowing is by bank loans, mainly in anticipation of tax collections, but partly for interim financing in anticipation of bond issues. On occasion short-term tax—or loan—anticipation securities are sold to the public, and in dire emergency governments have floated loans to the public by payment in scrip.

Long-term borrowing of states and local governments is now almost exclusively done by the issuance of serial bonds. Suppose, for example, that a government needs to borrow $1 million for a capital project. A straight twenty-year serial issue would provide for maturity of one-twentieth ($50,000) of the total obligation each year. Serial bond issues have several advantages. Although classed as long-term bonds, they appeal to investors of fairly short-, intermediate-, and long-term funds, thus utilizing nearly the whole spectrum of capital offerings. By varying the proportion of the issue maturing at any one time it is possible to tailor the issue to special situations in the capital markets. They provide a built-in program for orderly retirement without recourse to a sinking fund, and thus appeal both to investors and to government.

The figures presented in Table 15 include all local governments in the United States. Detailed information on the debt structure of local governments is available only for cities with populations over 25,000. The debt of these cities represented in 1958 about two-fifths (17/43) of the debt of all local governments. Although smaller units have somewhat different financial problems, the information on these larger units is instructive.

The backing given to state and local issues of long-term debt can be of three types. The securities may be "general obligation" securities. This means that the bond is not tied to specific revenues, but to the whole resources of the issuer. Second, the issue may have specific revenues pledged for principal and interest payments, but if these are insufficient the general resources of the issuing government can be drawn upon. Thus, the specific revenues may not be used for other purposes until obligations are met, but support is not limited to these specific revenues. Finally, the issue may be "non-guaranteed"; specific revenues are pledged to the bonds, but if these are insufficient the creditors may not, under the bond contract, expect deficiencies to be made up out of general funds. The bond market will normally rate issues in the order given above.

At the end of the fiscal year 1957, long-term debt of states and cities fell into these categories as follows (in $ million).[23] The magnitude of non-

	Long-Term Debt	Full Faith and Credit		Non-Guaranteed
		General Obligation	Payable Initially from Specified Non-Tax Revenues	
States	13,522	4,585	1,905	7,032
Cities over 25,000	15,227	10,440		3,997

guaranteed debt calls for some comment. The growth of non-guaranteed debt reflects mainly the expansion of governmental activity into areas where benefits are more obviously individual and therefore justifiably more self-supporting. Toll highways, university dormitories, and the like are cases in point with respect to the states. For cities, power, water, and sewer developments have long been built by self-liquidating debt. A second factor has been—particularly in recent years—the pinch of debt limits. Since debt limits usually exclude self-liquidating debt, it may be possible to finance a structure outside the debt limit by creating an autonomous agency which borrows in its own name and services the debt out of its own revenues. Even school building has been financed by creating special authorities, which borrow outside the local debt limit and rent schools to the local government.

In general, one would expect that the rapid growth of the last decade in state and local expenditures would be accompanied by rising debt. But another factor has become inherent in the situation in recent years. When the proportion of capital outlay in total expenditures rises, the debt will rise more than proportionately with total expenditure. For capital outlays, whose benefits are spread over a period of years, are more likely than operating expenses to be financed by borrowing. A rise in operating expenses will usually be accompanied by rising taxes; this is far less likely to occur when long-term capital projects are undertaken.

[23] From Bureau of the Census, *Compendium of State Government Finances in 1957*, p. 38; and *Compendium of City Government Finances in 1957*, p. 112.

Default. A debtor who fails to meet principal or interest on its obligations is said to be in default. At no time has the federal government defaulted on its obligations.[24] There are few cases of default by state governments even on floating debt, but the record of local governments is not good. It is estimated that 1,120 local governments were in default on bonded obligations on February 1, 1933; only six states were without defaulting local governments.[25] The cause of default was inability during depression to meet high fixed claims out of diminished revenues, at times made more acute by the failure of banks carrying government deposits.

Mention must be made of the favored position of the federal government on account of its currency and credit powers. The power to issue currency clearly represented a useful federal revenue instrument during the Civil War. It may be that federal default was avoided at that time by the issue of "greenbacks." The elasticity in bank reserves made possible under the Federal Reserve System offered a useful source of borrowed funds for the federal Treasury which proved to be a great boon during World Wars I and II. State and local governments can avoid defaults only by taxation or by new borrowing from capital markets which they cannot control.

What happens in case of default? In the case of private debt, foreclosure results. Foreclosure of government property is not only infeasible, but unthinkable except in the possible case of revenue bonds issued for the purchase of public utilities. It is, however, feasible to provide for municipal receivers, who take over the fiscal affairs of defaulting local governments, and operate them with a view to eventual repayment of creditors and rehabilitation of local finances. The failure of many state receivership laws lies in excessive subordination of receivers to local legislatures. In cases of receivership, receivers should be given powers to levy and collect taxes under authorization and control of the state government; too often the receiver's revenue powers are limited to borrowing.

Problems of Debt Management

Fiscal policy discussions usually run in terms of the relation of receipts to expenditures, the proper allocation of expenditures, and the proper pattern of taxation, all within the general context of the objective of stable economic growth. It is less frequently realized that, apart from these cen-

---

[24] In a very narrow and technical sense the abrogation of the gold clause (refusal to pay in gold as the bond contract specified) in 1933 can be characterized as default. Failure of the United States government to assume the debts of the Confederacy following the Civil War cannot be considered federal default.

[25] Evans Clark, *The Internal Debts of the United States,* New York, Twentieth Century Fund, 1933, p. 270.

tral questions of fiscal policy, the manner in which public debt is managed may have important economic impact. We are not here concerned with the budgetary question of whether a deficit should be created, making necessary an increase in public debt. The question facing us is, given the debt, or given budgetary situations which increase or decrease debt, how can we accomplish the inevitable debt turnover or refunding and the flotation or retirement of debt in order to gain the greatest economic advantages or the least economic disadvantages?

Three general principles of debt management can be identified: (1) The policies pursued must be able to extract from the public, without undue coercion, the necessary loans to finance a deficit or to replace maturing securities, and this should usually be done at the lowest feasible interest cost. (2) The extraction of loanable funds from the market, and the repayment of funds to the market when debt is retired, should serve and not frustrate the economic objective of stable growth. (3) The debt should be so placed as to minimize the need to enter the market when it is inconvenient or unpropitious to do so. There are potential conflicts among these aims, as separate consideration of them will demonstrate.

1. Clearly, debt management must be capable of providing the necessary funds from the lending market. Otherwise tax-expenditure policies will be thwarted, and fundamentally necessary confidence in fiscal management may be lost. But in addition, it is desirable that funds be procured at reasonable cost to government. Interest is a budgetary expense, and it represents a transfer payment that when injected into the income stream has a relatively low income-generating leverage effect. Though exceptions can be made, the generalization is widely accepted that taxation in order to make interest payments converts higher leverage dollars into lower leverage dollars, and thus detracts from the rate of growth. In general, governments can usually find many uses for funds that they would prefer to the payment of interest on the public debt. This first objective of debt management requires an arsenal of debt instruments capable of tapping loanable funds where they are. It also requires freedom to maneuver within debt limits and freedom to offer the terms (including maturities and interest rates) which the market demands. It requires reasonable cooperation from the monetary authorities in creating favorable money market conditions, consistent with the overriding responsibility of these authorities to serve the monetary needs of stable growth.

2. To manage the debt in the service of stable economic growth requires extreme flexibility in policy. In a situation of underemployment, new or refunding debt issues must be placed so as to have minimal contractive

effect upon private demand for goods and services. This means that funds cannot healthily be withdrawn from those with high spending propensities. It probably means that the funds going into debt instruments should not be taken from anyone, but should be newly created in the banking system. The reverse is true when the problem is one of overspending. There the objective should be that of restricting monetary demand, transferring funds from potential spenders (although this will mean high interest rates to attract funds), and certainly not creating new funds in the system. Failure to serve the objective of price stability—by debt management policy as well as by other policy—is destructive of the first principle described above. If the public fears devaluation of its savings, the fixed dollar interest and fixed dollar capital value of government bonds make them among the least attractive forms of saving, and it becomes increasingly difficult for government to borrow on these instruments. This has been clearly evident in the behavior of Savings Bond holders during the price rises of 1956–1959, when redemptions of these bonds greatly exceeded sales of new bonds.[26] Even a sweetening of interest terms in early 1957 failed to stem the tide of redemptions, indicating that the public had become aware of the inadvisability of holding assets in fixed dollar terms in the face of price increases.

3. Taken by itself, the third principle can best be served by lengthening public maturities. The ideal public debt from this point of view would be made up of instruments like the British Consols which never mature. Then the Treasury would retire or replace them only at its own choosing, taking action only at those times when lower interest or stable growth dictated. Retirement and refunding would then take place at the choice of the Treasury, and would not be dictated—often at inconvenient times—by contractual maturity dates. It is to a great extent the compulsion to replace debt instruments which has required the Federal Reserve to walk the tightrope between support of the government securities markets and the pursuit of stabilizing monetary policy.

Few would quarrel with any of these principles if they could be considered alone. The rub comes when conflict among them appears. While the Eisenhower administration almost worshiped at the shrine of longer maturities, the average maturity persistently shortened—more rapidly than the simple passage of time accounts for. Why? Two reasons were given,

[26] In 1956 for the first time since the beginning of the United States Savings Bond program, redemptions measured by sales price were greatly in excess of sales. It is important in this comparison to measure redemptions less accrued interest, for the interest accrued would tend to inflate the redemption figure. The measure we use here indicates that holders of Savings Bonds were holding fewer of these bonds after 1956. See *Treasury Bulletin*, June, 1959, p. 40.

one quite acceptable and one far less so. The first was that in a period of high interest rates—usually higher for longer than for shorter maturities—conversion of the debt into longer maturities would increase budget expenditures for interest, thus postponing the time when budget surpluses could justify tax reductions. The second was that in a period of strong business demand for investment funds, stability was best served by keeping the Treasury out of the long-term capital market, and leaving the function of control to the Federal Reserve. Thus, by not floating long-term securities, the Treasury claimed to be "staying out of the way of the monetary authorities." Actually, by influencing bank reserves, the impact of Federal Reserve policy is first upon the shorter-term money market, though in time the impact may be transferred to the long-term capital market.[27] However, the absorption of long-term funds by the Treasury through the issuance of long-term securities would have had immediate impact in that market at a time when the particular need was to limit the private investment boom. Thus, a lengthening of public debt would have effectively supplemented Federal Reserve policy in 1956–1957.[28]

A little reflection will turn up many situations in which it is impossible to serve all the stated principles or objectives of debt management at the same time. Cheap borrowing means issuance of short-term securities more often than not. Cheap borrowing on short term will usually contravene stabilization objectives when a boom is in progress. Short-term borrowing, while serving stabilization goals when the problem is one of underemployment, commits the Treasury to early replacement of this debt, quite possibly at a time when it is inconvenient to do so. A large debt not only forces the Treasury into the money markets frequently; it makes the Treasury's actions a significant force in establishing conditions in the markets. Thus, a large debt makes appropriate debt management policies both more necessary and more difficult.

[27] See Winifield W. Riefler, "Open Market Operations in Long-Term Securities," in *Federal Reserve Bulletin*, November, 1958.

[28] At the same time, such a policy would have made funds for residential construction and for state and local borrowing more scarce at a time when high long-term interest rates were already adversely affecting housing starts and school and other construction. This reason for preferring short- to long-term borrowing by the Treasury was less frequently offered than the two mentioned above. Special relief of housing from tight capital conditions could have been provided through existing federal programs, but the relief of state and local governments would have been more difficult, presumably through a variety of federal grant programs.

RECOMMENDED READINGS

Hansen, Alvin H., *Fiscal Policy and Business Cycles,* N.Y., Norton, 1941, Chapter 9.
Valuable treatment, not only of the conditions under which debt has
grown, but of changes in attitude toward debt.

Jese, Gaston, "Public Debt," *Encyclopaedia of the Social Sciences,* N.Y., Macmillan, 1934.
Good general discussion of the nature and management of debt. Essentially
descriptive representation of thinking and practice with respect to debt before
the depression decade of the thirties, without benefit of more recent analysis.

Murphy, Henry C., National Debt in War and Transition, N.Y., McGraw-Hill,
1950.

————, "Debt Management," Chapter 4 in Poole, K. E., *Fiscal Policies and the
American Economy,* N.Y., Prentice-Hall, 1951.
The first is historical in orientation, with considerable analysis of debt
management problems as they arose. Chapters 8–17 are especially useful for
elaboration of material in this chapter. The second is a good, short essay
on principles of debt management.

Studenski, Paul, "The Nature and Functions of Public Loans," in Fagan, E. D.,
and Macy, C. W., *Public Finance,* N.Y., Longmans, 1934, pp. 667*ff.*
Discussion at an elementary level of the nature of public credit and its
development. Though not recent, it is good description.

Treasury-guaranteed securities:

Hargreaves, H. W., "The Guaranteed Security in Federal Finance," *Journal of
Political Economy,* August, 1942, pp. 559*ff.*
Excellent discussion of the provisions for capital of government corporations
between 1932 and 1942. Good detail concerning debt practices and significant
analysis of the contingent debt problem.

CHAPTER 9

Public Debt and the Money Supply

The methods by which government borrows may have significant effects upon the economy through change in the amount of money available for use. It is not uncommon to hear it said that public borrowing is inflationary. That is, the issuance of debt securities by government has an inflationary effect additional to that inherent in the budget deficit which makes borrowing necessary. This is the question for analysis in the present chapter—how increasing or decreasing public debt may have an effect upon the supply of money in the economy.

Before considering the mechanics by which public debt may affect the money supply, we should investigate the possible effects that change in the money supply can have upon the rate of expenditure in the economy. By the "money supply" we mean the quantity of those things which do the work of money by acting as a medium of exchange. Included in the money supply are the quantities of "cash"—coin and paper money—and banking deposits subject to check. These are the things which pass as the means of payment in a modern economy.

The propensity to buy becomes effective in the market only when it becomes an offer of money. Combined with other factors influencing aggregate demand, the quantity of money (currency and checking deposits) may have an important impact on the level of economic activity and the distribution of wealth and income. It has these results through the influence it may have upon monetary demand for goods and services. And in the aggregate, monetary demand will be permitted to rise only through (1) an increase in the money supply, or (2) an increased rate of turnover of the money supply. This is not to say that changes in monetary demand are dependent only upon money supply or its velocity. For many other factors will be present in any decision to make a money offer for goods and services.

Through any given period of time the supply of money will be used either for transaction purposes—buying—or for liquid balances, either in

cash or bank balances, or in other liquid assets. If the demand for money
for transaction purposes (i.e., for consumption or investment) should rise,
and the money supply remains unchanged, the interest rate will tend to rise,
though it will rise more slowly if the velocity of money increases than
if it remains constant. A rise in interest rates, other things given, will have
a limiting effect upon investment spending, and also upon that part of
consumption spending which is made out of loans. This suggests the fundamental reasoning behind tight money policy under conditions of excessive
demand: If the money supply is not permitted to increase to accommodate
a tendency toward higher monetary demand, the resulting rise in interest
rates will tend to moderate further rise in transaction demand. The policy
could, of course, be thwarted or partially thwarted by a rise in velocity, in
the control of which monetary measures have had little force.

If monetary demand is falling below that required for full employment,
a stable money supply will increase liquid balances and lower interest
rates. Velocity of use of the money supply will also fall somewhat, strengthening deflationary pressures. The problem in this situation is to create
monetary ease, (1) providing money in the system adequate to satisfy the
desire for liquidity on the part of the public, and (2) lowering the interest
rate enough to strengthen the inducement to invest and borrow for consumption. In a recession the intent will be to prevent a decline in the money
supply[1] and if possible to increase it.

So far, our discussion has focused upon the role of the money supply in
promoting full employment conditions. But the question of stability in the
price level is also important. The classic case of inflation is that in which
monetary demand is excessive in relation to the capacity of the economy to
produce real goods and services. In this case, "too much money is chasing
too few goods," and the price level seeks an equilibrium where the money
value of goods equals the aggregate monetary spendings. Prices in general
rise. An intensification of monetary demand will not normally induce general price increases while there are significant unused resources; inflationary
pressures become great when aggregate demand continues to increase after
full employment of resources has been reached. Then the demand pull upon
prices creates profit opportunities which encourage competitive bidding for
scarce resources; costs are increased and seem further to justify price increases. Thus, a boom in demand in one sector (e.g., investment) creates
cost increases in other sectors (e.g., consumer goods) using similar re-

---

[1] Money supply tends to decline in recession by the inclination to pay off bank loans,
thus reducing aggregate demand deposits which make up by far the largest and most
volatile element in the money supply.

sources, even though little demand pull may have been evident in the latter sectors.

It has become fashionable in recent years to emphasize other types of inflation than the classic demand-pull type (such as wage-push inflation and administered-price inflation). But whatever the germinal element in inflation, it is fairly obvious that no general price increase can occur unless at least accommodated by adequate monetary demand. And if, as we have seen above, an important component of monetary demand is the money supply, it follows that change in the money supply is a relevant factor in price increases. We see, therefore, that the supply of money, because it affects monetary demand, affects both the level of economic activity and the level of prices. We turn now to a review of ways in which public borrowing can influence the money supply.

Monetization of the Public Debt: Currency Expansion

Study of the inflationary potentialities of public borrowing thus involves consideration of the monetization of the debt in terms of both currency and credit. The former is discussed in this section, the latter in the section following.

The man in the street normally considers monetization of the public debt to mean simply printing new money and requiring the government's creditors to accept it as legal tender. The popularity of this view finds its explanation in the experience of the United States prior to World War I. American history offers two striking examples of such monetization, and many more less striking. The outstanding examples are those of the continental currency during the Revolution and the greenbacks of the Civil War.

The Continental Congress began its issues of "Bills of Credit" in 1775, and between that date and 1779 there were forty issues[2] totaling approximately one-fourth billion dollars. It is to be noted that the Congress was newly formed, it had no tax resources separate from the willingness of individual colonies to contribute from their revenues, it had no credit standing either at home or abroad, and there was little free capital in the colonies available for borrowing. The Bills, or "Continentals," were promises of the Congress to pay, based upon the credit of the colonies, which were expected to provide redemption for their apportioned shares. The Bills were simply non-interest-bearing promises to pay, issued as money and supported by various colonial legal tender acts. Beginning in 1776 the Bills depreciated in value. By the end of 1779 they were exchangeable for silver money in the

[2] See Davis R. Dewey, *Financial History of the United States*, 12th ed., New York, Longmans, 1934, pp. 36–43.

market at about 40 to 1. This depreciation reflected both a loss of confidence in this particular type of money and the inflationary effects of the issues upon prices. In November, 1779, the Congress advised the colonies to fix prices at not over 2,000 per cent of the prices of 1774, a figure which reflects a current estimate of the extent of inflation,[3] but the depreciation of paper money had gone so far that such an attempt at stabilization was hopeless.[4]

The greenback inflation of the Civil War took place under somewhat similar circumstances. Although the federal government was well established, its credit standing was quite inadequate and its tax system unproductive. The United States Notes (greenbacks) were issued in small denominations for common circulation and paid out by the Treasury as money for war expenses. In 1862 and 1863 they represented 20 per cent and 40 per cent, respectively, of total Treasury receipts.[5] Professor Mitchell concludes that the effect of the greenbacks upon prices was out of all proportion to their importance as a revenue measure, and that they were very largely responsible for the war inflation.[6]

History is replete with examples of government issue of circulating notes to meet emergency demands upon the public treasury. The experience of Germany during and after World War I is a classic example of monetization of public debt in the form of currency. China and some of the Balkan countries went through similar experiences in World War II. In all such cases the inadequacy of taxes and the inability or unwillingness to borrow through usual channels on interest-bearing securities led to the issue of paper money.

It is well to note, however, that the over-all effect of such currency monetization of public debt is similar to taxation; for government gains purchasing power while individuals lose it. It involves a forced contribution to government, though it is inferior to most systems of taxation in that its allocation of burdens is entirely haphazard, offering little possibility of directing burdens to those who should contribute. It almost inevitably inflates profit incomes at the expense of other types.

Monetization of the Public Debt: Credit Expansion

A more sophisticated method of monetizing the public debt is that of using the securities issued as the basis for credit expansion. The average

---

[3] Chester W. Wright, *Economic History of the United States,* New York, McGraw-Hill, 1941, p. 221.

[4] Concurrent issues of paper money by many of the colonies assisted materially in the inflation.

[5] Wesley C. Mitchell, *A History of the Greenbacks,* Chicago, University of Chicago, 1903, p. 129.

[6] *Ibid.,* p. 279. Wholesale prices had risen by 1865 to an index of about 230 (1860 = 100). *Ibid.,* p. 277.

man is frightened by the prospect of currency inflation, and regards it as a departure from governmental respectability. Bank credit, on the other hand, is something about which he understands little, and credit inflation has been the subject of far less popular discussion. Thus, although the effects are the same, expansion of credit has received far less public condemnation than has expansion of currency.

Mechanics of Credit Expansion. An understanding of the techniques by which public borrowing may increase the credit supply requires some insight into the mechanics of bank credit expansion. The commercial banks which belong to the Federal Reserve System (hereafter called member banks) are required by law to maintain *as deposits in Federal Reserve Banks* their legal reserves against the deposits which they hold. The amount of reserves required is stipulated by the Board of Governors of the Federal Reserve System, within limits established by law. The Federal Reserve Banks (as distinguished from member banks) also have required reserves which they must maintain against deposits of the member banks which they hold and against the notes (currency) which they issue.

Legal reserves required against deposits are stated as a percentage of those deposits. Deposits, however, arise as a result of loans; when a bank makes a loan the borrower deposits it to his account and a new deposit is created. When a Federal Reserve Bank lends to a member bank a deposit is credited to the account of the borrowing member. Thus, by restricting the amount of money that can be lent out, legal reserves act as a brake on deposit creation.

Only Federal Reserve Banks issue notes, and reserves are required against these issues. The total of potential reserves which the Federal Reserve Banks possess must therefore be divided between their deposits and their note issues. An increase of required reserves against the one reduces reserves available for the other. Thus, an increase in public demand for Federal Reserve notes as circulating money pulls out into circulation funds which could serve as reserves against member bank deposits with the Federal Reserve Banks.

An individual member bank can increase its reserves by deposits of cash with the Federal Reserve Bank, by presenting to the Federal Reserve Bank for clearing checks drawn on other banks in excess of checks drawn on itself and presented for clearing by other banks, and by borrowing from the Federal Reserve Bank in the form of a deposit credit. A flow of cash into a member bank in excess of its day-to-day requirements would normally result in deposit of this surplus cash with the Federal Reserve Bank. Since the Federal Reserve Banks perform the check-clearing function for members,

checks are automatically sent there at the end of the business day. Federal
Reserve Banks then clear checks of the members against one another, debit-
ing the deposit account of the bank on which the check is drawn and credit-
ing the deposit account of the bank presenting the check for clearance. Thus
individual member bank reserve balances with the Federal Reserve Banks
rise and fall daily through the operation of check clearing. Loans by the
Federal Reserve Banks to members may be in the form of "advances" or of
"discounts." Advances are loans made on members' promissory notes, secured
by collateral. Discounts are loans which result when the Federal Reserve
Banks purchase from members endorsed "commercial paper" (notes, drafts,
bills of exchange) of the types which normally arise out of member bank
lending to businesses.

The factors which affect the magnitude of reserves of the individual
bank are not identical with those which affect reserves of all member banks
taken together. An excess of cash flowing into one bank, increasing its reserves, may be offset by an equivalent loss of reserves by another. And although check clearing causes the reserves of individual banks to rise and
fall, it does not affect combined reserves of all banks. Loans by Reserve
Banks to member banks increase combined member bank reserves; withdrawal of cash from banks for general circulation, or its reverse, decreases
or increases aggregate reserves.

Changes in total member bank reserve balances may result from conscious policy on the part of the Federal Reserve Banks to increase or decrease those balances. The open market operations of the Reserve Banks are
the purchase and sale of government securities in the open market on their
own account. Suppose, for instance, that it is desired to increase member
bank reserves, so as to loosen bank credit to government or business. The
Reserve Banks can purchase securities from individual investors, corporations, or member banks. The effect is an increase in member bank reserves,
accomplished in the following manner: If the Federal Reserve Bank buys
these securities from non-bank investors, paying for them by check, the
seller of the securities normally deposits the check in his bank. The member
bank then forwards the check to the Federal Reserve Bank for payment, the
proceeds of the check being credited to the member bank's deposit account.
The member bank's deposits (reserves) with the Federal Reserve Bank are
in this manner increased. If the Federal Reserve Bank buys the securities
from the portfolios of member banks, these member banks find themselves
in possession of checks which are deposited with the Federal Reserve Banks.
It is thus seen that open market purchases by the Federal Reserve Banks
result in increased member bank reserves, increasing their lending power.

Conversely, open market sales of securities by the Federal Reserve Banks decrease member bank reserves. If sales are made to non-bank investors, they are paid for by purchasers' checks drawn on member banks. When these checks are cleared the reserve balances of member banks are drawn down. If sales are made to banks, these sales are paid for by reduction of member bank reserve balances.

Open market purchases and sales by the Federal Reserve Banks are undertaken for the purpose of manipulating member bank reserves, and therefore the easing or tightening of bank credit. It should be noted, however, that this instrument is likely to be more effective in tightening than in loosening credit. A decrease in member bank reserves, if more than sufficient in magnitude to eliminate excess reserves (existing reserves in excess of legal requirements), *will* bring about a reduction in member bank loans in order to reduce the deposits against which the reserves are maintained. On the other hand, increase in bank reserves *may* encourage further lending but does not force it. During the middle nineteen-thirties open market purchases increased bank reserves, but the result was principally an increase in excess reserves and relatively little increased lending. Federal Reserve policy can thus urge lending, but can neither force banks to lend nor customers to borrow.

Supply and Use of Member Bank Reserve Funds.[7] The following outline shows all possible sources of funds that can be used for member bank reserves, and all possible uses of the funds, including, as one among several, their actual use as member bank reserves. Available funds will be apportioned among these uses by market forces and by Federal Reserve action.

1. Sources of supply of potential member bank reserve funds.
    a. Credit extended to member banks by Federal Reserve Banks:
        I. Discounts and advances.
        II. United States securities held by Federal Reserve Banks.
    b. Amount of cash available for bank and other uses:
        I. Monetary gold stock.
        II. Treasury currency outstanding.
2. Uses of potential reserve funds by banks and by others.
    a. Deposits with Federal Reserve Banks:
        I. Member bank reserves (deposits with Federal Reserve Banks).
        II. Non-member deposits with Federal Reserve Banks.

[7] See *Federal Reserve Bulletin*, November, 1943, p. 360 *ff.*, for discussion of this subject.

    b. Uses by others than banks:
        I. Money in circulation.
       II. Treasury cash holdings.
     III. Treasury deposits with Federal Reserve Banks.

The sources of supply of potential reserve funds represent funds which may or may not become member bank reserves. Within this category, credit extended by Federal Reserve Banks does become member bank reserves, because the credit is extended for that purpose. Member banks do not discount paper with the Reserve Banks or secure loans from them except to provide desired reserves. The United States securities held by the Reserve Banks represent open market purchases for the purpose of building up member bank reserves.

The amount of cash available is only partly used for bank reserves, the remainder being in the hands of non-bank users. The monetary gold stock arises out of domestic purchases or imports of gold. On purchase or import this gold typically first enters member banks as deposits. Under the gold nationalization policy it is immediately redeposited with the Reserve Banks and turned over to the Treasury. In this process both member and Reserve Banks gain reserves against which they may hold new deposits.[8] Treasury currency outstanding may be held by the Treasury, by the Reserve Banks, or may be in circulation. If it is in circulation it is either held by the banks for till money or by the public generally. Only that part of Treasury currency outstanding which is held by the Reserve and member banks actually serves as member bank reserves.

Member bank reserves (2, A, I in the outline above) at any time represent only a portion of the supply of potential reserve funds. This is because of competing needs for funds by the Treasury, the banks, and the public. Those items in 1, A in the outline above are subject to Federal Reserve control. Discounts and advances are controlled by persuasion of the member banks to rediscount and borrow or not to do so, and by rates of discount charged the member banks on discounts and advances. Government securities held by the Reserve Banks are principally the result of their open market purchases; the total of such securities held reflects Federal Reserve policy of purchase or sale in the open market.

On the other hand, items in 1, B in the outline are not subject to bank control. The size of monetary gold stock depends upon the inflow or out-

---

[8] Since metallic gold must by law be held by the Treasury, it is represented by non-circulating gold certificates which can be held by the Federal Reserve Banks as reserves against their own notes issued (Federal Reserve notes) or as cash reserves against the member bank and Treasury deposits which they hold.

flow of gold determined by conditions of international trade or finance. It is further determined by government policy with respect to the freedom of its movement internationally. Treasury currency outstanding, in so far as it is subject to control, is subject to non-bank (principally Treasury) control.

Let us observe how the sources and uses of potential reserve funds behaved during and after World War II. By noting changes in the figures we may see more clearly the interrelations of the various items, and also note some of the results of Federal Reserve policy. Table 16 is cast in the form of the outline presented on page 213, and presents statistics representing the situation at the end of July in the last prewar year (1940), the last war year (1945), and at the end of May in a recent year (1959). These dates are selected in order to portray changes during World War II and through the postwar inflationary years.

The column in the table showing changes from 1940 to 1945, roughly the war period, shows the extent to which debt was monetized during that period. The Federal Reserve Banks increased their holdings of Treasury securities by an amount in excess of $19 billion. The Federal Reserve was thus pumping a very large volume of new reserves into the member banks through its practice of open market purchases. At the same time, the item of "Member Bank Reserves" shows no such increase. The explanation of this is to be found in the $19 billion increase in "Money in Circulation." The public was thus withdrawing potential reserve funds from the banks almost as rapidly as new reserve funds were being created. The easy money policy of the Federal Reserve was necessary to offset the drain of money into circulation.

But does this mean that deposits of member banks did not increase during the war period? At first glance it would appear that, if reserves against member bank deposits (item 2, A, I in Table 16) had not materially increased during the period, then deposits against which reserves were held could not have increased. This was not the case. The last item added to Table 16 shows that almost half of the reserve balances in June of 1940 were in excess of requirements; i.e., although *required* reserves for the average of all banks in 1940 were just under 20 per cent of deposits, the banks were maintaining a reserve ratio of almost double that amount. The decline of *excess* reserves by the end of July, 1945, amounted to almost six billion dollars. At an average reserve requirement of 20 per cent against deposits, this transfer of reserves from the excess category to the required category would provide legal reserves against an increase of close to thirty billion dollars in deposits. The fact is that between June 29, 1940, and the first half of August,

TABLE 16

SUPPLY AND USE OF MEMBER BANK RESERVE FUNDS, 1940, 1945, 1959*

(in millions of dollars)

	July 31, 1940	July 25, 1945	Change, 1940–1945	May 27, 1959	Change, 1945–1959
1. SUPPLY OF POTENTIAL RESERVE FUNDS:					
A. Federal Reserve Credit:	2,484	22,129	+19,645	27,548	+5,419
I. Discounts and Advances	4	229	+225	675	+446
II. U.S. Securities Held by F. R. Banks	2,448	21,570	+19,122	25,905	+4,335
B. Cash Available:	23,487	24,356	+869	25,456	+1,100
I. Monetary Gold Stock	20,461	20,212	−251	20,188	−24
II. Treasury Currency Outstanding	3,024	4,144	+1,120	5,268	+1,124
TOTAL SUPPLY OF POTENTIAL RESERVE FUNDS	25,939	46,485	+20,546	53,004	+6,519
2. USES OF POTENTIAL RESERVE FUNDS:					
A. Deposits with F. R. Banks:	14,870	16,238	+1,368	19,037	+2,799
I. Member Bank Reserves	13,498	14,699	+1,201	18,393	+3,694
II. Non-Member Deposits	1,382	1,539	+157	644	−895
B. Uses by Others:	11,089	30,249	+19,160	32,724	+2,475
I. Money in Circulation	7,883	26,926	+19,043	31,473	+4,547
II. Treasury Cash Holdings	2,250	2,279	+29	708	−1,571
III. Treasury Deposits with F.R. Banks	694	594	−100	543	−51
TOTAL FUNDS USED	25,959	46,487	+20,528	53,005	+6,518
(Member Bank Excess Reserves)	6,514	994	−5,520	355	−639

* Figures from *Federal Reserve Bulletin*. Figures do not always add to subtotals because some very minor items are eliminated.

1945, member bank demand deposits subject to reserve requirements increased by approximately thirty-four billion dollars.[9]

Over-all developments between 1945 and 1959 closely parallel the trends of 1940–1945. However, the trends were not consistent throughout the period. The supply of potential reserve funds increased by almost $7 billion

[9] $27,877 million on June 29, 1940 (*Federal Reserve Bulletin*, November, 1940, p. 1199) and $61,562 million average for the first half of August, 1945 (*idem.*, October, 1945, p. 1028). The fact that actual increase in deposits was greater than that shown in the rough calculation above does not mean that in 1945 reserves were below legal requirements. For (1) the calculation above is on the basis of 20 per cent reserve requirements, while actual requirements were almost certainly not exactly 20 per cent, and (2) total member bank reserves showed a net increase of $1,201 million between the two dates, which would support approximately five times that amount in deposits.

between 1945 and 1952, but remained about constant after 1952. This increase in reserve funds was mainly the result of purchases of securities by the Federal Reserve (up by about $4.5 billion) and increase in Treasury currency outstanding (somewhat over $1 billion). On the uses side, member bank reserves (+ $3.7 billion) and the increase in money in circulation (+ $4.5 billion) more than account for the total increase, being partly off-set by decreases in other items. The increase in member bank reserves and the decline in excess reserves by $.6 billion, which occurred while the percentage of required reserves against deposits was falling, permitted an increase in adjusted demand deposits of some $42 billion. Thus, the long period between 1945 and 1959 should really be divided into two parts. Three-fourths of the increase in money supply since World War II had occurred by 1952. At about that time, the freeing of the Federal Reserve from a primary obligation to promote a market for federal securities and the acceptance of its primary obligation as that of promoting economic stability, greatly slowed down the rate of growth in the money supply.

Having analyzed the important factors determining potential lending power of the banking system, we turn to the experience of the last two major wars in which the United States was a participant, to note how the banking system was instrumental in furnishing to government the financial sinews of war.

Credit Expansion in World War I. The Federal Reserve System, which had been established in 1913, provided elasticity in reserves which made possible during World War I generous participation by the banks in Treasury borrowing. An amendment to the Federal Reserve Act in 1917, requiring that all legal reserves of member banks be deposited with the Federal Reserve Banks, provided maximum elasticity in the use of reserves. The same amendment reduced reserve requirements, and thus liberated bank funds for direct purchase of Treasury securities or for loans to customers who wished to invest in the expanding government debt.

One technique by which bank credit was made available to government was that of lending by commercial banks to security purchasers at rates of interest which corresponded with interest rates paid by the securities they bought. The impecunious citizen who, by his patriotic spirit and the pressure of his fellow citizens, was urged to buy bonds during liberty bond campaigns could borrow at his bank, deposit the bond purchased as security for the loan, and pay to the bank the same interest on the loan which the Treasury paid to him on the bond. When bank reserves approached the danger point as the result of such (or other) loans, the bank could redis-count the note, with the bond as security, at the Federal Reserve Bank, thus building up its reserves. A second method was that of direct purchase by banks of Treasury Certificates of Indebtedness. The funds borrowed by the Treasury on these certificates were then deposited by the Treasury in the banks. The required legal reserves against these Treasury deposits were acquired through borrowing from the Federal Reserve, with the certificates as collateral.[10] By either of the two methods mentioned the funds were eventually provided to the Treasury by the Federal Reserve Banks, with little necessity for reduction of member bank loans to private individuals and businesses. On April 2, 1917, two weeks after declaration of war by the United States, the Chairman of the Federal Reserve Board addressed a letter to the Federal Reserve Banks in which he said, ". . . and the Federal Reserve Banks may be counted upon by offering liberal terms of rediscounting. . . ."[11] The rediscount rates established were 3½ per cent on notes secured by Treasury Certificates or Liberty Loan Bonds,[12] and 3 per cent on fifteen-day obligations of member banks secured by certificates.[13] The latter provision was to induce banks to buy certificates for their own account; the fifteen-day maturity of the loan was little hindrance, both because it was easily renewable and because within that time the Treasury would have spent a large part of the proceeds of its short-term borrowing, and funds would flow back into the banks from depositors, restoring their reserve position.

By the middle of 1919 it was estimated by the Federal Reserve Board that the banks held in Treasury securities and in paper secured by Treasury securities something over one-third of the total governmental debt outstanding.[14] But such a snapshot does not tell the whole story, as the banks purchased nearly all of the successive issues of loan-anticipation certificates which provided immediate funds to the Treasury prior to popular subscription through the liberty loans. For example, the banks purchased over 99 per cent of the 1919 Victory Loan-anticipation certificates, their purchases amounting to over $6 billion.[15]

Although the extent of monetization of the public debt in World War I was relatively modest, the inflationary effect of new credit created was great, as any student of the behavior of prices during that period is aware.

[10] See Jacob H. Hollander, *War Borrowing*, New York, Macmillan, 1919, Chapter 4, for an excellent discussion of this procedure.

[11] *Federal Reserve Bulletin*, May 1, 1917, p. 338.

[12] *Op. cit.*, June 1, 1917, p. 429.

[13] *Op. cit.*, July 1, 1917, p. 497. At this time the certificates bore a rate of interest higher than 3 per cent to the holder.

[14] *Op. cit.*, October 1, 1919, p. 943.

[15] *Op. cit.*, June 1, 1919, p. 609.

During the period of wartime shortages of goods the effect was not so evident as it became during the reconversion period of 1919–1920.

Credit Expansion in World War II. The United States entered World War II after almost a decade of dull business activity, during which the excess reserves of commercial banks were high. By 1941, however, it appeared that prospective Treasury war deficits would be so great, combined with growing needs for capital expansion of industry, as to press eventually upon reserve limits. It should be borne in mind that by 1940 member bank policies with respect to the Federal Reserve Banks had undergone change from the World War I period. In the first place, under the existence of large excess reserves and pressure from the Reserve Banks themselves, member banks had come to look unfavorably upon the practice of being in debt to the Reserve Banks. Borrowing and rediscounting, though approved in temporary emergencies, had come to be frowned upon as a general practice, indicating something less than sound bank management. Further, operation under the existence of large excess reserves had developed a heavy dependence by bankers upon excess reserves. Serious reduction in *excess* reserves came to be regarded as an unhealthy sign. The combination of these two developments meant that some re-education of bankers was required, both to encourage the use of excess reserves and to encourage borrowing from the Federal Reserve Banks to replenish reserves.

The policies under which tremendous expansion of bank credit took place during World War II are listed and discussed in the following paragraphs.

1. *Use of Excess Reserves.* Recognizing that the banks had become dependent upon the existence of excess reserves as an indicator of sound banking practice, both the Board of Governors and the Federal Reserve Banks used their persuasive powers to urge that the banks utilize their excess reserves before turning to the central banks for replenishment of those reserves. The president of the Federal Reserve Bank of New York stated in a letter to all member banks in its district in late 1942: "The policy of continuing to hold substantial amounts of idle excess reserves is no longer appropriate nor desirable when such huge amounts of funds are required to finance this country's participation in the war."[16] At about the same time the principal federal and state bank supervising agencies issued a joint statement in which it was pledged that bank examinations would be less strict with regard to bank purchases of Treasury securities and loans to individual subscribers to the public debt.[17]

[16] Reported in *Federal Reserve Bulletin*, December, 1942, p. 1190.
[17] *Op. cit.*, pp. 1174–75.

2. *Open Market Operations.* Whereas prior to the war open market operations were carried on primarily for maintaining stability in the market for government securities, after America's entry into the war the primary purpose of such operations was to supply additional reserves to needy banks.[18] A ninefold increase in Reserve Bank holdings of government securities between 1940 and 1945, mainly of short-term maturity, was shown in Table 16. A major factor in this increase was the pegging of the price of Treasury Bills by open market action. On April 30, 1942, it was announced that all Reserve Banks stood ready to buy from member banks all Treasury Bills offered, at a discount rate of ⅜ of 1 per cent. On August 7 it was directed that banks selling Bills to the Reserve Banks could, if they desired, sell on the stipulation that they be allowed to repurchase the same amount of the same maturity at the same rate of discount at any time prior to their maturity.[19] This had the effect of making Bills highly liquid assets of the member banks; temporary excess reserves could be invested in these securities with the certain knowledge that they could be quickly liquidated at fixed discount when the need for additional reserves arose, and repurchased at the same discount should excess reserves reappear.

3. *Loans and Advances.* In order to replenish reserves, the Reserve Banks announced at the outbreak of war that they would make advances to all banks on government securities as collateral at par.[20] The discount rate on such advances was established at 1 per cent at all Reserve Banks by April, 1942. By the end of 1942, the Reserve Banks in the large cities had established a preferential discount rate of ½ of 1 per cent on advances to member banks secured by government securities callable or payable in one year or less.[21] It is thus evident that the Reserve Banks were going the limit to provide the reserves necessary for banks to purchase government debt for their own account and to lend to individuals on the security of government obligations.

4. *Reduction in Reserve Requirements.* By October, 1942, the reserve requirements of New York and Chicago member banks had been reduced from 26 per cent to 20 per cent.[22] Relief was provided for this particular group of banks because their reserves were peculiarly limited. They were the heavy buyers of Treasury Bills; the country banks had not been attracted by such low-interest investments. Further, the large flow of cash out of the

[18] *Op. cit.,* September, 1942, p. 872.
[19] *Ibid.*
[20] Reported in *Federal Reserve Bulletin,* January, 1942, p. 2.
[21] *Op. cit.,* December, 1942, pp. 1190–91.
[22] *Op. cit.,* October, 1942, p. 982.

banks and into circulation was particularly marked in the large financial centers. Finally, Treasury spending did not pour funds into these centers as rapidly as Treasury borrowing removed them; the consequence of this was that New York and Chicago banks lost reserves to banks elsewhere.

A Congressional amendment to the Federal Reserve Act on April 13, 1943, removed the requirement of any legal reserves against so-called "war loan accounts."[23] These were government deposits "arising solely as the result of subscriptions made by or through such member banks" for bonds issued for war purposes.[24] This amendment had the effect of greatly reducing reserve requirements during war loan drives. For when bank depositors purchased bonds their deposits, against which reserves must be maintained, were transferred within the same bank to the account of the government, against which no reserves were required. The liberated reserves could then be invested by the banks in short-term bills, for which the Reserve Banks maintained a pegged market. It is true, of course, that as government spent from its war loan deposits, a reverse substitution of private deposits for reserve-free deposits occurred, requiring a gradual increase in reserves. Nevertheless, this provision relaxed the rigidity of reserve requirements precisely at the time when it was desired to provide easy credit. The amendment led to the same result when banks bought bonds for their own account. Prior to the amendment, such purchases drew down member bank reserves as the proceeds of loans were transferred to the Reserve Banks. Subsequent to the amendment, bank purchases had no effect upon reserves, since the war loan deposits were retained at the purchasing banks and required no reserves.

We have so far discussed the creation of new bank reserves during World War II only with respect to the member banks. It must be recognized, however, that increased reserves of the member banks (held as deposits with Federal Reserve Banks) imply larger amounts of reserves held by the Federal Reserve Banks against those deposits. In fact, the creation of reserves for member banks through loans or through open market purchases of securities implies that the Federal Reserve was required to provide funds to create member bank reserves in the form of deposits, and at the same time to hold required reserves against these increased deposits. And the vast increase in Federal Reserve currency (notes) going into circulation during the war required larger total legal reserves against those notes. How were these apparently almost inexhaustible Federal Reserve Bank reserves provided?

[23] *Op. cit.*, May, 1943, p. 378 and pp. 369–75.
[24] The amendment also eliminated the deposit insurance tax on these deposits.

The answer is to be found principally in the fact that the Federal Reserve Banks entered the war period with tremendous excess reserves. At the end of May, 1940, although the reserve ratio required of Federal Reserve Banks against their combined deposits and note issues was just under 40 per cent (35 per cent against deposits; 40 per cent against notes), the actual ratio of total reserves to deposit and note liabilities was 88.4 per cent.[25] This provided a very large margin for expansion without additional reserves. But the expansion which took place in the interim period brought this combined reserve ratio down to 45.1 per cent by the end of May, 1945,[26] suggesting possible future inadequacy of Federal Reserve Bank reserves, and possible interference with the easy money policy. The following month Congress amended the Act to reduce Federal Reserve Bank reserve requirements against both deposits and notes to 25 per cent, thus creating extensive new excess reserves. We see, therefore, that although new reserves in the Federal Reserve Banks were not required until late in the war, when tightness approached the reserve requirements were relaxed. In this way no scarcity of Federal Reserve Bank reserves was permitted to obstruct the free flow of bank credit to the Treasury.

By way of summary of the results of heavy Treasury borrowing during the war and the reserve-expansion policies of the Federal Reserve System, the changes in important money and credit data are presented in Table 17.

TABLE 17

Changes in Important Money and Credit Items, 1940–1945[*]
(in millions of dollars)

Item	End of 1940	End of 1945	Change	% Change
Deposits (all banks in U.S.)	65,021	151,547	+86,526	+133.1
Loans (all banks in U.S.)	23,741	30,355	+ 6,614	+ 27.8
Investments (all banks in U.S.)	30,448	109,872[a]	+79,424	+260.8
Excess Reserves (member banks)	6,615	1,213	− 5,402	− 81.7
Fed. Reserve Credit Extended to Member Banks	2,274	24,172	+21,898	+963.0
Money in Circulation	8,732	28,515	+19,783	+226.5

[*] All figures taken from *Federal Reserve Bulletin*.

[a] United States Government securities held by banks at end of 1945 amounted to $101,295 million. Government securities held thus increased by an amount considerably greater than the change in total investments between the two dates, which indicates an increasing proportion of governments held to total bank investments.

We shall not analyze the items individually, as their significance has been analyzed or suggested earlier in this chapter. It is evident, however, that the banks as a whole not only came out of the war holding over one-third of

[25] *Federal Reserve Bulletin*, July, 1940, p. 685.
[26] *Op. cit.*, July, 1945, p. 657.

the public debt, but that they provided a prodigious increase in money in circulation[27] and possessed necessary reserves for an amazing increase in deposits. Only a small part of these increases was accomplished by reduction of excess reserves existing at the beginning of the period; the major part was the result of new reserves created for the purpose. Some of the consequences of this vast credit increase, due largely to monetization of the public debt, are indicated by an increase in gross national product in constant dollar terms from $100 billion in 1940 to $153.4 billion in 1945,[28] and by an increase in the Consumer Price Index from 100.2 in 1940 to 128.6 in 1945.[29]

Credit Expansion Following World War II and the Treasury-Federal Reserve Controversy. The Consumer Price Index, which had been at 128.6 in 1945, had risen to 189.6 by June, 1952, a 48 per cent increase. This increase occurred in two spurts, the first between 1945 and 1948, and the second between 1950 and 1952. The first of these two inflationary periods accounted for about three-fourths of the total increase in the price level. It reflected very heavy demand for consumption and investment goods under conditions of full employment. This heavy demand was financed in part by high current levels of income, in part by the large amounts of liquid assets in the hands of the public inherited from the war period, and in part by easy money policy. Though Federal Reserve policy was not markedly inflationary, it was by no means anti-inflationary, and gold imports in significant volume were adding to the money supply. Moderation of price increases could probably have been accomplished by demonetizing public debt by sale of securities in the open market. Between the end of 1945 and the middle of 1948, total reserves of insured commercial banks rose by $1.5 billion and demand deposits by $7 billion.

A mild business recession in early 1949 brought an abatement in inflationary pressures, but the last half of 1949 showed significant recovery, and by early 1950 it was clear that without anti-inflationary monetary policy upward influences upon prices would reappear. The outbreak of fighting in Korea in June, 1950, added highly volatile psychological fuel to the inflationary fires, and frightened the monetary authorities into taking bolder anti-inflationary steps.

The controversy which came to a head in late 1950 between the Treasury and the Federal Reserve had been developing since about 1948. Its occur-

---

[27] Practically the whole of the increase was in Federal Reserve notes, issued on the basis of Federal Reserve Bank holdings of gold and Treasury obligations.

[28] Totals for the year. From *Survey of Current Business, January,* 1951, p. 9.

[29] Averages for the year. From *Monthly Labor Review,* April, 1952, p. 479.

rence resulted from the realization of the essential incompatibility between monetary policies designed to moderate inflation and Federal Reserve maintenance of "orderly conditions" in the markets for Treasury securities. In the last chapter we noted the heavy responsibilities imposed upon the Treasury by the size and composition of the federal debt. Maturity of something over a billion dollars' worth of Treasury Bills weekly, combined with the frequent but irregular maturities of longer-term securities, imposes the need for replacing maturing debt at an average rate of something over $2 billion weekly. And if new debt is being incurred through an excess of governmental expenditures over receipts, new and additional funds must be borrowed. Under the pressure of needs of such magnitude, it is not remarkable that the Treasury should become hypersensitive to instability of the money markets. In addition, the Treasury rather naturally is concerned with the size of interest payments on outstanding debt; a minor change in interest rates on public debt can cause significant change in expenditures for interest.

In inflationary periods the principal technique for stabilizing market prices of government securities, for providing available funds for investment in new issues of securities, and for holding interest rates low, is the purchase of securities in the open market by the Federal Reserve Banks. The Federal Reserve, by offering to buy (or sell) at given prices for securities can pretty well establish market prices for those securities. During inflationary periods the maintenance of stable government security prices would require fairly constant and fairly heavy buying by the Federal Reserve. As we have seen, however, Federal Reserve purchases create new reserves for the member banks, thus expanding the basis for loans to government and to individuals and businesses. The action in holding security prices up and creating new reserves for the banks moderates interest rates.

During the depression years of the nineteen-thirties, the Treasury was borrowing in large volume to finance its deficits and the Federal Reserve was anxious to ease credit conditions. Purchases of securities by the Federal Reserve thus served both its own purpose of easing money and the purpose of the Treasury in promoting favorable markets for its securities. The same identity of objectives existed during World War II; the orderly financing of the war effort in years of heavy deficits required and enlisted the wholehearted cooperation of the Federal Reserve in using its open market purchases to create favorable conditions for the flotation of new securities.

Immediately after the war, the Federal Reserve continued to regard as its prime responsibility the maintenance of orderly conditions in the market for government debt. The Reserve authorities were apparently so appalled at the magnitude of the problem of debt management that they gave this objective priority over that of price stabilization in the formulation of their policies. Gradually, however, this attitude changed. By the end of the third full year of persistent inflation (1948), and with the happy occurrence of a large Treasury surplus, the attitude of the banking authorities had begun to change, and the objective of stabilizing the security markets was giving way to the objective of stabilizing commodity prices. The mild recession of 1949 raised the market prices of government bonds, forcing the Federal Reserve—in pursuit of its policy of pegging bond prices—to sell in the open market. This selling had a tightening effect on bank reserves, creating precisely the wrong monetary conditions for the time. And with the reappearance of inflationary forces in late 1949 and 1950, further purchases of securities by the Federal Reserve were required for security-stabilization purposes, at the same time creating new bank reserves and feeding the inflationary fires. In August, 1950, the Federal Reserve announced that the Open Market Committee were "prepared to use all the means at their command to restrain further expansion of bank credit consistent with the policy of maintaining orderly conditions in the Government securities market." Subsequent statements and actions indicated that since the two policies were fundamentally inconsistent with one another, the former was to take precedence over the latter.

The declaration of the Reserve authorities that they would emphasize economic stabilization in monetary policy over stabilization of government security prices led to a period of unpleasantness with the Treasury which ended in the Federal Reserve-Treasury "accord" of March, 1951. The monetary authorities freed themselves of a primary obligation to peg interest rates and the prices of long-term securities in the market through buying and selling securities. With a change in administration in 1953 the freedom of the Federal Reserve to pursue practices conducive to stabilization of employment and commodity prices was made a central feature of executive policy. This did not mean that officials in the executive department always agreed with the monetary authorities as to what monetary policy should be. Nor did it mean that the monetary authorities ignored the realities of debt management policies. On two occasions (in 1955 and 1958) the Federal Reserve bailed out the Treasury on issues of new securities when it seemed probable that terms were not attractive enough to satisfy the market. In these cases the Federal Reserve bought the issues in the market, and offset the undesired expansive effect of these purchases upon bank reserves by selling approximately equivalent amounts of other securities in its portfolio. Since the "accord," therefore, cooperation between the Federal Reserve and the Treasury has been notable, but it has been cooperation in a context of fluctuating interest rates and security yields. The budget item for interest on the public debt rose from $5.6 billion in fiscal 1951 to $7.6 billion in fiscal 1959, while the principal of the debt had increased about 11 per cent. Thus, debt managers have accommodated themselves to the money market rather than expecting the monetary authorities to provide a favorable money market for placement of securities. Monetary policy has given priority to the longer-term objectives of economic stability and growth, and in the short run has emphasized preventing serious disorderliness in the money market rather than pegged orderliness.

Our consideration of public debt and the money supply has been directed toward the possibility or the avoidance of monetary increase resulting from borrowing. What about the possibilities of reducing the money supply by debt retirement? Let us assume that a cash surplus exists, through an excess of current taxation over current payments (other than debt retirement). The excess of taxation over payments will, taken by itself, shrink potential money supply by transferring funds from the commercial banks to the Federal Reserve Banks, where the Treasury keeps its checking accounts.

If the Treasury were able to select for retirement securities which are held by the Federal Reserve Banks, the retirement of these securities would transfer funds within these banks from the Treasury to the banks, increasing the latter's reserve funds. The retirement operation does not increase the money supply (barring separate action by the Federal Reserve to use these funds), and the total taxing-debt-retiring operation will have reduced the money supply.

If the Treasury were to employ its cash surplus to retire securities held by the commercial banks, we should expect a less deflationary and essentially neutral result. The excess of taxation transfers reserves from the commercial banks to the Federal Reserve in amounts equal to the cash surplus. If the commercial banks were previously holding deposits up to the limit permitted by reserve requirements, the loss of reserves would require a multiple reduction of deposits. The retirement of bank-held debt in the amount of the surplus would re-transfer reserves from the Federal Reserve to the commercial banking system in an amount equal to the earlier loss of reserves, and deposits could be increased by a multiple of the regained reserves. Thus, the effect in the aggregate is neutral.

Finally, if debt held by the non-bank public were to be retired, the combined effect of the surplus taxation from the public and equivalent debt repayment to the public would be the same as in the paragraph above. Thus, of the three cases, only that in which the debt retired is held by the Federal Reserve Banks reduces the money supply. If we eliminate from consideration the surplus taxation effect, the act of debt retirement taken by itself is neutral when Federal Reserve-held debt is retired and expansive of money supply when debt held by the commercial banks or the public is retired. It is hardly conceivable, however, that particular debt-holders could be selected in a retirement operation as assumed in the examples here. But it may be important to note that it will make some difference to the money supply whether retired debt securities are held by the Federal Reserve Banks or by others.

Public Debt Monetization: Summary. Public debt becomes monetized when it is dealt with by the banks in such manner as to provide an increase in the money supply. Debt monetization may result in an increase in circulating currency, as occurs when bank reserves created by central bank purchase of securities are drawn out of banks in cash for circulation by the public. Newly created bank reserves find their more efficient use, however, when they support demand deposits in the banking system. Other things being equal, a new dollar of aggregate bank reserves permits a dollar in cash to be withdrawn from the banking system; a new dollar in reserves, however, permits an increase of five dollars in demand deposits when the reserve requirements are 20 per cent. Total money supply, including both circulating cash and demand deposits, increased from $63 billion to $102 billion between the end of 1940 and the end of 1945, and further to $139 billion by mid-1959.

It would be a major error to attribute the whole of these increases to Federal Reserve policy alone. The bringing of excess bank reserves into use, the addition of gold importations to bank reserves, and the reduction of Treasury deposits and cash holdings, contribute to an expansion of bank credit quite independently of debt monetization through Federal Reserve action. In view of the fact that these things were happening during and after World War II, their neutralization by tighter monetary policy—demonetization of the public debt—was indicated after the war if strong inflationary tendencies were to be countered. As we have seen, however, on balance Federal Reserve policy was expansionary, permitting net new monetization of debt. The experience after 1946 indicates clearly the inflationary bias imposed upon monetary authorities by the existence of large public debt. Orderly management of the debt calls for active participation by the central bank in monetary policies which are inconsistent with those required for price stabilization. Open market sales of securities when recession pushes security prices upward will have restrictive effects upon bank reserves and thus tighten money when it should be eased. Open market purchases when inflation weakens security prices will expand reserves and thus help to "boom the boom."

Our analysis of the process of debt monetization and its effect upon the price level has centered principally around an inflationary period, when anticipations are high and rising, and the propensity to spend for consumption and investment is high. We have pointed out in Chapter 5 that when anticipations are low the auxiliary spending to create income should be from borrowed funds. Further than this, the borrowed funds should represent new money, created for the purpose. In this phase of the cycle, therefore, it is desired that the debt be monetized—that public borrowing create new money from newly created bank reserves.

Three possible sources of borrowed funds for depression deficit spending exist. The first source is that of current private hoarding (current excess of private saving over investment) or past hoards (accumulated in the past through an excess of private saving over private investment). The second source is existing *excess* bank reserves. The third source is that of current net additions to excess bank reserves. Of these three possible sources, the third is least likely to create a further decline in anticipations.

Current hoarding when anticipations are low arises largely out of the desire of businesses and individuals to increase their liquidity. This being the case, if government were to finance additional expenditures by taxes or forced loans from current hoarding, it is virtually certain that accelerated private hoarding would occur in order to replace liquid hoards being taken by government. Acceleration of the rate of private hoarding is precisely the course to be avoided. A policy intended to halt the downswing and induce recovery must both substitute public spending for the deficiency in private spending and encourage private spending.

We have seen in this chapter that during the low income-low anticipations era of the thirties, the banks came to depend upon the existence of *excess* reserves as a factor in safe and sound bank operation. This being the case, attempts of the Treasury to borrow away excess reserves from the banks would probably encourage them to replace these excess reserves. This replacement of excess reserves would be likely to come about by increased limitations placed upon private borrowing, including higher (at least not lower) interest rates. Such action by the banks would operate to further discourage spending on investment and consumption, and thus to make more difficult the attainment of desired results in the recovery program.

We are thus left with the necessity of using newly created bank reserves as the principal source of borrowed funds with which to finance depression expenditures. The techniques to be employed are some of those utilized during the World War II period. Particular dependence will be placed upon open market purchases to create new reserves. Lower legal reserve requirements will be a necessity, particularly if a significant rise in reserve requirements has occurred in the previous boom period. It is to be noted that a reduction of reserve requirements does not in itself increase the total reserves, but by decreasing the proportion of existing reserves actually required against deposits a larger portion of these reserves is transferred into the excess category. If open market purchases of securities by the Federal Reserve Banks and lowering of reserve requirements are inadequate to provide the desired quantity of additional reserves, liberal offerings of Federal Reserve advances and discounts may be employed. This method is probably the least satisfactory of the three because such borrowing is voluntary on the part of individual bankers. The inhibitions of banking conservatism do discourage member bank borrowing from the Federal Reserve Banks, while open market purchases and reduction of reserve requirements inevitably create free bank reserves independent of the choices of individual bankers. It may be that direct Treasury borrowing from the Federal Reserve Banks would accomplish the desired results most simply and effectively.

RECOMMENDED READINGS

Chandler, L. V., *Inflation in the United States, 1940-1948*, N.Y., Harper, 1951.
> Probably the best detailed account of monetary and fiscal policies and their effects during this important period. Chapters with particular applicability to debt monetization are 9, 13, and 14.

Donovan, C. H., "Debt Management and Federal Reserve Credit Policy Since 1945," *Southern Economic Journal*, January, 1954, pp. 231*ff.*
> A mainly factual study of experience, 1946–1954, with the integration (or lack of integration) of monetary policy and debt management policy.

Fellner, William, "War Finance and Inflation," *American Economic Review*, June, 1942, pp. 235*ff.*
> Excellent treatment of the problem of inflation in wartime, with special reference to conditions, 1939–1942.

Goldenweiser, E. A., *American Monetary Policy*, N.Y., McGraw-Hill, 1951.
> Chapter 11 is particularly pertinent to the subject at hand; other sections will be found useful in clarification of the role of the central bank and of the history of central bank policies.

Hansen, A. H., "Inflationary Potentialities of the Public Debt," Chapter 5 in *Curbing Inflation Through Taxation*, N.Y., Tax Institute, 1944.
> Particular emphasis upon the relation between debt and propensities to spend, rather than upon the monetization of debt. A useful addition to the material in the text chapter.

Hollander, Jacob H., *War Borrowing*, N.Y., Macmillan, 1919, Chapters 4, 5.
> Analysis of the heavy dependence of the Treasury during World War I upon short-term borrowing. Particular emphasis in these chapters is upon the effect of such borrowing upon the money market and upon the price level.

Robinson, R. I., "Monetary Aspects of National Debt Policy," in *Public Finance and Full Employment*, Washington, Federal Reserve System, 1945, pp. 69–83.
> A recommended summary statement of essentially the area covered in the text chapter.

CHAPTER 10

The Burden of Debt

A public debt constitutes some economic burden upon the society incurring it. The nature and severity of the burden have, however, frequently been improperly understood, largely because of the temptation to think of public debt in terms of private debt and to apply identical standards to both. It will be the principal purpose of this chapter to explore the similarities and differences between public and private debt, and to analyze the nature of the burden of public debt upon the economy.

The Obverse of Debt: Credit

For every dollar of debt outstanding there is a dollar of credit. The liability of the debtor to the creditor is matched by the asset value of the creditor's claim. This is a routine fact which is frequently overlooked when considering the nature of debt. The canons of financial morality generally deplore the condition in which the debtor finds himself while extolling thrift and its economic virtues in the person of the creditor. Yet one cannot occur without the other, unless thrift merely results in hoards.

The essence of debt—public or private—is the use by one person of the savings of another. If by transfer of funds from lender to borrower these funds are more effectively utilized, there is no doubt that the circumstances which produce the debt are economically desirable. In this sense there is real point to the assertion that the existence of debt is an indication of economic vitality. Prosperity is accompanied by an increase in private debt, while its decrease typically occurs in depression. It should be clearly evident why this is so: an increase in consumption and investment (spending) necessitates both the borrowing of existing spendable assets and the borrowing of new money. Net decrease in debt to the banks implies the destruction of money, while net decrease in debt to others normally reflects less active use of funds in the market. The consequence is declining national income.

Government borrowing of idle funds in the hands of individuals or of new funds from the banks is likely to be income-inducing, and therefore desirable when underemployment exists. This was the point of the argument advanced in the late nineteen-thirties, that although federal debt had greatly increased since 1929, the total of public and private debt had not increased.[1] The income-maintaining potentialities of public borrowing—spending to offset the decline in private spending—should not require further elaboration here.[2] The leverage effects of both public and private borrowing are similar, and they may logically complement one another—the former being substituted as the latter declines.

To the extent that public debt is held by citizens of the debtor government, "we owe it to ourselves." This is equally true of private debt when viewed in the large. If, on the other hand, the debt is owed to citizens or governments of other societies, payments on the debt represent deductions from national product, and the standards of national welfare are thereby reduced. This does not mean that funds borrowed from abroad are unproductive to the borrowing economy. It means simply that investment of funds borrowed from abroad produces less net return to the borrowing economy than would similar investment of funds provided at home. The fact that internally held debts are owed to ourselves is significant in terms of the level of national income. The incurring of debt involves simply transfer of funds within the society; national income at the disposal of the society is not made smaller by debt, but may well be made larger by the expenditure which borrowing allows.

But debt has its individual as well as its national aspects. Although we owe internally held debt to ourselves, those constituting "we" are not necessarily the same individuals as those constituting "ourselves." This is perfectly obvious in the case of private debt, where, although both debtor and creditor may be fellow-citizens, the debtor and the creditor are not the same individual. In the case of public debt the ultimate debtors (taxpayers) may be, to a greater or less degree, the creditors (bondholders). But it would be coincidental indeed if distribution of ownership of the public debt were identical with distribution of the tax burden, eliminating in one stroke both the advantage to creditors and the burden to taxpayers.

We cannot, therefore, breezily assert that because we owe an internally held debt to ourselves, there is no burden of debt. For ours is, after all, an

---

[1] Chairman Eccles, of the Board of Governors of the Federal Reserve System, made this point in a letter to Senator Byrd dated December 23, 1938. *Cf.* Weissman, *Economic Balance and a Balanced Budget*, New York, Harper, 1940, p. 176.

[2] See Chapters 4, 5, 6.

economy of individuals; economic burdens are largely of a subjective and individual nature, and must therefore be analyzed in terms of individuals. But it is equally true that individual welfare is dependent to a great degree upon group welfare. Most individuals are far better off at a high than at a low level of employment and national income, and the causation frequently runs from general welfare to individual welfare. The danger is that we become either solely *macro*-economists, concerned with total or average data alone, or *micro*-economists, limiting our observations solely to the individual. To take either position to the exclusion of the other is to develop half-truths. To identify individual debt with public debt in all respects is as wrong as to declare that because we owe it to ourselves an internally held debt imposes no economic burdens. When indebtedness represents funds productively invested, there is no net burden, but a net benefit to society as a whole, for that society is better off than it would have been had the investment not occurred. But the debt itself sets up a system of transfers of principal and interest which may impose specific burdens upon individual members of the society.

The Benefits of Public Debt

Before analyzing the debt burden, we may consider some mitigating benefits to be derived from the existence of public debt. We shall dismiss very briefly the almost unlimited potential benefits of the ability to borrow. For respectable governments cannot permanently bind themselves to pay-as-you-go policies. Thus the existence of a strong public credit is highly advantageous to society, and the use of public credit is one of the pillars upon which fiscal policy must stand. Without it the financing of public emergencies would be impossible.

The political advantages of a widely held public debt, though impossible of measurement, are none the less real. The same arguments which support at least token tax payments by all citizens support widely held public debt. A government which derives its powers from the consent of the governed requires an interested as well as an informed electorate. Both interest and information are encouraged by financial contact. It is unfortunate, indeed, that so small a proportion of the electorate has traditionally been directly and recognizably affected by governmental fiscal operations. The morale effects of popular war bond drives are a case in point.

The economic advantages of a widely held public debt are considerable in the maintenance of a high level of consumption. Holdings of highly liquid government bonds by small income receivers represent accumulated assets which may be liquidated for expenditure in emergencies or for purchase of durable consumers' goods. Even if holders have no intention of liquidating bond holdings for consumption expenditure, their very existence as liquid reserves against contingencies will obviate to some degree the need for saving from current income to build up such reserves. Thus, the fact that bonds are held can be assumed to increase for low income spending units their propensity to consume from current incomes. In a potentially inflationary period the increased propensity to spend is by no means desirable; in the long run, however, there is little doubt that the economy requires the highest level of consumption consistent with savings adequate to meet new capital needs.

Estimates of the ownership of United States government securities are given in Table 18 below. During the war period, all groups markedly in-

TABLE 18

OWNERSHIP OF U. S. GOVERNMENT SECURITIES, SELECTED YEARS, 1941–1959[*]
(in billions of dollars)

End of December	Total Securities Outstanding	Banks	Individuals	Insurance Companies	State & Local Gov'ts	Other Corps. & Asso.	U. S. Gov't Agencies
1941	64.3	27.4	13.6	8.2	.7	4.9	9.6
1945	278.7	125.8	64.1	24.0	6.5	31.3	27.0
1952	267.4	97.6	65.2	16.1	11.1	31.6	45.9
1958	283.0	100.8	63.8	12.4	17.3	34.7	54.4

[*] Federal Reserve Bulletin, June, 1959, p. 622.

creased their ownership of government bonds. After the war, holdings by banks and insurance companies dropped, as other and more attractive securities came on to the market. Holdings of individuals and of other corporations have held relatively constant since the war, while holdings by governments and their agencies have continued to rise. The use of the Savings Bond had helped very greatly in encouraging individual ownership of public debt at the end of 1945; 67 per cent of individual holdings were in Savings Bonds, and by the end of 1959 this proportion had increased to about 75 per cent. But Savings Bonds have never been really widely held by the population. At the end of 1945, 37 per cent of spending units in the United States held no Savings Bonds, and another 37 per cent held less than $500.[3] By 1958 the situation had worsened—72 per cent held no Savings Bonds, and another 16 per cent held less than $500 worth.[4] This does not suggest a sufficient dispersion of ownership to accomplish by any means the full advantages of widely held public debt.

[3] Bureau of Agricultural Economics, National Survey of Liquid Asset Holdings, Spending, and Saving, Part One, Washington, June, 1946, p. 6.

[4] Federal Reserve Bulletin, September, 1958, p. 1055.

A further potential advantage in public debt lies in its provision of safe and liquid securities in which to invest funds. Investment in the public debt in recent years by all groups of holders reflects their need for high grade, liquid objects of investment. Circumstances being what they are, it is inevitable that federal securities should be of higher grade than those of corporations. From this it follows naturally enough that insurance companies, trust and thrift organizations, and state and local sinking funds should be compelled to invest a considerable portion of their assets in federal debt. And it is not surprising that, where safety of investment is the paramount consideration, such institutions should choose to purchase public securities in the absence of legal compulsion. The investment of federal trust funds presents a special situation. Safety of investment is essential. In addition, in what else than Treasury securities could such funds be invested? Investment in state, foreign, local, or corporate bonds would establish a federal government financial interest in the borrowing agency which is inconsistent with the concept of sovereignty. It might subject government to charges of gross favoritism and, in case of default, would involve the establishment of government as claimant in a potentially embarrassing manner. The possibility of exercise of control as creditor might generate fears or situations which are better avoided.

The conclusion is inevitable that public debt is desirable, no matter what its burden, when incurred for the purpose of securing benefits which outweigh the burden. In this sense debt is a necessary evil, like costs of production; if the benefits could be secured with less burden the alternative would be preferable. But as we go on to consider the burden of public debt, it is well to keep in mind that there are mitigating advantages. Alexander Hamilton's belief that a widely held public debt "will be a powerful cement of Union" is still pertinent. The consumption-inducing potential of the ownership by the public of liquid securities may be an important though by no means the only factor aiding in the maintenance of a high and stable level of national income. And finally, the existence of a large volume of safe and liquid government securities has provided desirable outlets for the savings funds of banks, individual and institutional investors, and governments. It amounts to government guarantee of the safety and liquidity of a major portion of private savings.

The Burden of the Debt as Related to Its Principal

The burden of a public debt is represented by the economic hardship which it imposes. This hardship may take the form of waste of productive efficiency for the economy as a whole or undesirable economic burdens imposed upon particular classes. The former involves misdirection of production, and when it occurs is far more likely to result from spending than from deficit spending. That is, uneconomic diversion of productive resources to government functions rather than to private functions can occur as easily under a balanced budget as under an unbalanced one. The latter involves redistribution of wealth and income, which may frequently occur as a result of the decision to borrow and spend rather than to raise spendable funds by taxation. It is essential in any analysis of debt burden to limit our attention to the debt itself. The spending which creates the debt may or may not be justified; study of the burden of debt assumes the debt to be in existence—for whatever reason—and considers the effects of that debt upon the economy.

Although popularly too much significance is attached to the principal of the public debt, there are elements of burden which *may* vary with the size of the principal. So long as the public insists upon measuring debt burden in terms of the magnitude of the principal, fears and hesitations so inspired must be considered an element of debt burden.

The possibility of inflation resulting from the form of borrowing constitutes another element of burden. For if debt is purchased by the banks out of newly created reserves while the economy is operating near a level of full employment, price inflation will result in redistribution of real income which creates a real burden upon the fixed money income classes. And it is highly unlikely that such redistribution will simply redress a previous maldistribution. Further social cost is incurred through inflation when uncertainty as to further production costs discourages expansion or maintenance of a high level of production. It is well known that inflationary pressures work with varying intensity upon particular production costs at different times; where the bottlenecks will first appear is difficult to determine and upsetting to producers' calculations. Evidently if borrowing is inflationary, the heavier the borrowing (the greater the increase in debt principal) the greater the inflationary possibilites.

The urge to reduce debt principal may involve three kinds of burden: (1) The raising of taxes for debt retirement by a regressive tax system[5] will take funds from those less able to pay and transfer these funds to bondholders who gain relatively little benefit from their receipt. (2) Reduction of expenditure on useful governmental functions will impose burdens upon prior beneficiaries of those functions. (3) Taxes to repay debt held by the

---

[5] A system in which the burden of taxes is heavier upon low income receivers than upon those with high incomes. It does not mean that low income receivers individually pay more taxes, but that they pay more in relation to their ability to contribute.

banks may result in net destruction of a part of the circulating medium.[6] If reserves freed by repayment of debt to banks are not used as a basis for new loans to private enterprises, the purchasing power taken from taxpayers will not be replaced in the economy. In boom periods such destruction of purchasing power may be desirable, though in other periods it may have an adverse effect upon the income level.

Finally, it is apparent that an existing debt so high as to have largely exhausted government's borrowing power would make further borrowing difficult or impossible, with the resultant loss of benefits which could be gained by new expenditure in excess of current taxes.[7]

All of the above listed aspects of potential burden taken together are not impressive. Each is but a conditional burden, becoming real when accompanied by unwise policy which could be avoided. Retirement of public debt is in modern times very largely a matter of choice. The issue of government bonds without stated maturity dates is common with many foreign governments. Everywhere (with the exception of many local governments) the possibilities of refunding and conversion suggest that repayment can rather easily be postponed indefinitely. This being the case, the burden of the *principal* of debt is far more hypothetical than actual.

It is unfortunate that so much popular measurement of the assumed burden of debt is related to the magnitude of the principal.[8] For the real burdens are related to interest payments, and even their burdensomeness is a relative matter. The size of national income, the nature of the tax system, and the degree of dispersion of security holding are all significant determinants of intensity of burden.

The Burden of Interest Payments

Transfer Frictions. The main burden of debt is the total costs to the economy or segments of it incurred in connection with the transfers of purchasing power involved in interest payments. These costs are partly money costs, partly subjective costs, applicable to individuals. Most of the money

---

[6] *Cf.* C. R. Whittlesey, "Retirement of Internally Held Debt," *American Economic Review*, September, 1943.

[7] The rigidity of debt limits can create this situation for any government, though it is difficult to imagine exhaustion of the borrowing power of the federal government.

[8] It was common in the early 1930's to state as a rule of thumb that a federal debt of $50 billion represented a maximum that the economy could support. Later in the same decade the figure was not uncommonly set at $100 billion. Still more recently the rule of thumb has been stated in a somewhat more refined and elastic form as some particular proportion of the national income. All such rules rest upon quite unsatisfactory grounds; for they are related to absolute principal sums, ignoring the relativity of nearly all factors determining the burden.

costs of transfer relate to a comparison of the pattern of tax burdens for interest payments with the pattern of claims for interest upon government. If the interest receivers were, individually, the taxpayers, and if each taxpayer contributed the whole amount which government was to pay him in interest, the burden would be minor indeed.[9] But no such identity of taxpayers and interest-receivers is likely.

Although no particular taxes are earmarked for interest payment, Table 18 will suggest on the surface that the original recipients of interest payments on the public debt are not always the same people or institutions as the payers of taxes. And of course within each category of security holders very great variations in holding and in tax obligations occur. To the degree that lower income individuals contribute in taxes funds which are to be paid to more privileged groups and institutions, an upward redistribution of income occurs.

If taxes upon certain types of business concerns or certain lines of production are made abnormally heavy because of the necessity of meeting high interest charges, the impact of the transfer will be disproportionate. Current taxes upon corporate income in general may well represent this type of case. When corporate profits are taxed twice—as income to the corporation and as income to the stockholder—the burden is relatively severe.

The burden of taxation for interest payments will vary in severity in different phases of the business cycle. Since interest represents a fixed charge upon the Treasury, taxation to pay a given amount of interest in depression will be far more burdensome than in prosperity. The availability of borrowing in depression to meet interest (and other) expenditure can mitigate the peculiarly intense burden of taxation in depression. And it has been previously indicated that such a policy is desirable for counter-cyclical reasons, both to reduce the negative effects of taxation upon anticipations and to put unused savings into private circulation.

It should go without saying that, other things being equal, the larger the volume of interest payments on the debt the greater the economic burden of the debt. Let us note, however, that this is not to state that the larger the debt the greater the burden. For the relation of the size of debt principal to the annual payments has undergone constant change. Changes in interest paid per dollar of federal debt outstanding are shown in Table 19 below. Too much warning can hardly be given against overestimation of the significance

[9] The burden of interest payments would then consist of (1) the unpleasantness of tax payments *per se;* (2) the frictional losses incurred through the necessity of employing men to administer the transfer, which means passing tax laws, collecting taxes, handling disputes, and paying interest; and (3) the dashing of any hopes bondholders may have had that interest receipts would be net above taxes.

of debt principal. In the peak debt year of 1946, the effective rate of interest was less than one-half that in 1924, which is to say that the interest burden (other things equal) resulting from debt of twenty billion dollars in 1924 was equal to that resulting from debt of forty-two billions in 1946.

TABLE 19

FEDERAL INTEREST-BEARING DEBT OUTSTANDING, COMPUTED INTEREST CHARGE,
COMPUTED RATE OF INTEREST, SELECTED YEARS, 1924–1959*

End of Fiscal Year	Interest-Bearing Debt ($ billions)	Computed Annual Interest Charge ($ millions)	Computed Rate of Interest (%)
1924	21.0	877.0	4.18
1932	19.2	671.6	3.505
1940	42.4	1,094.7	2.583
1946	268.1	5,350.8	1.996
1951	252.9	5,739.6	2.270
1959	281.9	8,066.0	2.867

* *Annual Report of the Secretary of the Treasury*, 1951, p. 813, and *Treasury Bulletin*, February, 1960, p. 25. Computed interest includes coupon interest on Treasury Bonds, Notes, and Certificates; on Savings Bonds and Notes at rates effective if held to maturity; and discount on Bills.

Minimizing the Debt Burden

The only way to avoid debt burden is to avoid debt. Such a suggestion is hardly pertinent, however, in view of the existence of large public debt, incurred, in the main, for essential purposes, and in view of the severe burdens which too rapid retirement would entail. The debt cannot be passed off as burdenless on grounds that "we owe it to ourselves." Nevertheless, that burden is a relative burden; a given amount of purchasing power transferred on account of payments on the debt will under varying conditions represent different real burden upon the economy. In the final analysis the burden of interest transfers is really a question of the economic burdens of taxes. Some of the variables have been suggested above and will be repeated.

Borrowing vs. Taxation for Debt Service. The method used in raising funds to be paid as interest will have important bearing upon the intensity of the transfer burden. In periods of marked underemployment the burden of raising funds for interest or repayment of debt will be less if these funds are borrowed. This is, of course, true of an *immediate* burden, and will hold true so long as the conditions of underemployment continue. We must not overlook the fact, however, that borrowing for payment of interest increases the principal of the gross debt, and therefore (other things being equal) increases the amount of interest to be paid on the total debt. In periods of full employment the reverse is likely to be true; taxation of a high income economy may well be less burdensome than borrowing from individuals, and will be less inflationary than borrowing from banks.

1. The Type of Borrowing. Borrowing from banks whose reserves are increased to provide the funds will always be immediately less burdensome than borrowing from individuals, since borrowing from banks out of newly created reserves implies the placing of "new money" into the hands of recipients of governmental expenditure and of interest receivers. If the current level of national income is such as to require the introduction of new money, this procedure makes the "transfer" almost completely burdenless. On the other hand, at a nearly full employment level of national income, such a procedure will accentuate boom tendencies, and is inferior both immediately and in the long run to borrowing from individuals. In fact, taxation to raise funds for interest payments is in most instances of high employment preferable to borrowing, either from banks or from individuals. As a general rule, therefore, indicated policy is to tax in periods of high employment and to borrow from banks in periods of low employment.

2. The Type of Taxation. A tax system which falls heavily on the low income receiver will impose greater burden per dollar collected than will a tax system which falls upon incomes in excess of consumption requirements. Thus, if funds are raised to meet interest payments by sales taxes upon common articles of consumption, the burden is necessarily heavier than it would be if such funds were taken by progressive taxes upon net income with a reasonable personal exemption. The problem of raising tax revenues with minimum burden upon the economy will be a major consideration in our later study of taxation. For the present it is important only to state the evident fact that while other things remain the same a given volume of tax revenue can be raised by good or bad taxes, and whether they are good or bad depends very largely upon how burdensome they are upon taxpayers.

Dispersion of Debt Ownership. The burden of taxes paid for debt service may be mitigated by receipt of interest by the persons who pay the taxes. Except for the frictional loss involved in the transfer, the burden would then be the subjective one of failure to receive net interest income after taxes. By and large, except for the possible effects upon business incentives, the program providing greatest redistribution of income from rich to poor would accomplish ownership of securities by the lower income classes and provide a tax system receiving its principal contributions from the high income classes. The former aspect of the ideal is hardly attainable under any conceivable circumstances; the latter characterizes the present federal tax system, though not the tax systems of states and cities. It may be noted that tax exemption of the income from government securities points toward this ideal *if* public debt is held by the lower income classes. But since the public debt tends to be held by individuals in the higher income groups and by investing institutions, tax exemption in fact tends to accentuate rather than to mitigate the debt burden.

National Income and Debt Burden. Probably the most important variable determinant of the intensity of the debt burden is the level of national income. This is an extremely important fact to be kept in mind in discussion of deficit spending to promote a high level of national income. For, if successful, such a program, while increasing the debt principal and probably the annual interest charge, carries its own mitigation of debt burden. Looked at from the point of view of the economy generally, although the interest charge on the federal debt was eight times as great in 1946 as it was in 1932,[10] the national income was four times as large in the former as in the latter year, which means that the proportion of income devoted to public debt interest was less than twice as great in 1946 as in 1932. Actually, however, if we allow for operation of the economic principle of diminishing marginal utility,[11] the burden of transferring 1/31 of a 165 billion dollar national income in 1946 might well be less than the burden of transferring 1/60 of the 40 billion dollar national income in 1932.[12]

A high national income will by sheer weight of proportion reduce the burden of debt. The extent to which this reduction in burden is shared by individuals depends upon the distribution of income among individuals as compared to the incidence of the tax or borrowing system and the distributive pattern of interest payments. Nicer adjustment of the dollar burden among individuals actually reduces the real burden, while increase of national income at a rate more rapid than the increase of dollar burden will reduce real burden, independent of the nicety of its distribution. As Mr. Evsey Domar has said: "If all the people and organizations who work and study, write articles and make speeches, worry and spend sleepless nights—all because of fear of the debt—could forget about it for a while and spend even half their efforts trying to find ways of achieving a growing national income, their contribution to the benefit and welfare of humanity—and the solution of the debt problem—would be immeasurable."[13]

[10] See Table 19.

[11] The larger the income the less utility attached to the marginal (or last) unit of that income. Consequently the larger the income the less the subjective sacrifice involved in giving up a given dollar to the tax gatherer.

[12] Such a comparison assumes reasonable similarity in the two years chosen for our example of tax systems, sources of borrowed funds, dispersion of debt-holding, and method (taxation or borrowing) of raising the necessary funds. It is probable that in the two years selected these factors were reasonably similar. But even if not, the principle stands.

[13] E. D. Domar, "The 'Burden of the Debt' and the National Income," *American Economic Review*, December, 1944, p. 823.

Reduction of Debt Burden by Manipulation. The burden of debt can under certain conditions be reduced by the artificial creation of markets for government securities bearing lower interest or no interest. By the National Banking Acts of 1863 and 1864, state bank notes were taxed out of existence and national banks were allowed to circulate their own notes upon the purchase and deposit of Treasury bonds. This system created an artificial market in the banks for government debt which previously could be sold only with difficulty. Although this was by no means the only reason for establishment of the national banking system, it was a potent one. The circulation privilege was valuable to the national banks, and under the refunding act of 1900, only new refunding 2 per cent bonds were made eligible for the support of note circulation. The effect was replacement of 3, 4, and 5 per cent bonds by 2 per cent bonds. This is clearly the use of an artificially created market to reduce the interest burden on the debt.

In recent years favorable hearing has been given in some quarters to a system which would require commercial banks to maintain secondary reserves against the deposits which they hold, in the form of government bonds. The scheme would require higher reserves, some part of which would be held in Treasury debt. Though the principal objective would be to tie up bank funds and thus tighten bank lending, some consideration has been given to the fact that such a requirement would help to create an artificial market for these securities, and interest arrangements somewhat more favorable to government might be secured. Though such action would presumably reduce receipts of interest by the banks from the Treasury—depending, of course, upon the volume of secondary reserves required and the ultimate effect upon the banks' lending policies—it is justified by its supporters on grounds that in easy money periods banks are beneficiaries in the form of interest receipts on investments which they purchase out of funds handed to them gratuitously by the Federal Reserve. On the whole, however, plans of this sort have had little public support; although the Board of Governors of the Federal Reserve System recommended establishment of a secondary reserve plan after World War II, it was motivated by a desire for more effective control of inflationary bank expansion and not by a desire to mitigate the interest burden on the public debt.

Borrowing and the Cost of War

Many of the realities concerning the burden of public debt are more clearly evident in connection with the challenge presented by the necessities of war finance: to tax or to borrow. The proportion in which each is used is to a considerable degree determined by day-to-day opportunities. Nevertheless, the facing of the problem urges establishment of definite ideals in wartime fiscal policy, and criticism of practice in terms of those ideals. Because the problem is huge and calls for some sort of immediate answer in wartime, and because idealism is given somewhat freer rein in the surge of patriotic sentiment, tradition in public finance is likely to offer somewhat less resistance to radical change than in peacetime.

Inevitably, short-term borrowing will play an important part in war finance. Even though the decision may be to pay the greater share of war expenses by taxation, legislation of new taxes takes time and some further time will elapse before collection of new taxes will begin. There must therefore be tax-anticipation borrowing. And to the extent that the war is financed by long-term loans there will likewise be loan-anticipation borrowing. The major financial policy decision is thus between taxation and long-term borrowing.

Postponement of War Costs. Let us dispose immediately of the popular notion that borrowing to finance a war transfers the burden of war cost to a later generation. If we talk of cost in real terms, it is evident that the war is fought with goods produced during the war. The real cost is in labor performed, materials used, and equipment depreciated, and this is a matter not related to the method of finance. It is not possible to fight a war with materials produced by the postwar generation, except to the extent that depreciating equipment is not replaced during the war and must be replaced by postwar labor, and that war dissipation of resources makes production in the postwar period more costly in terms of the real effort required to attain a given output.

In the purely monetary sense it is likewise true that the burden of war cost cannot by borrowing be postponed to a later generation. For funds borrowed during the war to pay current costs are funds given up by the war generation. And when in the postwar period the loans are repaid, they are repaid to the current postwar generation holding the securities. Since the postwar generation inherits the assets as well as the debt liabilities it is hardly possible to conclude that this generation is paying money war costs. Thus, although it may seem attractive that a postwar generation which inherits the benefits of victorious war should bear a part of its cost, this is possible only to a very limited degree. And to the degree that cost is transferred to a later generation, this occurs not at all because a policy of borrowing was pursued but because of the partial exhaustion of productive resources. The transfer is the result of the nature of war and not of the method of its financing.

Distribution of War Costs. Although the bearing of war costs cannot be postponed by the method of financing, their distribution among members

of society can. The analysis of Professor Davenport may be briefly para-
phrased as follows.[14] Since a large part of total wartime production is not
available for civilian use, labor's standard of living during the war cannot
rise in proportion to the effort which labor puts forth. As prices rise, with
wages lagging, *real* wages fall while profits rise. If government taxes profits
heavily enough to remove all windfall profits due to the lag of costs and
enough of normal profits to reduce the living standard of profit-makers in the
proportion by which labor's living standard is reduced, all classes will have
shared proportionately in war costs. If, on the other hand, government
finances war by borrowing, the principal buyers of bonds will be profit-
makers, who have war-produced surplus incomes to invest. The purchasers
of bonds thus establish claims to postwar production. Davenport's point is
that, when war is financed by borrowing under typical war circumstances of
production and prices, labor pays twice: once in loss of real income during
the war and again after the war in taxes to repay the government debt.
Profit-makers, on the other hand, experience only net gain. The disparity in
contribution is accentuated if prices fall in the postwar period so that
the claims of bondholders represent increased real claims upon postwar
production.

The two classes concerned might better be more broadly termed as
those whose money incomes lag behind and those whose money incomes
run ahead of prices during wartime. This preserves all of the truths of the
analysis while at the same time eliminating terminologies which carry over-
tones of "class warfare." And it is undoubtedly true that individuals within
any class may fare quite differently during a war period. What assumptions
are inherent in Davenport's argument? The first is that inflation occurs and
that certain incomes lag behind prices so that others increase more rapidly.
He would be a blind optimist indeed who would deny that this assumption
conforms with actual war experience. The second assumption is that the
postwar tax system is more regressive than is bondholding. This is likewise
not widely at variance with the facts, even though the tax system may not
be truly regressive.

Even though the inequities involved may in any war period be less severe
than Davenport implies, the analysis points to distinct social evils of typical
wartime financial policy of two sorts: heavy dependence upon loans rather
than taxes, and inadequate efforts to prevent inflation.

Commission of the former error almost inevitably leads to commission
of the latter. For failure to tax away inflationary incomes leaves as the only
alternative the borrowing of these inflationary incomes. Lacking compulsion,

[14] H. J. Davenport, "The War-Tax Paradox," *American Economic Review*, March,
1919, pp. 34–46.

however, borrowing can hardly hope to close the inflationary gap. Suppose that during a war year the national product is 150 billion dollars, represented by half civilian and half military goods. The problem of inflation control centers around the necessity of transferring nearly 75 billion dollars of private income to government. The proportion of the approximately 75 billion dollars not transferred to government by taxation should be transferred by borrowing. But the desire to increase consumption from increased income and the desire or inertia which results in increased liquid bank deposits will probably thwart government's desire that these funds be wholly invested in war loans. The deficiency must be borrowed by the Treasury from the banks, since it must have the money to buy military goods, and this borrowing will inevitably be from "new money" out of created bank reserves.

Forced lending of untaxed surplus income to government could accomplish the same immediate anti-inflationary results as would taxation. This could be done by measures similar to taxation in coerciveness, but allowing postwar credits against amounts paid in.[15] Under such a scheme a large share of incomes would be taken in taxes, and a further share would be taken for which bonds are given the payer. These bonds would have postwar maturity dates and would not be redeemable prior to these dates. Such a plan would not only remove inflationary pressure during the war, but would provide widespread holding of public debt, with all the postwar advantages accruing therefrom. Sensible as this scheme seems, it was very little used in the United States. England provided for postwar refunds of a considerable proportion of income taxes on low income receivers,[16] and of the top 20 per cent of the 100 per cent excess profits tax under certain specified conditions. In the United States the only use of the scheme was in connection with the excess profits tax during the years 1941–1943. Ten per cent of the tax could be deducted from tax paid if (within limits) it was used for retirement of the corporation's debt, and if not so used it could be taken in non-interest-bearing bonds maturing two to six years after cessation of hostilities.[17]

It is clear that in the absence of forced saving, principal reliance should be placed upon taxation in wartime. Though the proportion of war expendi-

[15] An excellent discussion of the policy of "deferred pay" is to be found in J. M. Keynes, *How to Pay for the War*, New York, Harcourt, Brace, 1940, Chapters 5 and 6.

[16] ". . . in 1941–42 income tax had been extended to 5½ million workers, who contributed 125 million [£]; but of this amount some 60 million was treated as credits, i.e., was credited to the taxpayer in a savings account to be repaid after the war." (*Annual Report of the Bank for International Settlements*, March 31, 1942, reprinted in *Federal Reserve Bulletin*, January, 1943. Quotation from p. 19.)

[17] The amount of such bonds outstanding at the end of fiscal 1945 was just over $1 billion. *Annual Report of the Secretary of the Treasury*, 1945, p. 528.

tures met by taxation cannot in a major war be 100 per cent, since production incentives must be kept strong, the nearest possible approach to this figure is desirable. The records of the various warring nations in this respect are not good, though some records are better than others. Table 20 shows the experience of principal belligerents during the earlier years of the war.

TABLE 20

PER CENT OF TOTAL EXPENDITURES MET BY CURRENT TAXATION, WORLD WAR II*

Country	Fiscal Years Covered	Taxes as % of Total Expenditures
United States	1940–44	41
United Kingdom	1939–44	47
Canada	1940–44	50
Japan	1943–45	27
Germany	1939–45 (first half)	40
France	1940–44	32

* Computed from the following sources: Bank for International Settlements, *Fourteenth Annual Report*, 31 March, 1944: U. S., p. 170; United Kingdom, p. 180; Japan, p. 193; Germany, p. 200; France, p. 214. Canadian figures from H. L. Seligman, "Patterns of Wartime Borrowing in the United States, the United Kingdom, and Canada," *Federal Reserve Bulletin*, November, 1944, p. 1057. Figures for Germany and Japan must be used cautiously, both because they are subject to considerable error and because their meaning for inflation is not parallel with those of other countries. In the case of other countries the difference between 100 per cent and the per cent listed represents the proportion of borrowing. In the cases of Germany and Japan, levies in money and in kind upon conquered territories represented considerable amounts which have effects similar to taxation.

It is outside the province of this book to analyze the whole problem of price control in wartime. It should be clear, however, that the effectiveness of taxation (and the form of borrowing) in preventing inflationary pressures is a basic aspect of the problem. The more successful the methods of war finance in preventing inflationary pressures, the greater the effectiveness of direct price controls.

Conclusions Concerning Public Debt Burdens

For a society as a whole the burden of debt of given size is greater when the evidences of debt (securities) are held by persons outside that society than when held by members of the society itself. This follows from the fact that payments on the debt represent deductions from the gross social product, thus diminishing social income. But the fact that a society as a whole owes debt to itself does not eliminate debt burdens. The real burden of internally held debt is the sum of the burdens upon individuals in that society resulting from the transfer of income from taxpayers and lenders for the purpose of meeting interest and retirement obligations. It is the loss of opportunity to use realized income for want satisfaction.

The intensity of burden of internally held debt of a given size at a given time will depend upon several factors. The pattern of taxation as related to the pattern of debt ownership is significant. Were these two patterns identical—so that individuals simply paid to themselves—the burden would be minor indeed. If the pattern of taxation is less progressive[18] than the pattern of debt ownership, a redistribution of income from those of lower income to those of higher income occurs. This is undesirable from almost any point of view, and tends to maximize the social burden of debt. On the other hand, if the pattern of taxation is more progressive than that of debt ownership, the redistribution of income which takes place is in the direction of greater equality. Such redistribution involves relatively smaller net burden, and may well provide benefits in an improvement of the level of consumption which create net social gain. When we look at the facts, however, it appears that present patterns of federal debt ownership and federal taxation show the first to be somewhat more progressive than the second. In the cases of state and local governments the pattern of taxation is typically regressive, while the pattern of debt ownership is highly progressive. The burden per dollar of state and local debt is thus comparatively great; from the point of view of debt burdens, therefore, it is fortunate that the great bulk of public debt is at the federal and not at the state and local level.

Certainly the most important single determinant of debt burden is the level of national income. The existing high level of public debt makes this the overriding consideration in minimizing debt burden. For the prospect of major reduction in debt in the near future is relatively unpromising, since even relatively large budget surpluses can accomplish only small proportionate reduction in a debt of $280 billion. Major reduction being unlikely, and levels of interest on existing debt offering little or no potentialities for reduction,[19] the essentiality of high employment and income levels becomes apparent as the only method by which the debt may be made easily bearable.

Sensible approach to the analysis of debt burdens requires that the size of debt principal be de-emphasized. For as we have seen, not only are the transfers of income which constitute debt burden principally those which relate to interest and not principal payments, but the size of principal is an inaccurate measure of the magnitude of these transfers. The principal de-

[18] That is, payments to debt holders in the higher income brackets are more than proportional to their tax contributions, and thus the proportion of tax payments by the lower income classes is greater than their proportion of total receipts of interest and principal on the debt.

[19] As we have seen, the trend of interest rates on the public debt has been upward since World War II. This is characteristic of inflationary conditions, when government borrowing comes into sharp competition with business investment for loanable funds.

terminants of debt burden are thus: (1) the magnitude of annual transfers for debt service, (2) the pattern of debt ownership within the economy, (3) the type of tax system, and (4) the level of national income.

RECOMMENDED READINGS

Domar, E. D., "Public Debt and the National Income," in *Public Finance and Full Employment,* Washington, Federal Reserve System, 1945, pp. 53–68.

> A simple and informative discussion of the influence of debt upon the level of national income.

Eccles, M. S., Letter to Senator Byrd, reproduced in Weissman, R. L., *Economic Balance and a Balanced Budget; Public Papers of Marriner S. Eccles,* N.Y., Harper, 1940, Chapter 10.

> A clear statement of the relation of the level of income to the severity of debt burden.

Fairchild, F. R., "The National Debt After the War," *Proceedings, National Tax Association,* 1943, pp. 268-84.

Hansen, A. H., "Federal Debt Policy," *ibid.,* pp. 256-67.

> The above two papers taken together, and including the ensuing discussion, constitute a full-dress debate on the subject of the federal debt.

Wright, D. McC., "The Economic Limit and Economic Burden of an Internally Held National Debt," *Quarterly Journal of Economics,* November, 1940, pp. 116 ff.

> A discussion of economic factors in debt burden. Essentially the same discussion appears in his *The Creation of Purchasing Power.*

CHAPTER 11

Public Revenues:
Grants, Gifts, and
Administrative Revenues

Chapters 8, 9, and 10 have discussed the principal non-revenue receipts of government—public borrowings. In this and following chapters, we shall be concerned with the revenue receipts of government—those receipts which increase the funds over which the Treasury has control without a comparable increase in debt obligations. The most important type of revenue receipt is the tax, though there are other types with varying revenue significance.

CLASSIFICATION OF REVENUE RECEIPTS

Much energy can be wasted in an attempt to set up categories within a classification which are so carefully and finely drawn up as to be unassailable on logical grounds. In fact, it is questionable whether any classification of revenue measures now in use can be constructed which is not open to criticism in terms of hairline distinctions. In practice, measures which originally were distinct tend to borrow techniques from one another, and the tireless seeking after new revenues tends to produce measures which straddle conventional categorical boundaries. We shall here use the broader categories of revenues, recognizing that although these categories are distinct from one another in major characteristics, the lines of demarcation cannot be followed rigidly for all characteristics.

The four classes of revenue receipts are:

1. Grants and gifts
2. Administrative revenues

3. Commercial revenues
4. Taxes

1. Grants and Gifts. We have earlier (Chapter 3) discussed the growth of grants-in-aid, by which one government provides financial assistance to another, usually in the performance of a specified function in a specified manner. Educational and highway grants have long been made by state governments to localities. The federal government has for a long time made grants to state governments for highway construction and maintenance, and for vocational education. Many state universities were originally established with the assistance of grants of land by the federal government.

Grants are seldom made from one government to another for general and unspecified purposes in the United States, though they are important in a few states and in several foreign countries. At present the only grants of this type are relatively minor ones made by states to their localities. A historical curiosity was the federal grant to the states for undesignated purposes in 1836. The revenues from sales of public lands and from the customs duties had been so great that by 1836 the federal debt had been completely retired and embarrassing surpluses were piling up in the Treasury. It did not appear feasible to reduce those revenues. The surplus of approximately $28,000,000 was therefore distributed to the states for use by them in any way they saw fit. Although subsequent similar distributions had been anticipated, the financial difficulties of 1837 again created deficit and debt, and no such embarrassing surplus has since reappeared.

Federal grants to the states for specified purposes were greatly increased both extensively and intensively during the nineteen-thirties. In the early part of this decade fairly generous relief grants were made. As the decade progressed, there were large grants for public works, and, under the social security program, for assistance to particular groups of persons and for administration of unemployment compensation. The period since the nineteen-thirties has been characterized by persistent increase in some of the older grants—notably for highways and public assistance, and the addition of a variety of grants in essentially new areas. These latter include housing, urban renewal, airports, health and hospitals, schools in areas whose costs are affected by federal activities, national resource development, and school lunches. Federal grants to state and local governments totaled $139 million in 1927, $1.3 billion in 1940, and $6.3 billion in 1958.[1] State grants to local governments have not been markedly broadened in function over recent

[1] *Historical Statistics on State and Local Government Finances, 1902–1953*, p. 17, and *Budget of the United States Government, 1960*, Special Analysis G, p. 988.

decades, except in the area of public welfare. The major purposes for which grants are made continue to be education and highways. Total grants by state to local governments were $596 million in 1927, $1.7 billion in 1940, and $7.9 billion in 1958.[2]

Grants-in-aid are, of course, cost payments of the grantor government and revenue receipts to the grantee, since no obligation to repay is established. This is true whether or not the grants are typically made for specified purposes.

Gifts are voluntary contributions from non-governmental donors, generally for specified purposes. Such contributions are likely to increase out of the fullness of patriotic fervor during war,[3] but even in normal times similar contributions are received from interested, grateful, or conscience-stricken persons. The total of gifts (as distinguished from grants) is never significant in amount.

Grants and gifts as a category of receipts are characterized by their voluntary nature, and by the absence of any expectation of direct benefit to the donor. In the case of grants the donor government gives financial aid in the performance of a governmental function at another level. The grant is made by the donor government in preference to direct performance of the function either because of constitutional limitations or because the grantee government is the logical administrative agency. Private gifts are also purely voluntary and provide no direct benefit to the donor except personal satisfaction in promotion of desirable activities.

2. *Administrative Revenues.* Those receipts placed in the category of administrative revenues include fees, licenses, fines, forfeitures, escheats, and special assessments. They are characterized by more or less free choice on the part of the payer as to whether or not he will pay, and more or less direct benefit (or penalty) conferred upon him. The amount of the payment does not necessarily, however, bear close relation either to the value of the benefit or the cost of conferring that benefit. A further and peculiar characteristic of administrative revenues is that they generally arise as a by-product of the administration of a control function of government— hence "administrative revenues."

As examples demonstrating the above characteristics of administrative revenues, let us consider incorporation fees, registration of motor vehicles,

---

[2] *Historical Statistics on State and Local Government Finances,* 1902–1953, p. 19, and *Summary of Government Finances in 1958,* p. 14.

[3] Between 1942 and 1945 the federal Treasury accepted donations of money totaling over $6 million, in addition to several millions of dollars worth of materials and equipment, mostly for recreational use by servicemen. (*Annual Report of the Secretary of the Treasury,* 1945, pp. 107, 108.)

barbers' licenses, and permits to operate automobiles. In the case of each, the individual is not exactly coerced into payment. But if he wishes to incorporate a business, use an automobile, or work as a barber, he must pay the necessary fees. The nature of the benefit conferred upon the fee-payer is to be found in the legal and practical advantages of incorporation over other forms of organization, the ability to operate his automobile under a system in which both the vehicle and the driver must meet certain standards of safety, and the advantage to the barber of maintaining certain standards in his profession. In none of these examples, however, is there any real attempt to equate the amount of the fee to the value of the benefit. There is more nearly an equation between the fee paid and the pro rata direct cost of administering the regulation, though even this equation is frequently disregarded.[4]

We shall have occasion to discuss administrative revenues more fully later in this chapter. Their distinguishing characteristics are (or originally were) more or less voluntary payment occasioned by the conferring of a privilege or the performance of a regulatory function.

3. *Commercial Revenues.* The revenues which we call "commercial" are received in the form of prices paid for government-produced commodities and services. They include payments for postage, tolls, interest on funds borrowed from government credit corporations, tuition to public educational institutions, prices paid for liquor in government stores, surplus war materials, electricity distributed by publicly owned utilities, and the like. The characteristics which distinguish commercial revenues from those in other categories are: direct receipt of a commodity or service in return for payment, and adjustment of the amount of payment at least roughly to cost (or benefit).

We must recognize that there is not always an equation of price of a government-produced good with average or marginal cost of production. General social policy may conflict with business policy, as in the case where postage rates or subway fares do not cover costs. In such instances it is

---

[4] When fees are used for purposes of outright restriction, as in the cases of excessive license fees for permits to sell oleomargarine or unconscionably high registration fees for motor trucks, the objective is to discourage competition, and neither benefit nor cost of administration is the controlling factor. In such cases the principal beneficiaries are not the fee-payers. This is an obvious case of using a revenue measure for control purposes. An important exception of a different type is use of an administrative revenue measure as a tax. Automobile registration fees are a case in point; here the trend has been toward raising revenues by registration fees which are far in excess of requirements (in terms of cost or value of the *regulatory* function), these surplus revenues to be used for highway construction. In this case there is little if any distinction between the objectives of the registration *fee* and the gasoline *tax.*

usually desired that the service—for social reasons—be more widely available to the public than would be possible if price were equal to cost. In other instances government monopolies in the distribution of certain goods are established largely to make monopoly profit which can be covered into the general funds. The French tobacco monopoly is an example of this; state liquor stores fit into this category also, although in this field monopoly operation for purposes of control may be as important as the prospect of profit.

Government may enter into the production and/or sale of commodities and services for several reasons. In some cases private enterprise will not or cannot perform the service (e.g., the postal system or the Panama Canal). In others it is believed that the service can be better or more cheaply furnished by government (e.g., production and distribution of electricity). In still other cases government may find resources or goods on its hands which ought to be used by the public (e.g., surplus war products or electric current as a by-product of flood and erosion control and of navigation). We shall study government industrial operations more fully in the following chapter. For the present it is important to note that the commercial revenues are similar in nature to prices paid to private producers of goods and services.

4. Taxes. Taxes are compulsory payments to government without expectation of direct return in benefit to the taxpayer. We should probably say "more or less" compulsory payments, since the degree of coercion varies with different taxes. A poll tax is paid simply because the taxpayer has reached taxable age. An income tax can be avoided only by failure to receive taxable income; property taxes can be avoided only by not owning taxable property; taxes on purchase of a particular commodity can be avoided only by refraining from purchase of taxed goods within the taxed area. Although some choice appears to exist, by and large the exercise of choice is not feasible and we conclude that for practical purposes taxes are coercive.

And although we say that taxes are by nature contributions to the *general* funds of government and not for specific benefit of the taxpayers, we have seen something of the growth of the tendency to earmark particular tax revenues for particular expenditures which benefit the payers of the tax. The major taxes still conform to the strict definition. Federal income tax receipts are covered into the general funds and allocated to objects of expenditure by appropriation; property and business taxes are treated similarly by the states, as are property taxes by local governments.

In summary, the characteristics of the four categories of public revenues may be compared as in the chart below.

Revenue Category	Extent of Coercion in Imposition	Specific Benefit Granted in Return	Payment Covers Cost or Value of Benefit
Grants and Gifts	(−)	(−)	(−)
Administrative Revenues	(∓)	(+)	(+)
Commercial Revenues	(∓)	(+)	(+)
Taxes	(+)	(−)	...

It must be recognized that any classification of a miscellaneous list of revenue measures will defy clear-cut and mutually exclusive categories. The classes discussed above have shown typical characteristics of the several categories. Nothing is to be gained by quarreling over minor exceptions, for it is admitted that any exact classification would require a separate category for each revenue measure.

It is necessary to record the existence of a trend at the state level toward emphasis upon administrative and commercial revenues in public finance. There has been a growing tendency to argue that a new tax can best be justified by a showing of benefit to the payers as a class. Gasoline taxes have shown this tendency to a marked degree. It must be recalled, however, that the functions of government are basically those of promoting general welfare. Measurement of the degree of welfare provided for a given individual through a general function is impossible in most instances. Furthermore, many of the most important governmental functions must provide benefits which accrue primarily to the less-privileged classes in order to raise the level of general welfare. Thus the major part of government revenues must be taken from citizens on a basis other than that of benefits derived from the expenditure. Otherwise government tends to exist more and more as a commercial entity, providing services for those individuals who can pay for them directly.

Table 21 below presents statistics showing the relative importance of the categories of revenue receipts in terms of the amounts produced in 1957. It will be noted that commercial and administrative revenues are combined in the table; separation of these revenues is impossible on the basis of existing statistics. The evidence is clear that taxes are by far the most productive of all revenue sources for all governments. For the federal government they constituted approximately 94 per cent of all revenue receipts in 1958; for state and local governments combined they made up 60 per cent of revenue receipts. Grants contributed more than one-fourth of combined state and local revenue receipts, while commercial and administrative revenues constituted about one-sixth of their revenues. The "other" revenues of the federal government are principally commercial revenues, of which those of

TABLE 21

FEDERAL, STATE, AND LOCAL REVENUE RECEIPTS FROM TAXES, GRANTS AND
OTHER CATEGORIES, 1958*

(in millions of dollars)

	Federal	State	Local
Taxes	65,921	14,919	15,421
Grants-in-Aid	———	4,764	8,220
Other	3,196	3,835	4,948
TOTAL	69,117	22,830	28,052

* From Bureau of the Census, *Governmental Finances in the United States*, 1958, p. 14, and *Monthly Statement of Receipts and Expenditures of the U. S. Government*, June 30, 1958.

federal credit agencies are the major items. The "other" revenues of states and cities in Table 21 are principally administrative revenues.

Grants and Gifts

It is presumed that gifts to governments require no further specific discussion. Grants-in-aid, however, loom rather large in the public finances of the United States, and certain problems of policy which they raise justify our giving them further attention. The rationale of grants from governments at "higher" levels to governments at "lower" levels proceeds from the belief that functions can frequently be more effectively administered on a decentralized basis even though the objectives to be accomplished are broad and therefore of concern to higher levels of government. The problem is to accomplish the performance of functions at essentially uniform standards among the decentralized administrative units.

Let us set up a hypothetical example which will clarify the nature of the problem of appropriately allocating grants among the various recipients. Suppose that within a state there are two towns of essentially equal size, economic status, and public school population. Town A operates good schools, at considerable tax burden to its property-taxpayers. Town B has poor schools, with comparably lower per-pupil expenditure and consequently comparably lower property taxes. The interest of the state in promoting uniformly high educational standards will probably lead it to concentrate its attention upon B, which is substandard. The simple solution will be to grant state funds to B until B's expenditures for education measure up to those of A. (This makes the questionable assumption, of course, that the quality of education is a simple function of per-pupil expenditures.) Though such a simple formula for distribution of grants will accomplish standardization in our example, it will be unpopular with citizens of Town A, and rightly so. What this system has done is to reward the town which has neglected its schools and to penalize the town which has shouldered its educational duties responsibly. On the other hand, a formula which favors A over B in the allocation of funds will create even greater differences in performance. Probably the most satisfactory solution to this problem is to establish first a measure of "standard effort," which must be met before the town is eligible for any grant. Standard effort should probably be defined as a uniform percentage of income payments in the town to be spent for local education. (Assessed valuation of property in the town would be an inferior, but possible, substitute for income payments if there is reasonable equalization of assessments throughout the state). A local governmental unit must then bring its school expenditures up to the standard effort level before it can qualify for a state grant. This will penalize the town which is remiss in its educational responsibilities, and if withholding of grants will not push the town into greater effort, this may be done by imposition of minimum standards by law.

How might grants be reasonably allocated among those local governments qualifying by having met minimum requirements? Since the object of the grants is to make the quality of performance of the function more uniform, the major share of funds will be granted to those whose economic potential is lower. In general, however, the objective should be to use money to help those who are willing but unable to afford high quality performance, and not those able but unwilling. Such an ideal approach to the management of grants will frequently have to be qualified to meet the political realities inherent in the composition of legislative bodies. It is a fairly typical legislative phenomenon in the United States that smaller towns are relatively over-represented in state legislatures, with consequent influence upon the allocation of funds to local governments.

Though our example above relates to state-local relationships, the reader will recognize that the same problems and the same principles apply in federal-state relations.[5]

Administrative Revenues

H. C. Adams[6] has given a useful description of a fee as a charge imposed on the occasion of a special service, the service arising incidentally in con-

---

[5] For a recent brief and thoughtful analysis of the problems of grants-in-aid, see James A. Maxwell, *Federal Grants and the Business Cycle*, New York, 1952, National Bureau of Economic Research. Chapter 3 is especially recommended for elaboration of the discussion above.

[6] *The Science of Finance*, New York, Holt, 1906, p. 226.

nection with some comprehensive governmental function. This description may be applied broadly to include all those revenues which we have classed as administrative revenues. Government performs certain general functions for society, such as the protection of persons and property, the regulation of trade, and certain fundamental facilities for the comfort and convenience of society. Sometimes the general regulatory function requires the issuance of permits to perform certain acts. At other times the administration of regulations requires punishment for infraction of rules. On occasion particular benefit, within the general benefit conferred upon society, is bestowed upon individuals. The contributions collected upon these occasions of contact with individuals may be justified on grounds of benefit, of cost, or of penalty. Practically, however, the amount of the contribution is seldom measured with any degree of accuracy by the justification.

A few examples may clarify the picture. Conduct of foreign relations is a general function of government. In the performance of this function the issuance of passports is an essential detail. The receiver of a passport pays a fee on its issuance; the amount of the fee paid bears little or no relation to the benefit to the traveler or the cost of issuance. For the protection of society those who practice medicine must meet certain standards of competence. A qualified physician is given a permit to practice medicine; the fee which he pays bears little or no relation in its amount either to the benefit so conferred upon him or to the cost of issuance of the permit. The health and convenience of residents of a municipality may require a sewage system. The owner of a new house will be charged for connection with the sewer, the amount of payment measuring only very roughly the benefit or cost of the connection. Finally a motorist who parks his automobile overtime on a city street may be required to pay a fine which measures neither benefit to him nor his pro rata cost of maintaining traffic control.

These examples demonstrate that administrative revenues are collected when government comes in contact with particular individuals in the course of administering its general functions. There is little fundamental reason why special charges should be imposed when these contacts occur. They do, however, provide occasions for revenue collections, and government seizes upon these opportunities for making additions to its revenues. Charges for permits bear no relation whatever to the individual permittee's ability to pay; they are flat sums charged to all who seek them. And charges for permits to undertake specified activities bear little or no relation to one another. By and large we may say that charges are fixed with a view to providing adequate revenue for a special administrative commission. In such cases the amount charged is determined by what the traffic will bear without undue exclusion from the profession or activity and without generating too much objection from permittees. In other cases exclusion is a primary objective, as in the case of excessive charges for permits to sell oleomargarine in some states, and excessive registration fees for motor trucks in others. There may be pressure by a profession to impose payments for permits which are high enough to discourage new entrants into the profession, though there are generally better and more direct methods which would accomplish this purpose more effectively. In still other cases excessive charges for permits are imposed in order to provide a maximum of net revenue to government. Motor vehicle registration fees in many states reflect this objective.

Most administrative revenues are dedicated to expenditure for particular purposes. The administrative branch of government which collects the charges usually has first claim on the receipts. In some cases a share of motor vehicle operators' license collections is paid directly to the county official issuing the license, who thereby works on a "commission" basis. Very frequently an administrative commission has earmarked for its use all collections from the issuance of permits and licenses by the commission. This is generally true of motor vehicle fees (registration fees, drivers' licenses, dealers' permits, etc.) which are dedicated to the highway fund, and of collections by special boards and commissions issuing permits to engage in trade or professions (i.e., boards issuing permits to barbers, cosmeticians, embalmers, doctors, dealers in oleomargarine, etc.).

The result of such dedication may well be to provide small and specialized agencies of government with funds far in excess of their requirements. The favored agency may be pressed to find opportunities to spend its income. To end the fiscal year with a surplus might well cause real trouble, either in pressure to transfer surplus to the general fund, which would raise objections by fee-payers to "diversion," or in pressure to reduce the amount of annual payment. The consequence of dedicating receipts to the particular use of the agency collecting them is practically to remove that agency from effective budgetary control.

Fees, Licenses, and Permits. We shall attempt no distinction among these terms, for there is no real distinction. We speak of "filing fees," "operators' licenses," and "permits to sell oleomargarine." They all give rise to government revenues of essentially the same sort; the terms used are likely to have been originally accidental and this original usage persists. They all arise out of a government grant of permission to be or do something. In general, the permission is required because a general governmental function could not be adequately performed without the sort of control implied in the grant of permission. But although a system of permits must be utilized, it does not necessarily follow that the permittee should be required to pay for the permit. The imposition of a fee as a prerequisite to receipt of a permit does not, in general, improve the system of administration by permit. The fee system of financing government is, as it has grown up, largely an opportunistic system of collecting funds where possibilities present themselves. Why should automobile owners have to pay a license fee before they can use the highway, while no such permit is required of pedestrians using public sidewalks, or persons using public parks? Why should barbers and tree surgeons be required to operate under permit while teachers in private schools do not?

The fee system has, in some instances, been pushed far beyond any logical reason for it. In one state, for example, operators of motor vehicles were required to purchase a driver's license every two years. No examination was required of drivers prior to receiving their original permits to drive. By paying forty cents each two years a person was permitted to drive his automobile. A large share of the payment was pocketed by the county official issuing the license. And the person who was caught driving without a license was subject to fine. It is impossible to see how this permit system can improve the administration of the safety function. The license is required to collect funds and pay administrators of the system. But the system is simply one of issuing licenses. A driver is penalized for failure to have a license whose only function is to create an occasion for paying a fee to the issuer of the license. One is reminded of the farm tenant who explained to his landlord that a certain wooden tub was kept in the farm yard "to keep water in so it won't leak."

A much greater danger in extension of the fee system is in its tendency to justify payments to government in terms of specific benefit to the payer. The obverse of this tendency is to justify payments to government only where a specific benefit is conferred. Such an emphasis obviously runs counter to the ideal of contribution to government on the basis of ability to pay. And it encourages departure from the concept of government as promoter of the general welfare and movement toward government as a dispenser of benefits to particular individuals and groups at a price.

Fines and Forfeitures. Fines are imposed as pecuniary penalties for infractions of law. It is obvious that they bear no real relation to the cost of administering the protection or control functions of government. They are presumably related in a loose sort of way to the severity of the infraction, though fines whose amounts are fixed and uniform weigh with varying severity upon persons with different incomes. Forfeitures of bail or of bond are similar to fines in that they are penalties for failure to appear in court, to complete contracts as stipulated, or to safeguard valuable assets. Fines and forfeitures are quantitatively unimportant as revenue measures, they are almost entirely unpredictable, and they are—in the revenue sense—pure by-products of the administration of larger governmental functions.

Escheats. Escheat refers principally to the claim of the state to the property of persons who die without legal heirs. It is the duty of the state to guarantee distribution of the estates of deceased persons to heirs specified in wills, or in the absence of a will to persons declared to be lawful heirs by common or statute law. If no such heirs exist, the property reverts to the state. Escheat may include governmental rights to unclaimed bank deposits or property of dissolved educational corporations. As a source of revenue escheat is obviously of no great importance, and raises few problems of fiscal control.

Special Assessments.[7] Certain public improvements, such as the construction of streets and sewers, confer specific benefit upon particular property owners in addition to their general community benefits. Special assessments are charges imposed upon property benefited by such improvements, the amount of the charge being determined by pro rata cost or pro rata benefit. Special assessments are thus similar in many respects to prices, since property owners are buying improvements from local government. On the other hand, there is a large element of general benefit to the community, and the scale on which the improvement is undertaken must conform to community plan as well as to the desires of peculiarly benefited property owners. We are thus justified in classing special assessments as administrative revenues rather than as commercial revenues. The contact with the individual property owner occurs in connection with the performance of the general function of urban physical development, and special revenue impositions upon individuals justifiably arise out of these contacts.

The combination of general and specific benefit in those improvements which give rise to special assessments is not peculiar only to them. As we have seen, payments for permits of all kinds involve the same combination. Nevertheless, special assessments present special problems because the payments required from individuals are commonly large in amount. This being the case, property owners are entitled to a voice in determination of what projects are to be undertaken, and how elaborate the improvements will be. Furthermore, the system of payment must be made as convenient to the

---

[7] For a detailed study of special assessments the reader is referred to A. R. Burnstan, *Special Assessment Procedure*, Special Report No. 1 of the New York State Tax Commission, Albany, 1929.

individual payer as is possible. The project is undertaken by government, and the financial obligations to contractors are assumed by government.

Recognizing that orderly and planned physical development of the community is the paramount interest, what voice should property owners have in initiating improvement projects? Procedures vary among the states which impose procedural regulations upon their local governments, and among local governments when no such state regulation is imposed. In practice, projects are usually proposed by government, and property owners are given some power of veto after public hearing. Since the interests of government are paramount, however, the veto cannot be exercised except by a substantial majority of property owners. The larger the share of cost borne by government, the greater should be the power of government to override the veto. Although in practice a project is less frequently proposed by property owners, this right is generally provided. When property owners recommend projects they should be, and generally are, empowered to state the upper limit of cost which they are willing to bear. If a respectable majority of property owners request an improvement, and are willing to assume substantially the whole cost, the veto power of government is properly limited, and will normally be exercised only when the project is out of line with city plans or when the city's interest would require performance on a more elaborate standard than contemplated by property owners. For it is possible that a street or sewer which would be adequate to the needs of existing residents in a new development would be quite inadequate to the needs of future expansion. In such a case the total cost of the improvement on a scale desired by government would be considerably in excess of the cost which the petitioners are willing to assume. As a general rule in matters of conflict the authority of government must be stronger than that of petitioners. This is not to imply that conflicts normally develop, for typically arrangements for special improvements are completed by cooperation between both interested parties in the accomplishment of projects desired by both.

Determination of the amount to be assessed against individual property owners presents another set of problems. Most state laws allow local governments to assess against benefited property the whole cost of the improvement, including, in addition to actual construction cost, the costs of land acquired and of engineering and supervision by city departments. In some states local governments are by law limited in assessment to only a portion of total cost of property improvements (e.g., one-half or two-thirds). This is statutory recognition of the element of general welfare in such improvements, requiring government to bear its share of cost. However, regardless of legal right, the common practice is for government to assume a share of the cost. The amount of assessment permitted is everywhere subject to the overriding limitation that no property owner shall be required to contribute an amount in excess of the value added to his property by the improvement. This obviously raises difficult problems of measurement, both of the amount of property value increase and the proportion of the appreciation which should be attributed to the improvement in question as distinguished from other appreciating influences.

Within the limits of apportioned cost or increment to property value the amount actually assessed is determined by local practice. If the improvement is in a low-income district the assessment of substantially the whole cost or value appreciation against parcels of property may meet with inability to pay and consequent transfer of property.[8] This factor will determine the extent to which government participates in cost, and may result in assumption by government of varying proportions of cost of different types of improvements and in different sections of the city.

The substantial assessments against property for improvements must in the normal case be spread over a period of years. It is common practice for local governments to borrow funds to pay contractors by the issuance of special assessment bonds. These bonds are guaranteed by government, but special assessment revenues are dedicated to their retirement. In this way, government advances funds for the improvement, and property owners are allowed to pay off the obligation gradually. Special assessment borrowing on an individual project basis is probably most desirable for most projects, though some larger cities have borrowed to create a revolving fund from which the costs of substantially all such projects are met and into which special assessments for all projects are paid.[9]

Conclusions with Respect to Administrative Revenues

The administrative revenues constitute a miscellaneous collection of individually small revenue streams. These revenues arise in connection with the performance of general administrative functions. When, during this performance, specific contact with the individual occurs, such as in the issuance of permits to engage in regulated activity, the imposition of penalties for failure to abide by laws or agreements, or the construction of improvements beneficial to specific items of private property, it is common for government to seize upon the occasion to exact a revenue. With the excep-

---

[8] The difficulty arises out of inability to raise the necessary amount of cash when payment is due. Although the assessment is limited to the appreciation in value, that appreciation can be realized in cash only by sale of the property. Transfers of ownership for tax reasons are to be avoided whenever possible, particularly in the case of residential property.

[9] See Burnstan, *op. cit.*, pp. 77–83, for discussion of these and other plans for financing special improvements.

tion of fines and special assessments, it is difficult to see how cost, benefit, or the improvement of regulation justifies a charge. Actually, such charges are badly adjusted to ability to pay and therefore hardly recommend themselves on grounds of acceptable revenue theory. In addition the automatic earmarking of such revenue receipts to their administrative departments tends to establish limits to expenditure quite out of step with acceptable budget procedure.

When these shortcomings are added to relative inflexibility of such revenues,[10] and thus the inability to adjust them to current needs, we are presented with a fairly complete logical condemnation of the fee system. Logical or not, however, the fee system is firmly rooted in governmental practice and thoroughly established in the fiscal experience of the public. In view of the public acceptance and the relative unimportance of fees, licenses, and permits in the general revenue picture, it is difficult to become violently exercised over their continuance. But further encroachment upon the field of taxes is a different matter, and should be vigorously opposed.

What we have said above regarding the fee system is not applicable to the other types of administrative revenues—fines, forfeitures, escheats, and special assessments. The fine and the forfeit are based upon other than revenue considerations, and so long as those responsible for the punishment of infractions regard them as satisfactory instruments there are slim grounds indeed for the student of public finance to recommend their qualification or abandonment. Escheats place the state in a position of residual legatee, standing at the end of the line when the property of deceased or lost persons is finally distributed. Under existing safeguards it is impossible to designate anyone who has as good a claim to this position as has the state. In regard to special assessments, there are clear grounds for upholding the principle that property owners contribute their fair share of the cost of improvements which confer financial benefits upon specific parcels of property. And the special assessment frequently serves as a useful preventive to excessive demands for semi-public improvements. What constitutes a fair share of the cost to be collected from individuals is a problem for administrative determination, though the fact should not be ignored that such improvements are not solely in the individual interest but to a considerable (and varying) degree in the public interest. The public's share presents a logical claim upon the general revenues.

The reader will recognize several reasons why the administrative revenues do not lend themselves to counter-cycle adjustment. Being minor in

---

[10] Inelastic because of (1) difficulty of forecasting revenue results with a change in fee rates, and (2) the fact that the amount of the fee is determined on grounds other than revenue considerations.

amount, variations in rates during the different phases of the business cycle can have little effect upon the levels of consumption and investment, and therefore on the level of income. Further, since there is less coercion in their application than in the case of taxes, those subject to the application of administrative revenues are presented with a respectable area of voluntary counter-cycle operation. Finally, the very nature of most such revenues implies that counter-cycle manipulation would vitiate other and more important considerations. Some exception to these conclusions should, however, be stated with respect to special assessments. Programs of public improvements in this class do offer real possibilities for counter-cycle scheduling. (This is an expenditure and not a revenue consideration.) And since to special assessment payers such levies are likely to be of major proportions, some elasticity in the schedule of payment should be provided in order to take account of fluctuations in income caused by cyclical influences. This would not only affect locally the level of expenditure for consumption and investment, but would help to avoid tax delinquency problems which have so frequently embarrassed local governments in periods of underemployment and low community income.[11]

RECOMMENDED READINGS

Additional reading in the classification of revenues is likely to be of little profit. Samples of classification may be found in H. L. Lutz, *Public Finance*, N.Y., Appleton-Century, 1947, Chapter 10, and in M. H. Hunter, "The Problem of Classification: Public Expenditures and Revenues," *American Economic Review*, March, 1930.

Administrative revenues:

Pigou, A. C., *A Study of Public Finance*, London, Macmillan, 1951, Chapter 4.
Analytical treatment of the usefulness of fees for purposes of appropriate allocation of resources in the economy.

Grants-in-aid:

Maxwell, James A., *Federal Grants and the Business Cycle*, N.Y., National Bureau of Economic Research, 1952.
A short, excellent monograph presenting both detailed fact with respect to federal grants and realistic analysis of problems.

[11] Such a program would call for postponing during depression special assessment payments on projects already completed, and probably increasing payments during prosperous periods. Such action would be difficult under present financing procedures whereby issues of special assessment bonds advance the funds and are to be repaid from annual special assessment collections. That is, it would be difficult as long as segregation of special assessment finance is rigid. Were such elasticity provided, it would imply willingness to refund matured special assessment bonds into general Treasury issues in order to stretch the life of the debt over the longer period of collections required by the postponement of revenue collections.

CHAPTER 12

Commercial Revenues:
Government Business Enterprises

NATURE OF COMMERCIAL REVENUES

Commercial revenues of governments are received in the form of prices paid by the public for goods and services produced by government-owned enterprises. These government commercial enterprises exist for the production of goods and services which provide specific benefit to users. The goods providing specific benefit are not typically by-products of the performance of a general governmental function, as in the case of administrative revenues, but are primary products whose production justifies the existence of the governmental agency. The goods produced for sale by government may be and usually are "necessary" items of public consumption. As such, the alternative to sale at a price might be to finance production out of general revenues (taxes), and to distribute the goods without relation to ability to pay for them. The decision to sell rather than to donate these goods results from the ability to identify almost completely the benefits they confer with the individuals who use them. Where the benefits are preponderantly individual there is strong argument for making their production self-supporting; i.e., if the individuals using the goods will not pay their cost there is strong *prima facie* argument against their production. From the selling point of view there are important "commercial" aspects to production and sale, and thus a strong tendency to apply commercial practices in this commercial segment of government.

From the buyer's point of view, government-produced goods are like privately produced goods. He can take them or leave them, to exactly the same degree that he can take or leave goods in the market place of the private economy. There is nothing inherent in municipally produced electric power to distinguish it from the same good when produced by a private corporation. State-sold liquor is the same as privately sold liquor. The buyer reacts to these government-produced goods through the typical rough market place calculus which relates utility of the good to its price. If the former is at least equal to the latter he will buy; if not he will not buy. Thus, specific benefit to the buyer is clearly recognized by him and he is willing to pay a reasonable price for it.

A commercial revenue is thus centrally characterized as a *quid pro quo*. It does not follow, however, that government price policy is *necessarily* identical with that of private industry. For government may exclude private enterprise from a given commercial field and operate the business as a monopoly, with the principal intent of receiving monopoly profit.[1] Or government may operate a business under the conscious policy of selling at less than cost in order to encourage wide utilization of the product. We shall have more to say about government price policy later in this chapter. The important point to note is that government prices differ from administrative revenues and from taxes on grounds of more complete identification of the benefit conferred with the amount paid.

Reasons for Government Operation of Commercial Enterprises

Purely revenue considerations are seldom of major importance in explaining why goods are sold by government in a free enterprise system rather than by private business. The reasons for government commercial enterprises are almost always extra-fiscal. The most usual reasons are related to promotion of public welfare—to provide goods which private industry could not or would not provide, to provide these goods more cheaply to individual users than they could or would be provided by private industry, or to accomplish needed regulation of production and distribution of certain goods. Fundamentally, therefore, public ownership and operation of commercial enterprises normally arise out of the inability of the private profit motive to promote adequately the public good. This means that the interests of private owners frequently collide with the interests of consumers, and in such instances government takes over production in the interest of consumers.

Ineffectiveness of Regulation in the Public Interest. Government regulation of public utility enterprises proceeds from requirements inherent in

---

[1] The French tobacco monopoly is a case in point, as are state monopolies in the retail distribution of liquor in the United States. In the case of the latter, however, the monopoly profit objective may be subordinate to the desire for effective control through government operation.

the nature of their production and distribution that they be local monopolies, from the fact that the goods and services they sell are important elements of the standard of living, and that their operation implies grants of public privilege. Since their services are important in an unusual degree, their monopolistic position is fraught with danger to consumers if they are left unregulated. Consequently elaborate systems of controlling rates and practices have developed. In many localities, however, and for many reasons, the discussion of which lies outside our scope, regulation has proved an unsatisfactory safeguard of public interest. In such circumstances pressure for public ownership of the means of production and distribution of the service has been frequent, resulting in substitution of public ownership for public regulation.

Public grievances against private utility concerns have commonly centered around price; over-all rates have been thought to be excessive, rate schedules have frequently imposed relatively heavy burdens on small users, and profits have been considered more than ample. In some cases, however, public ownership has been recommended to improve service. And particularly in the electric utility field integration into large systems and the related complications of corporate ownership have created confusion in the public mind which is conducive to suspicion that the interests of owners are by no means identical with those of consumers.

It is of real significance that local government has entered the business field precisely in those areas where public regulation has long existed—i.e., electric power, water supply, and to a lesser degree illuminating gas and street railway transportation. The conclusion must be that ownership has been thought preferable to administrative regulation of private concerns in promotion of the public interest. In industries where monopoly is "natural," improvement of regulation has frequently called for public ownership in place of private ownership. Where monopoly is not "natural," government competition with private enterprise has at times been recommended. The use of TVA as a "yardstick" for the measurement of the fairness of private electric rates is a case in point. The federal government's Inland Waterways Corporation operates barges on inland waterways in competition with private concerns, a purpose of which is to establish and maintain reasonable competitive rates. The continuance of depression-born federal credit corporations can be explained partially as a government attempt to force down the price of loans from private financial institutions, an attempt which has been markedly successful. In 1874 when Congress was searching for techniques of maintaining low competitive rates for railroad transportation, its Windom Committee recommended that government purchase and operate its own competing lines. No such plan was carried out, partly because severe railroad competition soon accomplished a marked reduction in rates. With the exceptions noted, government industry is principally monopolistic industry.

Unwillingness of Private Capital to Assume Risk. A second aspect of the conflict between consumer interest and the profit motive is the unwillingness of private capital to venture into fields of production where return is either questionable or long delayed. The failure of private capital to complete the Panama Canal is a case in point. In this case government could afford to gamble a part of its larger resources on a project which, although financially risky, promised compensation in national security and cheaper transportation in addition to some financial return. In view of its regard for returns in terms of general welfare, the risk of inadequate financial returns was of less consequence to government than to private capital.

Many of the federal lending corporations set up during the depression years of the thirties were created to make loans which banks and other credit institutions regarded as too risky. In depression the banks established high requirements for borrowers of mortgage capital and for business borrowers who needed funds because their assets were largely frozen. And if borrowers could qualify for loans, the risk involved made interest rates high. Government's entrance into the lending field at comparatively low interest was possible as a part of its recovery program, a program which private capital could not be expected to undertake.

The function of promoting rural electrification was undertaken by the federal government in the middle thirties partly as a recovery project to stimulate activity in construction and in the purchase of electrical supplies and equipment, partly to reduce labor costs on farms, and partly to provide to rural dwellers comforts of living which had long been available to urban residents. The cost of distribution of electric power to farms in less populous areas had been prohibitive under private operation principally because of the heavy investment required per customer in distribution lines. Government undertook the project through locally organized cooperatives and through public bodies, lending long-term funds at low interest for construction of lines. The program has made electric power available at relatively low cost to millions of farms. Here is a case where services were made available by government on terms which made electrification of less populous areas possible, and this represents government entrance into a commercial field (loans) which to a considerable extent private capital was unwilling to enter.

The relative venturesomeness of government capital accounts for the expansion of government commercial enterprises in various fields. In many instances the experiments have proved so successful as to create later friction between private capital and government. For once governmental enterprises were established the investments were demonstrated to have been less risky than was anticipated. Two recent examples demonstrate this. After the depression of the thirties, there was feeling among the banks that "government credit agencies should be taken out of the banking field." These agencies entered the field to assume risks which the banks would not assume at all or that they would accept only at prohibitively high interest. The long-run effect was to bring about an alteration of conditions in the capital markets; banks were now willing to accept these risks at lower interest after demonstration that the risks of loss were not so great as earlier assumed. The second example is that of rural electrification. The success of the Rural Electrification Administration led to fear on the part of the private electric utilities that this area of expansion would be permanently closed to them. They therefore proposed an agreement under which certain areas would be developed by the REA and certain areas by the private utilities. The REA refused to enter into such an agreement, on grounds of danger that only those sections of the private territory which could afford to pay high prices would be developed by the private concerns, leaving the sparsely settled and low-income areas unserved in a preserve from which government had excluded itself. Such competition is productive of recriminations and bad feeling; it is evident, however, that government can withdraw only on the assurance that private capital is in fact willing to accept the risks necessary to provide service on the desired scale, and not simply "skim the cream" from the market.

If further examples are required to demonstrate that areas exist where private capital is unwilling to accept risks at necessarily low price, government insurance upon the lives of soldiers and sailors in wartime is instructive. Private insurers could not have shouldered these extraordinary risks except at extraordinary rates. Yet the rates must be low if substantially complete coverage on a voluntary basis is to be attained. With general revenues acting as a reserve for contingencies, government accomplished broad coverage at low rates, and the broader the coverage the lower the risk per insured individual.

Conflict between the private urge to exploit for profit and the public interest to conserve resources has at times justified public ownership, with or without public operation. The profit urge is not always consistent with the national security or the orderly exploitation of national resources. Retention by government of title to forests, selling timber to private producers, has proved far more successful in terms of the objective of conservation than has sale of timber lands. Likewise, for reasons of national security, government has retained control over certain petroleum and nitrate deposits, on the principle that if left free for private exploitation the more productive deposits would be exploited first for commercial purposes and would thus be unavailable in a situation of national emergency.

The threat of public regulation, by competition or otherwise, may create an element of risk discouraging private capital investment in useful types of production. Even assuming that private capital could make the necessary investment to operate a nation-wide postal system, recognition of government's interest in maintaining low postal rates would be a strong deterrent. For the postal system is bound up with the whole governmental function of promoting the dissemination of intelligence, and must therefore in the public interest maintain rates which will expand the service on the broadest feasible base. Private operation would thus inevitably by subjected to severe rate regulation, the prospect of which would almost certainly make private investment on the required scale unattractive. Likelihood of governmental competition effectively checks private investment in commercial parks and playgrounds, toll bridges, and similar projects. Generally speaking, where the general benefits to be derived from an enterprise are large in relation to the benefits to particular individuals, there is probability of governmental regulation or competition which so dampens profit anticipations as to discourage private investment.

Sales of Government Surplus Goods. Entrance of government into certain commercial fields can be accounted for as attempts to dispose of useful goods through sale rather than to hoard them or destroy them. Sales of public lands during the nineteenth century are an important example. The nation came into possession of huge areas of useful lands. These lands could not, under the political and economic philosophies obtaining, be worked by government or worked by lessees for government. The only possibility was transfer to private ownership. Land was sold to settlers (and speculators) at low prices and given as subsidies to railroads. It could not feasibly have been given away, because this system would not have encouraged the type of settlement desired. Furthermore, it was reasonable that those who became landowners should pay at least a nominal sum for it, and that the proceeds be used to retire public debt. In this way the particular beneficiaries of land policy would pay for their benefit, while taxpayers in general would be benefited by debt reduction from the proceeds of sale of public property.[2]

Government may be required, out of considerations of economy or promotion of welfare, to enter competitive business fields in the sale of by-products of its other noncommercial functions. For example, TVA was originally planned as a flood control, erosion control, and navigation project. Accomplishment of these objectives required a system of dams in the Tennessee Valley. With relatively small additional investment, power could be generated, part of which was useful in development of government-owned nitrate deposits, but most of which was available for sale to the public.[3] It would obviously be uneconomic not to make cheap power available under the circumstances, just as it would be uneconomic to destroy surplus war products at the war's end solely to avoid competition with private enterprise. If the goods are useful and available in a period or area of need, they should be put to use.[4]

Our analysis concludes that government may, and sometimes does, enter into business fields primarily to make profit for itself. But this motive has not been strong in the establishment of most public industry. The major reasons may be classed under the general heading of conflict between the profit motive and the public interest. This conflict may produce government ownership in place of private ownership because of unsatisfactory public regulation of prices, profits, or service. Or it may produce government ownership and operation because of unwillingness of private capital to engage

[2] By 1836 the federal debt had been completely retired, owing in no small measure to receipts from sales of public lands. Subsequent to that time, proceeds of sales of public lands were frequently allocated to debt retirement. It has been estimated, however, that there was no net revenue received from land sales, since total receipts from sales were less than calculated cost of original government purchase and administration of the land policy.

[3] Much difference of opinion has developed over the order in which these various objectives appeared. TVA insists that power production is a by-product of flood control, erosion control, and navigation facilities. The private utilities insist that production of cheap power was the paramount objective, clothed in the respectable raiment of general welfare in terms of flood control, etc. If, as appears true, power is the by-product and not the principal product, and the costs of its production are calculated simply as the additional costs incurred for its production, rates which will cover these additional costs cannot accurately be used as a "yardstick" to measure the reasonableness of rates charged by private concerns whose primary and only product is power.

[4] It happens that TVA power historically is a by-product. But even if it were not, and government were to develop cheap power for no other reason than to utilize natural resources for the public good, its entrance into a competitive field could be justified in circumstances under which private capital was unwilling or unable to exploit those resources in the public interest.

in production of desired things. Finally, government may more or less accidentally enter a commercial field because it finds in its possession goods and services which society wants and for which individuals should pay because their benefits are largely individual and the society should not be required to furnish them gratis.

Business Enterprises of the Federal Government

The area in which federal governmental business enterprises operate is interstate or international. Where government business is of a character which requires uniform operations within the various states, federal administration is almost inevitable. (The reader should not interpret the statements above to mean that all interstate and international business is or must be carried on by the federal government; rather, *governmental* business enterprises whose operations are interstate or international require management by that government whose powers are coextensive with the commercial area involved.)

The postal system and the Panama Canal are the two federal business enterprises which most frequently come to mind. This is largely because they are the oldest in continuous service. The former enjoys the status of a federal department, while the latter is under the cognizance of the Secretary of Defense. Both, although they sell services at a price, contain very large elements of general benefit and thus reflect the meager extent to which earlier government philosophy justified entrance into commercial operations.

Marked expansion of federal commercial enterprises took place after 1931, and again during World War II. During depression many federal corporations and "administrations" grew up to act as lenders of cheaply borrowed government funds to individuals and businesses requiring liquid funds at attractive rates in order to check further deflation, or to guarantee such loans when made by private financial institutions. Loan agencies and loan-guaranteeing agencies were set up to assist in the financing of agriculture, electric power cooperatives, imports and exports, housing, banks, railroads, and many other business fields. The commercial enterprises of the federal government which developed during the thirties overshadowed earlier corporations in importance, and thus characterized federal business enterprises as being predominantly credit enterprises. During World War II the new business corporations created were given responsibility for promotion of production in many lines, accumulation of reserve supplies, and vital wartime construction. On June 30, 1945, the following government business corporations with assets of over one hundred million dollars each were in operation.[5] Date of origin is given in each case, and the postal system and Panama Canal are excluded.

Under Cognizance of Foreign Economic Administration:
   Export-Import Bank of Washington (1934)
   United States Commercial Company (1942)
Under Cognizance of the Department of Agriculture:
   Banks for Cooperatives[6] (1933)
   Federal Intermediate Credit Banks (1923)
   Federal Land Banks[6] (1916)
   Production Credit Corporations (1933)
   Commodity Credit Corporation (1933)
   Farm Credit Administration (1933)
   Farm Security Administration (1937)
   Federal Farm Mortgage Corporation (1933)
   Rural Electrification Administration (1935)
Under Cognizance of Federal Loan Agency:
   Reconstruction Finance Corporation (1932) and these of its affiliates:
      Defense Plant Corporation (1940)
      Defense Supplies Corporation (1940)
      Metals Reserve Company (1940)
      Rubber Reserve Company (1940)
      War Damage Corporation (1941)
Under Cognizance of National Housing Agency:
   Federal Home Loan Banks[6] (1932)
   Savings and Loan Insurance Corporation (1932)
   Home Owners' Loan Corporation (1933)
   Federal Public Housing Authority (1941)
   Federal Housing Administration (1934)
Independent Agencies:
   Federal Works Agency (1939)
   Federal Deposit Insurance Corporation[6] (1933)
   United States Maritime Commission (1936)
   Smaller War Plants Corporation (1942)
   Tennessee Valley Authority (1933)
   War Shipping Administration (1942)

Since World War II a large proportion of the agencies listed above has been liquidated, having served the special purposes for which they were created. But a new list of activities of a commercial type has grown up in its place. These activities are largely concerned with the provision or guarantee of credit in segments of the private economy. A list of these credit activities, with the amounts of loans and investments outstanding or guaranteed at the end of fiscal 1958, follows (amounts in millions of dollars):[7]

[5] *Annual Report of the Secretary of the Treasury,* 1945, pp. 645–57.
[6] Capital funds partially furnished from private sources.
[7] *Budget of the United States Government for 1960,* Special Analysis E, Table 4.

Agency or Program	Direct Loans and Investments	Guaranties and Insurance
Housing and Community Development:		
Residential Mortgages (Federal National Mortgage Association)	2,503	
Urban Renewal and Community Facilities	455	131
Housing	386	26,518
Farmers' Homes	858	172
Veterans' Administration	852	50,727
Rural Electrification	2,774	
Ag. Price Support Activities	1,172	428
Maritime Administration		79
Civil Aeronautics		1
Expansion of Defense Production	244	351
Small Business	232	48
Treasury Loans to Foreign Governments	3,470	
Export-Import Bank Activities	2,978	56
Other Foreign Loans for Economic Development	2,521	
TOTALS	18,454	58,515
GRAND TOTAL	76,969	

It is evident from the table that the federal government has participated heavily in the provision of funds, either directly or indirectly, for a variety of purposes. Of outstanding importance is housing, where capital scarcities and tight money policies are likely to make loans unavailable or available only at high interest, unless governmental assistance is provided. Capital aids to foreign governments appear second in volume, while the remainder of the items constitute aids to particular groups—farmers, veterans, small businesses, defense business, and shipping, where for various reasons special assistance is appealing.

In the fiscal year 1958, budget receipts from the federal government's commercial activities were (in millions of dollars):[8]

Interest	745
Dividends	674
Rents and Royalties	2
Sale of Products	303
Charges for Services (including postal revenues)	2,591
Sale of Gov't. Property	345
Realization on Loans and Investments	323
Recoveries and Refunds	451
TOTAL	5,434

This figure compares with tax receipts in the budget for the same year of $65.9 billion. But the commercial revenues in the budget accounts do not tell the whole story, since many commercial and quasi-commercial receipts

[8] *Budget of the Government of the United States,* 1960, Special Analysis B.

are handled in trust and revolving funds. It may be estimated that some $2 billion of additional commercial receipts accrued to these funds in 1958.

Business Enterprises of State Governments

Charges for services and other commercial revenues of the states amounted to $266 million in 1932.[9] By 1957 these revenues had increased to about $3 billion,[10] and represented about 14 per cent of total state revenue receipts. The reasons for the striking increase in importance of commercial activities by state governments since 1932 require investigation.

It is not difficult to see why state enterprises were unimportant in earlier years. State government is too far removed from those immediate and local situations which may create governmental enterprise to meet local needs. There are minor instances of ferries, irrigation projects, port facilities, and the like. Since local governments are in effect administrative arms of the state, they tend to assume the responsibility for providing local services, while the function of state government becomes more and more that of encouraging uniformity of practices among local governments. At the same time the scope of state government is not broad enough to embrace the larger regional or national field. The furnishing of goods and services generally requires administration in an area broad enough to be interstate, or in an area narrow enough to be better performed by local government. In short, state boundaries frequently are not identical with market boundaries. The commercial activities of state governments are almost exclusively confined to those intrastate and interlocal enterprises which are auxiliary to the performance of general state functions—i.e., regulation of the liquor traffic or the operation of toll facilities on the state highway system.

The marked increase in state commercial revenues between 1932 and 1957 is the result both of expansion in traditional activities for which charges are made—prices charged in performance of educational functions and for health and hospital services—and of the introduction of important new charges. Toll roads are a recent innovation which, in 1957, produced a quarter of a billion dollars in receipts. Sixteen states have state monopoly systems for distribution of alcoholic beverages. The gross revenue from these state liquor stores in 1957 was just over $1 billion. Those which set up state monopoly systems undoubtedly decided to do so largely in the belief that regulation by that method would be most effective. On the other hand, the expectation of monopoly profit was certainly not ignored. In 1957 the net

---

[9] Bureau of the Census, *Historical Statistics on State and Local Finances, 1902–1953*, p. 19.

[10] *Ibid., Compendium of State Government Finances in 1957*, p. 6.

income of seventeen state systems was about 21 per cent of sales revenue, amounting to $229 million. In terms of gross receipts, the sale of liquor is by far the largest business-type enterprise of the states. This is followed, in order, by earnings on property and securities, charges for higher and specialized education, and charges for highway use.

Business Enterprises of Local Governments

Detailed information concerning public enterprises of local governments is available only for cities with population over 25,000. The statistical picture for these cities will not necessarily reflect the situation for all local governments, for the aggregate population of the 481 cities over 25,000 comprises only about two-fifths of the population of continental United States. Data for utility enterprises in these cities are given in Table 22. The gross

TABLE 22

ENTERPRISES OPERATED BY CITIES OF OVER 25,000 POPULATION, 1957*

Type of Enterprise	Number of Cities	Gross Revenue (in millions of dollars)
Water Supply Systems	394	654
Electric Light and Power Systems	67	412
Transit Systems	19	369[a]
Gas Supply Systems	22	60
Liquor Stores	3	15
TOTALS	505	1,510

* Bureau of the Census, *Compendium of City Government Finances in 1957*, p. 79.

[a] The total is given undue importance by the fact that gross revenues of the New York City transit system alone account for $264 million.

revenue from these enterprises ($1.5 billion) may be compared with tax revenues of the 481 cities of approximately $4.8 billion, showing a considerable amount of commercial contact between the citizen and his local government.[11]

The two fields of widespread local government business enterprise are those of public water supply and the generation and distribution of electric power. Water supply systems lend themselves to public ownership and operation for several reasons: sources of supply are frequently a part of the public domain; operation and administration are essentially simple; readiness to serve increasing municipal population frequently requires recourse to

[11] The $1.5 billion of gross revenue from utility services in 481 cities over 25,000 population compares with $2.4 billion of gross utility revenues to all cities of whatever population size. The aggregate population of cities with less than 25,000 is about one-third that of the larger cities included in Table 22. Thus, on a per capita basis, the gross revenues from publicly owned utilities in cities under 25,000 is at least as large as that for the larger cities, indicating very roughly that such activities are widely spread over the cities of the United States.

distant sources of supply at higher cost, while rates may not be allowed similar increase; purity of water supply requires close supervision and constant check by public health authorities; the product is an absolute necessity, urging public policy designed to encourage widespread use by all income classes; its distribution and the exploitation of distant sources of supply may require the right of eminent domain.

Generation and distribution of electricity are not so clearly a "natural" public function. In this field the growth of public systems has largely taken place through the displacement of private firms—by public purchase of private plants. In such cases public ownership has almost always resulted from dissatisfaction with rates under private operation and public regulation.[12] At the same time, development of huge power resources by the federal government since 1930 has stimulated public ownership of distribution systems. Federal policy has been consistent in granting priorities in the purchase of wholesale electric power from its projects to municipal systems and to cooperative enterprises. Thus, availability of low-cost federal power has encouraged both the purchase of private local distribution systems by municipalities and the construction of new systems in communities not previously served with electricity. In cases of the latter, construction has been materially aided by federal loans at low interest, principally by PWA and by the Rural Electrification Administration.

Nonetheless, public ownership of electric light and power systems is not really widespread. Table 22 showed that of 481 cities of over 25,000 population, only 67 were served by publicly owned systems in 1957. John Bauer estimated that in 1939 about two thousand municipalities (of all sizes) were served with public power, and that only about 7 per cent of total electricity sold was sold by municipal systems.[13] The significance of public ownership, however, is not fully indicated by these figures. Though small at present, a trend toward substitution of public for private power has been evident. The rate of substitution accelerated during the thirties, principally under encouragement from federal projects. Local government revenue from public service enterprises in the states of Kentucky, Tennessee, Alabama, and Mississippi increased 173 per cent between 1932 and 1941, as against an

---

[12] The La Guardia administration accomplished electric rate reductions in New York City by threatening to construct a city system in competition with the private system when rate reduction through the state public utility commission appeared impossible. Such competition would, in most cities, be highly uneconomic, since it would duplicate by extremely heavy investment existing distribution lines already capable of providing adequate service. Thus in almost all cases, if public ownership is to supplant private ownership economically, the existing system should be purchased by the public.

[13] John Bauer, "Public Ownership of Public Utilities in the United States," in *The Annals of the American Academy of Political and Social Science*, January, 1939, p. 50.

average of 71 per cent for local governments throughout the country.[14] This unusual gain was due primarily to increased revenues from municipal electrical utility systems in the area, which, in turn, were encouraged by TVA.

Marked expansion of municipal industry in the future can hardly occur in the field of water supply, approximately 90 per cent of that field being already publicly owned and operated. Expansion of municipal commercial activity in local transportation is likely only in those large cities requiring mass transportation facilities. It would appear that any marked substitution of public systems for existing private systems would occur only if the inroads of the private automobile and the suburban shopping center upon the demand for street railways, buses, and subways become so great that existing private investment in those lines becomes critically unprofitable. In such a case local government might be required to take over in order to provide a necessary service. Of the types of public enterprise listed in Table 22, there appears little probability of substantial growth relative to private enterprise.

By concentrating upon utility-type public enterprise, we have ignored a large category of property and services for which prices are charged. Charges for services and sales of property have been a growing item of gross revenue over a period of time, though amounting to somewhat less than that of utility revenue. Principal items are charges for services auxiliary to education (e.g., school lunches), for services in city-owned hospitals, for airports, for parks and recreation, and for use of highways. Rental receipts from public housing are a recent item of commercial revenue, and the growth of reserve funds for various purposes has increased interest earnings.

Determination of Public Prices

Without entering into the intricacies of the matter, prices of privately produced goods in the market tend to represent both the utility of the good to the marginal buyer and its average cost of production plus a profit to the producer. The position of the buyer of government-produced goods is not different from that of the buyer of privately produced goods. He is urged to buy only by the utility of the good; if it is not worth its price to him he is free not to buy. It is true, of course, that the commercial fields into which government has entered are those which produce goods of wide usage. They constitute principally "necessary" goods of high utility, leaving little room for consumer choice as to whether at least some quantity will be purchased. But although "necessary" goods have highly inelastic demand for small quantities, the demand may be highly elastic for quantities beyond the mini-

[14] Bureau of the Census, *Financing Federal, State, and Local Governments: 1941*, 1942, p. 45.

mum required. We are safe in concluding that the buyer is no more coerced to buy government-produced goods than he is to buy privately produced "necessities," such as bread, meat, gasoline, and medical services.

Supply prices—prices at which various quantities will be offered by sellers in the market—may be determined quite differently by private industry than by government. Private industry must, in the long run, receive prices which will cover total costs (including taxes) and provide sufficient net return to attract adequate venture capital. Government, on the other hand, may allow extra-commercial considerations to enter into determination of its supply prices, and is constrained at all times to conduct its operations with a view to promotion of general welfare. For these reasons government prices may be at a level above those which would be charged by competing private firms, though more frequently prices are comparatively low because government does not intend that the enterprise shall be self-supporting.

Arguments concerning private *versus* public enterprise frequently ignore this fact, in implying that public enterprise can justify its existence only when its receipts cover its costs and contribute to the general fund amounts which are substantially equal to what private enterprise would contribute in taxes. The implication is that public business must be as efficient as private business *in terms of private business objectives.* A public business enterprise which operates at a loss may well make contributions to community income through cheap water, cheap electricity, cheap transportation, cheap loans, or cheap postage far in excess of its operating deficit. For many reasons it is a desirable *general* rule that government commercial enterprise be self-supporting, although departure from the general rule must be liberally allowed when extra-business considerations are important. There is general willingness to have efficiently run government enterprises operate at planned losses. However, the prices which produce such losses should evidently not be used as a "yardstick" to measure the reasonableness of prices charged by privately owned enterprises operated at a comparable level of efficiency.

The interests of government are inevitably broader than those of private enterprise. The consequence to cost calculation of broader public interest is that almost every government-produced good is more than one good—it is a good providing individual utility to the buyer, while at the same time providing utility to the community in terms of more general welfare. The second is normally regarded as a by-product of the first,[15] and although

---

[15] If community utility were considered the principal product and utility to the individual the by-product, the service would likely be distributed free as a general governmental service, or at nominal administrative charges imposed upon contact with benefited individuals.

there can be no exact science of allocating joint costs among multiple products, it is logical that the by-product bear some share. It is upon this type of analysis that operation of some public industries at less than cost (the remainder to be made up by the general fund) can be justified. It follows, however, that no such justification exists for long-run operation of private business at less than cost, since no outside source of revenue—comparable with taxes—exists for it.

The allocation of a share of costs of production to society in general, by covering deficits of commercial enterprises from tax receipts, results in subsidies to consumers of the product. Subsidies to producers are also sometimes embodied in prices set or permitted by government. Financial assistance to civil aviation has been given through intentional overpayments to carriers of air mail. Ocean mail contracts have included elements of subsidy to shipping. These subsidies are considered as items of cost of operating the postal service, and when postal revenues equal postal expenditures, the subsidies are paid by purchasers of postal service, i.e., the general public.

We have pointed out that government price determination may differ from that of private business by differences in factors influencing supply price. In analyzing the factors which may make government cost different from that of private enterprise, the impression may have been given that public enterprises typically are not self-supporting. Such a generalization cannot fairly be made. Public water supply systems are typically self-supporting, as are municipal electric light and power systems and most other municipal enterprises. In the narrow field of local transportation the record is spotty, the outstanding example of operation at less than cost being that of New York City. In the area of state enterprise, liquor monopolies have profited well, while other minor enterprises have in general made an acceptable financial record.

Among federal enterprises the postal system has consistently—except during war—operated at a deficit since 1920. This has been owing principally to the introduction of subsidies, not only to carriers but to third class mail (principally magazines and newspapers), and to free mailing service for government departments. Both of these contributors to deficits are evidently non-business costs. The direct revenues of the Panama Canal have by no means repaid its money costs for construction, maintenance, operation, fortification, and interest, in direct revenues. The Canal's military character, however, places it far outside the category of pure commercial enterprise, though its present value as a going concern would, in any business accounting sense, be at least equal to its construction cost, and thereby justify the conclusion that as a business enterprise it has been reasonably successful. Of the many government corporations created more recently no simple generalizations can be made. Some were set up as corporations for purely administrative reasons, with no intention that they be self-supporting. The Commodity Credit Corporation, for example, at the end of fiscal 1958 had an accumulated earned deficit of 7.1 billion dollars.[16] The Corporation was not, however, established as a self-supporting enterprise but rather as an agency of government to administer subsidies to agriculture. Price-supporting activities are essentially relief activities, which are not by nature self-supporting. Most other federal corporations which have built up large earned deficits are in the same category of organizations created to administer subsidies or to provide necessary war materials that would not have been provided by private concerns.[17] On the other hand, some corporations have been financially successful, even though they were created to enter fields of risky enterprise. The Reconstruction Finance Corporation had, at the time of its termination in 1953, an earned surplus just over one-fourth billion dollars. Other enterprises with outstanding earned surplus are the Federal Land Banks, the Intermediate Credit Banks, and the Farm Mortgage Corporation.

Our interest here is not to discuss the perennial question whether private or public industry is more efficient or productive of the public good. We have limited ourselves to a description of the fields from which price revenues are received, and have indicated general reasons why government is found operating in certain commercial fields. Consideration of the principles of public price determination leads to the conclusion that when government enters a "commercial" field—producing goods and services for sale—many extra-commercial influences may be involved. To the extent that these influences are involved, more or less disparity between public and private prices may result. Any attempt to compare the efficiency or desirability of public operation with private should begin by analyzing similarities and differences in the goods and services sold, to determine whether a real basis for comparison exists.

RECOMMENDED READINGS

Barnes, I. R., *The Economics of Public Utility Regulation,* N.Y., Crofts, 1942, Chapter 24.
> Discusses public ownership in the electric utility field. The chapter is largely descriptive and thus requires little knowledge of public utility regulation.

---

[16] *Budget of the United States Government,* 1960, p. 369.

[17] Those corporations with large deficits include: Federal Crop Insurance Corporation, Defense Plants Corporation, Defense Supplies Corporation, Metals Reserve Company, Rubber Reserve Company, U. S. Commercial Company, Rubber Development Corporation, and various housing corporations.

Jacoby, N. H., "Government Loan Agencies and Commercial Banking," *American Economic Review Supplement, March,* 1942, pp. 250–60.
> Best available short treatment of a field meriting far more exhaustive study.

May, Stacy, "Government Ownership," *The Encyclopaedia of the Social Sciences,* N.Y., Macmillan, 1934.
> An excellent source of theoretical and descriptive information.

Troxel, C. E., *Economics of Public Utilities,* N.Y., Rinehart, 1947, Chapter 29.
> A very good discussion of municipal electric utility systems.

CHAPTER 13

Taxes:
Allocation of Tax Burdens

Seligman's definition of a tax as "a compulsory contribution from the person to the government to defray the expenses incurred in the common interest of all without reference to special benefits conferred,"[1] will serve well as a starting point in our consideration of the nature of taxes. Compulsion is a general characteristic of taxes, though this compulsion may be subject to qualification when, for instance, a tax is applied to the sale of one good while sale of a competing good is tax-free. A special tax upon the sale of oleomargarine while sales of butter, lard, and vegetable shortening are untaxed leaves a large area for tax-avoidance which is not entirely consistent with the notion of compulsion as a tax characteristic.

The implication that taxes are or must be used exclusively for common benefit without reference to special benefit is, in marginal cases, a too narrow prescription. It would be difficult to argue that tax deductions from workers' weekly pay for old-age annuity purposes are entirely "without reference to special benefits conferred," especially when the amount of such taxes is based upon actuarial calculations. On the other hand, even this example may lead to an impatience with the definition in terms of general benefit which overlooks the large element of "common interest" involved in old-age security (maintenance of a high level of consumption), the contributions of employers to the plan, and the fact that normally some of the employer's contribution and some of the employee's contribution is eventually passed on to the buyers of products.

A rewording of Seligman's definition, changing "without reference" to "with little reference," would give a definition of a tax which leaves small room for exception. The important facts are that taxes are essentially coercive

[1] E. R. A. Seligman, *Essays in Taxation*, 10th ed., New York, Macmillan, 1925, p. 432.

and that they are collected as general funds to be budgeted among the various governmental functions. The earmarking of particular taxes for particular functions (e.g., gasoline taxes) short-cuts normal budget procedure, but does not change the nature of the tax as a general contribution. As governmental functions expand, there are inevitably services undertaken primarily for segments and not the whole of society, and a consequent tendency to designate as new classes of taxpayers those who can be identified with benefits from the new functions. Some social security taxes demonstrate this tendency, as do gasoline taxes to a degree, and some business taxes.

Revenue Importance of Taxes

In terms of financial contribution, taxes are by far the most important of the various classes of revenue receipts at all levels of government in the United States. In 1957, 88 per cent of federal gross revenue receipts were contributed by taxes. Excluding grants from other governments, taxes produced 83 per cent of revenue receipts to the states and 85 per cent to local

TABLE 23

RELATIVE CONTRIBUTIONS OF CLASSES OF TAXES, U.S., 1957*
(Percentage of tax revenues of each type of government)

Taxes on:	Federal	State	Local	Combined
Individual Income	51.2	11.9	1.4	38.4
Corporation Income	30.4	7.5	b	22.8
Property	—	3.6	87.5	13.5
General Sales and Gross Receipts	—	25.5	4.6	4.1
Selective Sales and Gross Receipts	14.6	38.5	2.6	16.3
Customs	1.0	—	—	—
Deaths and Gifts	2.0	2.6	c	1.7
Others[a]	.8	10.4	3.9	2.6
TOTAL	100.0	100.0	100.0	100.0

* Computed from *ibid.*, p. 23. Payroll taxes are not included.
(a) Includes also licenses and permits, except motor vehicle and operators' licenses.
(b) Included in individual income taxes.
(c) 5/100 of 1 per cent.

governments.[2] A preliminary view of the pattern of tax allocation is given in Table 23. We shall have much more to say on this subject as we study individual taxes in subsequent chapters. The table indicates roughly the

[2] Computed from Bureau of the Census, *Summary of Governmental Finances in the United States in 1957*, Table 1, p. 22. The figures of total revenue receipts from all sources are not entirely accurate. Trust fund revenues for retirement and similar insurance purposes are deducted as non-revenue receipts, but the figures include other trust fund items which are unidentifiable. The federal figures do not tally with budget figures because of the above and because postal gross receipts are here included among revenue receipts whereas the budget treats postal figures on a net basis.

decisions of governments at different levels as to appropriate distribution of contributions among various classes of taxpayers. Upon what basis have governments arrived at these decisions? How acceptable are the decisions in terms of application of the principle of equity among taxpayers, productivity of the tax system, and the effects upon the level of national income? These are questions on which tax theory must offer guidance, and they constitute the problems with which we shall deal in the remainder of this chapter.

Objectives of Taxation

The time-honored objective of taxation is to raise revenue. Although government is not limited to the use of taxes for revenue purposes alone, this objective has generally been uppermost. The introduction of new tax measures, or the "strengthening" of existing measures, means in most cases an increase in government income, to finance normal expansion of governmental activity. Adjustments in existing tax measures to provide a greater degree of equity among taxpayers have frequently come about slowly, if at all, because of the decline in revenue productivity which such adjustments often entail. Although the ease of borrowing frequently softens the desire to tax in order to pay current expenses, there is little reason to expect that the revenue objective will seriously diminish in importance in the future.

A second objective of taxation may be that of regulation or control. This is "sumptuary" taxation. Although technically the term "sumptuary" refers to the regulation or control of private expenditures, in public finance usage it has come to represent all extra-revenue objectives of taxation. The protective tariff is a revenue measure in the sense that it does produce governmental revenues, but in the United States its particular objective has historically been to limit imports of various products. The practice of governments of imposing high consumption taxes upon liquor and tobacco can be partially explained by a desire—at least in the early stages—to discourage use. The taxing out of existence of state bank notes during the Civil War, the abortive attempt to eliminate child labor by heavy taxation of the products of child labor, the imposition of discriminatory special business taxes upon chain stores, and various tax barriers to the sale of oleomargarine are examples of the use of what had traditionally been revenue measures for non-revenue or sumptuary purposes.

The question naturally arises why revenue tools should have been frequently used to accomplish the regulatory purpose. The most ready answer is to be found in the fact that use of revenue tools may accomplish regulation while at the same time serving a revenue purpose. A second explanation lies in the easy availability of tax machinery, while direct regulation would require establishment of new regulatory agencies. In the cases of some sumptuary taxes one is forced to the conclusion that regulation was desired through subterfuge—the desire to regulate or prohibit traffic in certain goods without implying that the principal objective was, in fact, regulation or prohibition.

It has frequently been argued that the regulatory function should be administered directly by regulatory agencies, and not by fiscal measures. As a general rule, this appears sound. For the mixture of revenue collection and regulation may well mean that neither function is administered as well as it might be. In addition, limitations upon purchase which are imposed through price-increasing taxes make the limited goods available only to those who can afford them. We are not concerned here with matters of trade policy. Whether or not it is economic to restrict imports into the nation or into a state or community lies outside the scope of our present study. But if some such policy is being followed, we are interested in the question whether it should be administered through direct prohibitions or quotas or through tax laws. In general, direct regulation is indicated except in those instances where a genuine revenue consideration is present. In such instances the treasury must set up machinery for tax collection, and may, with little additional effort, administer regulatory laws.

The third objective of taxation is in fact an extension of the second. When the sumptuary motive is expanded to the point where it refers not to the flow of a single good, but to the flow of national income, the regulatory method of accomplishing the objective is not available as an alternative. We know that taxes, which transfer income from individuals to government, are capable of altering the pattern of private consumption and investment, and thus of the level of national income. At a given level of incomes, taxes which are added to price tend to discourage purchase. Likewise, those taxes which are taken from surplus income reduce funds available for private consumption and investment. This all suggests that government's objective in using its tax measures may well be primarily regulation of the level of income and not the production of treasury revenue. In low income periods the national income necessity for heavy expenditures and light taxes clearly subordinates revenue objectives to sumptuary objectives. Similarly, in periods of threatened inflation at the full production level, public policy calls for heavy taxation and a minimum of spending, the principal fiscal objective being sumptuary. It is clear, therefore, that national income objectives, as they relate to taxation, frequently call for policy which is directly opposed to that which would normally be pursued if the revenue objective were paramount.

A small group of economists, led by Mr. A. P. Lerner, carries this conflict in objectives to the extreme point where revenue considerations are ignored completely. They insist that public finance must be "functional finance," in which every other consideration must give way to that of maintaining an adequate level of national income. On the side of taxation functional finance takes the position stated in the following quotation:

The effects that the government should consider are primarily the effects on the *public*, in whose interest the government is supposed to be acting. The effects on the *government* are always relatively unimportant.

. . . For example, two effects of any tax payment are that the taxpayer has less money and that the government has more money. The first of these effects is important, so that the tax should be imposed if there is a good reason for wanting the taxpayer to have less money. The effect upon the government, namely that the government will have more money, is not important because the government can always get more money quite easily without impoverishing any taxpayers. . . .

From this it follows that taxes should never be imposed simply because the government needs money. Economic transactions, . . . should be taxed only when it is thought desirable to discourage these transactions. *Individuals* should be taxed only to the extent that it is desired to make the taxpayer poorer.[3]

As a general statement of the purpose of taxation—to take money away from individuals—this "functional" view appears radical in the extreme. It seems to deny the validity of taxation as a means of providing for public goods, except when, incidentally, pursuit of the desire to reduce purchasing power in the hands of the public puts this money in the hands of government. It seems, also, to ignore the dangers of inflation, providing for public expenditures by monetizing public debt. A closer view, however, makes the principle appear less radical. If we think of "functional" taxation as operating at the margin, requiring small deviations up and down from a "normal" amount of taxation, the proposal is less startling. This is actually what compensatory use of taxes implies. The basic strength of the economy permits substantially full employment at a fairly high rate of taxation. In periods when business activity tends to fall away from full employment, the failure of tax revenues to meet the level of expenditures justifies borrowing and not higher taxes. But in this situation of deficient demand, borrowing is not likely to be inflationary. And in periods when booming demand presses upon capacity production and encourages price increases, the "functional"

---

[3] A. P. Lerner, "An Integrated Full Employment Policy," *International Postwar Problems*, Quarterly Review of the American Labor Conference on International Affairs, January, 1946, p. 70. The same position is taken in Lerner, *The Economics of Control*, New York, Macmillan, 1946, pp. 307–8.

use of the tax instrument provides adequate revenues to meet public expenditures. If we think, therefore, of a "normal" level of federal taxation as producing $70 billion, and the "functional" use of taxes as varying that total by $10 billion up or down, the tax system is substantially serving both principles—that of paying for public goods and services and that of taking funds out of the pockets of taxpayers or leaving funds in their pockets. Marginal or fractional variations of tax levels will serve the functional purpose—when used with other available compensatory instruments. It is not necessary for functional reasons to reduce the level of taxation from $70 billion to zero (or to increase it from $70 billion to $140 billion). Thus, the functional (marginal) use of tax levels for stabilization purposes can be expected to produce a nearly balanced budget over the period of a business cycle. This being so, functional finance will not produce wide swings either in expenditures or in public debt.

Government has a rightful claim upon the income of individuals. It has often in the past chosen to exercise that claim unwisely in terms of the business cycle—both increasing and decreasing tax rates at the wrong times. This has been due principally to the exaltation of the revenue objective in taxation. The adoption of counter-cycle sumptuary objectives need not mean renunciation of government's right to a share of individual income or relegation of the revenue objective to a position of insignificance. In the short run the compensatory objectives will be supreme, while revenue objectives justify a norm of taxation for revenue purposes, to be departed from when the exigencies of cyclical fluctuations in income require it.

Allocation of Tax Burdens

We now proceed to a consideration of principles which will guide in the construction of particular tax measures and of an over-all tax system. This implies both the selection of the types of taxes to be used in preference to other possible types and the determination of the amounts which different individuals should contribute under a given tax.

Two Fundamental Considerations. Before entering further upon tax theory it will help to clarify our thinking and to avoid pitfalls if we emphasize two basic facts. They are:

1. All taxes are eventually paid out of income, and in the last analysis out of the income of individuals. The only exception to this generalization is that if taxes exceed income they must be paid out of capital.

2. Many taxes do not finally rest upon the person upon whom they are first imposed.

The significance of the first lies in its ability to simplify what at first glance is a highly complex picture. It enables us to see that by whatever route it follows, a tax must finally transfer individual income to government. It makes possible generalization in terms of the flow of economic income and therefore of the larger aspects of the economic effects of particular taxes. Further than this, if we see that in a private property economy all income is finally individual income, we are in a position to detect and avoid discriminatory multiple taxation of a given individual's income.[4]

Recognition that the burden of a given tax does not necessarily fall upon the person who originally pays it will help us to avoid logical errors in analysis of the burden of particular taxes. Superficial assumption that the person who writes the check to the treasury is necessarily the person who bears the tax burden will lead to conclusions which are far from the facts concerning the real effects of a given tax. Tax theory begins with ideals of justice which are hopefully to be reflected in specific legislation. Whether those ideals are actually accomplished depends, of course, upon our ability to trace tax burdens to their final settlement. In our analysis of particular taxes in relation to general principles of tax-burden allocation, we shall be required to trace out these burdens to the greatest practicable degree.

Possible Bases of Tax-Burden Allocation. Before any particular tax measure can recommend itself, some fundamental decision must be made as to the basis upon which tax burdens are to be allocated among various payers. That tax burdens should be distributed "fairly" or "justly" is taken for granted, but what, specifically, do fairness and justice imply? We postulate the need for governmental performance of certain functions for the benefit of the society. It is for this reason that contributions cannot be left on a voluntary basis, allowing each to contribute what he thinks is "right" or "fair." But if coercive power is to be used to extract contributions, some positive basis of allocation must be determined upon.

It is inevitable that in allocation of burdens society must be thought of as being composed of broad classes. No possible legislation could distribute real burdens equally among all individuals, principally for the reason that, though burden is an essentially personal thing, it can be measured for tax purposes only by external indications which are themselves somewhat inaccurate. Tax measures thus consider society as made up of classes: income

---

[4] For example, we are able to see that income to a corporation is only on its way to becoming income to owners of the corporation, and is not a separate income stream. Thus, taxation of corporate income plus taxation of individual income is double taxation of that individual income which comes through the corporation. If individual income from other (noncorporate) sources is not doubly taxed en route, tax discrimination against corporate-produced income occurs.

classes, propertied classes, producer classes, and consumer classes. Within any class by no means all the variables can be taken into account if the measure is to be administratively workable.

But as among classes of taxpayers, what does "fairness" mean, and what measures of fairness can be found? It means equality of burden among taxpayers. The poll tax implies that equality requires the same taxes to be paid by all, excluding minors. At a later stage equality of burden has implied payment in proportion to some outward indication of faculty, such as the amount of property owned or the amount of income received. Until late in the nineteenth century it was taken for granted that the only fair system of taxation was that which called for proportional rather than equal contribution. This is, in itself, an admission that the burden of a dollar of taxes is unequal as between persons of different incomes. But how unequal? If equal taxes mean unequal burdens, do proportional taxes mean equal burdens? While there is some disagreement over this point, the weight of opinion would hold that burdens are equalized only when the amount of the tax increases progressively with income. We shall discuss this point more fully later in this chapter.

But the analysis of appropriate tax-burden distribution goes somewhat beyond the matter of fairness between individuals. Questions concerning the welfare of the economy as a whole must be raised, and these questions seem to be of two sorts: What is the effect of the tax distribution upon the operating level of the economy? And what is the effect of the tax system upon the kinds of goods and services the economy is called upon to produce? The first of these questions recognizes that inequalities in the treatment of individuals may be justified—or at least will be less objectionable—if each individual's position in an absolute sense is improved. That is, I may be left a smaller piece of pie than you, but if allocation results in an increase in the size of the total pie so that my relatively smaller piece is absolutely larger than it would be under a more equal distribution, I may be better off under the system of individual inequality. The second question follows from considerations alluded to in Chapter 7. Social welfare involves not only the quantities of goods and services produced, but the kinds as well. Thus, whatever the individual's preferences, some goods are socially more desirable than others. At this preliminary stage in our analysis it may be adequate to state the proposition boldly: The society will regard the production of staples and modest comforts more highly than the production of frivolous luxuries, and a system of taxation which encourages demand for the former and discourages demand for the latter through the pattern of after-tax income which it creates, will be serving a social function.

The amount of tax to be paid is the product of the tax rate times the tax base.[5] Questions of appropriateness must, therefore, deal not only with how heavily a thing should be taxed, but also with what things should be taxed. What handles are there to grasp? What outward indicators of capacity to pay can be found? At one time in England it was thought that ownership of a residence with glass windows indicated peculiar tax capacity. The poll tax assumes that arrival at the age of majority implies capacity to pay taxes. The property tax carries on the colonial presumption that ownership of property is a good measure of tax faculty. In modern times the trend is toward use of income as the tax base. Actually, income is the only source of taxes, and therefore exists as the only really reliable starting point for allocation of burdens upon which to compare the faculties of various taxpayers. All other tax bases mentioned above were nothing more than attempts to measure income by external appearances, and were (are) subject to wide error.

If income, the source of tax payments, is accepted as the appropriate tax base, the problem of equalizing the intensities of tax burden becomes one of determining appropriate rates of tax on incomes. But when several tax bases are used, the problem is complicated by the necessity of comparing not only the burdens among payers of the particular tax but also comparing burdens on those subject to the particular tax with those not subject to it. When the tax system applies to a multiplicity of bases, the difficulty of measuring the burdensomeness of that system upon individuals is increased.

Cost and Benefit. Among the oldest of principles followed in allocation of tax burdens are those of cost and benefit. The former implies that whenever governmental costs are incurred for the benefit of particular individuals, such costs should be borne by them. The latter proclaims the desirability of allocating taxes upon individuals according to the benefits which they enjoy from governmental action. The two are essentially alike, in that both place the state in a semicommercial position with respect to citizens, though the first carries implications of budget balance not necessarily implied by the second. The two fundamental faults in cost and benefit as general bases

---

[5] The tax rate is the multiplier in calculation of the amount of tax. The tax base (e.g., value of property, value of income) is the multiplicand. In the case of *ad valorem* taxes the tax base is measured in terms of value and the rate as per cent or cents per dollar. *Specific* taxes measure the tax base as physical quantity (e.g., one bushel of wheat, twenty cigarettes, one automobile), while the rate is measured as an absolute number of dollars or cents per physical unit of base. Examples of *ad valorem* taxes are: sales taxes, income taxes, property taxes, and many excises where the base is expressed in dollars. Examples of *specific* taxes are many customs duties (42c per bushel of wheat), gasoline, cigarette, and most liquor taxes.

for allocation are (1) the difficulties to be found in measurement of cost and benefit, and (2) the undesirable limitations which they place upon the scale of government services.

Obviously, neither cost nor benefit can be allocated among citizens with any degree of accuracy. Most government costs are of the "overhead" variety, involving difficulties of allocation. And benefits are, to a major degree, general. Who, specifically, benefits from the operations of the judicial branch of government? What part of the cost of fighting a war is my rightful share, as distinguishable from yours? And even when benefit at first glance appears to be reasonably allocable, careful investigation generally shows secondary and tertiary beneficiaries. For instance, relief recipients clearly draw special benefits from relief allowances, but how about the butcher, the baker, and so on back to the farmer? The automobile driver benefits from good highways, but so do the automobile and petroleum trades and the economy generally. It is clearly not "fair" that only the primary beneficiaries bear the cost, and yet beyond the primary beneficiaries, how can benefits be quantitatively allocated? On grounds of the impossibility of proper allocation alone, cost and benefit as general bases must be rejected.

But the rigidity which these requirements would impose upon government also demands their rejection. For cost and benefit as the bases for distributing tax obligations would rule out many of the general functions which government must perform. Relief of the needy, for example, could not be undertaken; for by definition the primary beneficiaries cannot assume any part of the cost of the function. Public education could be made available only to those able to pay their way. Clearly, the objectives stated in the Preamble to the Constitution of the United States would be impossible of any reasonable degree of attainment if government were, by the cost or benefit principle of taxation, relegated to the status of purveyor of services at a price.

There are, of course, situations in which cost and benefit are relatively easily allocable, and the principle of cost or benefit may reasonably be applied. The state highway department may build a highway in front of my house, and may be willing to pave my driveway leading to it. In such a case I should obviously pay the cost. Likewise, when costs can be allocated to groups of beneficiaries who are clearly almost the exclusive beneficiaries (e.g., municipally produced electricity), there is good reason for them to pay their way. But these are actually and reasonably price, not tax, payments. When cost or benefit cannot be scientifically allocated, or when such allocation would restrict the performance of socially desirable service—in short, in the vast majority of instances—these bases are quite unacceptable.[6]

Ability to Pay. Allocation of tax burdens among individuals on the principle of ability to pay *is* equalization of the tax burden. For ability to pay, correctly determined, brings us as close to the real tax base (income) as it is possible to be. The ability principle implies (1) a tax base which is capable of measuring ability to carry burdens, and (2) schedules of rates which truly equalize those burdens. Ability to pay refers to the relative (among individuals) real sacrifice involved in tax payment. That individual who can with least personal sacrifice give up a dollar from his income is the individual among all individuals who has the greatest ability to pay the next dollar in taxes. He is by no means necessarily a person who would otherwise spend his dollar for real estate, for liquor, for gasoline, or for movies. And he is not necessarily a person who would otherwise hoard his dollar. What he would otherwise do with his dollar unfortunately cannot tell us much about how much it hurts him to be forced to transfer it to government. The only way to be sure that government would take next the least useful dollar of private incomes in the whole society would be to have an infallible measure of subjective utilities. This measure would need to be quantitatively exact as applied to different individuals, and measurable in an objective manner, free from the vagaries of individual reporting on the basis of introspective searching. Clearly, subjective utilities and dis-utilities are not accurately measured in the market place. Two persons who spend a dollar each for the same quantity of the same good do not neces-sarily derive the same subjective enjoyment.

The problem is to select the outward measure which will most closely approach subjective utility and disutility. This is net money income. This measure is obviously more acceptable than purchases of a given commodity, current purchases of all commodities, ownership of physical goods, or just being alive and over twenty-one years of age. Yet it is by no means a perfectly just measure. For two individuals with the same net money income may differ in number of dependents, financial commitments, expectation as to future income, habits of consumption, and consumer tastes. Taking a dollar in taxes from each may therefore cause quite different sacrifices. Par-tial mitigation of such inequities may be accomplished through specific provisions in tax legislation. Number of dependents is typically a datum in determining tax liability from any income. But even so, to allow a fixed tax credit for each dependent assumes a uniformity among dependents which

---

[6] In spite of the fact that large elements of the benefit principle are now being imple-mented in property taxes, business taxes, and sales and excise taxes. (See Table 23 in this chapter.)

does not exactly exist. Debt position can be taken into account in framing income tax laws by granting tax credits for interest paid. Expectations respecting the duration of income at a given level may be roughly allowed for by treating labor (temporary) incomes and property (permanent) incomes differently, and by allowing a carry-over or carry-back of credits. But hardly anything can be done to mitigate inequities caused by different habits of consumption or different tastes. Even so, income is the best available measure of the subjective ability to pay. And it possesses the administrative merit of avoiding moral judgments upon individual choices, such as are implicit in purchase taxes.

Sacrifices and the Rate of Taxation. The paragraphs immediately preceding have dealt with the selection of that tax base which most closely approximates the basic determinants of ability to pay. We find that base to be net income to individuals. But the choice of the best tax base can be vitiated by application of improper rates to that base. In this section we analyze the intensity of tax burden in terms of the type of rate schedule which fairness in taxation demands. And again we are forced to use burden in the sense of the subjective sacrifice which tax payment entails.

We shall classify rate schedules under three general categories. A schedule of _proportional_ tax rates is one in which the rate of taxation remains constant as the tax base changes. A schedule of _progressive_ tax rates is one in which the rate of taxation increases as the tax base increases. A schedule of _regressive_ tax rates is one in which the rate of taxation decreases as the tax base increases. Thus, recognizing that the amount of tax payable is the result of multiplying the base by the rate, in the case of a proportional tax the multiplier remains constant with changes in the multiplicand; in a progressive tax the multiplier increases as the multiplicand increases; in a regressive tax the multiplier decreases as the multiplicand increases. Dia-

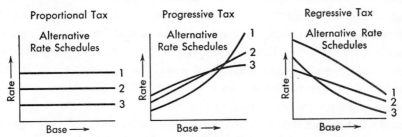

Figure 8. Diagrammatic representation of possible proportional, progressive, and regressive tax rate schedules.

grammatically, the differences are as shown in Figure 8. By definition a proportional rate schedule can be established at any level, provided the rate remains constant at that level. A progressive rate schedule offers many slope patterns, all of which represent progression so long as any increase in the base is accompanied by an increase in the rate. The same is true of regression, provided the rate decreases when the base increases. A tax rate schedule may combine more than one of the types shown. It is common for income tax rates which we say are progressive to progress by brackets; variations of income (tax base) within a given bracket carry proportional rates, while rates progress by brackets as income increases. The curve of the schedule would thus look like a profile view of an irregular set of stairs, where the risers may be higher and the treads broader as we look from bottom to top.

Correctly used, the terms "proportional," "progressive," and "regressive" refer to the relation between the tax rate and the tax base. Commonly, however, we refer to the "regressive effect" of a tax which may not be technically regressive at all. For instance, a sales tax is typically a proportional tax, because its rate is constant no matter how large or small the base. The usual sales tax rate is 3 per cent, whether the purchase is large or small, and the federal tax on cigarettes is eight cents per package no matter how many packages are purchased. But if the *amount* of the tax is related to the buyer's income, such a tax may be regressive *with respect to income*. If two persons of different incomes purchase the same quantity of taxed commodity, the tax paid bears a higher relation (rate) to the smaller income than to the larger. Thus, a tax which is proportional with respect to its base may be regressive with respect to income. The latter use, though technically less correct, often carries so useful a meaning that we would be unwise to ban it. And the dual use should cause no analytical difficulty, once our attention is directed to it.

Of the major tax measures now in use by governments in the United States,[7] property taxes, sales and excise taxes, payroll taxes, customs duties, and some business taxes carry rate schedules that are proportional with respect to their bases. Taxes on individual incomes, some corporation incomes, estates and inheritances, and on some specific businesses are typically applied at progressive rates with respect to their bases. There are no examples of regressive taxes used in this sense. It is rather generally agreed that the federal tax system is as a whole progressive, because of the preponderance of progressive tax measures (personal and corporate income taxes) in it. The typical state and local tax system is regressive with respect to income in the sense that a larger share of *income* is taken from the low

[7] Cf. Table 23.

income receiver than from the high income receiver. State and local systems are preponderantly composed of proportional taxes on things (i.e., property and consumption taxes), which are actually regressive in terms of income.

Our general theory of taxation must tell us whether appropriate distribution of burdens requires proportional, progressive, or regressive tax systems. If the cost theory of taxation were acceptable, we should probably adopt the practice of the market place, charging each beneficiary of government service his proportionate share of the cost. And under the benefit theory individuals would probably pay in proportion to benefit derived. Since we have rejected cost and benefit as general bases upon which taxes should be allocated, and recommended the ability principle, we shall investigate the implications of ability as related to rate schedules on the income base.

Adam Smith's first maxim of taxation was, "The subjects of every state ought to contribute towards the support of the government, as nearly as possible, in proportion to their respective abilities; that is, in proportion to the revenue which they respectively enjoy under the protection of the State."[8] Here is clear recognition that, in the last analysis, what an individual ought to contribute should be determined with reference to his income, and not to some external and haphazard indication of his income. But more important for our present purpose is his emphasis upon *proportion*. Contribution "in proportion to their respective abilities" can undoubtedly be interpreted as favoring progressive taxation, if it can be shown that the increase in ability is more rapid than the increase in income. But Smith was not acquainted with the more recently developed principle of diminishing utility; consequently, "in proportion to their respective abilities" carried for him a meaning identical with "in proportion to the revenue which they respectively enjoy." Up to the end of the nineteenth century, the essentially unanimous opinion of writers on the subject supported the view that fairness or justice in taxation calls for taxation at proportional rates. (The exceptions were those few "radicals" who advocated taxation for purposes of equalizing wealth and income rather than for revenue.) Proportional taxation unquestionably carries surface implications of justice and equality.

About 1870 the almost simultaneous but independent discoveries of the principle of diminishing marginal utility by Jevons, Menger, and Walras introduced a new economic concept which, through refinements, has profoundly altered the general view concerning the comparative sacrifices involved in different tax rate schedules. To be sure, until World War I a wide disparity existed between theory and practice, but since that time experi-

---

[8] *Wealth of Nations*, 1776, Modern Library Edition, p. 777.

ence with progressive taxation has immensely bolstered the theory in the public mind.

The Case for Progressive Taxation. Progressive taxation is a fact of our time, both in advanced societies and in those less advanced. The average man instinctively accepts the principle of progression as an article of faith, and governments implement this principle in the formulation of rate schedules for important tax measures. A curious aspect of the matter has been the broad acceptance of progression in practice while the preparation of a rational case for progression has lagged. The case for progression employs or has employed four component justifications:

1. Revenue productivity
2. Optimum individual allocation of tax burden
3. Promotion of stability and growth
4. Optimum social allocation of resources

1. The revenue productivity justification is the simplest of all, since it is a matter of simple arithmetic. Rising requirements for public goods, coupled with a general desire for budget balance, have called for rising aggregate revenue. The national inclination is to look for large streams of income as the source of higher tax payments, following the simple stratagem of taking the money from where it is. If the rates of proportional taxes continue to increase, there develops sooner or later a pressure upon low income groups which, for humanitarian as well as political reasons, cannot be ignored. Protestations from the lower income groups—comprising the bulk of the population—reflect resistance to further increases in proportional taxes, while there still remains a reservoir of taxable resources in the hands of higher income groups. The natural inclination is then to concentrate new rate increases upon the upper groups where the money is. There is no denying the fact that, given a level of national income and a degree of inequality in its distribution, more revenue can be derived with less outcry under a progressive system than under a proportional or regressive one. The revenue justification for progression is an intensely practical one, and rests upon the fact of income inequality. But it is an incomplete justification, lacking dependable basis for judgment as to whether the complaints of the lower income groups are rooted in real sacrifices or are the empty protests of self-interested avoiders of their just share of tax burdens. It is this lack which the second component of the case has sought to fill.

2. The almost simultaneous but independent discovery of the principle of diminishing marginal utility about 1870 by Carl Menger, Stanley Jevons and Leon Walras introduced a new economic concept which profoundly

altered the view concerning comparative sacrifices involved in different tax rate schedules. The principle of diminishing marginal utility of a good states the subjective fact that, after a certain point, as additional units of the good are consumed, the utility or satisfaction derived from each additional unit declines. If this is true of a single good, is it not also true of all goods taken together? And if it is true of all goods taken together (including savings), is it not therefore true of realized income? Thus, we move from diminishing marginal utility of a good to diminishing marginal utility of income, and giving up a marginal dollar from a large income involves less sacrifice than giving up a marginal dollar of a small income. Stated in another way, tax burdens are equalized by taking a proportionately larger number of marginal dollars from the large than from the small income.

Now this simple progression from an original fact or principle to a generalized rationale for progressive taxation will raise many an eyebrow. Is there any dependable outward indication by which we can measure the rate at which utility of a single commodity declines for a single individual? The answer must be negative. Lacking such a measure, can we conclude that all individuals are alike in their schedules of marginal utility for this particular good? Tastes differ between individuals, and the development of habits of consumption will markedly alter utility schedules. These are embarrassing questions, but if our reply to them is simply to look the other way—to ignore the limitations which they place upon our argument—there are still further embarrassing questions to be faced. Suppose we assumed the income utility functions of all individuals to be measurable, to be downward sloping, and to be identical. Could we then conclude that equal sacrifice of utilities calls for a progressive rate schedule?

The answer depends upon how rapidly the marginal utility of income falls as income rises. There are three areas of possibility as to the rapidity of decline in marginal satisfactions from income. The first is the special case where utility falls proportionately as income increases. This we shall use as our bench-mark case, with which other families of situations can be compared. The second area of possibilities is that in which the decline in marginal utility is less than proportional to the income rise. There are, of course, many quantitative possibilities here. The third area of possibilities includes all those situations where the utility decline is more than proportional to the rise in income.

We take first the bench-mark case where it is assumed that the utility of marginal units for all persons uniformly falls in exact proportion to the rise in income. For example, a 50 per cent rise in income is accompanied by a 50 per cent fall in the utility of the marginal unit of income. If the income of B is twice as large as that of A, B derives satisfaction from the last unit of his larger income exactly half as great as that which A derives from his last income unit. Thus, if we wish to accomplish equal sacrifice of utility from the two taxpayers, and we take the marginal dollar of income from B, we can take only one-half of his marginal dollar from A. A's income is half as large as B's; A's tax is half as large as B's. In this special case, therefore, tax rates *proportional to income* are required to accomplish equality of sacrifice.[9] The fact that marginal utility diminishes does not, in this case, justify progressive taxation.

Our second area of possibilities includes all of those where marginal utility is assumed to fall at a rate less rapid than income rises. Here, assuming the same income situations of A and B given in our first example, though B's income is twice as high as A's, the utility of his marginal dollar is more than half that of A. If we are to take B's marginal dollar away in taxes, we equalize sacrifice by taking more than half of A's marginal dollar. A's income is half that of B, but his tax is more than half that of B. This means that A's tax rate is higher than B's, and in this family of cases, where marginal utility falls less than proportionately with income, regressive tax rates are indicated if equality of sacrifice is to be attained.

In the third set of cases—marginal satisfactions falling more than in proportion to the rise of incomes—only progressive tax rates will produce equal sacrifice. B's income is twice as large as A's, but the utility of his marginal dollar of income is less than half that of A. If, then, we take away B's last dollar in taxes, we equalize sacrifice only by taking less than half of A's marginal dollar. This means that the marginal tax rate on A's income must be lower than that on B's, and indicates progression in the tax rate schedule.

But we have still not plowed through all of the theoretical problems. The paragraphs above, which indicate that progression is valid only when the marginal satisfactions from income fall more rapidly than income rises, proceeded under the assumption that we wish to attain equal sacrifice of utility from taxpayers in different income groups. But is equal sacrifice the bench mark we wish to use in a "fair" allocation of tax burdens? If we wish to think of taxes simply as a necessary evil in a society whose pattern of income distribution before taxes is the "right" pattern, we shall probably lean toward equality of sacrifice as our prime objective.[10] An alternative

---

[9] "Income" in this case means taxable income. An untaxed minimum of income may be allowed to both taxpayers. The rates would then apply to that income above the exempt minimum.

[10] See Walter J. Blum and Henry Kalven, Jr., *The Uneasy Case for Progressive Taxation,* University of Chicago Press, 1953, pp. 43–45, for a useful analysis of this question.

basis is that of distributing tax burdens so as to attain sacrifices from individuals *in proportion to* their incomes before taxes. In this case the sacrifice required from an income receiver would be only half that required from a person receiving an income twice as high. Assuming our first case above, where marginal utilities decline proportionately as income rises, if A, with a before-tax income of $5,000, is required to sacrifice the utilities represented by a tax payment of 10 per cent, then B, with a before-tax income of $10,000, would be asked to sacrifice utilities represented by 20 per cent of his income. B's tax would be four times that of A. In the first case, therefore, the proportional sacrifice rule calls for progressive taxation, while the equal sacrifice rule was seen to justify proportional taxation. In fact, if proportional sacrifices are sought, proportional taxes are indicated only in the very special situation when marginal utility does not decline at all. If A and B in our examples above experience the same marginal utilities from their different incomes, A will be asked to sacrifice half as much utility as B. Since A's income is half as large as B's, a proportional tax rate on income is required. Therefore, under the assumption that equity requires proportional sacrifice, any assumption that income utility diminishes justifies some degree of progression, the progression becoming steeper the more steeply the utility function diminishes. The proportional sacrifice rule thus possesses two possible virtues as compared with equal sacrifice: it reduces after-tax inequalities in total utilities, and its justification of some degree of progression is less dependent upon knowledge of the degree of diminution of the marginal utility of income. With regard to the latter, any assurance that marginal utility declines justifies progression; the steeper the decline the steeper the progression justified.

There is a third possible bench mark of justice among taxpayers—progressive sacrifice. Under this rule the sacrifice of utilities would be more than proportionate to income before tax. Here the marginal utility of income must be presumed to *rise* as income rises in order to justify proportional taxation, and a still wider range of possible cases justifies progression.

As we stand off and survey from a distance the role of diminishing marginal utility in the case for progressive taxation, what judgment can be made? The impossibility of measuring the utility function, of comparing the utility functions of different persons, and of determining relevant connections between the utility of a particular good and the utility of income, together with the difficulty of selecting among the bench marks relating sacrifice to equity, make diminishing utility a very weak reed upon which to lean the case for progression. At the same time these problems, while weakening the support which utility theory can give to progression, do not strengthen the case of proportional or regressive taxation. While they do not argue strongly for progression, neither do they argue for alternative bases for allocation of tax burdens.

3. In recent years the objectives of economic stability and growth have made a strong appeal for progressive taxation. Of principal importance has been the peculiar service of a progressive tax on income as an automatic counter-cyclical instrument. As money incomes rise, marginal dollars of income push into higher tax rate brackets, raising both the marginal and average tax rates on these incomes. If money incomes fall, both marginal and average tax rates fall. Two points are particularly noteworthy. The first is that because of progression in the rate schedule, taxes rise and fall more rapidly than income. At proportional rates, the tax "bite" would change in proportion to income, and at regressive rates less than proportionately. Of the three rate possibilities, progression thus has the largest counter-cyclical effect of all. The second point is that this effect is entirely automatic and almost immediate, requiring no legislative action. To be sure, the automatic and immediate reaction is not the result of progressive rates, but the result of having income as the tax base. But since the individual income tax is progressive, it is regarded as a total instrument reacting favorably, quickly, and strongly in the interest of stability.

There are other grounds on which progression serves stability and growth. By taxing relatively lightly the incomes of the mass of consumers—because the mass of people are at the lower end of the income scale—the economy tends to be undergirded with a mass of persistent consumption demand. Being rather stable over short periods, consumption provides a floor under economic declines and a brake to serious overinvestment or serious price inflation. As such, it is a powerful stabilizer. From the point of view of growth, high and persistently rising consumption over a period of time helps both to minimize the economic setbacks so restrictive of growth and to justify expansion of productive capacity. The opponents of progression argue that it is an enemy of growth by destroying investment incentives and by drying up the funds from which investment is made. One cannot escape the obvious fact, however, that the postwar period of high and progressive taxes has also been a period of rapid investment expansion —even including periods of overinvestment. On the face of it, something has encouraged investment growth in a high progressive tax period; surely the behavior of consumption has been of strategic significance in this.

4. Finally, the case for progression rests upon a value judgment by the society, in which certain goods are regarded as socially preferable to others. This amounts to an insistence that the pattern of income distribution be

such as to allocate—through individual demands—scarce resources toward the satisfaction of wants which it regards as real and worthwhile rather than trivial or indifferent. The problem of measuring the utilities of goods to individuals is eliminated, for it makes little or no difference how badly a person wishes to provide for a frivolous want. A social judgment is substituted in some degree for individual preference. And since it may be assumed that, among reasonably rational human beings, large incomes permit the satisfaction of frivolous demands more easily than small incomes, a case is made for relatively heavier taxation of large incomes. So long as the progressive rate schedule does not erode production incentives seriously, it accomplishes a redistribution of income and resources in a society which is productive of broad social welfare. This view of the problem of tax allocation is called by Professor Elmer Fagan the "sociopolitical" theory.[11] It make redistribution a major aim of policy, and one may guess that the wide public acceptance of progressive taxation is rather firmly rooted in this view.

Taken as a whole, the case for progressive taxation has been characterized as an "uneasy" one.[12] This is surely true of the historical tendency to rest the case upon diminishing marginal utility. But it is well to keep in mind that the weakness of the marginal utility basis for progression is its inability to prove a case; it does not disprove the case for progression. For the principle of diminishing utility makes no stronger case for proportion or regression than for progression. In fact the case is stronger for progression if we asume as the basis for proper allocation any but equal sacrifice. But the revenue productivity of a progressive tax, the facility with which it lends itself to compensatory use, and the redistribution argument present a strong case for progression, even with little or no help from diminishing utility. The question has become not whether progression is appropriate in an over-all tax system, but rather how severe a degree of progression is desirable.

Distribution of Burden in Sumptuary Taxation

There is no "theory" of sumptuary taxation distinct from the theory of the particular control function itself. If taxation is used to raise the price of a particular good (liquor, for example) with the purpose of discouraging consumption, the basis of allocation of the burden is simple. The person

[11] Elmer D. Fagan, "Recent and Contemporary Theories of Progressive Taxation," *Journal of Political Economy*, August, 1938, and reprinted in Musgrave and Shoup, *Readings in the Economics of Taxation*, Homewood, Illinois, R. D. Irwin, 1959.

[12] Blum and Kalven, *op. cit.*

taxed is the person whose potential consumption is to be discouraged. The tax must be so high as actually to discourage consumption, without reference to its revenue aspects. Obviously, in such a case, the more effective the tax weapon in accomplishing its sumptuary purpose, the less effective it is as a revenue measure. And if the commodity were taxed out of existence there would be no tax burden at all.

In the more general sense of sumptuary taxation—taxation to remove spendable or hoardable funds from the market—the theory of the tax is likewise the theory of control. It is not a question of "fairness" in the usual tax sense of the term, but a question of expediency. The burden of such taxation is not a necessary evil arising out of the need for revenue, but the means to a desired end. That is, stabilization of national income at a high employment level requires that income be taken from certain persons. The "burden" is therefore intended as the prime immediate objective of the tax, and the usual questions of fairness in distribution of the "burden" cannot arise.

What can we conclude with respect to the proper principles upon which to distribute counter-cycle tax burdens? The principle of expediency (if, indeed, it can be called a principle) will be dominant. That is, the major tax measures will possess large elements of elasticity, making possible quick and effective increase or decrease in tax burdens upon those segments of the economy whose disposable income after taxes is to be decreased or increased.

The proper allocation of tax burdens under a counter-cycle program will at any time depend upon the particular objectives to be accomplished. If the objective is an encouragement of investment, a lightening of tax burdens upon the income from risk capital is indicated. If encouragement of consumption is desired, reduction of taxes on lower incomes (and of course on consumption goods) will be desirable. The important point to be kept in mind is that conditions to be combated will vary at different times. The tax measures which provide for counter-cycle allocation of burden will thus lend themselves to expedient application to the circumstances.

Summary

In preparation for consideration of particular tax measures, we have considered the general foundations upon which the tax system as a whole should be built. We have noted that taxation for revenue purposes cannot utilize generally the principles of benefit and cost in determining the proper distribution of burdens among individuals. The reasons are that benefit and cost cannot often be reasonably allocated on an individual basis, and if they could, many important governmental functions would necessarily be discontinued.

The matter of fairness as between taxpayers evidently implies comparison of sacrifices involved. But no valid method exists by which these comparisons can be made with any degree of precision. This does not mean that the principle of fairness will be abandoned; it means that evident inequities will be avoided, and that any instinctive suppositions concerning justice which are widely held will tend to be implemented. However, there are other grounds upon which a system for distributing burdens can be built, notably the maximum contribution to economic stability and growth in the usual sense, and growth in terms of maximum social advantage in the kinds of goods and services produced. The matter of revenue productivity cannot be ignored in the long run, though the problem is to raise sufficient revenue without excessive cost in terms of discrimination, instability, or economic stagnation.

The principal necessary ingredient of a tax system designed to promote the required level of employment in a dynamic economy is flexibility, or ability to adjust quickly to changing requirements without violent overhaul. This use of the tax system will, from time to time, conflict with accepted notions of equity. As an example, an inflationary situation essentially caused by investment may require for its control heavier taxes on consumers, some of whom are underprivileged from any humanitarian point of view. As in all areas where the budget principle operates, choices are required both among ends and means. Those ends which are more immediate and more pressing can be expected to receive high priority. And when the society feels that it knows what it is doing—when the ends can be rationally justified and the means are dependable—it is likely to move ahead. For this reason the allocation of tax burdens will be largely determined by considerations of revenue productivity, stability and growth, and a reasonable degree of redistribution. The equity objective is likely to be served principally by not changing the rules radically with respect to a distribution system to which income groups have become accustomed.

RECOMMENDED READINGS

Blum, Walter J., and Kalven, Henry, Jr., *The Uneasy Case for Progressive Taxation,* Chicago, Univ. of Chicago, 1953.

    An effective attack on some traditional bases for progression.

Chapman, S. J., "The Utility of Income and Progressive Taxation," *Economic Journal,* March, 1913. Reprinted in Musgrave and Shoup (Eds.), *Readings in the Economics of Taxation,* Chapter 1.

    An early critique of the assumption that the case for progressivity can be based entirely on the principle of diminishing marginal utility.

Dalton, Hugh, *The Principles of Public Finance,* Third Edition, London, Routledge and Kegan Paul, 1952, Chapter 9.

An extensive analysis of various possible bases for tax-burden allocation on the assumption that the principle of equity is being pursued.

Fagan, Elmer D., "Recent and Contemporary Theories of Progressive Taxation," *Journal of Political Economy,* August, 1938. Reprinted in *ibid.,* Chapter 3.

Evaluation of the major bases for justification of progressive taxation, concluding that progressivity must finally rest on a sociopolitical judgment.

Lutz, Harley L., *Guideposts to a Free Economy,* N.Y., McGraw-Hill, 1945, Chapter 9.

In opposition to progressive taxation, by one of its most articulate opponents. Reprinted in H. L. Groves, *Viewpoints on Public Finance,* N.Y., Holt, Chapter 8.

CHAPTER 14

Tax Incidence and Other Effects

In Chapter 13 we pointed to two fundamental facts which must be borne in mind in any intelligent discussion of tax policy. The first is that, with minor exceptions, taxes eventually are paid from the streams of individual income. This led us to the conclusion that as far as possible the tax base should be individual income. Any alternative tax base is certain to be a less reliable measure of the income from which taxes are paid. The exceptions to this rule arise out of sumptuary taxation, where the control function may require more limited and specialized tax bases.

The second fundamental fact to which we referred was that the person upon whom the tax is originally imposed is not necessarily the person who bears its burden. This being the case, tax theory must offer conclusions as to who finally bears the burden resulting from imposition of a given tax. Unless this is done, undesired results will frequently be obtained. It is the purpose of this chapter to analyze in general terms the conditions under which the person on whom the tax is originally imposed can transfer its burden to others. The incidence of particular taxes will be considered in later chapters, as these taxes are described.

The Meaning of "Incidence"

When a tax is levied, its first impact will be felt by the *subject* of the tax, the person who actually makes the tax payment. He may be an income receiver, property owner, or a buyer or seller of goods and services. He may absorb the tax himself (bear it), or he may be able to shift the burden to someone else. In either case, there will be a series of secondary effects of more or less economic significance. Acceptance of the burden of the tax by the original subject will affect his disposable income, and therefore his demand for productive factors and for other commodities. Shifting the burden to someone else implies a change in disposable income of others. If the tax results in a higher price, the buyers will bear it, and will have less disposable income to spend for other products. If shifting the tax results in lower physical volume of transactions in the taxed commodity, the productive factors engaged in producing the good will experience lower total income. Thus, wherever the incidence of a tax is—whether it is shifted or not—a chain of economic effects is set in motion.

Our first problem is to select a concept of "shifting" and "incidence" which is meaningful and at the same time amenable to analysis. There is much to be said for defining incidence narrowly enough to exclude some part of the whole array of tax effects. We exclude first those effects which result from the expenditure by government of the taxed funds. Our study so far has given considerable attention to the effects of those expenditures taken by themselves. We exclude also the array of effects upon demands for products resulting from the fact that someone's income has been transferred to government through the operation of the tax. This is done primarily to avoid excessive complication of the analysis. We are left, then, with a definition of incidence as the locus of direct burden of the tax. If the subject of the tax does not shift it to someone else, the incidence is upon him. If he partially shifts it, the burden is upon others as well as himself. If he wholly shifts it, he escapes its burden entirely.

But even within this definition, two possible meanings are embraced. The first is to identify incidence with the subject of the tax and to equate the burden with the dollar value of the direct tax payment. If the tax (or some part of it) is shifted, the subject contributes the funds to government, but in the process of shifting there may be a net decline in the income of someone else. This latter person makes no direct financial contribution to government, but he incurs a loss of income he otherwise would have had. This second meaning is the more common usage of the term "incidence," though it still excludes a variety of indirect effects which would not have occurred had the tax not been imposed.

The Conditions of Tax Shifting

The Role of Price in Tax Shifting. As we turn our attention to tax incidence, we are interested in determining the conditions under which the original payer (subject) of the tax can reimburse himself by shifting its amount to others. If he can reimburse himself only partially, the incidence of the tax will be divided between him and others. The more closely we examine the conditions of tax shifting, the more clearly we see that shifting can occur only in connection with a price transaction. For in our economy there is no vehicle—except gifts—for reimbursement other than prices. By prices, of course, we mean not only the prices of goods and services but the prices of the factors of production (wages, salaries, interest, rents) as well. Thus, if a tax is shifted, some price will be changed to include the tax; i.e., it will be different from what it would have been if the tax had not been levied. This change in price may, however, be accomplished by a change in quality; the quality of the good may be altered while the price remains as before.

The inclusion of shifted taxes in price is a well-known market phenomenon, and constitutes a popular and reasonable argument against those "hidden" taxes which are readily shiftable.[1] In general, other things being equal, there is strong argument for promoting awareness of tax payment. It makes the taxpayer conscious of his contribution to government, and it removes from the seller the onus of responsibility for price increases due to taxes. Interesting attempts to make the buyer aware of taxes shifted to him are apparent in the gasoline tax, where price is typically calculated on price signs as basic price plus federal tax plus state tax; and in many sales taxes, where the law encourages either collection of the tax separately at the end of the transaction or the posting of prices exclusive of taxes.[2]

Forward and Backward Shifting. The shifting of a tax will involve a change in the price of something from what it otherwise would have been. When the tax is shifted *forward,* the price which constitutes the vehicle for shifting will increase. When a tax is shifted *backward,* the price which constitutes the vehicle for shifting will decrease as compared with what it would have been. There are some situations in which the buyer of the product upon which taxes will be levied at a subsequent stage can shift a part or all of it backward to the seller in the form of a lower buying price. It is essential to distinguish real backward shifting from inability of a seller to shift the tax forward. Suppose that after the shifting process is completed we find that a part of the incidence is upon the buyer and a part on the seller. To determine whether the tax was partially shifted forward from seller to buyer, or partially shifted backward from buyer to seller, we must

[1] The terms "direct" and "indirect" taxes, which have cut such a figure in court decisions in the past, are finally distinguishable in meaning only in terms of shiftability. Direct taxes are not shifted, while indirect types are. The decline in use of these terms can be accounted for by inability to make such broad generalizations with respect to many tax measures. As we shall see, a given tax may be shifted under certain conditions, while under other conditions it may be shifted only partially or not at all. To denominate particular taxes as direct or indirect is to oversimplify the question of incidence.

[2] On the other hand, there have been occasions due either to intent to mislead or to ignorance, when propagandizing efforts to emphasize the tax element in price have included both shifted and non-shifted taxes. Clearly, the price of a pair of overalls includes many shifted taxes on its production, but many taxes imposed upon makers or handlers are not shifted and thus do not enter into the price.

know upon whom government originally imposed the tax. If originally imposed upon the seller, we conclude that it was partially shifted forward; if originally imposed upon the buyer it was partially shifted backward.

We shall consider as examples two cases where real backward shifting may occur: unemployment compensation taxes on employers and processing taxes under the old Agricultural Adjustment Act. The taxes which create the reserves from which unemployment compensation benefits are paid under the Social Security Act are originally paid by employers. It is highly unlikely, however, that in the typical case any considerable part of the incidence of these taxes is upon the employer. Some part is normally shifted forward to the buyers of the employer's product, but a typically larger part is shifted backward to the employee in the form of lower wages than would otherwise be paid. When market conditions are brisk and when labor's bargaining power is strong the tendency would be to shift substantially the whole tax forward to buyers. But if demand for the product is not strong and the bargaining position of labor is weak, there will be a strong tendency to shift substantially the whole tax backward to labor. The employer against whom the tax is assessed thus is presented with two directions in which shifting may occur. The price of his product to buyers constitutes one vehicle for shifting, while the prices paid to his labor (and other factors) constitute another. Whether one or the other vehicle is the more available in given circumstances will depend upon the strength of demand for his product and the consequences to him of attempts to reduce wages. If both vehicles are unavailable he will bear the tax himself.

Under the Agricultural Adjustment Act of 1933, producers of various agricultural products were encouraged to pledge a reduction in production in return for governmental benefit payments. The fund from which benefits were to be paid was contributed by special taxes upon the processors of the commodities to be controlled. These taxes were thus originally paid by processors. The theory was that processing taxes would be shifted to consumers of processed agricultural products, and the justification for such an arrangement lay in the reasoning that, since consumers had long benefited from the low agricultural prices which worked hardship upon the farmer, relief of the farmer should be largely carried by consumers. A study by the Bureau of Agricultural Economics in 1937 drew the following conclusions with respect to incidence of these taxes:[3]

[3] Bureau of Agricultural Economics, *An Analysis of the Effects of the Processing Taxes Levied Under the Agricultural Adjustment Act, Washington,* 1937, pp. 4–7. This study represents an excellent example of the empirical approach to tax shifting and incidence, but it evidently adopts a much broader definition of shifting than we use here, for the expenditure of tax funds is a part of the analysis.

1. No processor of any of the commodities finally bore any appreciable part of the tax.

2. No distributor of any of the commodities finally bore any appreciable part of the tax.

3. When the demand for the processed good was relatively inelastic (i.e., wheat, rye, cotton products, corn products, cigarettes, and chewing tobacco), the major incidence was upon consumers. When demand for the processed good was relatively elastic, or subject to special control (i.e., hog products, cigars, smoking tobacco, and sugar), the tax was not shifted forward in appreciable degree.

4. The major part of the taxes on hog products, cigars, smoking tobacco, and sugar was shifted backward to farm producers.

The processing taxes demonstrate clearly the possible directions in which taxes may be shifted. Whether a tax is shifted forward or backward depends upon the relative strength of the resistance to transfers of the burden. The very fact of low agricultural prices due to overproduction testifies to the weakness of the farmer's position in resisting backward shifting. Those processed commodities for which consumer demand was relatively elastic found greater resistance to forward than to backward shifting, while those goods sold under inelastic demand conditions found less resistance to forward shifting.[4]

A special, though not unusual, type of backward shifting is what is called *tax capitalization*. It occurs in cases where the good is a durable good, and thus is subject to a series of successive annual taxes during its lifetime. If the whole series of future taxes on the good is to be shifted backward at time of purchase, the future taxes must be capitalized and deducted in a lump sum from price offered. For there will be no later opportunity—no price vehicle—for backward shifting. The only difference between backward shifting of the taxes on a durable good and backward shifting of the tax on a nondurable good is in the computation of the dollar amount to be

---

[4] A relatively elastic demand is one in which a small change in price will meet with a relatively large change in quantity taken. In such a case, given a quantity to be marketed, forward shifting of the tax (with consequent price increase) would mean a considerable unsold surplus, and the farmer's position would be relatively weak. The whole quantity of his products ready for market would not be taken by processors. A relatively inelastic demand is one in which a given change in price meets a relatively slight change in quantity taken. Here the conditions are reversed, and consumer defenses against forward shifting are weak, since price increases are accompanied by little shrinkage of the market. (If under conditions of inelastic consumer demand the processed product is sold under highly monopolistic conditions, it is presumed that the consumer price is already at a maximum, and consumer demand, though inelastic, will strongly resist further price increase. In such a case it is the expected outcome that considerable backward shifting will occur and quite likely some considerable absorption of the tax by processors.)

deducted from the price offered. In all cases of backward shifting the buyer pays the tax to government, but the seller bears the burden of incidence.

Suppose I were to consider purchase of a piece of agricultural land, and my estimates as to average annual income and expense were as follows:

Value of gross annual product	$5,000
Total cost of production, excluding property taxes	3,500
Net income before property taxes	1,500
Annual property taxes	300
Net income	$1,200

By purchasing this piece of land, therefore, I would be making a capital investment which I calculate would return me net $1,200 per year. If I am willing to invest my savings at a rate of return of 5 per cent per year, I would be willing to pay $24,000 for the land.[5] The annual net return of $1,200 would then be the required 5 per cent on my investment, and I could pay no more than $24,000 for the land unless I either revise my estimate of probable net income upward or my required rate of return downward.

But suppose there were no property taxes anticipated. According to the calculations, net income per year would then be $1,500, and I could afford to pay $30,000 for the land, still receiving 5 per cent on my investment. Thus, because property taxes are estimated to take $300 yearly, the price I am willing to pay for the land is $6,000 less than it would be if no taxes were anticipated. And $6,000 is $300/.05, or the capitalized value of the annual tax. Because the tax has reduced the price which I am willing to pay by $6,000, the tax of $300 per year for all time has been shifted backward to the seller. Of course the seller may not sell the land to me because someone else offers a higher price. Any higher price offered, however, must be due to (1) an estimate of higher net income before taxes than $1,500, and/or (2) a lower rate of return on investment than 5 per cent, and/or (3) an estimate of annual taxes lower than $300 per year. But whatever the alternate buyer calculates these figures to be, the tax will be capitalized and the price offered will on that account be less than would have been offered if no taxes were anticipated. Unless they can shift the new taxes forward, current owners of land will bear the incidence of any additional taxes imposed subsequent to or unforeseen at the time of purchase.[6]

We have pictured tax capitalization in terms of a simple example. There

---

[5] The capital value of a "perpetual annuity" is: annual net income/rate of return required. In this case: $1,200/.05=$24,000.

[6] Land used for business purposes generally offers opportunity to shift new and unanticipated property taxes forward as a part of the price of the product. Land used for consumption (e.g., residential) purposes offers no such opportunity; taxes not capitalized and thus not shifted backward at the time of purchase of the land have their incidence upon the owner.

are, however, wide applications of the same principle. Capitalization occurs at the time of purchase of real estate, and of many durable consumers' goods. It may also occur on the occasion of purchase of investment securities and durable producers' goods.

Of particular interest is tax capitalization in connection with the purchase of investment securities. The purchaser of a share of corporate stock will determine what he can pay by a calculation exactly like that in our agricultural land example. He will obviously capitalize the tax unless he is willing to pay for an opportunity to pay annual taxes. This is particularly true if he buys for investment (to receive income), but if he buys for speculation he must recognize the future level of income taxation (corporate and personal) as being an important determinant of the price at which he can sell in the future.[7]

We are dealing here with a principal reason for exemption from taxation of the income from state and local government bonds.[8] For if government bond coupons are tax-exempt, there is no tax capitalization and the capital value of the bonds is higher than it would be if taxed. This is particularly true when the income from other investments is taxed; government bonds are given "especial" price support in the market. The consequence is that with the tax exemption advantage the demand for a government bond would be strong—other things being equal—even at lower rates of coupon interest than non-tax-exempt bonds pay. But though tax exemption will result in interest savings to the treasury of the issuing government, there may be serious question whether exemption is on the whole fiscally desirable. For if income taxes are steeply progressive and government bonds are largely held by the high income classes, the tax loss to the treasury from exemption may be greater than the gain in lower interest. Recognition of this fact is largely responsible for the abandonment during the last three decades of tax exemption of its bonds by the federal government. Here is a case where the fact of tax capitalization has become an important determinant of policy.

[7] When the tax is so general as to apply to all incomes, investment or otherwise, the total effect may be to lower generally the rates at which individuals are willing to invest. For if all income is subject to the same rate of taxation, given the propensity to save, the effect will be to generate a general willingness to invest at a lower return after taxes. Considerable saving does occur regardless of the income available from investments. Given savings, there is little choice under general taxation as to whether one purchases securities whose income is taxed. Thus, the long-run effect will probably be a lower required rate of return to bring forth investment. If such occurs, prices of investment securities may not permanently fall in spite of tax capitalization, prices being supported by a lower effective rate of return.

[8] Also exemption of the bonds themselves from property taxes.

We have seen that there are three distinct, though not mutually exclusive, possible incidence results when a tax is imposed. It may be shifted forward from seller to buyer in the form of an increased price. Capitalization does not enter into forward shifting because when the seller disposes of title to the thing sold he retains no future tax liability related to it. The tax may be shifted backward from buyer to seller in the form of a decreased price. When purchase involves nondurable goods or services, the amount of the single tax payment establishes the maximum amount to be shifted. If a durable item is purchased, the amount which the buyer attempts to shift backward is the capitalized value of future tax obligations related to ownership of the item. The person upon whom the tax originally falls will attempt to shift it either forward or backward. He can do neither if there is no price which can be used as a vehicle for shifting the tax, and the incidence will be upon him. If vehicles exist for either forward or backward shifting, he will follow the path of least resistance, which will be measured in terms of all the foreseeable effects upon him which shifting in either direction would set in motion. Obviously, then, some taxes are not shifted at all, some are shifted forward, some backward, and in the cases of some the incidence is divided. The state of the market will, in the short run, be the important determinant of the degree and direction of shifting.

General Analysis of Tax Shifting and Incidence

In this chapter we shall deal with the problem of shiftability in rather general terms, postponing discussion of shifting of particular tax measures in connection with later chapters dealing with those taxes. For the present we discuss shifting in terms of general categories of taxes: those imposed upon net income, those imposed upon property ownership, and those imposed upon the production or sale of goods.

1. Taxes Imposed on Net Income. A tax imposed generally upon individual net income is typically not shifted. If we assume that personal incomes before taxes—whether composed of salaries, wages, rent, interest, or profit—are at a maximum justified by the productivity of the factors of production, there is nothing in the imposition of the tax which permits raising before-tax incomes.[9] In the longer run, if the tax were to apply only to particular incomes over a broad area or if it were to apply to all incomes in a narrow geographical area, the migration of labor, capital, or natural

[9] As noted earlier, we exclude from our analysis the effects of government spending of the tax receipts, which could increase aggregate demand for products and thus increase value-productivity of some factors. This could justify increases in some before-tax incomes.

resources to untaxed employments or to untaxed geographical areas would create scarcities in the taxed areas which would tend to raise before-tax incomes there.[10] But if we assume a personal income tax broadly applied to all net incomes in all geographical areas, the prospects for shifting the tax are very slim.

This conclusion rests crucially upon the assumption that particular incomes were already at their maximum justified by the market situation before the tax was imposed. If not, bargaining by some income receivers for a larger share of the aggregate may be successful. But this means a reduction of incomes to others, and is a matter of distribution alone. If these observations appear to rest upon too static assumptions with respect to aggregate income and its distribution, let us assume that a rise in incomes occurs over a period of time. In this case, is there reason to believe that the tax will alter the distribution of that rising income from what it would have been without the tax? If the tax is general in application, there is no reason to believe that the tax itself gives any income group a bargaining position it would not otherwise have had. Thus, there is no reason to believe that individuals will be able to shift the tax backward.

The conclusion that a general personal income tax does not change the prices of productive factors and thus is not shifted is implicit in most policy discussions. In those discussions the economic dangers of high personal income taxation are not that prices will thereby be raised. If demand for the product is being fully exploited, how can higher payments to the factors be reimbursed to the business in higher prices? The principal danger is that the tax may change the balance between productive effort and leisure, by encouraging the subject of the tax, who also bears it, to put forth less effort. This would reduce the productiveness of the economy and slow down the rate of growth. But the possibility of this outcome may easily be overstressed. When persons receiving higher incomes are in a constant competition with those lower in the scale who would be happy to receive more income, the former cannot afford to lie down on the job.[11]

The consequent reduction in output could result in higher factor pay-

[10] But presumably not all incomes in these taxed areas could rise; some would rise at the expense of others, if the expenditure effects of tax revenues are excluded. For there is nothing in the picture to lead us to expect that the sources of total income in taxed areas would rise. Thus, some incomes would rise at the expense of others, and presumably profit incomes would suffer. But even this could not continue indefinitely without the disappearance of unprofitable firms and a worsening of employment in the taxed area.

[11] This assumes, of course, that the marginal rate of taxation is less than 100 per cent, so that some part of additional income is always left to the income receiver after taxes.

ment rates, and thus in higher prices, if aggregate monetary demand were to remain the same. In the long run, then, some shifting of the tax to buyers of products would occur. Our conclusion must be that, since the personal income tax provides the income receiver no implement for the increase of his before-tax income, the imposition of the tax will not change costs of production and therefore will not urge price increases.[12] But in saying this we must recall our assumption that optimum price-quantity relations are in effect before imposition of the tax, and that optimum distribution of factor payments is also in effect. If there were unexploited possibility in the market for increasing pretax profit, and if there were unexploited power in the hands of one factor to increase its share of total return, the firm or factor might well be encouraged to take advantage of this unexploited margin.

We turn now to the shiftability of a tax imposed upon the net income of a business firm.[13] Our analysis must be pursued in terms of the factors affecting price, quantity of output, and profit of the business firm. We begin with the assumption that, given the conditions of demand and of competition facing the firm, it will be maximizing its net income before imposition of the tax. The question is whether, after the tax is imposed, a different price-quantity relationship will maximize income. If so, shifting of the tax will occur.

The net income of a firm will be maximized at that price-output point where marginal revenue and marginal cost are equal. Since marginal revenue is the additional gross revenue received as output sold is increased, and marginal cost is additional gross cost as output is increased, it follows that if net income is to be at a maximum the firm should sell all units for which marginal revenue exceeds marginal cost and no units for which marginal cost exceeds marginal revenue. Let us take a hypothetical example of the marginal cost, revenue, and profit of a given firm, as presented in Table 24.

The 200th unit adds $7 to net income (ignoring fixed costs); the 300th unit adds $4.67; the 400th unit adds $2.33; and the 500th unit nothing. Thus, to maximize net income (or minimize net loss), all units up to 500 should be produced and sold, and none beyond the 500th unit. The sale of 500 units at a price of $6 maximizes net income. Now let us assume the imposition of

[12] It may reduce demands by reducing disposable individual incomes, and thus prevent price increases. But this sort of consideration we have ruled out of our discussion as an indirect effect of the tax and thus not relevant under our definition to the matter in hand.

[13] Federal and state net income and excess profits taxes on corporations are of this type. Net income taxes have not been applied to unincorporated businesses, primarily because of the difficulty in pursuing a consistent definition of net income for such a heterogeneous collection of firms.

TABLE 24

MARGINAL COST, MARGINAL REVENUE, AND NET INCOME OF A HYPOTHETICAL FIRM

1	2	3	4	5	6
Quantity of Output	Demand Price Per Unit	Total Revenue	Marginal[a] Revenue	Marginal Cost[a]	Marginal Add'n to Total Net Income
100	$10	$1,000	$10		
200	9	1,800	8	$1.00	$7.00
300	8	2,400	6	1.33	4.67
400	7	2,800	4	1.67	2.33
500	6	3,000	2	2.00	0.00
600	5	3,000	0	2.33	−2.33
700	4	2,800	−2	2.67	−4.67
800	3	2,400	−4	3.00	−7.00
900	2	1,800	−6	3.33	−9.33
1,000	1	1,000	−8	3.67	−11.67

[a] Average unit revenue or cost for marginal increments of 100 units.

a tax upon net income at the rate of 10 per cent. The marginal additions to net income *after tax* will be as follows:

Quantity of Output	Marginal[a] Tax	Marginal Addition to Net Income After Tax
200	$.70	$6.30
300	.47	4.20
400	.23	2.10
500	0	0

[a] 10 per cent of column 6, Table 24; or, the amount by which the total tax is increased by selling the marginal unit.

A comparison of the last column with that in Table 24 indicates that the tax moderates the additions to net income. But the important fact is that after-tax income is still at a maximum (or after-tax loss at a minimum) with the output of 500 units. The firm could raise its price by reducing output, but this would reduce its net income both before and after tax below the maximum possible in the market. It is often said that net income taxes are a cost to a corporation, that these taxes will be added to price, and that the tax thereby will be at least partially shifted. The tax may be incorporated as a cost, but even so the profit maximizing price-quantity relationship will remain unchanged. Thus, if the firm consistently operates in such a way as to maximize net income, the price-quantity relationship will not change and the tax will not be shifted. The above treatment may be checked by noting that so long as the marginal tax rate on net income is less than 100 per cent, maximum net income before taxes will always give maximum net income after taxes.

In the short run, with demand and other costs given and profit-maximization assumed, a tax on business net income is not shiftable. The maximum net income is reduced by the tax, and its incidence is upon the firm's claimants—proprietors, partners, or shareholders—to net income. In the longer run, any changes in demand or cost not attributable to the tax will not alter this conclusion. For if at a later date the figures in columns 2 or 5 of Table 24 have changed (for nontax reasons), the analysis above continues to apply. The profit maximizing price-output relationship may change, but the existence of the tax will not make this relationship any different from what it would have been without the tax.

But also in the longer run the fact that incidence of the tax is upon profit receivers may create a shift in the demand schedule facing the firm. If inadequate profit after tax forces some firms from the market, the remaining firms may be able to sell larger quantities at the same prices, or the same quantities at higher prices. Here the tax—over a period of time—has created a situation in which net income claimants have become reimbursed through higher maximum profits than they had immediately upon imposition of the tax. In this situation, shifting of the tax or some part of it has occurred through higher prices brought about by realignment of the industry. Indirectly, therefore, the tax has been shifted over a period of time.

Some evidence that corporation taxes have been shifted in the longer run is given by the fact that the rate of return after taxes on invested capital in manufacturing corporations has remained more or less constant since 1927. Lerner and Hendrickson[14] found this to be true, if cyclical fluctuations are eliminated, in spite of an increase in the effective rate of tax from 11.7 per cent in 1927 to 54.6 per cent in 1952. The conclusion, however, should be accepted with caution, for, as these authors point out, other changes than the rise in tax rate occurred during the period. The first was a vast increase in output per unit of capital investment, resulting from technological improvements. Second, the continued prosperity during and following World War II meant an almost consistently high utilization of plant capacity. Third, profits are made on current dollars, while investment tends to be carried at original cost, and a period of price inflation will increase the rate of return on investment so measured. The first of these explanations would seem to imply that since the tax is not shiftable, the firm reaches for cost-cutting techniques to increase its profits per dollar of investment in order to offset the tax bite on prices. The second and third explanations suggest that fortunate circumstances have produced enough increase in before-tax profit to offset the rise in tax rates on that profit. At the same time, however, the second explanation refers to conditions of strong demand

[14] Eugene M. Lerner and Eldon S. Hendrickson, "Federal Taxes on Corporate Income and the Rate of Return on Investment in Manufacturing, 1927 to 1952," *National Tax Journal*, September, 1956.

in which it is most likely that a tax could be shifted. It would be rash to conclude that the constancy of the rate of return on investment proves that the tax is completely shifted. Lacking knowledge of what prices and profits would have been today had not corporate taxes risen makes such a simple generalization impossible. But it is difficult to escape the conclusion that, since a theoretical possibility of long-run shifting exists, some shifting should have occurred through a period of high and rather persistent prosperity.

2. Taxes Imposed on Property Ownership. The principal tax in this category is the local tax on real and personal property. In the same category are recurring licenses and permits and some minor taxes on the use of items of property. An annual tax on durable property used for consumption—e.g., a residence lived in by its owner—cannot be shifted except as the tax is capitalized and shifted backward at the time of purchase, because no recurring price vehicle exists for the purpose of shifting. The same is true of a recurring registration fee or tax on a pleasure automobile. Any amount of tax on property used for consumption which was not foreseen and capitalized when the property was purchased will fall upon the property owner and cannot be shifted.

Taxes on property used in the production and sale of goods are a different matter, however, for recurring opportunities to shift the tax are present. If such a tax is in the nature of a fixed cost, i.e., if the tax is imposed upon a building, a machine, or fixtures, the amount of the tax is independent of short-run variations in sales. (A property tax on inventory would not be a fixed cost, assuming inventory to vary with sales.) A firm which wishes to select a profit-maximizing price-quantity relationship within the capacity of its plant would select that relationship where marginal revenue and marginal cost are equal. But fixed costs do not affect marginal costs after the first unit of output, and the price-quantity relationship which produces maximum profit before tax would produce maximum profit after tax. We conclude, therefore, that such a tax, though it raises total costs, will not be shifted in the short run, provided a policy of precise profit-maximizing is pursued. There is, however, a real possibility that under popular business practice, the tax would be shifted to some degree. It is widespread practice for firms to treat fixed costs as a fixed percentage addition to variable costs of production—treating them, in fact, as if they were variable with volume of output. If this is done, the point of equality between marginal revenue and marginal cost would show maximum profit at a smaller output, and call for a higher price. In such a case forward shifting would occur. How much of the tax would be shifted would depend upon the direction of miscalculation. For the point of maximum profit has been miscalculated if fixed costs are treated as variable, and an increased addition to marginal costs when the tax is imposed continues and may compound the miscalculation. The whole question of mishandling of costs (or incorrectly estimating demand) contravenes our assumption of profit maximization; if that assumption is discarded an entirely different type of analysis of shifting is required.

In the long run, however, as in the case of the corporate income tax, property taxes affecting fixed costs are at least partially shiftable. For a rise in fixed costs is a rise in real costs to the firm. If the profit after taxes is inadequate to justify continuance in business, some firms will eventually leave the market. Assuming stable aggregate monetary demand for the product, the demand functions facing remaining firms will be higher, and quite possibly steeper. This would permit price rises by the remaining firms and some recouping from buyers of taxes paid by producers. How much of the tax can be shifted forward in the long run will depend upon a variety of factors, most of which can be embraced by the concept of the elasticity of demand and cost.[15]

3. Taxes on the Production or Sale of Goods. Sales and excise taxes are the most common forms of taxes found under this category. The tax is imposed only once, at the point of production or sale, and thus capitalization does not enter into our analysis. But either forward or backward shifting is possible.

The unit taken for the analysis is the individual business firm, upon which the tax originally falls and in which price and production policies are determined. We assume again the objective of maximized profit for the firm, given a demand situation determined outside the firm and a cost situation largely influenced by externally determined factor prices. The case selected for diagramming is that of imperfect competition, where the seller or producer is one of a sufficiently small number so that a change in his output will have an effect upon the price he can get.[16] We shall assume a specific tax levied at a constant rate per unit produced or sold. An *ad valorem* tax

[15] Demand elasticity is the relationship between the percentage change in quantity of the good taken and the change in its price. Cost elasticity is the relationship between the change in output and the change in cost. An inelastic demand is characterized by a relatively small change in quantity taken with a given change in price. In an inelastic cost function, a small change in output will be accompanied by a larger percentage change in cost. When demand is highly elastic, a small rise in price will result in a large decrease in quantity taken. An elastic demand therefore discourages (with other things equal) attempts to shift a tax forward through a price increase. An elastic cost function also discourages forward shifting, for a decline in output resulting from a price rise lowers marginal costs only slightly. These concepts are developed and applied more fully in the next section.

[16] In a case of pure competition the individual seller is so insignificant in total market output that changes in his quantity of output will have no measurable effect upon the market price.

would take a constant per cent of the price per unit. If the firm faces a downward-sloping demand curve, a larger output would bring a smaller unit price, and therefore a smaller dollar tax return per unit.

If the firm wishes to maximize its net return it should produce to the output where its marginal revenue and marginal cost are equal—where it is selling every unit which adds more to total revenue than to total cost, and no units beyond this quantity. On the diagram, this is 500 units, for MC_1 is the marginal cost before tax, and MR the marginal revenue as derived from the demand curve labeled DD'. The tax is $1 per unit, and when we add this tax to MC_1 we get a new marginal cost MC_2. Now the new equilibrium quantity of output is less than 500 units (about 457 units) and the equilibrium price has risen from P_1 to P_2 (from $6 to about $6.43). Let us see what has happened with respect to the incidence of the tax when the firm adjusts to the new equilibrium resulting from the addition of the tax to former costs.

We note first that the price has risen, but by less than the amount of the tax. We note also that the quantity sold has fallen. Finally, the marginal cost exclusive of the tax (MC_1) is lower at the new equilibrium than it was at an output of 500 units before the tax was imposed. The original impact of the tax was upon the seller of the good—he advanced the tax to government. He then proceeded to shift the tax, as far as possible, to the buyer of the product by raising its price. But the elasticity of demand is such that if he were to raise the price by the whole amount of the tax, the number of units he could sell would be so severely reduced as to cost him heavily in profit. So he raises the price to P_2, where he maximizes profit under the new conditions, partially reimbursing himself for the tax advance he has made. But he does not completely reimburse himself, for his total profit after tax will be less than it was before. The incidence is thus divided between the seller and the buyers of his product.

With the reduction in output, marginal cost of the factors falls somewhat. That is, the distance from the base axis to MC_1 is shorter at 457 units than at 500 units. His total outlay to the factors of production is less for the smaller output than for the larger. This does not, however, imply that some part of the tax is shifted to the factors of production. They bear a burden, to be sure, of disemployment, but this results from a reduction of output and only indirectly from the payment of the tax. The factors do not reimburse the seller for a tax advanced; they lose income because the attempt to shift the tax to buyers reduces the number of units sold. If the factors were to assume part of the tax, the curve MC_1 would fall, reflecting lower rates of payment to them. This does not occur in the short run, though in the longer

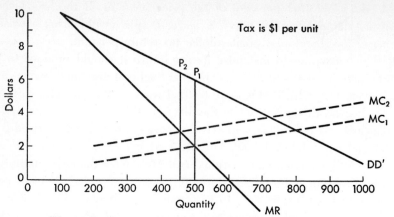

Figure 9. Tax as constant addition to variable costs.
(imperfect competition)

run disemployment of factors could push their rates of remuneration downward.

Figure 9 pictures a situation of partial shifting which may well be a fairly common case in the short period. There are, of course, a multitude of other cases which might be considered. The differences, however, boil down to differences in the elasticity of demand and/or cost facing the individual firm. In Figure 10 we take a marginal cost function (MC_1) exclusive of tax, and indicate the effects which different demand elasticities will bring about. Demand curve D is more elastic throughout than demand D', and the marginal revenue curve for each of these demands (MR and MR', respectively) is shown. If a seller is intent upon maximizing net income, he will press output to the point where marginal revenue and marginal cost are equal. This is point E_1, with respect to both demand functions. Under demand D, the equilibrium price before tax is P_1Q_1 ($4) and the equilibrium quantity OQ_1 (400 units). Under demand D', the price is P'_1Q ($9) and the quantity OQ_1 (400 units).

The imposition of the excise at a rate of $1 per unit will raise marginal cost for all quantities by $1, giving a cost curve MC_2 including tax. The equilibrium points under the two conditions of demand are now different (E_2 and E'_2). The new equilibrium under the more elastic demand (D) gives a price P_2Q_2 and a quantity OQ_2. Under the less elastic demand (D'), the new equilibrium price will be at $P'_2Q'_2$ and quantity will be at OQ'_2. The price increases by a smaller amount when the demand is more elastic, but the quantity decrease is larger. Thus, the tax is more easily shiftable forward to buyers when the demand is less elastic. It is evident that resist-

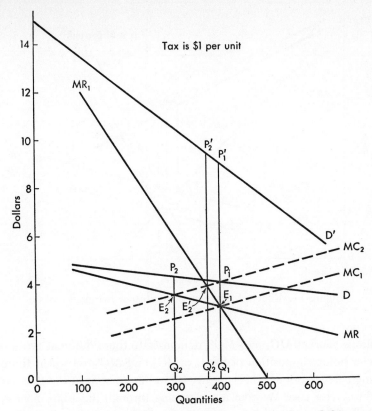

Figure 10. Effect of different elasticities of demand on shifting.

ance of buyers to forward shifting of the tax has meaning only in terms of the elasticity of demand. Resistance is great when demand is highly elastic; high elasticity means that for a given amount of price increase, the quantity taken falls off by a relatively large amount. And a large decline in taking has an adverse effect upon the total net income of the seller. The extreme case would be that in which elasticity is infinite—when the demand curve is horizontal. In this case, any increase in price would, in the short run, reduce the quantity taken to zero. On the other hand, inelasticity of demand reflects the inability of buyers to do without the product; they do not significantly withdraw from the market at higher prices. This makes them fair game for forward shifting.

The behavior of costs in the firm—the rate at which the unit cost of production changes with changes in output—will also affect the shiftability of a tax on the production or sale of a good. Figure 11 shows two quite different marginal cost curves under given demand and marginal revenue

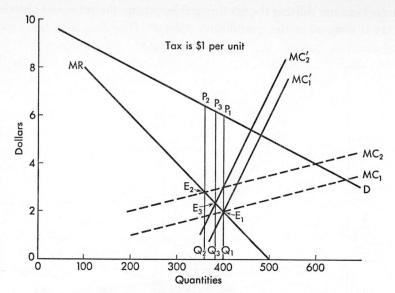

Figure 11. **Effect of different elasticities of marginal cost on shifting.**

conditions. Curves MC_1 and MC'_1 demonstrate these different types of cost behavior before imposition of the tax. MC_2 and MC'_2 represent the corresponding cost situations when the tax (equal in amount in the two cases) is added to factor cost. Without again tracing through the adjustment process in detail, the price under cost conditions MC_2 rises from P_1 to P_2, while under cost conditions MC'_2 the price rises only from P_1 to P_3. While the price increase is greater when marginal unit cost rises less abruptly, the decline in quantity sold is also greater. The reason for this is that the firm producing under rapidly rising marginal cost is adding very much more substantially to its total net income as the last few units are sold than is the firm producing under more gradually rising marginal cost. (These additions to total profit are measured by the vertical distances between marginal revenue and marginal cost.) Thus, as the firm with a steep marginal cost function raises its price, these highly profitable marginal units are sacrificed, and the firm's total profit falls relatively fast.[17] This firm is discouraged from raising its price markedly, because inherent in the quantity reduction which accompanies even a slightly higher price is a rapid loss of profit. The best com-

[17] Note that the angle E_2, which is equal to the corresponding angle at E_1, is considerably smaller than the angle E_3, which is equal to the corresponding angle at E_1. Thus, as we reduce output by falling back to the left of E_1, the loss of profit is much more rapid for the firm producing under cost conditions MC' than for the firm producing under cost conditions MC.

promise between shifting the tax forward by raising the price and absorbing the tax is realized at the equilibrium point E_3. The firm with less rapidly rising marginal costs can better afford to accept the consequences of forward shifting through a higher price. Thus, with other things equal, the less elastic the marginal cost function the greater the resistance to forward shifting of the tax.

The preceding paragraphs have considered the possible incidence of a tax imposed upon the production or sale of a good in the short run. We find that upon its imposition—or an increase in rate of a tax of longer standing—the normal presumption is that the original subject of the tax partially shifts it forward in the form of a higher price, and partially bears the incidence himself. The extent to which he will shift it forward will depend upon the degree of resistance met, both from the demanders of the product and from internal cost conditions of his firm. The more elastic the demand, the greater the resistance to forward shifting. And the less the rate of change in marginal cost the greater the resistance. The reader can prove to himself that if, in a very special case, the demand were infinitely elastic, no forward shifting could occur in the short period. And if the marginal cost were zero in elasticity—the curve being perfectly vertical—no forward shifting could occur in the short run.[18]

In the long run there may be opportunities for both forward and backward shifting which are not present in the short period. Any partial absorption of the tax by the seller in the short run will reduce net return below what it was before the tax was imposed or below what it would have been in the absence of the tax. Firms which had been or would have been marginal will incur losses. As they disappear from the market, the demand facing the remaining firms strengthens—i.e., the demand curve rises. And as this occurs, price may be raised without a fall in quantity sold, thus permitting forward shifting over a course of time.

To the degree that short-run forward shifting reduces the quantity sold, there will be some disemployment of factors of production. If these factors are not absorbed elsewhere, they may tend to force down the rates of remuneration to employed factors. This would, in time, lower the marginal cost function and—other things being equal—create a new profit-maximizing equilibrium at a larger output and a lower price. To the extent that this occurs, the tax tends to be shifted backward to the productive factors.

The reader may have already observed that in the analysis of short-run incidence we have been entirely concerned with movements along given

---

[18] In this case there would be no point in incorporating the tax into the marginal cost, for such a curve implies only one technically possible quantity of output.

curves of demand and cost. When we concern ourselves with questions of long-run incidence we look for factors which change the slope or position of the curves themselves. This is not very startling when we realize that the concept of the short run has implicit in it demand and cost conditions which are given and unchanging. The longer run is properly defined as a period long enough to permit changes in demand and cost structures.

The matter of short-run incidence is one of adjustment by the taxed seller within strictly limited circumstances. He can raise his price at the expense (in most cases) of smaller output within fixed demand and cost structures. In the longer run there is more room to maneuver. He can alter his productive capacity through depreciation or otherwise. He can alter the productivity per dollar of investment in his plant through improved technology, thus affecting his cost structure. He may be able to influence demand for his product through product improvement or mere salesmanship. And beyond the changes which he can himself bring about, there may be changes outside his control in the business cycle, public tastes, income, products, the prices of factors of production, and even population.

Other Influences upon Tax Shifting

We have observed the nature of internal factors in the market which affect the degree and direction of tax shifting. These are: (1) whether any price vehicle is available by which the tax can be shifted, (2) whether the incorporation of the tax into cost changes the price-quantity equilibrium under which profit is maximized, and (3) the elasticities of demand and supply for the taxed seller.[19]

But there are other factors which should be noted as playing some part in the shifting process, some of which have been implied in our discussion of long-run incidence. The type of tax law can have real effect upon the shiftability of a tax. For example, the advertising or posting of prices less tax assists in the forward shifting process. The unsophisticated buyer decides to buy on the basis of advertised or posted price, and does not frequently change his mind when the tax is added. Likewise, the collection of sales taxes at the cash register after parcels are wrapped helps to break down buyer resistance to forward shifting. The imposition of taxes upon some items while leaving substitutes untaxed strengthens resistance to forward shifting of these taxes.

The existence of customary prices in the market militates in the short

---

[19] The term "supply" is used here to refer generally to cost conditions. While marginal cost and supply are identical under purely competitive conditions, there is no such thing as a supply curve in the literal sense in imperfect competition.

run against forward shifting to the consumer. The custom of a five cent cigar, a five cent candy bar, or a dollar watch means that the seller stands to lose valuable good will by raising his price.[20] This is particularly true in cases where the price has traditionally been a small, round sum, or where the seller has stressed price in his sales campaign. To raise the price of what had come to be known as a "dollar watch" to $1.10 would have far more serious consequences to demand than would raising the price of a $24.95 watch to $27.45, though both would represent a 10 per cent increase. And after the successful expenditure of millions of dollars of advertising budget to sell smoking tobacco *because of its price,* the seller will be extremely hesitant to discard the good will so engendered by raising the price to shift a new tax.

Closely allied to the fact of customary price is the size of the tax in relation to price of the good. If the tax were at the rate of 5 per cent imposed upon the manufacture of a good, this tax might well be shifted forward. The manufacturer's bulk price for large quantities sold to wholesalers will generally permit of a percentage increase. But suppose at the retail level the commodity has been selling at five cents per unit, and the quantity commonly purchased at retail is one unit at a time. If the tax were completely shifted down to the retailer and he were to shift it on the consumer, the retail price should be more than five cents and less than six cents. In such a case the retailer is frequently wise to absorb the shifted tax himself, and to resist shifting to him as far as is possible.

The geographical coverage of the tax law can be an important determinant of shiftability. The administrative authority of a city or a state extends to the boundaries of that city or state. In the nineteen-thirties, when considerable variation in the level of state gasoline taxes existed, one could travel from a low-tax state to a high-tax state without experiencing an immediate change in the price of gasoline. If the tax had been completely shifted in each state, there would have been an abrupt change in price as the state line was crossed. The fact that this was not the case indicates that resistance to shifting was great, and was due to the availability of a lower-priced substitute (gasoline bearing lower tax) in a neighboring market. In the interior of the high-taxed state, prices were typically higher, because of insulation from low-price competition, and the tax was almost completely shifted. At the border, where forward shifting was impossible without seriously reducing sales, it is nevertheless unlikely that any major share of

[20] But the tax can frequently be shifted forward just as effectively by reduction of quantity or quality of the goods' content, so that the five cent candy bar may be made smaller or of poorer quality.

the tax was borne by the individual retail distributor. The major share was typically borne by refiner-wholesalers, who were able to maintain gallonage of output at retail only by quoting lower base prices to their retail distributors.[21]

The size of the taxed area will always affect shiftability of a tax on the production or sale of a commodity. When the good can be bought in near-by untaxed markets, an attempt at forward shifting will meet vigorous resistance, caused by the availability of untaxed competing goods. Although the size of the taxed area does not typically affect the *shifting* of income taxes or taxes on the ownership of property used for consumption (e.g., residences), it does encourage the avoidance of these taxes by transfer of residence or the situs of taxable property.[22]

Finally, there is good reason to believe that those taxes which are shiftable at all are more easily shiftable over a period when demand is rising than when it is stationary or falling. Thus, a booming industry can more easily shift a tax forward than one which is static or declining. The rise in demand for a product may result from a general business boom, or it may result from special causes affecting demand for a particular product. In the latter case, a shift in tastes may be the major cause, or it may be that the government spends the tax funds in such a way as to strengthen demand for the taxed product. The use of gasoline taxes for the improvement of highways is a case in point. And if, as demand rises, it also becomes less elastic, the chances of forward shifting are improved. This could come about through product differentiation, through price leadership in an oligopolized industry, or simply through the existence of sellers' markets in a business boom.

Other Effects of Taxes

Our analysis of tax incidence has proceeded in terms of a definition of incidence as only one segment of the total range of tax effects. We have limited our meaning of incidence to the final resting place of the burden of

---

[21] It would be instructive to investigate the effect upon the price of gasoline in state A when contiguous state B raised its gasoline tax rate. Retailers in B at the border could not pass on the tax increase without experiencing serious loss of business to retailers across the line in A. But B's new tax does change conditions in A. If the wholesale distributors lowered base prices to absorb only a part of the tax applied to sales in state B, they could conceivably raise base prices to sellers in A. If this were done, a part of the tax would be shifted to consumers in both states.

[22] Clear distinction must be made between *avoidance* and *evasion* of taxes. The first is perfectly legal, placing one in a position where he is not legally liable for payment of a tax. The latter is illegal, and means failure to pay a tax which is payable. A poll tax may be *avoided* by moving to a state with no poll tax; it may be *evaded* by keeping out of sight of the tax authorities.

the amount paid to government. But we have also noted that there are effects other than incidence, and these effects may be vastly more important in the long run than incidence itself. These "other effects" we have previously classified as (1) those (other than incidence) created in the process of shifting, and (2) those resulting from incidence.

Effects Created in the Process of Shifting. When a tax is not shifted, it is evident that effects of this type do not result. But when a tax is shifted there are typically concurrent effects (other than incidence) of varying types. Assuming as typical a demand curve which slopes downward from left to right, and a marginal cost curve sloping upward from left to right (increasing cost), forward shifting of a tax on a salable good will reduce the number of units sold. This reduction of quantity sold will decrease employment of some factors of production by the firm. The disemployed factors are clearly worse off immediately than they would be if required to bear a part of the incidence, and in the long run may experience lower income as a result of their general oversupply.

Taxes may have important effects upon the structure of industry. A general sales tax, which is imposed upon each transfer of a good from one stage in production to another, may well urge vertical integration of industry. The fewer the transactions prior to marketing the end product, the smaller the amount of tax to be included in the final price. Tomatoes raised on a farm, sold to a canner, then to a wholesaler, then to a retailer, and finally to a consumer, would change hands four times. If each stage in production were independently owned, there would be four price transactions from raw material to final consumption. If each of these transactions were subject to a general sales tax, the retail price would include four taxes, and each of the last three would be taxes computed upon prices including previous taxes. The complete shifting of such a tax would be increasingly difficult as the retail level is approached, and the pyramiding of such taxes could be avoided by integrating the processes into fewer firms so as to reduce the number of transactions. A retail grocery chain, by owning its own truck gardens, canneries, and wholesaling facilities, would gain a retail price advantage over its independent competitors by eliminating all price transactions except the last, and thus being subject to taxation only once. Such integration would be a clear case of tax avoidance, making shifting easier or making the incidence easier to bear if the tax could not be shifted. Clearly, a general sales tax would create a great comparative advantage to integrated firms, and would be a strong force promoting further integration.

Effects Resulting from Incidence. Every tax involves sacrifice of purchasing power on the part of those upon whom the incidence falls. It is this fact which makes a tax system an instrument for the allocation of resources between government and private uses, and for the allocation of resources among individuals and groups. An important consequence is that a considerable amount of ingenuity and effort are constantly directed toward the avoidance of incidence. Interstate and interlocal competition for residents and for business firms is widespread, and often results in the adoption of tax policies which are less than rational on other grounds. The calculating individual manages his affairs to take advantage of opportunities for avoidance or for minimizing the incidence. Thus, all kinds of contortions with respect to mergers of profitable corporations with others whose accumulated losses can be deducted from current income, the translation of income into capital gains in order to qualify for a lower tax rate, the substitution of business expense accounts for personal income, and the substitution of stock options for higher salaries, can avoid the incidence of taxes by avoiding the taxes. Not the least troublesome in this respect is the persistent drive by interest groups for modification of the tax laws to permit greater tax avoidance on their part. This kind of piecemeal erosion of the tax base has the effect of increasing burdens on others if the revenues are to be maintained, and in time a crazy quilt pattern of burden allocation may result.

To bear the incidence of a tax is to have one's disposable income reduced below what it would have been in the absence of the tax. This will, of course, have an effect upon the consumption or saving of the taxed individual or upon the investment or hoarding of the business firm. Thus, the allocation of incidence affects aggregate consumption and investment, and affects the relative strength of demand in segments of the aggregates. Incidence is thus very much at the center of the allocation problem.

Concluding Observations on Shifting and Incidence

A recent empirical study of who finally pays the taxes in the United States[23] draws certain pragmatic conclusions with respect to the incidence of taxes in 1954. These conclusions are: that taxes on personal incomes are not shifted; that taxes on corporation net income have two-thirds of their incidence upon shareholders and one-third upon consumers; that sales taxes, excises, and customs duties are borne by consumers; and that the incidence of the property tax on owner-occupied residences is upon the owners, while most of the tax on business property is borne by consumers. These are ad-

[23] Richard A. Musgrave, "The Incidence of the Tax Structure and its Effects on Consumption," in *Federal Tax Policy for Economic Growth and Stability: Papers Submitted to the Joint Committee on the Economic Report,* Washington, 1955.

mittedly rough generalizations made by a leading student of the subject. An interesting fact, however, is that these expert conclusions are essentially in line with the views of the man in the street.

Working assumptions with respect to incidence must, inevitably, play a major role in the determination of tax policy. It is extremely important to know who pays the taxes, and what the implications of this knowledge are for the major objectives of fiscal action. In Chapter 13 we considered several bases for judgment of the appropriateness of the allocation pattern of tax burdens. The first was elemental justice or equity among citizens, based upon a reasonable distribution of sacrifices. The second was the revenue objective of taking revenue from where funds exist. Third, the objectives of economic stability and growth are to be served to a maximum extent. And fourth, an optimum pattern of allocation of resources with respect to social values must be maintained. Now, all these ideals in tax allocation become meaningless or useless in the absence of any knowledge of who finally pays a particular tax. For allocation on the basis of the original impact of a tax does not necessarily tell us anything about justice, compensatory usefulness, or social advantage.

At the same time that we note the importance of incidence knowledge in the formulation of tax policy, it is necessary to observe that although we can be quite precise in analysis of factors which affect shifting, quantitative conclusions as to the distribution of final burdens in any tax system cannot now be made with great precision. We thus tend to fall back on rough generalizations like those noted at the beginning of this section. But this is not all. What is wanted is an applicable general theory of fiscal effects, including not only incidence in the narrower sense but the whole range of effects resulting from a particular fiscal system. Such an accomplishment would permit judgment between alternative systems which can now be made only piecemeal and based upon rather large areas of assumption.

RECOMMENDED READINGS

Boulding, Kenneth E., "The Incidence of a Profits Tax," *American Economic Review*, 1944, pp. 567–72.

This is an instructive analysis of incidence when assumptions other than profit maximization are made.

Brown, H. G., *The Economics of Taxation*, N.Y., Holt, 1924.

A reliable, standard work on tax incidence. Though it does not have the benefit of the later developments in the theory of imperfect competition, it is a challenging and impressive study. No chapters are specifically recommended, for the various chapters analyze the incidence of particular tax measures.

Bureau of Agricultural Economics, *An Analysis of the Effects of the Processing Taxes Levied Under the Agricultural Adjustment Act,* Washington, 1937.

   An excellent example of empirical determination of incidence.

Ferger, W. F., "The Measurement of Tax Shifting: Economics and Law," *Quarterly Journal of Economics,* May, 1940, pp. 429*ff.*

   A valuable contribution to incidence literature, high-lighting the practical factors of business practice and legal influences.

Goode, Richard, *The Corporation Income Tax,* N.Y., Wiley, 1951.

   Chapter 4 discusses incidence and effects of a corporation net income tax, demonstrating an integration of pure theory and practical fact and reaching useful conclusions. Recommended not only for its balanced judgment but as a useful type of approach to incidence studies.

Hicks, U. K., *The Finance of British Government, 1920–1936,* London, Oxford, 1938, Chapter 15.

   A sprightly, unqualified statement of conclusions with respect to incidence, with special application to Britain.

CHAPTER 15

Property Taxation

Property taxes are used only by state and local governments in the United States. The constitutional prohibition of direct taxation by the federal government except on the basis of census enumeration would largely rule out federal property taxation even if this tax field had not been pre-empted by state and local governments. Its revenue importance to state governments has shown marked decline, as indicated in Table 25; it is no longer a major contributor to the revenues of the states. This is due both to the abandonment of state property taxation in several states and to the rise of other revenues at the state level. As the states reduced their dependence upon

TABLE 25

PROPERTY TAXES AS PER CENT OF TOTAL GENERAL REVENUES (EXCLUDING GRANTS), SELECTED YEARS, 1902–1958*

Year	States	Local Governments	Combined
1902	44.8	78.2	71.9
1913	38.9	77.4	70.0
1922	31.2	83.8	71.2
1932	15.2	85.2	63.8
1942	4.8	80.9	40.5
1952	3.4	71.0	38.2
1958	3.1	70.3	38.6

* Sources: Bureau of the Census, *Historical Statistics on State and Local Government Finances, 1902–1953*, pp. 19, 21; and *Summary of Governmental Finances in 1958*, p. 13.

property taxation, local governments took up much of this slack until World War II. The decline since the war has been due largely to a tendency of larger local governments to look for sources of general revenue other than the property tax. The states largely abandoned property taxation during the decade of the nineteen-thirties, with the primary intention of leaving this revenue source to local governments. While state property tax revenues declined slightly in absolute amount between 1922 and 1942 (and declined very markedly as a percentage of general revenues), local property tax revenues increased by almost 50 per cent during the same period. Rapid urbanization of the population since 1942 has made the cities a more important factor in the aggregate local picture. And while, in 1958, the property tax accounted for 70 per cent of general revenues of all local governments taken together, it accounted for only 58 per cent of the general revenues of cities with population over 25,000. These cities account for two-fifths of aggregate local general revenues.[1] On the other hand, three-fourths of county general revenues come from the property tax, and seven-eighths of the general revenue of small cities, towns, townships, school districts, and special districts is produced by taxes on property.

The property tax is one of the oldest forms of taxation. And it is still an important element of the American tax system. At the same time, there is little to recommend it on grounds of theory, and in practice the quality of its administration throughout the country varies from fairly good to bad. In short, it is a bad tax made worse in its effects by indifferent administration.

Steps in Administration of the Property Tax

There are four steps in administration of the property tax: assessment, equalization, apportionment, and collection. We shall discuss each of these steps at some length, to show something of the types of problems which arise and the quality of administration to be found. We postpone analysis of the theory until later in the chapter.

Assessment. The tax base in property taxation is the assessed value of the property against which the tax is levied, and the amount payable is this base times a flat tax rate. The first step is to determine the value of taxable property—i.e., to assess it. The assessment function involves two steps: (1) bringing taxable property into the tax rolls, and (2) placing a value upon it for tax purposes. Neither of these steps is as simple as might be assumed. Bringing taxable property into the tax rolls involves knowledge on the part of the taxing authorities that such property exists. The typical practice has been to depend upon the taxpayer himself to report items of taxable property. This method makes unnecessary a detailed search by the assessor, but leaves wide openings for tax evasion.

The personnel requirements of annual assessment at the site by a representative of the assessor's office are usually prohibitive. Most assessment is therefore done at the assessor's desk, by copying or slightly amending the

---

[1] Bureau of the Census, *Summary of Governmental Finances in 1958*, p. 13, and *Compendium of City Government Finances, 1957*, p. 6. Throughout, general government revenues are exclusive of grants from other governments.

return of the previous year. It would appear that real property (land and buildings) could be brought into the rolls with little escape. Nevertheless, investigations have quite uniformly turned up fairly large tracts of land which had entirely escaped assessment. Comparison of aerial survey photographs with tax maps offers a useful method of bringing real property into the rolls. But the problem of bringing real property into the tax rolls is minor compared to that with respect to movable personal property. We may distinguish two types of personal (movable) property: tangible and intangible. Tangible personal property includes machinery, materials, furniture, clothing, jewelry, and the like; in short, all tangible things except land and buildings, which are classed as real property. Intangible personal property includes securities and bank deposits, and such intangible assets as "good-will" and patent rights.[2]

How nearly possible is it to bring tangible personal property within the cognizance of assessors? A good job would involve a much larger corps of investigators than is usually available, much greater determination on the part of assessing officers than is typically the case, and legal authority to enter premises and conduct a thorough search. Experience has shown that the gains to the taxpayers from evasion are so great, and the likelihood that evasion will be detected and punished so small, that dependence upon the property owner to report his holdings is highly unsuccessful. Likewise, experience has shown it to be infeasible to provide assessors with sufficient personnel and sufficient power to do the job without dependence upon self-reporting.[3] The consequence is that a large proportion of tangible personal property escapes taxation through evasion, and the tangible personal property tax falls heavily on business concerns whose property is readily included in the rolls and upon those unfortunate individuals who are burdened either with a vigorous conscience or a groundless fear of legal consequences. It should be added, however, that some items of tangible property offer little opportunity of escape from the tax rolls. The ownership of automobiles, for example, is easily detected because state motor vehicle registration records

---

[2] The reader will do well to realize that not all property tax laws contemplate taxation of all real, tangible personal, and intangible personal property. The exemption or special treatment of some items of property in particular tax laws may result from recognition that in theory a "general property tax" under the "uniform rule" is undesirable, or far more likely that reasonably good administration of the "general property tax" is impossible. We shall discuss this matter later in the chapter.

[3] In a few instances, states have used "tax inquisitor laws" which give the assessor the right to search. Use of this power, however, makes the job of the assessor an unpleasant one, especially if he is an elected official. Further, such laws are highly unpopular, conflicting with the principle that "a man's home is his castle." Such laws have thus been both short-lived and ineffective.

are available to assessors. Where licenses to own or operate items of tangible property are required, e.g., automobiles, such property typically represents a major portion of the base of this tax.

The problem of evasion is generally even more serious in the case of intangibles than in the case of tangibles. The assessor cannot walk (or drive) down the street and see them, and voluntary reporting can be evaded with the greatest of ease, except in the case of local bank deposits. The industrious assessor *can* thus make a good record in including real property in the rolls; he will be quite unsuccessful with respect to tangible personal property (with the exception of some items), and almost wholly unsuccessful with respect to intangibles. In the case of intangibles, however, back taxes may be collected at death, when a transfer of the estate is made.

But bringing property into the rolls is only the first step in assessment. If property is to represent the tax base, some value for tax purposes must be placed upon it. The only true value of a thing is the price it will bring in the market. But most taxable property is not for sale, and thus has no objectively determinable value. The value of a merchant's inventory of goods for sale is not easily determined, and partly-manufactured goods, much real estate, and most used consumers' goods require pure estimate on the part of the assessor. Much litigation therefore has arisen over assessed valuation, and much more would arise if general assessment below market value were not the usual rule.

Property tax laws typically require assessment at some proportion of "true" value. Where the property is not for sale by a willing seller to a willing buyer, some substitute for "true" value is required. But this substitute for true value is not true value, and the taxpayer would thus in many cases have recourse to judicial review of the assessment. Under conditions of general underassessment, however, judicial review might well raise the assessment rather than lower it. This is true because when the judicial spotlight is thrown upon the particular assessment it may be clear that, although the assessment under consideration is high in relation to others, it is low in relation to the level of assessment required by law. It is thus frequently desirable to let well enough alone, and to accept existing inequity in assessment as the lesser of two possible inequities. One reason for underassessment is to avoid litigation. Another will be discussed in connection with equalization.

Intangible property by and large lends itself to valuation more simply than either of the other two classes. There is, of course, no problem in placing a true value on bank deposits. Many stocks and bonds offer regular market quotations, while other stocks, bonds, mortgages, patent rights, etc., and even good will, have a calculable book value which is reasonably dependable for tax purposes. The chief assessment problem with respect to intangibles consists therefore in bringing them under scrutiny, not in attaching a value to them.

Tangible personal property, because of its great variety, is most difficult to value for tax purposes. Standard trade-in values typically exist for used automobiles, and their rule-of-thumb valuation is not difficult. But most other items in this property class lack standardized used-market values and require expert appraisal. The small amount typically reported, however, makes the employment of expert appraisers impracticable, and the typical appraisal is a rough guess generally erring on the low side. For this class of property we find a high degree of evasion and a low degree of expertness in determination of value for tax purposes.

Real property escapes inclusion in the tax list only with difficulty, and being more or less homogeneous in nature is subject to comparison with actual market prices and to slide rule methods of valuation. For these reasons the property tax has come to be in fact very largely a real estate tax, whether or not the law has kept pace with tax practice and offered exemption or other special treatment to the other classes of property.

What possibilities exist for improvement of property tax assessment? The first requirement would seem to be outright exemption of those classes of property which defy either inclusion in the rolls or simple and objective processes of valuation. This would mean almost complete exemption of tangible and intangible personal property. When the degree of evasion is admittedly high, it is generally the better part of discretion to make it legal by exemption. This removes the premium upon disobedience of law and the penalty upon the law-abiding citizen. The sacrifice of revenue would be relatively small, while the danger inherent in the probable carry-over of the propensity to evade from a poor tax to a good one is considerable. The morale effects upon taxpayers in general of retaining a disreputable tax may easily carry over into other tax fields, so that the continued encouragement of evasion morality by the property tax may have serious repercussions upon the administrative effectiveness of, say, the income tax.

Wholesale evasion of tangible and intangible personal property taxes has long been recognized. The solution to the problem lies in exemption. But some states have shown considerable reluctance to take this drastic step, partly because of unwillingness to sacrifice even a small amount of revenue, partly because of the belief that property is property, whether real or personal, and partly because exemption of personal property would give legislative sanction to discrimination against real property. Consequently, they have alternated between the policies of the carrot and the stick, at times attempting to entice intangibles into the rolls by special low-rate treatment (thus narrowing the gap between the gain from evasion and the penalty of prosecution), and at other times increasing penalties for evasion or arming assessors with search warrants. The policy of the carrot has produced little additional revenue and has reduced evasion but little. The policy of the stick has been equally unsuccessful, while generating new antagonisms toward government.[4]

Exemption of certain items of property from taxation does not represent a radical departure from traditional tax practice. States have typically provided exemption of a minimum amount of property (e.g., a round sum exemption of combined types of property or exemption of minimum amounts of separate categories of property such as furniture, musical instruments, etc.). Traditionally a special exemption has been granted to war veterans These exemptions follow from the principle of an untaxed minimum of sub sistence or the principle of the continuing bonus. Government property is generally exempt from taxation, for obvious reasons. Property used by non-profit charitable, educational, and religious organizations in the direct performance of their functions has always been exempt from taxation. Three reasons have been given for this. The first is that these are functions which government would be required to perform if private agencies did not, and a minimum of government assistance can be given through tax exemption. The second is that the performance of their functions by these private agencies actually increases the capacity of other property to pay taxes, and thus exemption is no burden upon taxed property. (It is difficult to see why a railroad or any other economically desirable concern could not justifiably use the same argument.) The third reason is that, being non-profit organizations, they possess no net income and thus no capacity to pay taxes. (Any unprofitable business concern might well claim exemption on the same grounds.) The first of these reasons is the controlling one, although the traditional financial difficulties of most such organizations probably justify a departure from strict logic in the public interest.

The second requirement for improvement of assessment is to provide for more centralization of assessment than now exists. The state should exercise active cognizance over local assessors, whether elected or appointed. This means far greater emphasis upon uniformity in techniques, and particularly far greater uniformity in the proportion of real value at which property is assessed. Competitive underassessment is destructive of justice among taxpayers in different assessment districts.

---

[4] In later discussion of the theory of property taxation we shall show that justice (in addition to expediency) requires exemption of intangibles from property taxation.

The third requirement for improvement is to eliminate a great deal of fossilization, both in assessment personnel and in assessment procedure. This latter becomes much more possible if the classes of property (tangible and intangible) which cannot be assessed properly are given complete exemption. Then the tax becomes a real estate tax, and taxable property can be brought into the lists by industrious searching on the part of the assessor. Once all taxable real property is listed, the problem of valuation can be reduced to formula. In some cities "scientific assessment" has been developed to a point where it is both easily administered and amenable to proper adjustment. Scientific assessment implies the development of formulae by which the assessed value of a piece of property can be determined simply, and yet is subject to change with variations in market value.

The Cleveland system, for example, provides for the assessment of urban land by the multiplication of a front foot value factor by the frontage of the lot. This is then modified by a depth formula for lots of varying depth, a triangle formula which allows adjustment for lots of irregular shapes, and a corner influence formula for corner lots. The formulae are themselves derived from actual sales of land which indicate corner influence, depth influence, and shape-irregularity influence upon market values. Once determined, these formulae are subject to little change over long periods. The factor which does change, however, is the value of the location per front foot. Constant observation of changes in site values is required to keep the front foot factor up to date. Buildings are assessed by the multiplication of floor area by a square foot factor. This factor varies with different types of buildings and with different kinds of construction. The formulae, however, are developed from data of actual costs of construction, and the square foot factor is subject to change with building values. The assessed value of a piece of real estate is then the sum of the formula-determined land assessment and the formula-determined building assessment.

Under such assessment procedures, three types of assessment personnel are required: researchers to keep the formulae and factors up to date, "outside men" to gather original information as to dimensions and types of property and to record improvements or changes in particular parcels, and clerks who will apply the formulae to the property description to determine the assessment. Possibly only the large cities can afford such a staff. But there is no reason why the state cannot perform much of this service for its administrative subdivisions. There are two fundamental requirements for such a change. The first is determination to correct as many of the present abuses as is possible. This means a change in attitude from hopeless surrender to a bad tax badly administered. The second is introduction of realism into tax laws. Such scientific assessment does not tell what the actual value of a piece of property is when that property is not for sale. It merely determines a tax base which is a reasonable and equitable substitute for a true value which is unknown. And property tax laws should recognize this fact realistically. They too frequently call upon the assessor to perform an impossible task—to assess at true value when true value cannot be determined. In the field of public utility regulation a similar problem has been met. Clearly, the true "value" of public utility property depends upon the rates which the regulatory commission will allow. It is absurd, therefore, to use the "value" of property to test the adequacy of rates. The circle is broken by the adoption of a useful "rate base" independent of value. Similar adoption of a fair "tax base" is required, without insisting that it be identical with "true value."

Our discussion of improvement in assessment should not be taken as an indication that, if properly administered, the property tax is a good tax. In spite of its theoretical undesirability, which we will explore later in this chapter, it is likely to be with us for a long time. Inertia is a powerful factor in preventing an identity between what might be and what is. If we are going to live with a bad tax, the least we can do is to raise the quality of its administration to the highest possible level.

Equalization. The purpose of equalization is to iron out injustices in assessment. It is in line with democratic procedure to provide some appeal from the assessment to permit judicial determination of its fairness. Boards of review or equalization exist in all property-taxing jurisdictions, to hear the complaints of property owners dissatisfied with their assessments. Since the city tax rate is applied to assessments appearing on the grand list of the city, a city board will pass upon the justice of local assessments. Since the county tax rate will be applied equally to all assessments in the county, dissatisfaction may arise over the relative levels of assessments in two cities in the same county. Hence, there may be a county board of equalization. And the state, if it employs a property tax, will be likely to apply its tax rate equally to all assessments in the state, and thus a state board is desirable. When different governments tax the same property, they do not assess independently. City or town government does the assessing (by districts if the city is large enough). City grand lists are made up of combined assessment district lists in the city. County grand lists are made up of combined lists of all towns (townships) in the county. And the state grand list combines the county grand lists. Since one assessment serves for all participating governments at various levels, inequality in standards of assessment may occur. Thus, provision must be made for review of assessments at all levels.

The service of equalization is not, however, of much significance in practice. In some states the property owner has no recourse to review unless he has voluntarily made his return. This provision is designed to encourage voluntary listing, since the failure to list subjects the offender to arbitrary assessment without recourse.[5] The principal reason why boards of review have little work to do is that when there is general underassessment it is dangerous to request investigation. Suppose that state law requires that all property be assessed at 100 per cent of true value. Suppose that in city A property is generally assessed at 70 per cent of value, while in city B in the same county the level is 50 per cent. So far as the county tax is concerned, property owners in A are required to pay more heavily per dollar of actual value than are those in B. But if the property owner complains to the board of review he may find that his assessment is raised to 100 per cent, while those of others in cities A and B remain as before. In such a case he would pay more heavily after review than if he had made no complaint. And finally, a board can ease its duties by discouraging applications for review with a "tough" attitude.

It may be asked why underassessment occurs so generally. The first reason is that underassessment forestalls complaints. If the assessor is required to guess at a proper assessed value it is safer to guess low and not be required later to substantiate his guess in terms of "true value." In addition, there are political advantages in not only assessing low, but below the assessments in other districts. If the assessor is elected to office there may be a real urge to perform favors for those who elected him. If assessments in city A are below those in city B, it makes no difference *so far as city taxes are concerned* how far property in A is underassessed.[6] But in county and state taxation greater underassessment in A reduces the county and state tax bill to property owners in A. And if the assessor is appointed to office it may be a policy of the administration to keep assessments low relative to those in other areas, and for the same reasons as are given above.

Perhaps we have emphasized too much the urge to underassess. While assessment statistics reflect very general valuation below market value, there are influences operating to weaken this tendency. The surrender of property taxes by states to local governments removes a strong incentive to competitive underassessment, by removing one of its major advantages. If state grant-in-aid formulae are not tied to grand lists, another reason for under-

---

[5] Much more effective in encouraging voluntary listing is a tax penalty payment for failure to list voluntarily.

[6] This is true because the lower the general level of assessment, the higher the tax rate must be in order to raise the required revenue. So long as assessments within a city are at a uniform level, so as to avoid discrimination between parcels of property, it makes no difference whether assessments are low and tax rates high or assessments high and tax rates low.

assessment is removed. Furthermore, the rapidly rising need for local government funds in recent years has forced heavier property taxation and more borrowing. If the tax on a piece of property is to be increased, the public seems to have preferred that the whole rise not be concentrated in the tax rate but that some of it be accomplished through upward assessment. And because local debt limits are often based upon grand lists, an appropriate way to relieve the pinch of the debt limit is to increase assessments generally.

Apportionment. We have hinted several times in previous discussion at the nature of apportionment. It is the process of determining the rates of property tax to be imposed by various levels of government upon a given piece of property. The device by which the property tax burden is apportioned among taxpayers within a tax jurisdiction is the mill rate. This rate says the total tax need is a proportion of the total value of property. Taxpayer A's property is a share of total property. His tax liability share is the same proportion of the value of his property as the total tax need is of the total value of property. When assessment and equalization are completed, it is possible to determine the proper tax rates to be applied by various governments participating. If more than one government is involved, each knows how much it wishes to raise by property taxation, and each has its grand list. When the former is divided by the latter, the result is the tax rate. Let us follow the process in tabular form.

Taxing Government	Grand List (Assessed value of property) (1)	Desired Revenue (2)	Tax Rate (2 divided by 1)
City A	$ 50,000,000	$1,250,000	25 mills (2.5%)
County 1 (includes City A)	200,000,000	800,000	4 mills (.4%)
State I (includes County 1)	1,000,000,000	4,000,000	4 mills (.4%)
Total tax rate on property in City A			33 mills (3.3%)

Property in city A will pay 33 mills (3.3 per cent) per dollar of assessed valuation. Actually our example is oversimplified, and particular parcels of property in city A may pay considerably more. There may be special district (school district, fire district, sewer district, etc.) property taxes imposed as special assessments and included in the annual tax bill. The tax rate which any government may apply will depend upon the property tax revenues required, the amount of tax delinquency which may result from given tax rates, and legal tax rate limits, if any, imposed upon it. Clearly, however, the amount of tax payable depends as much upon the assessment (tax base) as upon the tax rate. The level of assessments in practice is therefore as significant a datum to the prospective property owner as is the level of tax rates.

Collection. The final stage in administration of the property tax is that of collection. Once apportionment is completed and the rates determined for various governments and districts, tax bills can be forwarded to property owners. Evidently the ease of collection depends upon the burdensomeness of the total tax in terms of ability of the property owner to pay. And this will depend upon how heavy the tax is in terms of the income of the property taxpayer.

If assessments are not adjusted to the decline in true values in depression periods, a high proportion of delinquency will follow. It is here that we see clearly the nature of the fiscal problem resulting from a combination of heavy local dependence upon the property tax and debt limitation. In business depression, property values fall because the income from property falls. This calls for reduction in assessed valuations without (in the majority of cases) opportunity for increase in tax rates. If the basic functions of local governments plus the unusual relief functions of depression are to be maintained, deficits are inevitable. The enforcement of debt limits means that expenditures must be reduced to conform to the reduction of property tax revenues. Inelasticity of local revenues goes a long way to explain why the financing of the previously local function of relief was necessarily taken over by the federal government in the early nineteen-thirties.

Tax delinquency is an embarrassing fact for government to face. It frequently involves eventual foreclosure of property for unpaid taxes, giving government title over property for which it generally has no use. The taking of private property for tax debts is an action which government would like to avoid. There are two ways of avoiding it: either allowing delinquency to continue indefinitely without foreclosure action, or adjusting assessments and tax rates to the changing ability to pay. The first obviously does not solve the long-run problem, and encourages delinquency on the part of those who otherwise could and would meet their tax obligations. The second clearly is the only satisfactory long-run solution, though some delinquency will occur even under the best conditions of assessment and apportionment. If the steps of assessment, equalization, and apportionment were properly taken, most tax delinquency would not occur. If there were more elasticity in local tax systems, and particularly in local fiscal policy, a principal barrier to assessment revision and reasonable rates would be removed. Then a vigorous delinquency policy could be adopted without hardship to taxpayers and without great embarrassment to government.

Theory of the General Property Tax

The "general property tax" contemplates taxation of all items of property —real, tangible personal, and intangible—at a uniform rate and at a uniform percentage of true value. It is frequently referred to as property taxation under the "uniform rule."

In the essentially simple local economies in which property taxation was nurtured, ownership of property was, and with reasonable accuracy could be, taken as a satisfactory index of ability to pay. As the economy has become more complex, it has become a very bad index. For ability to pay is measured basically in terms of income, and there is very poor correlation between the amount of income and the amount of property owned. The production of income in some lines (e.g., manufacturing) requires the use of a considerable amount of wealth. But the production of income of comparable size in the professions requires relatively little wealth. The comparison suggests that the property used in production measures only very inaccurately the amount of income produced.

Further, the disposal of income reflects very inaccurately the size of that income. Some may prefer to spend income upon durable things (e.g., estates) which represent large property tax bases. Others may prefer to purchase securities, whose taxation as property is contemplated by the uniform rule, but the difficulty of whose assessment means almost complete escape. Still others may prefer a high level of current consumption of nondurable goods and services, which results in the ownership of relatively little property for tax purposes.

Finally, the ability-to-pay principle implies the existence of available income for tax payments. The large family should have a large house, and yet the capacity to pay taxes is clearly not indicated by the size (assessed value) of the house. So long as property ownership is taken as an outward and objective indication of ability to pay, different treatment of individuals with the same assessed value of property (but quite different taxable capacity) is impossible. Fundamentally, the trouble arises because ability runs in terms of income, and there is no close relationship between the amount of property owned and the amount of income.

In a simple agrarian economy, where income is mainly income from wealth, reasonable justice in terms of ability to pay can be accomplished through the taxation of wealth. With the increased complexity of the economy it was hoped to eliminate inequities by taxation of intangibles uniformly with wealth. The results have not been good. However, rather than exchange the tax for something better the line of less resistance has been to change the justification. Consequently, justification for the property tax has come to run principally in terms of benefit.

Let us see how well the benefit theory justifies property taxation. The typical modern apology for the property tax lists such benefits as police and fire protection, streets, sidewalks, sewers, garbage and snow removal, and public education as representing peculiar benefits to property. Undoubtedly benefits do accrue to property from these services. But can any equation be set up between the benefits to a particular piece of property and the amount of taxes it pays? We have previously justified special assessments upon property when the cost of a peculiarly beneficial improvement enhances property value by at least as much as allocated cost of the improvement. Special assessments, however, represent a minute share of local revenues, and the improvements for which special assessments are made are those in which special benefit is clearly conferred upon the property and its owner. In 1958, approximately 70 per cent of local revenue (exclusive of grants) was derived from the property tax. On the other hand, nearly all expenditures of these same governments were for functions whose cost can hardly be identified with particular pieces of property. The important objects of expenditure of local governments in 1957 were education, highways, public welfare, health and hospitals, sanitation, and police, in that order. Of these expenditures few can be claimed to have important direct beneficial effects upon property *per se*. Further than this, their ownership of taxed property very poorly measures the extent of these benefits to particular individuals. Without laboring the point further, we reiterate that the benefits of public functions are by nature principally general. The identification of benefits received with property owned is very largely arbitrary and incapable of acceptance on logical grounds.

Ability, Benefit, and the Incidence of Property Taxes. The theories of ability and benefit as applied to property taxes generally ignore the fact that a considerable portion of such taxes is shifted. Backward shifting in the form of capitalization imposes upon the seller of the property the anticipated future property taxes. This means that in the case of a residence, for instance, the seller bears a large part of the tax. The justification for property taxes has been based upon the taxable capacity of the present owner or the benefits of government to him, while the tax burden is in fact largely upon someone else.

When taxed property is used for business purposes, there may be forward shifting in the form of increased price of the product. (This is less common than backward shifting, for, as we have seen, such an increase in fixed cost does not result in higher price and smaller quantity in the short run.) When forward shifting occurs, the real bearer of the tax is not the property owner, but the buyer of his product. To the extent that such shifting occurs it is absurd to justify the tax in terms of the property owner's ability to pay or of the benefits which accrue to his property.

Nevertheless, not all property taxes are shifted either forward or backward; a large part must be borne by the owner himself, especially when taxes are rising. In such a case it is incumbent upon the authorities to justify the tax in terms of some theoretical basis. Unless this can be done, the only defense of the property tax is the practical one of tradition. And this is really the only justification remaining for it—society has become so accustomed to it that its burden is taken for granted. Other things being equal, this is a desirable attribute of a tax, but other things are not equal. When theoretical justification is on such questionable ground and administration so poor, there is little consolation in retaining the tax on grounds that to discard it would terminate a long life and require adjustment to a new (though almost inevitably better) tax, unless it is argued that partial or complete abandonment of the property tax would involve a cost, in the nature of a sacrifice of local autonomy. For almost inevitably a substitute for it would be administered at a higher governmental level.

Theory of Taxation of Intangibles. Taxation of stocks, bonds, mortgages, bank deposits, and other possible forms of intangible property can hardly be justified in terms of benefit. For the direct benefits to bondholders from education, police protection, snow removal, garbage collection, and sewer construction are meager indeed. Taxation of intangibles stands entirely upon the principle of ability to pay, and reflected a grasping at straws when it became apparent that the ownership of tangible property was not a completely satisfactory measure of taxable capacity. For although the property tax was a tax on the thing (property), it was supposed to be measured by the ability of the person (owner). When, therefore, it appeared that many persons with income, and therefore taxable ability, did not own physical property in proportion to that ability, intangibles were added to the property tax lists.

This assumes, however, that intangibles represent a capacity to pay distinct from the physical property that they represent. The fallacy will be clear if we use an example. Assume two farms producing exactly equal net income. Let us say that each is worth $10,000. A buys his farm outright by the payment of $10,000 cash. B buys the other farm with a cash payment of $5,000 and a mortgage of $5,000. The capacity of the two farms to pay taxes is the same (though the capacity of the two *farmers* to pay taxes may not be equal). A and B are taxed on an assessment of $10,000 each. But C, who holds a $5,000 mortgage on B's farm, is taxed upon his mortgage at the uniform rate. The income from which C's mortgage tax will be paid is the income from his mortgage, which is income from B's farm. In effect, therefore, income from B's farm is taxed 50 per cent per dollar more than is income from A's farm.

If no thought is given to incidence, it may be argued that B should be taxed only upon his equity in the farm ($5,000), while C is taxed upon his equity ($5,000). Then income from the two farms would be taxed with equal severity. This would be reasonable (shifting aside), but it is not the way property tax laws are drawn. When we introduce incidence considerations, it is almost certain that the mortgage interest which B pays to C includes C's tax. Thus the tax borne by B is actually 50 per cent greater than that borne by A, ignoring the possibility that taxes were shifted backward at time of purchase of the farm.

It is thus seen that double taxation occurs through the taxation of wealth *and* the taxation of rights to that wealth. The principal argument against double taxation follows from the fact that it is not uniform. If everything were taxed twice the effect would be no different than if everything were taxed once at double the rate. In our farm example above we found that two farms exactly alike were treated quite differently, as shown below.

	Real Estate Tax (at 3% tax rate)	Intangibles Tax (at 3% tax rate)	Total Property Tax
A's Farm	$300	none	$300
B's Farm	$300	none ⎫	
C's Mortgage on B's Farm	none	$150 ⎬	$450

Two alternative methods present themselves for elimination of this injustice. The first would be to provide for uniform double taxation, by taxing all rights to wealth whether or not actual documents exist. The effect would be as follows, assuming that because of uniform double taxation the tax rate could be halved.

	Real Estate Tax (at 1½%)	Intangibles Tax (at 1½%)	Total Property Tax
A's Farm	$150	none ⎫	$300
A's Equity in his Farm	none	$150 ⎬	
B's Farm	$150	none ⎫	
B's Equity in his Farm	none	$ 75 ⎬	$300
C's Mortgage	none	$ 75 ⎭	

This would represent a highly cumbersome administrative approach to the problem of achieving justice in the treatment of A and B. The same result could be accomplished much more simply by the outright exemption of intangibles, which would require both A and B to pay a real estate tax of equal amounts ($300) on their farms.

The usual objections to such exemption center around the fact that C, who holds property in a mortgage of $5,000, is required to pay no tax on it. But any tax on C's mortgage will almost certainly be shifted to B as the borrower, and not borne by C.

Granted that taxation of mortgages results in undesirable double taxation of some property, is the same true of other intangibles? Examples similar to that which we have used in analyzing the double taxation of a mortgaged farm could be set up showing discrimination between a corporation whose stocks and bonds are taxed in the hands of their owners in addition to taxation of the physical property, and an unincorporated business having no stocks or bonds outstanding. Stocks are indications of ownership of wealth, and not wealth itself. Clearly, the income to stocks represents distribution of the income of the corporation; if the real and tangible property of the corporation is taxed as representing ability of the corporation to pay (or benefit enjoyed), ownership of stock does not represent a separate capacity. And bonds are debts of the corporation, similar to mortgages. Taxation of the one is taxation of the other, and taxation of both is double taxation. Here again elimination of discriminatory treatment involves either complete double taxation of all wealth or exemption of intangibles. The latter is administratively the more sensible.

Property taxation of intangibles is thus open to condemnation on the counts of both theory and practice. Intangibles do not constitute a separate ability to pay nor do they derive significant benefits separate from those accruing to the wealth which they represent. Clearly, there are no theoretical grounds upon which their taxation can be justified. The incidence of such taxes is almost inevitably upon the physical property, which makes for highly undesirable concentration of the double burden upon one person. On the side of administration, intangibles largely escape the tax lists, so the persons upon whom their double burden falls are principally those few who are the victims either of admirable honesty or pitiful unsophistication in the ways of evasion. When we combine these criticisms with the fact that this major tax is proportional (as are all property taxes) and consequently does not stand up under the principles of appropriate tax allocation, it is difficult to imagine a more completely damning case against any tax. The unsuccessful efforts expended in attempting to bolster administration of taxation of intangibles in view of its lack of logical justification is one of the sadder commentaries upon state and local fiscal wisdom.[7]

Classified Property Taxes

Classification of property for tax purposes has been frequently practiced among the states. Under a classified property tax it is intended to treat

[7] In 1951 only thirteen states legally exempted all intangibles from property taxes. (*Tax Systems,* 13th ed., Chicago, Commerce Clearing House, 1952, pp. 173–79).

different types of property differently. Differential treatment may be accomplished in either of two ways: by applying different tax rates to different classes of property, or by applying the same rate to all classes and assessing the different classes at different proportions of full value. Three reasons for property classification are evident in the experience of the states. The first is to accomplish greater justice among types of property by adjusting the tax liability to differential capacity to pay. The second is a surrender to expediency—granting concessions to those types of property which, in fact, largely evade taxation under the uniform rule, or to those underprivileged types which possess little opportunity for evasion. The third is to grant tax concessions to favored classes of property, irrespective of ability or of benefit (e.g., improved land, farm property, favored industries).

Do different types of property actually possess different capacities to pay property taxes? It is of course true that some property produces greater net income than does other property, and that much property produces not money income but satisfactions. These differences are, however, reflected in capital values of the various property items. The value of a piece of property is determined by capitalization of the amount of the expected net return by the rate of return required upon investment in such property. There are thus three variable determinants of capital value: the amount of annual net income expected, the rate of return required on investments carrying given estimated risk, and the time factor involved in expected return—i.e., the period of time expected to elapse before receipt of income, and the duration of the stream of income. Capital values of the various types of property thus take account of the variables presumed to indicate differences in ability to pay. If, then, all property were assessed at full market value, the capacities to pay per dollar of assessed value of all property would be equal.[8] We thus see that differential capacities to pay taxes do not exist in terms of true property values, though failure to assess accurately will frequently give tax bases which apply the tax quite unequally among property types.

Granted that under proper assessment capacity to pay per dollar of assessed valuation is equal for different items of property, there are other capacities which justify special treatment of particular types of property. Specifically, we note differential capacities to shift the tax and differential capacities to evade the tax. The tendency to shift taxation of intangibles to

---

[8] This is true of the capacity of *property* to pay, but obviously not true of the capacities of the *owners* of property. In the last analysis property ownership is clearly not a good measure of personal capacity to pay—real taxable capacity must be measured in terms of individual income (from property and other sources).

the debtor imposes double taxation upon the physical property carrying the debt obligation. The tendency to shift some business property taxes to buyers of the product results in incidence far different from that contemplated by the tax itself. The total effect, therefore, of shifting is to impose tax burdens which are inconsistent with the notion of capacity of property or of its owner to pay taxes.

The capacity to evade property taxes is high in the cases of intangibles and of much tangible personal property. This being the case, the only practicable alleviation of inequities among property owners of these classes is to place such property types in an exempt class. Such exemption may be considered a type of classification for tax purposes.

There is a further class of real property which offers practical difficulty from the point of view of public policy. Lands containing mineral or other exhaustible resources and lands used for production of timber cannot be taxed like farm land or residential land. The difficulty lies not in the theory of property taxation, but in practical conflict between tax policy and conservation policy. Land containing mineral resources, if taxed annually on a base representing its true current value, encourages the rapid and often wasteful use of those resources. Since their quantity is limited, the total amount of taxes imposed on them over the period of their existence will vary inversely with the rapidity with which they are used. In the interest of conservation and orderly use of such deposits, it is desirable to grant special treatment which will remove the tax premium upon rapid exhaustion.

Taxation of forest land presents a somewhat similar problem. The economic use of forest resources requires that timber be cut only at the age most appropriate for lumber production. And conservation policy requires that cut timber be replaced with growing timber. Application of the usual property tax to timber lands would assess annually those lands at values which include the current value of standing timber on them. The long period required to grow timber to economic size would thus involve payment of a succession of annual taxes before any return is realized from sale of the product. Clearly, this places a premium upon early cutting and discourages the planting of replacement timber.

Proper taxation policy should remove the urge to waste and at the same time impose tax obligations upon such property which are in line with those imposed upon other taxed property. It is generally agreed that the logical solution is to combine low annual taxes upon such property with special yield taxes when the product is marketed. Such an arrangement would involve special classification of such lands for property tax purposes.

Our general conclusion with respect to classified property taxes is that, if the property tax is to serve reasonably well, abandonment of the general property tax (uniform rule) is essential. Exemption of intangibles is indicated because they possess no taxable capacity and enjoy no benefits distinct from the wealth which they represent, and because practically it is impossible to bring a sufficient quantity of them into the tax lists to avoid serious injustice among taxpayers. When they represent indebtedness they are typically shifted to the debtor-owner of wealth, and when they represent ownership the wealth which they represent is twice taxed. It is difficult to believe that such discrimination can have been consciously intended.

Exemption of tangible personal property is necessary to avoid the injustices arising out of evasion and the practical impossibility of proper assessment. It may be desirable for special reasons to impose special property taxes upon certain items of such property which can be brought into the rolls by recourse to registration records and can be reasonably assessed by reference to market prices of standardized items. Motor vehicles and boats represent virtually the only types of tangible personal property items which possess these characteristics.

Classification for exemption of such large areas of general property would limit the property tax to real estate—land and buildings. Such delimitation would reduce property taxation to administrable proportions. More scientific assessment methods could then be widely adopted under state authority, and the assessment task would be greatly simplified. Within the area of such limited applicability of the property tax the only special classification required would be that of lands bearing exhaustible mineral and timber resources. Land in this exceptional category would be assessed for annual tax purposes as if it possessed no such resources, while at the time mineral resources are extracted or timber resources marketed a special yield tax in lieu of additional property taxes would be imposed.

Taxation of the "Unearned Increment" from Land

This would seem to be the appropriate place to discuss a special theory of property taxation, which has had public acceptance in practice almost in inverse proportion to the enthusiasm for it in some quarters. It is the theory of the "single tax," propounded in its modern form principally by Henry George during the last quarter of the nineteenth century. The theory is based upon two major beliefs: (1) Land is peculiar among the factors of production in that it is non-reproducible. Therefore the return to land of any given quality is in the nature of a monopoly return to those fortunate enough to possess it. For this reason, in a growing economy, "rent" returns to owners of land are likely to produce large private fortunes. (2) These returns are not the result of anything the landowner does. All he needs to do is to sit tight while the demand for the products of land rises with rising population and rising standards of living. The greater the necessity to bring less productive lands into use in order to satisfy public demand for products, the higher the price must be to cover marginal cost on the less productive land. This creates large surplus returns from the better land. Thus, it is the society which creates high land values, and not the landowner. It is therefore elementary justice that this "unearned increment" be taxed away for use of the society which created it.

In George's view, the whole of this increment should be taxed away, leaving the owner of land a fair return upon his improvements on the land. It is not, of course, necessary that the whole of the increment be taken, but the theory would seem to justify higher property taxes on land than upon other items of real and personal property. There are further arguments in justification of the proposal. Taxes on items of cost of production are, in general, more easily shiftable than taxes upon surplus returns over those required to bring forth production. Thus, a tax on profits which are only sufficient to attract entrepreneurship in proper quantity and quality is a tax on cost of production, and is usually shiftable forward in the long run. But a tax on surplus profit—a differential return over the going rate—is much less easily shiftable. Since the rent return is a surplus over cost of production, there is reasonable assurance that its incidence would be upon the person upon whom the tax is originally assessed. Furthermore, a landowner who wishes to escape the tax by selling the land will find the tax capitalized and deducted from the selling price, and therefore no escape is possible. And finally, inability of owners to realize "unearned increments" in value would seriously limit the likelihood of land speculation.

How might such a tax be administered, if it is to accomplish the social results intended? An annual tax on land values (as distinguished from the value of improvements) not only raises difficult assessment problems, but does not easily accomplish the desired result. To be applied consistently with the theory, not land value, but the increase in land value should be taxed. Thus, a parallel to a capital gains tax is called for, with the difference that increases on paper would be taxed as well as realized gains from sale. This would, presumably, force sales or at least force the application of land to its most remunerative use. A landowner who had to pay a high tax based upon the increase in its potential market value could not afford to hold it in a less profitable use.[9] Land would thus be more efficiently used.

The theory of the unearned increment tax as applied to land has the weakness of ignoring other similar surplus returns. As Alfred Marshall pointed out in 1890, "quasi-rents" may accrue to any of the factors of production, provided they are differentiated enough to prevent free entry of competitors. Surplus returns may accrue to patented processes, to monopolistic organization of industry, to performers gifted with distinguished beauty or other natural traits. A land tax would not touch these surplus returns. One could effectively argue that such socially created gains could be more effectively mopped up wherever they are by the use of an income tax.

Probably the most effective method of taking away the "unearned increment" from land would be to nationalize all land, and lease it to the highest bidder at a rental equal to its current use value. This has been done in parts of Australia. Other attempts to apply the principle in moderation have occurred in Australia, in some Canadian provinces, and in a few United States cities, by applying a higher rate to the assessed value of land than to other real or personal property. This means, in effect, that a classified property tax is employed. But on the whole, special taxation of land values has had little popular appeal. Since in the United States the general outlines of property taxation are determined by state and not local governments, the tendency has been to avoid a tax practice which would be discouraging to farmers.

Counter-Cycle Use of Property Taxes

Counter-cycle tax policy can make little or no use of property taxes. Annual assessment and collection of property taxes offers little opportunity for the type of immediate adjustability in payments required to serve counter-cycle purposes. In addition, the local nature of property tax administration militates strongly against the possibility of coordinated national counter-cycle property tax policy. And finally, the poor correlation of prop-

[9] While there might be economic gains from frequent changes in land use, rather serious social problems might well be created. For example, a farmer on the edge of a growing city could not afford to continue farming his land; he should sell it for urban use. But he could not retire on the proceeds because they would be taxed away. The more rapid the changes in land use, the more rapid the obsolescence of structures on land, and the economic gain is not unmixed. Likewise, a retired person, living on land which is rising in value, could not longer afford to live where he had spent his working years preparing to live. These examples indicate that a program designed to make things less easy for the idle and often absentee landlord, and for the family which through good luck had had ancestors with foresight, would make life more difficult also for many persons for whom there is considerably more public sympathy.

erty ownership with personal income suggests relatively little effect upon consumption and investment were it feasible to build counter-cycle elasticity into the tax. In fact, the continued existence of the property tax either in its present form or in the limited form suggested herein discourages adoption of state-collected, locally shared personal income taxes which would offer far brighter prospects for effective counter-cycle use.

The Property Tax: Conclusion

Of the total value of property in the United States as assessed by local governments in 1956,[10] four-fifths was real estate, about one-fifth tangible personal property, and less than 1 per cent intangibles. Local governments in all states taxed real estate; in all but three, tangible personal property was taxed in some degree, and in thirty-five states intangible property was exempt. The trend has been toward the exemption of intangibles, and toward at least partial exemption of tangible personal property. In general, this trend has resulted from difficulties in assessing these kinds of property, though in many cases the exemption of intangibles has occurred as states have adopted personal income taxes. In spite of the erosion of the property tax base, the property tax is still the most important in aggregate state and local tax systems, and overwhelmingly so in the case of local governments. Both assessed values and mill rates have risen rapidly and generally since World War II.

We have seen that the property tax, even with general abandonment of the uniform rule, falls far short of justifying itself as a good tax on grounds of theory. The ownership of taxable property cannot serve as a reasonable measure either of the benefits of local government or of the ability of individuals to contribute to government. Thus, it is impossible to allocate tax burdens rationally with this tax measure. By and large, the administration of the property tax by local governments leaves much to be desired. Heavy reliance is still placed upon self-assessment, and auditing personnel and procedures are quite inadequate. But there is a further difficulty with the property tax as the revenue mainstay of local governments. This has appeared particularly in recent years, as local educational costs have skyrocketed and very great pressure has been put on the property tax in many localities to meet these costs. It is the competitive attempt of one locality to increase the grand list at the expense of another and to increase its grand list at the expense of local planning. Local governments have feverishly attempted to attract industry by temporary tax rebates and by provision of

[10] Bureau of the Census, *Property Tax Assessments in the United States,* 1957, p. 13.

facilities at governmental expense, and often on the firm's own terms. The particular appeal of industrial units is their immediate swelling of the local tax base. Closely related is the fact that if the property tax on a business is shifted, it may be shifted to buyers in other localities, thus transferring some of the burden of schools from citizens in Town A to citizens of towns B, C, and D. Zoning laws which protect the residential character of a locality are under constant pressure for change in order to attract big tax-payers. And recently, a rash of local ordinances excluding trailer parks has broken out; they add many children to the schools but little taxable property. The important point is that increasingly, as heavier burdens are thrown upon the property tax, these actions have been taken for the wrong reasons. They tend to create an artificial pattern of industry and residential location, not justified by basic economic factors. They tend, also, to compromise the ideal of freedom in residential location. When concessions are made, local governments may well be laying the basis for fiscal trouble in the future, when new plants become old. Finally, the scramble for a broader property tax base threatens the character of localities, since intelligent planning and zoning may be required to play second fiddle.

In spite of these criticisms of the property tax as the principal source of local government funds, one can hardly expect the property tax to decline in importance or its problems to moderate. There is a very large element of tradition or of customary acceptance of property taxation. This is one of the oldest forms of taxation in the United States. But if its role were to be significantly reduced in local finance, what would the alternatives be? The other major forms of taxation—on incomes and on sales—do not lend themselves to local use except in the largest municipalities. Bad as property tax administration is, an income tax requires even more competent adminis-tration, which smaller local governments, at least, are unable to provide. And where governmental boundaries are narrow, as they are for cities, towns, townships, school districts, and the like, a host of troubles would arise over taxing jurisdictions. The few existing problems between states, as to whether incomes shoud be taxable by the state of residence or by the state in which the income is earned, would be multiplied manifold if local income taxes were to be substituted for the property taxes. And the prob-lems raised by interlocal competition for taxable property would be equally great if interlocal competition for incomes were substituted.

Local government sales taxes can hardly be substituted for property taxes. While the larger cities can effectively supplement revenues by sales taxation, suburban and rural communities would be left high and dry for revenue. Large items, such as automobiles, furniture, clothing, and building materials, produce large amounts of sales tax revenue. These are usually purchased in retail centers, in the core cities, which are the larger cities within reach. A small residential town would gain little revenue from such purchases, and might well be forced to impose a sales tax on food at the nearby grocer's in order to produce the necessary revenue.

In areas where local governments are pushing the property tax toward its critical limit,[11] the reduction of relative dependence upon this tax can be accomplished only by more generous state aid to local communities. When income or sales taxes are applied by state governments, these difficulties are nowhere nearly as serious as when local communities attempt to apply them. In fact, these are already principal revenue measures of the states. The greatest pressure for property tax relief currently comes from groups suffering special property tax disadvantages, such as farmers, whose income-earning requires an inordinately large amount of taxable property; from older people, whose fixed and limited income places them in real trouble as property taxes rise; and from the low income groups in general, who realize from bitter experience that the value of one's residence or one's automobile bears little dependable relationship to the amount of one's income. And the pressure for property tax relief usually has taken the form of agitation for the assumption of a larger share of fiscal responsibility by the state or the federal government. One may expect this to be the pattern for the future. Though property tax revenues will continue to rise absolutely with natural growth of the base, the proportion of local expenses carried by the property tax will probably fall.

RECOMMENDED READINGS

Bird, Frederick L., *The General Property Tax: Findings of the 1957 Census of Governments,* Chicago, Public Administration Service, 1960.

> An up-to-date, factual description of property tax practices in the United States in 1957. Deals mainly with assessment, but includes material on the present character of the tax, its revenue productivity, and its administration.

Jensen, J. P., *Property Taxation in the United States,* Chicago, Univ. of Chicago Press, 1931.

> Property taxation in practice has changed rather little since this book was published. Though it is not recent, it is suprisingly current. Chapters should be selected according to the phase of the subject in which the reader is interested.

---

[11] Meaning, of course, not some explosive collapse of the property tax or of local government, but forcing more and more of its citizens into a situation of real hardship, while others whose taxable property is small in relation to their incomes are touched only lightly.

Leland, S. E., *The Classified Property Tax in the United States,* Boston, Houghton
   Mifflin, 1928.
   A considerable part of the book is now out of date. Nevertheless, Chapters
2, 4, 5, and 6, dealing with the theory of classification, will be instructive.
"Report of the Committee on State Equalization of Local Property Tax Assess-
ments," *Proceedings, National Tax Association,* 1958, pp. 315–65.
   Analysis of the need for equalization in the interest of equity, and methods
of approach to the problem.
Tax Policy League, *Property Taxes: A Symposium,* N.Y., Tax Policy League, 1940.
   The papers cover a variety of subjects related to property taxation. Espe-
cially recommended are Chapters 1 ("Importance of the Property Tax in State
and Local Tax Systems"), 7 ("Some Observations Concerning the Classified
Property Tax"), 10 ("The Property Tax as a Measure of Ability"), 11 ("The
Property Tax as a Benefit Tax"), 13 ("Capitalization and Shifting of the
Property Tax"), and 16 ("Improvements in Personal Property Tax Adminis-
tration").

CHAPTER 16

Personal Income Taxation

Taxes imposed upon the incomes of individuals constitute the most important source of federal revenues and a growing source of state revenues. In addition, nearly all recommendations for overhaul of tax systems call for even greater scope for these taxes. For these reasons we shall give particularly careful attention in our analysis to taxes upon personal net income. In this chapter we shall describe existing personal income taxes, their history, and their current revenue importance. In the three chapters following we consider problems of income taxation, indicating several suggestions for improvement.

Our earlier discussion has emphasized the importance of two basic facts in our tax thinking: (1) nearly all taxes are eventually paid out of personal income, and (2) intelligent use of taxes implies knowledge of their incidence. The personal income tax recommends itself on both counts. Since the base of the tax *is* personal net income, it aims directly at the income streams from which taxes are eventually paid, and thus avoids the vagaries of indirect approaches through property ownership or purchases of particular goods. We have further noted (Chapter 14) that the incidence of a personal net income tax is relatively simple and well known—it is generally upon the income receiver and cannot be shifted.

Revenue Importance of Personal Income Taxes

Table 26 indicates the relative importance of personal income taxes in the revenues of the federal government for selected years since 1910. The statistics are not entirely accurate, and tend to err by attaching less relative importance to personal income taxes than they deserve. This error arises from the fact that in varying degrees in earlier years the federal corporation income tax—not included in personal income tax collections in the table—

TABLE 26

FEDERAL PERSONAL INCOME TAX RECEIPTS, SELECTED YEARS, 1910–1958*

Fiscal Year	Individual Income Tax Receipts ($ million)	Net Budget Receipts[a] ($ million)	Individual Income Tax as Per Cent of Budget Receipts
1910	0	900	0
1917	180	1,449	12.4
1925	845	4,380	19.3
1930	1,147	4,883	23.2
1940	982	5,114	19.1
1945	17,594	44,475	39.6
1950	15,745	36,495	43.1
1955	28,747	60,390	47.7
1958	34,724	69,117	50.3

* Sources: 1910–1930: *Annual Report of the Secretary of the Treasury*, 1935, p. 323; 1940–1945: *Annual Report . . .*, 1958, pp. 390, 454; 1950: *Budget of The United States Government from 1958*, Special Analysis L; 1955–1958: *Budget . . .* 1960, Special Analysis L.

[a] Net budget receipts are gross receipts less refunds of taxes and less transfer to trust fund accounts in the case of social security taxes. The tax receipt figures from 1950 on are adjusted for refunds. Those before 1950 are not so adjusted in the sources. However, since there was no withholding prior to 1945 in the table, refunds were extremely small during those years. In 1945, however, refunds were large, but not allocated among taxes in the statistical data available. Therefore, an estimated allocation of refunds to the personal income tax has been made for 1945, based upon more recent proportions. These differences suggest that the percentage figures for years before 1950 are not precisely comparable, but it is believed that errors are small.

represented collection at the source of personal income taxes on corporate dividends.[1]

The relative revenue importance of the federal personal income tax shows almost a persistent increase through the period from its beginning in 1913. When variations from this trend occur, they are the result either of temporarily heavier reliance upon other tax measures or the accident of

[1] Full discussion of this point must be postponed until we discuss the federal corporation income tax, in the two following chapters. Briefly, until 1936, individuals did not pay a normal tax on cash dividends from corporate stocks, because the corporation had already paid a tax on the earnings from which dividends were distributed. However, individuals did pay surtaxes on dividend income. In 1936 individuals were subject to both normal and surtaxes on dividend income, in spite of the fact that the corporation paid an income tax on its earnings before distribution. It is therefore clear that (until 1936) some part of corporate income taxes represented personal income taxes paid at the source.

cyclical change in the economy which changes, for a short period, the base of the income tax more markedly than that for other taxes in the system. In 1940, and for the major part of the nineteen-thirties, heavy reliance was placed upon excises on commodities. This was done because of the shrinkage of the income tax base during that period, a consequence of low national income levels. The 1958 figures reflect a recession decline in personal income tax liability. In this year, total budget receipts had increased since 1950 by a greater proportion than income tax receipts. However, the individual income tax has for some time produced approximately half of federal budget receipts.

Use of personal income taxes by state governments has shown a gradual increase. Twenty-nine of forty-eight states were using such taxes in 1959. The rates are comparatively low in comparison to federal rates; minimum rates ranged in 1959 from ¾ of 1 per cent to 3 per cent, while maximum rates ranged between 3 per cent and 11 per cent. Personal exemptions are relatively high in most states. The revenue produced by state individual income taxes in 1958 was $1.5 billion. This represented only 10 per cent of total tax revenues of the states, and indicates the relative unimportance of personal income taxes among the states as a group. Among the states employing them, these taxes produce amounts ranging from less than 10 per cent to about one-third of total tax receipts.

Use of personal income taxes by local governments is virtually nonexistent. Though information is scattered and incomplete, it appears that not more than eight or ten cities employ this form of taxation, including the District of Columbia; Philadelphia; Louisville and Paducah in Kentucky; and Columbus, Dayton, Toledo, Youngstown, and Springfield in Ohio. With one exception (District of Columbia) these cities apply a low, single tax rate, and with the exception of the Kentucky cities, none is located in a state employing a personal income tax.

Early History of Federal Personal Income Taxation

The Civil War Income Tax. The first federal tax upon personal incomes was legislated in 1861, to be payable in 1862. It was imposed upon all individual income, at a flat rate of 3 per cent and with exemption of the first $800 of income per year. In 1862 rates and personal exemptions were altered, and fragmentary progression was introduced into the tax. Under this tax, income between $600 and $10,000 per year was taxed at 3 per cent, and income over $10,000 was taxed at 5 per cent. A further increase in rates occurred in 1865, when incomes between $600 and $5,000 were taxed at 5 per cent and all over $5,000 at 10 per cent. The 1865 law represents the most intensive application of the Civil War income tax. In 1866 some 460,000 persons paid personal income taxes of approximately 73 million dollars.[2] The tax was repealed in 1872, having produced revenues totaling approximately 350 million dollars since 1861.

The question of constitutionality was inevitably raised against the Civil War income tax,[3] although by and large it was accepted almost whole-heartedly during the period of war need. The constitutional issue was raised under Article I, Section 9, which forbade federal levy of a "capitation or other direct tax" unless it was levied "in proportion to the census or enu-meration." Since the tax in question was levied according to income and not according to census enumeration, the nub of the problem was whether a personal income tax is a direct tax. The plaintiff maintained that the tax was direct, and cited an imposing list of then-eminent economists, including Adam Smith, John Stuart Mill, and J. B. Say, whose writings unquestionably testified to the directness of the tax in the economic sense. The Court found, however, that ". . . *direct taxes*, within the meaning of the Constitution, are only capitation taxes, as expressed in that instrument, and taxes on real estate; and that the tax of which the plaintiff in error complains is within the category of an excise or duty."[4] A personal income tax was thus found to be legally an indirect tax, and its use declared to be within the federal power.

The Income Tax of 1894.[5] Congress enacted a personal income tax law in 1894 which was to tax personal incomes in excess of $4,000 annually at a fixed rate of 2 per cent. The law was passed with the support of western and southern legislators over the virtually unanimous opposition of the east. The tax, with its high personal exemption, would have been borne almost exclusively by residents of the eastern states, and was regarded as a discrim-inatory attack upon the wealthy classes.

In *Pollack* v. *Farmers' Loan and Trust Co.*,[6] the Supreme Court deter-mined the law to be unconstitutional with respect to the taxation of the income from real estate and the income from municipal securities. With

[2] Most of the facts concerning the Civil War income tax are taken from Davis R. Dewey, *Financial History of the United States,* 11th ed., New York, Longmans, 1931, pp. 305, 306.

[3] *Springer* v. *United States,* 102 U. S. 586.

[4] *Ibid.,* p. 602.

[5] Cf. Dewey, *op. cit.* pp. 456–58.

[6] *157 U. S. 429* (1894).

respect to the first point, the issue was whether a tax on the income from real estate was a direct tax, and therefore unconstitutional unless levied according to a census enumeration. The Court found that usage both in tax literature and in English judicial practice identified such a tax as being direct. Nevertheless, as in *Springer* v. *United States,* the Court was compelled to accept not general usage but the intent of the framers of the Constitution as to the meaning of the term. The opinion stated:

> Nothing can be clearer than that what the Constitution intended to guard against was the exercise by the general government of the power of directly taxing persons and property within any state through a majority made up from other states.[7]

Thus a tax on property would contravene the constitutional protection of the minority against the majority, and "we are of the opinion that the law in question, so far as it levies a tax on the rents or income of real estate, is a violation of the Constitution, and is invalid."[8]

Concerning the validity of a tax on the income from municipal securities, the Court concluded that such a tax is "a tax on the power of the states and their instrumentalities to borrow money, and consequently repugnant to the Constitution."[9] On a rehearing of the case in 1895[10] to rule upon two points in the original case upon which the Court was equally divided, it was determined that the tax on the income from personal estates was a direct tax, and that the law did not meet the constitutional requirement of uniformity.

The 1894 tax was therefore abortive; the decision of the Court—a complete reversal of the decision in *Springer* v. *U.S.*—closed the way to federal taxation of personal incomes except through amendment to the Constitution.

The Corporation Tax of 1909 and the Sixteenth Amendment. In the *Springer* case the Court had declared that the Civil War tax was an excise (an indirect tax) and thus the constitutional rule of apportionment was not applicable. This conclusion with respect to excises was reiterated in the *Pollack* decision, though in that decision the personal income tax was declared to be a direct tax and not an excise. In 1909 a federal excise upon corporations for the privilege of doing business was enacted, imposing a 1 per cent rate upon the net income of corporations in excess of $5,000. This tax was interpreted to be an excise *measured by net income,* and thus was held to be an indirect tax.[11]

---

[7] *Ibid.,* 583.
[8] *Ibid.*
[9] *Ibid.,* 586.
[10] *158 U. S. 601.*
[11] In *Flint* v. *Stone Tracy Co., 220 U. S. 107.*

Modern taxation of personal incomes in the United States dates from ratification of the Sixteenth Amendment in 1913. The Amendment reads:

The Congress shall have power to lay and collect taxes on incomes, from whatever source derived, without apportionment among the several States, and without regard to any census or enumeration.

A personal income tax law was passed immediately after ratification of the Amendment (1913), largely to offset the revenue losses anticipated from reduction of certain tariff rates by legislation of that year.

The principal features of the Act of 1913 were the following: (1) A *normal tax* of 1 per cent on net income over $3,000 per year ($4,000 for a married couple); (2) a *surtax* (in addition to the normal tax) upon higher incomes, at progressive rates of 1 per cent on incomes between $20,000 and $50,000 and reaching a maximum of 6 per cent on incomes over $500,000; (3) treatment of capital gains (realized gains from the sale of capital assets) as income, and capital losses as deductions from income; (4) use of the corporation income tax as an instrument for collection of taxes on dividend income at the source. By this arrangement the 1 per cent tax on corporate income was a substitute for the 1 per cent normal tax on individual income derived from corporate dividends. The individual did not pay a normal tax on dividend income because the corporation had paid it for him.[12]

Outline of Federal Income Tax Computation

We shall briefly and broadly outline the steps in calculation of the amount of personal income tax payable under present law, primarily to give the reader an impression of the nature of net income for federal tax purposes, and to lay the foundation for later analysis of problems in income tax theory and practice.

It is necessary to keep in mind that a tax imposed upon personal net income requires uniform definition of net income. The law must so define net income that it means essentially the same thing to many different taxpayers, deriving their incomes from different sources and in different forms. This definition of net income must, for practical reasons, be spelled out in terms

[12] Actually, collection at the source was more widely employed than is indicated above. The Act of 1913 required all persons and corporations to deduct the tax of 1 per cent on all rent, interest, and salaries over $3,000 paid to other persons. The income recipient was then excused from payment of normal tax on such income upon which the tax had been paid at the source. We shall be interested in the problem of integration of corporate and personal income taxes; it is for this reason that we have above pointed particularly to collection of the tax on dividend income at the source.

of the items included in and excluded from gross receipts, and the specific items deductible from gross income, to arrive at a uniformly determined figure of net income. In the discussion which follows we shall be interested in broad categories of items, and not in the intricacies of unusual cases.

1. Adjusted Gross Income. The gross income of the individual represents his receipts during the year in money and in kind. These receipts are of two general sorts. Receipts from personal services, such as wages, salaries, commissions, fees, and tips, are entered as their gross amounts before any payroll deductions. Receipts from ownership of property, such as dividends, interest, rents, royalties, and profits, are entered net of the expenses incurred in earning them. Capital gains from the sale of property during the year are also a part of gross income, though they may be segregated and given particular tax treatment at the taxpayer's option.[13] If the individual's income is received partly in money and partly in kind (e.g., the inclusion of living quarters or board as part of wages), both are included as gross income. Gross income is "adjusted" by the deduction of the expenses of earning it and by the exclusion of the first $50 per taxpayer of dividends received.

Major items of receipts excluded from gross income are:

1. Insurance settlements, since premium payments on insurance are not deductible for tax purposes, or because the payment is made for an equivalent loss incurred.

2. Gifts and bequests received, because they are but transfers of funds upon which the tax was paid by the owner when it was earned.

3. Interest on state and local debt obligations under an exemption of long standing, quite probably required by the Constitution.

4. Reimbursement for expenses incurred in performing duties for an employer.

5. Certain payments to military personnel, largely as a legislative favor to this class of public servant.

The exclusions from gross income are thus designed to avoid double taxation of the same income, and to exempt certain types of income for special reasons.

2. Deductions from Adjusted Gross Income. Having determined adjusted gross income of the individual, various deductions are permitted before arrival at the tax base. The principal deductible items are:

(1) Contributions. Payments made to a charitable, educational, or re-

---

[13] Full analysis of the treatment of capital gains and losses will appear in a later chapter.

ligious organization are in general deductible if the organization does not carry on propaganda or legislation-influencing activities to any substantial extent. These contributions may not be deducted if any consideration or benefit accrues to the donor. In general, such charitable deductions may not exceed 20 per cent of adjusted gross income.

(2) Interest. When payments of interest on personal debt are made, these payments are deductible in the year in which they are made. (Payments of interest on business or professional debt are excluded from adjusted gross income.) Payment of principal on a personal debt is not deductible, for the proceeds of the debt when the funds are borrowed are not counted as income. The presumed reason for permitting deductions of interest on personal debt is that it reduces the "netness" to the individual of his wage or other gross income, though it is difficult to make a case for this deduction.

(3) Taxes. In general, state and local taxes, licenses, and fees are deductible, but federal taxes are not.

(4) Medical and dental expenses. Expenses for diagnosis, treatment, medicines, health and hospital insurance premiums, and such things as eyeglasses, hearing aids, seeing-eye dogs, and false teeth are deductible in the year in which the expense is incurred. The extent of the deduction, however, is limited to any amount in excess of 3 per cent of adjusted gross income, except for persons over sixty-five, for whom there is no limit.

(5) Casualty losses and thefts. To the extent not covered by insurance the depreciated value of the loss may be claimed as a deduction. Such loss represents impairment of the capital of the individual which was presumably accumulated out of income formerly subject to tax.

(6) Alimony paid. This deduction avoids double taxation of income used for alimony payments. Congress has transferred its sympathies in the matter of broken marriages. Formerly, alimony received was excluded from gross income, and the payer was subject to tax on that part of his income used for alimony payment. Alimony is now deductible by the payer and taxable to the receiver.

(7) Standard deduction. The taxpayer is given an option of listing his items for deduction or of taking instead a standard deduction in lieu of listing. If he has a small income and uses the short form, a standard deduction of 10 per cent is built into the rate structure. If the long form is used, the taxpayer may either itemize deductions or take in lieu thereof a lump deduction of 10 per cent of adjusted gross income or $1,000, whichever is the smaller. The larger the income the more likely the taxpayer will be to

itemize deductions. Persons with incomes under $15,000 overwhelmingly utilize the standard deduction.[14]

3. Taxable Income. After subtracting the deduction(s) from adjusted gross income, personal exemptions of $600 each for the taxpayer and his dependents are subtracted in order to arrive at the taxable income, or the base of the tax. An additional $600 exemption is allowed to a taxpayer or his wife if he (she) is over sixty-five years of age or blind. Determining who is a dependent is a very complex question, and more errors are made with respect to dependency on tax returns than with respect to any other item. In general, a dependent must receive over half of his support from the taxpayer, may not receive gross income in excess of $600 unless he is a student, is a member of the taxpayer's household, or is a reasonably close relative. But there are many variants upon these rules.

Allowance of personal exemptions provides a tax-free amount of net income supposedly adequate for the maintenance of a minimum level of living. Clearly, some allowance for living expenses must be made if the tax is to reflect ability to pay. On the other hand, the law obviously could not allow the taxpayer to determine the amount necessary for living expenses, nor could it use actual living expenses as an index of necessary expenses. The amount of the personal exemption has varied frequently through the history of the federal income tax, as shown below, but the variations by no means reflect changes in the cost of living—the trend of exemptions has usually been downward or stable as the price level has risen over a period of time.

Date Law Enacted	Exemption for Husband and Wife
1913	$4,000
1917	2,000
1921	2,500
1926	3,500
1932	2,500
1940	2,000
1941	1,500
1942	1,200
1944	1,000
1948	1,200

4. Application of Tax Rates. For some years, separate rate schedules have applied to single persons, married couples filing joint returns, and unmarried or separated persons qualifying as heads of households. All are progressive schedules, beginning at 20 per cent for the first dollar of taxable income, and rising as high as 91 per cent. The blocks of income subject to these progres-

---

[14] For the year 1956, 35 per cent of taxable returns with adjusted gross income under $15,000 itemized deductions, while 76 per cent of those over $15,000 did so. Computed from United States Treasury Department, *Statistics of Income . . . 1956, Individual Income Tax Returns*, pp. 23, 35.

sive rates are twice as large on a joint return by a married couple as on a return by a single individual. That is, a single individual pays 20 per cent of the first $2,000 of taxable income, while for husband and wife the 20 per cent rate applies to the first $4,000. And a single taxpayer pays 91 per cent on taxable income over $200,000, while on a joint return this rate applies to income over $400,000. In between are unmarried or separated persons who qualify as "heads of households." Their brackets of income are about the same as for single taxpayers, but the rates progress somewhat more slowly as the income brackets rise.

The changes in rates at the extreme ends of the progressive rate schedule since the beginning of federal individual income taxation in 1913 are shown in Table 27.

TABLE 27

BOTTOM AND TOP RATES AND INCOME BRACKETS:
U.S. INDIVIDUAL INCOME TAX, 1913–1959
(Joint return, husband and wife)

Year of Enactment	Starting Rate (%)	Net Income to Which Starting Rate Applies[a] ($0 to $:)	Maximum Rate (%)	Net Income to Which Maximum Rate Applies (over $:)
1913	1.0	20,000	7.0	400,000
1916	2.0	20,000	5.0	2,000,000
1917	2.0	2,000	67.0	2,000,000
1918	6.0	4,000	77.0	1,000,000
" (eff. 1919)	4.0	4,000	73.0	1,000,000
1921	4.0	4,000	67.0	200,000
1924	2.0	4,000	46.0	500,000
1926	1.5	4,000	25.0	100,000
1928 (eff. 1929)	.5	4,000	24.0	100,000
" (eff. 1930)	1.5	4,000	25.0	100,000
1932	4.0	4,000	63.0	1,000,000
1936	4.0	4,000	79.0	5,000,000
1941	10.0	2,000	81.0	5,000,000
1942	19.0	2,000	88.0	200,000
1944	23.0	2,000	94.0	200,000
1945	19.0	2,000	86.5	200,000
1948	16.6	4,000	82.1	400,000
1950	17.4	4,000	84.4	400,000
1951	22.2	4,000	92.0	400,000
" (eff. 1954)	20.0	4,000	91.0	400,000

[a] Between 1913 and 1945, the starting rate was the *normal* tax rate. For most of the period the normal tax rate was a flat rate on all income. The figure in column 3 was that beyond which the progressive rates began to apply, or at which a slightly progressive normal tax rate applied. By the 1945 act, both normal and surtaxes were combined into a single schedule.

The complete schedule of rates currently applicable to a joint return of husband and wife is as follows:

If the Amount of Taxable Income Is:		The Amount of the Tax Is: (Cumula- (Marginal tive) rate)					And the Average Rate on ª:	
Over—	But not over:							
0	$4,000	20% of income					$2,000 is	20.0 %
$4,000	$8,000	800	plus 22% of excess over			4,000	6,000 is	20.67%
8,000	12,000	1,680	"	26%	"	"	8,000	10,000 "	22.0 %
12,000	16,000	2,720	"	30%	"	"	12,000	14,000 "	23.71%
16,000	20,000	3,920	"	34%	"	"	16,000	18,000 "	25.55%
20,000	24,000	5,280	"	38%	"	"	20,000	22,000 "	27.45%
24,000	28,000	6,800	"	43%	"	"	24,000	26,000 "	29.46%
28,000	32,000	8,520	"	47%	"	"	28,000	30,000 "	31.53%
32,000	36,000	10,400	"	50%	"	"	32,000	34,000 "	33.53%
36,000	40,000	12,400	"	53%	"	"	36,000	38,000 "	35.42%
40,000	44,000	14,520	"	56%	"	"	40,000	42,000 "	37.24%
44,000	52,000	16,760	"	59%	"	"	44,000	50,000 "	40.60%
52,000	64,000	21,480	"	62%	"	"	52,000	58,000 "	43.45%
64,000	76,000	28,920	"	65%	"	"	64,000	70,000 "	46.89%
76,000	88,000	36,720	"	69%	"	"	76,000	82,000 "	49.83%
88,000	100,000	45,000	"	72%	"	"	88,000	94,000 "	52.47%
100,000	120,000	53,640	"	75%	"	"	100,000	110,000 "	55.58%
120,000	140,000	68,640	"	78%	"	"	120,000	130,000 "	58.80%
140,000	160,000	84,240	"	81%	"	"	140,000	150,000 "	61.56%
160,000	180,000	100,440	"	84%	"	"	160,000	170,000 "	64.02%
180,000	200,000	117,240	"	87%	"	"	180,000	190,000 "	66.29%
200,000	300,000	134,640	"	89%	"	"	200,000	250,000 "	71.66%
300,000	400,000	223,640	"	90%	"	"	300,000	350,000 "	76.75%
400,000		313,640	"	91%	"	"	900,000	400,000 "	78.41%

ª The average is the total tax divided by the total taxable income.

In Figure 12 the average and marginal tax rates effective in 1960 under the individual income tax (unchanged since 1954) are plotted. This chart

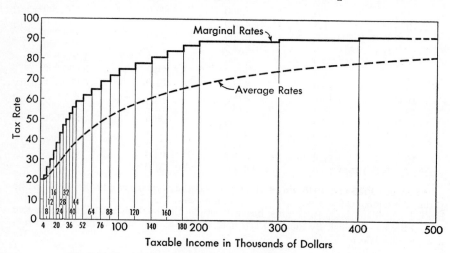

Figure 12. Marginal and average tax rates: U.S. individual
income tax, 1959.
(rates on joint return)

is instructive, for several reasons. The marginal rate structure shows that there is no possible dollar of income for which the rate is 100 per cent or more. Some part of every marginal dollar is left to the taxpayer, no matter what the size of his income. This part decreases as income increases, but it never reaches zero. The larger the income before tax the larger the income after tax. Though what is left of a marginal dollar of large income is small and might not be worth the effort required to earn it, it is always something. A second important observation is that no matter how high the marginal rate on a large income is, the earlier portions of that income are subject to the same lower marginal rates as smaller incomes. It has been too often believed by the uninitiated that when an income is subject to a marginal rate of 91 per cent, the whole income is subject to this rate. This is quite wrong; the first $4,000 pays the same 20 per cent rate as an income totaling $4,000. This is why the average rate rises less rapidly than the marginal rate in the chart.

A third important observation is that progression in the rate structure is more rapid at lower income levels than at higher income levels. This is true both because the increase in marginal rates from step to step is constant or decreases, and because the income brackets to which the marginal rates apply become broader as income increases. Thus, the average curve flattens out as income rises. The reason for this is a very practical one. Since there are so many more incomes at the bottom of the scale than at the top, the rates must be rather high where the most incomes are in order to raise large amounts of revenue.[15] Also, a look at the chart will indicate that if marginal rates kept on rising after $32,000 at the same rate as before, they would rather quickly reach 100 per cent.

A special problem of equity has arisen because of the way some states have historically treated the income of married couples. In "community property" states the law provides that income to one spouse is regarded as belonging one-half to the other spouse. It was possible in those states for separate returns of husband and wife to be made, although only one spouse received the income. The advantage of separate returns and income splitting was, of course, that each would pay a marginal rate lower in many cases than would have been paid if the income were not divided. In other states, the income tax law required that if the income was received by one

[15] For the calendar year 1956, 78.3 per cent of aggregate adjusted gross income reported in all personal income tax returns was reported by persons with gross income of less than $10,000. Ninety per cent was reported by persons with adjusted gross income under $20,000. U. S. Treasury Department, *Statistics of Income . . . 1956: Individual Income Tax Returns*, p. 20.

spouse, it was a single income subject to standard progressive rates. The community property provisions gave a distinct federal income tax advantage.

In an attempt to eliminate this geographical discrimination, Congress in 1948 granted the privilege of income-splitting on a joint return to all. In calculating the tax, the taxable income was divided by two and the progressive rate schedule applied to half the income. Then the tax so calculated was multiplied by two. This practice has continued to the present, though the effect is now frozen into a special rate schedule for joint returns. Though the geographical discrimination has been eliminated, a new and very serious discrimination has taken its place. It is between the unmarried or widowed taxpayer who is not the head of a household, and the married person who can file a joint return. If the marginal rates for an individual were plotted on Figure 12 beside those for joint returns, the stair-step curve for the individual would have the same number of risers as the curve for the joint return, and the risers would have the same height, but the steps themselves would be only half as wide. In terms of actual tax liability, the following samples of the difference may be instructive:

Taxable Income	Tax on Joint Return	Tax on Individual Return
$4,000	$ 800	$ 840
6,000	1,240	1,360
8,000	1,680	1,960
10,000	2,200	2,640
20,000	5,280	7,260
40,000	14,520	19,740
100,000	53,640	67,320

A heavy penalty is imposed upon bachelorhood and widowhood. Before 1948, when rates were roughly the same as in 1959, the married person was granted an additional personal exemption for his spouse, but this was taken to measure roughly the difference in basic living costs. Since 1948, income splitting has placed a great premium upon marriage and imposed serious discrimination upon the single person,[16] particularly upon the person who becomes widowed, and the tax may force a sharp readjustment of personal budgets.

The question may be raised whether the marginal or the average rates of taxation are the more significant for analytical purposes. This may seem

[16] For the year 1956, of a total of about 46 million taxable personal income returns, about 14 million were made by single persons not heads of households or surviving spouses. They paid over $6 billion of total tax receipts of about $32 billion. The problem here is thus not one to be ignored, for single persons made 31 per cent of all returns and paid 19 per cent of total tax. The discrepancy is presumably due to the fact that a large proportion of single taxpayers are at the lower ages among employables, or in the high age groups. Their gross incomes are thus below average.

to be raising an artificial distinction, since, of course, the two are simply different measures of the same tax burden situation. However, in terms of the tax burden upon whole incomes, the average rate is a very useful and simple device. In Figure 12 one can tell at a glance the proportion of taxable income taken by the tax by comparing for any income the vertical distance from the base to the average rate curve with the distance to the horizontal 100 per cent line at the top of the chart. On the other hand, the marginal rate is the critical one in analysis of incentive effects of the rate structure. For the question is usually one of whether the tax rate encourages additional effort or investment. And this is normally more closely related to the additional tax incurred with additional income received—a function of the marginal rate—than with the average tax per dollar on the whole income. For a given income, it would be possible to arrive at the same average tax rate with a high but flat marginal rate schedule, or with one which starts lower and rises higher. The latter would probably have much more serious incentive effects.

5. Credits Against the Tax. Our digressions into rate structure problems may have caused us to lose sight of the fact that we were outlining the steps in determination of the amount of the tax under the federal law. To return to this matter, we had applied the appropriate rate to taxable income. The result, however, may not be the final tax. For there are two possible credits that can be subtracted from the tax so computed. The first of these is a special credit of 4 per cent of dividends received, provided the credit does not exceed 4 per cent of taxable income. This is another "break" given to dividend receivers—the other was the $50 dividend exclusion from gross income noted in the discussion of adjusted gross income. These "breaks" are given on grounds that dividends are derived from corporation profits, upon which the corporation has had to pay a federal corporation income tax. Only corporate profits are subject to this "double taxation" among the streams of income, and we shall have more to say about this in a later chapter. The second tax credit is for 20 per cent of retirement income up to $1,200 per year which has been included above in taxable net income and which is determined by law to be untaxable. Social security benefits up to $1,200 per year are not taxed, and the retirement income provision takes care of equivalent amounts under private retirement schemes and property incomes for those who do not qualify for up to $1,200 of social security benefits. It is taken as a 20 per cent tax credit rather than as an exclusion, a deduction, or an exemption, in order to prevent the tax saving to a high-income person from exceeding that to a low-income taxpayer.

The amount remaining after applying the tax rate to taxable income and then subtracting any tax credit is the amount of tax payable. The long form procedure described here is simply the process of "cleaning up" at the end of the tax year. Most taxpayers are subject to regular withholding during the year. The remainder are required to estimate their tax at the beginning of the year (actually by April 15) and pay this estimated tax in quarterly installments during the year. The final calculation we have described is therefore in practice a process of determining whether an additional tax beyond that paid by withholding or by estimating is due, or whether a refund is due from the Treasury.

Coverage of the Federal Personal Income Tax

It was not until early in World War II that the federal personal income tax was extended to include a major portion of the income receivers of the United States. This extension of coverage was dictated by great need for revenue and by the anti-inflation program. Continuing postwar revenue needs, a realization of the desirability of taxation by means of the personal income tax, and the remarkable increase in personal incomes have brought about a continued broadening of the popular base upon which the tax rests.

TABLE 28

PERSONAL INCOME TAX COVERAGE, SELECTED YEARS, 1916–1957*

Year	Total Returns (thousands)	Taxable Returns (thousands)	Total Tax ($ million)	Tax Per Return ($)	Proportion of Population Paying Tax (%)
1916		429	173	403	.4
1919		5,333	1,269	238	5.2
1929	4,137	4,044	1,002	248	3.3
1934	4,198	4,094	511	123	3.2
1939	7,715	7,633	928	122	5.5
1942	35,973	27,285	9,046	331	20.6
1945	49,965	42,651	17,050	400	30.8
1948	52,072	36,411	15,442	428	24.8
1957	59,825	46,865	34,394	575	36.5

* Figures of returns and taxes paid taken from Treasury Department, *Statistics of Income;* population statistics used in the calculation are census figures. Nontaxable returns were not reported prior to 1929.

Table 28 presents certain data demonstrating personal income tax coverage for selected years between 1916 and 1957. In a very real sense, the federal income tax, before World War II, was a "rich man's tax." In 1948, on the other hand, some 83 per cent of the total labor force made returns, and

58 per cent paid personal income taxes.[17] Though the average tax per return in 1945 and in 1948 was almost identical with that in 1916, it should be understood that this average tax was paid in the two later years by persons on the average much farther down in the real income scale.

The proportion of the population making returns or paying taxes in any given year will depend principally upon two variable factors: (1) the size and distribution pattern of personal income, and (2) the provisions of the tax law itself respecting the amount of income exempt from taxation. The increased number of returns since 1939 has been due both to increased incomes and radically reduced personal exemptions. The decrease in the number of taxable returns in 1929 and 1948 resulted from increased exemption, while that in 1934 was caused by lowered income levels in spite of the offsetting effect of a lowering of exemptions by the Act of 1932.

The total tax paid depends upon the level of income, the amount of the personal exemptions, and the schedule of rates applicable in the law. Of the two selected years (1934 and 1948) shown in the table in which there was marked decline in total taxes paid, the 1948 reduction was due to rate reductions and raised exemptions, while in 1934 to reduced national income. The amount of taxes paid per return through the period considered suggests little with respect to the variables involved. Generally speaking, a high tax per return indicates high rates on taxable income. This may result from concentrating taxes on relatively high incomes, as was the case in 1916,[18] and to a lesser degree in 1929, or from imposition of heavy rates on the majority of incomes, as in 1942, 1945, 1948, and 1957.

An important determinant of the number of persons subject to taxation is, of course, the amount of individual income granted exemption. Because the income distribution pattern is such that the large majority of individuals receive net incomes (as defined by the tax law) in the lower income brackets, a relatively minor change in personal exemptions will cause marked change in the number of persons subject to tax. Estimates showing variations in probable income tax coverage and revenues with minor varia-

---

[17] The "labor force" in 1948 was estimated to have been 62.7 million persons. (*Statistical Abstract of the United States,* 1949, p. 174). The "labor force" is made up of all persons 14 years old or over who are in the labor market, including, in addition to those involuntarily unemployed and those with jobs, persons who are self-employed. It should be recognized that the relation of tax returns to the labor force does not give the exact proportion of income receivers making returns. Some returns were made on income from sources other than employment by persons not in the labor force. Nevertheless, the relation is a useful ready approximation.

[18] Personal returns in 1916 were principally surtax returns (at relatively higher rates), since a large part of the normal tax (typically at low rates) was collected at the source through the corporation income tax. See p. 361.

tion in exemptions under conditions obtaining in early 1947 are given in Table 29.

TABLE 29

ESTIMATED NUMBER OF INDIVIDUAL INCOME TAXPAYERS AND REVENUE
UNDER VARIOUS EXEMPTIONS, 1947*

Exemptions { a. Single Persons b. Married Couples c. Additional Dependents (each)	Number of Taxpayers With Net Income Under $3,000 (000)	Number of Taxpayers With Net Income Over $3,000 (000)	Total Number of Taxpayers (000)	Total Expected Revenue ($ million)
1. a—$500; b—$1,000; c—$500	40,813.1	7,731.5	48,544.6	16,692.0
2. a—$600; b—$1,200; c—$600	36,232.4	7,584.4	43,816.7	15,046.1
3. a—$700; b—$1,400; c—$700	30,748.6	7,268.4	38,017.0	13,658.3
4. a—$800; b—$1,600; c—$400	31,811.4	7,680.2	39,491.6	13,383.2

* The estimates are made on the assumptions of tax rates effective in 1947 under the Revenue Act of 1945, and national income of $166 billion. Adapted from Table G, accompanying the testimony of the Secretary of the Treasury, *Individual Income Tax Reduction*, Hearings, House Committee on Ways and Means, on H. R. 1, Eightieth Cong., 1st Sess., 1947, p. 32.

Much may be said for broad coverage of incomes for tax purposes. This is particularly true if the extension of personal income taxation takes place at the expense of other less attractive tax measures. For as we have seen, the objectives of taxation, in terms of known incidence and controlled allocation of burdens, are far more nearly possible of accomplishment under the personal income tax than under other tax instruments. There is the further morale advantage of direct taxation, in which tax payment is a separate act on the part of the payer. The taxpayer is then aware of the taxes he pays, and the act of tax payment is generative of an interest in the financial affairs of government. No such morale advantages inhere in tax schemes which hide the tax as an indefinite and unknown element of the price of a good.

Collection at the Source[19]

Payment of the tax on income at the time of its realization has for a long time been an integral part of the British system. Collection at the source has been utilized by the federal government of the United States to a greater or lesser degree since the beginning of the modern income tax in 1913. Of those states employing personal income taxes, only a small minority

[19] A condensed and very useful treatment of the use of collection at the source is George E. Lent, "Collection of the Personal Income Tax at the Source," *Journal of Political Economy*, October, 1942, pp. 719–37.

utilize collection at the source. The British plan dates from 1803, and has been applied to investment income and to salaries paid by the government and by the railroads since that time.[20] Collection at the source involves deduction of the tax from an income payment by the maker of the payment. The tax is thus withheld on the occasion of the realization of income, and the income receiver is thereafter exempt from a personal tax upon this tax-paid income. The objective is to make tax collections from relatively few sources, obviating a large number of small individual returns.

The 1913 federal income tax in the United States provided for extensive use of collection at the source by two methods. The first required any person or concern making payment of wages, salaries, interest, etc. (except dividend payments) to any individual in excess of $3,000 to deduct the 1 per cent normal tax at the time of payment. The receiver of the income was then not taxed under the 1 per cent normal tax upon the income so received, but he was required to pay a surtax if his total net income was large enough to be subject to it. The second method of collection at the source worked through the 1 per cent corporation net income tax. The corporation paid this tax on its net income, and dividends received by the individual were exempt from the 1 per cent normal tax. Thus, many individuals had all or a part of their normal tax paid at the time of receipt. Those whose incomes were of the business type, from the sale of goods or services, were subject to payment of normal taxes, since there was no vehicle for deduction at the source.

This extensive use of collection at the source was not to continue long. By an amendment of 1917, those making payments of wages, salaries, interest, etc. (except dividends) were relieved of the obligation to deduct the tax at the source except for payments to non-resident aliens. The receivers of such incomes were then required to pay the normal tax. Having abandoned collection at the source on such income payments to most individuals, Congress by the Act of 1918 adopted "information at the source," requiring those making substantial income payments of these types to report the amount and recipient of the payment. This scheme was adopted to provide information against which individual returns could be checked. The substitution of information at the source for collection at the source (except in the case of corporate dividends) continued until 1942.

The use of the corporate income tax as the vehicle for collection of the personal normal tax at the source began disintegrating with the Act of 1918. By that Act, dividends in the hands of individuals continued to be exempt from the normal tax on the grounds that this tax was being collected from

[20] Cf. Lent, *op. cit.*, p. 720.

the corporation through the corporate income tax. However, the corporate tax may be considered an acceptable collecting instrument only when the corporate tax rate is identical with the personal normal tax rate. Lacking such identity, dividend incomes become subject to treatment different from that applied to other types of income. By the Act of 1918, the corporate tax rate was established at 12 per cent, while rough progression was introduced into the personal normal tax rate: 6 per cent on the first $4,000 of taxable income, 12 per cent thereafter. Thus dividend income as a part of total taxable income not greater than $4,000 was taxed (through the corporation) at 12 per cent, while other types in an equal total income were subject to a rate only half that severe. This departure from identity in corporate and personal rates began a series of modifications which eventually resulted in complete disappearance of the original intent to utilize the corporate tax as a vehicle for collection at the source. By the Act of 1936, corporate income was taxed at progressive rates ranging from 8 to 15 per cent without exemption of dividends distributed. (No such exemption has ever been allowed.) At the same time, dividends received were taxed in the hands of individuals under *both* the normal tax (4 per cent) and the surtax (4 to 75 per cent). Dividend incomes thus were required to pay the corporate tax as corporate income and later the personal taxes as personal income, while other types of income were taxed only in the hands of individuals. With this Act, therefore, we may say that the original system of collection of personal taxes at the source had completely disappeared. Corporation income was regarded as separate and distinct from individual income.

The reasons for collection at the source were originally purely administrative—to reduce the number of personal returns to a minimum and to collect the major part of the tax through centralized responsibility for payment. At the same time, however, there was the advantage of partial collection at the time the income was realized, providing some current tax payments. This was beneficial both to government and to the taxpayer. However, when income tax burdens are not heavy, such advantages are relatively minor. The reasons for abandonment of collection at the source by 1936 are varied. In the first place, only under proportional rates was collection at the source simple and not administratively burdensome upon the payers of income. Thus, the scheme worked to reduce the number of returns only with respect to the normal tax; those individuals with large incomes were still required to make a surtax return. Further, in the case of incomes other than from corporate dividends, the sources from which collection was made were many, and the advantages in fewer returns were not marked. Thus it is doubtful that the total administrative problem was greatly simplified by collection at the source. So far as taxation of dividends at the source is concerned, its abandonment can hardly be accounted for on grounds other than that corporate income appeared to be too easy a target for productive additional taxes, regardless of the discrimination involved.

In the early years of World War II, conditions required the introduction of collection at the source on a broad scale. Extension of the coverage of the income tax by radical reduction of personal exemptions brought, as we have seen in Table 28, almost five times as many returns in 1942 as had been required in 1939. This meant a great many returns on small incomes, with the danger of widespread evasion which could be curbed, if at all, only by unusual administrative diligence and at heavy financial cost. Thus, it was desirable to require payment by those who could have little motive for participating in evasion, since they were the payers and not the receivers of the income. In addition, the great extension of coverage brought under the tax for the first time many persons who were unsophisticated in the ways of income taxation. Their personal income records were typically quite inadequate, and many of them would have experienced great difficulty in correctly computing their taxes payable, even with the assistance of the tax return form. The administrative advantages of collection at the source were thus great.

But there were other advantages to collection at the source during the war period, both to taxpayers and to government. Prior to the Current Tax Payments Act (1943), the income tax return was made on March 15 on the income of the preceding calendar year. Payment could then be made in equal quarterly installments beginning with March 15. This meant that payment of the tax on the income of a given year was made during the following year. There were three great disadvantages in this during the war period. The first was that with broad coverage at relatively high rates, persons would be required to prepare for relatively large cash payments on quarterly tax dates. The tax on a given year's income was typically actually paid out of the following year's income, since few persons anticipated tax payments far enough ahead to prepare for them by current saving. It was thus apparent that much heavier taxation under the old scheme of delayed payment would impose serious hardship and possibly a high degree of tax delinquency. This would be particularly true in the case of fluctuating incomes. It was thus a service to the taxpayer to collect the tax in the manner least burdensome to him—in small amounts on paydays. The second great disadvantage of single annual payments was that to government, which would receive the revenue return from its heavier taxes only approximately a year after they were legislated. Under the system of current tax payments, revenue from the heavier levies became immediately available, and government had ample immediate use for them.

The third disadvantage in continued use of the old system of delayed tax payments lay in its inability to perform the necessary anti-inflation tax function during the war. The severe taxes were imposed partially to take spendable funds from the public and thus reduce the upward pressure upon prices. During a period of rapidly increasing national income and growing scarcities of consumable civilian goods, it was obviously essential to remove excess incomes from the market as they were earned.

Granted the benefits to all concerned in the institution of a scheme of current tax payments, the question may be raised why such a scheme implied collection at the source. The reasons are administrative. Weekly returns by income receivers who receive their incomes on a weekly basis would create a frightful burden both upon the taxpayer and upon the Treasury. The simplest way to administer the plan was clearly to collect the tax at the source and to require the employer to furnish a statement of taxes withheld to the employee at the end of the income period.

The inauguration of a scheme of current tax collections at the source was not without its difficulties and disadvantages. The principal difficulties were: (1) the difficulty involved in initiating current tax payments in any year while payments under the old delayed-payment scheme were being made on the previous year's income; (2) the difficulty in application of progressive rates to incomes from several sources; and (3) the difficulty involved in current collection arrangements applicable to those incomes received not in large amounts from few sources but in small amounts from many sources. We shall discuss these difficulties and the techniques adopted separately.

When the current tax payment scheme was inaugurated in 1943, most taxpayers had made but one or two quarterly installment payments on the tax on their 1942 incomes. Had all paid up their 1942 taxes in a lump sum on March 15, 1943, the current tax payment scheme could have been inaugurated later that year with little inconvenience. But most individuals planned to pay their 1942 tax quarterly out of 1943 income, and a doubling-up of 1942 and current 1943 taxes upon 1943 income would have been unbearable. There were thus only two possible solutions to the dilemma. One was to excuse all taxes on 1942 personal income except the first quarterly payment made March 15, 1943. The other was to postpone (actually, drop) the current tax payment plan. Clearly the advantages of the plan were so great as to dictate adoption of the former solution, and all but the first quarterly installment on 1942 income were cancelled or, in cases where they had already been paid, returned. The Treasury thus lost a major part of the revenue on 1942 incomes, though its 1943 personal income tax receipts were greater than they would have been under the old system.

The application of progressive rates to withheld taxes (i.e., taxes collected at the source) presented a problem never before faced. The reader will recall that earlier experience with collection at the source had been related only to the proportional normal tax. But under a progressive tax, it became necessary for the withholder to apply the proper exemptions and deductions granted to the income receiver. The withholding tax was applied to salaries and wages; the wage earner was required to deposit with his employer a statement of his withholding (personal) exemptions. The amount of tax withheld for the pay period was determined by withholding tables which allowed for a round sum of deductions from gross income regarded as standard for income receivers in general. At the end of the year, therefore, the total of taxes withheld on wages or salaries for the year would approximate, but probably not exactly equal, the tax payable when calculated on an annual basis. For the deductions allowed the individual taxpayer might vary from the standard deductions provided for in the withholding table. Or the taxpayer might have received gross income for part of the year below the amount of personal exemption, and thus pay no tax, while for the remainder of the year his income might have been high enough to subject him to withholding tax. For the whole year, therefore, his income would have been such that if computed on an annual basis he would have paid less total tax than was actually withheld. The solution to this problem was to require a return covering his whole income for the year by the following March 15, calculating the tax payable on an annual basis. If the tax so computed was in excess of the total of tax withheld as shown on his withholding receipts, he paid the difference in a lump sum. If the total annual tax so computed was less than taxes withheld, he was entitled to a refund. The plan thus works to collect approximately the amount of the tax currently, and to settle the difference at the end of the year.

The third difficulty in current tax payments related to those incomes to which the withholding plan could not feasibly be applied. Such incomes included those in the form of interest, dividends, rents and royalties, and those created by the sale of goods and services to miscellaneous buyers in the market. To take an extreme example, it would be clearly impracticable to require the consumer to withhold the income tax on that income of the independent corner grocer created by the purchase of a dozen eggs. It would be impossible to establish standard tables of withholding rates, even if administration of such a scheme were possible. And in the case of interest, dividend, and similar incomes, it is likely that fewer returns would result if income were reported and the tax paid by the income receiver than if withheld at the source. Further, since such incomes commonly come to the receiver from several sources, it is much simpler to apply progressive rates, personal exemptions, and deductions to such incomes in their totality. These types of income were therefore excluded from the withholding plan, and taxed in the hands of their receivers. How, then, could current tax payments upon such incomes be accomplished? The Act required all persons not included under the withholding plan who anticipated taxable income to file a declaration of their estimated income and estimated amount of tax on that income at the beginning of the year or portion thereof during which such income is anticipated.[21] The estimated tax is payable during the year in which it is earned, in equal quarterly installments.[22] Since the estimated tax is paid, over- or underpayments are adjusted by a final return for the year showing actual income and actual tax liability.

By the provisions of the Internal Revenue Code, substantially all personal incomes are subject to tax during the year in which they are received.[23] The degree of currency depends somewhat upon the pay period. The withholding tax collects weekly from incomes received weekly, and monthly from incomes received monthly. Those not subject to withholding pay their tax quarterly through the calendar year. The advantages of such a plan, both to taxpayers and to government, are clearly evident. There are, however, certain costs connected with it which are worthy of note. It represented a radical departure from earlier tax procedures, and therefore required a re-education of all taxpayers. Other things being equal, such radical changing of the rules is undesirable, particularly in the case of the income tax, which is by nature complex and difficult for the individual taxpayer to learn. It embodies an element of uncertainty, both to the taxpayer with

---

[21] This requirement applies to persons not subject to withholding and persons receiving income in the form of interest, dividends, rents, and royalties, whose gross income from such sources is expected to exceed $100 for the year. Further, persons whose wages are subject to withholding are required to file a declaration if their estimated gross income exceeds $5,000 for the year. This requirement results from the fact that they are liable to taxation in excess of the amount withheld at the source.

[22] If the declaration is made during the second quarter of the year, the tax is payable in three equal installments; if made during the third quarter, in two installments, etc.

[23] In 1959, of individual income tax collections totaling $40,729 million, approximately 70 per cent represented taxes withheld, 30 per cent not withheld.

respect to the amount of tax which he will finally pay, and to the Treasury.[24]

Two types of administrative burden are imposed by current tax payments. The plan places great responsibility upon the employer, who is required to act as agent for the taxpayer. The record-keeping responsibilities, the accumulation of data on withholding exemptions of employees, and the issuing of withholding receipts, impose relatively heavy burdens. Accounting by the Treasury is likewise made more onerous with the great increase in number of individual collections and the increase in number of refunds.

With the increased costs involved in administration of a system of current tax payments and collection at the source, the balance is still heavily in favor of the system. It is doubtful that the severe taxes of the war and immediate postwar period could have been administered without some such plan. Experience with the withholding and current payment plan has obviously accustomed taxpayers to it, and reduced the adjustment frictions involved. Simplification and perfection of techniques can reduce some of the present uncertainties and improve administration, thus reducing other costs involved. It is probable that there will never be a return to the old system of "year-late" payments, partly because of satisfaction with the present system and partly because of the difficulties involved in transition. In fact, it was largely the transition problem which held up introduction of the current tax payment system until wartime fiscal needs demanded it.

State Personal Income Taxes

We are concerned in this section with taxes imposed by state governments upon the general personal incomes of individuals. In 1959 there were thirty-one states employing such taxes including Alaska and Hawaii. This count does not include all states which use what they may refer to as "income taxes," for many apply business taxes to the net income of certain types of business enterprises, and some states employ special taxes on the income of certain intangibles as a substitute for the taxation of these intangibles under the property tax. This latter group includes the states of New Hampshire, Ohio, and Tennessee. The Massachusetts income tax began in this manner, but the base has been so broadened as to make of it a general personal income tax.

Of the twenty-nine states currently employing individual income taxes, excluding Alaska and Hawaii, thirteen adopted this form of taxation prior to 1930 and the remaining sixteen between 1930 and 1937. Three other

---

[24] In fiscal 1958 the Treasury made refunds of tax overpayments amounting to approximately $3.8 billion. *Annual Report of the Secretary of the Treasury*, 1958, p. 13.

states employed individual income taxes at some time during the thirties, but subsequently abandoned them. A very considerable stability in the use of this form of tax is evident from the information given above. Adoption of the personal income tax by a state, whatever its original intent, has meant its permanent use.

In general, we may say that those states which enacted personal income tax laws prior to 1930 did so out of a desire to improve their tax systems in the direction of greater justice. Although in a few cases taxation of incomes began as an attempted new approach to the property taxation of intangibles, the major portion intended substitution of the income tax for the property tax at the state level. Motives for enactment of state income tax laws during the thirties were principally two: (1) To substitute new revenues for ailing property tax revenues during depression, and (2) to provide net new revenue to finance the state contribution required to qualify for federal grants-in-aid, principally for aid to the needy and specifically for the Old Age Assistance program. These late-comers were guided more by the pressures of expediency than from the conscious desire for long-range improvement in their tax systems.[25]

Of the thirty-one states with personal income taxes in 1937, more than half devoted substantially the whole of the revenues from this tax to the general funds of the state. This means that revenues were not shared with local governments, and were not earmarked for particular governmental purposes. In seven more states the revenues were used by state government, but dedicated to specific purposes. In three such cases the revenues were dedicated to public schools, in two others to relief of the needy, and in the last two they were divided between the general fund and school funds. In four states the revenues were divided between state and local governments, and in two others substantially the whole revenue was returned to local governments. In the six states last mentioned there is strong suggestion that the tax had its origin as a substitute for property taxation of intangibles. By and large, however, a survey of the personal income taxes now in force indicates an intent to reduce the tax burden upon property. As indicated above, in some cases this decision resulted from free choice on the long-run merits of the case, and in others resulted from the failure of property tax revenues to hold up in depression.

---

[25] Indeed, the special tax commission of 1933 in Connecticut recommended the emergency use of a sales tax to supply the revenue deficiency rather than a personal income tax, partially on the grounds that the former, being an inferior tax, would be more likely to be repealed at termination of the emergency than would an income tax, whose desirable qualities might well establish it as a permanent institution.

In general structure the state income taxes follow the pattern of the federal tax. The definition of gross income, the list of deductions, and the types of personal exemptions (though not the amounts), are similar to those of the federal tax. All but two[26] of the states employing general personal income taxes in 1959 taxed incomes at progressive rates. The rates themselves and the degree of progression are very mild compared with the federal income tax, though the income blocks to which particular rates apply are typically small and maximum rates are reached rather quickly. The majority of rate schedules begin at 1 or 2 per cent and apply to taxable incomes below one or two thousand dollars. The maximum rate varies between 3.75 per cent (one state) and 11 per cent (one state), with greatest concentration between 5 and 8 per cent. Great variation exists in the size of the income bracket to which the top rates apply. This variation ranges between incomes in excess of $4,000 (Iowa and Utah) and those in excess of $100,000 (New Mexico), with a concentration between $10,000 and $25,000.

The moderation shown by the states in the taxation of personal incomes is probably explainable in terms of the general belief that the federal government has "pre-empted" the personal income tax field, leaving relatively little "free" income available for other governments to take. Curiously enough, the very holding of this belief makes it true in a sense. For although all taxes fall on income and therefore there is as much income available for taxation by one measure as by another, failure to realize this simple truth tends to establish a *political* limit to income taxation well before the economic limit is reached. On the other hand, since state income taxes are deductible in calculating federal income tax, it is somewhat surprising that more states have not adopted income taxes during the postwar period of high federal tax rates. The larger income receiver, who benefits from itemizing deductions when calculating his federal income tax, thus finds that the state tax represents a considerably smaller net share of his income than is indicated even in the modest rates applied by state income tax

[26] These two states are Maryland, which imposes a flat tax rate of 5 per cent on the income from investments and 2 per cent on other income, and Massachusetts, where various rates are applied, but not progressively. The Massachusetts tax distinguishes four types of income and applies a different rate to each. These types and their rates are:

1. Annuity income	1.5%
2. Income from employment or business	2.5%
3. Capital gains from sale of intangibles	6.0%
4. Dividends and certain interest	6.0%

Here is a real curiosity in the field of income taxation. In part it reflects the evolution of the tax from an intangible property tax. It is a "classified income tax."

laws.[27] To the degree that payment of the state tax saves on the federal tax, revenue is in effect transferred from the federal government to the state government.

In this chapter we have centered our attention upon the descriptive aspects of personal income taxation. Little has been said about its theory. The broad outlines of income tax theory have been suggested at several points in our previous discussion. The taxation of incomes is clearly founded upon the principle of ability to pay. It recognizes that all taxes are eventually paid from the stream of personal income, and that intended allocation of burdens is more likely to be accomplished by direct levy upon income. The federal income tax and most state income taxes (on individuals) employ progressive rate schedules. This is in line with the principles governing proper allocation of tax burdens discussed in Chapter 13, though we have seen that deductibility modifies the combined effect of the two taxes.

RECOMMENDED READINGS

Ecker-R, P. L., "The Place of the State Income Tax in a Period of Expanding Federal Needs," *Proceedings, National Tax Association,* 1941, pp. 552–59.

    One of few discussions of the possible separate use of the personal income tax by federal and state governments.

Lent, G. E., "Collection of the Personal Income Tax at the Source," *Journal of Political Economy,* October, 1942, pp. 719 *ff.*

    A good description of the use of this device in various countries, with analysis of its benefits and shortcomings.

---

[27] When the state tax is deducted from the base of the federal income tax (as is permitted by the Internal Revenue Code), the *net additional* burden of the state tax is less than the state tax rate times its base. Let us take two examples: (1) An income receiver is subject to a marginal state income tax rate of 5 per cent and a federal marginal rate of 20 per cent. The two combined do not produce a burden of 25 per cent on the marginal dollar. He pays $.05 of his marginal dollar to the state. He deducts this tax from the federal tax base, which means that $.95 of his marginal dollar of income is subject to the federal rate of 20 per cent. The federal tax on this is $.19. The combined tax on the marginal dollar of income is $.24, and the combined rate is 24 per cent. (2) Assume a high income receiver whose marginal income is subject to a state tax rate of 10 per cent and a federal rate of 80 per cent. On his marginal dollar of income he pays $.10 to the state. After deducting this, the federal tax on his marginal dollar of income is .80 x $.90, or $.72. The combined tax is $.82, while had there been no state tax he would have paid $.80 of his marginal dollar to the federal government. The net additional burden of the state tax is thus 2 per cent on his marginal dollar, not 10 per cent. The larger the income, under progressive federal rates, the smaller the tax impact imposed by a given state tax rate.

For the small income receiver, who does not itemize deductions under the federal tax, but takes the standard deduction, the extra impact of the state tax is at the whole of the state tax rate. The combination of high marginal federal rates for large incomes and the inability of small income receivers to deduct state taxes from the base of the federal income tax makes it very difficult to construct a state income tax with any significant degree of progression. This matter is discussed more fully in Chapter 24.

Penniman, Clara, and Heller, W. W., *State Income Tax Administration*, Chicago, Public Administration Service, 1959.

As the title suggests, the emphasis is upon administration. Chapter 1, however, is an excellent historical study of state income taxes, and Chapter 10 makes predictions as to their role in the future.

Sigafoos, R. A., *The Municipal Income Tax*, Chicago, Public Administration Service, 1955.

The six chapters of this small book contain most of what is known about an interesting area of income taxation.

Strayer, P. J., *The Taxation of Small Incomes*, N.Y., Ronald, 1939.

Chapters 1 ("Introduction"), 2 ("Revenue Aspects"), and 3 ("The Theory of the Personal Exemption") are especially recommended for collateral reading.

For detail concerning the federal income tax law and its interpretation, one of the "tax courses" published by Prentice-Hall or Commerce Clearing House is almost essential, though it is possible to use the Bureau of Internal Revenue handbook *Your Federal Income Tax* or J. K. Lasser's *Your Income Tax*, both published annually.

CHAPTER 17

The Nature of Net Income for Tax Purposes

If a tax is to be imposed upon the "net income" of individuals, it is essential that net income be defined in such a manner as to accomplish the theoretical and practical objectives of the tax. More specifically, the definition must be precise in its inclusiveness; it must lend itself to consistent application to the various types of income; it must be logical or "correct," so that its application accomplishes justice among taxpayers; and it must define a magnitude which is possible of objective measurement.

It is common in economics to use the term "income" in the sense of a flow of satisfactions from capital or labor. This is *real* or *psychic* income, and doubtless for purposes of analyzing individual or general welfare represents income in its truest sense. But although basically income is satisfactions, use of the term in this sense for tax purposes presents difficulties of various orders. In the first place, it is useless in income taxation unless translated into monetary terms, for the tax base must be stated in dollars. But to take this step involves some loss of preciseness and accuracy in the relation between real income and money income. For if real income represents a flow of satisfactions, money income is the market values of the goods and services which provide those satisfactions. But what guarantee have we that the expenditure of ten dollars on goods by one person actually provides the same satisfaction to him as the expenditure of the same amount of money by another? By taking a dollar in taxes from each of these persons, therefore, we cannot be certain that both have sacrificed exactly the same amount of satisfaction. Were there some dependable, objective measure of the amount of satisfaction yielded, this measure could be used as the clearly proper income tax base. Lacking such a measure, we are forced to accept the closest approximation to it—money income—fully recognizing that in taking a step away from real income we use a measure which is somewhat inaccurate.

The economic definition of income as real income raises problems in determining at what stage it is to be measured for tax purposes. We have already seen that it cannot be measured at the stage of realization—the creation of enjoyment. But if we use money income, shall we measure it at the stage of use for purposes of enjoyment? It is often assumed that since real income is psychic, money income must be measured at the point nearest to the realization of that psychic income. For this reason it is frequently presumed that the most accurate money measure of true income is the money value of the goods and services producing true income. But this is too frequently taken to mean the value of *consumers'* goods purchased. A little reflection will show, however, that satisfactions are not only consumer satisfactions. For real income (satisfaction) can be gained from saving for future enjoyment or from giving away a part of one's money receipts. In fact, saving and giving frequently occur because the satisfaction so derived is actually greater than the satisfaction which would otherwise have been realized by expenditure on consumption. Suppose that two individuals are in the same personal situation and receive salaries of the same size. If one spends more on consumption than does the other, it is by no means clear that the first derives more immediate satisfaction from his salary than does the second.

The point at which money income should be measured is that point at which it comes into the hand of the receiver—when it is available for disposal by him for consumption or saving. For the disposal of income must be presumed to follow the principle of maximizing satisfactions, whether that income is used for consumption or saving. It is over the question of savings that a considerable amount of disagreement has arisen. Are savings income? If real income is narrowly defined as the enjoyment derived from consumption alone, savings are not income, and money income must be measured after division into the consumption and saving streams. On the other hand, if real income is broadly defined to include all satisfactions derived from the disposal of monetary receipts (after deductions of cost of production of those receipts), it is measured before disposal, and savings are income. The broader definition is preferred because it measures more accurately current ability to pay taxes, and the tax is levied at the time when ability to pay first exists. It relates ability to pay to what the receiver could get in satisfaction from the use of his net receipts, rather than what he did get from their disposal. And the definition preferred here places government's claim on a par with those of personal consumption and saving, rather than to place government in the position of residual claimant after disposition of income between consumption and saving has been determined upon by the individual.

The question whether savings should be considered income for tax purposes implies a possibility of discriminatory taxation of savings. Clearly, if that part of receipts which goes into savings is taxed before saving takes place and again when dis-saving (expenditure) occurs, discrimination results. The alternatives are to tax savings and exempt dis-savings, or *vice versa*. Such discrimination can obviously be avoided by definition of income in the tax law. Administratively, however, there is a clear preference for the former method (the method used by all income taxes at the present time). The latter method would require exemption of savings in the individual's tax return, and would require both detailed personal accounts of the disposition of income and great difficulty in checking the accuracy of returns. It would require also the inclusion in taxable income of such troublesome items as withdrawals from bank deposits and the proceeds of sales of securities and other personal capital assets. On practical grounds, therefore, there is distinct preference for defining income as personal net receipts from capital and labor prior to disposal. And on the grounds of theory there are elemental aspects of justice in taking the position that two persons with the same net receipts before disposal and in the same personal situation have equal capacity to pay taxes.

By defining income for tax purposes as net receipts before disposition for consumption and saving, we impose taxation upon funds destined to become a part of the individual's capital. But to say that this *is* the taxation of capital is to deny that capital is created out of income, a denial obviously not square with the facts. For capital is a fund (of money or goods) created out of savings from income. But there is another aspect to the problem of distinction between capital and income. The income tax is not intended to be paid out of capital, and thus reduce the capital of an economy. It is essential, therefore, that the definition of income exclude that portion of receipts which are themselves capital. The simplest example is that of depreciation. If depreciation were not deducted, part of "national income" would not be income from capital, but the capital itself. In the process of production specific items of capital are used up, some in a short period and others over a longer period. This using-up, or loss of service value, is depreciation. If replacement (or creation of reserves for replacement) does not take place out of gross output—or gross receipts—the fund of capital moves toward depletion. Net additions to the fund of capital will occur out of income, but existing capital is not maintained out of income.

To deal adequately with the necessity for distinction between capital and income in the flow of gross receipts (in the case of a national economy, a firm or an individual) the definition of income for tax purposes must lay down a general principle for exercising the distinction in practice. Mr. J. R. Hicks' "central criterion" of income will serve us well for tax purposes: ". . . a person's income is what he can consume during the week and still expect to be as well off at the end of the week as he was at the beginning."[1] Stated more generally, and in monetary terms, the income of an individual for any period of time is the money value of that part of his gross receipts (in money and in kind) which can be used up without impairing the prospects of equivalent gross receipts in any following similar period. Quite clearly, according to this definition, depreciation is not income, while net additions to capital occur from income. We shall see in later applications of the definition to questions of income tax policy that some such definition of net income is essential to the practice of justice among taxpayers.

We turn now to several problems of personal income taxation which have been and continue to be troublesome. Our specific interest will be in application of the definition of income to these problems, and in discussion of the possibilities of applying the definition in tax practice.

What Is an Individual Income?

The individual income tax need not utilize the individual person as the object of taxation. As a matter of fact, the rationale of the ability-to-pay principle would seem to utilize the notion of ability to pay not of the individual, but of the income-receiving and income-spending unit, generally composed of a group of individuals. Other things being equal, a single person without dependents has greater capacity to pay taxes per dollar of income than does the head of a family. Thus, we may say that ideally it is the income of the spending unit and not that of the individual income receiver which should constitute the tax base. The joint income provision operative since 1948, which was discussed in Chapter 16, is a sort of recognition of the income-receiving, income-spending unit concept. As pointed out in the preceding chapter, the allowance of income splitting on the joint return gives married couples a decided advantage with respect to income tax rates. This is a fault, however, of the rate structure as between the two groups, and not an inevitable consequence of treating the household's common income as a single taxable income. Differences in family size, and other household unit differences within a given income bracket, are more

[1] *Value and Capital*, Oxford, 1939, p.. 176. Cf. also H. C. Simons' definition (b), *Personal Income Taxation*, Chicago, University of Chicago Press, 1938, p. 49.

appropriately treated through deductions and exemptions than through the rate schedule.

The Income Period for Tax Purposes

The federal law requires the return to be made on the basis of a twelve-month period, though this need not necessarily be the calendar year—it may be any twelve-month period corresponding with the taxpayer's system of maintaining accounts. The important fact is, however, that the personal income tax operates upon a cash basis rather than on an accrual basis. Thus, an income is presumed to be earned when it is received. Although this is generally acceptable in the case of wages, salaries, interest, and dividends, it is frequently quite unacceptable with respect to profit and royalty incomes.

The selection of the year as an arbitrary period during which incomes are presumed to be earned may cause serious practical injustice among personal income taxpayers. It is accepted as typical in the business community that the first few years of a new business involve relatively low net income, and in many cases losses. The costs of starting a business are partially those of building up good will. Later income which results from good will is not, therefore, allocable solely to the twelve-month period in which it is received. A doctor or a lawyer may well be required to live frugally while he builds up his clientele to the point where respectable net income is received. Of course, during the years when he makes no income he pays no tax. But this does not affect the size of the tax which he eventually pays out of then current income.

Suppose we take the case of a writer, who struggles along for a period of, say, three years during the writing of a novel. During the three-year period he either lives on his savings, on charity, or takes time out to write bits here and there from which he earns enough to finance himself while preparing his major work. Let us assume that he has no taxable income during the three-year period. During the fourth year his novel is published and is successful, bringing in royalties in that year which give him taxable net income of $60,000. If he is taxed as if the whole amount were earned in the one (fourth) year, his tax would be approximately $26,440, calculated at 1959 rates on a joint return. If this net income of $60,000 were allocated over the four years actually required to earn it, the total tax for the four years would have been about $14,480. We here face a basic problem in ability to pay. In the example just cited, the real ability to pay taxes in any one year for the novelist's income of $60,000 is considerably less than the ability to pay from an income of the same size which is consistently at that level from year to year, yet a tax which assumes income to be earned in the twelve-month period in which it is received does not take account of such differences in ability to pay.

It is not often feasible to take account of these differences by the calculation of income on an accrual basis, for two reasons. The first is that it is generally impossible accurately to forecast the amount of income eventually to be received. Our novelist, our doctor, or our lawyer cannot know with any degree of accuracy what his future income is to be, and cannot therefore accurately calculate a tax on accrued income during the years before cash income is received. The second objection to taxation of accrued income is that in the early years before cash income is received, the taxpayer might be subject to great inconvenience in raising the necessary cash for tax payment.

The same objective may be accomplished by the operation of a "carry-back" system of computing the final tax. When the income is actually received, the tax liability could be computed on the basis of what it would have been had it been received in equal installments during the period while it was being earned. Such a system overcomes both difficulties mentioned in the paragraph next above.[2] But there is as much reason for carrying forward as for carrying back. What we have said about those incomes which represent a long period of production can equally be said for incomes which fluctuate from year to year for any cause. Losses of one year must be met by income of another, and it is impossible to say that losses are always met out of prior income; they may be and are met from future income. And even if net losses do not occur, the tendency under conditions of fluctuating income is to use income from high income periods during low income periods.

Aside from the justice aspect of carry-over and carry-back provisions,

---

[2] Since 1948 there has been some provision for spreading certain lump-sum compensation over the period of production. The conditions are, however, restrictive, for (1) the work involved must have covered at least a 3-year period, and (2) at least 80 per cent of the total compensation must have been received in the year in which it is taxable. Our author in the example above would qualify under (1), but probably not under (2), for his $60,000 income might well be less than 80 per cent of the total of royalties to be received from the novel. If he did qualify, he would spread the $60,000 equally over the four-year period and pay the tax which would have been due in each of the four years. The income allocated to a previous year would be taxed at the then existing rates on this amount when added to whatever other income was taxable in those years. This provision is, of course, too restrictive to include very many cases of irregular income. The widely noted case of General Eisenhower's tax saving on receipts from his book, *Crusade in Europe,* involved an entirely different matter. On that occasion it was ruled that the General was not by profession an author, and his receipts were in return for the sale of property. He was thus subject to capital gains tax, discussed later in this chapter.

there is the incentive aspect. Any economic pioneering venture involves relatively high risk of loss, along with the possibility of unusually high gain. If, therefore, losses in periods of low income are to be ignored while gains in periods of high income are heavily taxed, the prizes to be gained from economic venturesomeness are made less attractive while loss possibilities are made no more so. A dynamic economy, with heavy dependence upon risk-taking investment, will do well to avoid unnecessary burdens upon risk-takers. The calculation of income for tax purposes over a period longer than a year would almost certainly encourage the type of new and more risky investment which is required in order to maintain a high level of national income. The question may be raised whether this is not a matter more properly applicable in the taxation of businesses than in the taxation of individuals. The answer is that it applies to both. The net income of unincorporated business and professional ventures is taxed by the individual income tax, and corporations have no monopoly upon investment and the acceptance of business risks.

We have not so far been concerned with the mechanics of a carry-over provision in the tax. But it is a problem which must be met if the principle is to be adopted. Professor Simons recommends "a simple averaging device" by which the carry-over and carry-back provisions would be applied.[3] If income were computed on the basis of a five-year moving average, with annual settlement of over- and underpayment, a great deal of progress could be made toward justice to the recipients of fluctuating income. Such an averaging device could not be "simple" in an absolute sense, but minor corner-cutting such as is characteristic of the "short form" at present would eliminate many complications which present themselves.[4]

Carry-over and/or carry-back provisions have frequently been employed, both in the United States and elsewhere. These have applied only to the carrying over of *losses* from year to year, and have related only to net *business* losses. Thus the averaging of income over a period of years—as suggested here—has not been attempted, and even the carry-over or carry-back of losses has not included losses in general. The carry-over of net business

[3] Henry C. Simons, "Federal Tax Reform," in *International Postwar Problems*, Quarterly Review of the American Labor Conference on International Affairs, January, 1946, p. 27.

[4] Under any system it would be necessary for the taxpayer to retain records of taxable net income reported and tax paid. Other recommendations in this chapter, particularly with respect to treatment of capital gains and losses, would somewhat simplify the problem. It is believed that the precise arithmetic formulae by which the "simple averaging device" would be applied are beyond the scope of our discussion here. But it seems reasonable to believe that at some sacrifice of meticulous refinement, and by use of modern record-keeping methods, such a plan could be devised.

losses has been allowed under both the personal income tax (personal incomes from unincorporated business) and the corporation income taxes. Under present law net business losses can be carried back one year, and any losses not so carried back can be carried forward for a period of five years, though losses must be carried back before they are carried forward. If there is virtue in permitting business losses to be deducted from business net income over a period of years, why should not the same principle be applied to all individuals? The individual should be permitted to carry over an excess of deductions and exemptions over his adjusted gross income in any year, and apply this excess against later (or earlier) taxable income. In the interest of justice to those with highly variable incomes, it appears reasonable to take the further step of averaging taxable income over a reasonable period of years.

The system of averaging incomes over a period of years is clearly to be recommended for reasons of justice among individual taxpayers, eliminating the present discrimination against the receivers of widely fluctuating incomes. On the other hand, however, the system of averaging has disadvantages in terms of counter-cycle use of income taxes. Under boom conditions, where taxation is to be used to remove excess purchasing power tending toward price inflation, an averaging scheme would allow the high income receiver to carry back a portion of currently high income to bring former incomes to the average level for the period. If former losses are to be made up in this way, considerable amounts of currently received income may escape the high anti-inflation rates of the current year; if currently received income is to be allocated to earlier low income years, it will be subject to lower rates. In either case some part of the objective of anti-inflation taxation is unrealized, although by upward adjustment of rate schedules some part of these tax-freed funds could be recaptured.[5]

Exclusion of Capital Items from Income

Recalling our definition of income as receipts which can be used up without impairing the prospect of equivalent receipts in any following

[5] Some detail in explanation of the averaging plan is in order to explain the above statements. Two kinds of variation are contemplated: variation from year to year in income and variation from time to time in tax rates. The averaging plan would eliminate variation in incomes (for tax purposes) by allocating a portion of income in a high income year to years with lower income. This does *not* mean, however, that income so allocated would then be taxed at tax rates current in the year to which it is allocated. Thus when for counter-cycle reasons tax rates are increased, income realized in a high rate year would be subject to those rates even though allocated to former years. The difference would be that the total tax bill is lowered by allocating income, which in the absence of averaging would reach a high rate bracket, to lower brackets.

period, we are forced to the conclusion that any part of receipts which if used up would impair this prospect must be capital or its equivalent in capitalized human earning power. Income tax laws have been quite meticulous in exempting capital itself from taxation. The same cannot be said concerning human assets. The individual who receives his income from personal service experiences with the passage of time the wasting of his principal asset—the ability to earn. The human being typically reaches at some age a cessation of earning power, due to age, infirmity, or death. In more technical terms, his service life is limited. While he is earning, therefore, the whole of his earnings (salaries or wages) cannot be considered as income, since a part of these earnings represents the gradual loss of the human equivalent of capital value in a machine or building. Capital which produces an interest income to its owner is presumed to be permanent, since the amount of that income is everywhere recognized to be determinable only after depreciation has been deducted for the purpose of replacing the particular capital instrument with another when its service life has ended. True income from personal service, by the same reasoning, is determinable only after deduction of an amount from current receipts adequate to replace the capitalized earning power of the human being at the end of his service life. It is, of course, unthinkable that this accumulated reserve should be used to purchase another human being, as is done with the depreciation reserve for capital instruments. The earning power of the individual must then be replaced by a fund of his savings, which savings perpetuate his earning power. It is no more reasonable to expect a machine to create its replacement fund than to expect a human being to do it. If it be pointed out that when the laborer dies he not only loses his earning power, but also his need for earning power, it can be argued with equal force that neither are the wants of the owner of capital more permanent than he himself.

The common sense of deducting depreciation of capital in arriving at taxable net income for business-income tax purposes has been consistently implemented in the tax laws. Following the same reasoning, the federal law permits rather generous deductions for depletion by owners of mineral and petroleum deposits and timber. The more general nature of the problem is pointed up by a letter in 1952 to the Commissioner of Internal Revenue by a group of fashion models who requested some income tax relief on the grounds that their principal assets (beauty and shapeliness) would be lost over a period of time and that they were therefore entitled to reasonable allowance for "obsolescence" or "depletion."[6] The force of their claims will

---

[6] *The New York Times*, October 4, 1952.

be recognized not only by the worshipers of beauty but by the champions of elementary justice. The case for similar treatment of other incomes from personal services should also be evident, where the wasting asset is not personal attractiveness but capacity to perform personal service. It should be clear that wage receipts of $4,000 per year are not as pure income as are interest receipts of the same amount. The latter is income after depreciation allowance, while the former is not. It follows, therefore, that the capacity to pay taxes from an annual wage of $4,000 is less than the capacity to pay taxes from an annual interest income of $4,000.

The federal income tax has in the past provided a special deduction for income from personal service. When utilized, it has been referred to by the law as the "earned income credit." The terminology has been unfortunate, and has tended to obscure the rationale of the deduction. For income from personal service has been called "earned income," while that from property or wealth has been termed the opprobrious opposite, "unearned income." The public has been (naturally) led to the feeling that the latter is in some way less useful to society, and less justifiable economically.

This deduction first appeared in the 1924 Act, and was retained through successive acts until 1932 as a 25 per cent deduction from the normal tax. (It was not applicable to surtax.) It was completely repealed by the 1932 Act, but restored again in 1934 as a 10 per cent deduction from net income as computed without this deduction, and again only for normal tax purposes. Furthermore, all net income up to $3,000, whether from personal service or from property, was considered earned, and all net income over $14,000, from whatever source, was considered unearned. This was a far more niggardly credit than the previous 25 per cent of normal tax. The earned income credit was repealed in 1943 and has not been resurrected.

Why has depreciation of capital been consistently allowed in the tax laws, while the allowance of an earned income deduction has come and gone? The first explanation lies in the fact that the rationale of the earned income credit was never generally understood. The receiver of an "earned income" credit regarded it as a windfall, probably resulting from legislative concern for the little fellow, while the receiver of "unearned income" typically regarded it as class discrimination based either upon the desire for re-election or as a pronouncement of social condemnation of property income. The misunderstanding was not reduced by Congressional wavering in application of the principle itself. Congressional confusion was added to public confusion in 1934 by failure to distinguish earned incomes from small incomes (all net income of $3,000 or less was considered "earned") and unearned incomes from large incomes (all net income over $14,000 was considered "unearned"). The consistent application of the earned income credit to normal tax alone reflected indecision as to the nature of earned income.

The second suggestion in explaining the indecisive policy is the usual one of revenue need. Tax history is replete with demonstrations that when the chips are down, revenue considerations supersede those of justice. Repeal of the credit in 1932 and again in 1943 suggests that the special treatment of personal service incomes is largely a fair weather matter. In extenuation of the 1943 action, it may be pointed out that a particular tax objective in that year was the control of inflation in the consumer goods markets, and the receivers of "earned incomes" were then behaving badly from the anti-inflationary point of view.

Were not the two explanations given above so broad as to account by themselves for this curious and inconsistent Congressional behavior, a third might be put forth seriously. With a rather large proportion of the receivers of personal service incomes brought under the provisions of the Old Age and Survivors' Insurance scheme of the Social Security Act, the individual worker was no longer required to provide his own retirement income. Those workers covered by the Act thus could consider their wages (after social security tax deductions) as true income. It is not seriously suggested that this is a genuine explanation for Congressional action in removing the earned income credit. And if it were, it would not be a logically acceptable excuse. For many receivers of "earned income" do not come under social security coverage. In the second place, such coverage does not provide treatment equivalent to that provided in depreciation deductions, for the coverage does not make labor incomes permanent, but only for life subsequent to attainment of legal retirement age. Finally, social security taxes taken out of his pay are not deductible for income tax purposes from the employee's income, indicating conclusively that social security could not have been seriously considered by Congress as a substitute for the earned income credit.

Capital Gains and Losses

Nature of Capital Gains and Losses. One of the most difficult and unsettled problems of federal income taxation has been the treatment of capital gains and losses. By a capital gain we mean a financial gain resulting from the sale of a capital asset at a higher price than was paid for it. The gain arises out of an appreciation of capital value, and creates in the hands of the receiver a clear capacity to pay taxes.[7] We must recognize, however, two administratively different types of gains arising from the sale of assets. The first is typified by the usual gains from mercantile enterprises, where goods are sold for prices higher than were paid for them. Such gains are clearly business income, and should be treated like other income for tax purposes. The second type of capital gain is of the irregular or unusual sort, occurring outside the normal course of earning one's income. It is this latter type with which we are dealing when we speak of the treatment of "capital gains and losses" in income taxation. It is perhaps best typified by the physician whose regular income arises from the practice of his profession, but who may pick up gains now and then through the purchase and sale of bonds and stocks.

The federal income tax law describes capital gains and losses to the individual as the gains or losses from sale of certain types of property. These types of property include assets held by the taxpayer other than (1) "stock in trade" held primarily for sale to customers in the ordinary course of his business, (2) real property used in trade or business, (3) depreciable property used in trade or business, or (4) the securities of governments in the United States.[8] The intent is clearly to specify for treatment under this head gains and losses on sales of property outside the area of one's normal trade or occupation. Thus, a grocer's gain from the purchase and sale of groceries would be taxed in the same manner as are salaries and wages; but any gain from the sale of his residence would be regarded for tax purposes as a "capital gain," and given somewhat special treatment. A capital gain or loss can be "realized" only through actual sale or exchange[9]—paper gains are not recognized. In practice, the principal capital assets subject to this special tax treatment are investment securities and real estate.

We are thus treating here a class of taxable incomes which have certain striking peculiarities, among which are: (1) their basically fluctuating character, (2) their susceptibility to manipulation in order to gain tax advantage, and (3) their special incidence among larger income receivers. Being outside the normal course of income-earning activity, capital gains or losses are

[7] A *net* appreciation of capital value is meant. Property may increase in value because of the investment of capital in its improvement. The capital gain would then be the appreciation in capital value less any direct cost incurred in improvements.

[8] *Internal Revenue Code,* Section 1221.

[9] With the following exceptions: (1) worthless stocks or bonds, which create realized loss though not sold, (2) retired bonds, where comparison of matured value with price originally paid may establish capital gain or loss, and (3) dividends declared in liquidation of a corporation, constituting distribution of their equities among the owners. (*Internal Revenue Code,* Section 23 (g) (2), (k) (2); Section 117 (f); Section 115 (c).)

realized infrequently by the average person, though it should be pointed out that they are typically realized more frequently by the "speculator" than by the "investor." Capital gains and losses are further heavily dependent upon the course of prices and the business cycle. The experience of the Treasury with respect to revenue collections from capital gains and losses shows their widely fluctuating character. From 1926 to 1940, the average yearly revenue from capital gains was about $120 million. However, in 1928, the highest year, the revenue was $576 million, while in the years 1930, 1931, and 1932, the Treasury actually lost revenue on account of an excess of capital losses deducted from other income.[10]

The following tabulation of reported capital gains or losses in 1956 income tax returns shows a heavy concentration of such items in the upper income classes.[11]

Adjusted Gross Income Class	Number of Taxable Returns With Capital Gain or Loss (thousands)	Total Taxable Returns (thousands)	Returns Having Gain or Loss as % of Total Returns
$600–$5,000	979	26,970	3.6
5,000–10,000	1,103	16,179	6.8
10,000–25,000	735	2,651	27.8
25,000–100,000	265	435	60.8
100,000 and over	20	23	88.2

Survey of Federal Treatment of Capital Gains and Losses.[12] As in the case of other troublesome problems of income taxation, the treatment of capital gains and losses by the federal government has been changeable and lacking in consistency with regard to any central principle. The first modern federal income tax (1913) included net capital gains with other income and taxed the whole at uniform normal and surtax rates. *Net* capital losses (i.e., capital losses in excess of capital gains) were not recognized; capital losses could be deducted from capital gains, but no excess could be deducted from other income. At the beginning, therefore, gains were assumed to be the equivalent dollar for dollar to other income so far as taxable capacity was concerned, although Congress was not ready to go the whole way in consideration of all capital losses as negative income—they were only negative capital gains.

In the 1918 law, capital losses were deductible in full from both capital

[10] See testimony of Randolph Paul before House Committee on Ways and Means, concerning the *Revenue Revision of 1942*, Vol. 1, p. 255.

[11] Computed from United States Treasury Department, *Statistics of Income . . . 1956, Individual Income Tax Returns*, pp. 23, 54.

[12] No attempt is made to catalogue all changes in treatment of capital gains and losses. Only those provisions significant to discussion of the nature of the problem are included.

gains and other income. We find, therefore, adoption of the consistent principle that capital gains and losses are full-fledged (positive and negative)
incomes. In 1921 a new treatment appeared. Capital losses were fully
deductible from capital gains and from other income, but a receiver of
capital net gain was given a choice. He could pay a tax of 12.5 per cent,
or he could include capital gains as regular net income, subject to normal
and surtax rates. If he chose the former alternative, however, the total tax
paid could not be less than 12.5 per cent of total net income including
capital gains. Only gains from the sale of property held over two years were,
however, entitled to the alternative computation. The implication of this
action is that capital gains are not on all fours with other income. If they
were a part of high incomes, the alternative method provided some relief.
Under the 1921 law, however, capital losses were fully deductible from
capital gains and from other income.

The 1924 law reinstated limitations upon the use of capital net losses for
reduction of taxable income. From the tax as computed without regard to
capital loss, a deduction of 12.5 per cent of capital net loss was allowed,
provided such deduction did not reduce the total tax by more than 12.5
per cent. Capital net losses in any year in excess of the amount used in that
year to reduce the tax were permitted to be carried over for a period of two
years. Curiously enough, such losses carried over were deductible from
"ordinary net income" in subsequent years, and not from subsequently
realized net gains.

The developments in the early nineteen-thirties were essentially continu-
ations of the trend toward limiting capital losses for tax purposes. The significant change was the distinction between short-term and long-term gains
and losses. The latter were given more favorable treatment than the former.
Short-term gains were held to be essentially speculative in character, and
thus (for non-tax reasons) entitled to less consideration. The mood of the
times, largely the result of the speculative excesses of the late nineteen-
twenties, was distinctly unsympathetic to speculation. Another reason has
far more solid foundation in tax theory: long-term gains and losses may be
considered as accruing over a period generally longer than one year, and
to tax them as if they represented income for the year in which they were
realized would involve application of undesirably heavy tax rates in many
cases. A third reason for more harsh treatment of short-term gains and
losses lay in the realization that such gains and losses were peculiarly sus-
ceptible to manipulation for purposes of controlling the amount of income
tax payable. Short-term losses could easily be arranged so as to cancel
capital gains and to reduce other net income for tax purposes. This was

done particularly by those in the higher income groups, and thus partially negated the high surtax rates of the period. It was further evident that in some cases sales to establish losses were not *bona fide* as contemplated by the Congress, but represented end-of-year exchanges within the family or among friends for the purpose of establishing losses. In some instances these exchanges were found to be only temporary, the securities finding their way back into the hands of the original owners soon after the tax date.

By the 1932 law, short-term losses were deductible only from short-term gains, eliminating the possibility of any reduction in other income through net short-term losses. The carry-over of net short-term losses to subsequent years was terminated in 1933. In 1934 gains and losses were classified by an elaborate schedule, the longest-term gains being those on securities held over ten years, and the shortest-term less than one year. The former were entered at 30 per cent of their amount, the latter at 100 per cent, with several gradations between. Capital losses were allowed to the extent of capital gains plus $2,000, but the carry-over of losses to subsequent years was disallowed. Further, the flat 12.5 per cent rate on gains was eliminated, which made them again subject to regular tax rates. Succeeding laws have not radically changed the method of treatment, though percentages, holding periods, and the extent of net loss allowances have varied.

Under the currently applicable Internal Revenue Code of 1954, capital gains or losses are considered short-term if the assets have been held six months or less. All others are long-term gains or losses. The treatment of gains and losses is very complicated, but its main outlines may be discussed under six possible circumstances. We first subtract long-term gains from long-term losses to determine *net long-term gain or loss*. Similarly, the difference between short-term gain and short-term loss gives *net short-term gain or loss*. By putting these long- and short-term *net* figures together we may get any of six results. They are:

1. Net gain possibilities:
    a. Net long-term gain *minus* net short-term loss *equals* net gain.
    b. Net short-term gain *minus* net long-term loss *equals* net gain.
    c. Net long-term gain *plus* net short-term gain *equals* net gain.
2. Net loss possibilities:
    a. Net long-term loss *minus* net short-term gain *equals* net loss.
    b. Net short-term loss *minus* net long-term gain *equals* net loss.
    c. Net long-term loss *plus* net short-term loss *equals* net loss.

It is convenient to discuss treatment of these possibilities in the law as they are numbered and lettered above.

1. Net gain possibilities: (a). If the net gain is a surplus of long-term gains over short-term losses, as in (1, a) above, the gain may be taxed in either of two ways, at the taxpayer's option. But in either case, being long-term in character, only 50 per cent of the net gain enters into the tax computation. The taxpayer may enter 50 per cent of the net gain as gross income on his tax return, and proceed to compute the tax as described in the last chapter. Or, alternatively, he is permitted to pay a tax at a flat rate of 50 per cent on the 50 per cent of this net gain, as a separate tax added to the tax as computed on other income. Obviously, if his marginal rate of tax on income is over 50 per cent, he would use the second alternative. This alternative is clearly a favor to larger income receivers who have net gain of a long-term variety.

(b) If the net gain is an excess of net short-term gain over net long-term loss, as in (1, b), the net gain thus established is treated like any other income. It is wholly included in gross income, and subject to whatever tax rates are applicable to the taxpayer's income, including this gain.

(c) If the net gain is the result of both net long-term and net short-term gains, the taxpayer must separate them. The former are treated as in (a) above, while the latter are treated as in (b) above.

2. Net loss possibilities: (a), (b), (c): The law does not distinguish between long- and short-term net losses. The net loss of any year may be used to offset other income to the maximum extent of $1,000. Any excess over $1,000 may be carried over for a period of five years, to be subtracted from net gains, and from other income to the extent of $1,000 in any one year.

In summary, net capital losses are permitted limited deductibility from other income in any year, but may be carried over for five years. Net capital gains are divided into two categories, depending upon how long the assets were held before the gains were realized. If they result from sales of assets held more than six months, the taxpayer usually elects to have them taxed at a flat 25 per cent rate (50 per cent of gains taxed at a 50 per cent rate). If, however, the taxpayer finds his taxable income, including 50 per cent of such gains, to be in an under-50 per cent rate bracket, he will elect not to tax them separately but to include them with other income. If the net gain results from sale of assets held six months or less, the gain is treated on all fours with other income.

In the welter of changes attending the treatment of capital gains and losses, certain general patterns stand out. In summary, we note a general tendency to tax capital gains as income, though for a major part of the modern period the taxpayer has been offered an optional flat-rate tax on such gains. The implication is that although capital gains are income, they do not possess precisely the same capacity to pay taxes as does other income—at least in the higher brackets. The treatment of capital losses is even less consistent. They have always been given some consideration as negative gains, but typically they have been deductible from other income only in limited amounts. Only between 1918 and 1924 were they fully deductible; before that period they were not deductible at all, and since that period they have been deductible generally only in nominal amounts. Finally, the distinction between long- and short-term gains and losses has grown up in recent years, with comparatively favorable treatment granted the former.

Are Capital Gains Income? It has sometimes been asserted that capital gains have no place in an income tax, because capital gains are not income. This position rests upon a definition of income as a flow of receipts from a fund of capital, human resources, or natural resources. Appreciation of capital value may result from the capitalization of an expected larger stream of income from it, but the appreciation of capital is not itself income. Thus, in this view, it is appropriate for an income tax to be imposed upon the rising stream of income, but not upon the rise in capital value. It has even been argued that taxation of capital gains under the income tax is double taxation; the tax takes away from income upon which capital value is based, and if, in spite of this, capital value rises, a second tax is imposed upon the appreciation in value. But it may well be that appreciation itself should be considered a flow of value, separate from the maintained fund of capital itself. Also, the difference between capital as a fund and income as a flow tends to break down if pushed too far. For example, the goods of a retailer appreciate in value between their purchase and their sale. Part of this is value added by factors of production, including labor, storage, packaging, and advertising, which change the product and increase its value. But a part of the appreciation (mark-up) is also return to ownership or entrepreneurship—true capital appreciation not accounted for by costs incurred for services to the product. Is this element of profit not income but capital? Should this stream of receipts not be taxed under an income tax? Clearly, this stream is income and should be taxable.

But the case for inclusion of capital gains as income is clear on other grounds. In the first place, the definition of income we have used before— receipts which can be disposed of without impairing the possibility of equal receipts in a subsequent period—would clearly justify the classification of capital gains as income. So long as capital remains intact, its productivity is not reduced by the taxation of net appreciation in its market value.[13] In the second place, it is pretty clear that capital gains are regarded by their receivers as additional income available for disposal. In fact, such gains may be regarded as windfall income when they are infrequent, and as such represent income with an abnormally high capacity to pay taxes.

If we view capital gains as disposable receipts, we find that they clearly represent ability to pay taxes at the time of their realization. They represent liquid funds which can be spent or saved (or taxed) without disturbing the prospect of continued income from capital at the same level as before. That they are irregular must be admitted, but that their utilization worsens the capacity to receive future income must be denied. To the professional speculator, capital gains are clearly his only income; to argue that he receives not income but capital premiums and therefore should not be taxed is to make a distinction where no significant difference exists. Thus we may see that the annual receipts of the salaried worker are not different—for tax purposes—from those of a merchant whose income arises from appreciation in value of the goods he sells, except that the former may be somewhat more regular. The nature of the merchant's income is not different from that of the professional speculator. And is the income of the professional speculator different from that which the amateur and part-time speculator receives for doing the same thing? It is impossible to find differences in the taxable capacities of the following three men: A, who receives $10,000 salary per year; B, who receives $5,000 per year from legal practice and $5,000 per year in capital gains from the sale of assets; and C, who receives $10,000 per year solely from capital gains. (We assume by saying "per year" that an averaging process has ironed out year-to-year fluctuations in all incomes.) We conclude, therefore, that for purposes of equity all should be treated alike by the income tax, and we are driven to this conclusion in full view of the storms of controversy surrounding the issue.

Common Objections to Capital Gains Taxation. The objections to capital gains taxation may be segregated into two classes: those which object to any inclusion of capital gains and losses in income taxation, and those which object to particular methods of treatment. The objection to any income taxation of capital gains and losses centers around the question whether they are truly items of income. This is not an idle question of theory; it has im-

---

[13] The method of computing a capital gain is such as to measure this gain as an excess over maintained cost value. Ignoring the intricacies of individual situations—and there are many—the general method of computing a capital gain is: Depreciated value of the asset at time of sale *minus* the sum of cost or value at time of acquisition, cost of improvements, and cost of sale *equals* capital gain. Changes in the general price level between time of purchase and time of sale are not taken into account, as they should be if real capital value is to be maintained. But price level changes are ignored throughout the operation of the income tax, so capital gains are not peculiar in this respect.

portant practical applications in the realm of discriminatory double taxation. For example, is it logical to tax as income an appreciation in capital value which is the result of capitalizing anticipated increases in income from capital, and then later to tax this increased income when realized? The answer would be in the negative, provided *paper gains* were taxed as income. But since gains must be realized through sale of the asset before they are taxable, the capital gain accrues to one person (and is like his other income) while the higher anticipated interest, dividend, or rental accrues to another. It would be difficult to label this as discrimination or double taxation.[14]

A second objection to subjecting capital gains to income tax is that there is a tendency for this practice to interfere with the free purchase and sale of corporate securities. This is generally referred to as the "locked-in" problem. It suggests that stockholders whose stocks have risen in the market find it impossible—for tax reasons—to sell these stocks and realize gains as they normally would. They are locked in because the tax makes it unwise to dispose of a stock which has risen in the recent past, and transfer funds to something more promising.[15] The adverse consequences which, it is claimed, follow from this are: (1) the tax tends to accentuate instability in the prices of securities, and (2) the immobility of investment funds makes for a less than optimum allocation of resources. With regard to the first, the argument runs that if a stock is rising in price, the inability of holders to sell reduces the supply of the stock in the market and permits the strong demand to push the price of available shares higher than would otherwise be the case. If there were no capital gains taxation, holders of stock could afford to sell and take profits, and thus to counter upward pressure on prices. This argument is also reversible, for if capital losses can offset other income to any extent, stockholders would be more inclined to sell in a falling mar-

[14] A special situation which causes discriminatory double taxation through taxation of capital gains is that in which corporate income is reinvested by the corporation. The corporate earnings are reinvested after having paid corporate income taxes. However, the very reinvestment is likely to increase the market value of securities outstanding; if such securities are subsequently sold, capital gains are likely to result. The income and the appreciation of capital created by its reinvestment are both taxed (finally) against the same person.

This kind of discrimination, however, occurs even when corporate earnings are distributed to stockholders. Personal income which arises through corporate activity is thus taxed twice—once as corporate income and again as personal income. The fact of such double taxation is due not to the taxation of capital gains but to the taxation of income to the corporation as if it were a separate stream of income.

[15] This problem of "locking-in" is treated at length and from opposite points of view by Jonathan A. Brown and Walter W. Heller in papers in: *Federal Tax Policy for Economic Growth and Stability: Papers Submitted . . . before the Subcommittee on Tax Policy,* Joint Committee on the Economic Report, Washington, 1955.

ket, thus adding to the downward pressure on prices. Thus, if gains and losses were ignored by the tax system, stockholders would be more inclined to sell in a rising market and not sell in a falling market. With regard to the mobility of investment funds, the argument says that if the possessors of capital funds were not locked into their present holdings, these funds would move to the support of new and promising ventures more quickly.

There is reason to suspect, however, that the seriousness of the locked-in problem has been greatly overstated. Heller[16] throws doubt on the arguments given above, principally on the following grounds: As to the market stability argument, would not receipts realized from the sale of stock A normally be used to buy stock B? If so, the downward selling pressure on A would be offset by upward buying pressure on B. Further, if capital gains taxes were reduced, market funds which are now diverted to government through the tax would remain in the market, looking for investment in securities, and strengthening over-all demand. And finally, the differential and favorable treatment of capital gains as compared with other income already favors income derived through capital gains. If this differential were widened, would not more funds flow into the securities markets, thus creating the basis for a more robust demand for stocks and a stronger boom in prices?

With respect to the desirability of making investment funds more mobile, an important question of perspective arises. While gains taxation would seem to produce immobility when compared to a situation with no tax, the differential treatment of gains, as Heller suggests, "makes the long-term gains tax one of the lowest sections of the tax wall." If a greater differential were provided, the flow of funds into the stock market would probably be enlarged further, but is this kind of "mobility" desired? The sort of mobility desired, in which the flow of funds is influenced by non-tax decisions, might well be improved by eliminating the differential—by lowering the tax rates on other income or by raising the rates on long-term gains.

There are many different objections to specific methods of taxing capital gains. Heading the list of such objections is that which opposes the taxation of capital gains in full while capital losses are not given full and equal treatment as deductions. There has never been a disposition to disallow capital losses as deductions from capital gains. But government in recent decades has shown quite consistent determination to stand firm against a significant amount of deduction of net capital losses from other income. This practice

---

[16] *Op. cit.* Concern over the locked-in problem is also somewhat suspect on grounds that those who are loudest in their concern over it are the stock exchange and its member firms, whose incomes depend largely upon the rate of turnover of stocks.

can be explained—though not justified—on two counts. When capital losses are fully deductible, the large investor can frequently create capital losses by proper selection of securities for sale with the purpose of avoiding high taxes in the upper brackets. The effectiveness of the high rates in bringing in large revenues from other income is in this manner largely vitiated. And whether or not losses are intentionally realized for tax purposes, the downward swing of the business cycle will inevitably create large capital losses, as well as a lower level of "ordinary income." The downswing thus normally brings a severe reduction in income tax revenues, and this reduction is intensified through capital losses, when losses are deductible from other income. The reader will note that the revenue objection to full deductibility of losses does not take account of the desirability of severe reduction of tax burdens during the downswing of the cycle. But we are here endeavoring to explain why the Treasury and the Congress have favored limited deductibility, and experience so far has shown too great concern by these agencies for high levels of revenue during such periods.

The second explanation of the rather consistent limitation of capital losses to the approximate extent of capital gains runs in terms of the morale effects upon taxpayers. Those who can best afford to pay taxes are precisely those who—because they own assets upon which capital losses can be realized for tax purposes—can effectively escape heavy taxation when full deductibility is allowed.[17] When in 1933 it was demonstrated that many persons whose names were identified with great wealth had been paying little or no income tax by taking advantage of capital losses, the man in the street roundly condemned them for doing something which the tax law gave most of them every right to do. The Treasury and the Congress will naturally wish to avoid such animosities, and the most easily available instrument is that of limiting the allowances for capital losses. It may be observed that had government followed a low-tax policy in the middle thirties rather than a high-tax policy, lower income earners would have been largely taxexempt, and the animosities would almost certainly have been far less intense.

It is presumably evident from our earlier discussion that capital net losses should be fully deductible from other income, not in the year in which the losses are realized, but over a period of years through the averaging process. No other procedure is logical in terms of equity. But there is another reason for advocating such action. The major part of capital gains and

[17] This problem is clearly outlined in H. M. Groves' article, "Yachts Without Income," in the *New Republic*, July 19, 1933.

losses results from transactions in corporate securities, principally common stocks. These securities represent largely venture capital, and arise out of investment. As we have seen in earlier chapters, the level of investment is an important key to the level of national income. But if capital gains are to be heavily taxed while capital losses are unequally treated, a discouragement of venture capital investment may exist.[18] Indeed, this aspect of the problem is considered so important in some quarters that equal treatment of losses with gains is regarded as only a beginning. In this view, capital losses should be given more than equal treatment; they should be fully deductible, while capital gains should be segregated from other income and subjected to low and proportional rates. This view appears to assume too much frailty in the spirit of venture capital, especially if counter-cycle tax policy were earnestly pursued. For when a deficiency of investment occurs, it is presumed that tax rates will fall, accomplishing some real relief to capital gains along with other income.

On balance, it appears that the arguments for special treatment of capital gains and losses are by no means entirely convincing. Such treatment would lighten the tax burden on gains and discriminate against other types of income which have no greater ability to pay. It has not been demonstrated that equal treatment would seriously discourage investment, particularly if capital losses were fully deductible. This latter would, however, represent a major change in tax treatment which is wholly desirable on grounds of equity, and would remove the major current discouragement to invest in more venturesome enterprises. The second major change indicated is that of averaging incomes over a period of time. With respect to capital gains and losses, such averaging would eliminate the need for segregation of long- and short-term gains and losses, and treat all as if they were of the long-term variety. This is entirely consistent with the proposal to measure the ability to pay of fluctuating incomes as if they were constant. Ideally, of course, income should be taxed over the period of its accrual. Short-term gains accruing over a period of less than a year should, in strict logic, be taxed as income of that year, while those accruing over a period longer than a year should be considered for tax purposes as having been realized over the longer period, and the proper portion should be taxed as income realized in each year of the accrual period. In the absence of a general averaging

---

[18] It is, of course, difficult to assess the extent of this discouragement in actual practice. But it is so frequently iterated by representatives of the financial community that a presumption of its reality must be accepted, even though it contains some characteristics of special pleading. Cf. H. M. Groves, *Postwar Taxation and Economic Progress*, New York, McGraw-Hill, 1946, p. 222.

scheme for unstable current incomes, it is difficult to argue for the application of averaging to gains and losses alone. But a workable and simple scheme can be applied to gains and losses—that of differentiating long-term from short-term gains and losses by holding periods, and taxing varying amounts of gains depending upon the holding period. The present method is, however, not entirely satisfactory. The shortest period should be one year rather than six months. Beyond the shortest period there should be several identifiable periods involving different proportions to be included in the tax base. And while different percentages of gain or loss, depending upon the period held, can be justified on grounds of equity, the application of a special rate to long-term gains cannot. While the inclusion of 50 per cent of net gain from sales of long-term assets may be a proper rough-and-ready substitute for income averaging, there is no justification except favoritism for the flat 50 per cent rate applied to them.

There are other substantive problems connected with treatment of capital gains and losses, whose proper discussion would unduly extend our treatment of the subject. In the following summary, therefore, we not only recapitulate the implications of matters already discussed, but introduce very briefly other points which should not be ignored but which can only be alluded to.

Improvements in Taxation of Capital Gains and Losses

The following proposals grow largely out of our analysis in this chapter. Some would be opposed bitterly in some quarters, partly because they violate minority beliefs with respect to the nature of capital gains and losses, and partly because they would tend to eliminate special advantages now enjoyed. But the logic of the issue indicates their desirability.

1. Capital gains and losses, being no different from other irregular incomes, should be given treatment consistent with that of other incomes.

2. As irregular incomes, gains and losses should ideally be subject to an averaging plan. But in the absence of a general averaging scheme for all incomes, there is still reason for proceeding with a substitute applicable only to capital gains and losses, because in this category irregularity is typical. The substitute is that of differentiation by holding periods. The shortest holding period cannot logically be less than one year, for income irregularities within a year's period are automatically ironed out, but beyond that period as many as three or four additional periods would be desirable. The difference in holding periods would be reflected in differential proportions of gains or losses to be included in income in the year realized. These differ-

ing amounts would serve as nearly as possible to produce over the years the same tax "bite" as would an averaging plan.

3. Capital losses should be treated symmetrically with gains, eliminating the present loss limitation. Differentiation of the amount of losses to be counted, based upon holding periods, would seem to be both possible and reasonable.

4. Since gains are not to be differentiated from other income, to the extent to which they are included they should be subject to ordinary progressive rates. The alternative method of taxing long-term gains by the application of a flat rate should be withdrawn.

5. Assets transferred at death or by gift should be subject to taxation on their capital gain or loss up to the time of their transfer. The practice has been to exempt that portion of the gain that accrued to the decedent or donor while he held it. For capital gains purposes, an heir, if he later sells the asset, computes the gain or loss as the difference between its value when he received it and that when he sold, thus permanently exempting gains to the decedent from the tax. In the case of a gift of assets to a charitable institution, the donor deducts as a contribution not the cost of the asset to him but the value at transfer. Here, also, the capital gain to him permanently escapes. In the case of other gifts the tax is not permanently lost but postponed until the recipient sells the asset. Then he computes the capital gain on the basis of the donor's cost.

The proposals for improvement here made would undoubtedly increase the bite of the capital gains tax, and would stir up vigorous opposition in some quarters. But if logical they should be implemented, gradually if not all at once. They could be most easily implemented concurrently with an easing of general income tax burdens if and when such a change becomes advisable. But the objective is not punishment of particular taxpayers who have been favored in the past. It is to reconstruct an area of income taxation in the direction of equity, and to create a tax structure more nearly neutral in its influence upon the allocation of resources within the economy. But there is a further value in reconstruction. Experience has shown that a loophole invites pressure to enlarge the loophole. The history of capital gains taxation has been one of very strong pressure to have income on the fringe of the loophole defined as a capital gain. This results over a period of time in an illogical, opportunist definition of capital gains to include more and more items of income. The broader the definition becomes, through exception, the less the resistance to still further erosion of the definition. This process can be checked only by the complete closing of the loophole, and the sooner the better.

RECOMMENDED READINGS

Brown, Jonathan A., "The 'Locked-in' Problem," and Heller, Walter W., "Investors' Decisions, Equity, and the Capital-Gains Tax." Joint Committee on the Economic Report, *Federal Tax Policy for Economic Growth and Stability (Papers Submitted by Panelists before the Subcommittee on Tax Policy)*, Washington, 1955, pp. 367–80 and 381–93, respectively.

These two papers present the two sides of the question whether taxation of capital gains seriously affects the mobility of capital in the economy.

Groves, H. M., *Postwar Taxation and Economic Progress*, N.Y., McGraw-Hill, 1946, Chapters 7 and 8.

Discussion of policy with respect to income tax base, rates, yield, and the possible treatment of tax-exempt securities, capital gains and losses, and irregular incomes.

Simons, H. C., *Personal Income Taxation*, Chicago, University of Chicago, 1938.

A bright, readable analysis. Chapters 2, 7, 10, and Supplementary Note are especially applicable to the material of this chapter.

Surrey, Stanley S., "Definitional Problems in Capital Gains Taxation," Joint Committee on the Economic Report, *op. cit.*, pp. 404–18.

Highly recommended for the reader who has a taste for the myriad problems of distinguishing capital gains from ordinary income. Suggestions for improvement, given at the end of this selection, are well worth the attention of the serious student of the subject.

CHAPTER 18

Taxation of Personal Income from Business Corporations

It cannot be too frequently repeated that (1) taxes are finally paid out of the stream of personal income, no matter where their original impact is felt, and (2) we cannot judge the acceptability of a given tax measure unless we know with reasonable accuracy where its incidence lies. On both counts the personal income tax recommends itself above all other measures. It makes personal income (the final source of tax payments) the immediate base of the tax and thus avoids the vagaries of indirect approach to the source. The incidence is essentially clear, for little shifting occurs. In consequence, it is evident that both simplification and improvement of the tax system suggest greater emphasis upon personal income taxes and less emphasis upon other tax forms. This being the case, the reason for particular concern for proper methods of personal income taxation is evident. In Chapter 17 we considered some details of conformity in tax practice to the proper definition of income. In this chapter we shall be concerned with the relation of personal to corporate income taxation.

The Federal Corporation Net Income Tax

Federal taxation of corporation net income began with the Act of 1909, and has continued to the present. In 1958 it was second to the individual income tax in revenue production, furnishing $20 billion while the individual income tax provided almost $35 billion. In fact, since its introduction the corporation tax has been a major element in the federal revenue system. Though its revenues have never exceeded those of the personal income tax, it has outproduced the excises consistently except during the period 1933–1941, when corporate profits were at depression lows and great emphasis was placed upon excise taxation. In times of war emergency, the corporation

TABLE 30

U. S. CORPORATION INCOME TAX, SELECTED PROVISIONS, 1909–1959

Date of Act	Normal Tax Rate(s) (%)	Max. Normal Rate (%) if Total Net Income Is Over ($)	Net Income Exempt from Normal Tax	Surtax Rates* (%)	Max. Surtax Rate (%) if Surtax Net Income Is Over ($)	Exempt Surtax Income ($)	Excess Profits Tax Rate(s)** (%)
1909	1.0		5,000				
1913	1.0						
1916	2.0						
1916	1.0, 4.0, 2.0						
1918	12.0		2,000				20–60
1918 (on 1919, 1920 income)	10.0		2,000				20–40
1921	10.0		2,000				30–65
1921 (on 1922, 1923 income)	12.5		2,000				20–40
1925	13.0		2,000				
1925 (on 1926, 1927 income)	13.5		2,000				
1928	12.0		3,000				
1928 (on 1929 income)	11.0		3,000				
1928 (on 1930, 1931 income)	12.0		3,000				
1932	13.75						
1936	8.0–15.0			[a]			
1938	12.5–19.0					[a]	
1940	14.85–36.9	24%; $38,566					
1941	15.0–37.0	24%; $38,642		6.0–7.0			35–60
1942	15.0–31.0	24%; $50,000		10.0–22.0	16%; $50,000		90
1943	15.0–31.0	24%; $50,000		10.0–22.0	16%; $50,000		95
1945	15.0–21.0	24%; $50,000		6.0–22.0	14%; $50,000		
1950	23.0			19.0		25,000	30
1951	28.75			22.0		25,000	30
1951 (on 1952, 1953 income)	30.0			22.0		25,000	30
1951 (on 1954 income)	30.0[b]			22.0		25,000	

* Surtax net income may be larger than normal tax net income by inclusion of interest on certain United States obligations issued prior to 1941.

** Does not include war profits tax, 1917–1921, or declared-value excess profits tax, 1932–1946.

a Surtax on undistributed corporate profits only; repealed in 1938.

b Scheduled reduction to 25 per cent at end of 1953 has been postponed annually to the present (1960).

income tax has been regularly supplemented by an excess profits tax on corporations. Steady growth in importance of corporation income taxation is discernible; since 1950 its revenues have held to a high plateau caused by high corporate profits and little change in provisions of the law. Its relative importance in the total federal revenue structure has followed a course quite parallel to that of the individual income tax.

A summary of major rate and base changes in the corporation income tax law since 1909 is given in Table 30.

The tax was essentially a flat-rate tax until progression was instituted in 1936. (The only exception is that minor progression was used in the 1916 amendment to the 1916 law). During World War I a progressive element was provided by the excess profits tax. But since 1936, progression has been consistently applied, sometimes by separate normal and surtax rates (1950 to the present), sometimes by progressive rates within each category (1940–1945), and sometimes by progressive normal rates (1936–1938). Net income for corporate tax purposes is gross income from all sources less specified deductions. The principal deductions are for costs of production, charitable contributions, depletion, net operating losses carried over from previous years, and dividends received from other taxed corporations. We shall not pursue the description of the tax further at this point, for our interest is in noting the relationship of the corporation income tax to the individual income tax. It is sufficient for our present purposes to note that the federal government singles out corporations among all business firms as the subjects of a special net income tax, and that that tax is based upon the whole net income of the corporation, uniformly defined for all.

Relation of Personal to Corporate Income Taxation

The separation of the corporation income tax from the personal income tax without imposing a comparable tax on the net income of unincorporated business enterprises raises some difficult questions about the double or additional taxation of personal income created by corporations.

An income or an income payment is a receipt or a payment for a productive service. The income may be received for the performance of a service by a person, as in the case of wages and salaries, or it may be received by a person for the performance of a service by some non-human factor of production owned by him, as in the case of interest, rents, royalties, and pure profits. The important thing, however, is that the income is a payment for a contribution to production—the creation of output. But there are other money flows which are, taken by themselves, unrelated to production. Gifts, bequests, deposits to and withdrawals from bank accounts, borrowing and lending, and the payment of taxes—all have in common the transfer of funds or other valuable goods without the performance of productive services. These may be regarded as "transfer payments," as distinguished from "income payments." But the danger is that they will not be distinguished for tax purposes. And if they are not, double or extra taxation is likely to occur.[1] The question is not whether transfer payments may be properly subjected to taxation, for it is quite proper to impose a tax on gifts and bequests. It is whether a personal income tax of a general character, attempting to blanket all streams of income, should tax some transfer payments as well.

It is essential to the analysis that we see clearly the relation of corporate to personal income. The corporation is simply a business organization, differing only in certain matters of legal status from other types of business units. If a person operates a corner grocery business of which he is sole proprietor, the net income of the business is never seriously considered as distinct from the grocer himself. If his grocery business earns net $5,000 for a year, that is the equivalent of saying that the grocer earns $5,000. It would be absurd to claim that the grocer and the grocery together receive income of $10,000. No known income tax has ever taxed such income once to the business and again as income to the individual proprietor of the business.

Let us assume the case of three lawyers who combine their talents and create a "legal firm," a professional partnership. The partnership itself, however, is but an organizational shell within which they practice their profession. During the year the firm receives net income over and above its out-payments to persons and firms outside the partnership. At one stage this appears as income to the partnership (firm), but in reality it is, of course, income to the partners, and is distributed among them according to the terms of the partnership agreement. Income to the firm is but individual income of the owners of the firm, caught in an accounting snapshot prior to its distribution among those who are entitled to it. Even before distribution it is income to which the partners as individuals have economic title. If the partnership earns $20,000 net during the year, and this amount is subsequently distributed to the partners, there would be neither reality nor utility in claiming that the partnership and the partners combined netted $40,000 for the year. In income tax matters there is complete agreement upon these conclusions with respect to business incomes derived through the individual

---

[1] If there is any useful meaning to the term "double taxation," it is that the same governmental jurisdiction (federal, state, or local) taxes the same thing (income, property, or a purchase) more than once in the same period through the same form of tax instrument. The problem is, of course, one of equity, and even "double taxation" of the sort implied in the definition is not widely objectionable provided it is done across the board. But single taxation of some while others are taxed doubly is discrimination.

proprietorship or through the partnership. But though the logic of the conclusion extends naturally to the corporation as well, tax practice since 1936 has denied it.

Net income to the corporation is income available for distribution to the owners (stockholders) of the corporation. If it is not distributed, it is nevertheless income of the owners which they choose not to take out but to put back into the corporation. But the act of distributing corporate income to its owners (or of reinvesting it for its owners) is not an act creating additional income. Clearly, then, if under the income tax we impose a levy upon the income to the corporation and again upon the distribution of that income to those entitled to it we are guilty of double counting of a single income. From the point of view of equity among taxpayers, double counting is undesirable only when it is not complete. If all incomes were taxed twice at comparable rates, no single taxpayer could reasonably complain against injustice, though he might reasonably complain of the intensity of the double tax burden. But to impose a tax on corporate income before distribution at rates ranging from 30 per cent to 52 per cent, and then to impose an individual income tax at 20 to 91 per cent[2] after distribution, is to practice gross discrimination against such incomes. For profits derived from other forms of business organization are subject to no separate tax before distribution. Wage, salary, interest, rent, and royalty incomes are subject only to individual taxes. Profit incomes are taxed in the same manner if they are derived from an individual proprietorship or a partnership.[3] Profit incomes derived from a corporation are subject to individual income taxes, but in addition are singled out for special penalty in the form of the 30–52 per cent corporate tax. This discrimination involves the false assumption that the income of a corporation becomes a second income when distributed to its owners. This theory becomes completely confused, however, when we try to apply the principle of ability to pay separately to corporate and personal incomes. For if the ability to pay implies the ability to sacrifice—to give up utility—then the corporation, being not a natural person but a legal entity existing only "in contemplation of law," cannot experience utility or disutility, and its whole income can be given up without one iota of sacrifice *to the corporation*. Were we to follow strict logic, and on these grounds tax corporate profits at 100 per cent, it would become immediately evident that the income to the corporation *is* the income of the owners of the corporation, and that the owners bear the burden of corporate income taxation.

---

[2] These rates were applicable to 1959 income.

[3] Unless it is a "limited partnership," in which case it is subject to tax as if it were a corporation.

The History of Integration and Dis-Integration. We have seen (Chapter 16) that by the 1913 Act the corporate net income tax of 1 per cent provided for collection at the source of the 1 per cent normal tax on dividends received by individuals. Dividends received by individuals were exempt from normal tax but subject to surtax. Such an arrangement can work quite satisfactorily so long as the rates are identical and not progressive. Obviously, a progressive schedule of rates on the corporation's net income cannot be related to individual ability to pay. Under progressive schedules, two corporations with net income of identical size will pay at the same effective tax rates, though the one may be closely held by a few owners with large incomes while the other is widely held by many owners with small incomes. If progressive taxation at the source, based upon net income of the corporation and not the individual, is employed, the final effect is to brush aside all consideration of ability to pay as a personal fact. When identical proportional rates are applied to corporate and personal incomes, the area of injustice is greatly reduced, though not eliminated. For even the 1913 Act, by taxing corporate income at 1 per cent, reduced by that amount the dividend incomes of small income receivers whose personal exemption should have made their whole incomes free of tax.[4] Even granting an exempt minimum to the corporation does not serve the same purpose as an exempt minimum to individuals.

In spite of the inequity to low income stockholders in collection of taxes on dividends at the source through the corporation tax, Congress began in 1918 a series of further departures from equitable treatment of dividend incomes. By introducing in that year graduated personal normal tax rates (6 per cent to $4,000, 12 per cent above) while the corporate tax rate was 12 per cent on its income, the inequity to small income receivers was not only continued for those who would pay no normal tax whatever, but extended to those whose taxable income was not greater than $4,000. Thus, by collection at the source, a person whose taxable income was not over $4,000 would have paid 6 per cent on individual income, while the corporation was paying the tax on his dividends for him at the rate of 12 per cent. The purpose of the corporation normal tax on dividends is badly served when the rate schedules cease to be identical.

The period 1918–1936 represents persistent refusal to treat individuals and corporations alike with respect to rates. After 1918 corporate rates continued higher than normal tax rates on individual income. In 1935 a system

---

[4] The personal exemption for a single person under the 1913 Act was $3,000, and the 1 per cent normal tax applied only to income above that exempt minimum. A stockholder in, say, the $2,500 income class, would find that the corporation had paid a tax of 1 per cent on his share of the corporate earnings, though if his share had been subject to personal rather than corporate taxation he would have paid no tax at all.

of graduated (progressive) corporate rates was introduced, though the normal tax to individuals had (in 1924) settled back to a flat rate of 4 per cent. Though until 1936 individuals were exempt from normal taxes on dividend income on the grounds that these taxes had been collected through the corporate tax on its net income, the rates in 1935 were as follows:

Individual Normal Tax Rate	*Corporate Tax Rates*
4%	Corp. net income up to $2,000—exempt
	$2,000–$15,000—13%
	$15,000–$40,000—14%
	Over $40,000—15%

The dividend receiver whose income was small could derive little comfort from exemption of his dividends from normal taxation at 4 per cent on the grounds that the corporation had already paid his tax for him at a rate of 14 per cent.

In 1936 Congress abandoned completely the use of the corporate tax as an instrument for collection at the source. This year marks complete acceptance of the fallacy that the stream of corporate income is distinct from the stream of individual income. The whole question of the relation between individual and corporate income taxes was reviewed at length in connection with the 1936 Act. The opportunity was presented to return to basic principles, but instead, a long backward step was taken. In the hearings and debates over the bill an unusual amount of heat was generated, and the action taken shows little conformity to the logic of the issue.

The President recommended to Congress the following action, with the dual objective of introducing greater equity into the system and closing an important tax loophole of long standing:

1. Repeal of the existing corporate income tax.

2. Taxation of dividends in the hands of individuals at rates identical with those applied to other income.

3. Imposition of a new corporate tax on net income not distributed as dividends, at rates comparable as nearly as possible with personal rates applicable if such income had been distributed.

The first recommendation was based upon the principle that corporate income is not distinct from the income of the individuals who own the corporation. It was also made in recognition of the fact that the scheme of collection at the source (even when corporate and personal normal rates were identical) worked injustice upon the small dividend receiver. The second recommendation would complete the change-over from collection at the source to collection from the individual at rates which are presumably gauged to individual ability to pay. The third recommendation was made in view of the generally recognized fact that in many cases corporate earnings were withheld from distribution in order to avoid personal taxes. This was obviously done in the interest of the large income receiver and constituted an important loophole for the avoidance of income taxes. All income tax laws, beginning in 1913, had provided penalties for "fraudulent" or "unreasonable" withholding of corporate income from distribution. The loophole had always been recognized, but it had been impossible in practice to close it. It was therefore suggested by the President that undistributed corporate income be taxed to the corporation as if it had been distributed, at rates as nearly as possible in line with existing individual normal and surtax rates. The rates would, of course, show only a rough-and-ready equality with personal rates, since persons in many tax brackets and therefore subject to different tax rates would be entitled to undistributed income.

Though clearly a logical solution to the problem of the proper relation of personal to corporate income taxes,[5] the President's recommendations raised a storm of protest both in and out of Congress. The discussion quite consistently emphasized political points of view, and the real points at issue were all but lost.[6] The Act as passed could hardly have satisfied anyone, for it met neither the requirements of a logical system nor the desires of taxpayers.

By way of recapitulation and demonstration of the issues, let us outline the original role of the corporate tax, the proposal of 1936, and the law as passed in that year. We are interested, of course, only in the treatment of personal income derived through the corporation.

THE 1913 ACT

Personal Income Tax	*Corporate Income Tax*
Normal tax (1%)—Dividends exempt, since the tax had been collected at the source.	Normal tax (1%)—Corporate net income subject to tax, as a tool for collection of tax on dividends at the source.
Surtax (1–6%)—Dividends subject to surtax at rates applicable to brackets in which total income falls.	Surtax—no such tax.

[5] The essentials of the plan recommended by the President had been urged as early as 1920 by Professor F. R. Fairchild ("Federal Taxation of Income and Profits," *American Economic Review,* 1920, p. 785).

[6] For example, Professor A. G. Buehler imputes motives to the President suggested in the following quotations: "The censured wealthy classes would be taxed more heavily, but there would be no opposition among the masses toward selecting the corporations and their wealthy stockholders for new taxes." "The tax would permit the President to give expression to his well-known bias against large corporations as well as to his animosity toward the concentration of wealth. In this role, he would be the champion of the small enterprises against their large rivals and of the small man against the millionaire." (Reprinted by permission from pages 23–24 of *The Undistributed Profits Tax,* by A. G. Buehler, copyright 1937 by the McGraw-Hill Book Co., Inc.) Here is no indication that the proposal was anything but political in nature.

Two alternatives were open: to tax dividends only in the hands of individuals, and eliminate corporate taxes entirely, or to utilize the corporate tax as a mechanism for collection of the tax on dividends at the source. The latter alternative was chosen in 1913 as part of a general enthusiasm for collection at the source to reduce the number of individual returns and to minimize evasion. (It will be recalled that taxes on wage, salary, and interest incomes were also largely collected at the source under the 1913 law.) Collection at the source applied only to normal tax, however, and the personal normal rate was identical with the corporate rate. By choice of this method, inequity occurred only with respect to the small income stockholder, for whom a tax was paid by the corporation, even though without collection at the source his total income would have been small enough to be entirely exempt from income taxation. Since cases of this sort were not numerous, and since the tax rates were low, the extent of inequity was not so great as to offset the supposed administrative advantages of source collection.

THE PRESIDENT'S RECOMMENDATIONS, 1936

Personal Income Tax	*Corporate Income Tax*
Normal tax (4%)—Dividends to be subject to normal tax, like other income.	Normal tax—to be eliminated entirely.
Surtax (4–75%)—Dividends subject to surtax, as before	Surtax—*On undistributed corporate income only,* at rates comparable with personal normal and surtax rates in "typical" brackets.

Under this proposal collection at the source was to be abandoned, and dividend income was to be taxed exactly like other income. With the increase of rates, particularly under the existing corporate tax, and more extensive stock ownership by the lower income classes, the inequity inherent in the existing system was regarded as serious enough to warrant elimination. The recommended tax on undistributed corporate profits was intended to close a loophole of long standing, and was to be imposed at rates which would make it a matter of indifference (so far as taxation was concerned) whether earnings were paid out or put into corporate reserves. Accumulation of reserves was not to be penalized in an absolute sense, though closing a loophole through which income had generally avoided taxation would create an immediate relative penalty by removing favored treatment. An incidental effect of the closing of this escape route would probably be to encourage dividend distribution. Consequently, not only would tax revenues probably increase, but encouragement of distribution was thought desirable both to raise the level of consumption by dividend receivers and to slow down the accumulation of idle corporate balances thought to be already excessive. It will be recalled that higher employment was an important objective of federal policy in 1936.

THE 1936 ACT AS PASSED

Personal Income Tax	*Corporate Income Tax*
Normal tax (4%)—Dividends subject to normal tax.	Normal tax (8–15%)—On all corporate net income, as before.
Surtax—Dividends subject to surtax, as before.	Surtax (7–27%)—On undistributed net income only.

The law represented a compromise which departed as far as possible from both logical alternatives in accomplishing a proper relation between personal and corporate taxes. The existing loophole was closed by the surtax on undistributed corporate surplus, but the limit was attained in discrimination against personal incomes realized through the corporation. Instead of eliminating the minor discrimination against small dividends inherent in previous acts, it instituted severe discrimination against all dividend incomes. The effect was to tax dividend incomes twice (under corporate and individual normal taxes) at rates which would typically total approximately 15 per cent, while interest incomes, not subject to corporate tax, would pay no more than 4 per cent normal tax. The undistributed corporate surplus tax was abandoned in 1939 under great political pressure, and the tax loophole was again opened.[7] The ultimate result of the 1936 fiasco was (is) thus serious discrimination against profit incomes realized from corporate sources, unmitigated by any improvement in the earlier situation of major tax escape.[8] The discrimination was made complete by inauguration in 1941 of a surtax on most corporate income.[9]

While the Congress has, largely for revenue reasons, brought about almost complete dis-integration of the original and logical relation between the individual and the corporation tax, there are islands of reasonableness

[7] In 1939 the principle of taxing undistributed corporate surplus, as embodied in the 1936 Act, was abandoned, and the pre-1936 plan of imposing a penalty tax upon "unreasonable accumulations of surplus" was re-established.

[8] It was estimated by the Treasury in 1936 that, if undistributed profits were allowed to escape taxation at rates applicable to individuals in that year, the loss of revenue would be something over one billion dollars. (Total federal revenues in 1936 were $8.9 billion.) This would not, of course, be entirely and permanently lost, since earnings plowed back would presumably be realized by individuals at some later date either through capital gains on sale of stocks whose values were increased by plowed-back earnings or through later distribution of plowed-back funds. To the extent, however, that earnings were left undistributed *for tax reasons,* their later distribution could be expected only in periods of low personal income or under lower-rate tax laws. A significant revenue loss was inevitable.

[9] The tax, ostensibly to reach tax-exempt federal securities held by corporations, applied to all net income except dividends received from other taxpaying corporations. Rates in 1941 were 6 per cent and 7 per cent; in 1942 they were made to range from 10 per cent to 16 per cent; in the 1945 Act rates were made 6 per cent to 14 per cent.

within the law. The first example is to be found in the long-standing provision of the law which permits the deduction by a corporation of substantially the whole of dividends received from other domestic corporations in computing its taxable income. Thus, while the law imposes a tax upon the corporation's income and also upon individual income derived from the corporation, multiple taxation of the same *corporation* income is largely avoided. This implies that the legislature is aware that corporation A should not be subject to corporate income tax on that part of its income derived from corporation B after B has paid the tax. In this case of a transfer type of payment, therefore, the position is logical. But the logic is not extended to the final distribution to stockholders.

A second example of partial logic is to be found in Subchapter M of the Internal Revenue Code of 1954,[10] dealing with "regulated investment companies." These are securities investment trusts of whose gross income at least 90 per cent is derived from dividends, interest, and capital gains on securities, and 90 per cent of whose net income is paid out in dividends to shareholders during the taxable year. The principle involved here is often referred to as the "conduit principle." These companies serve as conduits for distribution of corporate income to final claimants. Corporations create net income upon which they pay corporation income taxes. Some part of the remainder is paid in dividends to investment trusts which hold securities of the corporations. Trusts then distribute substantially the whole of their income to their own shareholders. The income which only passes through investment trusts from corporations to stockholders of the trusts is not subject to taxation in the hands of the trusts, which serve only as conduits. So far, so good, but the same reasoning which avoids triple taxation would argue for the avoidance of double taxation by regarding the original corporations as conduits.

The third example is that of the dividend credit and exclusion first applied in 1954 under the personal income tax. By this provision, the first $50 of dividends from domestic corporations subject to the corporate tax are excluded from gross income. (One hundred dollars are excludable for a couple if each receives at least $50 in dividends.) In addition, a credit against the tax of 4 per cent of dividends received (up to 4 per cent of taxable income) is allowed. While the examples in the paragraphs above illustrated avoidance of triple taxation, this provision faces the issue of double or extra taxation squarely, permitting a small degree of integration between the personal and the corporate tax. Indeed, the legislative hearings on this provision

[10] Sections 851–855 of the Code.

clearly indicate its intent to reduce the burden of double taxation and suggest that this is but a start toward the gradual elimination—as the budget permits—of double taxation.

It is unfortunate, however, that in attempting to reduce double taxation by the dividend exclusion and credit, the Congress pulled the wrong one of two possible levers. A better alternative than dividend exclusion and credit would have been to reduce the corporation's tax on dividends paid out. This method leaves the progressive rates on individual incomes intact. Thus, of every dollar saved on the corporate tax and paid to stockholders, each individual stockholder would pay on his share of the increased dividends at the marginal rate applicable to him. But the dividend exclusion granted to stockholders under the personal income tax is now worth more to the stockholder with a higher marginal rate than to one with a lower.[11] This would not, however, be true of the tax credit provision. It is to be hoped that if, in the future, progress can be made toward further elimination of the double taxation, the concessions will apply to the corporate and not to the individual tax.

Possible Methods of Eliminating Both Double Taxation and the Undistributed Earnings Loophole. Daniel Holland, in a study of the extra burden upon stockholders of the combined individual and corporate income taxes, has calculated these extra burdens for 1950.[12] He finds that average stockholders in the $2,000 gross income class paid 34 per cent more in personal and corporate taxes combined than they would have paid if distributed earnings had been taxed only as personal income and not as corporation income. This extra burden declined to 30 percentage points for the $25,000 gross income class and to about 11 percentage points for the $500,000 gross income class. With respect to undistributed corporate earnings the corporation tax was 29 percentage points higher than it would have been if these earnings had been distributed to stockholders in the $2,000 gross income class. But the extra burden for retained earnings fell to 2 percentage points for the $50,000 class and to *minus* 33 percentage points for the $500,000 class. In general, then, the extra burden on small stockholders is very large, whether or not earnings are retained. But for the high incomes this burden declines, and for some at the top of the scale represents a tax advantage,[13]

[11] See Carl S. Shoup, "The Dividend Exclusion and Credit in the Revenue Code of 1954," *National Tax Journal*, March, 1955, p. 136.

[12] Daniel M. Holland, *The Income-Tax Burden on Stockholders*, Princeton University Press, 1958. Materials referred to here are found in Table 4, pp. 36 and 38.

[13] Assuming that the alternative to the present arrangements would be the taxation *pro rata* of retained earnings to the stockholder.

depending upon the proportions of corporate earnings paid out or retained.[14]

The first step in proper integration of federal personal and corporate income taxes is to eliminate the tax on corporate income in general. This step would accomplish real progress in improvement of the system of income taxation. But if this were done, the second step would be to bring undistributed corporate profits under the income tax in the year in which they are earned, subject, of course, to any averaging scheme in use.

Three techniques for achieving integration present themselves.[15] The first possibility is revival of something similar to the 1936 undistributed corporate surplus tax. The corporation would pay a tax upon that part of individual income reinvested by it, measured by the amount of income undistributed. This possibility has several weaknesses, however, and cannot strongly be recommended in view of the existence of preferable methods. Rates of tax would need to be determined which at least approach typical rates which would have been paid by individuals if income had been distributed. Under present conditions—a wide range of progressive personal rates and distribution of corporate shareholding among nearly all income classes—any schedule of rates selected could only very roughly approximate the appropriate personal rates. If rates on undistributed income were made progressive with respect to the amount of income withheld, or the ratio of withheld income to total capital, they would operate on quite a different base than do personal tax rates. When we add the requirement of averaging personal income over a period of years (including undistributed corporate income), the roughness of the approximation of a tax paid by the corporation to the appropriate levy upon the individual is evident. It is of course true that the roughness would be ironed out in the end, by refunds of overpayments or additional collections in cases of underpayment.[16] But the extent of such year-end adjustments would be so great as to argue strongly for adoption of another alternative.

The second possible treatment of undistributed corporate income is to

---

[14] The matter of appropriate taxation of retained earnings is not a minor one. During the decade 1949–1958, on an annual average about 50 per cent of corporate profits after taxes were retained, ranging from 34 per cent in 1958 to 60 per cent in 1950. *Economic Indicators,* August, 1959, p. 8.

[15] Some of the possibilities here considered are suggested by H. M. Groves (*op. cit.,* Chapter III, and *Production, Jobs and Taxes,* New York, McGraw-Hill, 1944, pp. 29–48). Groves' discussion of the problem is highly recommended. It is suggested, however, that in the references cited above no such rigorous distinction is made between corporate taxes as income and business taxes as is assumed here.

[16] Presumably the individual would include undistributed earnings as a part of his income in his year-end return, and submit receipts for taxes paid for him by the corporation when he settles up for the year. Such year-end adjustments are already numerous under the present system of current tax payments.

tax it as capital gain to the stockholder when realized through later sale of his securities. This is probably the least attractive of all. In essence it involves waiting until the security is sold or the stockholder dies before collecting the tax, if, indeed, capital gains do exist at that time. As Groves says, "The timing of taxation is exceedingly important, and it is doubtful if any burdens imposed upon the dead can make up for immunities allowed the living."[17] This proposal is so out of harmony with the ideals which have brought about the system of current tax payments that it should be discarded on those grounds. In addition, if this treatment were applied to reinvested corporate earnings it should in justice be extended to those of unincorporated businesses.

The third possibility possesses the merits of both equity and simplicity. It is to treat the whole income received through the corporation exactly like that received through the partnership or the individual enterprise. With respect to distributed income, this would be accomplished through the action previously suggested—repeal of the present corporation income tax. With respect to undistributed profits, the corporation would notify stockholders of record at the end of the tax year of the amount of earnings on their holdings not distributed. Negative earnings (net losses) per share would be reported in the same manner, and similar information submitted to the Treasury for the purpose of checking individual returns. His share of undistributed corporate earnings would then be reported by the stockholder on his individual return, and the rates appropriate to his whole net income (including undistributed profits) would be paid by him. Such a plan would operate equitably in all individual cases. It would eliminate the tax loophole now present by removing from corporate management any *tax* influence in the determination of dividend policy. The needs of the corporation for reinvested earnings would predominate in decisions to distribute or not to distribute, and not the desires of individual large stockholders to avoid personal income taxes.

The difficulties of such a plan are not great. Obviously, if income previously untaxed is to be brought under taxation, some further accounting and reporting will result. It has been suggested that the taxpayer might find himself liable for a tax on undistributed profits when he has actually realized no available cash with which to pay the tax. If such embarrassment were to materialize—which is entirely possible—a system of collection at the source is not unthinkable. The corporation now withholds taxes on wages paid, the

---

[17] Reprinted by permission from page 61 of *Postwar Taxation and Economic Progress* by Harold M. Groves, copyright 1946 by the Committee for Economic Development, published by McGraw-Hill Book Company, Inc.

amount withheld being determined by the wage earner's individual tax liability. It is likely that the same could be done to an extent which would take care of possible financial embarrassment to small stockholders. Groves suggests that the corporation could distribute enough of the earnings as cash dividends to cover the tax liability, though he recognizes that stockholders embarrassed by illiquidity are likely to be those small holders who carry little weight in determination of dividend policy. Finally, we may note the criticism that any taxation of undistributed profit is a burden on saving. This is of course true. But it is as great a burden upon the saving of unincorporated businesses and other individuals as upon those who own the corporation, and to date only corporations have been especially favored. It would seem that discouragement of savings by an effective tax on undistributed corporate profits would be largely offset by elimination of the present corporate normal taxes and surtaxes.

Our discussion of the proper relation of personal to corporate income taxes has proceeded in terms of equality of burden of such taxes upon the various tributaries which make up the personal income stream. We have seen that the current system of double taxation of personal income derived through the corporation imposes a peculiar burden upon this type of income. The principal objective in elimination of the corporate income tax is that of accomplishing elementary justice among income receivers. But an additional evil resulting from such discrimination is its discouragement of investment, since the net returns from the type of investment which carries the major share of economic risk are subject to discriminatory treatment.

Our analysis of the problem brings us to a simple conclusion with respect to the most desirable method of attaining the objective of eliminating this discrimination. Elimination of the corporation income tax in its entirety is the first step. This corrects a fundamental fallacy in current income tax practice—the presumption that income derived through the corporation is both income to the corporation itself and to the owners of the corporation, while other business incomes are simply incomes to the owners of those businesses. It is not evident why, either in theory or in practice, undistributed corporate income should not be treated exactly like undistributed income of a partnership or an individual proprietorship.

An inevitable practical objection is raised against any reform proposal which would reduce the total revenue derived from the income tax. The corporate income tax has been a heavy revenue producer to the federal Treasury, and the sacrifice of this revenue, under conditions of high budgetary expenditures and high public debt, is not to be taken lightly. It should be evident, however, that adoption of the proposals above would not result in the net loss of the whole of present corporate income tax revenues. In the first place, the taxation of undistributed corporate income to the individual would offset some revenue loss from abandonment of the corporate income tax. In the second place, elimination of the corporation tax would increase personal incomes derived through the corporation, and thus increase the personal income tax revenues. Let us observe the revenue effects of the proposed changes, when we assume that: (1) over-all, 30 per cent of corporate income is reinvested, (2) the average tax rate on corporate income is 50 per cent, and (3) the average effective individual rate on income derived from corporations is 50 per cent.

Present System:

Corporate taxes per dollar of corporate income	$.50
Personal taxes per dollar of corporate income ($.50 remaining after corporate tax; 70% of $.50 actually distributed and subject to individual tax at 50%)	.175
Total revenue per dollar of corporate income	$.675

Proposed System:

Corporate tax per dollar of corporate income	none
Personal tax per dollar of corporate income (all corporate income taxed as if distributed, at 50% rate)	$.50
Total revenue per dollar of corporate income	$.50
Net revenue loss per dollar of corporate income	$.175

Under the assumptions of our example, which, if not exactly square with the facts, at least is probably not rigged in favor of the proposal, there is a 26 per cent revenue loss from the proposed change. If the applicable personal tax rate were 40 per cent the net revenue loss would be 24¢ per dollar of corporate income; if it were 60 per cent, the loss would be 11¢ per dollar. Professor Holland has estimated the current revenue effect if corporations had been taxed similarly with partnerships during the period 1944–1955.[18] The effect would have ranged from a gain of $.2 billion in 1947 to a loss of $6.5 billion in 1951. The annual average loss during the period 1950–1955 would have been $5.1 billion, which could have been recovered by a percentage point rise in personal tax rates of 3.9 in the average year. The crux of the revenue question in such a revision in tax practice is to be found in the relation of effective personal income tax rates to effective corporation tax rates. When corporate tax rates are relatively high, abandonment of this tax would involve significant revenue loss. But when corporate rates are high the inequity of double taxation is extremely onerous.

In spite of revenue loss, abandonment would appear to be justified in terms of the gain in equity and the long-run encouragement it would give to the investment of venture capital. And though it is revenue, and not

[18] *Ibid.*, p. 232.

equity, which pays government costs, once equity is attained we are on much firmer ground in proceeding toward tax rates which will meet revenue needs.

Elimination of the corporate income tax, and the taxation of corporate profits—whether distributed or not—as individual income, would solve a problem which has caused an inordinate amount of trouble throughout our income tax history. It is the problem of using the corporation as a personal tax dodge. The receivers of very large incomes have at times "incorporated themselves" to avoid payment of high personal surtaxes. The top-bracket corporate rates being considerably below top-bracket personal surtax rates, by making what is actually personal income become income of a corporation for tax purposes the individual can considerably reduce his immediate tax obligation. Suppose an extreme case in which the net income of an individual is one million dollars per year for a period of one year. The effective rate on such an income would be approximately 90 per cent. Thus in a single year he would be obligated to pay approximately $900,000 tax. By making the major part of this income an income to his corporation, the corporate tax rate applicable would be 52 per cent. Suppose $100,000 were to be taken as personal income, and the remainder made income of the personal corporation. The personal income tax payable would be approximately $70,000. The income to the corporation ($900,000) would be taxed at approximately 52 per cent, making the corporate tax $520,000. The total tax in the year in which the million dollar income is earned would thus be about $590,000, as contrasted with a tax of $900,000 if the whole income were taxed as personal income. The final difference is, however, less marked, for when at some future date he draws funds from the corporation he will be subject to personal income tax. Nevertheless, he will be likely to draw funds from the corporation at a time when his current income is low and will thus fall in a lower surtax bracket, or when tax rates in general have been reduced. Or, by dissolving the corporation at a later date and distributing the assets to himself, he would pay only a capital gains tax of 25 per cent. If the corporation were dissolved at death there would be no capital gains tax.

Such avoidance is clearly not contemplated in the theory of the income tax.[19] It arises out of the complexity of recent tax practice, and to attempt to check it as a peculiar loophole not only adds to the pieced-up and patched-together character of the modern income tax, but runs the risk in the patching of adversely affecting some other taxpayers whom it is not intended to disturb. If income to the corporation is treated as income to the

---

[19] It clearly vitiates any logic in terms of ability to pay which a schedule of progressive rates embodies.

individual, this simple return to essentials eliminates the patchwork character of the system. It is frequently both cheaper and more satisfactory to tear down an old house and build a new one than to undertake a program of perpetual repair and renovation.

RECOMMENDED READINGS

Goode, Richard, *The Corporation Income Tax*, N.Y., Wiley, 1951, Chapters 1–3.
> A strong position is taken in favor of independent taxation of corporations. Comparison of Goode's argument with that presented in this chapter is recommended.

Groves, H. M., *Postwar Taxation and Economic Progress*, N.Y., McGraw-Hill, 1946, Chapters 2 and 3.
> On the integration of personal and corporate income taxes.

Holland, Daniel M., *The Income-Tax Burden on Stockholders*, Princeton, Princeton Univ. Press, 1958.
> A technical analysis of the "double-taxation" problem, with particular emphasis upon measurement of the extra burden. It will be rather hard going for a beginner, but rewarding to one with some background.

Keith, E. Gordon, "Economic Impact of the Corporation Income Tax," Joint Committee on the Economic Report, *Federal Tax Policy for Economic Growth and Stability (Papers Submitted . . .)*, Washington, 1955, pp. 658–68.
> A good summary statement on the incidence of this tax, the significance of incidence conclusions, and the place of the corporation tax in the federal tax structure.

Shoup, Carl S., "The Dividend Exclusion and Credit in the Revenue Code of 1954," *National Tax Journal*, March, 1955, pp. 136ff.
> An analysis of methods of reducing the "extra taxation" of stockholders under the combined personal-corporate income taxes.

Simons, H. C., *Personal Income Taxation*, Chicago, Univ. of Chicago, 1938, Chapter 9.
> A plea for taxation of undistributed corporate surplus as personal income.

CHAPTER 19

Strengthening the Personal Income Tax

The title to this chapter suggests an inevitable conclusion from the material presented in the previous two chapters: that the personal income tax is and promises to be the most important in the arsenal of revenue measures. But the meaning attached here to the word "strengthening" does not necessarily suggest persistent rate increases over a period of time. Nor does it necessarily suggest that the role of personal income taxation in the total revenue system will or should be expanded. What it does mean is that the structure of personal income taxation should be improved so that the tax can do its assigned task more efficiently and more equitably.

In the abstract, the personal income tax is admirably qualified to fulfill the requirements of a good tax. In fact, no other tax approaches its qualifications in simple theory. The policy-maker can know what he is doing with a personal income tax, because (1) the stream of income out of which all taxes must be paid is, or can be made to be, identical with the base of this tax. A tax relating income to income is a much more precise instrument than one that tries to estimate income from property ownership or from purchases out of income. And (2) dependable conclusions are more nearly possible with respect to incidence—the locus of final burden as between individuals and groups—in the case of the personal income tax than in the case of any other major tax measure. Policy consequences under the income tax can, therefore, be more accurately foreseen than under any other general tax instrument.

Also, the personal income tax is the only tax under which any rational form of progression can be practiced. This is not to say that, in the abstract, other taxes cannot be made to have a progressive effect. But largely for reasons suggested in the paragraph above, only the income tax can apply progression meaningfully in terms of the case for progression—equity, stability and growth, and general social welfare.[1] In particular, there is no other general tax measure which qualifies as thoroughly for counter-cycle or growth use as the progressive personal income tax. Its basis in income makes it capable of almost instant reaction to changes in income, so that its stabilizing power is automatic.

It seems almost inevitable, therefore, that the role of personal income taxation will expand over a course of time. This makes it the more necessary that the tax in practice realize its possibilities in the abstract. But whether or not it is given an expanded role in the future, its present importance requires that it be generally and uniformly applied—that it be a general tax on personal incomes and not a collection of more or less related taxes, each with its own rate schedule and each with its own specially defined base.

There are other reasons why special attention should be given to the "strengthening" of this most important tax measure. For reasons evident to any observer, compliance with an income tax law depends more heavily upon voluntary assessment than almost any other tax. Uniformity in treatment under the law is essential to voluntary participation and the minimizing of evasion. A widespread attitude that "one must keep up with the Joneses" in matters of evasion would be disastrous. And the income tax rates are "high" (at least in the historical sense), offering real prizes to the successful evader. It is almost a truism that the propensity to evade is increased by a feeling that one's tax is high because someone else is evading. But essentially the same is true of legal avoidance. The progressive creation of legal loopholes, or redefinition of concepts to favor pressure groups, generates even more widespread agitation for special treatment, and uniform treatment under the law is seriously endangered. Professor Heller has referred to this tendency as the "most favored taxpayer principle"—that any concession to one group, whether justified in theory or not, tends to raise a clamor for more widespread concessions.

In Chapters 17 and 18 we discussed at length some major areas in which strengthening of the income tax would be in order, and suggested the form of improvement required. A fairer treatment of unstable incomes would provide for establishment of an income averaging plan. Favored treatment of capital gains, and discriminatory treatment of capital losses, should be

---

[1] In a narrow field of operation, other taxes may be made very roughly progressive with income or progressive with respect to the base of the tax if it is feasible to set specific rates item by item. A sales tax of 5 per cent on Ramblers and 25 per cent on Cadillacs is possible, but is suggestive of real complications. The British purchase tax (sales tax) has been successful in discouraging the consumption of less necessary imports, and can be made progressive with import cost. But none of these really relates the amount of the tax to the income of the individual buyer if he chooses to depart from the pattern of buying considered standard for his income group.

eliminated. The heavy discrimination against single persons should be corrected. And double taxation of corporate earnings should be eliminated. These matters need not be discussed further, but in the remainder of this chapter we look at other, and often somewhat more detailed, areas of potential improvement.

Income Tax Changes to Promote Uniformity and Equity

1. **Exclusions from Adjusted Gross Income.** Since the definition of adjusted gross income largely defines the tax base, permitted exclusions of money receipts from gross income can create opportunities for serious erosion of the base. The present list of exclusions is, on the whole, reasonable. Nevertheless, if the objective is to begin with a clean slate, to wipe out inequities or practices which may be regarded as inequitable, there are some improvements to be made. The first proposal is to eliminate the exclusion of combat pay and mustering-out pay for members of the armed services. The point is not, of course, that these payments are undesirable or that they are excessive. The point is that they are receipts which may possess a capacity to pay taxes, depending upon the income status of the individual. Even though making them subject to taxes might necessitate an increase in the level of payment in order to provide appropriate after-tax receipts to the individual, this would be a preferable procedure, in order to maintain uniformity in the tax law.

The exclusion of the first $50 of dividends received was discussed in the last chapter. This exclusion would, of course, be eliminated from the personal tax if, as recommended in the last chapter, the present corporation tax were eliminated and undistributed profits brought under the personal income tax. The dividend exclusion is a partial attempt to eliminate the double taxation of income received through the corporation. If this were done wholesale by ceasing to tax income to the corporation, the problem of double taxation would be solved.

Whether or not the exclusion of 50 per cent of net capital gain from the sale of long-term assets should be kept would depend upon the type of averaging plan applied in the tax. Insofar as this exclusion is taken to be a substitute for a more complex averaging plan, it would be kept. But insofar as it represents a favor to capital gains receivers, it should be eliminated. And if capital gains and losses were treated as income, and taxed uniformly with income as recommended in Chapter 17, the problem of definition of gains and losses would disappear. There would no longer be pressures to define other income as capital gains, as has occurred in the past, for favorable treatment could not be gained thereby.

Finally, although it is entirely proper that the cost outlays for earning net income should be excluded from taxation, there are two areas in which improvement would need to be made: the treatment of depletion allowances and the "expensing" of research and experimental outlays. The percentage depletion provision is one which permits special deductions from gross income for the depletion of wasting assets by the owners of mineral and other natural deposits. This allowance permits firms to subtract from gross income a fixed percentage of gross income per year without limitation of the number of years.[2]

It is, of course, quite appropriate that capital wastage in economic exploitation of natural resources be deducted as costs in the process of production. But it is difficult to justify a provision in the law which permits, over a period of time, depletion in excess of the value of the original deposit. And it is also difficult to justify depletion allowances more rapid than the actual depletion of the resource. It is noteworthy that percentage depletion is related to gross income and not to the value of the deposit, and therefore bears no relation to actual depletion. It seems clear that, in order to eliminate subsidy to natural resources industries under the tax, the depletion deduction[3] should relate to the value of the deposit being depleted. Thus, however calculated, the sum of allowances over a course of time should not exceed the original value of the deposit. But more than this, assuming total depletion allowances equal to actual value depletion, the allowance for tax purposes should not deplete the resource more rapidly than the asset actually is depleted. Otherwise, taxes are postponed, and the concern has the use of the money saved through the period of postponement. In general, then, a return to the original method of allowing depletion on an actual cost basis in any year is indicated, in order to eliminate tax favors to particular individuals who have been very effective in agitating for subsidies.

Section 616 (a) of the Internal Revenue Code permits research and experimental outlays to be "expensed," i.e., to be considered as a cost wholly in the year incurred rather than entering into capital accounts and being subject to annual amortization.[4] Expensing of research and experimental outlays gives a business the advantage of an immediate and total deduction

---

[2] There is a limitation, however, upon the percentage depletion allowed, in that the allowance may not be more than 50 per cent of taxable income computed without the depletion allowance. But this still does not limit the number of years during which the percentage can be applied.

[3] While it is a "deduction" and not an "exclusion" under the corporate tax, for unincorporated firms it is subtracted from gross income and is thus similar to an exclusion.

[4] The same treatment applies to development and exploration costs with respect to many sorts of mineral deposits.

rather than a fractional deduction annually over a period of time. The present value of the tax saving when such costs are expensed is greater than its discounted value over a course of time, and expensing therefore contains an element of tax subsidy of research and experimentation. This subsidy could be eliminated by a return to earlier practice requiring amortization of such expenditures over their useful life.

2. **Deductions.** This is the area in which the largest number of subsidies occur, and in which the erosion of the personal income tax base is most serious. Upon close investigation many of the deductions which have been allowed from the early years of personal income taxation are found to represent grants of encouragement or subsidy to special groups. The purpose of the personal exemption (now $600 each for the taxpayer and his dependents) is to make tax-free an amount of family income necessary to meet minimum living requirements. If the amount of the personal exemption is inadequate, the figure should be changed. But this is the item in which uniform taxpayer subsidies are intended to reside. Deductions were not originally designed for this purpose, but some have gradually assumed an aspect of this function.

A deduction for up to $600 of the cost of care for the dependents of a working woman or widower, provided the parent earns no more than $5,100 of adjusted gross income, appeals on humanitarian grounds but hardly in terms of income tax theory. While child care may logically be regarded as an expense of earning an income, it is singled out for special treatment, and contravenes the principle of uniformity. Commuting costs to one's work are not permitted as a deduction. And if the theory of the deduction is that child care may be necessary if the parent works, why the limitation on the adjusted gross income to which it applies? It may be just as necessary to working parents or a working widow earning $100,000, but it is not allowed as a deduction in such a case. The limitation to lower incomes clearly suggests that this is a use of a deduction to take care of a situation which should be treated through the personal exemption or through lower rates on lower incomes.

Consider, next, the deduction permitted for interest paid on personal borrowing. A major deduction in this category is that of interest on residential mortgages. This is clearly a subsidy to home ownership, and available only to those who can afford to buy a home. In the case of other installment credit the effect again is to subsidize it. These are all matters of personal expenditure, which is not generally taken into account in the theory of the tax. Normally, the tax is assumed to be placed uniformly upon persons in an income class, with distinctions within the class made by total personal exemptions. What the person does with his income after taxes is not a matter for income tax consideration. Yet, the amount of the tax is permitted to be altered by the spending choice of the individual. Again, the law appears to be motivated largely by concern for the little fellow, a matter which should be handled through personal exemptions and rate schedules. But in addition, the motive is badly served by the deduction, for the tax saved through the deduction is larger per dollar of interest paid for the larger income than for the smaller, the former being subject to a higher marginal rate.

Much the same thing needs to be said about the deductions permitted for state and local taxes. The deduction of local property taxes represents another subsidy to home ownership. The person who lives in his own home is permitted deductions for interest on his mortgage and his property taxes, and at the same time is not required to include the imputed rental value in his income. The renter, on the other hand, pays a rental which presumably covers taxes and mortgage interest, and is not permitted to deduct any part of his rental from gross income. The discrimination is clear and by no means inconsiderable. The deduction for state excise and sales taxes has the effect of making luxury taxes less progressive with income and general sales taxes more regressive with income. For the deduction, per dollar, provides a greater saving from the federal income tax for the large income than for the small. The same must be said of the deduction for state income taxes, except that here there is a very special need for some deduction. For without deduction a maximum federal rate of 91 per cent and a state rate of more than 9 per cent will give combined marginal rates in excess of 100 per cent on the last units of income.[5]

The best that can be said for permitting deduction of charitable contributions in arriving at the personal income tax base is that it provides a sort of monetary ointment to salve the strain of charity. Again, the ointment provides more relief to the large income donor than to the small. There is little doubt that charitable contributions would be reduced, particularly for large-income givers, if the deductions were eliminated. But one can assume that a decline in giving would also occur if the deduction were maintained and tax rates lowered. In general, it is a highly questionable practice to use a tax measure to prod philanthropy, particularly when philanthropy is made cheaper for one income group than another.

In the cases of deduction of extraordinary medical expense, uninsured

[5] See Joseph A. Pechman, "Erosion of the Individual Income Tax," *National Tax Journal*, March, 1957, p. 7. On the subject of this chapter in general, the Pechman article is excellent supplementary reading.

losses, and bad debts, government is sharing in the cost of these unusual setbacks. It is difficult to argue against the practice in principle, though it is obvious that in the case of the latter two, government is absorbing a penalty for individual imprudence, and the benefits are greater to the wealthy imprudent person. While the limitation of the medical deduction to expenditures in excess of 3 per cent of adjusted gross income applies the deduction properly to extraordinary costs, permitting those aged sixty-five or over to deduct *all* medical expenses is inconsistent with this objective. Perhaps the best that can be done with these deductions is a minor cleaning up of exceptions to the principle of extraordinary expense.

Finally, the standard deduction of 10 per cent of adjusted gross income, not to exceed $1,000, presents problems. The standard deduction may be taken by the taxpayer instead of itemizing the particular deductions allowed, and the major purpose of the standard deduction is to simplify record-keeping and preparation of the tax return. Analysis of personal income tax returns for 1956[6] shows the following use of the standard deduction by income classes:

Adjusted Gross Income Class	Total Returns (thousands)	With Standard Deduction (thous.)	% with Standard Deduction
$ 0–$ 5,000	39,744	31,215	78.4
$ 5,000–$10,000	16,343	8,323	50.9
$10,000–$15,000	1,919	917	47.8
$15,000–$25,000	732	224	30.6
over $25,000	458	60	13.0

Both taxable and nontaxable returns are included, though the nontaxable returns fall almost entirely in the first income class. Two conclusions are fairly obvious from the table. The first is that the standard deduction does simplify record-keeping and the preparation of returns for the large bulk of persons making returns. The second is that, to a considerable though undeterminable extent, the standard deduction provides a tax saving to a large number of persons in the lower and middle income groups.

If elimination of a large proportion of the itemized deductions were to occur, as suggested in paragraphs above, a very substantial reduction in the standard deduction would be in order. It should probably be reduced to the smaller of 2 per cent of adjusted gross income or $200. Otherwise, the standard deduction would grant a large tax benefit to nearly all taxpayers, which, if desirable, should be accomplished by adjustment of the rate schedule or by adjustment of the personal exemptions. If, on the other hand, the present itemized deductions are retained, there is still logical basis

⁶ *Statistics of Income . . . 1956, Individual Income Tax Returns,* pp. 45–49.

for reduction in the standard deduction. A reduction to the smaller of 5 per cent of adjusted gross income or $500 would take away a considerable portion of the tax advantage which the present law gives. Many more returns would find it advantageous to itemize deductions than at present, total deductions would be considerably reduced, and the stated purpose of the deductions would be more nearly realized. At the same time, only the smallest incomes would, in general, gain the simplifying advantages of a standard deduction.

3. **Exemptions.** In general, the law now permits an exemption of $600 for the taxpayer and for each of his dependents. A dependent, in general terms, is one who is related to and receives more than one-half of his support from the taxpayer. Except for the years 1945–1948, when the exemption was $500 per dependent, the personal exemption is now the lowest in the history of the income tax. And this is true in spite of a Consumer Price Index for 1958 which was 61 per cent higher than in 1945 and 103 per cent higher than in 1940. Since the purpose of the personal exemption is to permit an untaxed minimum of income presumably necessary to subsistence or minimum comfort, it is clear that the present provision makes a more niggardly real allowance for basic expenses than it did even at the end of World War II. Furthermore, the personal exemption has always been the same in all geographical areas, even though the cost of living has been by no means identical in all sections of the country. In addition, the value of home-produced food or other articles is not included in income, making the $600 cost of living exemption much more adequate for persons who are fortunate enough to be in this situation than for others. While it would be administratively very difficult to make these distinctions in the law, there would seem to be good reason for adjusting exemptions for major general increases in the cost of living. And although this might necessitate higher rates somewhere in the scale to provide necessary revenue, such action would protect the progressiveness of the tax by being somewhat more lenient with the low income groups.

Exceptions to the general rule of $600 exemption per dependent are the additional exemptions of $600 each permitted to a taxpayer or his wife for age in excess of sixty-five and for blindness. Also, a child who is under nineteen or a student, but who earns over $600, is entitled to be counted as a dependent by the parent and to receive a $600 exemption on his own tax return. Additional exemptions for the aged and the blind are hardly justified in terms of the theory of exemption, so long as deductions for abnormally large medical expenses are permitted. These are clearly given on the supposition that incomes of these persons are low, but they apply no matter how large the income and it would be far better to take account of differences in incomes by an adequate exemption applied regardless of age. With respect to students, the double exemption should be eliminated by giving a choice between withdrawing the parent's exemption when the student makes a return, and granting the exemption to the parent and including the student's income (above some practicable figure, say $200) with that of the parent.

4. Tax Credits. There are two tax credits which require a change in treatment if a general uniformity in tax treatment is to be accomplished. The first is the credit against the tax of 4 per cent of dividends received. This would, of course, be eliminated if the corporate income tax were eliminated, for its purpose is a partial adjustment for the "double taxation" which is applied to personal income derived through a corporation. Of the two methods now used for reducing double taxation of dividends, the dividends-received credit does not possess the discriminatory features of the $50 dividend exclusion. The latter is a larger tax saving per dollar of dividends excluded for the large income than for the small. But since the credit is 4 per cent of dividends, the savings per dollar of dividends are equal for all taxpayers. Thus, if the corporate tax were not to be altered, the dividend tax credit is a more equitable provision than the dividend exclusion.

The second major tax credit is that of 20 per cent of retirement income from pensions, annuities, interest, rents, and dividends, with an upper limit of $240 (20 per cent of $1,200). This provision is intended to give privately provided retirement income equal treatment with untaxed social security benefits. In practice, this credit is applicable principally to persons over sixty-five years of age. Again, therefore, we are dealing with a matter which in the interest of uniformity should be dealt with through the amount of the uniform personal exemption, or through the rate schedule. If $1,200 of social security benefits is exempt from tax, then it is reasonable to exempt $1,200 of private retirement income to those who do not qualify for social security. But neither is equitable with respect to other incomes; a minimum income for living requirements should be exempt, but this should be true regardless of age. To single out older people for the benefit is not only to grant the benefit to older people with larger incomes, but to discriminate against younger people with equally small incomes.

The Effect of Proposed Changes upon the Tax Base

In previous paragraphs it has been suggested that if we were to eliminate special treatment for certain types of income and for certain groups of individuals, greater uniformity and thus greater equity as between individuals could be accomplished. This would involve the elimination of some exclusions from gross income, notably the exclusion of special pay to armed services personnel and the exclusion of a portion of dividends received. Also, practices with respect to certain especially favorably treated costs of earning incomes should be changed, such as percentage depletion and the expensing of research, exploration, and development costs. The exclusion of the portion of long-term capital gains in excess of that required to make an averaging plan work should not be permitted, and in the absence of a general averaging plan, to create more than two holding periods for capital assets would seem desirable.

We have suggested that most of the permitted deductions are illogical, and should be cancelled, so as to leave as deductions only those extraordinary and necessary outlays by the individual (such as large medical expenses) which make his gross income produce less net income than that of another. The standard 10 per cent deduction, if not cancelled, would be brought into line with the above changes. It has also been indicated that a realignment of personal exemptions and elimination of credits against the tax would make for desired uniformity in the tax treatment of individuals in substantially the same income and expenditure situations.

The reader who has followed the suggestions thus far will probably view them with mixed feelings. Some are so obviously desirable in eliminating favoritism that little objection would be heard. But many of the proposals would, taken by themselves, operate to increase the tax on the lower and lower-middle income groups, and these may be harder to accept. The important point is, however, that to define the tax base logically, simply, and uniformly by the elimination of special treatment will permit a substantial reduction of rates and still raise the same revenue. Increase in the income tax base would obviously result from the removal of exclusions, deductions, extra exemptions, and credits. But there are further advantages in promoting compliance when the base is simplified. Each one of these special treatments creates a situation increasing the possibilities of evasion. And while the Internal Revenue Bureau politely refers to these as "errors," the fact is that far more of these "errors" result in underpayment than in overpayment of taxes. Inability to audit all returns means that many "errors" will not be spotted. If many complicating provisions which multiply the opportunities for evasion were eliminated, it seems clear that two advantages would be gained: several instruments for evasion would no longer be available, and the task of auditing would be eased. And if, at the same time, the collection of the tax at the source on interest and dividends income were inaugurated, a very substantial increase in the tax base at any level of aggregate personal income would result.

Pechman[7] has estimated the effect of elimination of "leakages" in the form of exclusions, deductions, extra exemptions, tax credits, and rather poor enforcement upon income tax revenues in 1956. He concludes that had these leakages not been permitted, tax rates averaging almost 25 per cent lower than those in effect in 1956 would have raised the same amount of revenue. Pechman further concluded that if the income-splitting provisions for married couples using joint returns were eliminated, rates about one-third lower could have been applied to raise the same revenue. It is pretty clear that new life could be breathed into the personal income tax by the elimination of a variety of special treatments not justifiable in income tax theory. The substantial rate reductions made possible by these alterations, if wisely used, could promote public acceptance of the revolutionary changes.

Tax Rates

Let us suppose that illogical and tax-base-eroding provisions in the law were removed. The base would substantially rise, permitting substantial reductions in rates. As indicated above, Pechman estimates that in 1956 a uniform and uneroded base at the then current rates would have produced revenues of $44.5 billion—$12.0 billion higher than the $32.5 billion of actual revenues in that year. If the advantages of income splitting were eliminated, by applying to joint returns the same rates and the same income brackets as to individual returns, the additional revenue in that year would have been still larger—$48.5 billion or about $16 billion more than was actually received. This would give considerable leeway for the alteration of the rate schedule. On the average, rates could be reduced by 33 per cent, but this need not be a horizontal decrease, applicable to the same degree throughout the rate schedule.

One change which we have previously recommended—elimination of the general corporation income tax and substituting a tax at personal rates on undistributed surplus—would, it is estimated, involve a revenue loss of nearly $5 billion. By subtracting this from the $16 billion to be gained by broadening the personal income tax base, there remain about $11 billion for use in reducing personal income tax rates.[8] A considerable amount of

[7] "Erosion of the Individual Income Tax," *National Tax Journal*, March, 1957, pp. 24–25.

[8] See p. 424 for the Holland estimate of revenue loss resulting from the corporate tax changes. Since both the Holland and the Pechman estimates are based upon 1956, the subtraction is justified.

pulling and hauling over the locus of rate reductions in the schedule would be expected. At one extreme are those who would concentrate upon the top rates in the structure, setting the maximum marginal rate much below the present level of 91 per cent. Such proposals usually imply a scaling down of rates below the present maximum, though one of long standing would set the maximum rate at 25 per cent. If this were done, it is fairly obvious that the revenue loss would be so staggering as to require at the very least the raising of rates below that level up to 25 per cent. Most proposals for reduction of maximum rates are, however, more responsible and more modest. Several authorities have proposed in recent years the reduction of the maximum rate from 91 per cent to 60–70 per cent.

Those who emphasize reducing rates at the top of the schedule usually base their argument upon the importance of investment and of executive management to economic growth. It is widely believed—especially in high income circles—that the high marginal rates are a deterrent both to executive effort and to investment. With respect to investment, the high tax rates are seen as a two-edged sword. One edge, by reducing investment funds in the hands of potential investors, reduces the financial capacity for investment. The other edge, by threatening a heavy sharing by government in any proceeds of successful investment while accepting no share of possible losses, is seen as dulling investment incentives for those subject to high tax rates. This argument has strong appeal on abstract grounds. That is, it appears to rest upon sound assumptions as to how individuals "would" or "should" react. The difficulty with it is that there is so little evidence that individuals do react in that way. The postwar period of very high tax rates is one of almost persistent prosperity and a respectable rate of growth. The problem has, in part, been one of generally excessive pressure of demand upon the capacity of the economy to produce output, and a considerable share of this demand pressure has been for investment purposes. Thus, it may be argued that to have strengthened incentives during this period would have intensified the inflation problem without significantly improving the rate of growth.

Whether or not high income tax rates have deterred investment and executive effort, it would seem probable that a marked and immediate reduction of tax rates would provide a fillip to these incentives. This push would presumably last until people had adjusted to them—until tax burdens under the new rate schedule had come to be regarded as normal. Given the postwar tendencies toward inflation, it would seem desirable to institute a major rate reduction over a period of time and under conditions where monetary and other fiscal policies can be employed effectively to offset the expansive effect of the tax reduction upon demand.

To question that there have been real disincentive consequences of the high tax rates is not necessarily to oppose reduction of those rates. There are good reasons why these rates should be reduced. The first reason is that high rates encourage a spirit of evasion which can be corrected only by greater expense in enforcement. More important, when rates are believed to be confiscatory, avoidance is encouraged, both by taking advantage of existing loopholes and by pressing for the inclusion of more and more loopholes in the law. In some sense the incentive argument is misleading, for it is commonly based upon the published marginal rates on regular income, while the actual results are those flowing from the rates actually paid, and these involve the variety of special treatments now incorporated into the legislation.

A reduction in rates—particularly in the higher ranges—is probably a necessary precondition to the acceptance of reforms recommended in this chapter. This is particularly true of the treatment of capital gains as regular income. For a reduction in rates would reduce the differential between present rates applicable to capital gains and those applicable to other income. And once the reforms were accomplished, lower rates would tend to forestall intensive efforts to erode these reforms by writing new provisions for special favors into the law.

There is a further gain to be had by reducing the rates in the higher ranges. It would partially eliminate the widespread reference to the 91 per cent figure in rate discussions as if it were far more widely applicable than it is. In 1956, with a marginal rate of 91 per cent, the average rate paid on taxable income of taxpayers in the over $1 million adjusted gross income class was 65 per cent. Among this group, those who paid taxes at regular income rates paid an average rate of 82.6 per cent, while the larger number, who used the alternative method of taxing capital gains, paid an average rate of 61.3 per cent on total taxable income including capital gains.[9] Given these facts, it is obvious that the 91 per cent figure, whose mention seems to bring more gasps from those in low income groups than from those in higher, plays a much more significant propaganda role than it deserves. To reduce the top marginal rate to, say, 65 per cent, would eliminate this tool of obfuscation in rate discussions, and at a revenue cost which is not great. Most estimates place the revenue loss, if the maximum rate were reduced to 65 per cent, at considerably below $1 billion. This would leave

[9] *Statistics of Income . . . 1956, Individual Income Tax Returns*, p. 44.

about $10 billion of revenue under the expanded tax base, after elimination of the general corporate tax and the reduction of top rates, for rate adjustments elsewhere in the scale.

At the other extreme are those who would concentrate the rate reductions at the lower end of the schedule. The reasons given for this are usually the encouragement it would give to a constantly expanding consumption base for the economy, and the relatively harsh treatment of lower incomes during and following World War II. With respect to the latter, the number of taxable returns rose from $4.1 million in 1934 to $7.6 million in 1939, $27.3 million in 1942, $42.7 million in 1945, and $46.3 million in 1956. The rapid increase during the war was of course partially due to the rise in incomes, but it was mainly due to the reduction in personal exemptions.[10] The exemption for husband and wife fell from $2,500 in 1939 to $1,200 in 1942 and further to $1,000 in 1944. Thus, millions of persons who had paid no tax at all prior to the war were now subject to it. And the starting rates rose from 4 per cent in 1940 to 19 per cent in 1942 and 23 per cent in 1944. Therefore, not only were large numbers of people made newly liable for taxes but they were made liable at historically very high starting rates. The postwar drives to settle back to a "normal" level of taxation have to date resulted only in an increase in the personal exemption for husband and wife to $1,200 and a decrease in the starting rate to 20 per cent. In the meantime, of course, inflation has made the real value of the exemption fall; the deflated values of the married couples' exemption for selected years are as follows:

Year	Money Value of Exemption	Consumer Price Index (1947–1949=100)	Deflated Value of Exemption
1939	$2,500	59.4	$2,500
1942	1,200	69.7	1,023
1944	1,000	75.2	790
1958	1,200	123.5	577

By contrast people at the top of the rate scale, while they have been minutely affected by the reduction in personal exemptions, have seen the highest marginal rate rise from 79 per cent in 1939 to 94 per cent in 1944 and drop back to 91 per cent at present. But also, the income splitting provision introduced in 1948 raises the income to which the maximum rate applies in the case of a joint return from $200,000 to $400,000.

Any desire to "do something" for the lower incomes through tax rate reduction is confronted by the simple fact that even a small change in

---

[10] The institution of withholding undoubtedly brought in some returns which had previously evaded.

rates at this level produces a heavy loss of revenues. This is partly due to the fact that such a large proportion of total taxable income is in the hands of the very numerous lower income groups. (The Joint Committee on Internal Revenue Taxation estimated in 1958 that 56 per cent of aggregate adjusted gross income on taxable returns falls in the under $7,000 class.)[11] But a second reason why it is costly in revenue to reduce the rates on lower incomes is that whatever is done automatically applies to the first units of large incomes as well.

The two major proposals for tax relief primarily for the lower incomes are an across-the-board increase in the personal exemption, and reduction in the rate applicable to the lowest bracket of taxed income. Though the two may appear to accomplish the same purpose, there are reasons for preferring the rate reduction over the exemption increase. One reason is that raising the exemption would remove persons entirely from the tax lists, and there are political as well as economic reasons for wide citizen participation in the duty of financing federal functions directly through a major tax instrument. Another reason for preferring rate reduction is that all taxpayers would receive the same dollar benefit, while the tax saving if the exemption were increased would be larger for the large income. If, for example, the lowest bracket rate were reduced from the present 20 per cent to 15 per cent, a tax saving of 5¢ per dollar of taxable income *in that lowest bracket* would be granted uniformly to all taxpayers. On the other hand a rise of $100 in the personal exemption would provide a tax saving of $20 to a taxpayer whose whole taxable income is in the first bracket, but would provide a $50 saving to one subject to a 50 per cent marginal rate.

Let us recapitulate and then carry forward our description of the major possibilities in revision of the personal income tax structure, looking toward simplification and uniformity, and consequent rate reductions.[12]

1. We began with Pechman's estimates of the revenue-increasing consequences of sweeping elimination of tax favors to particular groups in the present law. His estimate, including the removal of income-splitting benefits

[11] Joint Committee, *Alternative Plans for Tax Relief for Individuals*, Washington, 1958, p. 1.

[12] Estimates of the effects of tax changes upon revenues received is a very tricky business, in which very few persons are expert, and the pitfalls are so numerous that even the experts prefer to keep their estimates as private as possible. It will be evident, of course, that any estimate of the revenue effect of a given tax change will be relevant only to a fairly narrow range of aggregate personal income in an economy, and will be relevant to a given distribution pattern of that income. When estimates are made in the text here, they should, unless specifically indicated to be otherwise, be understood as approximations which are relevant to income levels of the late nineteen-fifties. For published estimates of the revenue effects of various tax changes, see Tax Foundation, "What Next in Taxes," *Tax Review*, May, 1957.

to married couples, showed a potential increase of personal income tax revenues of about $16 billion. This is the revenue cushion which we can "play with" in considering rate reductions.

2. We have suggested the elimination of the general corporate income tax and the application of personal income tax rates to undistributed corporate profits. By rounding Holland's estimate we would expect a revenue loss from this of about $5 billion. This would reduce our cushion to $11 billion.

3. A reduction in the top rates to a ceiling of 65 per cent we estimated, generously, would involve a loss of about $1 billion. This leaves about $10 billion which can be absorbed in further rate reductions.

4. If personal exemptions were to be increased, each increase of $100 (eliminating additional exemptions for the aged, the blind, and minors who earn, removing income-splitting advantages, and reducing top rates) would cost in the vicinity of $2.8 billion. Thus, the $10 billion cushion remaining could be largely used up by increasing the personal exemption from $600 to $900 or $950.

5. If rate reductions in the lowest bracket were substituted for exemption increases, a reduction of one percentage point (assuming elimination of the income-splitting advantages) would probably reduce revenues by $1 billion to $1.5 billion. Thus, if the whole $10 billion revenue cushion were to be absorbed in first bracket rate reductions, it would seem possible to reduce the first bracket rate from 20 per cent to roughly 13 per cent. But nothing would be left for the middle incomes, and an awkward jump in marginal rates from 13 per cent to 22 per cent would occur as taxable income moves over the $2,000 level.

6. Clearly no Congress would exhaust its resources for tax reduction in relief for only the very lowest and the very highest income taxpayers. A considerable part of aggregate taxable income under present law is subject to rates above the minimum and below the maximum, and in any major move toward tax rate reduction the middle incomes can hardly be ignored. This is particularly true since the proposed extensive elimination of deductions and the withdrawal of the income-splitting advantage would have heavy impact upon this group. Furthermore, many of them would be affected by a more severe treatment of capital gains. A simple way of distributing relief among all classes is to permit a percentage reduction to all taxpayers. For example, we have left in our calculation a cushion of $10 billion for further tax rate relief, having already accounted for the revenue loss involved in reducing the top rates to 65 per cent. This $10 billion would permit, by rough estimate, about a 20 per cent reduction in all rates

except the maximum rate.[13] This would mean that the bottom 20 per cent rate could be lowered to 16 per cent, the 30 per cent rate to 24 per cent, and the 50 per cent rate to 40 per cent. This would provide some rate reduction for everyone, but it might be objected to on grounds that it reduces the rate of progression and is therefore relatively unfavorable to the lower incomes.

A possible variant would be the reduction in all rates (except the 65 per cent top rate) by a fixed number of percentage points. The $10 billion revenue margin might well permit a reduction in each rate in the schedule by 3 percentage points, so that the 20 per cent rate would become 17, the 30 per cent rate would become 27, and the 50 per cent rate 47. This would more nearly maintain the rate of progression than a constant percentage reduction throughout the rate schedule.

A third possibility would combine special treatment of low incomes and a flat percentage point reduction for all. As an example, if all rates below the top one of 65 per cent were reduced by 2 percentage points, there would still be room for a special reduction for the first bracket to, say, 15 per cent. This would leave an awkward jump from 15 per cent to 20 per cent as we move from the first to the second brackets, and another from 62 per cent to 65 per cent at the top. These should probably be smoothed out by adjustments elsewhere.

The rate-reducing possibilities which have been outlined suggest something of the range of policy decisions which could be made if the base were simplified and broadened. The total program of base increase and rate decrease has been discussed in the context of revenues from the personal (and corporate) income tax comparable with those now realized. The consequence of these revolutionary changes would therefore be no significant change in the revenue received, and thus taxpayers as a whole would continue to pay the same amount. But considerable changes would occur in the amounts of tax paid by particular individuals. Some would gain and others lose from the changes. However, the individual adjustments would all be in the direction of greater equity. Those previously favored would lose their advantage, while those previously discriminated against would have the discrimination removed.

[13] In 1958 the personal income tax produced $34.7 billion. After adjustment for provisions in paragraphs 1, 2, and 3 above, we estimate that this amount would have been about $10 billion higher, or $44.7 billion. The $10 billion expendable for further tax relief to bring the revenue back to $34.7 billion under the broadened base represents a 22.5 per cent reduction in revenues. Thus, if each taxpayer were allowed a reduction of about 20 per cent in his tax, the total revenues would be reduced by the same proportion.

The alternative to making basic changes in income tax is the continuance of the past practice of gradually eroding the base. Experience has shown that once a "loophole" is established and strict uniformity abandoned, there is little likelihood that it will be closed. Rather, the loophole is likely to be broadened, extending favors to others than those originally favored. As additional revenues are needed, rates are raised (or at least not lowered as economic growth expands the base) for those who cannot get particular loopholes established for themselves, and those who are not in a position to evade—those, for example, who are caught in the withholding system. Furthermore, specific erosions of the base vastly complicate and render less effective the enforcement of the law. That evasion is more than a hypothetical problem under the personal income tax, which must depend heavily upon self-assessment, is attested to by the miserable record of compliance in many countries of continental Europe and Asia. A spirit of competitive evasion very seriously undermines the whole personal income tax program. There is much experience over the world to indicate that when income taxation breaks down, regressive taxes on sales tend to be substituted for them.

Counter-Cycle Adjustments in the Personal Income Tax

Aside from the matter of equity among taxpayers, the inevitability of counter-cycle use of the income tax recommends its fundamental strengthening. In general, the personal income tax offers a major opportunity for influencing private spending in the economy. But in order to use the tax wisely for compensatory purposes, it is important that it be simply defined and uniformly applied to persons in similar circumstances. Every complication in the definition of the base makes more complex and less dependable the estimating of the economic effect of a change for compensatory purposes. In addition, public acceptance of the wide use of the income tax as a compensatory measure requires that individuals feel that the tax is uniformly applied. That is, if a rise in tax rates is to be employed as an anti-inflationary device, the taxpayer whose obligation is increased has a right to feel that he is not singled out to fight alone an inflation for which he alone is not responsible. During the Korean rearmament boom of the early nineteen-fifties, for instance, organized labor showed a much greater willingness to accept higher income tax rates without wage increases than they would have shown if the anti-inflationary instrument had been a sales tax. If the latter had been used, labor would have interpreted the use of this regressive tax as an attempt to throw the burden of anti-inflation taxation largely upon a particular class. By the same token, if the income tax becomes further eroded by special dispensations, the distrust of this instrument for compensatory purposes will make its use less possible.

If income tax obligations are to be varied to conform to the needs of cyclical stability, three possibilities for action offer themselves. Rates may be raised or lowered. Personal exemptions can be raised or lowered, or, following the lead of some of the states, specific and temporary percentage increases or reductions of the tax may be employed. The last would involve the addition or subtraction of a given percentage of the tax as computed. It would leave the tax measure essentially intact, and emphasize the temporary nature of the variation. By leaving the measure intact, familiarity with standard rates and practices is promoted, and this, over a period of time, is desirable in promoting compliance. Changes in rates and exemptions are relatively difficult to reverse as conditions change, both because the legislative process is complex and because taxpayers tend to regard lowered rates or raised exemptions as a vested right. It would even be possible to accomplish a differential compensatory change in tax burdens within the rate schedule by the use of differential percentage reductions or increases. Suppose that economic conditions seemed to call for a tax adjustment to give temporary support to consumption. While one would normally expect such an adjustment to be made through a lowering of rates at the lower end of the scale—to affect the tax obligations of the bulk of incomes and those with higher propensity to consume—this could also be accomplished by granting a larger percentage reduction to those whose tax is small.

On the whole, the personal income tax lends itself best to those kinds of compensatory adjustment which are very broad and designed to influence disposable income without differentiation as to its source. That is, variations in the impact of the personal income tax can affect disposable income in general, and can be made to have varying impact upon incomes of various size, but the tax is a rather clumsy instrument for producing selective impact upon particular streams of income. And the proposals made in this chapter for strengthening the income tax would reduce the opportunities for selective use. The elimination of the corporate income tax, for instance, would destroy an instrument for limited compensatory use when it might be desirable to curb or to foster a corporate investment boom. It is fairly evident that the more general and uniform and simple the base of the income tax, the fewer the opportunities for variation in tax treatment of particular segments of the economy. It is doubtful, however, that this is a great loss. For tax action which influences disposable income in general, without differentiation as to source, will cover most compensatory requirements in practice. If more narrow objectives are to be accomplished through tax changes they can be accomplished either by use of other existing taxes or, in a very pressing situation, by the legislation of a special tax.

In the last four chapters we have given far more attention to the personal income tax than we shall give to any other single type of tax. This has been done because it is the most important tax now in use, because it promises to increase in importance in the states, and because its qualities are such as to recommend its use as the major fiscal instrument in the kit of revenue tools. We are led to the conclusion that a proper tax system will make the personal income tax the great central bulwark, while other taxes will be relegated to the role of complementary measures when particular sumptuary objectives, particular revenue objectives, or divided governmental sovereignty make their use desirable or necessary.

RECOMMENDED READINGS

Hellmuth, William F., Jr., "Erosion of the Federal Corporation Income Tax Base," Joint Committee on the Economic Report, *Federal Tax Policy for Economic Growth and Stability (Papers Submitted by Panelists Appearing before the Subcommittee on Tax Policy)*, Washington, 1955, pp. 888–916.

Though the subject of this paper hardly qualifies it for reading in connection with this chapter, anyone who studies the Pechman paper below may wish to round out his investigation with this paper. Some of the same points are covered.

Pechman, Joseph A., "What Would a Comprehensive Individual Income Tax Yield?", in Committee for Economic Development, *Essays in Federal Taxation*, 1959.

This is a revision of Pechman's "Erosion of the Individual Income Tax," *National Tax Journal*, March, 1957. It measures the erosion over a period of time of the individual income tax base, and suggests improvements in the direction of equity and greater revenue productivity.

Shere, Louis, "Federal Tax Revision to Promote Economic Growth and Stability," testimony presented in *Hearings . . . Joint Economic Committee: January, 1957, Economic Report of the President*, Washington, 1957, pp. 424–66.

An encyclopedic statement of what should be done with the federal tax system. Shere deals mainly with the problem attacked by Pechman in the selection above, but includes also possible rate changes and corporate and excise adjustments.

CHAPTER 20

Taxes on Sales

Types of Taxes on Sales

Taxes imposed upon the sale or use of goods take several forms, some of which are clearly intended to fall upon the consumers of those goods, while others, though apparently intended to fall upon sellers, are generally shifted to buyers. We shall class as taxes upon sales all those taxes which are imposed upon sellers or buyers of products when the base of the tax is the amount of sales (or purchases). The tax may be applied at the point of sale or on the occasion of production. Particularly noteworthy are many state taxes imposed upon business enterprises, called taxes upon the "privilege of doing business," but levied upon the volume of sales. Such "business" taxes are, in effect, sales taxes. We shall consider separately (1) customs duties, (2) taxes on the production, sale, or use of particular goods, (3) turnover, or general sales taxes, and (4) retail sales taxes.

Customs Duties. Tariff duties imposed upon goods imported into a country are in all mechanical and economic aspects like taxes imposed upon the sale of goods produced and sold within a country. The duty is collected from the importer at the time the goods enter the country, and becomes an element of cost of the goods to him. The intent of the import duty is generally to discourage importation of a good by an artificial tax addition to its price, while the objective of an internal sales tax is almost always to raise revenue. Nevertheless, a tariff for protective purposes incidentally produces revenue, unless duties are so high as to stop importation completely, while a tax upon the sale of a home-produced good possesses inevitable elements of discouragement of its sale.

Though customs duties are and have been imposed with the primary intent to protect home industry against foreign competition in the home market, such duties can also be and at times have been used for revenue purposes only. If the purpose is revenue, the import duty should impose no price disadvantage upon the imported good. The objective of a revenue tariff will be to maximize the revenue received; i.e., to establish the duty at a level which will make the duty per unit times the number of units a maximum. If the good is not produced at home, the duty will be relatively low in rate, particularly if it is a good of relatively elastic demand. In the case of goods of relatively elastic demand, a high duty would cause major reduction in the quantity imported, and thus provide less than the maximum amount of revenue. When demand for the good is highly inelastic, the quantity imported would be far less affected by high rates.

The typical case, however, will be that in which the good is both home-produced and imported. In such a case the use of a tariff for purely revenue purposes requires imposition of a comparable tax burden upon the home-produced good. Thus, a tariff duty imposed for purely revenue purposes will be accompanied by an equal tax upon the sale of the home-produced good, and if it is desired to raise revenue by imposing a tax on the sale of a good produced at home it is reasonable that an import duty of comparable severity be levied upon similar foreign-produced goods. Prior to World War I, England used some import duties in this way, in a manner entirely consistent with her "free trade" policy.

Whether imposed for revenue or protective purposes, however, the customs tariff is a tax upon the sale of a good. Its behavior with respect to shifting is exactly like that of taxes imposed upon sales of goods produced internally. This being the case, we are justified in applying to customs duties the same conclusions with respect to incidence and effects as are drawn with respect to other sales taxes.

Taxes on the Production, Sale, or Use of Particular Goods. Under this heading we consider a miscellaneous group of tax measures which appear on the surface to be distinct types, but possess common basic characteristics. These common characteristics are: (1) they are applied specifically to a selected list of products or sellers, and (2) they are so applied as to make available a price vehicle for forward shifting to buyers of the product and are thus actually taxes upon sales. We shall describe briefly three groups of such taxes: those on the gross receipts of particular businesses, those upon the use of particular commodities, and those upon the sale of particular commodities.

The first group comprises taxes upon business gross receipts which are imposed by some states as part of the general scheme of state business taxation. Frequently such "business taxes" are not intended as commodity or sales taxes, but as taxes to be borne by businesses out of their net incomes. For example, many state business tax systems apply different measures to different types of business. Corporations in general may pay business taxes imposed upon their net incomes as a proper measure of their supposed business ability to pay, or in return for benefits conferred upon them. But since miscellaneous unincorporated businesses do not possess uniform accounting systems, and thus do not determine their net income by uniform methods, business taxes upon them are frequently measured by their gross receipts or gross income. State business taxes on public utilities are generally levied upon gross receipts. But taxes on gross receipts can easily be allocated as variable costs per unit of output, and shifted forward as an addition to price. Thus business taxes on net income are generally not shifted in a short time-period, while those on gross receipts generally are. Though the intent of the two measures may be identical—imposition of the tax upon business, to be paid from business net income—the results are quite different. A *business tax* of 1 per cent on gross receipts, though called by a different name, is exactly like a *sales tax* of 1 per cent whose base is gross sales of the business. If we are to be realistic, therefore, we must class many so-called business taxes with taxes on sales.

"Use taxes" are a form of excise imposed not upon the purchase or sale of the good, but upon its use. The federal government, for example, imposed a tax in 1942 of five dollars per year upon the use of motor vehicles and boats.[1] Some states with retail sales taxes accompany these measures with a tax imposed upon the use of goods purchased at retail outside the state. The use tax is employed as an instrument to discourage avoidance of the sales tax by purchases outside the state, and to eliminate the competitive disadvantage imposed upon home sellers by the introduction of a tax on sales. Use taxes thus are clearly like taxes on sales so far as their economic effects are concerned. Though they are quite widely employed, they constitute a minor element in any tax system,[2] partly because most of them present real administrative difficulties in promoting compliance.

Taxes imposed upon the sale of particular commodities are generally termed "excises" or "selective sales taxes." They are utilized extensively by both the federal and the state governments. Customs duties are actually of this type, though we have chosen to discuss them under a separate heading because their use is commonly dominated by the objective of protection. The time-honored federal excises are those upon tobacco products, playing cards, and alcoholic liquors. State governments since 1930 have selected for excise taxation certain goods of wide consumption, such as gasoline, cigarettes, and liquors. Federal and state taxes upon that group of commodities mak-

[1] Repealed as of the end of 1945.
[2] In economic effect annual motor vehicle licenses are identical with use taxes.

ing up the established and permanent "excise list" have generally been levied on the manufacturer or primary distributor. The tax is frequently paid by purchase of tax stamps, which must be affixed to the product before it enters distribution channels.[3] The reason for applying the tax at an early stage in distribution is to simplify administration and compliance. The tax stamp system is used to check compliance with the tax law which forbids subsequent sale of the commodity within the taxing jurisdiction unless it bears the stamp.

As the federal excise list has been lengthened since 1932 and was especially developed during World War II, collection by the Treasury of the many taxes on specific goods has been applied at various distributive levels. The principal manufacturers' excises (collected from manufacturers) include those imposed upon gasoline and oils, automobile parts and accessories, sporting goods, luggage, household appliances, musical instruments, and electrical energy. The principal retailers' excises are those on furs, jewelry, and toilet preparations. Dues and initiation fees, admissions and luxury entertainment, rental of safe deposit boxes, and the use of telephone and telegraph facilities are taxed by special excises at the retail level, but these do not normally flow through the manufacturer-wholesaler-retailer channels. The types of goods and services taxed by wartime additions to the excise list are not generally such as to permit use of the tax stamp system.

The federal excise laws employ both specific and *ad valorem* taxes. In general, the items in the traditional or permanent excise list—tobacco, playing cards, liquor, and gasoline—are specific taxes; i.e., the tax is a fixed amount per physical unit of the product, without regard for the value of the unit. For example, the federal war rates on some of these products were:

Distilled Spirits:	$9.00 per proof gallon ($10.50 in 1959)
Gasoline:	1½¢ per gallon (4¢ in 1959)
Cigarettes:	$3.50 per thousand ($4.00 in 1959)
Playing Cards:	13¢ per pack

On the other hand, most of the newcomers in the federal excise list were taxed *ad valorem;* i.e., the tax is a fixed per cent of the selling price of the product at whatever distributive level the tax is collected.[4] In general, the *ad valorem* tax is preferable to the specific tax. A specific tax falls more heavily upon the cheaper brand of taxed article, since it represents a higher

---

[3] Gasoline taxes, for obvious reasons, cannot be administered by use of the stamp system.

[4] The provision that stamps be affixed to taxed articles is feasible only in the case of specific duties, for variations in price require variations in the amount of tax under the *ad valorem* system, and stamps of various denominations would be required. When prices are changing it would frequently be impossible to determine at time of purchase of stamps the precise denominations required.

percentage of selling price. If the specific tax rate charges what the traffic in cheaper brands will bear, potential revenue is lost on the more expensive brands. If the rate charges what the more expensive brands will bear, the cheaper brand is driven from the market, and the cost of the commodity to the low income buyer is increased both by the tax and by the disappearance of the cheaper article. On the other hand, the ease of administration of the specific tax is considerably in its favor.

Turnover Taxes. The "turnover" or "general sales" or "occupation" tax is intended to cover not only all commodities and services,[5] but transactions at all stages of distribution. Use of this type of tax has not been extensive in the United States. Agitation for its adoption as a federal tax was found among the "Townsendites" in the nineteen-thirties to finance their proposed old-age pension plan. In 1952 a general sales or gross income tax, though usually labeled as an occupation tax or as a tax on the "privilege of doing business," was operating with varying degrees of inclusiveness in seven states.[6] Of these seven, only three—Indiana, New Mexico, and West Virginia —applied the tax so inclusively as to make it a general turnover tax. The others exempted fairly large blocks of business institutions. No general pattern of rates is noticeable in the experience of these several states, except that sales at retail are generally subject to the highest rates.

The differences in rates applied to sales at the various distributive levels appear to follow very roughly differences in mark-up policy employed by distributors at those levels. These differences, however, recognize the principal economic peculiarity of general sales taxes: the tendency to pyramid one tax upon another. If the tax collected at one stage in distribution is shifted forward by being added to the price of the commodity, the distributor at the next stage will find the cost to him increased by the amount of the tax. He proceeds to apply his mark-up to this cost to determine his selling price, and when the good is resold a sales tax is again paid. The base of the second tax includes the first tax, and the more transactions before retail sale the larger the element of pyramided tax in retail price. But the effect upon the magnitude of retail price is possibly less critical than the premium such a tax places upon the vertical integration of business. For when an additional tax is imposed with each transaction, it is of competitive advantage to avoid as many independent transactions as possible in the process of distribution. The integrated firm which is in possession of the good from its

[5] Specific exemptions may, however, be made.

[6] Arizona, Indiana, Mississippi, New Mexico, Virginia, Washington, and West Virginia. In addition, gross receipts taxes were applied as business taxes to specific industries in nearly all the states, but the intent was not to accomplish taxation of gross sales generally. *Tax Systems,* 1952 Edition.

raw material stage to retail sale will find only one tax—at retail—included in its price. The good passes through as many stages in the process of production and distribution, but all except the last are intramural. The consequences of such an urge to integration may well be quite inconsistent with the general desire to promote competition.

If it is assumed that the whole tax is shifted forward in any case, a given amount of revenue could be raised by a retail sales tax alone at less cost to consumers than by a general sales or turnover tax. This follows from the fact that under a general sales tax a part of the retail price covers distributors' mark-ups on the taxes paid at earlier stages in distribution. This can be demonstrated numerically by a hypothetical example. Suppose three transactions are involved in distribution of a product, and a 10 per cent turnover tax is applied to the selling price at each transaction. Suppose further that each seller sells at a mark-up of 20 per cent over cost to him. The following results will be obtained, assuming the whole tax to be shifted forward at each transaction:

Cost plus Mark-up (Seller A)	$10.
Plus Tax at 10%	1.
Cost to Seller B	11.
Plus 20% Mark-up	2.02
Selling Price (Less Tax) of Seller B	13.02
Plus Tax at 10%	1.32
Cost to Seller C	14.52
Plus 20% Mark-up	2.90
Selling Price (Less Tax) of Seller C	17.42
Plus Tax at 10%	1.74
Price to Final Buyer	$19.16

The total tax collected in this set of transactions is $4.06 ($1 + $1.32 + $1.74). Now let us see what the price to the final buyer would be under identical circumstances except that the tax is collected only at the final (retail) sale. The tax is again completely shifted forward.

Cost plus Mark-up (Seller A)	$10.
Equals Cost to Seller B	10.
Plus 20% Mark-up	2.
Cost to Seller C	12.
Plus 20% Mark-up	2.04
Selling Price (Less Tax) of Seller C	14.4
Plus Tax at 28.2% (to Provide Revenue Equal to That Received under Turnover Tax)	4.06
Price to Final Buyer	$18.46

The difference ($.70) in price to the final buyer under the two types of tax is due to the cumulative effect of applying fixed mark-ups to tax ingredients of cost.

Retail Sales Taxes. We have assumed a retail sales tax in our second numerical example above. It is applied only at the point of final (retail) sale, and thus avoids differential advantage to integrated systems of distribution, reduces the administrative difficulties of collection by reducing the number of original taxpayers,[7] and can collect a given amount of revenue with less increase in the final price of the product. The retail sales tax, by applying the whole tax at the point of final sale, typically promotes greater consciousness of the amount of tax paid than does the turnover tax. On the other hand, the turnover tax obviates the difficulties inherent in defining firms subject to the tax, since it applies the tax at all levels of sale.[8]

It is possible to provide exemption from sales taxation to almost any selected group of buyers under any type of sales tax. The simplest method of providing tax exemption is to exempt certain sellers from paying sales taxes. If, for example, it is desired to exempt foodstuffs from taxation (as is not infrequently done), sellers of foodstuffs can be exempt from all provision of the tax. If, however, it is desired to exempt certain buyers (e.g., governments, and charitable, educational, and religious organizations) of any product, the mechanics of exemption become more complex. Probably the plan which comes closest to precise accomplishment of this type of exemption is that employed by Ohio, which requires the seller to give the buyer a cancelled receipt for the tax paid at the time of purchase. Buyers entitled to exemption can then forward these receipts to the treasurer for reimbursement.[9] The plan is, however, cumbersome and it seems quite likely that the effort of compliance militates against its satisfactory operation.

Extent of Excise and Sales Taxation

The Federal Government. The federal government has utilized customs duties since its origin. The sumptuary intent (protection) of the tariff has so dominated its use as to make revenue results almost wholly incidental and to place it largely outside the scope of our study. Excises on particular commodities, however, have played a continuing role as an important elastic revenue element in the federal system. It is difficult to know to what extent

[7] A sales tax on manufacturers and processors or on wholesale distributors would provide greater ease of collection than a retail sales tax, since it would collect from a smaller number of firms. On the other hand, it would present problems in defining those subject to taxation because of the variety of firms engaging in the first (or an early) stage of distribution, and would allow the pyramiding of mark-ups on the tax in successive distributive steps.

[8] This is true only if all transactions are subject to taxation at the same rate. If different rates are applied at different levels of sale, the problem of defining these levels is not simple.

[9] This system is described in greater detail (and with more feeling) in Hearings, Committee on Ways and Means, *Revenue Revision of 1942*, Vol. 2, p. 1788.

sumptuary motives have influenced the excise list. The sumptuary persuasion is clearly suggested by the principal items on the historical and permanent excise list—liquor, tobacco, and playing cards. On the other hand, the demonstrated inelasticity of demand of these "luxury" items makes them fair game for taxes intended for revenue purposes, for the tax addition to price results in relatively slight tendency to decrease consumption. Perhaps we may say that excises on these commodities provide large and stable revenues without disquieting the consciences of legislators and tax-gatherers.

Sales taxes on liquor, tobacco, playing cards, and more recently gasoline have provided the solid and stable core of the federal excise system. In modern times these items have been consistently taxed extremely heavily—with the exception of gasoline, which is more heavily burdened by state excise taxes—and thus leave little room for increase in revenue production by rate increase in emergencies. The real revenue elasticity in the federal excise system has been gained by lengthening and shortening the list of commodities subject to taxation. The commodities taxed typically possess three characteristics: (1) widespread consumption, (2) relatively inelastic demand, and (3) status in the range of goods somewhat above the group of accepted "necessaries" of life.

Revenue productivity of the federal excise system is shown in Table 31. The years selected in the table will show the element of controlled elasticity in the system in response to revenue needs. We begin with 1912, at which time we find only those standard items of excise taxation subject to the levy.

TABLE 31

FEDERAL EXCISE TAX COLLECTIONS[*]
(in millions of dollars)

Items Taxed	1912	1926	1932	1936	1945	1951	1958
Liquor	220	26	9	505	2,310	2,547	2,946
Tobacco	71	371	399	501	932	1,380	1,734
Other Stamp Taxes[a]	—	50	32	69	66	93	109
Manufacturers' Excises[b]	—	—	87	383	783	2,384	3,974
Gasoline	—	—	—	177	406	589	1,637
Other	—	—	87	206	377	1,795	2,337
Retailers' Excises[c]	—	—	—	21	424	457	342
Misc. Excises[d]	—	253	3	44	1,168	1,423	1,583
Admissions and Dues	—	34	11	45	372	419	158
TOTAL EXCISES	291	734	452	1,547	5,945	8,704	10,814

[*] Sources: *Statistical Abstract of the U. S.*, 1920, pp. 718, 720; *Idem*, 1926, pp. 172–73; *Annual Report of the Secretary of the Treasury*, 1958, pp. 455–58.

[a] Major items are issues and transfers of capital stock, etc., and playing cards.
[b] Major items are motor vehicles, parts, and tires; household appliances.
[c] Major items are jewelry, furs, toilet preparations, and luggage.
[d] Major items are telephone, telegraph, cable, and transportation.

Two periods of extension of the excise list stand out. During the depression of the nineteen-thirties, specifically in 1933, nearly all the modern manufacturers' excises were inaugurated. This was a period when the base of the income tax was behaving badly from the revenue point of view, and the more stable excise base was resorted to. The second period of extension was during World War II, when a major objective was discouragement of demand for scarce goods and services by substantial tax additions to prices. During this period nearly all the retailers' and miscellaneous excises were introduced. The effect of the Prohibition Amendment of 1920 and its repeal in 1933 is evident in the liquor excise figures. There have been relatively few changes in the excise list or in rates since World War II, except that *ad valorem* rates above 10 per cent were cut back to 10 per cent in 1954, manufacturers' excises on gasoline and some motor vehicle items were increased under the Defense Highway Act of 1956, and the exemption on admissions was increased in 1957.

During the last quarter century, excises have been consistently regarded as an important foundation stone of the federal revenue system. They constituted 19 per cent of internal revenue collections in 1933, 35 per cent in 1940 after the excise list extensions of the depression decade, and 14 per cent of the much larger total tax collections in 1945 associated with wartime increases in the income tax. In recent years the proportion has tended to decline, following an immediate postwar increase, and in 1958 the excises accounted for 15 per cent of internal revenues. The decline of recent years reflects again the stability of the excise tax base when the excise list and its rates remain essentially constant. Excises react more slowly to income changes than income taxes; the prosperity of the nineteen-fifties has reduced the relative importance of the excises by increasing the yield of personal and corporate income taxes. Nevertheless, the excises are consciously used as a revenue anchor to windward, more dependable in revenue productivity than are income and profits taxes, and amenable to notable increase and decrease, especially through the simple expedient of subjecting a larger or smaller number of items or sellers to the tax.[10]

State Governments. The experience of the states shows very marked

[10] We should not lose sight of a special emergency use to which the excises can be put. They lend themselves to finely focused sumptuary use. During the World War II period, for example, it is clear that several items were brought into the excise list to discourage their purchase or use. The taxation of automobiles, automobile parts, lubricating oils, and tires was easily justified in terms of the scarcity of these items and of motor fuel. The same may be said of taxes upon electrical energy and telephone and telegraph service, while heavy taxation of items such as luggage and jewelry reflects the clear purpose of channeling increased incomes away from the markets for luxury consumption goods.

increase in the use of commodity taxes since 1930. This increase has occurred along two lines: new excise taxation of specific commodities—principally liquor, cigarettes, amusements, and gasoline—and the imposition of
retail sales taxes. Repeal of the Prohibition Act is of course the principal
cause of the rise in liquor tax revenues in recent years. The regulation of
traffic in alcoholic liquors devolves principally upon the states, and it is not
surprising to find taxation (or state liquor stores) accompanying the imposition of regulation. Sales of gasoline had been taxed in all states prior to
1930, but between 1930 and 1936 twenty-one states increased rates at least
once. The average tax per gallon among all states in 1936 was 3.85¢; by
1951 the average had risen to 5.3¢ per gallon; and by 1959 the average for
the same forty-eight states was 6.04¢. The states were somewhat slower in
enacting taxes on cigarettes and other tobacco products. Twenty-one states
had specific cigarette taxes by 1937, and in 1959 the number had grown to
forty-two. Other excises in rather wide use by the states are those on horse-
racing and pari-mutuel betting, registration and transfer of securities, and
chain stores.

Excises, representing principally those on motor fuels, alcoholic beverages, and tobacco but excluding gross receipts and more general sales taxes,
produced 35 per cent of total tax receipts of the states in 1958.[11] When we
add general sales and gross receipts taxes, we find that taxes on commodities
and services constituted 63 per cent of tax revenues of the states in that
year.[12] While during the last quarter century the proportion of special excise
revenues to total tax revenues has shown a modest decline, the proportions
of combined special excises and general sales and gross receipts revenues to
total tax revenues has risen markedly. This is due to the major substitution
over this period of general sales taxes for the property tax in state revenue
systems.

At the end of World War II, twenty-four states had taxes which should
be characterized as sales tax measures, as distinguished from specific excises.[13] Of these twenty-four states, only one had employed a sales tax prior
to 1930. Twenty-two adopted the sales tax during the five years 1933–1937
to expand their depression revenues and qualify for federal grants, while at
the same time largely abandoning property taxation in favor of local governments. The second period of expansion in the use of the sales tax was the
late nineteen-forties and early nineteen-fifties. Not only did tax rates rise
during this period in the states which had earlier adopted this form of tax,

[11] Bureau of Census, *Compendium of State Government Finances in 1958*, p. 11.
[12] *Ibid.*
[13] *Tax Systems*, 1946.

but eight more states inaugurated sales taxes as major elements in their revenue structures. At present, therefore, there are thirty-two states with retail sales and gross receipts taxes general enough to qualify them as "sales tax states."

Rates of taxation on retail sales among the states currently (1959) vary between 2 per cent and 4 per cent, with distribution as follows:

2 per cent—13 states
2½ per cent—1 state
3 per cent—16 states
3½ per cent—1 state
4 per cent—1 state

Of the thirty states which had sales taxes in 1952, eleven have increased the rate of taxation since that date, one has reduced the rate, and twenty have left it unchanged. Rates of sales taxation are rather resistant to upward change, partly because no state wishes to get "out of line" with respect to its neighbors and thus put its border retailers at some disadvantage. For this reason there appears to be a good deal of regional uniformity in rates. But also the general conclusion that the tax is regressive, imposing relatively heavy burdens upon the lower income groups, makes rate increases infrequent and unpopular.

How burdensome or how regressive a retail sales tax is will depend to a considerable extent upon the exemptions provided in the law. A retail sales tax imposed upon all consumption expenditure without exemption will be at a higher rate per dollar of the consumer's income if his income is small than if it is large. The reason for this is that consumption expenditure tends to represent a lower proportion of income as incomes rise. A hypothetical example will show the point involved here, assuming a 3 per cent sales tax without exemptions.

Disposable Income	Average Propensity to Consume	Taxable Consumption Expenditures	Tax at 3%	Tax as % of Disposable Income
$ 5,000	.95	$ 4,750	$142.50	2.85
$20,000	.75	$15,000	$450.00	2.25

If we now exempt food from sales taxation, and assume that the first family spends $125 per month for food while the second family spends $200, the figures become (using the headings above):

$ 5,000	.95	$ 3,250	$ 97.50	1.95
$20,000	.75	$12,600	$378.00	1.89

The introduction of a food exemption has made the tax very nearly proportional with respect to income as between these two selected income levels.

Less than one-third of the sales tax states exempted food from taxation in 1959.[14] This is a surprisingly small number, in view of the importance of this exemption in maintaining a semblance of proportionality of burdens with respect to income. A primary reason for taxing food is the revenue reason. Food represents a large and essentially stable element in family budgets, capable of producing considerable amounts of revenue. But another factor in the niggardliness of states in exempting food is the belief rather widely held that the extreme progressiveness of the federal personal income tax will make the inclusion of some degree of regressiveness in state taxes tolerable. Our study of the federal income tax, however, shows it to be considerably less progressive in practice than is indicated by a cursory look at the rate schedule. It is highly doubtful that regressiveness in state taxation can be regarded as a virtue.

Another common exemption under state sales taxes is that of most or all services. Many states impose sales taxes upon specified services, such as room rentals by transients and admissions to entertainments, but in general the tax is imposed upon the sale of tangible property. It is a well-known fact that as incomes rise beyond some rather moderate level, an increasing proportion is spent for services. This means that for high income economies, services offer a generally untaxed area which might be taxed as a source of revenue, though some significant administrative problems would arise. But beyond this, it is quite certain that the exemption of services from sales taxation makes the tax highly regressive with respect to large incomes.

Most states exempt from sales taxes those goods upon which special excises or special gross receipts taxes are already imposed. Thus, gasoline and cigarettes are widely exempted from sales taxes, for rather obvious reasons.

Sales of newspapers are generally exempt, and to a lesser extent sales of magazines. There is usually good reason for this, for newspapers and to some extent magazines sell at prices below the minimum above which the seller is permitted to collect a tax from the buyer. Thus, if the seller cannot charge a tax to the buyer on sales below 20¢, but the seller is liable to sales taxes on his gross receipts from sales, he is singled out as one seller who would have great difficulty in shifting the tax. But the conclusion is inescapable that general exemption of newspaper sales is due in some degree to propaganda fostering the notion that liability to taxation somehow limits the freedom of the press. This is apparent by the fact that other sellers of

[14] Summaries of state tax provisions may be found in Commerce Clearing House, *State Tax Guide,* a loose-leaf service which keeps well up to date on the changes in the states. The term "food" in the text sentence means groceries, not restaurant meals. The latter are exempt in still fewer states.

goods with unit prices below the exempt minimum on which taxes are chargeable to buyers have not received the same consideration as have newspapers.

Specified exemptions in state sales tax laws tend generally to single out farmers for particular treatment. Logically, feed, seed, fertilizers, and insecticides used in agricultural production should not be subject to retail sales taxes, for they are but ingredients of production used in the creation of some final finished good upon which sales taxes will be imposed or which will receive special exemption. But farmers are not alone in this; other producers have usually not received similar exemption for purchases of machinery or other ingredients of final products.

Finally, exemption of medicines and prescriptions is fairly common, exemption of sales to public, educational, and charitable institutions is general, and a few states single out items like children's clothing for special exemption. The reasons for these exemptions would seem to need no elaboration.

Local Governments. Use by local governments of sales, gross receipts, and specific excise taxes has increased somewhat since World War II, but not markedly if measured by the relative revenue importance of these taxes. It is necessarily true that use of such taxes will be limited to the larger population and trading centers. In 1957, local governments raised $654 million from general sales and gross receipts taxes, and another $279 million from selective excises.[15] These represented 6.3 per cent of their total tax revenues. But if New York City is eliminated, the figures become, respectively, $287 million, $232 million, and 3.9 per cent. And if we eliminate all cities over 250,000 population,[16] general sales tax revenues were $162 million and special sales tax revenues $95 million, giving a combined total which is 2.3 per cent of their total tax revenues.

The use of these taxes by local governments is spotty by size of city, but also spotty geographically. Cities in some ten states imposed general retail sales taxes in 1957, with heaviest use in California, Illinois, and Mississippi. Most city sales taxes are at low rates, for they generally occur in cities whose state government employs the sales tax as a major revenue measure.

Use of selective sales and gross receipts taxes are much more widespread. The more common objects of these taxes are public utilities, tobacco products, amusements, motor fuels, and alcoholic beverages, in that order. It is noteworthy that when cities utilize selective sales and gross receipts taxes, they tend to concentrate upon products and services already specially taxed

[15] Bureau of the Census, *Summary of Government Finances in 1957*, p. 23.
[16] Bureau of the Census, *Compendium of City Government Finances in 1957*, p. 28.

by the states, and also taxed under special excises by the federal government. The consequence is very heavy commodity tax burdens upon gasoline, tobacco, alcohol, and amusements almost everywhere, with particularly heavy burdens in those areas where local governments also single out these items for special excises.

Shifting of Taxes on Sales

The popularly accepted conclusion with respect to the incidence of taxes on sales is that such taxes are completely shifted forward as an addition to the purchase price. This assumption is, indeed, an integral part of consumption tax theory. Sumptuary use of a consumption tax—to discourage purchase and use of a good, as in the case of a protective tariff—could hardly be expected to produce the desired results unless forward shifting were taken for granted. The selection of items for special excise taxation for revenue purposes generally favors goods of wide and less elastic demand, thereby taking for granted that the tax addition to price will reduce consumption relatively little. And it has even been argued that adoption of a sales tax is desirable to offset excessively steep progression in the federal personal income tax and to adjust the burdens of the whole tax system more equitably with respect to ability to pay. Clearly, this implies that the burden of "consumption" taxes is upon consumers, who are predominantly in the lower income groups.

A tax per unit upon production or sale of a good adds to the seller's cost of production or sale. If the tax is specific (a stated amount per physical unit of the good produced or sold), it is a constant addition to cost per unit, whether cost is measured marginally or as an average. If it is an *ad valorem* tax of a given per cent of the price of the good, it becomes a decreasing addition to variable cost per unit, since typically the larger the quantity sold the lower the price per unit. Taxes imposed upon gross sales or gross income of the seller are also of this type. The general effect of tax additions to cost is the reduction of supply—i.e., quantities offered for sale at given prices are smaller than they would have been without the tax. In terms of our general discussion of incidence (see Chapter 14), marginal cost is increased by the tax, with consequent sale of a smaller quantity of the good at a higher price. Under conditions of imperfect competition the intersection of marginal revenue and marginal cost, which determines the optimum output of the seller, moves to the left, and the market price rises. Under pure competition the decrease in market supply raises prices, and thus raises the horizontal demand line facing the individual seller. It is clear, therefore, that in the general case an increase in price will result from imposition of the tax. It is upon this type of observation that the general conclusion with respect to forward shifting is based.

Limitations upon Forward Shifting. To show that imposition of a commodity tax typically results in an increase in price is not to show that the tax is shifted forward *in toto*. What proportion of the tax is shifted depends upon the elasticity of demand and the elasticity of supply (cost). If the demand facing the seller were completely inelastic (a vertical line, where quantity taken would not decrease at all with an increase in price) the tax could be completely shifted.[17] At the opposite extreme, if the demand were infinitely elastic (a horizontal line, where no quantity would be taken at a higher price) the tax could not be shifted forward at all. In this case the incidence of the tax would be completely upon the seller, though other important economic effects would be the disemployment of some of the factors of production—incident to the decrease in production—and the reduction in quantity consumed.

The typical situation would lie somewhere between these extremes of zero and infinite elasticity. And in the typical situation a part of the incidence is upon the buyer, while the other part is upon the seller. The more elastic the demand—other things being equal—the greater the proportion of incidence assumed by the seller. But other things (principally the elasticity of supply) are not necessarily equal. When supply is relatively inelastic—i.e., marginal costs rise steeply with an increase of output and fall steeply with a reduction in output—the saving in cost (other than the tax) increases rapidly as the scale of output declines. This means that the tax can be covered with a relatively small reduction in output and a small rise in price.[18] Thus, under conditions of relatively inelastic cost, a smaller proportion of the tax is shifted to buyers than is the case when costs are elastic.

Recalling our earlier analysis of incidence, however, we find that in the long run, forward shifting possibilities may be strengthened. The disappearance of marginal firms, the effect of salesmanship upon demand, and the institution of changed techniques of production can rebuild profits after taxes, by affecting either demand or cost or both. This is particularly true in a period of strong and rising demand over a course of time, as has been the situation since World War II.

Institutional factors will affect the degree of shiftability of a tax on commodities. Among these we mention specifically the coverage of the tax. Coverage actually affects shifting by its influence upon demand. If the tax is imposed within a small geographical area and it is not difficult to buy

[17] Assuming that the price was not already at the upper limit of demand.
[18] See Figure 11, page 322.

outside the taxed area, it will be relatively difficult to shift the tax. When the good is readily available from an untaxed source, a rise in price in the taxed area will encourage purchases outside. This means that the demand facing sellers in the taxed area is relatively elastic, and the resistance to shifting is great. Obviously, the more insulated the market in which the tax is imposed, the less elastic will be the demand.[19] Recognition of the difficulty of shifting sales taxes applied in a narrow geographical area has led to adoption by many sales tax states of "use taxes." These impose approximately equivalent burdens upon goods purchased outside and brought into the taxed area for use. The intent is both to bolster revenues by removing the tax urge to buy outside the area or to collect revenue from such purchases, and to eliminate the tax-created competitive disadvantage to the home seller. In the same manner, taxation of a narrow list of commodities while leaving substitutes untaxed will make forward shifting difficult. An attempt to increase prices to shift the tax would result in defection of buyers to substitutes.

Price theory clearly indicates a significant amount of forward shifting of taxes on commodities, though how large a part of the tax in a given instance actually is shifted will be determined by a number of factors varying among different products, different markets, and different sellers. It is naive to assume, except as a very rough generalization, that the whole tax is always shifted in the short run. The intense opposition of merchants to the imposition of sales taxes can hardly be explained solely in terms of the costs to them of compliance and shifting;[20] as a group they realize that a portion of the incidence, at least temporarily, falls upon them. Nevertheless, though

[19] It will be noted that we have not said an attempt to shift the tax will make the demand more elastic. The demand facing sellers in a given market is a schedule of the quantities which will be taken from those sellers at various prices, and these quantities assume the existence of similar products available in competing markets. Imposition of the tax and subsequent attempts to shift it by increasing prices will demonstrate the elasticity of demand, but will not create it.

[20] Some states recognize the cost of compliance to the seller. This is done by requirement that the seller pay a tax equal to the sales tax rate times slightly less than 100 per cent of gross sales, by permitting the seller to keep the first few dollars of the tax which by strict computation would go to the state, or, more commonly, by setting up a schedule of tax charges to the buyer averaging a little more than the amount of the tax for which the seller is liable. Thus, the Connecticut 3 per cent sales tax directs the seller to collect taxes from purchasers as follows:

Sales of 20¢ to 38¢ .... 1¢
Sales of 39¢ to 70¢ .... 2¢
Sales of 71¢ to $1.19...................... 3¢

Note that amounts of sales on which the collection would be exactly 3 per cent (33¢, 67¢, and $1.00) are nearer the top than the bottom of the bracket. In the aggregate, this should collect from buyers more than the seller is required to forward to the tax collector.

there is a good deal of diffusion of incidence and other effects, a tax system which depends heavily upon consumption taxes inevitably falls with heaviest force upon the class of consumers. Such a tax system, therefore, because the largest share of consumers are in the low income classes and the consumption tax itself is proportional, has a regressive effect in terms of the relation of the incidence to the ability of the incidence-bearer to pay, unless, of course, generous exemption of cost-of-living items is granted. Enthusiasm for sales taxes must be catalogued as a retrogression from the principle of tax payment according to ability.

Legal Aids to Shifting. Commodity taxes are almost uniformly intended by legislators to be shifted forward to consumers. Recognition of economic and other obstacles to shifting have frequently led to inclusion in the law of provisions to facilitate shifting. One of these provisions is the enactment of a use tax, mentioned above, to remove the premium on buying outside the taxed area. Another legislative technique employed by some states is to impose the tax upon each transaction separately rather than upon the gross sales of the seller. The intention is to specify that the tax is a cost of sale, not a general cost of doing business, and is to be paid at the time of purchase. This may aid in focusing the attention of both buyer and seller upon the legislative intent that the tax be shifted. It may forestall objections by purchasers to addition of the tax to price, and impress upon the seller the importance of shifting. To facilitate precise shifting, some states have printed or struck off "tax tokens" in denominations of one, two, or five mills. This makes possible the collection of taxes precisely equal to the rate times the base, even with small purchases. The token plan, however, is not widespread; it adds to the cost of administration and is inconvenient to purchasers. The usual method is simply to assess the tax to the nearest cent at the time of purchase.

Finally, in a few states the sales tax law specifically requires that the whole tax be shifted forward to the consumer. The intent of such a provision goes beyond the requirement that (say) 3 per cent be collected in addition to the price at the time of sale. For although a "tax" is collected it is perfectly possible for some part of it to be absorbed by the seller in the form of a selling price lowered by the amount of the tax. Thus the price plus the tax may be no higher than the price would be if there were no tax. If such were the case, the tax would not be shifted. A legal requirement that the tax be shifted would appear to be difficult of enforcement. It is intended, however, to avoid granting any competitive advantage to the seller who might hope to attract business by announced absorption of some part of the tax.

The Case for the Sales Tax

We have seen that a frantic search for new revenues resulted in a large crop of state commodity taxes—both excises and sales taxes—during the decade of the nineteen-thirties. During the same period there was strong agitation for adoption of a federal sales tax. Again during 1942 and 1943, when government sought additional revenues, the federal sales tax drive became intense. Although the intensity of the agitation for federal adoption diminished with the end of the war, it is still strong in some quarters. Two objectives appear uppermost in recent agitation: to provide revenues for war debt reduction, and to reduce the burden of federal income taxes. But though agitation for a federal sales tax virtually disappeared with the choice to tax incomes more heavily, the sales tax, since the war, has again become a lively issue among the states. High postwar price and wage levels have sent the states on a new search for new revenues, and the sales tax is again a formidable contender. The choice appears to be principally between sales and income taxes, and justifies careful analysis of the case for the sales tax.

Professors Haig and Shoup have pointed out that the most vocal opposition to the adoption of sales taxes by the states has come from retailers.[21] This is not surprising, in view of the typical immediate absorption of a portion of a retail sales tax (the type most widely used) by the retailer. In addition, however, a large share of the costs of collection and nearly all of the considerable cost of compliance with the provisions of the law fall upon the seller. Two other classes—consumers and labor—have shown weak opposition in view of the tax obligation which they bear under a sales tax. Weakness in opposition on the part of consumers is not surprising, as they have seldom been effective in impressing their interests upon legislators. Haig and Shoup account for labor's weak opposition on the grounds that, during the early thirties when the issue was being decided, labor was comparatively impotent, and that, since in most states the revenues to be raised were largely destined for education and unemployment relief, it would have been difficult for labor to have effectively opposed enactment of the tax. This view seems to be borne out by the greater effectiveness of labor opposition to sales taxation in recent years, as labor organization has become stronger and more politically oriented.

The groups principally agitating for state sales taxes during the thirties were those who stood to gain from a lightening of the property tax burden.[22] Specifically, farmers and real estate interests were enthusiastic for the sales

[21] *The Sales Tax in the American States*, New York, Columbia, 1934, pp. 16–24.
[22] *Ibid.*

tax. The authors cited above mention as vocal proponents the highway trans-portation interests, who feared "diversion" to emergency use of the large highway fund revenues when general funds were unable to support general functions. The supporters of a federal sales tax generally see in the sales tax a possible opportunity for reduction of steeply progressive and high income tax rates—principally incorporated businesses and individuals in the high personal income brackets. In addition, there are those individuals who favor a federal sales tax on grounds of objective tax theory, while others, from desperation over the magnitude of the public debt and the belief that exist-ing taxes cannot be pushed further, accept the sales tax as a last necessary resort.

Ignoring the fact that much agitation for adoption of a sales tax is moti-vated by the desire to transfer existing or future tax burdens to some other group, the case for the tax made by its proponents runs in terms of the following:

1. The stability of commodity tax revenues.
2. The relatively low cost of collection.
3. The regressiveness of the tax.
4. The sumptuary possibilities in the tax.
5. Its ability to produce revenue immediately.
6. Its promotion of tax-consciousness.

1. Stability of Revenues. Sales tax revenues are generally considerably more stable than are income tax revenues. The level of consumption is more stable over a period of time than is the level of income, and thus the base of the consumption tax is more stable than that of the income tax. In addi-tion, while the consumption tax is proportional with respect to its base, the income tax is typically progressive. Fluctuation in the income base results typically, therefore, in even more violent fluctuation in income tax revenues. This is true because an increase in national income means some increase in average individual incomes, making many individual incomes subject to higher rates in the progressive schedule. The reverse is true when national income falls. From the purely revenue point of view, ignoring the principle of ability to pay and the burdensomeness of the tax system, an advantage exists for the sales tax. On the other hand, it would be incorrect to assume that commodity tax revenues are entirely stable. Although it is impossible to demonstrate the instability of sales tax revenues accurately by comparing revenues actually received (because of frequent changes in the extent to which sales taxes were used), the level of total consumption in the economy increased by approximately 50 per cent between 1920 and 1929 and fell by approximately 20 per cent between 1929 and 1932.[23] The stability of sales tax revenues over the business cycle will depend to a considerable extent upon the exemption list. If food and other "necessaries" are exempt, the tax becomes more nearly a tax on "luxuries," and a relatively wide fluctuation in revenues will result.

From the point of view of general economic well-being, stability of revenues is on balance highly undesirable. For stability of revenues means that tax *burdens* rise as incomes fall, and fall as incomes rise. The consequence of such behavior to the levels of income and employment will be clearly evident to readers of earlier chapters in this book.[24] If fiscal policy is to be integrated into general economic policy, controlled instability of revenue is not a vice.

2. Cost of Collection. It is commonly assumed that the sales tax "collects itself," and thus involves relatively slight cost of collection. If so, this would be a real merit of the tax. Apparently, however, so far as available figures show, the sales tax is relatively costly to administer. Professor Due[25] reports that the costs of administering state sales taxes range from 0.67 per cent to 2.5 per cent of receipts, with the average about 1.5 per cent. It must be borne in mind, however, that this represents only the cost to *government* of administration. Actually, the cost of collection and compliance which is imposed upon the sellers may be considerably greater than that of administration by the state.[26]

Comparison of various taxes in terms of their administrative costs is likely to be quite unsatisfactory and inaccurate, since it is frequently impossible to allocate administrative expense to particular tax measures. Estimates in a few states studied show the costs of administration of the property tax to range on the average from 2 per cent downward.[27] The cost to property owners of compliance with the tax is of course extremely small. The Secretary of the Treasury reports that for fiscal 1951 the administrative costs of the Bureau of Internal Revenue were one-half of 1 per cent of the revenue collected. Of the nearly $50 billion in revenue, nearly 80 per cent was income and profits tax. As in the case of sales taxes, a considerable

[23] Ohio sales tax collections varied between $40 million and $63 million per year during the period 1937–1941. Cf. Hearings, House Committee on Ways and Means, *Revenue Revision of 1942*, Vol. 2, p. 1788.

[24] Specifically, Chapters 4 and 5.

[25] John F. Due, *Sales Taxation*, Urbana, University of Illinois Press, 1957, p. 306.

[26] Some few states allow the seller to withhold a small part of his tax liability as payment for performance of the collection function. Illinois and Arkansas allow approximately 2 per cent; Missouri, 3 per cent; Michigan, $600 per year. Blakey, *op. cit.*, p. 12.

[27] *Studies in Current Tax Problems*, pp. 120–24.

portion of total "costs" of collection fall upon those responsible for withholding taxes from wages and other incomes and upon individuals required to prepare returns. Furthermore, the administrative cost of any tax, when expressed as a percentage of receipts, varies directly with the effectiveness of its administration, and varies inversely with the tax rate imposed and therefore with the gross tax receipts.

In view of the scarcity of dependable figures it is impossible to arrange the various tax measures in the order of the expensiveness of their collection and administration. It does appear, however, that so far experience does not show the sales tax to possess any marked advantage in this respect. It has frequently been suggested that should the federal government adopt a sales tax, it should be collected at the wholesale level. Should this be done, the cost of collection and administration would probably be lower than is typical for state retail sales taxes.[28]

3. Regressiveness of Sales Taxes. Although technically a proportional tax, the sales tax, whose incidence falls principally upon consumers, is regressive with respect to the personal income from which the tax is paid. The reader may well wonder that regressiveness is regarded as a virtue, in view of general acceptance of ability to pay as the proper basis for allocation of the tax burden. Those who favor sales taxes because of their regressiveness do so upon the assumption that the tax system is already too steeply progressive,[29] and requires counterbalancing by taxes which fall heavily upon lower incomes. The argument is obviously founded upon an assumption that income tax rates are too steeply progressive in terms of ability to pay. This assumption is not subject to proof—one way or the other—and is essentially a matter of opinion. If we accept this assumption, there is still little logic in enactment of a regressive sales tax to counterbalance overenthusiastic application of progression in the income tax. If this is used as an argument for a federal sales tax, it has little force. For the legislative body which would accept the sales tax has legislative authority over the rates of the income tax. If, therefore, income tax rates are too steeply progressive, the

[28] Generally, the larger the revenue and the broader the application of the tax, the lower the percentage cost of administration. Even a federal retail sales tax would probably be more efficiently administered than are state sales taxes.

[29] Cf. testimony of F. R. Fairchild before Committee on Ways and Means, *Revenue Revision of 1943*, p. 639: "What we now need to counterbalance these strictly progressive taxes on incomes, estates, and so forth, is some tax of the other sort, so that the balanced picture may give us a reasonably well-rounded tax system." Also, "This regressive distribution of the burden of the [sales] tax would not be material so long as the rate of the tax was low and would be counterbalanced by the highly progressive distribution of the federal personal income and estate taxes." (*Report of the Connecticut Special Tax Commission of 1933*, p. 583.) See also National Association of Manufacturers, *Facing the Issue of Income Tax Discrimination*, 1955, pp. 5, 6.

logical step is to make this progression more gradual, either by lowering rates at the top, by raising rates on lower incomes, or by lowering personal exemptions. The argument has more force as applied to the states (assuming federal taxes to be too steeply progressive). For state governments can do little to bring about change in federal tax rates, and may thus more reasonably adopt for themselves new taxes which in their judgment round out a system whose incidence is still moderately allocated according to ability.

4. Sumptuary Possibilities. Specific excises offer an instrument for rather precisely affecting sales of particular goods. There can be little question that items on the early federal excise list—liquor, tobacco, renovated butter, filled cheese—were selected partially for the purpose of discouraging their consumption on moral grounds. In the same category are the abortive 1918 tax on commodities produced with child labor,[30] the state excises upon the sale of oleomargarine, now largely repealed, and the taxes imposed upon chain stores in several states. During World War II, to discourage consumption of certain goods and services and thus reduce the resources used in their production, federal excises at relatively high rates were newly imposed on appliances, jewelry, furs, toilet preparations, luggage and handbags, telephone service, and railway and bus transportation. At the same time, rates on many items in the older excise list were raised. These excise increases were accompanied, of course, by much higher rates on personal income and corporate profits, which served to limit disposable income in general.

When the objective is a narrow sumptuary one, affecting a few commodities, the specific excises are extremely useful. Like the customs tariff, the objective is to discourage purchase and not to raise revenue. On the other hand, the general retail sales tax has few if any advantages for general sumptuary purposes over the income tax, and it has more disadvantages which will be discussed below in connection with compensatory possibilities in the use of the sales tax.

5. Immediate Revenues. One of the more popular arguments for the sales tax points to its ability to produce revenue in a very short time after enactment. This is generally a very desirable characteristic of a tax. Payment of an annual tax in small amounts through the year is generally less burdensome upon the taxpayer. And as we have seen, counter-cycle tax policy clearly implies the use of taxes whose effects are immediately felt. When it is realized, however, that the issue is generally between sales taxes and income taxes, this advantage for the sales tax is seen to have disap-

---

[30] Declared unconstitutional in 1918.

peared with successful employment of the current tax payments provision in the federal income tax.

6. Tax-Consciousness. It is of course desirable that the taxpayer in a democratic society be aware of his contribution to the revenues of government. Income and property taxes accomplish tax-consciousness to a high degree. The argument is thus primarily defensive in nature when used in support of the sales tax. It is probable that a retail sales tax, as usually employed by the states, is productive of as much tax-consciousness as are income and property taxes, and all are preferable in this regard to selective excises.[31]

Compensatory Possibilities in the Sales Tax

Unintended Economic Effects. The combined federal, state, and local tax system in the United States has not resulted from any coordinated attempt to frame a complete system based upon a single theory of the proper allocation of tax burdens. Rather it has grown in an opportunist manner largely driven by the desire to raise additional revenue. Its over-all economic effects may therefore be characterized as unintended. The principal items in the system are the federal income tax, the local property tax, and the federal and state excises and sales taxes. The federal income tax, whose incidence is generally upon those on whom it is levied, is markedly progressive in rates. The incidence of property taxes is highly diffused; a considerable amount of backward shifting (capitalization) occurs when rates hold reasonably stable; the remainder, not shifted backward, may be shifted forward when property is used for business purposes, though this is not the case when property is used for consumption. The incidence of sales taxes and excises is principally upon consumers of taxed products; such taxes are thus generally regressive in effect, owing to the fact that expenditure for taxed items consumes a larger portion of low than of high incomes.

In order to show the degree of progression in combined federal, state, and local tax systems it is necessary to relate figures of tax liability to the income classes required to assume liability. This is by no means a simple operation. It is necessary first to accept hypotheses concerning the incidence of particular taxes. We have seen that in the cases of some taxes this is relatively simple, but in some others the facts as to their incidence are by no means clear in any precise, quantitative sense. The second requirement is to determine the extent of liability for the payment of particular taxes by

---

[31] On the other hand, if a sales tax is collected at the production or wholesale level it almost inevitably becomes one of the "hidden taxes," producing relatively little tax-consciousness.

persons in particular income classes. Statistics are by no means adequate to
permit the taking of this step without generalizing on the basis of frag-
mentary data. For these reasons, the figures available should be accepted
with some qualification, and it is not surprising that there should be some
disagreement on results as among various research studies. The results of
the major studies dealing with the distribution of tax burdens among income classes are presented in Table 32.

TABLE 32

EFFECTIVE RATES OF COMBINED FEDERAL, STATE, LOCAL TAXES BY INCOME CLASSES
FOR VARIOUS YEARS: A SUMMARY OF FOUR STUDIES

Income of the Spending Unit	Tarasov, 1938–1939[a] (%)	Adler, 1946–1947[b] (%)	Musgrave, 1948[c] (%)	Tucker, 1948[d] (%)	Musgrave, 1954[e] (%)
Under $1,000	18.0	19.6	20.2	18.7	} 22.8
$1,000–$1,999	17.5	15.1	17.5	20.8	
$2,000–$2,999	17.4	17.3	18.8	23.9	23.5
$3,000–$3,999	17.7	17.7	19.1	25.0	23.8
$4,000–$4,999	18.2	22.9	19.3	26.3	24.7
$5,000–$7,499	18.7	24.2	21.4	28.3	27.4
$7,500 and over	32.7	36.2	35.1	44.8	29.9–39.5
Total	20.2	24.2	24.0	29.7	29.4

[a] Helen Tarasov, "Who Does Pay the Taxes?," Supplement IV, *Social Research*, 1942,
p. 5.
[b] John Adler, "The Fiscal System, the Distribution of Income, and Public Welfare,"
in K. E. Poole, *Fiscal Policies and the American Economy*, New York, Prentice-Hall, 1951.
[c] R. A. Musgrave *et al.*, "Distribution of Tax Payments by Income Groups: A Case
Study for 1948," *National Tax Journal*, March, 1951. The Musgrave figures are calculated on the assumption that the corporate net income taxes have their incidence upon
profits and dividends.
[d] R. S. Tucker, "Distribution of Tax Burdens in 1948," *National Tax Journal*, September, 1951, p. 281.
[e] R. A. Musgrave, "The Incidence of the Tax Structure and its Effects on Consumption," in *Federal Tax Policy for Economic Growth and Stability, Papers Submitted by
Panelists, Joint Committee on the Economic Report*, Washington, 1955. The two figures
given for the $7,500 and over income group are given because Musgrave separates this
group into two classes. The first figure is for incomes $7,500 to $10,000 and the second
for over $10,000.

We cannot enter into the technical comparison of these studies with one
another to show differences in procedure or differences in assumptions as
to the incidence of particular taxes. What is important is to note the essential
similarity in pattern of effective rates as shown in all studies. The most significant facts are regression of the tax system as it affects the lowest incomes,
rough proportionality of tax burdens among the lower middle incomes, and
rather mild progression applied to high incomes. (The lumping together of
all incomes over $7,500 tends to present an effective rate for this group
which is unrealistically high for incomes near the $7,500 level, for the rate

shown for this group is an average for the wide range of incomes above this level.) A combined tax system which imposes an over-all rate of one-fifth to the smallest incomes and two-fifths to high incomes can hardly be characterized as a steeply progressive system. The implications of these facts are clear. The tax system has not notably applied the principle of ability to pay. It has borne heavily upon consumption, through sales and excise taxes, property taxes, and low personal income tax exemptions. The particular offenders in this respect are state and local governments, and the effect upon consumption is particularly vicious when, as has been true to a very considerable degree, use of the most regressive taxes has been expanded in periods of unemployment when consumption needs encouragement. The recent popularity of the sales tax, based largely upon its ability to produce large state revenues, has had unintended depressive effects upon consumption. In some phases of the business cycle this brake upon consumption may be useful, but in other phases it is seriously destructive.

Commodity Taxes as Intentional Compensatory Instruments. As a matter of long-run policy to encourage a high level of income and employment, the effect of commodity taxes is strongly deterrent. There are only very limited cyclical situations in which they may be used without injury. Professor Hansen claims that they may be properly employed to apply brakes to consumption during boom periods when productive resources are fully utilized and further consumption pressure can only induce inflation. This position appears more attractive at first glance than upon closer analysis. The alternative to commodity taxes is adjustment in personal income taxes, and their relative merits for counter-boom purposes will depend upon several factors.[32]

Professor Shoup lists for the sales tax the following particular advantages over the personal income tax as an instrument for fighting inflation during a period of boom. In the first place, a sales tax is likely to encourage overtime work somewhat more than is an income tax. The advantage here is that some elasticity in the labor supply is provided by a lengthening of the work day, increasing the volume of output and thus somewhat relieving the inflationary pressure of excessive demand. The reason why an income tax may be somewhat more discouraging of overtime work is that under a sales tax an individual may avoid a part of the heavier tax by judiciously controlling his consumption out of increased earnings, while it is certain that an increase in weekly pay will involve withholding of a larger income tax. Actually, it is doubtful that either a sales tax or an income tax will seriously deter the

[32] This question has been analyzed by Carl Shoup, *Taxing to Prevent Inflation,* New York, Columbia, 1943, pp. 92 *ff.* Much of what follows is taken from Shoup's study.

worker from accepting a reasonable amount of overtime work. In the second place Shoup concludes that a sales tax is less likely to induce laxity in management during a boom period than is an income tax. The point here is that with managerial wages and profits high in a boom period, additional effort to procure higher income will mean higher rates of personal income tax, and after a point the added income after high taxes does not warrant the added effort required. Furthermore, when income tax rates are high, wasteful outlays which can be deducted from gross income are less costly in terms of profits after taxes. Finally, the sales tax allows for regional variations in the cost of living, whereas the income tax does not. Thus, the sales tax tends to raise the cost of consumption by approximately the amount of the tax,[33] and regional differences are maintained. On the other hand, income tax exemptions are fixed for the nation as a whole, without adjustments to differences in the cost of living. In so far as this advantage of the sales tax exists, it is applicable to any phase of the business cycle.[34]

By comparison with the income tax, the sales tax is inferior for a number of reasons. First, it is hardly desirable to discard the principle of ability to pay, even in a boom period. Not all consumer incomes share equally in the boom; many incomes remain fixed over long periods. This being the case, the ability of the income tax to exempt completely a minimum standard-of-living income is decidedly in its favor. And the possibilities in the income tax for the practice of progression establish a clear preference for it in any phase of the business cycle. For no policy of compensatory taxation can logically attempt to combat booms by imposition of severe burdens upon those of low and fixed income. The upward pressure upon prices does not arise uniformly from all income classes. Quite obviously, the consumer pressure arises from demand on the part of those individuals who are anxious to increase purchases by the expenditure of income in excess of that required to provide their former levels of living. Heavy taxation of income in excess of that required to provide a pre-inflation level of living is far preferable to taxing all dollars of expenditure equally.

Second, the case for anti-inflation taxation of consumer purchases exclusively ignores the simple fact that investment expenditures are, dollar for dollar, equally inflationary with consumer purchases. Demand for structural steel or machine tools competes directly for scarce materials and labor with demand for automobiles or pots and pans. Buying for inventory (invest-

---

[33] In a boom period it is generally possible to shift a larger part of a consumption tax forward, as demand is high and rising.

[34] Shoup lists other potential advantages of the sales tax. They are ignored here because to the writer they appear of very minor significance among a list of advantages which altogether present a weak case for this type of tax measure.

ment) has the same price effect as buying for consumption. In the short run, therefore—and acute inflationary pressure is typically a short-run phenomenon—offers to purchase investment goods are equally price-increasing with offers to purchase consumer goods. This is true in spite of the fact that in the long run additions to the economy's capacity to produce, other things being equal, do effectively relieve inflationary pressures. Thus, though in the long run "the best cure for inflation is production," the immediate effect of additional investment in an inflationary period is the inducement of more inflation, a fact which seems to have been unquestionably demonstrated in 1946–1947 and 1956–1957. Herein lies a distinct advantage of income taxation over consumption taxation for counter-inflation purposes. For the income tax can be—almost automatically is—designed to take off the market private investable income as well as private consumable income, limiting overinvestment as well as overconsumption.

Further, there is a group of practical or institutional considerations bearing upon the choice of tax measures to combat inflation. The "cost of living" has come to represent an important datum in the field of wage bargaining. The boom period is that in which organized labor is particularly successful in realizing its demands. And whether reasonable or not, it is generally agreed that an increase in the cost of living will in practice drive labor to the bargaining table with demands for increased wages more quickly than will increased personal income taxes. This is partly due to a belief that a rise in the prices of consumers' goods has an effect which is discriminatory against the consumer (= labor) class, while an increase in income taxes typically affects everyone across the board. The certainty that consumption taxes increase prices, and that general consumption taxes increase the cost of living, creates a powerful urge toward wage increases and thus "builds into" the sales tax a peculiar inflationary pressure less likely to be present in a personal income tax.[35]

Comparable to the situation in the wage field is the situation in the field of agricultural prices. The "parity" formula has become generally accepted in the American economy, justifying a rise in agricultural prices when other prices rise. It is almost inevitable, therefore, that unless agricultural policies revert to those prior to 1933, a tax increase in prices of things bought by farmers will encourage further rise in farm prices. If this is a reasonable expectation, then the sales tax would become a more potent instrument for

[35] The Bureau of Labor Statistics Consumer Price Index, which is widely watched as the index of the "cost of living" and which is used in many labor contracts as the basis for automatic or escalator wage adjustment, includes consumption taxes but does not include income taxes. Thus, higher sales taxes are reflected in the Consumer Price Index, and automatically produce or "justify" higher wages.

promotion of inflation in agricultural prices (and thus increase the cost of living and the cost of many industrial raw materials) than would the income tax. Obviously, both a sales tax and an income tax would skim off excessive purchasing power, and to the extent that this is accomplished would reduce the upward pull of demand upon prices. But we must recognize also the potency of the upward push of increasing *costs* upon prices—the phenomenon commonly designated as the "cost-price spiral." With respect to the cost push we find that whether entirely rational or not, the forward-shifted sales tax has a marked influence upon costs, while the income tax does not. This difference would argue strongly in favor of the income tax for counter-inflation purposes.

A principal objective of inflation control is to avoid the redistributive effects which inflation imposes upon a society. That is, since not all individual incomes move upward together, uncontrolled inflation will tend to ration goods according to a pattern different from that which obtained before prices began their movement upward, favoring those whose incomes rise and penalizing those whose incomes remain relatively constant. The imposition of a proportional tax on consumption will raise the prices of the affected goods and services proportionally across the board. Thus, those whose incomes are not rising will be adversely affected by an anti-inflation sales tax much as they would have been affected had the inflation been permitted to go unhampered, except that the redistribution will not be permitted to go so far. The fixed income groups will be required to sacrifice either a portion of their consumption or a portion of their savings to check an inflation in the encouragement of which they would play no significant part. On the other hand, those whose incomes are rising can maintain or increase their consumption or saving. The burden of the program is thus largely misplaced, and we can see that labor opposition to consumption taxes for inflation control is essentially rational. For wages tend to lag behind prices, placing the labor group in the disadvantageous position mentioned above.

The personal income tax as an anti-inflationary measure might possibly produce essentially the same results that consumption taxes would produce in redistributing real purchasing power during a potentially inflationary period. This would be particularly true were income taxes to be increased by lowering personal exemptions. But if the income tax rates are raised by a given percentage throughout the progressive schedule, all income classes will participate in the sacrifice. Those whose incomes are high and rising, and who can easily escape a large part of the burden of consumption taxes by refraining from consumption, would be required under an income tax to pay on their current savings, and the major redistributive effects would be avoided both in the present and for the future. Anti-inflation tax policy will be unpopular at best. It will be more palatable and therefore politically more feasible if all classes have confidence that its burdens are widely and fairly distributed.

RECOMMENDED READINGS

Criz, Maurice, *The Use Tax*, Chicago, Public Administration Service, 1941.
  A short, thorough description and analysis.
Due, J. F., *Sales Taxation*, Urbana, Univ. of Illinois Press, 1957.
  For the beginning student in the subject, some or all of Chapters 1, 2, 3, 14, 15, 17, and 18 will probably be most useful. Most of the remainder of the book deals with experience elsewhere than in the United States.
Haig, R. M., and Shoup, C., *The Sales Tax in the American States*, N.Y., Columbia, 1934.
  Though not a recent study, this book is currently pertinent. Chapter 1 ("The Sales Tax Movement in 1929–1933"), Chapter 2 ("Reaction of Taxpayers to the Sales Tax"), and Chapter 4 ("Evaluation of the Sales Tax as a State Fiscal Measure") are particularly recommended for reading in elaboration of the text chapter.
Hall, J. K., "Excise Tax Incidence and the Postwar Economy," *American Economic Review Supplement*, March, 1942, pp. 83ff.
  A discussion of incidence and of effects in terms of both prevention of wartime inflation and long-run postwar needs.
Hansen, A. H., and Perloff, H. S., *State and Local Finance in the National Economy*, N.Y., Norton, 1944, Chapter 3.
  Excellent general treatment of the regressive effects of state and local tax systems, with special reference to sales and business taxes.
Wald, H. P., "A Comparative Analysis of Three Variations of Retail Sales Taxes," *American Economic Review*, June, 1944, pp. 280ff.
  This article should be very useful in defining objectives and in analyzing the effects of particular sales tax provisions. It will induce acquaintance with various types of sales taxation.

CHAPTER 21

Death and Gift Taxes

Death taxes are imposed upon the occasion of transfer of property at death. Under a system of private property it is almost inevitable that the individual possess some right to determine how his property shall be distributed upon his death.[1] In a primitive or thoroughly communized society, where property ownership resides in the group or society, the death of a member would involve no transfer of property ownership, since during his lifetime he was only using property of the society. The institution of private property, on the other hand, implies private right to the use and to the distribution of property, both during life and at death of the owner. However, the right to property is not a natural right; it is a creature of the social and legal system, and thus is legally established by common consent. There may be, and frequently are, established legal limitations to the rights of bequest and inheritance. A system of primogeniture may exist within a society in which property is regarded as individual; the system clearly limits the rights of bequest and inheritance. In many modern states the right of bequest is limited by standing legal claims of widows and children to some part of the property of the deceased father. Death taxes themselves are a recognition of a legally enforceable claim of the state against private property transferred at death.

The transfer of property in an organized society must take place under the aegis of government. This is merely an extension of the governmental function of protection, and is an essential feature of the distribution of estates according to the wishes of decedents and the existing laws of inheritance. It is upon the occasion of distribution that government presents its tax claims. Two types of death taxes are in use. One is the *estate tax*, imposed upon the estate before distribution to lawful heirs. The other is the *inheritance* or *succession tax*, using as its base the distributive share to the

[1] See G. D. H. Cole, "Inheritance," *Encyclopaedia of the Social Sciences.*

individual heir. Much controversy has raged over the relative merits of the two types. We shall have occasion to take note of the issues in this controversy as we discuss the theory of the death tax.

Theories of Death Taxation

Death taxes are among the oldest of tax measures.[2] During their long history they have not wanted for theoretical justification. Indeed, almost every conceivable tax justification has been used at one time or another.

1. Benefit. The benefit theory as applied to death taxation calls attention to the service which government performs in guaranteeing the distribution of estates to lawful heirs according to the wishes of the decedent. And when no will exists, government arranges for distribution of the estate according to society's wishes as expressed in the statutory provisions governing such circumstances. According to this theory, the tax is a payment to government for performance of this service. The benefit theory, however, hardly recommends itself beyond the justification of a probate fee. In modern times, when death taxes typically are imposed in addition to collection of probate fees, and are generally progressive in rates, the benefit principle falls far short of representing an adequate theoretical base for the tax.

It has frequently been asserted that since the laws of inheritance are state laws, and since the orderly distribution of estates at death is a function of an agency of state government, death taxes are "naturally" state taxes. By this reasoning, federal taxation of estates or inheritances is regarded as an invasion of a revenue field which belongs to the states. This can be regarded as acceptable only to the extent that the tax is based upon the benefit principle, and the inadequacy of the benefit principle as a justification for modern death taxes implies similar inconclusiveness of the argument that the tax belongs to the states.

2. State Partnership. A theory of minor importance advanced in justification of death taxes is that which claims that government is inevitably a passive and silent partner in the creation of all value.[3] This being the case, government is rightfully a major claimant in the distribution of estates, on grounds that what actually belongs to government cannot logically be given away by the decedent. Such a theory can hardly be tenable as justification for modern death taxation. If acceptable, it is equally applicable to income taxation, and if used to justify income taxation it cannot logically be used

---

[2] See William J. Shultz, "Inheritance Taxation," *Encyclopaedia of the Social Sciences*, for a brief history of these taxes.

[3] Andrew Carnegie is reported to have said, "The American republic is the partner in every enterprise where money is made honorably." (E. R. A. Seligman, *Essays in Taxation*, 8th ed., New York, Macmillan, 1913, p. 129 n.)

again in justification of a death tax. Furthermore, modern practice of exempting minimum estates and inheritances from taxation and application of progressive rates to those taxed do not appear to reflect the partnership principle. If government is a partner in the creation of wealth and property rights, it contributes to the creation of small as well as large estates. And it is unclear how the partnership theory can account for the taking by government of a larger portion of a large than of a small estate, or how it justifies sharing by the governmental "partner" in gains but not in business losses.

3. The Back-Tax Theory. This theory regards the death tax as an instrument for collecting taxes due but evaded by the decedent during his lifetime.[4] It has had particular reference to the evasion of property taxes, since in the United States the death tax was an early instrument of the states and the principal state tax at that time was the property tax. Recognition of the consistently high degree of property tax evasion has added support to the theory. However, as Seligman points out, death taxes have been imposed upon all types of property making up the estate or inheritance, whereas there has been relatively little evasion of the real property tax. Logically, therefore, if the death tax represents a final accounting for unpaid property taxes it should be limited almost exclusively to personal property. It is, of course, absurd to assume that large estates can be accumulated only through evasion of property (or other) taxes, and that therefore the existence of an estate is *prima facie* evidence of earlier tax evasion.[5]

4. Ability to Pay. The generally accepted principle justifying the taxation of transfers of property at death is that of ability to pay. It asserts that the inheritance of property places assets in the hands of the receiver which create an ability to contribute to government distinct from the ability to pay other taxes. This is undoubtedly true in the majority of cases, and the establishment of a minimum inheritance exempt from taxes can provide for cases of need. With respect to inheritance, ability to pay taxes per dollar received progresses in two directions. Other things being equal, the larger the inheritance the greater the capacity to pay per dollar, for reasons discussed at considerable length in an earlier chapter presenting the case for progressive taxation. In addition, the capacity to pay taxes from an inheri-

---

[4] Cf. Seligman, *op. cit.*, p. 135.

[5] There are in existence special taxes imposed at death whose function is that of collecting previously evaded taxes. An example was the Connecticut "Estate Penalty Tax," which required probate judges to report the items of property in estates which had paid local property taxes during the last taxing period. A special penalty tax was imposed upon those items upon which a property tax was due but unpaid. Such a special tax is to be regarded as a measure to improve enforcement of the property tax, and not as a tax on the transfer of estates at death.

tance varies with the extent to which the heir has depended upon its receipt. Pure windfall inheritances of a given amount possess very high capacity to pay per dollar received compared to inheritances of the same size received by dependent widows and children.

The ability principle thus points to progression of death tax rates in two directions: with increase in the size of the estate or inheritance, and with greater distance in relationship between the testator and the heir. With respect to the latter, many states classify heirs into at least three classes. Class A or "direct" heirs include spouse, children, parents, grandparents, and grandchildren, and enjoy high exemption and relatively low (though progressive) rates. Class B or "collateral" heirs include brothers, sisters, cousins, uncles, aunts, and children-in-law; both lower exemptions and higher (progressive) rates are applied to this class. The highest (progressive) rates and lowest exemptions are applied to Class C heirs or "strangers," which category includes all heirs not related by blood. It is, of course, possible to create a larger or smaller number of classes and to vary the definitions of the typical classes indicated above. The classification, however, results from the economic fact of greater ability to pay per dollar of inheritance by those who are not normally dependent upon the inheritance as a substitute for income.

It is the desire to tailor the tax to ability to pay which has led to quite general enthusiasm for the inheritance tax as opposed to the estate tax. The latter involves none of the complications such as life interests and contingent estates. The valuation for tax purposes of such special or deferred inheritances creates difficult problems of administration, frequently withholding inheritances from lawful heirs for long periods of time while the administrative machinery is in operation. Supporters of the inheritance tax believe this a small price to pay for a tax measure which lends itself to far greater precision in adjustment to ability to pay. It is true that two estates do not possess the same capacity to pay when one is granted wholly to a single heir while the other is divided among several. For ability to pay relates to the heirs and not to the estate, and to apply progression to the estate before division is at best but a rough and ready application of the ability principle. An estate tax thus ignores the important datum of ability of the heirs to pay taxes, both as to size of inheritance and as to relationship to the decedent.

On the other hand, a realistic view of how the inheritance tax operates raises several questions concerning the actual conformance of its burdens to ability of individual heirs to pay. In the majority of cases there is no practical difference in the effects of the two tax measures, for, most commonly, estates are passed directly to the surviving spouse. Under such circumstances an inheritance tax is in effect an estate tax. When estates are divided into shares and distributed among several heirs, it is supposedly the merit of the inheritance tax that it can impose upon each heir a tax which measures his peculiar ability.[6] Unfortunately, however, the testator may by his own choice (or lack of it) defeat the laudable purposes of the inheritance tax. Although it is true that inheritance taxes are generally paid out of each distributive share,[7] the testator generally has full knowledge of the impact of such taxes upon the various heirs, and can adjust his contributions to take account of them.

For example, suppose a testator expects to have a net estate (after payment of debts and expenses, but not taxes) of $50,000, and that the inheritance tax allows an exemption of $30,000 for direct heirs and none for "strangers."[8] He wishes to leave the bulk of his estate to his widow (his only direct heir), but would like to leave something to his secretary and to the widow of his former business partner. Let us suppose that if there were no tax he would choose to leave $40,000 to his wife and $5,000 each to the two "strangers." But on investigation of the inheritance tax law he finds that under such a distribution his widow would pay taxes of $200 (2 per cent on the excess above the exempt minimum), leaving her $39,800. Each of the others, however, would pay 10 per cent without exemption, or $500, leaving $4,500. Confronted with this situation, it is conceivable that he will provide $5,555 to each of the "strangers," so as to give each $5,000 after taxes. The consequence of this is a reduction in his bequest to his widow to just under $39,000. Obviously, some violence has been done to the notion that the inheritance tax can measure accurately the ability to pay of each heir. The effect of the differential rates and exemptions has been to throw the whole burden of the tax upon the widow. The "stranger" has after tax the amount he would have had if there were no tax, while the widow—whose ability to pay per dollar of inheritance is regarded as considerably less—has borne the whole burden. The point to be made, however, is only illustrated by this example; it does not depend upon the figures and actions assumed. The point is that, when we say the inheritance tax implements the ability to

[6] This means his peculiar ability only with respect to his inheritance, and not with respect to his over-all asset position. It is hardly conceivable that any death tax not completely integrated with an income tax could measure the whole ability to pay of the individual.

[7] Cf. T. W. Chrystie, "Division of Death Taxes Among Beneficiaries," *Proceedings,* National Tax Association, 1939, p. 411.

[8] These exemptions are approximately those effective under several state inheritance tax laws.

pay principle more precisely than does the estate tax, we assume no power of voluntary vitiation or qualification by the testator. That this assumption is unreal would be attested by those whose profession brings them into the confidence of testators.[9] We find, therefore, that the supposed economic merit of the inheritance tax is or can be very largely imaginary.

On the other hand, the inheritance tax offers an opportunity for reform of an important weakness of the estate tax. If, as not infrequently occurs among the wealthy, an heir participates in the distribution of several estates during his lifetime, it should be possible to cumulate these several as if they were a single inheritance. Second and third inheritances should pay taxes at the progressive rates that would have applied had these inheritances been parts of a larger single distribution. This is possible, however, only under an inheritance tax, which imposes the tax upon the receipts of the heir, and not upon the estate before distribution. Let us see how the inequities arise under the estate tax. Suppose an heir receives a whole taxable estate of $600,000. The tax under the progressive rates of the current federal estate tax is $180,700. Another person, who is sole heir to three net estates of $200,000 each, would pay combined taxes of $152,100. But this is not all. Each of the three estates in the latter case would get the $60,000 deduction in calculating the taxable estate; the former would receive it only once. Clearly, a great deal of inequity results, which cannot be corrected under the estate tax where each estate must be regarded as a separate entity. Inheritances to the receiver could, however, be cumulated over his lifetime and erase the inequity arising from multiple inheritances.

Though death taxes are frequently quite imperfect in precise implementation of the principle of ability to pay, it is nevertheless true that the ability principle constitutes the major modern theoretical justification of them. By any measure, ability to pay taxes does arise out of the institution of inheritance. This personal ability is quite distinct from that arising out of the receipt of recurrent income, and justifies the separate employment of the principle as the theoretical basis for both taxes.

[9] It is not meant to imply that this qualification entirely vitiates the supposed advantages of the inheritance tax, nor that, for the reasons indicated above, the estate tax is better tailored to ability to pay. Experience seems to show that practical factors very frequently shift the whole burden of the estate tax on to those least able to bear it, although it is generally assumed that all heirs share proportionally in the estate tax. Chrystie (*ibid.*) finds that in general, ". . . Estate taxes, whether federal or state, which are imposed upon the entire net estate as one unit, are to be paid out of the residuary estate." Since in practice specific grants are generally given to collateral heirs and strangers, while direct heirs are made residuary legatees, the tax sacrifice does not fall proportionally upon all heirs but most heavily upon those to whom the sacrifice per dollar is greatest.

5. Redistribution of Wealth. Death taxes are imposed at the time of transfer of property at death; the tax base is the property itself, and the rates applied are frequently high enough to take considerably more than the current income from the estate. Clearly, therefore, the death tax is intended to be a tax on wealth. A long-standing and widespread criticism of the private property economy concerns its propensity to create highly unequal incomes and highly unequal distribution of economic power. It is generally agreed that the development of an industrial economy requires the accumulation of large quantities of capital, and that this capital is formed primarily from the savings of those larger income receivers whose propensity to consume is relatively low. On the other hand, the consequences in terms of welfare of highly unequal incomes are so serious as to raise questions in the minds of many as to whether a system which produces so much inequality can justify its continued existence without the introduction of measures to mitigate its evils. One extreme view would favor major or complete elimination of the private property system. At the other extreme is the view which insists that with all its inequalities the situation of even those least favored by the system is better than it would be under any alternative system. The liberal, middle point of view in general favors the retention of the basic outlines of the private property system, but would introduce measures to mitigate the serious consequences of maldistribution of wealth and income.

Traditionally, the objection to wide inequality has been based upon a concern for the welfare of those least favored by the system. As such, it is based upon moral and ethical considerations, and in its less radical forms has advocated such mitigating measures as shorter working hours, minimum wages, social security, relief expenditures, usury laws, excess profits taxes, progressive income taxes, and progressive taxes upon property transferred at death. More recently, however, with the development of the income analysis of business cycles and secular stagnation, wide inequality is condemned on purely economic grounds. The newer analysis has emphasized the causative relation between the level of consumption and the level of national income. Poverty, therefore, is not only socially significant because of the low standard of living it creates; it is economically significant as an obstacle to economic progress. The importance of a high level of consumption in generating a high level of investment, income, and consumption argues strongly for a system of distribution in which the masses possess sufficient income to maintain high consumption. Granting the necessity of saving to finance a rapidly expanding economy, and granting that such saving comes largely from large incomes, the rate of expansion cannot be maintained unless consumption is to continue increasing. When consumption ceases to increase, the savings of the large income receivers turn to hoards, and stagnation sets in.[10]

Inheritance is but one among many factors contributing to inequality in the ownership of wealth. And of course inequality in the ownership of wealth is but one factor in the inequality of incomes. Nevertheless, inheritance is sufficiently important to have generated a considerable amount of radical and liberal agitation for its elimination or qualification. Progressive taxation of estates and inheritances has been persistently motivated by the desire to mitigate the recognized evils of inheritance in its purest form. It would be improper to assume, however, that death taxes are designed to make private inheritance impossible. The federal tax on estates has carried fairly high and progressive rates, but has allowed generous exemptions. The state taxes have generally granted lower exemptions, but have applied low rates. Obviously, a death tax system which appropriated substantially all of every estate to government would, in the majority of applications, create real hardship. For in the majority of cases estates transferred simply serve to maintain consumption for remaining family members at or below the former level.

The objectives of redistribution of wealth and of taxation according to ability to pay, both of which lie behind death taxation, are not in any important way in conflict with one another. In individual cases they may conflict, but those cases are relatively few and indicate the conflict which at times arises from the application of a tax measure uniformly to all members of a society whose members are in different circumstances. In general, however, it cannot be controverted that the greater the inheritance, the greater the capacity to pay taxes from that inheritance. And the application of a uniform set of progressive rates upon inheritances will meet the broad demands of the ability principle and at the same time mitigate some of the results of highly unequal ownership of wealth.

It is convenient at this point to analyze the observation not infrequently expressed that death taxes, since they are imposed upon wealth, actually decrease the stock of wealth in the economy. The observation appears to confuse wealth itself with the ownership of wealth. It generally cites the example of a large, closely held corporation, which on the death of one of its few large owners must be "broken up" to meet death tax obligations. Ignor-

[10] The influences which promote progress in a rapidly expanding economy in spite of serious inequality in incomes are principally: (1) population growth, (2) new lands, and (3) a high degree of competition accompanied by rapid technological change. When population becomes nearly stable, and new lands disappear, two major external factors in the expansion of consumption disappear. When the economy becomes non-competitive, the tendency is toward restriction of production and lowering of consumption.

ing whatever legal possibilities there may be for avoiding death taxes or avoiding the sale of stock to meet tax claims, let us assume that a portion of the estate (in shares of stock in the corporation) of the decedent must be turned into cash to pay the taxes. If these shares are sold to others among the small shareholding group, obviously no destruction of capital occurs and no dissipation of ownership occurs, although the decedent's heirs hold a smaller share of ownership than did the decedent. But more likely, if the corporation is large and closely held, stock must be sold on the market to meet tax obligations. Here again, though the number of owners of the corporation is increased, no destruction of capital has occurred. And even if the shares must be sold at a low price, no destruction of capital in the real sense has resulted, though the size of the inheritance after taxes has been reduced. Savings of outsiders have replaced savings of the decedent in the corporation, and government has taken that portion of the decedent's savings replaced. It would be impossible to generalize upon the long-run effects of such dispersion of ownership.

It has sometimes been argued that high death taxes are self-defeating as revenue measures, for they tend to dry up the stream of death tax revenue by discouraging the accumulation of taxable estates. This is undoubtedly true to a degree. But there are ways of moderating the death tax bite. Purchase of (partially) tax-exempt insurance offers one possibility. And there are various legal preparations which may be made to avoid death taxes, their types and their effectiveness depending upon existing law in different localities. Establishment of residence in low-tax states is sometimes possible; in community property states the amount of the estate actually transferred at death may be less because of the legal presumption that each spouse was owner of one-half of the assets before death; in some states the legal intricacies of joint tenancy will reduce death taxes by eliminating transfer of ownership at death; estates may be largely given away before death and thus avoid some taxation. Without question— ignoring the possibility of secular increase in number and size of asset accumulations in the society, and changes in the tax laws—death taxes heavy enough to encourage tax avoidance will reduce death tax revenues.

Should we expect high death taxes to discourage saving? It is impossible to answer the question inductively by reference to observed facts. Nevertheless, the question is of some importance, and when answered in the affirmative has been employed as an argument against the death tax. Death taxation is but one—and a minor one—of the influences upon the amount of saving. It would appear doubtful that individuals determine their choices to save or not to save during life in terms of estate or inheritance taxes.

Small savings and even savings of medium size have hardly been touched by these taxes, while it is almost certain that the comfort and economic power which go with substantial assets during life are far stronger motives for accumulation than is the privilege of making large bequests at death. If this is true, death taxes would be minor deterrents to saving. And it may be observed that in terms of economic stability, oversaving has as serious effects as undersaving. A counter possibility exists: that the death tax forces higher savings when the saver wishes to provide given amounts for his heirs after taxes.

Incidence of Death Taxes[11]

The popular but much oversimplified theory of incidence of the death tax places the whole incidence upon the successor or inheritor of the estate. It reasons that since the tax is assessed and collected subsequent to the death of the creator of the estate, and dead men cannot bear tax burdens, the decedent must be free of all incidence. Since there is no vehicle for tax shifting beyond the successor, the total incidence is upon him. Certain easily observable facts seem to support this analysis. The net estate is available for distribution according to will among designated heirs. Were no tax collected, the sum of the shares distributed would be larger by the amount of the tax. Therefore the heirs—or at least some of them—have contributed the tax from their shares.

This theory would be wholly acceptable were it possible to assume that those who create estates during their lifetime either (1) take no thought of death taxes, or (2) consistently during life save what they can for the purpose of estate-building.

In many instances these assumptions harmonize with the facts. They imply that the prospect of death taxes has no effect upon estate-building. There are probably those who are quite ignorant of the existence of such taxes, and set an estate goal—usually by purchase of life insurance—which is regarded as adequate. And there are others who, during life, are so conscious of their obligation to dependents that they follow a consistent program of self-denial for the purpose of maximum estate-building. Many such persons truly "save all they can," and the weight of taxation, though deplored, does not affect the size of the estate before taxes. In such circumstances the tax has but one effect—the size of the net estate being given,

---

[11] See James K. Hall, "Incidence of Death Duties," *American Economic Review*, March, 1940, p. 46, for an excellent short discussion of comparative theories of the incidence of these taxes.

the tax is but a deduction from the shares of the heirs, and the incidence is upon them.[12]

In many other cases, the program of estate-building is conditioned by anticipation of the death tax. Whenever the objective in estate-building is the creation of assets of a given amount *after taxes,* it is to be presumed that the rate of saving during the testator's lifetime was greater than it would have been without the tax. He has not only laid up an estate after taxes for his heirs, but he has also set up a fund for tax payment. The additional self-denial required to meet the tax represents the burden of the tax. How burdensome this incidence is depends upon the intensity of the sacrifice involved in additional saving. But the incidence in this case is clearly upon the decedent. The assumption that dead men cannot bear tax burdens is not strictly true. As dead men, of course, they experience no burdens. But the burden (incidence) can be borne prior to the date on which the tax is assessed. We conclude, therefore, that the incidence of death taxes may be upon the predecessor or upon the successor, or upon both. When anticipation of the tax has led to more rapid estate-building by the predecessor than otherwise would have occurred, to that extent the incidence is upon him. If the estate under the tax is what it would have been without the tax, the incidence is upon the successor. When the predecessor anticipates the tax but is able only partially to provide for it, the incidence is divided between predecessor and successor. Incidence is therefore largely a matter of personal choice of the testator. He may bear the incidence if he chooses (and is able by greater saving or greater industry) to do so, or he may place it upon his successors. As to what generally occurs it is foolhardy to guess and well-nigh impossible to determine by investigation.[13]

Recent History of Death Taxation

The modern era of death taxation in the United States began at about

---

[12] Some would insist that there can be no burden upon heirs, since inheritances are purely fortuitous—a net windfall gain. (Cf. Hall, *ibid.,* p. 58.) However, "incidence" does not necessarily mean "burden": it answers the question, "Who actually has contributed the tax?" The tax may conceivably be contributed without an attendant burden in the case of an heir whose inheritance is entirely of a windfall nature. What he gets is net gain, because he expected nothing. On the other hand, the incidence represents negative benefit in the sense that he would have had greater windfall gain without it.

[13] At a more detailed level it is evident in experience that incidence may be determined by purely legal factors. Suppose that the incidence is upon the successors—that the estate would have been larger had there been no tax. Suppose further that the tax is an estate tax, paid from the estate before distribution. Generally speaking, state inheritance laws require that designated amounts willed to designated heirs remain intact without tax deduction. The residual heirs then bear the incidence, while those granted designated amounts bear none. Laws of the states vary in this regard; although most follow the pattern described above, some make special provision for prorating the tax or especially favor close lineal heirs (who are generally residual heirs).

the beginning of the present century for state governments, while modern federal use began during World War I. Several states had employed rudimentary measures of this type during the nineteenth century, but it was not until the Wisconsin law in 1903 that the tax first included all heirs, all types of property, and progressive rates. Federal employment of death taxation occurred sporadically during the nineteenth century, principally during war revenue emergencies. Until 1924 death taxes were generally regarded as the peculiar property of the states. Previous to that date the federal taxes had been promptly repealed with the passing of the emergency. In 1924, however, the debate over repeal of the federal wartime death tax terminated in legislation designed largely to eliminate duplication of federal and state burdens upon estates and inheritances. This plan not only laid the foundation for a permanent federal tax, but greatly accelerated the movement toward uniform death taxation among the states.

The Federal Credit for State Death Taxes Paid. In 1916 the federal government levied an estate tax whose rates, though moderate by contrast with the present law, were considerably higher than those formerly applied by federal death taxes.[14] The maximum rate in the progressive schedule in 1916 was 10 per cent on the net estate; the rate schedule was increased to a maximum of 25 per cent in 1917. The imposition of a fairly heavy federal tax on estates, in addition to existing state inheritance taxes, imposed new and relatively severe burdens upon transfer of property at death. During the war this duplication was not regarded as onerous, but with the end of the war fundamental decisions were required about the problem of duplication of death taxes. State tax rates were low; in fact there was a good deal of competition among states to establish death tax advantage for their residents. Competition for wealthy residents was keen, on the principle that low death taxes would encourage establishment of residence, and annual property taxes and other revenues would be thereby increased.[15]

Subsequent to the war Secretary Mellon actively urged repeal of the wartime federal estate tax, and return of this revenue source to the states. The states strongly supported this solution of the problem. However, the legislation of 1924, far from eliminating the federal tax, increased its rates to a maximum of 40 per cent. Estates continued to be subject to both state

[14] Previous federal experience was confined to taxes on inheritances. A stamp tax on legacies at 2/10 of 1 per cent was levied between 1797 and 1802; a very moderate inheritance tax producing only 1½ million dollars per year was employed between 1862 and 1870; and the tax of 1898–1902 was levied at a maximum rate of 2¼ per cent on the inheritances of direct heirs.

[15] States with death taxes frequently countered with the claim that collection of death taxes made annual property and other taxes lower.

and federal taxation, but in 1924 20 per cent, and in 1926 80 per cent, of the federal tax could, in effect, be paid by showing proof that state taxes equal to this amount had been paid. The problem of double federal and state burdens was solved, since no state then taxed to the extent of the 80 per cent federal credit.

The intent of the federal credit provision, however, went well beyond the desire to eliminate the double burden. It was frankly designed to bring the states into line in death tax practice. It represented a conscious federal attempt to establish the death tax as a uniform nation-wide fiscal instrument and to put an end to death tax competition among states.[16] It was extremely effective, for the credit provision made very difficult state refusal to pass the necessary legislation to take for its own treasury revenue which would otherwise go to the federal government.

Forty-eight states now have some form of death tax.[17] While the simpler method of taking advantage of the federal credit would be for the states to adopt estate tax laws at rates 80 per cent of the 1926 federal rates, and with the same exemptions and graduation scale, very few have done so. In 1959 only eleven states had such laws. The remaining states use less precise devices for recouping federal death taxes. The popular state method of adjusting to the federal credit has been to tack on to the inheritance tax an estate tax which absorbs the difference between the inheritance tax and the federal credit. Thirty-five states and the District of Columbia employ such additional estate taxes.[18] The remaining states appear only more or less concerned with taxing only to the extent of the federal credit and eliminating duplication of death taxes.

By and large during the late twenties the states were quite content with this experiment in federal-state sharing of revenues. But in 1932, under pressure for increased revenue, the federal government superimposed an "Additional Estate Tax" upon the 1926 Act. The new law greatly increased the rates on estates and provided no credit against the additional estate tax for state taxes paid, though the 80 per cent credit against the 1926 tax was (is) retained. During the debates on the 1932 law it was suggested that the old (1926) tax be repealed and a new, heavier, and more steeply progressive tax be installed, with a credit of 16⅔ per cent against the new tax for state

[16] Florida in 1924 adopted an amendment to its constitution prohibiting inheritance taxation in that state. With the adoption of the federal credit this state unsuccessfully challenged its constitutionality before the Supreme Court. Finally, in 1930, the Florida constitution was again amended to permit death taxation, but only to the extent and for the duration of the federal credit.

[17] Nevada has no such tax. (Information is not at hand concerning Hawaii.)

[18] Commerce Clearing House, State Tax Guide, 1959.

death taxes paid. This suggestion was not accepted, however, and the additional estate tax was added to the 1926 estate tax.

The action of 1932 in leaving unchanged the participation of the states in death taxation while turning over the major share of such revenues from large estates to the federal Treasury has been described as a "tactical triumph of no small importance" on the part of the federal government.[19] This description implies, justifiably, that the federal attitude toward sharing death tax revenues had changed between 1926 and 1932. The 80 per cent credit under the 1926 Act was probably a necessary political compromise to avoid complete repeal of the federal tax.

The attitude of the states toward the 1932 shift is apparently one of extreme discomfort. This discomfort results because (1) the federal government is now in the controlling position with respect to disposition of a tax which was traditionally thought to belong to the states, and (2) the states are allowed only a small portion of death tax revenues currently being collected. What was described as generosity on the part of the federal government in 1926 has since 1932 been characterized as niggardliness. Though state death tax revenues did not decline as a result of the 1932 action, the position of the states changed from major to minor participation in revenues from large estates. Yet it is clear that the 1926 Act increased state death tax rates and revenues. And it is highly likely that if the federal government were to be completely generous and retire from the death tax field, the states would return to a considerable amount of undercutting one another's death taxes to bid for wealthy residents.[20] The consequence could very well be lower state death tax revenues than at present. From the point of view of revenue alone, the ideal situation for the states would be a heavy federal tax with a 100 per cent credit for state taxes paid. In view of the prospects of state finances and the relative unimportance of death tax revenues to the federal government, such a procedure deserves consideration. It would, however, nakedly reveal the indirect financial power which the federal government possesses over the states.

Until 1954 the federal estate tax was a combination of two estate taxes, computed by adding the tax due under the 1926 law to that due under the additional estate tax. With the Internal Revenue Code of 1954, however, the two taxes are combined into a single rate schedule, and the credit for state taxes paid is also treated through a schedule of credits which leave

[19] Eugene Oakes, "The Federal Offset and the American Death Tax System," *Quarterly Journal of Economics*, August, 1940, p. 573. This article is highly recommended for further reading on this subject.

[20] This tendency would probably be especially strong in view of the growth of state income taxation.

the actual amount of credit unchanged. The "net estate" forms the base of the tax. This is determined by deducting from the gross estate the expenses of burial, administration expenses, charitable bequests, and up to 50 per cent of the gross estate as a "marital deduction" for the decedent's spouse.[21] The net estate is subject to progressive rates of tax after exemption of the first $60,000 of net estate. Finally, there are credits against the tax, in the form of a gift tax already paid on assets given away by the decedent prior to death, and the credit for state death taxes paid. The rates of taxation range from 3 per cent of the first $5,000 of taxable estate to 77 per cent on amounts over $10 million of net estate.

As in the case of the federal personal income tax, the introduction of income-splitting for married couples in 1948 discriminates against the single person. By regarding half of the estate accumulated during the period of marriage as an estate belonging to the surviving spouse, and not therefore subject to taxation, the law permits many estates to pay marginal rates much lower than would otherwise occur. Assume a taxable estate of $500,000. If the decedent had no surviving spouse, the tax would be $145,700, and the tax would be imposed at an average rate of 145,700/500,000, or 29.1 per cent. But if there is a surviving spouse whose marital deduction is 50 per cent of the estate, the tax will be $65,700, and the average rate on the whole estate will be 13.1 per cent. Of course, in the latter case, when the spouse dies there may be a tax payable on her share. But if the spouse uses up the estate, partially or wholly, the sum of the two taxes will be much lower than in the case of a single decedent. If the spouse's estate remains intact until his (her) death, the combined taxes of the married couple are less than that of the unmarried person ($131,400 as against $145,700), and in addition the spouse has had the use of what would have been the tax on half of the estate.

Revenue Productivity of Death Taxes

Table 33 shows the relative importance over time of death taxes in the whole revenue picture of federal and state governments. Variations in revenue from year to year result from variations in some or all of three factors. The first is a group of technical elements inherent in the tax laws themselves, such as rates of taxation, specific exemptions, and the degree to which revenues are shared between governments. The rise in state death tax revenues in 1931 (see Table 33) is due largely to heavier state taxes

---

[21] Life insurance proceeds are excluded from the gross estate if the decedent retained no "incidents of ownership," such as the power to change the beneficiary or to borrow on the policy.

resulting from the federal action of 1926, while the severe decline in federal revenue from this tax reflects small federal participation in these revenues under the 80 per cent credit. The second factor is the current level at which estates and inheritances are valued for tax purposes. Both federal and state death tax revenues were lower in 1931 than they would have been under conditions of higher property values. This factor does not stand out in the figures as distinct from the other two, but it is unquestionably constantly in operation. The third factor is the purely accidental one of the number of large estates subject to taxation in a particular year. Other things being equal, this is likely to be a more significant variable to individual states

TABLE 33

DEATH AND GIFT TAX REVENUES AND PER CENT OF TOTAL TAX REVENUES FROM SUCH TAXES, FEDERAL AND STATE GOVERNMENTS, SELECTED YEARS, 1916–1958*

| | FEDERAL | | STATE | |
YEAR	Death and Gift Tax Revenues ($ millions)	% Total Federal Tax Revenues	Death and Gift Tax Revenues ($ millions)	% Total State Tax Revenues
1916	—	0.0	29	8.0
1922	139	4.3	66	9.1
1927	100	3.5	106	7.8
1931	48	2.0	183	10.2
1937	316	6.8	115	3.7
1940	360	6.8	113	2.1
1944	510	1.3	114	1.7
1951	730	1.4	195	2.2
1958	1,393	2.2	351	2.3

* Federal figures from *Annual Report of the Secretary of the Treasury*, 1945, p. 484, 1951, p. 723, and from the *Budget* for 1960; state figures from various volumes of the *Statistical Abstract of the United States*, and *Compendium . . .* , 1951, p. 11, and 1958, p. 11.

than to the federal government, because of broader federal coverage. The death of a very wealthy resident in a particular year may mean to a state the difference between budget surplus and deficit. On the other hand, the lower exemptions in typical state taxes provide a larger number of estates subject to taxation per thousand deaths, and thus work toward stability in state death tax revenues.

The facts displayed in Table 33 indicate clearly, however, that death and gift taxes[22] are of relatively minor importance to both federal and state governments from the revenue point of view. Furthermore, it is unlikely that they could be made to occupy a significantly more important position. Some increase in rates is of course possible without severe hardship, particularly in the lower and middle brackets touched by the federal tax (i.e.,

[22] The relation of gift taxes to death taxes will be discussed in the following section.

on gross estates between $100,000 and $500,000). But the small number of such estates would still mean relatively small revenues. It is probable that little lowering of federal exemptions or raising of state rates on smaller estates and inheritances could be justified. Such a move would produce considerable additional revenue, but would subject to taxation estates and inheritances typically essential to the security of dependent persons. Under present prices an estate of less than $50,000 possesses little ability to pay death taxes.[23]

Gift Taxes[24]

Federal and state taxes upon gifts are employed primarily to close an otherwise easily available opening for the avoidance of death taxes. Without such instruments it would be possible by transfers before death to accomplish substantially the equivalent of tax-free inheritance. If, therefore, there is theoretical and practical justification for death taxation, there is approximately identical justification for the taxation of gifts *inter vivos*. The principal difficulty in use of the gift tax to supplement the death tax has been to define workably those gifts which are made "in contemplation of death," and thus made for the purpose of death tax avoidance.

The federal Act of 1924 assumed that gifts made within a year prior to death were made in contemplation of death, and a tax was imposed upon gifts made during that year.[25] In 1926 this gift tax was repealed and a two-year presumption of "contemplation" was substituted. This presumption was, however, declared unconstitutional in 1932. In that year the separate gift tax was installed, imposing gift taxes at progressive rates approximately three-fourths as high as those of the estate tax.[26] With changes in rates and exemptions in line with changes in the estate tax, this tax is currently in operation. A peculiar aspect of the gift tax is that, although it is applied annually to gifts made in that year, it applies progressive rates on a basis com-

[23] This would be typically true no matter where the incidence of the tax lies. If it is upon the decedent during his lifetime, accumulation of an estate of less than $50,000 probably means rather severe skimping on expenditures in the representative case, because such estate-builders are not likely to be in the high income classes. If the incidence is upon the heir, likely as he is to be dependent upon the income (and capital) of his estate, there is likewise little taxpaying ability in what is taken to be the representative case.

[24] A useful treatment of this subject is C. Lowell Harriss, *Gift Taxation in the United States*, Washington, American Council on Public Affairs, 1940.

[25] Cf. C. Lowell Harriss, *Proceedings of the National Tax Association*, 1938, pp. 722 ff.

[26] Apparently the gift tax rates were made lower than the estate tax rates on the grounds that gift taxes are paid in the year in which the gift is made. Since they are regarded as prepayments of death taxes, the rate differential in favor of gifts represents discount for prepayment.

parable to those of the estate tax which is paid only once on a given estate.

A specific gift tax exemption is granted each donor for the period of his life. This exemption is comparable to—though somewhat lower than—the specific exemption under the estate tax.[27] An additional exemption, peculiar to the gift tax and not applicable to the estate tax, is an annual one of $3,000 to each donee. Although gifts (if large enough to be subject to the tax) are taxed annually, the rate of taxation applicable in any year is found by reporting a cumulative total of all gifts made since 1932 and applying the rate appropriate to the bracket reached by that total. For example, suppose that gifts of $25 thousand were made in 1959, and including 1959 the taxpayer had made a cumulative total of $450 thousand in net gifts since the act became effective in 1932. The rate of gift taxation on the $25 thousand of gifts made in 1959 would be 24 per cent, which is the rate on that part of the cumulative total of gifts between $250 thousand and $500 thousand. It is evident that some such cumulative plan is necessary in order to establish approximate indifference on the part of the donor as to whether he transfers his estate at death or over a period prior to death.

Clearly the gift tax of 1932 and subsequent years completely avoids the problem of segregating those gifts for taxation which are made in contemplation of death. All gifts (above exempt minima) are taxable. This implies that the gift tax has come to be not only a tool to prevent avoidance of death taxes, but also a tax in its own right, based quite properly upon the principle of ability to pay. There is no fundamental difference between gifts *inter vivos* and bequests made at death. Nevertheless, the mechanics of gift taxation, the stated intent, and the relatively high exemption carry the implication that bolstering the estate (or inheritance)[28] tax is the prime function of the gift tax. Those subject to gift taxes are quite likely to be those who would otherwise make substantial gifts during life to avoid death taxation.

Since the principal function of the gift tax is to provide support for the death tax, there is little significance to the relative revenue productivity of gift taxes. As a matter of fact the federal gift tax revenues have been far smaller than the estate tax revenues.[29] No attempt is made to uncover a comparison of revenues of the two taxes among the states, as the comparison

[27] In 1959 the estate tax specific exemption was $60 thousand, while the aggregate gift tax exemption was $30 thousand. Prior to 1942 both exemptions were $40 thousand.

[28] In 1959 only twelve states employed gift taxes. Most of these employed the inheritance tax, with an additional estate tax to absorb the federal credit (Commerce Clearing House, *State Tax Guide*, 1959).

[29] In 1957 federal gift tax revenues were approximately 47 per cent of estate tax revenues. No consistent relationship, however, appears evident over a period of years.

is of little importance. What is important it that without gift taxes, whatever their revenue productivity, revenues from death taxes would be lower than they are. Thus, the major revenue productivity of the gift tax is to be found merged in the death tax revenues.[30]

Integration of Death and Gift Taxes

We have seen that the primary purpose of the gift tax is to complement the estate tax by subjecting gifts *inter vivos* to taxes similar to those on property transferred at death. It would appear eminently reasonable, therefore, to consider both gifts and bequests as similar manifestations of a single process—the transfer of wealth from one person to another. From this point of view there are two inconsistencies in the modern application of these tax measures. The first inconsistency lies in the separate—and different—specific exemptions. The federal estate tax allows specific exemption from taxation of the first $60 thousand of the estate. The gift tax allows a lifetime exemption of $30 thousand plus an annual exemption of $3,000 per donee. Consistency would seem to require amalgamation of these into a single exemption, in addition to, say, an annual exemption of $500 to cover private gifts not likely to have been made in contemplation of death. Possibly the proper solution is a single, cumulative, over-all exemption of $60 thousand for both estates and gifts. The additional gift tax exemption of a given amount per donnee per year can hardly be justified on any grounds. Conceivably it encourages the breaking-up of large estates into widely dispersed gifts, which accomplishes a certain redistribution of wealth. But for smaller accumulations it is also conceivable that the urge to avoid taxes may result in too great dispersion for the benefit of dependents. On the whole, however, if the additional exemption per donee is logical under the gift tax it is equally logical under the estate tax. The simplest and most reasonable reform would seem to be the establishment of one general exemption to be applied to gifts and/or estates, as the donor chooses. The particular merit of such combination would be to integrate more closely the two complementary taxes.

The second inconsistency in modern practice is to be found in the separate application of progressive rate schedules to gifts and estates. If the two taxes are really one, the logical treatment would be to add *inter vivos*

---

[30] Why, then, do so few states have gift taxes? The explanation is to be found in the fact that in the brackets where death tax rates are high and the propensity to avoid is great, the federal gift tax is effective. Thus, the federal gift tax serves to discourage evasion by the gift route. On the other hand, *inter vivos* gifts are given some advantage over transfers at death in the absence of state gift taxes.

gifts to the estate transferred at death, and apply a single progressive schedule to this total. Gifts are now cumulated over the life of the donor. Administratively it would be simple indeed to treat the estate as the final item in a series of transfers.[31] Roughly speaking, at the present time, the wise possessor of a considerable estate would distribute approximately half by gift and half at death. In so doing he would be subject to the lowest total tax on the transfer of his wealth. Such separation does the same violence to the theory of progressive taxation as applied to death and gift taxes as do separate returns on a single family income under the personal income tax. It is indeed curious that two taxes which are really one and are generally so regarded should be treated as quite distinct taxes with respect to the application of rate schedules and exemptions. Present gift and estate tax practice may in many respects be considered comparable to the payment by a single individual of separate income taxes with separate exemptions and separate progressive rate schedules on income as wages, income as interest, income as rents and royalties, income as profits, and capital gains.

The Problem of Situs in State Death Taxation

Much hardship and confusion has resulted from the lack of uniformity in state taxation of inheritances and estates. The situs of property for inheritance tax purposes has been so variously defined by state laws as to create much duplication of taxation of the same property items. It seems to have been reasonably well established that the situs of real estate for tax purposes is its location. It is, however, movable property—particularly intangible property—which has caused the greatest difficulty with respect to multiple taxation. Suppose the decedent to have been a resident of State A. State A would probably impose its death tax upon all intangibles transferred at death, on the principle that "movables follow the owner" and have their taxable situs in the state of his residence. But suppose his estate includes securities of a corporation incorporated in State B and owning property in State C. Under some state laws both B and C would be entitled to death tax. Under the laws of some states, State D would file death tax claims against bonds held in safe keeping in that state, even though the decedent was non-resident and the corporation a foreign one.

---

[31] A practical difficulty would arise because the heirs at death would frequently be left but a small amount of the specific exemption, and the estate at death would frequently be subject to higher rates than would *inter vivos* gifts. This result would occur because gifts take place prior to transfer of the estate at death. Yet the theory of death taxes points to preference for direct heirs, who in the majority of instances are the principal heirs at death.

Such multiplication of inheritance taxation of the same property does, of course, increase unnecessarily the burden of death taxation. On the whole, it is probably true that the multiple tax is less expensive and annoying than the cost and delay in clearing the estate of tax liability before the shares can be distributed. Though taxes may not actually be multiplied, the administrator of the estate must obtain waivers of possible tax claims from several states before the estate may be divided. Litigation to avoid multiple taxation is likewise expensive and time-consuming.

It is probably too much to hope that uniform state laws can ever be established. It is, however, possible that the practice of reciprocity will accomplish essentially the same result. Under a reciprocity law State A does not tax the transfer of intangible property of decedent residents of State B if State B affords the same immunity to residents of State A. The reciprocity movement began after a few forward-looking states had repealed inheritance taxation of intangibles of non-residents only to find that other states refused to fall in line. In self-defense, therefore, they returned to their former systems.[32] A reciprocity law can be enacted, but it does not become effective with respect to another state until the latter state reciprocates. In 1939 approximately thirty states participated in the type of death tax reciprocity described here.[33] It is quite likely that the reciprocity movement can expand but little further. The reason is that the less populous and less wealthy states frequently derive more revenue from the estates of non-residents than from those of residents.[34]

Even if reciprocity were complete the determination of domicile of the decedent might present some problems. Such difficulties sometimes arise in the cases of persons of means who wish domicile in one state for tax reasons

[32] New York and Massachusetts repealed the tax on intangibles of non-residents in 1911 and 1912, respectively. In 1919 and 1920, respectively, these taxes were restored. (F. S. Edmonds, "Progress in Reciprocity in State Inheritance Taxation," *Proceedings, National Tax Association,* 1925, p. 247).

[33] F. S. Edmonds, *Proceedings,* National Tax Association, 1939, p. 406.

[34] "During the past year our committee has conferred with many state tax commissions, and has suggested that they join us in this reciprocity movement. In some cases, we have heard from states whose Tax Commission says, 'We would be glad to recommend reciprocity, but it happens that our state is the home state of a large corporation, most of whose stock is held by non-residents, and we get a very large income from these non-residents and it is very hard for us to give up that income. We do not know what we would do if we were obliged to give up that income.' And then there is quoted to us the stock example of the State of Utah which is the home state of the Union Pacific Railroad, and which received $780,000 by the death of Mr. E. H. Harriman, the great railroad builder, which sum was used to build the State Capitol. Visitors to this state are told, 'We built this Capitol from a non-resident's estate.' " ("Report of Committee of the National Tax Association on Reciprocity in Inheritance Taxation," *Proceedings, National Tax Association,* 1927, p. 414.)

and residence in another for business or personal reasons.[35] Adjudication of such problems involves purely legal processes, and is outside the scope of the present study. Death tax theory is bedeviled by the fact, however, that a person may maintain the legal fiction of domicile in one state while actually residing in another. The state of legal domicile lays claim to death taxes, while the state of residence frequently possesses no such claim.

Compensatory Use of Death Taxes

Death and gift taxes offer practically no counter-cyclical, compensatory, or functional possibilities. They touch at any one time an extremely small segment of the economy and thus cannot conceivably exercise noticeable leverage over the levels of consumption or investment. They are not amenable to timely use, for they are not continuing taxes but are applied only once. Raising or lowering of rates or exemptions through the business cycle could have essentially no effect upon the long-period saving or spending of estate-builders. And although raising rates to discourage lavish spending by the inheritors of windfall legacies might be desired at the moment, such actions would effectively reduce for all time the inheritances of those whose increased spending in some few months might be very desirable. Finally, the time elapsing between death and the final distribution of estates further negates compensatory objectives.

The death and gift taxes are highly desirable as revenue instruments. They produce some vital revenue according to genuine ability to pay. In addition, however, they perform a long-run economic service in their pressure toward redistribution of large concentrations of wealth. It is clearly desirable that these taxes be retained and improved, though they can hardly take a place among compensatory fiscal instruments.

RECOMMENDED READINGS

Eisenstein, Louis, "The Rise and Decline of the Estate Tax," Joint Committee on the Economic Report, *Federal Tax Policy for Economic Growth and Stability (Papers Submitted by Panelists Appearing before the Subcommittee on Tax Policy),* Washington, 1955, pp. 819–47.

An informative paper presenting a brief but long-range history of estate taxation, the faults of current practice, and a pessimistic view of the future.

Hall, J. K., "The Incidence of Death Duties," *American Economic Review,* March, 1940, p. 46.

A useful study, particularly as a summary of theories of death tax incidence.

---

[35] Cf., for instance, the Dorrance case (New Jersey and Pennsylvania), the Trowbridge case (New York and Connecticut), the Hunt case (California and Massachusetts), and the Green case (Texas, Florida, New York, and Massachusetts). Discussion of the issues in these cases may be found in *Proceedings,* National Tax Association, 1939, pp. 423–432.

Harriss, C. L., *Gift Taxation in the United States,* Washington, American Council on Public Affairs, 1940.

The following chapters are particularly recommended: 1 ("Why Gift Taxes?"), 2 ("Gifts in Contemplation of Death"), 4 ("Structure of the Federal Gift Tax"), 8 ("State Taxation of Gifts"), 11 ("Proposals for Change").

Oakes, E. E., "The Federal Offset and the American Death Tax System," *Quarterly Journal of Economics,* August, 1940, pp. 566*ff.*

The history and implications of this significant example of federal-state fiscal relations.

CHAPTER 22

Business Taxes

THE NATURE OF BUSINESS TAXES

Taxes are frequently not what they seem. By no means all the taxes imposed upon businesses or business transactions are technically "business taxes." We have seen, for example, that between 1913 and 1936 the federal corporate income tax was not regarded as a special business tax, but merely as an agency for collection at the source of the personal income tax upon that part of personal incomes derived from corporate profits. And sales taxes are levied upon business with the intention that they be shifted to buyers of products. The states frequently employ "in lieu" taxes, i.e., taxes which may be imposed upon business institutions, but in lieu of certain types of property taxes. For example, some state severance taxes are imposed upon business exploitation of forest or mineral resources, but for purposes of collecting delayed property taxes. At least one state imposes a tax upon the income from investments of insurance companies; this tax is, however, not regarded as a tax upon business as such, but rather as a tax on intangible property measured by the income from intangibles. We are concerned in this chapter not with all taxes applied to business establishments, but with those intended to be paid by business as such, either for the privilege of doing business or because of presumed distinct capacity of a business establishment to contribute to government. A brief survey of business tax proposals will help to clarify this concept.

The National Tax Association's "Model Tax Systems"[1]

The "Model Tax Systems" proposed by the National Tax Association have recommended three types of taxes upon which ideally state and local

[1] "Preliminary Report of the Committee Appointed to Prepare a Plan of a Model System of State and Local Taxation," 1918, *Proceedings, National Tax Association,* 1919, pp. 426 ff., and "Second Report of the Committee on a Model System of State and Local Taxation," 1933, *Proceedings,* National Tax Association, 1933.

tax systems should be founded. The three types are: a tax on tangible property, a tax on personal incomes, and a tax on "business carried on for profit." It is implied that each of these major taxes possesses its own separate justification. Although the special justification of the third is stated to be "for the benefits it receives," the special nature of this justification is so hedged as to suggest serious qualification. The Committee says:[2]

If the owners of the business are residents of the state, this principle may not be appealed to, since the ordinary methods of taxation may be considered to provide for such a case. If a considerable amount of real estate and other personal property is employed in a business conducted for the account of non-residents, again no appeal may be made to this principle, since here too the ordinary methods of taxation may be considered adequate. But if the owners are non-residents, and the business, though very profitable, employs little or no property subject to taxation in the locality, the states, to an increasing degree, demand that some method shall be devised for reaching such business enterprises.

Let us see what this means with respect to theoretical grounds for imposition of a special business tax. The general grounds for justifying it are "the benefits it [business] receives."[3] But according to the statement above, no payment need be made for these business benefits if (1) the owners are residents of the state or (2) the business owns a considerable amount of tangible property in the state. If the owners are residents of the state, state personal income taxes constitute adequate payment for benefits. If the business has considerable tangible property, property taxes will cover benefits received. We are forced to the conclusion that business benefits consist of property and personal benefits, else the exceptions to the business tax in cases where these other taxes are paid would not have been stated. If benefits to business are not distinct from benefits to property and to owners of business, upon what grounds can a state justify special taxation of those businesses owned by non-residents or owning tangible property outside the state? It appears that the Committee's recommendation is to impose unusual tax burdens upon interstate business; the state in which the owners have domicile will receive income taxes from them, the state(s) in which the business holds property will receive property taxes, while the states in which the concern does business (provided owners do not live there or the business owns little or no property there) will collect business taxes. This appears to carry a curious notion of benefit, for it implies that business receives special governmental benefits only when carried on by non-resident owners with non-resident property. However, our principal interest at this point is

[2] *Proceedings*, 1919, p. 430. The same statement appears in the revised report, *Proceedings*, 1933, p. 361.

[3] *Ibid.*

in describing the nature of a "business tax." Curious as its notion of benefit is in this case, the Committee's analysis serves to characterize the business tax as a tax imposed independently of other types of taxes and justified on grounds separate from those which recommend other tax measures.

More Recent Theories of the Business Tax

The large crop of miscellaneous business taxes imposed by both federal and state governments and increasingly by local governments has grown up far more as the result of the desire for revenue than of the development of an acceptable theoretical justification. Nevertheless, there are modern theoretical advocates. Another committee of the National Tax Association justifies business taxes on corporations on grounds of "(1) the special benefits enjoyed by corporations through the peculiar legal privileges granted them to exist and to conduct business in the corporate form and (2) the benefits enjoyed by corporations in common with other forms of ownership organization by virtue of numerous governmental activities contributing to the establishment and maintenance of a favorable environment in which to carry on business activity."[4] And a more elaborate and more recent statement of the theory of business taxation[5] justifies business taxes separate from those on property, personal income, and consumption on "one or the other" of these eight grounds: (1) special privileges (licenses, franchises, or charters) conferred by the state on certain types of business; (2) special services (inspection of dangerous equipment, special protection) rendered to certain businesses; (3) general services (protection of property, enforcement of contracts, public education, public improvements, etc.) rendered to all business; (4) social costs or losses (destruction of national resources, pollution, overcrowding, industrial accidents, technological unemployment, etc.) resulting from certain business operations; (5) impersonal tax-paying capacity of business; (6) general welfare (a means by which to tax the general public through the price system); (7) social expediency (revenue productivity, ease of administration, popular acquiescence); and (8) exercise of desired social controls (discouragement of imports, chain stores, excessive profits). Here the whole gamut of tax justifications appears: benefit, cost, ability, revenue productivity, and control. It is profitable to examine each separately as a justification for special business taxation.

The benefit principle is presumed to justify special business taxation on grounds that the state confers both special benefits upon certain businesses

[4] "Final Report of the Committee of the National Tax Association on Federal Taxation of Corporations," *Proceedings*, National Tax Association, 1939, p. 537.

[5] Paul Studenski, "Toward a Theory of Business Taxation," *Journal of Political Economy*, October, 1940, pp. 621 *ff*.

and general benefits upon the business community as a whole. Among the special benefits are: the privilege of conducting business under the corporate form; the privilege granted to public utilities to operate on the public domain (on, over, and under city streets); the privilege of conducting special types of business in which the public possesses a special concern for the quality of performance; and special protection of various sorts. It is easily granted that such benefits do exist. But it is quite another matter to justify general business taxes upon such grounds. The administrative revenues, such as fines, fees, permits, licenses, etc., represent payment for the receipt of special governmental benefits. Government is, therefore, "working both sides of the street" in imposing additional business taxes on grounds of special benefit. The privilege of incorporation is open to all under modern statutes; the administrative cost of issuing the charter is supposedly covered by the fee. In the case of public utilities, the franchise to operate on the public domain as a monopoly is frequently paid for, but the real *quid pro quo* is public regulation of rates and practices to secure for the society a desired service of good quality at reasonable rates. What special benefit remains to justify the imposition of a business tax? In those business fields where the public interest requires regulation of certain phases of operation, such as the inspection of elevators and control of the conditions under which milk, meat, drugs, medicines, and similar items are produced and distributed, the cost of inspection and administration are generally met by special license fees. The benefits of such inspection and regulation do not accrue to the business, but to the consuming public; it is difficult to justify taxation of the business on benefit grounds. Where special protection of property is needed, there is a growing tendency to provide such protection privately. Businesses frequently provide their own watchmen, police, and fire inspectors, build with fireproof materials, construct fences or walls, and provide facilities for safekeeping of valuables. When special protection is furnished by government, this is quite generally done at a price. Under such circumstances the justification of general business taxation on grounds of special protection is largely unreal.

The general benefits presumed to justify special taxation of business present somewhat similar problems of allocation. These general benefits are: protection of life and property, prevention of torts, enforcement of contracts, public improvements, public education, and all those conditions of a favorable business climate which are encouraged by the performance of general governmental functions. The translation of such general benefit into specific tax bills implies an ability to allocate such benefits which does not exist. Clearly, business does benefit from the maintenance of an orderly society. But business is merely an aspect of that society; society itself benefits from orderliness. Indeed, the benefit principle of taxation appears to foster the popular inversion of the facts by assuming that society exists for business and social stability is desired for purposes of business stability. In general terms, a desirable business climate is but a part of a desirable social climate—a productive economy is essential to a productive society. This being the case, we recognize protection of life and property, public education, and public improvements to be means to social objectives, with which economic objectives are merged. The attempt to allocate general benefits to individual businesses is thus both futile and unreal. The allocation of tax obligations must logically conform to the ability principle.

But does the ability principle support a separate category of taxes on business? In other words, do business enterprises possess tax-paying ability distinct from the abilities of those who derive income from business? The preponderance of expert opinion appears to answer this question in the negative, though there are staunch supporters of the belief that "business enterprises are producing organizations having a personality of their own,"[6] and thus have separate tax-paying capacity from that of the individuals who compose them. What is required here is a re-examination of the ability principle. Ability to pay is ability to give up; the less the sacrifice involved in transferring a dollar to government the greater that taxpayer's ability. It has no relevance for a business as such, but only for those who derive income from the business. Professor Studenski, a strong supporter of the belief that business does possess separate ability, appears to qualify his position when he says: "This ability, *except in personally conducted businesses,* is distinct from the personal abilities of the owners to pay taxes from their incomes."[7] The implication is that in personally conducted businesses the ability of the business and of the owner are identical. But does the corporate form of the separation of the functions of ownership and management create a new and distinct ability? If so, at what point does this distinct ability appear as we pass from the personally conducted to the impersonally conducted business? It would seem quite obvious that the business organization is but an instrument for the production of personal income, and that the form of business organization and the techniques of business operation do not alter that basic fact. We recall again our basic principle that taxes are paid from the stream of personal incomes. Taxes collected on incomes prior to their distribution to individuals reduce realized individual incomes by the amount of those taxes. Thus the tax burden is upon individuals, and in most cases is badly

[6] Studenski, *op. cit.*, p. 632.
[7] *Op. cit.*, p. 633. Italics added.

allocated among them because it is levied before distribution and therefore typically bears little relation to individual ability.

We may dismiss rather quickly the need for revenue and the desire to exercise control as justifications for business taxation. The need for revenue is a perfectly respectable need, provided it is sufficiently subordinated to the need for elementary justice and the objective of a high level of business activity. These primary objectives call for distribution of the revenue burden on the bases of ability and (when pertinent or possible) benefit. But a tax which does not qualify under the principles of ability or benefit can hardly qualify as an acceptable producer of revenue. The control function may be perfectly well accomplished through special types of business taxation. It cannot, however, justify general taxation of business *per se,* and therefore is hardly pertinent to the matter in hand.

The elaborate case for business taxation as a major pillar of the fiscal system is a shoddy one at best. Separately considered, the particular theories supporting such taxes are found to be either unacceptable or acceptable only when applied in limited and special situations. But to argue that there are many such special situations and that therefore general business taxation is justified on "one or the other" of several grounds is obviously an invitation to blind pursuit of revenue at any cost. It is comparable with an argument that with so many laws it is inevitable that each person must have broken at least one, and that therefore everyone should periodically serve a jail sentence.[8]

Types of State Business Taxes

As stated at the beginning of this chapter, it is frequently difficult to determine which taxes in a state system are intended as business taxes. Many states still utilize the property tax as a major contributor to revenues, and in its administration it is frequently desirable to impose property taxes on businesses measured by gross or net income. These are not intended as business taxes, but as property taxes. On the other hand, the recent rise in importance of consumption taxes frequently presents a problem in determining whether a tax upon gross receipts finds its justification in the theory of consumption or of business taxation. And finally, among those states employing the personal income tax as a major fiscal measure, several utilize corporate income taxes as adjuncts to personal income taxes. We are interested here in those taxes upon business which are given separate existence from property, per-

---

[8] The frail theoretical rationale by which general business taxes are "justified" falls apart completely when the incidence of particular business taxes is considered. This matter will be pursued later in the chapter, following description of major types of existing business taxes.

sonal income, and consumption taxes, and find their theoretical rationale in the arguments of special benefit or special ability discussed earlier in this chapter.

Attempts at uniform taxation of business enterprises early meet the basic difficulty that business itself is so hetergeneous as to offer few if any simple and uniform tax bases. And sooner or later in the process of constructing an acceptable business tax system it becomes necessary to grapple with the basic question whether the tax is in fact based upon benefit or upon ability. The principal types of business taxes are those based upon net or gross income and those based upon the amount of capital employed.

Business Taxes on Net Income. Were it not for two difficulties—one theoretical and one practical—it is highly probable that a general preference would exist for business taxes based on net income. The theoretical difficulty is found in the assumption that by and large the general benefit principle is material to business taxation. The benefits of a favorable business climate are extended to unprofitable as well as profitable concerns, while under a net income tax only the profitable concern pays for these benefits. Here is a clear conflict between the principle of benefit and the principle of ability. The practical difficulty in a general business net income tax lies in the lack of uniformity among business accounting systems. Quite obviously, if the base of the tax is to be net income it is important that all taxpayers compute net income by the same method. Yet the reader may look at the multiplicity of types of business establishments in his own community to observe the difficulties involved in imposing uniform and accurate accounting systems upon all businesses. In unincorporated retail trade and service establishments such a procedure is hardly imaginable. For this reason, those states which employ business net income taxes generally apply them only to incorporated businesses. The accounting systems of corporations are in general far superior to those of the average unincorporated firms, particularly in view of the standardization of corporate accounting methods made necessary by the long-standing federal corporate income tax. State corporate net income taxes almost uniformly employ flat rates. In some cases a minimum annual tax of a flat amount is assessed, to pay for benefits conferred, while a net income tax is paid when its amount exceeds the minimum tax. Here is the curious implication that the business pays its tax on the basis of either "ability" or "benefit," which ever is the greater.

"Business" Taxes on Gross Income.[9] Taxes levied upon the gross income of a business are actually sales taxes. The amount of the tax is measured

[9] We lump together taxes based on "gross income," "gross receipts," and "gross earnings," which, although they are not precisely the same, are generally similar in nature.

by the volume of sales, its imposition adds directly to variable costs of production or distribution, and its incidence is identical with that of a tax on sales. Failure to recognize this fact has led many state governments to assume that because the tax is imposed upon businesses as such, and because it is called a "business tax," it is therefore essentially similar to a tax upon the net income of a business.

"Business" taxes on gross income have generally been applied to unincorporated businesses and to public utility concerns, for two reasons. The first is that the business benefits provided by government are made available irrespective of the amount of *net* income earned by the firm, and that even unprofitable firms should bear their share of the cost. The second reason is that if net income were used as the base of the tax, it would be necessary to insist upon uniformity in accounting systems, so that net income would be determined by the same process in all of these miscellaneous unincorporated firms. Since imposition of uniformity in accounting systems upon small, miscellaneous firms is impracticable, the gross income base has been adopted.[10] Uniformity in the method of calculating net income does exist among corporations, since the federal corporation income tax has long required it. But a shift in tax bases from net to gross income, for whatever reason, involves basic change in the type of tax. The business net income tax on business is paid from the net income of the business, while a "business" gross income tax is a tax primarily upon consumers, and is not a business tax at all.[11]

Capital Stock Taxes. Nearly every state imposes some sort of tax on the capital stock or net worth of general corporations. It is difficult, however, to determine to what extent legislators have used these taxes as business taxes. In many instances they are producers of small revenue and they are undoubtedly used in many cases as a substitute for property taxes on corporations. But in several states this "corporation franchise tax" is a business tax, resting upon the justification of special benefit conferred on businesses operating under the corporate form of organization. If possible, this type of tax ignores "ability" even more completely than does the gross in-

---

[10] A further reason why the net income tax may not be practicable for unincorporated businesses is that, being closely held, it is possible to avoid the appearance of high net income by payment of a high salary to the owner.

[11] Business gross income taxes are generally applied by states to public utilities and railroads. This is done partly to avoid the use of net income, which is the principal datum in rate regulation, frequently because the tax is intended as a tax on consumers, and generally because gross income represents a base which is more easily proportioned to the intrastate operations of an interstate business than is net income. But whatever the reason, the tax is a tax on sales and is not a "business tax."

come tax, for the ratio of net income to capital will vary even more widely than does the ratio of net to gross income.[12]

Taxation of Special Types of Business. We have already noted widespread use of the gross income business tax upon public utility enterprises. This is due to the special nature of these enterprises. But there are other business areas in which special types of business taxes have been imposed. Notable among them are banks and insurance companies. The peculiarities of bank taxation by the states have been due primarily to federal legislation limiting the types of taxes which the states could impose upon national banks.[13] We shall not consider the intracacies of the legal limitations upon state taxation of national banks. But in general, the problem of state taxation of banks has been to steer a course between the desire to equalize tax burdens among various types of business on the one hand, and the tax limitations imposed upon the states by the National Banking Act on the other.[14]

The taxation of insurance companies raises special problems, not because of federal restrictions but because of the necessity for selection of special tax bases to provide business tax burdens comparable with those on other businesses.[15] The calculation of net income is difficult, in view of the uncertainty of the volume of reserves required to meet fluctuating insurance claims. Furthermore, the computation of net income for tax purposes in mutual companies is well-nigh impossible. The absence of capital stock in mutual companies rules out a popular base for the business franchise tax. The most popular type of insurance business tax is levied on net premiums, i.e., gross premium receipts less some or all of returned premiums, cancellations, dividends, and premiums on reinsurance. The typical base is thus similar to gross income, though qualified to take account of practices peculiar to the insurance business.

Productivity of State Business Taxes. Little precise information can be given concerning the revenue productivity of state business taxes. This is due partly to the difficulties involved in acquiring comparable data from the various states, but, to a more important degree, is due to the difficulty of distinguishing in the statistics true business taxes from other types. It is

---

[12] This is particularly true when the franchise tax uses as its base the par or paid-in value of capital stock. When the base is net worth, it is only slightly less true.

[13] For detailed discussion of bank taxation, see Ronald B. Welch, *State and Local Taxation of Banks in the United States*, 1934, Special Report to the (New York State) Tax Commission. No. 7.

[14] Specifically, Section 5219, Revised Statutes.

[15] See *Report of Connecticut Temporary Commission*, 1934, Chapter 13, for a good analytical treatment of insurance company taxation.

quite evident, however, that the business taxes contribute but a meager proportion of state revenue collections. The Federation of Tax Administrators reported that in 1939 state corporation income taxes produced 3.5 per cent of tax and license revenues of the states.[16] A part of this should be credited to source collections of personal income taxes, while small lump sum tax collections from unincorporated businesses should probably be added to arrive at a total of business tax revenues. In 1942 this figure had risen to 7 per cent of total tax and license revenues, and by 1958 it had reached about 10 per cent. The states draw more revenue from fees and license charges upon business than from general or special business taxes.

Federal Business Taxes

It is quite generally presumed that the field of business taxation represents a revenue preserve of the state and local governments. This presumption grows out of the benefit principle of business taxation—the benefits, both general and specific, conferred upon business are presumed to flow principally from state and local governments. In the light of recently developed interest in economic affairs by the federal government, it is doubtful that the creation of an economic climate can any longer be attributed principally to state and local governments. And the period (since 1930) during which the federal government established itself as a primary influence in economic and business affairs has seen rapid expansion of federal business taxation. This development is partly accidental and partly inevitable. The accidental aspects relate almost wholly to the war and the excess profits tax. The inevitable aspects relate to the corporation income tax; the inevitability is, however, accounted for by revenue needs rather than by any rationale with respect to federal benefits conferred upon business. These two taxes— corporation income and excess profits—represent the business tax measures employed by the federal government.[17]

The Federal Corporation Income Tax. We have seen in Chapter 16 how the corporation income tax was employed in 1913 simply as an instrument for collection of the personal income tax on dividends at the source. Although beginning with World War I the two taxes followed somewhat divergent courses, resulting in heavier burdens upon dividend incomes than upon other incomes, the separation was not complete until the Act of 1936. By this Act, it will be recalled, not only was the corporate surtax of the previous year continued, but dividends in the hands of individuals became

---

[16] Research Report No. 16, *Recent Trends in State Revenues,* Chicago (no date), p. 6.

[17] This ignores the federal capital stock tax and declared value excess profits tax, employed from 1933 to 1945. Both were troublesome, unpopular, and unproductive taxes, adopted in lieu of an increase in corporation income taxes.

subject to personal normal and surtaxes after having paid corporate normal and surtaxes as corporate net income. It can hardly be said that this fission of the income tax system which created a full-fledged federal business tax was the product of rational analysis. It was a purely opportunist action, motivated by the desire for revenue.

The corporation income tax applies essentially the same computations employed by the personal income tax. From gross receipts (or sales) of the corporation are deducted the costs of production, including interest on the firm's bonded debt, taxes, uncompensated losses, contributions, interest on tax-free government securities, and 85 per cent of dividends received from other taxed corporations. A special allowance for amortization of plant and equipment purchased for military production is provided in the 1951 Act. This permits deduction of 20 per cent of the cost of such equipment per year for a period of five years from gross income in arriving at net income.[18] Net capital gain is included as income and taxed at the rates applicable to ordinary net income, though if there is an excess of net long-term capital gain over net short-term capital loss, the alternative method of taxing this excess at a flat 25 per cent rate is available if a smaller tax will thereby result. There can be no net capital loss deductible in any year from other income, though an excess of capital losses may be carried forward for a period of five years and deducted from capital gains in those years. The corporate normal tax rate since the 1951 Act has been 30 per cent; the surtax at a flat rate of 22 per cent is applied to taxable income in excess of $25,000.[19]

Table 34 shows the revenue importance of the federal corporation income tax for selected recent years. The reader will recognize that the figures are not entirely comparable, for prior to 1936 a share of corporate income tax revenues represented collection of personal income taxes on dividends at the source. The severe decline in relative importance during World War II is due not to absolute decline in corporate tax revenues, but to marked increase in revenue from the personal income tax, the excess profits tax, and the miscellaneous excises. In 1945, for example, corporation income tax receipts were nearly $5 billion, and were exceeded by revenues from individual income taxes (ca. $19 billion), excess profits taxes (ca. $11 billion), and miscellaneous excises (ca. $7 billion).[20] The greater relative significance of the corporation income tax since 1945 is explainable on several grounds.

[18] This deduction is allowable only for plant and equipment acquired after December 31, 1949, and certified as necessary by the appropriate governmental authority.

[19] The normal tax base is the same as the surtax base except for the exclusion of minor amounts of interest on certain federal bonds from the former, and exclusion of the first $25,000 from the latter.

[20] *Annual Report of the Secretary of the Treasury, 1945*, pp. 724–26.

The corporate tax rates were essentially maintained through the postwar years of great expansion of corporate output and rising prices, making for marked increase in the absolute amount brought in by the tax. In addition, individual income tax rates were lowered in 1948 and the higher rates of

TABLE 34

FEDERAL CORPORATE INCOME TAX RECEIPTS AS PER CENT OF
TOTAL INTERNAL REVENUE, SELECTED YEARS*

Year	Corporate Income Tax Receipts ($ millions)	Per Cent of Total Internal Revenue Receipts [a]
1923	937	54.8
1928	1,292	46.3
1932	630	40.4
1939	2,151	41.5
1945	4,880	11.1
1950	10,854	27.5
1955	18,265	27.6
1959	18,092	22.7

* Figures taken from *Statistical Abstract*, 1924, 1933, 1940, 1946, 1947, 1951; Treasury *Annual Report*, 1956; and monthly *Treasury Statement*, June, 1959.

[a] Internal revenue is all revenue less customs and non-tax revenue.

the Korean War did not become effective until fiscal 1950; the wartime excess profits tax was repealed during fiscal 1946 and the new excess profits taxes of the Korean War had disappeared before 1955.

These figures indicate a heavy federal dependence upon the business income tax. Unfortunately, it is impossible to justify this dependence on rational grounds of tax justice, or the principles of benefit or ability. It is particularly to be noted that the federal business tax applies only to those businesses operating under the corporate form of organization. The share of business done and income received by unincorporated business in the United States is by no means insignificant; yet such concerns are freed from federal business taxation. It would seem that if the separate taxation of business is reasonable, comparable taxes should be placed upon all types of business. Yet this is done neither by the federal government nor by most states.

The Federal Excess Profits Tax.[21] The excess profits tax is essentially a wartime phenomenon. During peacetime the notion of taxing "excess" profits is generally regarded as inconsistent with the principles under which

[21] A readable and useful book, dealing principally with the historical and descriptive aspects of this subject is Kenneth J. Curran, *Excess Profits Taxation*, Washington, American Council on Public Affairs, 1943. For an analytical discussion, and for special reference to British experience, see J. R. Hicks, V. K. Hicks, and L. Rostas, *The Taxation of War Wealth*, Oxford, 1941. A. G. Hart and E. D. Allen, *Paying for Defense*, Philadelphia, Blakiston, 1941, presents a good short discussion, especially in Chapter 12.

the private enterprise system operates. For in peace, high profits when they occur are presumed to be the prize for successful acceptance of risk—not infrequently offset by heavy losses—or the prize for efficient management under competitive conditions. To impose a tax penalty upon temporarily high profits is to discourage both the assumption of risk and the drive to greater efficiency. If abnormally high profits exist over a long period of time in any business, the appropriate line of attack is probably through anti-monopoly legislation.

In wartime, however, conditions are quite different. The need for revenue —generally the overriding fiscal consideration in times of emergency—is acute. Further, it is generally regarded as unfair and destructive of war morale that excessive profits should be realized during a period of national emergency when heavy sacrifices are being borne by the major portion of the society. These two factors—revenue needs and public antipathy toward war "profiteers"—almost exclusively account for the imposition of excess profits taxes in the United States during World War I. While these same factors were dominant in urging profits taxation in World War II, certain economic refinements were added to the argument. The prevention of serious general price increase was strongly desired. This implied transfers of excess profit incomes to government, both to remove from private hands funds which could add to inflationary pressure and to absorb investment funds which might otherwise be placed in nonessential production and thus waste scarce productive resources. War profiteering was to be avoided not only on account of its social injustice but because of the opportunity it gave scarce and highly organized labor to drive for higher wages, both on grounds of elementary fairness and of the increase in living costs. Among experts, however, the function of excess profits taxation was regarded less as an anti-profiteer instrument than as one of many tools for the prevention of serious inflation.

During World War I excess profits taxation began in the United States as a pure *war profits* tax on munitions makers. By the Act of 1916, an excise was imposed upon net profits from the sale of munitions, very narrowly defined. It became evident rather soon, however, that war profits do not accrue only to the makers of some war instruments, and by two acts of 1917 profits taxation was made to apply to others than the sellers of munitions. The first of these two acts (March) applied only to partnerships and corporations, and was a *high profits* or *excess profits* tax since its base was those profits of any firm in excess of 8 per cent of invested capital. The second of these acts (October) provided essentially a *war profits* tax, whose base was profits in excess of the average of the "normal" years of 1911–1913. However, a high profits qualification was introduced by considering as normal profits only those up to 9 per cent of invested capital. The tax applied to all forms of business organization. By the Revenue Act of 1918 a new system, called the "War Profits and Excess Profits Tax," was inaugurated. It applied only to corporations; the war profits tax base was the excess of profit in the taxable year over the average 1911–1913 profit, while the excess profits tax base was profit in excess of 8 per cent of invested capital. The taxpayer was liable for the larger of the two taxes.[22]

The war and excess profits taxes were repealed in 1921. During the period of their operation (1917–1922) they produced total revenue of more than $7 billion, nearly one-fourth of all federal revenue receipts of that period.[23] Excess profits taxes exceeded income tax revenues during the war years 1917 and 1918. Curran's analysis of the "netness" of excess profits tax revenues points out, however, that without profits taxes, personal and/or corporate income taxes would have been increased, for three reasons: (1) payment of profits taxes reduced the magnitude of the stream of dividends, and thus reduced the personal income tax base; (2) profits taxes paid were deductible from net income for corporate income tax purposes, and for individual income tax purposes when profits taxes were assessed against individual enterprises; and (3) the high excess profits tax encouraged evasion and avoidance. Avoidance was possible by excessive expenditures on advertising and personnel relations, so as to reduce net income, and by postponing capital gains and realizing capital losses. Though the total revenue effect upon the income tax of such provisions and actions was probably considerable, it is nevertheless true that the excess profits tax was highly productive of net revenue.

Some brief mention should be made of the declared value excess profits tax, originated in 1933 and repealed by the Revenue Act of 1945. This measure should not be regarded, however, as a serious attempt to tax excess profits in peacetime, but rather as an adjunct of the capital stock tax, whose life span was identical with it. The capital stock tax was levied at the rate of 0.1 per cent on the capital stock of a corporation. To avoid difficulties of evaluation, the tax-paying corporation was allowed to place its own value upon its stock. And in order to forestall too low an evaluation for tax purposes the declared value excess profits tax was employed, placing a tax of 5 per cent upon all profits in excess of 12½ per cent of the declared capital

---

[22] Some of the more intricate problems of profits taxation will be considered in connection with excess profits taxation in World War II.

[23] Curran, *op. cit.*, p. 136.

stock value.[24] It is reasonable to conclude that in general the revenues produced by the declared value excess profits tax ($117 million in 1945) should in fact be considered as capital stock tax revenues ($372 million in 1945).[25] Professor Groves has characterized these two taxes in the following terms:

They add little to the tax system but complication, extra compliance costs, and occasionally capricious results, and they are essentially inimical to small companies. Calculation for these taxes is carried on in an artificial atmosphere all but divorced from reality; they are a lawyer's plaything rather than a producer's levy; and they serve principally as a monument to the misdirected ingenuity of taxmakers.[26]

The World War II excess profits tax was inaugurated in 1940. Although the United States was more than a year away from active military participation, her role as the "arsenal of democracy" created the type of war economic atmosphere to which an excess profits tax is a modern integral part. The taxpayer was allowed to choose whether to subject himself to a strictly war profits tax or a strictly excess profits tax. He had the choice of calculating his "normal" (and thus not "excess") profits as 95 per cent of his average profits for the years 1936–1939, or as 8 per cent of his invested capital.[27] Only corporations were subject to the tax, and the computation of net profits followed closely the computation of net income under the corporation income tax.

Rates were subjected to several changes during the war period; in 1940 they were graduated from 25 per cent to 50 per cent, while from 1944 on a flat rate of 95 per cent was imposed, with the over-all proviso that corporate income and excess profits taxes could not exceed 80 per cent of the corporation's surtax net income. The revenue produced by this tax during the war years is indicated below.[28] As in the case of the World War I profits tax, this cannot all be considered net revenue, though particularly in the later years the net revenue contribution was very substantial.

[24] The corporation which guessed wrongly as to its future earnings (it was assumed that the value of capital stock would be determined by capitalization of expected earnings) might well experience real penalty in this excess profits tax. It was not until 1942 that this situation was largely eliminated by allowing the corporation to revise the declaration of the value of its capital stock annually.

[25] *Annual Report of the Secretary of the Treasury,* 1945, p. 724.

[26] Reprinted by permission from pp. 82, 83 of *Postwar Taxation and Economic Progress,* by Harold M. Groves, copyright, 1946, by the Committee for Economic Development and published by the McGraw-Hill Book Company, Inc.

[27] Firms not in existence during the base period were of course required to compute their tax on the invested capital base. By an amendment of 1941, new capital invested was added to the base at 125 per cent of its amount, in order to encourage expansion. Firms which had shown marked increase in profits during the period 1936–1939 were allowed a normal profits base in excess of their average through the period.

[28] *Statistical Abstract of the United States,* 1946, p. 319.

Year	Revenue ($ millions)
1941	192.4
1942	1,670.4
1943	5,146.3
1944	9,482.2
1945	11,147.3

Certain features of the World War II tax are worthy of consideration. The earlier rate schedules were progressive with the size of excess profits net income. They were not, therefore, adjusted to individual ability to pay, as individual abilities are in no marked degree correlated with the magnitude of a corporation's excess income. In 1944, with the shift to a flat rate, consideration for the small enterprise (which would supposedly be more seriously affected by postwar adjustments) was introduced by raising the minimum of excess profits exempt from taxation from $5,000 to $10,000.[29]

As noted above, the taxpayer was given his choice between two methods of computing excess profits. The income method based "normal" profits on the average of net income plus all advertising expenditures during the base period 1936–1939. Ninety-five per cent of the average "normal" profit during the base period was regarded as "excess profits net income." The term is somewhat misleading, but represents the amount of profits regarded as not excessive. This reflects a presumption that actual profits during the base period were slightly above "normal." To the excess profits net income was added 8 per cent of additions to capital since the base period, to provide "normal" return on new capital (quite inconsistently, only 6 per cent of capital reductions since the base period were deducted from excess profits net income). The base of the tax in any year was net income for the taxable year less "excess profits credit" (the sum of excess profits net income and 8 per cent of capital additions), less unused excess profits credit carried forward or backward two years, and less the specific exemption ($5,000, $10,000 or $25,000 depending upon the year).

The invested capital method involved a quite different computation, to be used at the option of the taxpayer or in cases where the taxpayer was not operating during the base period.[30] This method looked toward taxation of "high" or "excess" profits, and determined the amount of excess by comparison of profits with a standard or appropriate return. Determination of the tax base by the invested capital method began with the net income of the firm for the taxable year. From this figure three deductions were made

[29] $25,000 after December 31, 1945.

[30] If the taxpayer was operating during a part, but not all of the base period, he was entitled to use 8 per cent of invested capital as base period income in any year during which he was not in operation.

to determine taxable excess profits: (1) the percentage[31] return on invested capital considered "normal" and not excessive; (2) the specific exemption of $10,000 or $25,000 (the latter for the year 1946); and (3) unused credit carried over from the preceding two years.[32] In an outline description of this sort numbers (2) and (3) require no elaboration, though the determination of "invested capital" should be explained. It consisted, in general, of the daily average of the net worth (capital, surplus, and undivided profits) of the corporation plus one-half of borrowed capital represented by written evidences of debt. The inclusion of 8 (6 or 5) per cent of but one-half of borrowed capital in the excess profits credit is more liberal than was the 1918 law, which made no provision for inclusion of borrowed capital. On the other hand, no more than one-half of borrowed capital was permitted on grounds that the allowed per cent of invested capital regarded as normal profit was in most cases far in excess of interest paid for the use of that capital. Without this limitation the profit position after taxes of the owners of a firm with a small proportion of equity capital and a large proportion of borrowed capital would be superior to that of a firm in the opposite circumstances. Such a provision would presumably encourage the retirement of debt out of net income, placing the firm in a somewhat stronger postwar position.

A further provision of World War II excess profits taxation is of special economic significance. Concerns constructing, acquiring, or installing "war emergency facilities" were allowed to amortize the cost of such facilities over a period of sixty months. The provision was included to encourage private provision of new war production facilities by considering their service life to be no longer than five years. The major risk in undertaking plant extensions lay in the possibility that they would represent excess capacity after termination of the war emergency. This amortization allowance was handled as a cost of operation deductible from gross income in arriving at the base of both the corporate income tax and the excess profits tax.[33] To the extent that it was utilized, corporations should have emerged from the war in a position to undertake peacetime production with lower plant overhead. Some three-fourths of war emergency facilities are estimated to have been provided by federal government corporations out of Treasury

[31] The percentages allowed were 8 per cent of the first $5 million of invested capital, 6 per cent of that amount between $5 million and $10 million, and 5 per cent of that amount over $10 million. The revenue objective is here evident.

[32] A carry-back for two years was also permitted. This would result in a refund.

[33] Computation of excess profits tax began with corporation normal tax net income. Thus the amortization deduction applied to calculation of both taxes.

borrowed funds,[34] the remainder representing private investment. Because of the tax provision for rapid amortization, and the liberality of prices paid by government for war materials, government actually paid for a large share of that portion of emergency facilities normally provided by private concerns. It is quite possible that in terms of over-all effect, the provision of emergency facilities would have been cheaper to government if it had furnished the whole and increased its tax revenues by avoiding the amortization deduction.

Finally, we have seen that the excess profits tax provided for a two-year carry-back or carry-forward of unused excess profits credit. Under the Revenue Act of 1945, which repealed the excess profits tax as of December 31, 1945, unused excess profits credits were allowed for a taxable year beginning before January 1, 1947. Thus, though there was no excess profits tax collectible on 1946 or 1947 profits, concerns were allowed to carry forward excess profits credits for those years. This meant that firms which in 1946 or part of 1947 failed to earn amounts equal to what would have been allowed as excess profits credit when the tax was in force, could receive rebates to that extent from excess profits paid in 1944 and 1945. The intent of this provision was to assist firms through the reconversion period. Corporate reports indicate that many firms which showed profits in 1946 actually made some part or all these profits out of excess profits tax rebates. The charge made by representatives of organized labor that the tax refund provisions of the Act of 1945 made it possible for strike-bound firms to delay coming to terms in 1945 and 1946 was undoubtedly true in some instances. By a curious twist of fate, in such cases a pro-labor government helped to finance employer opposition to labor's demands.

Evaluation of Excess Profits Tax Experience in World War II. The tax, designed to provide large war revenues, prevent the creation of "war millionaires," and combat inflation, was only moderately successful. Large revenues were produced, though they doubtless could have been larger without discouraging production. The record of corporate profits after taxes shows no absence of the stuff of which millionaires are made. This is explained in Groves' statement: "The war excess-profits tax is an example of the propensity of Congress to levy a tax at conspicuously high rates but with a relatively 'easy' base."[35] Certainly the man in the street is not satisfied

---

[34] A. D. H. Kaplan has shown that of a total of $22 billion in new industrial facilities created during the war just under $16 billion was financed with public, as distinguished from private, funds. ("Liquidating War Production," in S. E. Harris, *Economic Reconstruction*, New York, McGraw-Hill, 1946, p. 133.)

[35] Reprinted by permission from p. 75 of *Postwar Taxation and Economic Progress*, by Harold M. Groves, copyright, 1946, by the Committee for Economic Development and published by the McGraw-Hill Book Company, Inc.

that the creation of war millionaires was prevented; nor did labor's actions in the war and immediate postwar periods indicate official labor belief that war profits were reasonably moderated by the tax.

As for the prevention of inflation, although the war record was good, the credit is due far more to direct price controls and rationing than to taxation. Obviously, the excess profits tax alone could not hold the price line, even if it had operated perfectly. War experience indicates that what was needed was an effective companion to a more effective excess profits tax. A companion frequently recommended was a general "excess income tax," which would apply the excess profits tax principle to other types of income and to profits derived from unincorporated businesses.[36] It is probable, however, that a more vigorous increase in personal income tax rates, combined with severe lowering of personal exemptions, could have accomplished the same purpose effectively.[37] The question may logically be raised why with heavier personal income taxation the excess profits tax could not have been dispensed with. The answer lies principally in the ineffectiveness of the personal income tax as then and now constituted in preventing the escape of undistributed corporate profits from personal income taxation.

It is difficult to mourn the repeal of the excess profits tax. Its sole peacetime use, in view of the existence of other income taxes, would appear to be as an instrument for discouraging monopoly profits and thus discouraging monopolistic organization and practice. Yet, there must be more effective direct methods of dealing with the monopoly problem. The excess profits tax, if severe enough to confiscate monopoly profits, might at the same time discourage risk-taking and the furtherance of efficiency in production. And one might argue that the tax with which we have had experience favors the steady (though rather high) profit income which characterizes monopoly while burdening the fluctuating incomes typical of venturesome employment of capital in a competitive economy. If this is a fair observation a peacetime excess profits tax similar to that employed during the recent war might well encourage monopoly.[38]

The Excess Profits Tax of 1950. The outbreak of hostilities in Korea and the early participation of the United States in the fighting created immediate inflationary pressures and promised heavy military expenditures in the United States. The tax program presented by the President called for

[36] This recommendation was urged by (among others) Hicks, Hicks, and Rostas, *op. cit.*

[37] This is not to say that fiscal measures could have been substituted for direct controls, but that direct control could have been more effective and more simple with stronger fiscal support.

[38] Groves presents substantially this point, *op. cit.*, pp. 76–77.

increases in personal and corporate income taxes, and the reimposition of an excess profits tax. Experience during World War II had led rather naturally to the presumption that an excess profits tax is a proper component of the battery of war revenue measures. In addition, corporate profits had been high through the postwar period and the flash of inflation which followed the outbreak of hostilities in June, 1950, promised a further boost in business profits. Legislation of an excess profits tax was probably a condition necessarily attached to the popular acceptance of higher personal income taxes and direct wage controls.

The usual two alternative bases for determination of a corporation's "excess profits credit"—the portion of its profits regarded as "normal" and therefore not subject to excess profits tax—were employed. The first was 83 per cent of the average net income for the best three of the four years 1946–1949. Since these were, in general, profitable years for corporations, it was believed that the selection of the best three years would create a liberal base and eliminate many applications for special relief. If, however, the condition of a company's earnings was such in several of those years as to create hardship by the use of this average, the company might be permitted to adopt as its own a figure which was typical of the industry to which it belonged. If the average income base was used, and the corporation had made capital additions or had experienced capital reductions since the base period, it added to or subtracted from its three-year average 12 per cent of the additions or reductions. This rather high calculated rate of "normal" return on new capital appears to have been designed to reward expansion and penalize contraction of plant.

The second alternative method of calculating normal profits as a first step in determining excess profits was the invested capital method. By this method the law considered as normal profits a specific percentage return on the invested capital of the firm. (The determination of the invested capital figure was complex and would add unnecessary detail to our discussion here.) Profits in excess of 12 per cent on the first $5 million of invested capital, 10 per cent on the next $5 million, and 8 per cent on the remainder were defined as excess by this method. These generous allowances reflected the fact of high profits in the base prewar-period; they also reflected a desire to treat smaller and growing corporations with relative leniency.

The excess profits tax was imposed upon a base which was the net income of the corporation as calculated for corporation income tax purposes, less the excess profits credit for those profits considered normal. The excess profits were then taxed at a flat rate of 30 per cent, but the excess profits tax could not be greater than 18 per cent of net income before subtraction of the excess profits credit. The establishment of the 18 per cent ceiling meant that, with minor reservations, a return of 12 per cent on invested capital was permitted without regard to the size of the firm.

We have previously noted Professor Groves' observation made at the end of World War II that American practice is to apply high rates of excess profits tax to an easy base. The 1950 Act employed the "easy" base, but applied a comparatively low rate. Several reasons may be noted for legislative moderation in the passage of this law. A major reason was that the rates of taxation on corporation net income had already been significantly raised, and it was believed that relatively little scope remained for application of the excess profits tax. A second major reason was concern over the incentive effects of a high excess profits tax in an "emergency" which was far from being an all-out war. It may be that the Congress was unimpressed with the value of an excess profits tax as an anti-inflation tool, and was inclined to emphasize wage increases and heavy consumer expenditures as the principal inflationary forces. In addition, the excess profits tax had proved difficult to administer, with many individual applications for relief, and these difficulties multiplied as the tax became more pressing upon taxpayers. Finally, there had developed a general belief that high corporate taxes encouraged wasteful expenditure as deductible costs, and therefore waste of resources, and that consequently they not only contributed in this way to inflation but discouraged the efficient allocation of scarce resources in emergency production. The combination of these reasons explains the relatively moderate tax of 1950; the same reasons will explain the readiness to drop the excess profits tax at the end of 1954.

Incidence of Business Taxes

To this point we have presented the rationale of a category of business taxes separate from those on property, income, and consumption, and have briefly described the principal types employed by state and federal governments. These principal types are net income, excess profits, gross income, and capital stock taxes. Net income and excess profits taxes are typically not shifted in the short run for reasons developed in the analysis of net income taxes in Chapter 14. The demand for a firm's product being given, the imposition of a net income tax does not change that demand. This being the case, the firm's choice of the proper quantity to be produced at the price the market will pay for that quantity does not change with imposition of the tax. The total income—price times quantity—which produces maximum net

income before taxes will produce maximum net income after taxes.[39] The
fact of differential net incomes among various firms implies that even
temporary experimentation with attempts to shift the tax forward would be
discouraged because of unwillingness of nearer-marginal firms to go along.
This discouragement would presumably be stronger in the case of the excess profits tax than in the case of the net income tax, since many firms
would be submarginal in the *excess* profits sense.

Though in the shorter run we are confident that the net income tax and
the excess profits tax are not shifted, this fact in itself may, under certain
circumstances, make possible some long-run shifting. If the tax is general,
applying over a broad geographical area and affecting all business concerns,
some shifting will occur, because the long-run effect may be to decrease the
number of firms operating in the taxed area. This would tend to increase
demand for the remaining firms, creating possibilities for forward shifting.
Such conditions might well obtain particularly under uncoordinated state
business taxation—relative freedom from income taxation in neighboring
states might well encourage the migration of business to those states.[40] And
if the net income tax is imposed only upon certain classes of business (e.g.,
munitions manufacturers), the same type of shifting may occur. Such shifting is less likely when the net income tax is applied only to a given form of
organization (e.g., corporations). Although in some lines of business, particularly those with heavy capital investment per unit of output, the corporate form of organization is virtually a *sine qua non,* in other lines business
can be carried on by unincorporated concerns. We recognize, therefore, the
possibility of long-run exceptions to the general rule that net income and
excess profits taxes are not shifted.

Gross income taxes typically are shifted. For the tax on gross income is
essentially one which adds a decreasing amount to variable cost of production as quantity of output increases.[41] We thus see again that the gross
income "business" tax is merely an *ad valorem* sales tax. Marginal costs are
increased by the tax, and therefore the point of maximum net income
represents a smaller quantity and a higher price per unit. Consequently,
some part of the tax is shifted forward; when demand is inelastic the tax is

[39] This assumes, of course, that the firm was maximizing its net income before the
tax. It does not ignore the fact that sales policy—advertising, etc.—can change demand,
but assumes that the firm has or would have utilized such resources to maximize demand with or without the tax.

[40] It is presumed here that a state which taxes the net income of its own business
firms imposes equivalent taxes on foreign firms doing business in that state.

[41] Because the typical demand curve is downward sloping from left to right, gross
income *per unit* falls and the tax per unit decreases as quantity increases.

more completely shifted than under elastic demand conditions. But the gross income business tax is most notably applied by the states to businesses subject to public regulation (i.e., public utilities), and in this application the tax is virtually completely shifted. For under rate regulation the objective is generally to establish rates which will provide a fair net return on investment. And since such regulated businesses do not typically fully exploit their demand possibilities—making higher rates possible without significant loss of business—and taxes are considered an expense deductible before determination of net return, the regulated rates typically include the tax. We are justified in the conclusion that the gross income tax is largely shifted on to the buyers of products.

The capital stock tax bears little relation to the quantity of a firm's output. It is but an addition (and in practice a minor one) to the fixed costs of production. As such, it affects neither of the two determinants (marginal revenue and marginal cost) of the quantity of output productive of maximum net income to the firm. Assuming, therefore, that the firm is maximizing net income before the tax, there is nothing to be gained in changing either output or price. Under such circumstances the tax will not be shifted. On the other hand, there are minor long-run possibilities for shifting through migration, and the analysis follows the same pattern as is indicated in our discussion above of long-run shifting possibilities in the net income or excess profits tax. In addition, however, a capital stock tax, which falls indiscriminately upon profitable and unprofitable corporations, may cause elimination of marginal firms from the market, and thus increase demand facing those remaining. Under such circumstances some long-run shifting would occur. This is the major difference between net income and capital stock taxes, in terms of incidence. The marginal firm is free from net income taxes, while it is not free from the capital stock tax. The long-run possibilities of forward shifting would thus be somewhat greater in the case of the latter than of the former.

Incidence and the Rationale of Business Taxation

Earlier in this chapter we surveyed the bases upon which separate taxation of business is in some quarters thought to be justified. Aside from the blind groping for additional revenue, we noted that business taxation is based upon one or more of the assumptions of (1) special benefit to certain individual businesses or classes of business, (2) general benefits to all business flowing from governmental maintenance of a favorable business climate, and (3) the existence in business of a capacity to pay taxes distinct from the capacities of those who derive personal incomes from business. We have raised serious doubt as to the feasibility of using special benefit as a justification for general business taxation. And we find it necessary to reject the general benefit theory of business taxation. The grounds for such rejection are several. Thoroughgoing utilization of the principle of benefit taxation would require the elimination of many governmental functions regarded as of primary social importance, since the beneficiaries cannot pay their own way. Furthermore, it is highly artificial to allocate general benefits among individual taxpayers, since by their nature such benefits are not allocable on any scientific grounds. In addition, where benefits are specific and individual enough to justify allocation, it is likely that prices charged for services rendered by government business enterprises and administrative revenues from fees, permits, etc., have already exhausted legitimate benefit allocations. And even general benefits implied in functions such as protection and education have already been overworked in supporting the theory of property taxation.

With respect to supposed distinct capacity of business to pay taxes, we find that it rests upon a quite inaccurate view of the nature of income. No separate business capacity does exist, distinct from the capacity of those economically entitled to income from the business. Beyond this, however, is it not logically quite inconsistent to embrace both the principle of benefit and the principle of ability in constructing a theory of business taxation? As theoretical bases for the apportionment of the burdens of government costs among individuals, each largely excludes the other. We are guilty of "working both sides of the street" by combining two largely exclusive concepts of equity.

Having determined the equity basis upon which a tax is to be built, the second step is to determine the type of tax base which most properly implements the principle of equity in practice. A business tax measured by business net income almost completely denies the benefit principle, while the business tax bases of gross income, net insurance premiums, or the amount of capital stock almost completely deny the validity of the ability principle. Yet combinations of these bases are to be found in the "business tax system" of nearly every state.[42] This curious mixture of tax principles and tax bases results at times from practical difficulties in the application of an accepted "ideal" principle or tax base, but it is feared that in the majority of instances the mixture results from frustration in the development of generally acceptable business tax theory and consequent retreat to the haven of revenue opportunism.

[42] The federal government is consistent in its adherence to a fallacious ability theory of business taxation.

One of the more serious sins of omission in business tax theory is its failure to relate tax incidence to tax justification.[43] Business taxes whose incidence finally falls upon consumers of the products of business can hardly be justified in terms of special business benefit or ability. These taxes are found to be but consumption taxes in disguise, and can be rationalized only in terms of consumption tax theory. We see here a demonstration of the importance of a fact so frequently reiterated throughout this book—that unless incidence is reasonably accurately determinable, the consequences of a particular tax may be quite foreign to theoretical intent. We are driven to the conclusion that no separate field for the taxation of business *per se* exists.

RECOMMENDED READINGS

Curran, K. J., *Excess Profits Taxation,* Washington, American Council on Public Affairs, 1943.

Chapters 1 ("Fundamentals") and 12 ("In Retrospect") are recommended for general reading. The remainder of the book is description of specific measures.

Goode, Richard, *The Corporation Income Tax,* N.Y., Wiley, 1951.

A thorough and highly recommended monograph dealing with rationale, incidence, and other effects of the federal tax.

Shoup, C., "Business Taxes," *Encyclopaedia of the Social Sciences,* N.Y., Macmillan, 1934.

Short survey of the theory of business taxation.

Studenski, Paul, "Toward a Theory of Business Taxation," *Journal of Political Economy,* October, 1940.

A statement of the case for special business taxation. Should be read to gain the opposite point of view from that presented in the text chapter.

[43] A striking example of this is Studenski, *op. cit.* Studenski begins by stating that separate taxation of business "can be justified on one or another of the following several grounds." There follows a list of eight separate justifications, embracing the principles of benefit, ability, revenue needs, and control through taxation. One feels that his "one or another" should have been "one or more," and that it would be simply impossible to apply the various justifications in terms of a single over-all business tax. Nevertheless, a business tax measured by the value added by the firm—value of gross product less cost of materials—is recommended as best meeting the theoretical requirements. To this point in the analysis one has the uncomfortable feeling that he has been carrying water in a sieve. The discussion of incidence, however, shows that incidence would typically be largely on consumers, though it "would most likely vary greatly from industry to industry, depending on its nature and the relative elasticity of supply and demand and existence of competition or monopoly therein" (pp. 643–44). We cannot quarrel with the incidence analysis itself, but the incidence conclusions seem to have little relevance to the rationale of the tax. This tax is principally justified in terms of governmental benefits conferred upon business enterprises and the special tax-paying capacity of those enterprises. Yet, the incidence, so far as it is known, would fall largely upon consumers, whose benefits or whose ability are not regarded as entering into the tax justification. We are not disposed to single out this study for criticism. It does, however, fairly represent the thinking of supporters of separate business taxation, and illuminates the logical weaknesses inherent in that thinking.

CHAPTER 23

Taxes on Employment
and Miscellaneous Taxes

Our survey of major types of tax measures would not be complete without some attention to several miscellaneous taxes. Of these the employment taxes introduced by the Social Security Act of 1935 are of real consequence, both in revenue productivity and in economic effects. A major part of this chapter will be devoted to the *payroll taxes* created by the Social Security Act, which can be easily identified by the specific allocation of their revenues to old age and unemployment compensation reserve accounts. Those other elements of the social security program—old age assistance, aid to the blind, and aid to dependent children—which are financed by grants of federal funds matched by the states, are generally met from the general funds of the federal and state governments.[1] Since their financing has not generally given rise to special earmarked taxes,[2] we shall not be concerned with them here. We shall bring into this chapter a short discussion of the poll tax and of the federal "Unjust Enrichment Tax," two minor taxes which our survey of tax measures cannot completely ignore.

Taxes on Employment

The Old Age and Survivors' Insurance Taxes. The old age pension benefits of the Social Security Act are administered entirely by the federal government. Benefits are paid to qualified retired persons after reaching age sixty-five (sixty-two for women) and to their dependents. The amounts of

---

[1] The titles of the Social Security Act creating special earmarked taxes are that providing old age and survivor annuities (Title VIII) and that establishing unemployment compensation (Title IX).

[2] These social security expenditures from general funds have been partially responsible for increases in state gasoline taxes, and for the spread of state personal income and sales taxes. In a few cases new earmarked taxes have been created, e.g., Connecticut made of its poll tax an old age assistance tax.

benefits paid are not related significantly to the previous earnings of the beneficiary, but are essentially similar for all persons in the same status with respect to dependents. The plan operates roughly on the reserve principle, building up a reserve fund in the earlier years as tax collections exceed benefits, and using both current taxes and interest on the reserve fund as sources of benefit payments in later years.

The system of contributions employs wage and salary taxes rather than individual premiums. Actually, two taxes are employed: one upon the wages of the employee, usually withheld from his pay by his employer, and an excise of equal amount upon the employer. The taxes are imposed only up to a given amount of wage or salary for each individual; in the beginning the maximum amount subject to taxes was $3,600 per year, but it has been successively raised to $4,200 and to $4,800. Since benefit payments are not related to previous earnings, the taxes are not imposed upon total income. Each of the two taxes (upon employers and employees) was to begin at 1 per cent for each year between 1937 and 1944, to rise to 2 per cent in 1945, thence to 2.5 per cent between 1946 and 1948, and to become permanently established at 3 per cent in 1949. Eventually, therefore, the combined annual contribution of employers and employees was to be 6 per cent of taxable wages and salaries. But by a succession of amendments the 1 per cent rate was retained through 1949 and a new schedule of rates climbing to 2.75 per cent in 1960 and to 4.25 per cent by 1970 has been substituted for the original plan. The combined contribution of employers and employees in 1970 would thus be 8.5 per cent of taxable wages and salaries.

Aside from changes in tax rates and in the maximum amounts subject to these rates, two further changes in the program have occurred. One of these is extension of the program to self-employed persons. Because the self-employed individual is both employer and employee, only one payroll tax can be imposed, and this is imposed at a rate half again as high as the general rate upon employer or employee. Thus, while the rate in 1960 for employer or employee is 2.75 per cent, that for the self-employed is 4.125 per cent (150 per cent of 2.75 per cent). The second change was the provision of benefits for disability under the Social Security Amendments of 1956. A separate Disability Insurance Trust Fund was created, and a tax at one half of one per cent was imposed upon employers and employees for the Fund. This tax was combined with the Old Age and Survivors' Insurance Tax.

In the fiscal year 1959 the combined old age and disability taxes on employers, employees, and the self-employed produced about $8 billion for payment of current claims and additions to the reserve accounts. The two reserve accounts stood at about $23 billion at the end of that year. If government employees' and railroad retirement pension funds are added in, the tax receipts for 1959 total $10 billion, and the reserves stand at nearly $35 billion.

Unemployment Compensation Taxes. The unemployment compensation provisions of the Social Security Act place major administration of the system in the hands of the states, with reasonable uniformity in state action accomplished by federal influence. A federal unemployment compensation tax is imposed upon employers of four or more persons in non-exempt employments. The tax began in 1936 at 1 per cent of wages paid to employees subject to the tax, rose to 2 per cent in 1937, and reached the permanent level of 3 per cent in 1938. Federal influence working toward state uniformity is evident in the credit allowed against the federal tax in the amount of 90 per cent of state unemployment compensation taxes paid. Thus, for each $30 assessed by the federal tax against an employer in a state with an approved unemployment compensation system, $27 is credited to him for state unemployment taxes paid. If the state tax rate is 2.7 per cent (the federal rate being 3 per cent), this employer's total federal-state tax is $30, $27 going to the state and $3 to the federal government. If a state chose to enact no federally approved ᴊnemployment compensation law, the federal tax on its employers would be collected, but the funds would not be available for unemployment benefits to their employees. The effect of the credit provision has been enactment of approved systems by all states, with maximum tax rates generally at 2.7 per cent,[3] to receive the full benefit of the federal credit.

The unemployment compensation system, however, is intended less to provide for general unemployment caused by the business cycle than to ameliorate the effects of unemployment in particular firms, caused by seasonal production or the movement of individual workers from one job to another. Thus, most states have built into the system incentives to individual employers to improve their unemployment records. Under various "merit rating" or "experience rating" plans, forty-seven states and the District of Columbia grant unemployment tax relief in the form of lower rates to those employers with good records in regularizing employment. In such

---

[3] As of 1959, forty states and the District of Columbia imposed unemployment compensation taxes at a maximum rate of 2.7 per cent of payrolls. Nine states applied higher maximum rates; the highest was at 4 per cent. (Alaska is included in the listing, but Hawaii excluded). The taxes are applied up to a maximum wage of $3,000—the federal provision—in all but four states. We speak of maximum rates to take cognizance of lower rates permitted by merit rating systems in all but two states, discussed in the following text paragraph. (Commerce Clearing House, *State Tax Guide,* 1959.)

states the applicable tax rate may fall as low as zero for employers with the highest merit rating.[4] The federal act recognizes the merit rating plan by considering merit-abated state taxes as if they had been paid in calculating the federal credit. Suppose, for example, that the federal tax at 3 per cent on an employer were $3,000, and the standard state unemployment tax rate were 2.7 per cent. If the employer actually paid the standard rate, he would pay $2,700 to his state and $300 to the federal government. Suppose, however, that because of high merit rating with the state his unemployment tax rate were .5 per cent. He would actually pay $500 to the state and $300 to the federal government, the difference ($2,200) being credited to him as meeting the federal requirement even though not paid to the state. It is important to note that state merit rating systems must meet federal approval before merit abatements are deductible as part of the federal credit. In those cases where state tax rates are higher than 2.7 per cent, no part of the excess can be claimed as credit against the federal tax. For the federal credit is 90 per cent of the *federal* tax, not of the state tax. Those states which have adopted rates higher than 2.7 per cent of payrolls are not only employing merit incentives, but demerit penalties to encourage stability of employment in firms. Three states impose wage taxes upon employees as well as payroll taxes on employers. The federal law allows no credit for such taxes paid.[5]

State employment tax collections are deposited in the federal Unemployment Trust Fund. By the end of fiscal 1946 the balance in the fund was $7.4 billion, representing 73 per cent of cumulative deposits from the states since 1936.[6] During the war period of high employment, contributions to the fund were heavy (though reduced by almost inevitably high merit ratings) and withdrawals light. During 1946 unemployment due to industrial reconversion and demobilization of the armed services slowed down the wartime rate of accumulation of the fund. The rapid growth of the reserve fund generated some unsuccessful agitation for reduction of federal unemployment tax rates immediately following World War II. Merit rating schemes reduced contributions to the reserve account in most states during the high income years of 1947 and 1948; the recessions of 1949, 1953, and

---

[4] *Ibid.* The most popular minimum rates are 0 per cent (nine states), .1 per cent (fourteen states), .3 per cent (four states), and .5 per cent (eight states).

[5] This would be hardly possible without a federal unemployment compensation tax on employees. Those states which have adopted such taxes have apparently reasoned that the employee should make a contribution to reserves created for his benefit. This implies a sorry ignorance of the incidence of employer taxes, as we shall see in the next section.

[6] *Annual Report of the Secretary of the Treasury,* 1946, p. 572.

1958 considerably increased the magnitude of benefit payments and jeopardized the reserves of a few states which had lowered tax rates drastically during the good years. The recession experience has largely checked the enthusiasm for reduction in basic tax rates and at the same time generally raised effective tax rates under merit rating schemes. By June 30, 1958, the Unemployment Trust Fund balance was about $7.8 billion.

Incidence of Social Security Taxes on Employment.[7] We have noted three different taxes based upon employment introduced by the Social Security Act: the unemployment tax imposed upon employers; the old age benefits tax imposed upon employers; and the wages tax on employees. Since the provision of retirement income benefits and of unemployment compensation represent distinct projects, it is reasonable and almost inevitable that they be financed by distinct taxes. But the provision of two separate taxes to provide old age benefit funds suggests an intention that such funds should represent joint contributions from employers and employees. If this is a fair observation concerning legislative intent, it is reasonable to assume legislative expectation that the two taxes would carry separate incidence. It appears that incidence of the wage tax upon employees was expected to be upon employees, encouraged by the procedure of employer deduction of the tax from the employee's wages on pay day. On the other hand, the incidence of the payroll tax on employers was expected to be upon them, payment to be made out of the profits of the firm.

Such a view of incidence assumes, however, that neither of these taxes is shifted. Yet one or more price vehicles is available in the case of each of the social security taxes. The tax deduction from the worker's pay could conceivably result in an increase in basic pay, so as to shift this tax to the employer. Employer taxes based upon payrolls could conceivably be either shifted forward in the price of the product to the buyer, or backward in reduced payment to one or more of the factors of production. The problem of incidence is to determine which of the three possible groups—employers, employees, consumers—actually does (do) bear these taxes. We consider first the old age benefits tax upon the employee. Two and three-fourths per cent of his wages are deducted as earned; the impact of the tax is thus upon labor's wages in the first instance. There are several good reasons for believ-

---

[7] The appearance of the social security employment taxes in the thirties generated a great deal of interest in the question of their incidence, and consequently some significant additions to incidence literature. Notably good selections from that literature are the following: J. K. Hall, "Incidence of Federal Social Security Pay Roll Taxes," *Quarterly Journal of Economics*, November, 1938; Russell Bauder, "Probable Incidence of Social Security Taxes," *American Economic Review*, September, 1936; Eveline M. Burns, "Financial Aspects of the Social Security Act," *American Economic Review*, March, 1936; S. E. Harris, *The Economics of Social Security*, McGraw-Hill, 1941, Part III.

ing that little forward shifting occurs in the typical case. The first reason is that, the tax being quite general in application, there is practically no possibility of escape from it by migration to another job. Virtually the only possibility of avoiding incidence of this tax would be to migrate into a type of employment exempt from its payment. But well over 90 per cent of gainfully employed workers are now covered, and occupational and other aspects of labor immobility further prevent the likelihood of such migration. For this reason there is little probability of a decrease in the supply of labor in taxed employments. And it is especially unlikely that the tax would result in any noticeable withdrawal of workers from the market. Thus a long-run tendency for wages to rise in taxed employments as a result of migration or voluntary idleness is practically impossible.

The second reason is that the tax provides funds for retirement income of laborers, partially eliminating the need for private saving for old age. Recognition of this fact by the worker is likely to weaken any determination he might have otherwise had to try to shift the tax to his employer. In many instances the social security tax is but a substitute for private saving from current income, and thus the incidence of the tax involves no new or additional burden upon the worker. And even when voluntary saving had not occurred previously, the forced savings plan of social security may be accepted by the worker as coercion to do only what he should have been doing. Many workers consider the insurance to be worth more than its cost. Our point here is that the purpose for which the funds are used tends to weaken the urge to attempt to shift the tax to the employer.

A third reason for believing that the incidence of the tax is upon the worker is that the tax itself is small. A tax of less than 3 per cent on wages typically somewhat above a subsistence standard hardly justifies agitation for a wage increase. It is doubtful that even the eventual 4.25 per cent tax will generate much pressure to shift the tax to the employer. Certainly in a typical case the tax deduction from the worker's wages is like a net income tax, and it is hardly of sufficient size to encroach seriously upon his standard of living.

Over all, therefore, we find little possibility of escape from the impact of the tax by transferring to untaxed employment, accomplishing a long-run reduction in labor supply in those firms and thus raising wages. In addition, it is highly unlikely that the size of the tax, the manner in which it is imposed, the use to which the funds are to be put, and the gradual program of rate increases would encourage attempts to shift it. Further, it seems generally agreed that among all shares in distribution, wages are least resistant to tax bearing, and thus an attempt on the part of the worker to shift the tax forward would probably be unsuccessful.

The two social security taxes on employers—the unemployment compensation tax of 3 per cent of eligible payrolls, and the (now) 2.75 per cent tax on payrolls for old-age annuities—are similar in impact and in incidence. We consider them first as if they were but a single tax, later pointing out differences which may condition their incidence. Three possibilities of incidence present themselves: the wage vehicle is present for possible backward shifting, the price of the product to buyers constitutes a possible vehicle for forward shifting, and if neither were possible the burden of the tax would remain upon the employer as a deduction from his profits. Of these three possibilities it is least likely that the employer will bear the tax. Let us recognize that the combined excises impose upon the employer a tax of approximately 6 per cent of his payroll.[8] If the incidence of these combined taxes were upon profits of employers subject to them, a marked reduction in net profit would occur.[9] Since the tax would involve a burden upon profit incomes, it is unquestionably true that entrepreneurs would make every effort to shift it. It may be granted that, when the tax is a minor one, impact is likely to be an important determiner of incidence. For when the tax is insignificant the person who first pays it is likely to bear it rather than to undertake the process of shifting against inevitable obstacles. But when the tax is large, the effort of shifting is of lesser significance, and he will experiment with whatever possibilities exist for shifting.

Granted that the employer would be anxious to shift this tax, we will consider the probable success of the shifting effort. We will first consider possible forward shifting through an increase in the price of the product to the buyer. A tax on payrolls obviously bears close relation to marginal costs of production. Taxes paid on the wages of workers are similar to the costs of materials used in production. An increase in marginal costs is tantamount to a decrease in supply, and results in some increase in price. If the demand for the product is relatively elastic, an increase in price will entail major

[8] "Approximately," because (1) merit rating systems in use by most states may reduce the rate of the unemployment compensation tax of a given firm, (2) some minor group of employees may be in one of the several exempt classes, and (3) wages and salaries above $3,000 and $4,800 per year are untaxed for unemployment and OASI respectively.

[9] In 1951, employer contributions for social insurance were $4.19 billion. Net income of corporations, partnerships, and sole proprietorships (excepting farmers, who are excluded from the system) were $66.30 billion in that year. By this rough calculation, if employer contributions had had their incidence upon employers, their profits on the average would have been reduced by about 6.3 per cent (figures from *Survey of Current Business,* July, 1952, p. 17).

reduction in quantity marketable, and will almost inevitably decrease the seller's net income. The resistance of buyers to forward shifting is far less vigorous when demand is inelastic and but slight decline in quantity sold accompanies increased price.

It is doubtful that any serious resistance to forward shifting is to be found in competition from untaxed employers. It is sometimes argued that the existence of untaxed employments will make shifting difficult by taxed employers, since there is no urge to raise prices in the former. But the validity of this argument depends upon the effectiveness of competition between taxed and untaxed employers. In the case of the 2.75 per cent tax on payrolls for old age benefits, the only major exempt groups are doctors and casual laborers, though a few state and local governments and non-profit organizations have as yet not elected to be included. Clearly, there is substantially no opportunity for substitution of the products of untaxed employers for those in taxed lines. This observation implies that taxed employers will not to any important degree be inhibited from attempting to shift the tax forward for fear of losing their markets to untaxed employers who have no incentive to follow suit. There is a somewhat greater possibility of competition between taxed and untaxed employers in the case of the 3 per cent unemployment compensation excises on payrolls. For this tax not only exempts more employments than the OASI tax, but adds two other completely or partially exempt groups: those employing fewer than four employees,[10] and those whose records for stability of employment are such as to grant them the benefits of lower tax rates under the merit rating system. With the possible exception of the retail and service trades, the employers of fewer than four persons do not figure large enough in the total picture to offer a serious competitive threat, especially in view of the fact that any marked substitution of their products for those of larger employers would place them in the taxed class themselves. The possibility of competition from those employers with higher merit rating and thus lower tax rate is less clear. The merit rating of a given employer is not likely to be stable over long periods. The impact of cyclical and technological change will probably be stronger in the typical case than the merit rating incentive. It would seem reasonable to expect, therefore, that merit ratings will rise and fall more or less uniformly for large groups of employers. To the extent that this does occur, there is less competitive differentiation among employers at a given moment than might be expected. Furthermore, differences in merit rating at a given moment among competing employers, though they impose

[10] But the limit is lower than four employees under the laws of several states. Seventeen states apply the taxes to employers of one or more workers.

different rates of unemployment taxation, will frequently entail compensating expense to the highly rated employer. If in the face of cyclical or seasonal decline in sales, employment is maintained at a stable level, this stability (and high merit rating) may be attained by the incurring of expense which at least partially offsets the tax rate advantage. And if stability in employment is maintained by hesitancy in adopting technological improvements, it is likely that a differential in cost of production partially offsets tax benefits. On the whole, therefore, we conclude that in the case of neither of the employer payroll taxes does competition from lower- or non-taxed employers significantly discourage forward shifting.

It seems clear that employers typically will bear but a small part, if any, of the taxes on payrolls, since these taxes offer essentially the same forward-shifting possibilities as do general taxes on consumption. We have still to consider, however, the possibility that such taxes may be shifted backward to the workers in reduced "take home pay." The general consensus of those economists who have written on the subject appears to be that backward shifting of the employer taxes is the most likely of the various alternative possibilities. The reasoning leading to this conclusion is essentially the same as that which concludes that the incidence of the income tax on the laborer's wages rests with him. The first of these reasons is that workers cannot shift from taxed to untaxed employment in order to avoid acceptance of incidence. If such migration were possible the supply of labor in taxed employments would decline, and the wages of those remaining could rise to include the tax. But all the factors contributing to labor immobility militate against migration, particularly the fact that entrance into exempt employments is virtually impossible. Finally, migration to untaxed employment would mean migration to employment not covered by the benefits of old age insurance and/or unemployment compensation.

A further reason for believing workers to be liable to the incidence of payroll taxes is that these taxes do not increase the demand for goods in general. Thus, the demand for labor in general would not increase. On the other hand, attempts to raise prices to shift the tax forward would result in some decline in output and in employment. Under conditions of labor competition and typically inelastic labor supply the new equilibrium would be expected to occur at lower net wages, and the tax in the long run would be shifted backward.[11] There are always, of course, short-run qualifications of the conclusion that the employer payroll taxes are largely shifted to labor. Producers under cost-plus contracts (e.g., in wartime production for govern-

[11] Neither the size nor the duration of unemployment benefits is sufficient to encourage permanent unemployment in preference to absorption of the tax in slightly lower wages.

ment) can generally shift these taxes forward in the price of the good. Likewise, in boom periods of labor shortage and great demand for products there will be less resistance to forward than to backward shifting.[12] And at the time of institution of payroll taxes on employers, existing wage contracts will prohibit backward shifting for the duration of those contracts. Undoubtedly in the long run more effective bargaining organization by employees will shift a larger share of the tax to unorganized buyers of the product.

A final reason to expect general backward shifting of the taxes is found in the use to which the funds are put. Labor's resistance to backward shifting is weakened by the general feeling both by labor and by the public that the benefits of social security accrue to labor and that the major part of the expense should therefore be borne by labor. And if it is commonly agreed that the incidence of all such taxes *should* be upon workers,[13] there is greater likelihood that incidence *will* be upon them. In summary we find the incidence of the social security taxes to be principally upon employed workers. The wage (income) tax deducted at the time of wage payment is clearly upon the wage-earner. The major part of the incidence of the two excises paid by employers is also upon employed labor in the long run. The remainder of incidence is upon buyers of the products sold and upon the sellers, the major share of this remainder being upon buyers. These are generalizations which do not ignore the fact that the lines of least resistance to shifting vary among firms, among industries, and with changes in cyclical conditions. It is worth observing that historical conditions have been such as to strengthen the analytical conclusion that incidence is principally upon labor. The social security taxes originated during a period of rising wages and removal of governmental relief programs. Such conditions make absorption of the taxes by labor more likely. And once shifted, so that tax incidence is merged in going wage rates, the friction of tradition makes for permanence.

[12] Conversely, in depression periods, unless there are major public works and work relief programs in operation, labor's defenses against backward shifting are weak, while low demand for goods makes buyer defenses against forward shifting strong.

[13] The common assumption that the burden of financing social security should be wholly upon the worker is not to be taken as clear evidence that this is where the burden logically belongs. Since unemployment is likely to be a serious problem principally as an effect of the business cycle, such an assumption implies that labor as a class is responsible for its occurrence. This implication is clearly unreasonable. And it would be very difficult to demonstrate that old age dependency in the absence of retirement annuities is wholly the fault of labor. Maintenance of over-age and unemployable workers is obviously a cost to be borne by the economy which leaves them at termination of employment without adequate financial reserves of their own.

Social Security Taxes in the Revenue System. The titles of the Social Security Act providing respectively old age benefits and unemployment compensation have exclusively claimed our attention in this discussion because they provide special taxes for their financing. It is desirable, however, to outline briefly the larger connection between the tax collections, the payment of benefits, and the handling of funds, in preparation for study of the compensatory aspects of the social security system. The major part of unemployment compensation excises upon employers is collected by the states and deposited to the credit of the particular state in the federal Unemployment Trust Fund. The Unemployment Trust Fund is invested by the Social Security Board in United States government securities, and interest on these investments is paid to the fund by regular appropriation of Congress. The old age benefit system is wholly federal; the taxes on employers and employees are paid into the Old Age and Survivors' Insurance Trust Fund, and benefits are paid from the fund. This fund is likewise invested in Treasury securities.

Both plans aim to accumulate reserves in good times which may be later drawn upon for benefit payments. In the case of unemployment compensation it is admitted that unemployment is not an "insurable risk," since there is no such thing as an unemployment experience pattern which may be depended upon to repeat itself. The plan calls for payment of benefits only so long as the reserve funds are adequate, and although the federal government might feel compelled to carry on benefit payments if state funds became exhausted, the law does not provide for it. The reserve fund for old age benefits contemplates accumulations for a period in excess of withdrawals, so that as the average age of the population increases, benefits may be paid from the reserves to supplement current tax collections. Analogy with private insurance breaks down further when we recognize that benefits are not paid according to contract but according to law. The amount of the benefit paid is essentially uniform among beneficiaries and not determined to any considerable degree by individual contributions to the funds. (Since contributions are based on wages there is some rough relation of contributions to benefits, but the relation is by no means as precise as in private insurance.)

The absence of correlation between individual contributions and individual benefits suggests that these two social security programs have little in common with private insurance contracts. They are more logically considered as of the same pattern as state highway expenditures, where special taxes on motorists are covered into a special highway fund, which is then utilized for highway construction and repair. If the highway fund is inadequate to finance a road-building program, the difference is provided by appropriations from the general fund. Both social security programs provide for the building of surplus funds in favorable times and their use when required to meet legislated benefits. It is highly likely that the states would provide considerable amounts of general funds if the unemployment compensation reserve fund were depleted. And it is equally probable that deficiencies in the old age reserve account would be made up from the general funds of the federal Treasury before benefit payments were reduced.

In the case of Old Age and Survivors' Insurance, the failure in earlier years to raise tax rates as rapidly as originally planned must be interpreted as acceptance of a part of the obligations as a charge upon general revenues, though the 1956 amendments strongly reaffirm the principle of self-support. There are, indeed, those who oppose the accumulation of reserves for payment of old age benefits. They reason that each generation should and does take care of its aged. When current old age taxes equal current benefit payments this is clearly being done. But even under the reserve plan the same results occur. For a current excess of tax receipts over benefit payments increases the Old Age Trust Fund, which, like the Unemployment Trust Fund, is invested in Treasury securities at current interest rates. The borrowing of these surplus funds by the Treasury makes possible their use for the payment of general government expenses. As a matter of fact, therefore, collection of social security payroll and wage taxes in excess of current benefits provides funds for general expenditure, while in the future if current taxes are inadequate to meet benefit obligations the difference must come from general revenue sources.[14] Thus each generation does care for its aged and unemployed, whether or not reserves are accumulated. The reader will note that this is also true whether the social security scheme is governmental or private. For consumption at any time is made possible by current production.

Counter-Cycle Social Security Taxation

The social security payroll taxes, considered separately, apart from the benefit payments that they give rise to, are among the most regressive of all taxes. Their incidence is principally upon wage and salary earners, and to a much lesser extent upon consumers. The fact that the unemployment

---

[14] It does not follow, of course, that use of surplus funds for general expenditure represents a betrayal of trust. It has been argued that an irresponsible government has squandered social security reserves on "boondoggling" projects. If this is not true, why do the social security reserves contain nothing but government debt? The implication of fraud is, of course, absurd, for it could be made with equal force against all private insurance companies, whose cash holdings are always less than their legal reserves. So long as the obligation to pay benefits is honored and revenue resources are sufficient to support the obligation, it would be utter folly to accumulate huge reserves of cash.

compensation taxes are upon the first $3,000 of wages, and the old age and disability taxes are upon the first $4,800 of wages (without differentiation for dependents), means that the effective rate with respect to income is high for those whose total income is within these maxima and for those whose income is subject to the tax. The situation is one in which a flat rate of tax is imposed upon gross income below maximum taxable levels, and zero upon income above those levels. Apart from the benefit payments, the long-run impact of such taxes on consumption would be downward and perverse with respect to the cycle, and the system introduces a significant element of regression into the tax system as a whole.

Granted their persistent long-run downward pressure on the level of consumption, their burdens become more intense in depression than in prosperity. This is true in spite of the fact that no payroll taxes are paid by or for the unemployed worker. But little comfort can be taken from unemployment as an escape from the tax. And for those who remain employed, probably at lower wages or less overtime, the flat rate of taxation imposes a heavier burden. Added to this is the fact that in depressed markets and with extensive unemployment the resistance of consumers to tax shifting strengthens while the resistance of workers weakens. Thus less forward shifting and more backward shifting of the taxes onto employees is likely.

On the other hand, the old age security and unemployment compensation programs offer one of the few opportunities for reasonable application of the benefit principle in taxation. For a large share of the benefits of these programs accrues to individual insured workers. And since these individual benefits are in the nature of cash payments, there is no difficulty involved in measuring the amount of benefit in the individual case. In fact, it is reasonable to consider the social security tax payments as the approximate equivalent of prices paid for insurance services. So considered, the regressiveness of the payment is of less concern than would be the case if such taxes were simply covered into the general funds of government and used for general governmental purposes.

At the same time, there are important elements of general social benefit —as distinguished from individual benefit—in such social security programs. Prevention of dependence of the aged and the unemployed, and maintenance of a higher level of consumption, are objectives in the general good. It is therefore logical that something less than full reserves be accumulated out of payroll taxes, and that the remainder be a charge upon the general funds.

Though social security taxes upon workers' wages are regressive, their burdens are distributed roughly in accordance with the distribution of social security benefits. And there are definite morale advantages in making the worker feel entitled to his benefits because he has paid for them. Further, the assumption of a major part of the expense of the program by its beneficiaries may well serve to discourage irresponsible drives for extension of the benefit system beyond the limits established by the productivity of the economy. There thus appear to be reasonable grounds for continuation of the system of tax contributions by those who stand to benefit individually. However, such a system offers little opportunity for counter-cycle adjustment of the payroll taxes, except as employment and wages vary through the cycle and thus possess some elements of built-in adjustment. With respect to such adjustment it is fortunately not likely that tax collections in recession and depression will approach the volume of benefit payments, and therefore income-generating deficit spending will automatically occur. And in prosperity, tax collections will almost inevitably exceed benefit payments. Such further adjustment to cyclical conditions as is needed—and far more will be needed—should come from outside the social security program. That is, other governmental expenditures and other elements of the tax system must provide elasticity sufficient to offset the rigidities of the social security program and to bring the whole fiscal system into appropriate balance with respect to counter-cycle requirements.

We turn now to a brief description of two kinds of taxes whose importance earns for them only brief mention. Though of minor significance, they should not go unmentioned; on the other hand, each is peculiar to itself, defying classification along with any of the major taxes previously discussed. We therefore bring them in at this point, as miscellaneous taxes briefly discussed at the end of our survey of tax types.

Poll and Capitation Taxes[15]

The principal taxes of local governments in the early period of American history were those on "polls and rateable estates." The latter was the property tax, while the former was a flat amount levied upon persons. The term "poll tax" has become more common than "capitation tax" or "head tax," because it implies the usual limitation of the tax to those of voting age. At the time when the poll tax was established there were several reasons for limiting its application to mature males. In the first place, its proceeds were devoted largely to road construction and maintenance, and in a period when money was scarce, taxpayers were generally allowed to "work out" this tax in labor on roads. Mature males only could be expected to possess ability to pay in road work, ability being measured in terms of capacity for

---

[15] A good short description of these taxes, with bibliography, is presented in Carl Shoup's article, "Poll Tax," in the *Encyclopaedia of the Social Sciences*.

hard physical labor. The limitation of the tax to those of voting age suggests also a rough form of application of the principle of ability to those who would pay in money. For most persons under twenty-one would not be financially independent.[16] In the second place, taxation without representation was unpopular, and a person who was not old enough to vote could not justly be required to pay a personal tax. Finally, in some states, payment of the poll tax was prerequisite to possession of the voting privilege, and the intention was to deny the franchise to certain groups.[17] There was obviously no object in erecting a poll tax barrier to voting by those who were already denied the franchise on other grounds.

The poll or capitation tax is now employed principally by local governments, only nine states deriving state revenues from it. Frequently it is a principal source of county revenues, particularly in those states where the counties continue to exercise responsibilities for public roads. In general, however, it is regarded as a city, town, or village tax. The uses to which poll tax revenues are put have shown little change over a period of time. Earmarking of such revenues is still very common, and what began as a road tax has been devoted to few additional purposes. Substantially, the only purpose other than roads to which these revenues are devoted is that of public school operation.

With few exceptions the poll tax is badly administered by local governments. Its revenue productivity is small at best, generating little enthusiasm for careful administration. In many localities its administration has been so down at the heels for so long that evasion has become a major sport, in the supposedly harmless nature of "cops and robbers." The very tradition of poor administration has generated so general a disrespect for the poll tax that improvement of its administration is doubly difficult. And finally, in some sections of the United States, evasion of the poll tax is quite generally

[16] In approximately one-third of the states employing the poll tax, it can still be paid in cash or in road work. The latter, however, is attractive only to the very impecunious, since this labor carries very low value for tax purposes. In 1938 the highest maximum rate at which the tax could be "worked out" was $2 per day. Louisiana counted road work as worth fifty cents per day for tax purposes. Payment in labor is discouraged principally for the reason that modern methods of road construction and maintenance can hardly make good use of many miscellaneous, untrained, and out-of-condition laborers.

[17] Rates of the poll tax in 1952 ranged from a figure of $1 per poll in many localities to a maximum of $7.50 in one state. Several localities permit the duplication of the poll tax by different governmental units (counties and cities) and by special districts (road districts and school districts). The payment of the poll tax as a direct requirement for voting is now required in only six or seven states. This requirement remains only in Southern states, and poll tax rates are in general somewhat higher in Southern than in other states.

desired for political reasons, since failure to pay the tax disqualifies the person from voting.

Were it not for the political and social implications of its use to withdraw the franchise from large numbers of citizens, and for the fact that a spirit of evasion with respect to one tax is easily communicable to other taxes, the general failure of the poll tax would be cause for rejoicing. For in terms of tax theory it is a bad tax. Its base is the individual person, and not his income or any near or distant relative of it. All persons subject to the tax pay the same amount. It is thus regressive with respect to personal income. Its incidence is simple; the payer of the tax bears its incidence, as there is no price vehicle for either forward or backward shifting. But though its continued existence is anachronistic, its long history and the lightness of its burden upon those who principally mold policy combine to offer little hope of its complete abandonment.

The Unjust Enrichment Tax

The Supreme Court decision in *Butler* v. *United States* (1936) voided the first Agricultural Adjustment Act and the taxes imposed by it upon the processors of certain agricultural products. The decision created real confusion concerning the status of some $200 million of taxes impounded pending decision of the case, and some $1 billion of taxes collected since 1933 and spent for agricultural benefits under the Act. Almost immediately a series of court orders and decisions directed the return of impounded taxes to individual processors who had paid them under protest. Clearly a difficult situation was presented. In general, it was correctly assumed that substantially the whole tax had been shifted forward to consumers in increased prices. Thus, the processors legally entitled to a return of impounded taxes had, in general, already been reimbursed by buyers of their products, and the return of impounded taxes would create a nearly pure windfall.[18] Furthermore, those firms which had paid their taxes without protest were apparently not entitled to refund. The return of these impounded taxes would thus create grave injustices between producers and consumers, and among producers. Clearly, it was impossible to find those who had borne the incidence of the impounded taxes, even if return of the funds to them could have been made legal. And the same problems existed with respect to the billion dollars in taxes formerly collected and already spent, although their return had not been ordered.

At the request of the President, Congress passed the Unjust Enrichment

---

[18] One firm would have been entitled to a refund of approximately $4 million.

Tax, designed to recoup returned taxes, as well as to settle the larger problem of taxes paid without protest. The measure provided for a flat rate of 80 per cent upon the net income of any person or firm, arising from: (1) Any federal excise tax imposed but not paid (this was to recover taxes added to price prior to the court decision but not paid to the Treasury); (2) any reimbursements to a taxpayer by persons who sold goods to him when the taxpayer shifted the tax forward (such cases would infrequently occur; they might occur when a processor or wholesaler was a party to suit against the Act and had carefully arranged to bear the tax); (3) any refunds of shifted excise taxes improperly or illegally collected (this provision was to recoup impounded taxes as well as to forestall suits to recover processing taxes which had previously been paid without protest).[19] Although the law was drawn in general terms to cover all federal excises, it was specifically directed toward the processing taxes.

The law was probably effective in discouraging litigation which if successful would have created "unjust enrichment," though the tax produced little revenue. The Treasury estimated in 1936 that approximately $82 million in revenue would be received from the tax in 1937 (the only year in which it was expected to produce revenue),[20] though receipts were actually but $6 million in that year.[21] By Congressional resolution in 1937 the Commissioner of Internal Revenue was empowered to extend the period of payment, and in 1951 payments were not yet entirely complete. Nevertheless, the total of collections to the end of fiscal 1945 amounted to only about $43 million, and in that year payments had dwindled to $180 thousand. The meagerness of revenue collection under the unjust enrichment tax was due primarily to the fact that the major part of the impounded taxes was paid by firms which could show that the incidence was upon them. They therefore received refunds of processing taxes but were not subject to unjust enrichment taxes.

It may be inquired why we devote attention to a tax of such insignificance. with respect both to life span and to revenue productivity. Granted that the unjust enrichment tax has played a very minor role in the fiscal system, it is nevertheless interesting for two reasons. First, it represents a new departure in taxation, using a tax measure to pick up specific windfall incomes regarded as socially unjust or undesirable. As such, it may prove to be a useful tool with which to meet in the future a fairly wide range of situ-

---

[19] Cf. Title III, *Revenue Act of 1936,* for provisions of the law.
[20] *Annual Report of the Secretary of the Treasury,* 1936, p. 385.
[21] *Ibid.,* 1937, p. 298.

ations.[22] But more important, the use of such a tax involves application of specific conclusions as to the incidence of other taxes. The tax of 1936 was constructed upon the assumption that processing taxes were shifted by sellers. Any other interpretation would deny the "unjustness" of the enrichment. It is interesting to note the legal treatment of the economic concept of incidence, for the law was required either to accept a simple hypothesis with respect to incidence, or to set up a workable measure of the degree of shifting in the individual case. Actually it did the latter, though with reservations. The extent to which the tax was shifted was computed by comparing the seller's margin while the tax was imposed with his average margin on the same good in the same quantities for the six years immediately preceding imposition of the tax. The seller's margin was his selling price per unit less the cost of the good per unit to him. In the case of the manufacturer, cost meant cost of material only; in the case of goods purchased for resale, cost was simply the price paid for the good at the time of purchase. For example, suppose that during the period 1927–1933, the seller had had an average margin of twenty cents between the cost and selling price per unit of his product. Suppose that in 1935, his product then being subject to the processing tax, his margin had risen to twenty-three cents per unit, assuming comparable quantities in the two periods. The difference in margin is three cents and if the processing tax on the taxed-commodity-content of his good were four cents per unit he would have been assumed by the law to have shifted three-fourths of the tax and borne the other fourth himself. He would be entitled to keep one-fourth of these processing tax payments returned to him, but three-fourths of the refund (less cost of obtaining the refund) would be subject to the unjust enrichment tax. This was, of course, only a rough and ready measure of the degree of tax shifting. It takes little account of a host of variables affecting the firm's demand and costs. The improvement in the general demand situation between 1933 and 1936 might well have brought a natural increase of margins irrespective of the tax. But any less simple measure of shifting would

[22] For example, in early 1947 its revival was tentatively suggested in connection with the frightening portal-to-portal pay suits. Though the portal-to-portal flurry quickly disappeared, there was for a time concern lest the legality of suits claiming retroactive pay would severely affect the condition of the Treasury. For if wage claims totaling approximately $5 billion had been judicially upheld, the Treasury could have been affected in two ways. Firms required to pay heavy wage claims could in some instances establish claims for refunds under the excess profits tax, by carrying back loss credits against excess profits taxes paid during the war. Also, it is conceivable that some cost-plus war production contracts would require re-negotiation at higher prices on the findings of increased labor costs. The temper of the Congress would very likely have defined retroactive portal-to-portal pay as "unjust enrichment."

have multiplied administrative difficulties, and a recognition of its lack of precision is reflected in a tax rate of 80 per cent rather than 100 per cent.

RECOMMENDED READINGS

Burns, E. M., "Financial Aspects of the Social Security Act," *American Economic Review,* March, 1936.

A short paper dealing with the broader financial problems in allocation of social security burdens.

Hall, J. K., "Incidence of the Federal Social Security Pay Roll Taxes," *Quarterly Journal of Economics,* November, 1938.

Survey of theories, with readable analysis of incidence.

Harriss, S. E., *Economics of Social Security,* N.Y., McGraw-Hill, 1941.

Particularly recommended are Chapter 9 ("The Theory of Reserves"), discussing the economics of the method of financing, and Chapter 13 ("A Survey of Views"), outlining briefly various theories of the incidence of the social security taxes.

Rice, L. P., "Financing Social Security by Means of Payroll Taxes," in *How Shall Business Be Taxed?,* N.Y., Tax Policy League, 1937, Chapter 11.

A clear statement favoring application of the benefit principle in social security finance. Reprinted in Groves, *Viewpoints on Public Finance,* Chapter 70.

CHAPTER 24

State and Local Finance in the National Economy

Increasing economic attention is being paid to the matter of state and local finance, for two major reasons. The first is that the fiscal activities of these governments are increasingly significant to the behavior of aggregate demand in the economy. The second is that the principal functions of these governments are of crucial importance both to the maintenance of living standards and the provision of strategic instruments for economic growth.

One of the really startling developments in public finance has been the persistent growth of state and local outlays in recent years. Between 1946 and 1957, the expenditures made directly by state and local governments increased almost fourfold—from $11 billion to something over $40 billion. These expenditures, which were about 18 per cent of federal budget expenditures in 1946, were nearly 60 per cent as large as federal expenditures in 1957. In terms of the GNP, state and local purchases of currently produced goods and services rose from under 5 per cent of the total in the economy in 1946 to over 8 per cent of a more than doubled total in 1957. It is no longer possible, therefore, to ignore state and local fiscal action as insignificant in the total flow of funds in the economy.

Since World War II state and local outlays have marched forward at a rate of between $2.5 billion and $3 billion per year without interruption, for fiscal needs have left little choice to legislative bodies with respect to the support of local services. These governments since the war have been the most consistently dependable contributors to economic growth of all the components of aggregate demand, with the possible exception of consumers. In recession, state and local purchases of goods and services have, with consumer purchases, moved persistently forward, partially offsetting declines in domestic and foreign investment and in some cases in federal purchases. In recovery and expansion these purchases have held to their rate of growth.

This dependability is not the result of conscious acceptance of responsibility for economic stability and growth, but of the persistence of demand for expansion in the types of services which these governments perform for the public. Indeed, the states and localities have in general chafed under the fiscal "problem" created by this expansion, and have sought to reduce the financial burden whenever possible. But the imperative requirements for education of a rapidly expanding population, for removal of congestion on the highways, for the provision of basic facilities and services in new population centers, and for provision of services to the underprivileged in a wide variety of situations have overridden unrealistic attempts to "hold the line" on government expenditures. The consequence has been a noteworthy rise in state and local debt, from $14 billion in 1946 to $51 billion in 1958. In terms of aggregates, within which much individual variation has occurred, the increase in state and local expenditure has largely been paralleled by the increase in debt. This can be seen in tabular form as follows:[1]

Year	Biennial Increase in State and Local Expenditure ($ billions)	Biennial Increase in State and Local Debt ($ billions)
1946	1.8	−.5
1948	6.4	2.6
1950	5.1	4.4
1952	3.3	5.1
1954	4.6	7.6
1956	6.0	9.3
1958	8.3	8.9

Evidently, state and local governments in the aggregate have reacted to the service imperatives more quickly with respect to expenditure than with respect to taxation. However, much of the increase in expenditure has been for construction, which would normally be financed largely by borrowing. Even so, unwillingness to tax heavily has been characteristic of these governments, and this unwillingness is the result both of lagging adjustment to the realities of the situation and of the burdensome and inequitable character of major taxes employed by them.

[1] Expenditures are direct expenditures of state and local governments, including funds transferred from the federal government but excluding transfers between state and local governments. Figures from Bureau of the Census, *Historical Statistics on State and Local Government Finances, 1902–1953*, p. 19; *Summary of Governmental Finances in 1955*, p. 24, 1956, p. 26; 1958, p. 15; and *Economic Report of the President, 1959*, p. 194.

State and Local Governmental Relationships

The federal system in the United States contemplates a division of governmental sovereignty between two levels of government, federal and state. The area in which the federal government exercises sovereignty is that of foreign and interstate relations. A state exercises sovereignty in matters peculiarly confined within its own boundaries. There are, of course, areas of distinct overlapping between intrastate and interstate affairs, and the lines of demarcation between the two require frequent definition by the courts in cases of specific conflict.

Local governments, embracing county, city, town and village governments, and special districts possess no sovereign powers in their own right. Local governments are thus seen in American political practice as administrative agencies of state governments, on the one hand required by the state to perform certain functions, and on the other hand limited by the state with respect to ways and means. Local governments have rather frequently found themselves in the unfortunate position of the subordinate in a chain of command: required to carry out an order with insufficient freedom or authority to accomplish the requirement successfully.

Though this complaint of local government is frequently heard and frequently justified, there is another and opposite situation which cannot be ignored. It is that if local governments were unrestricted in their choice of services and the means of maintaining them, standards of performance would be highly varied. Some local governments have been inefficient and irresponsible, and the only solution to this problem may well be the centralization of authority in government at a higher and more inclusive level.

The responsibility for performance of local functions such as public education, construction, and maintenance of local highways and roads, and administration of certain personal welfare activities are, in the last analysis, the responsibility of the sovereign state governments. At the same time it is generally agreed that there are distinct advantages in local and more intimate administration of these activities. The personal interest of parents in the quality of public education offered their children is presumed to be a powerful motivating force in providing adequate facilities and good teachers. And because these same parents (and their neighbors) are required to foot the major part of the bill, it is believed that strong incentives to efficient school operation without undue frills are created. As to local highways, the theory is that local residents are in the best position to judge the necessity for road improvement and to distribute improvements fairly or sensibly throughout the locality. And it is reasonable to assume that local residents who know their neighbors and who have a personal interest in the height of local tax rates are in the best position to temper mercy with hard-headed evaluation of charitable and welfare expenditures.

The case for local administration of important state functions is a strong one. It is less strong in principle, however, if local governments simply spend funds passed to them by the state than if these local governments are required to raise the necessary money through their own revenue systems. It is this latter which imposes the important check upon wasteful expenditure. At the same time the sovereign state government cannot escape ultimate responsibility for assuring the performance of such important functions respectably. Direct or indirect coercion upon local governments is therefore necessary at times, when the locality attaches fiscal virtue to excessive niggardliness. The argument for decentralization, for "home rule" and local autonomy, is thus an appealing one, while the decentralization of responsibility opens the door to such a variety of standards of performance as to qualify one's enthusiasm for letting local government's "carry the ball."

Fiscal Problems of Local Governments

Most of the fiscal problems of local governments in the United States stem from the rigidity of their revenue systems and inflation in the costs of their principal functions. The solution of these problems lies in increasing revenues from their own sources, increasing the contributions of governments at higher levels, improving efficiency of operation, or curbing the expansion of outlays.

Promotion of Efficiency. There would appear to be only two ways to reduce expenditures by local governments: to perform given functions at a higher level of efficiency or to lower service standards. We deal with the former in this section.

There can be little doubt that the United States is over-organized at the local government level. The very multiplicity of levels of government within the local category implies that the performance of their functions is frequently spread too thin. Most experts would probably agree that county government is largely an anachronism in our system. In the Northeastern states this is particularly true; the county stands as an artificial geographical and political entity whose functions are the maintenance of certain courts and participation in provision for the aged and the indigent. The allocation of judicial responsibilities to the county as a unit appears to have resulted from a desire to give it something to do; it is not at all apparent that the county is a peculiarly appropriate district to perform the judicial function. Concerning the charitable services provided by the counties, the state governments have all but taken over these services in centralized provision for a variety of welfare services, and quite probably the complete absorption by the state of that part of this function not performed by the towns would markedly improve the level of welfare service.

Elsewhere in the nation the counties have traditionally played a major part in the administration of local highway systems, in addition to the performance of welfare services. But the rapid growth of state highway systems has transferred the responsibility for major highways to the state government. The remaining local roads beyond city boundaries, still the responsibility of the county, might profitably for all concerned be placed under the state. It is almost certain that the highway job can be done both more cheaply and with more acceptable quality by centralization. In general, therefore, the county stands as an essentially hollow governmental shell, and its disappearance would more often than not pass unnoticed except as improvement in quality of service became apparent.

The elimination of county governments would leave a multiplicity of local governments, ranging from town, city, and village governments to subdivisions in the form of school districts, fire districts, road districts, sewer and water districts, and the like. These latter subdivisions frequently possess a rather high degree of independence of city and town governments in matters of taxation and expenditure. The rationale for this independence has generally been either to vest special groups of particularly interested or qualified persons with power to carry on specialized functions as they see fit, or to create specialized boards of trustees over local debt incurred for specialized purposes. Though the objectives in creation of such subdivisions are frequently commendable, it is difficult to see why the same interests and talents cannot be mobilized under an integrated local government, with the specialized services participating in an integrated budget under legislative control. The present multiplicity of local governments seems to be largely historical accident strongly influenced by an indigenous tendency to over-organization.

The dispersion of local governmental functions among several independent or semi-independent "governments" may easily result in inefficiency through inadequate control. Much more important, in all probability, is the inefficiency inherent in the fact that the area to be governed is too small to justify the existence of governmental organization. When the job is big enough it justifies the employment of full-time personnel, it permits the selection of qualified administrators, and it allows effective organization. It may be useful to suggest, however, that "efficiency" is not simply a matter of total cost or cost per capita. It is cost per unit of service at a given level of quality. More and better services usually cost more per capita than fewer and poorer services, but this does not mean that the efficiency of performance is lower. In Table 6 (Chapter 3) we noted a consistent tendency for per capita expenditures to increase as the population of a city increases. But this is due, in general, to a larger variety of services made necessary by population congestion, and per capita costs rise even though the service may be performed at lower cost per unit than would have been possible in a smaller governmental area. When the governmental unit is below optimum size, expenditures in the nature of overhead are distributed among too few persons, while above optimum size the organization becomes too complex for maximum efficiency.

It seems clear that a major obstacle to efficiency in smaller local governments is inadequate population size. But the optimum size of the area for efficient administration of local functions varies with the function considered. Some functions, such as snow removal, annual property assessment, and home relief, may be highly efficiently performed in very small communities. But for other functions, such as highway planning and construction, major reassessment of property, and provision of secondary education, greater efficiency is to be accomplished only in larger units. This is clearly evident in the development of regional schools, which typically represent cooperative arrangements transcending local government boundaries so as to provide both an adequate number of pupils to justify the necessary outlay and to broaden the revenue base for performance of the service.

The representative local government in the United States is not of sufficient size to permit fiscal efficiency. At the same time, however, one would be extremely optimistic to suppose that a reshuffling of governmental boundaries is likely to come about in the near future. For the present system is deeply mired in tradition, in group loyalties, and in legal—even constitutional—arrangements. A realistic view of the situation leads to little optimism concerning the probability of significantly greater efficiency in the use of public monies among these governments. On the other hand, county government has fallen into some disrepute in the popular mind precisely because it is fiscally inefficient, and its abandonment or atrophy in sections of the United States appears but a matter of time. Furthermore, there is a noticeable trend toward integration of the relatively independent subdivisions of local governments with these local governments. The formal consolidation of townships into fiscally efficient communities is by no means an unreasonable expectation over a period of time, in view of the prevalence of fiscal crises among these inefficient units. More probable, however, is the creation of regional authorities which modern conditions demand, here and there taking important functions out of the hands of inefficient units (state as well as local) and depositing them with more or less *ad hoc* governmental institutions capable of meeting the needs of adequate and efficient performance. The more widely this is done the more the small, inefficient governmental unit becomes merely a repository of tradition and not a vital governmental institution. On the whole, however, there can be little hope that in the near future the fiscal pressures upon local governments can be significantly relieved by the accomplishment of real efficiency.

Lowering of Service Standards. It was suggested earlier in the chapter that the fiscal problem of local governments could be solved by increased revenues or by decreased expenditures.[2] The latter can be accomplished either by getting more for the dollar or by being satisfied with less. We have seen that in the short run the prospect of securing more for the dollar by inducing marked efficiency is considerably less than promising. What about lowering service standards? Can we expect that communities will be satisfied by a lower quality of service performance by their local governments? The evidence is clearly in the negative, for less adequate schools and less adequate highways would be quite inconsistent with levels of living in the United States, and it is reasonable to expect that higher standards will be demanded.

Let us examine recent trends in community requirements with respect to the major, and therefore the more costly, local services. The outstandingly important local governmental services are the provision of public primary and secondary education and of local roads and highways.

Table 35 on page 550 brings together pertinent statistical information concerning trends in public educational expenditures by comparing the school years 1939–1940, 1949–1950, and 1957–1958.

The factors causing the "school crisis" are clearly evident in the table. The first is, of course, the rapid increase in school population. This began to be felt in the elementary schools in the late years of the 1940's, following a mid-forties decline to figures below those of 1940. The explosive increase in birth rates during World War II proved to be not a temporary phenomenon, but has continued to the present. Thus, between 1950 and 1958, elementary school enrollments increased very rapidly. A marked decline in secondary school enrollments occurred between 1940 and 1950, attributable to the low birth rates of the nineteen-thirties. But following 1950, an increase of over 50 per cent in high school enrollments has occurred.

---

[2] By decreased expenditures we imply not necessarily an absolute decline below what they were at a previous time, but below what they would be without a conscious attempt to reduce standards of performance.

Although an aggregate increase in school enrollments necessarily increases school costs, the aggregates do not tell the whole story. Much the larger percentage of increase in enrollment has taken place at the secondary school level, where costs per pupil are comparatively high. Specialization in high schools, providing a choice of curricula and of electives within curricula; the need for teachers with specialized training; the provision of equipment for laboratory sciences, for shop, for athletics, and for

TABLE 35

COMPARISONS, 1939–1940, 1949–1950, 1957–1958: CERTAIN ASPECTS
OF PUBLIC DAY SCHOOLS*

	1939–1940	1949–1950	1957–1958	% Increase 1939–1940 and 1957–1958
I. Total Enrollment (000)	25,434	25,111	33,509	31.7
Elementary Schools	18,832	19,405	23,815	26.5
Secondary Schools	6,601	5,707	9,694	46.9
II. Average Salary of				
Classroom Teachers ($)	1,441	3,010	4,650	222.4
III. Current Expenditure per Pupil ($)	88.09	208.83	320.00	266.1
Capital Outlay per Pupil ($)	10.17	40.39	99.57	880.0
IV. Revenue Receipts of Public				
School Systems ($ million)	2,260	5,442	11,143	393.1
From Federal Government (%)	1.8	2.9	3.6	—
From State Governments (%)	30.2	39.6	40.6	—
From Local Governments (%)	68.0	57.5	55.8	—

* Sources: Federal Security Administration, Office of Education, *Statistics of State School Systems, 1949–1950*, Washington, 1952; and National Education Association, *Advanced Estimates of Public . . . Schools . . . 1957–1958*, Washington, 1958.

a variety of other activities—all these make for considerably higher per-pupil costs in secondary than in elementary schools. Finally, the increase in school population has not been a horizontal one; communities in general have not experienced the same rate of growth in enrollments. Along with the startling rise in the aggregate has been a considerable degree of population shift. Older communities have grown less rapidly than new suburban communities. Location of new industrial plants has imposed heavy education, sanitation, and other costs on new communities. The consequence has been to increase the need for new facilities beyond what would have been necessary if the population shifts had not taken place.

The second factor of note in the table is the significant rise in average salaries of teachers. An increase of more than half is seen in the table to have occurred between 1950 and 1958. In a situation of high employment in the economy generally, to attract and to hold the necessary number of teachers has required an increase in salaries more than double the rise in consumer prices during the same period.

Finally, the state and local governments, in the large, have maintained or improved educational standards in the crisis. With obvious exceptions, teacher-pupil ratios have not been permitted seriously to deteriorate, and may have been somewhat improved. Educational "frills" have not been eliminated, and the local communities have apparently insisted upon a quality of education consistent with rising standards of living. The per-pupil costs indicated in the table thus reflect a serious attempt to provide education of a better quality to a larger number of pupils, and under conditions of rising prices and wages.

This has been done substantially without federal financial assistance. With respect to current expenditures it has been done with only very minor increase per pupil in state aid, though the states have probably participated more heavily in school construction than in current expenses. The major burden has thus fallen upon the property tax. But it is important to keep in mind that the school crisis has had a widely variable impact upon communities, and this is not shown in Table 35. The differential impact is one reason why state fiscal systems have not absorbed a larger part of the educational burden. For population centers are characteristically underrepresented in state legislatures; overrepresented rural communities with lesser educational problems are slow to impose state-wide taxes to assist those communities where the impact of educational costs has been greatest.

Although other functions have contributed far less than public education to the "crisis" in local finance, several are important enough to deserve mention. In terms of direct expenditure by local governments, the construction and maintenance of highways and streets is the second most expensive local government function. Local highway direct expenditures have, however, increased somewhat less rapidly in recent years than their total direct expenditures. This is partly due to a tendency for states to take over local roads, both to produce greater uniformity in state highway systems and to take advantage of the more efficient state facilities for construction and maintenance. But another fact contributes to the moderate rise in road costs imposed upon the local governments: state grants for local road purposes have constantly increased. In 1957, of the $2.9 billion of direct expenditure by local governments upon highways, $1.1 billion of the funds were provided through state grants.[3]

Other major objects of local expenditure are public welfare, health and hospitals, and sanitation. The major increase in public welfare expenditures occurred prior to 1950, though modest increases have recently been rather persistent. Here again, however, a substantial part of the cost is provided

[3] *Summary of Governmental Finances in 1957*, pp. 27, 28.

through grants from higher governments. Local health and hospital expenditures have expanded rapidly, both before and after 1950, while grants-in-aid have remained rather small. This class of expenditure, therefore, has contributed rather substantially to rising local government financial responsibilities. Likewise, sanitation facilities have recently become a significant outlay item, resulting from population growth and population shifts. In this area also, state grants are still relatively small. On the whole, therefore, the "crisis" in local finance is mainly attributable to the demands of education. But other functions, individually relatively small but in the aggregate significant, have accentuated the fiscal problem. Among these, for the older and larger cities, is the prospect of major redevelopment outlays, so far rather small in the aggregate but promising major expansion.

Increasing Revenues. On the local revenue side, a remarkable increase has occurred, particularly since World War II. Two general sources of receipts have accounted for the increase: grants-in-aid, particularly from state governments, and local taxes. Table 36 shows the rise in annual receipts since 1922, and relative changes in the importance of revenue sources

TABLE 36

Main Components of Local Government Receipts, Selected Years, 1922–1957[*]

	1922	1932	1942	1952	1957
Total Receipts[a] ($ million)	3,866	5,690	7,122	16,952	25,638
Grants-in-Aid (% of total)	8	14	26	31	29
Taxes (% of total)	80	75	65	56	57
Charges and Miscellaneous (% of total)	12	11	9	13	14
Memorandum:					
Property Taxes as % of Total Taxes	97	97	92	87	87

[*] Sources: Bureau of the Census, *Historical Statistics on State and Local Government Finances, 1902–1953*, p. 21, and *Summary of Governmental Finances in 1957*, p. 22.

[a] Excludes utility and liquor stores revenue and insurance trust revenue.

through the period. A more than threefold increase in total receipts since 1942 is apparent, about half of which has occurred since 1952. The relative importance of state (and federal) grants has changed little since 1942, although the absolute amounts have, of course, markedly expanded. Charges and miscellaneous revenues have shown considerable relative increase between 1942 and 1957, but they remain less than half as important in the total as grants. Taxes as a proportion of the total have declined as the other two categories increased. In absolute amount, however, the tax revenues in 1957 were almost five times as large as in 1922 and over three times as large as in 1942. And as shown in the memorandum line of the table, property taxes have consistently produced an overwhelming proportion of total tax revenues.

Local revenue systems are characterized by a high degree of rigidity. While there are examples of the use of sales and even personal income taxes by local governments, these are by their nature necessarily limited to use by large and relatively isolated cities. Thus, even if local option in the selection of revenue measures were liberally permitted, few local governments would find the use of new forms of taxes practicable. But freedom to choose a form of tax structure is not liberally granted to local governments by the states. This is partly because the states themselves are in a fiscal crisis, and have wished to preserve revenue measures for their own use. In addition, the states have, in general, felt that their surrender of the property tax to local use has endowed the local governments with almost exclusive use of a productive tax measure, and that further fiscal provision is unnecessary. For most local governments, therefore, the property tax is the only available instrument for increasing tax revenues.

Charges and miscellaneous revenues have shown recent fairly large increases, though as a source of additional revenue for general purposes these items are not promising. This category comprises sales of goods and services, interest on investments, and special assessments. Of these, the last is principally responsible for the rise in revenues from this general category, and the receipts from special assessments are necessarily allocated to the cost of improvements beneficial to property. The recent wave of urbanization has made necessary very heavy expenditures for sewer and water extensions, and it is this development which has increased charges and miscellaneous receipts. But the special assessment is not useful for increasing the general funds of local governments, and it is the general funds which must be increased to pay the rising costs of education, health, welfare, police, and the like.

Local governments can expect in practice to meet rapidly rising costs of general functions either by property tax increases or by increased grants from the states. As shown in Table 36, grants to local governments increased rapidly as a proportion of local receipts between 1922 and 1942, and have substantially held this proportion since. The earlier period of expansion is associated with the depression years, and principally with public welfare. Since World War II the absolute expansion of state grants is to a considerable extent associated with education. But the amounts of state aid given to local governments for education purposes vary widely among the states. Estimates for the year 1957–1958 show that for the continental United States, 40 per cent of local receipts for educational purposes (excluding borrowing) were provided by state governments. But six states provided less than 20 per cent of education receipts to their local governments, while eight states provided over 60 per cent.[4] These differences tend to be reflected in differential burdens upon property under the local property tax.

It is worth repeating that an outstanding characteristic of the "fiscal crisis" of local governments is the lack of uniformity in its impact. It depends in some basic degree upon the rate at which demands upon particular local governments have increased. Those localities whose population has shown rapid growth through in-migration have been confronted with the most pressing problems. For in many of these localities the demands have been not only for expanded services but for the substantial improvement in their quality which accompanies urbanization. In most cases these increased requirements have occurred in localities where the use of alternative revenue measures to the property tax is not only impracticable, but also prohibited under the laws of the state. Borrowing in these localities has climbed rapidly toward or to the ceiling established by the debt limit, and a combination of upward revaluation of property assessments and increases in the property tax rate has created serious inequities.

As examples of the differential impact described above, let us consider the behavior of property taxes on the average dwelling in some selected Connecticut towns between 1950 and 1957.[5] In Town A, a large, old, and industrialized city, the tax on the average dwelling increased by 19 per cent between 1950 and 1957. This is a modest rise indeed, in view of the increase in the prices of goods and services purchased by local governments. But population remained relatively stationary, and city services over a long period had been performed at an essentially satisfactory level. Town B is a newly industrialized city, smaller than Town A. Here the tax on the average dwelling rose only 37 per cent, in spite of a rapid rise of population and a rise in the level of local services. But industry has swelled the grand list of taxable property, and large contributions by industry (the incidence of their taxes being largely on persons outside the town) have held local taxes on the average dwelling within reasonable limits. Town C is rural, small, and residential in character. Its population has increased gradually, and the town budget has not been relieved by the inclusion of industry within the tax rolls. The average dwelling in Town C had its taxes raised by 49 per cent between 1950 and 1957. In Town D—a rapidly growing rural town without industry and with large state institutions whose property is tax-exempt— the tax on the average residence rose 144 per cent during the period under

[4] National Education Association, *Advanced Estimates of Public Elementary and Secondary Schools . . . 1957–1958*, Washington, 1957, p. 29.

[5] Computed from State Tax Commissioner (Connecticut), *Information Relative to the Assessment and Collection of Taxes,* 1950 and 1957.

consideration. Town E is a new, suburban "bedroom town." The tax on the average residence here rose by 111 per cent.[6]

While the rate at which taxes have increased does not tell the whole story of burden, it is an important aspect of it. The percentage increase in tax in Town D is almost eight times that in Town A. This does not prove, of course, that the tax is eight times as large. But the rapid increase has two important implications. First, shifting through capitalization—or otherwise— cannot occur as effectively in a period of rapid change in tax levels as in a period of relative stability. Thus, the rapidly rising taxes tend to have a larger share of their incidence upon the current owner of property. Second, the town whose taxes per residence are rising rapidly is probably one in which many property owners cannot participate effectively in the rise in market values of property. The farmer in a boom town, and the older resident, may well find themselves in a situation where the rise in market (and assessed) values places them, willy-nilly, in a situation where the value of property owned is out of all proportion to their current income. Thus, while the tax may not be exorbitant in its relationship to the value of the property on paper, it may well be exorbitant in relation to the income of the taxpayer. This is a point already treated in our discussion of property taxation in Chapter 15. It is a source of very considerable inequity, and its impact is greatest where taxes rise rapidly.

While the high income person may regard as reasonable a property tax of forty mills (4 per cent) on an assessed value of 50 per cent of market value of property, this same tax is a very heavy burden upon those whose incomes have not kept pace with the inflation of property values. Newer residents as a group will find the tax reasonable, while older residents as a group may not. And it is on grounds of this sort of inequity that the tendency has been strong to look for relief in state grants-in-aid to relieve the property tax. For broader-based state taxes are not likely to be subject to as high a degree of inequity as the local property tax. At the same time, we should note that traditional formulae for the distribution of grants by the states do not deal effectively with the differential impact of the crisis upon localities. What is needed is a revision of these formulae to provide more than proportional aid to the rapidly growing locality where the impact of change is greater.

[6] While the tax per average residence is a simple and available measure of tax increases, it is an imperfect measure of tax burdens. The growing town will have in its tax rolls new residences, with relatively higher assessments for the same quality and size of construction. And in some of these growing communities—those of a suburban character—the new residences may well be larger and more elaborate than the older ones.

Fiscal Problems of State Governments

Much of what we have said concerning the crisis in local government finance can be applied with almost equal validity to state governments. The problem is to find the revenues to support established and expanding state functions in an inflationary era. One may assume, however, that the problem of bureaucracy is somewhat more acute at the state level than generally at the local level. Departmental operations are larger and more impressive; these operations tend to be somewhat less personal in the relationships they involve; administrative and research activities tend to be intermingled to a considerable degree; and over-all management, both by the executive and the legislature, is likely to occur at arm's length. It would be improper to assert that the consequence is a high degree of inefficiency; we simply imply that the degree of inefficiency may be greater than it needs to be.

As was mentioned in Chapter 3, the common practice among state governments of earmarking particular revenues for particular funds, to be used for the performance of particular functions, tends to weaken budgetary control over expenditures. For when a function is amply endowed with productive revenues which cannot be "diverted" to other purposes, the budgeting process merely rubber-stamps expenditures to the extent of these earmarked funds. Even the casual observer of state government operation is impressed with the lack of uniformity in facilities provided to different departments. One can almost identify the special funds of a state by observing the ratio of secretaries to executives, of telephones to employees, and the quality and quantity of office equipment. If funds which now support relatively high levels of living in some departments could be spread uniformly, more efficient use would usually result.

Expensive Functions of State Governments. Four functions dominated the general expenditures of state governments in 1958, excluding expenditures of state business enterprises and insurance trust funds. Taken together, expenditures for these four purposes constituted 81 per cent of total general expenditures. They were, in order, education (31 per cent), highways (28 per cent), public welfare (13 per cent), and health and hospitals (9 per cent).[7] These four types of function absorbed about $19.1 billion of expenditure. Of this amount, nearly 37 per cent represented grants to local governments for the performance of these stated functions.[8] In the case of education, the major part of state expenditures (61 per cent) goes directly to local governments for the operation of primary and secondary school

---

[7] *Compendium of State Government Finances in 1958*, p. 22.

[8] Computed from *Compendium, op. cit.*, p. 25.

systems. The remainder provides for state institutions of higher education, special technical schools, and a minor amount for libraries. To a large extent, therefore, state expenditures are made for education in order to relieve local governments of the fiscal burdens present-day school systems would otherwise impose upon them.

The situation with respect to highways is somewhat different. Only 17 per cent of state highway expenditures represented direct grants to local governments in 1958. The major share was used for construction and maintenance of the state highway system, comprising the principal intertown and interstate roads. The conditions requiring significant additions to the highway system since World War II have been referred to earlier. The phenomenal increase in highway construction costs has also been noted. The states have attempted to meet the situation by increasing rates of the taxes and other revenue instruments which have traditionally been channeled into special highway funds. For example, between 1946 and 1952 thirty-one states increased their gasoline tax rates by at least 1 cent per gallon, and between 1952 and 1959 twenty-five did so.[9] The average gasoline tax rate for all states in 1946 was 4.52 cents per gallon, while in 1952 the average had risen to 5.3 cents per gallon and in 1959 to 6.1 cents. The increased tax rates and the rise in motor fuel consumption are largely responsible for a significant increase in construction out of current highway funds after World War II. In 1950, expenditures from current state revenues for highway construction, maintenance, and administration were $1.7 billion. In 1957 this figure had risen to $3.2 billion.[10] In addition, federal grants to the states were $.4 billion and $1.2 billion, respectively. But even this increase in the expenditure of current funds has fallen far short of meeting highway requirements. Outstanding long-term debt incurred by the states for highway construction purposes increased from $1.4 billion in 1950 to $8.0 billion in 1958.[11]

By and large, however, it would be improper to say that highway requirements have caused a serious crisis in state finance. The identification of certain productive revenues for highway purposes has, until recently, provided reasonably adequately for highway needs. When requirements have risen, the tendency has been to increase highway revenues by raising rates of these identified highway revenue instruments, and in the case of a growing system of super-highways, to charge tolls. In general, the policy

[9] U. S. Bureau of Public Roads, *Highway Statistics*, 1950, p. 72, and 1957, p. 88.

[10] Bureau of the Census, *Compendium of State Government Finances*, 1950, p. 37, and 1958, p. 39.

[11] Comparison of rates in the 1946 edition of *Tax Systems* with those in the 1952 edition, and with Commerce Clearing House, *State Tax Guide*, 1959.

has been to cut the garment to fit the cloth, after a reasonable amount of elasticity in highway revenues has been taken up. The result is that many urgent highway needs remain unfulfilled, but the urgency of the need tends to be measured against a relatively high standard of excellence. The basis for judgment of the adequacy of highways is by no means austere; we tend to label a highway inadequate if it is unsafe at very high speeds, or if cross-traffic or traffic congestion imposes delay in reaching one's destination. Comparably luxurious standards are not applied to most state services.

The fiscal crisis of state governments is real with respect to the general funds of the states, involving those inadequately financed general services which must subsist upon what remains of state revenues after earmarked receipts are allocated to their particular functions. Of the more expensive categories of state functions listed earlier in this chapter, education, welfare, and health and hospitals are of this nature. These three functions, dependent upon the general funds of the states, make up over half of the general expenditures of the states (including highways). The general funds are also the source of payments for general governmental administration, and in addition, unusual new functions, such as the provision of state bonuses for soldiers, public buildings, and housing, usually fall upon the general funds. The consequence of this great pressure upon the general funds, financed principally by sales taxes, individual income taxes, business taxes, specific excise taxes, and some license revenues, has been a frantic search for new tax sources and federal grants, and a policy of austerity with respect to these general services. A feeling is current among state officials that the crisis cannot be solved unless the federal government renounces its "tax-greediness," leaving more potential revenue to the states. In the more wealthy states much is made of the federal "drain," represented by the excess of federal tax payments by citizens of those states over federal payments back to those states. But most of this is merely discontent; there appears to be little real expectation that much change in this respect will be forthcoming. The states thus talk a great deal of these federal "injustices," but their actions are largely concentrated upon trying to stem the tide of expenditure increase at home and getting a larger share of federal grants.

Possible Solutions to the State-Local Fiscal "Crisis"

In using the term "crisis" to describe the fiscal situation of state and local governments, we are mindful that the term does not apply with equal force to all state and local governmental units. Some of the more fortunate or more forward-looking continue to be in good fiscal condition. Indeed, the spottiness of the distribution of critical conditions has tended to work against determined attack upon the problems of those units which find themselves in trouble.[12] However, with the passage of time fiscal hardship has embraced larger and larger numbers of governmental units, and this has contributed to a more widespread feeling of urgency.

From the viewpoint of the governments affected, the "crisis" is budgetary —the inability to balance their budgets without severe limitation of expenditures for essential functions. Between 1950 and 1957, state and local debt in the aggregate increased by about $28 billion, an average of $4 billion per year. About three-fourths of this increase has been in local government debt. The remarkable increase in debt outstanding does not, however, reflect equivalent budget deficits on current account, for a large part represents capital expenditure on school buildings, sewer and water installations, and highways. If these capital outlays were, in fact, essentially nonrecurrent, the debt increase created by them would be less alarming to the issuing governments. That is, if these expenditures could be considered as unusual outlays to catch up with requirements, it would be prudent to finance them by long-term borrowing and amortize the cost out of current revenues. But in many cases these outlays must be regarded as recurrent—not to *catch up* so much as to *keep up* with persistently rising demand for facilities. Under such circumstances, the rise of debt does reflect something akin to current deficit, and the piling up of debt builds up an increasingly serious budgetary problem for the future. Governments faced with these circumstances would do well to provide immediately for major increase in current tax or other receipts.

Borrowing to cover the difference between expenditure and income has encountered critical problems in recent years. The condition of the economy, with temporary exceptions, has been one of pressure of demand upon resources. This has been particularly evident in the money and capital markets, where the large demand for funds, coupled with tight money policy, has forced up interest rates. The consequences to state and local borrowing governments are suggested in Table 37, showing yields on high-grade municipal bonds annually from 1950 to 1959.

---

[12] The 1959 crisis in state government finance in Michigan is a case in point. A series of poor automobile years, accentuated by the recession of 1958, had adverse effects upon both revenues and expenditures. The earlier prodigal assignment of a major portion of sales tax revenues to local governments, and the imposition of a constitutional limitation upon the sales tax rate, created a situation in which local use of the property tax was relatively meager while the state was unable to pay for current expenditures. A tight state debt limit precluded further borrowing, and the adoption of a state personal income tax was rigidly resisted by one house of the legislature. Fiscal crisis at the state level was thus apparently regarded as a cheap price to pay for local government affluence.

TABLE 37

MUNICIPAL BOND YIELDS, ANNUAL AVERAGE, 1950–1959*

Year	Municipal Bond Yields (% per annum)	Year	Municipal Bond Yields (% per annum)
1950	1.98	1955	2.53
1951	2.00	1956	2.93
1952	2.19	1957	3.60
1953	2.72	1958	3.56
1954	2.37	1959	3.95

* From Joint Economic Committee, *Economic Indicators*, Historical and Descriptive Supplement (1957) and January, 1960. The yield figures are averages of weekly data. The yield is not the interest rate at issue, but a computation showing the rate of return which would equate the present value of the provisions in the bond contract with the market price at which the bonds were selling.

A simple computation using the figures above will indicate the effect of a rise in interest rates upon the cost of a public project. Suppose a municipality were to borrow $1 million for a project by issue of twenty-year serial bonds, one-twentieth of the issue maturing each year. By a rough but reasonably accurate calculation,[13] we compute the total interest outlay to be the interest rate *times* half of the total bond issue for each of twenty years. The total cost of the project if the borrowing had occurred in selected years, using the rates of yield in Table 37 as the rates of interest on the bonds, would be:

Year	Yield (%)	Principal ($)	Interest ($)[a]	Total Cost ($)
1950	1.98	1,000,000	198,000	1,198,000
1955	2.53	1,000,000	253,000	1,253,000
1959	3.95	1,000,000	395,000	1,395,000

[a] $500,000 (average principal amount outstanding per year) *times* the interest rate for that year *times* twenty (years).

The total cost of the project if the borrowing had been done in 1959 would have been about $200,000, or 17 per cent, greater than if it had been done in 1950 and about 11 per cent higher than in 1955. States and local governments are quite sensitive to changes in interest rates, for higher interest charges will necessarily call forth higher tax rates. Though this sensitivity is difficult to demonstrate statistically, there is a tendency to translate borrowing costs into tax rates, voters are more hesitant to approve major bond issues when interest costs are high, and governments are more hesitant to float bonds in congested markets. Factors other than the interest rate will, of course, affect the volume of new issues in the market at any given time. Among these factors are the availability of room for further borrowing

[13] Ignoring the possibility that various pieces of the issue would carry different interest rates, and assuming annual interest payments.

within the debt limit, the public's feeling with respect to the remaining capacity of the tax system to produce more revenue without imposing "unbearable" tax burdens, and the immediacy and intensity of the need for the new facilities.

It may be worth noting that the prices of goods and services purchased by state and local governments rose rapidly during the decade of the 1950's. The index (1954 = 100) rose from 83.7 in 1950 to 117.7 in 1958. This is an average rise of about 4 percentage points per year, and can be compared with an average rise of about 1.5 percentage points per year in wholesale prices and about 2 points in the consumer price index. Substantial annual revenue increases are therefore required simply to permit state and local governments to buy goods and services on the previous scale.

There is an inclination in some quarters to rely upon the growth of the tax base, as economic growth occurs, to provide automatically the additional revenue required without increasing tax rates. But this is a forlorn hope, given the principal tax forms utilized by state and local governments. While revenues from sales, excises, and gross receipts taxes have shown approximately the same percentage increase between 1950 and 1957 as state and local expenditures from their own funds, this has been accomplished by substantial increases in the rates of these taxes. The necessity for rate increases reflects the fact that the aggregate base of these taxes has not increased as rapidly as expenditures (net of federal grants).

Not only have aggregate consumption expenditures in the economy risen less rapidly since 1950 than state and local expenditures from their own sources,[14] but the base of consumption taxes is considerably narrower than aggregate consumption expenditures. While aggregate consumption increased by 46 per cent, the service component of aggregate consumption rose by 71 per cent while the commodity component rose only 34 per cent. Services are, in general, exempt from state sales and excise taxation, and their growth thus adds little to the base of such taxes. Therefore, in order for revenues to keep up with the rise in expenditures, additional taxes in these categories have needed to be adopted and rates on existing taxes increased.

The property tax—the revenue mainstay of local governments—has behaved similarly. The base of the property tax expands *automatically* only as additional items of property are brought into the tax lists. Increases in

[14] Personal consumption expenditures in the aggregate increased by 46 per cent between 1950 and 1957. During the same period, state and local expenditures (exclusive of those from federal grants) increased by about 81 per cent and state and local revenues from sales, excises, and gross receipts taxes by about 76 per cent.

property values are incorporated into the tax base only by revaluation, which normally occurs only periodically as wholesale revaluations are made. Both of these factors for increase in the base have been at work in recent years. But the property tax revenue increase necessary to match the increase in state and local expenditures has required substantial tax *rate* increases in most localities. However, there is a peculiar barrier to continued upward revaluation and rate increases. It is the loose and undependable relation between income (taxable capacity) and property ownership. To raise property tax valuations and rates in order to extract higher contributions from those whose incomes are rising, it is inevitable that the same sort of increase will apply to those whose incomes are remaining constant or falling. Thus, the hardships involved in imposing higher property taxes on those whose incomes are stable, falling, or slowly rising effectively prevent local governments from raising these taxes at a rate which would keep pace with rapidly rising incomes.

Solutions Available to State and Local Governments. There is much to be said for requiring state and local governments to work out their own solutions to their fiscal crises. This is consistent with the notion of state sovereignty and of a maximum feasible degree of decentralization. It means, of course, that responsibility rests with the states, for constitutionally the local governments exist only as arms of the states. What are some of the actions which might be taken by these governments?

1. Promoting Efficiency in Expenditures. With respect to local government functions, the units performing them are in many cases incapable of performing them efficiently. These units are to a considerable extent historical accidents, and their boundaries are not natural boundaries within which efficient performance can be attained. Specifically, many localities are too small, and consolidation of contiguous units on a functional basis would offer real opportunity for both more efficient and higher quality service. This does not mean a wholesale reshuffling of local government boundaries, for the proper area within which a particular function may be more efficiently performed is not necessarily the proper area for another. The slow recent trend toward "regional" schools is an example of the establishment of governmental units transcending traditional boundaries. Regional planning is an attempt to rationalize land and resource use within the existing framework of local government. "Authorities" designed to develop integrated regional facilities, such as water resources, transportation facilities, and the like, have been successfully used. The point is that to assign to traditional political units the responsibility independently to provide their own services tends to multiply overhead unnecessarily and to prevent the realization of economies of scale.

There would appear to be many areas of local government operation which could be benefited by technical assistance from the state. In some cases, this would take form of research services, providing, for example, technical guidance in the efficient construction of school buildings, roads, and similar structures. There would seem to be no reason why states could not provide auditing services for their local governments. The state tax department could save local assessors considerable outlay for periodic property revaluation by providing this service free or at cost. State assistance to local governments in floating their securities would also seem to be feasible. The planning of issues to provide orderly access to the capital market, and to avoid disorderly competition for supplies of funds, is a function which the states could usefully provide. It might even be appropriate to establish a system of state guarantees of local bond issues, reducing risks on such issues and thus reducing interest costs.

At the state level, there are do-it-yourself possibilities capable of effecting some savings. A considerable lack of technical competence within state governmental agencies is apparent in recent years. Highway departments seem more and more to turn to private engineering firms for highway planning in its more technical aspects. Legal services are bought from private firms rather than being performed by state agencies. Advice on financing is too often received from private groups with a pecuniary interest in the financing, and the absence of such financial competence in state government means that the state is too much at the mercy of interested outsiders. Agencies concerned with economic growth tend more and more to publish elegant but banal brochures on the attractiveness of the state, and substitute for hard analysis the easy practice of hiring professional consultants to say the obvious for a price. The tendency to routinize departmental operations and hire the critical jobs done by outsiders is partly the result of a desire to escape responsibility for mistakes in planning, and partly due to the questionable assumption that outsiders are more objective. But principally it is the consequence of erosion of technical competence through unwillingness to pay for competence.

2. *Improved Practices in Fiscal Management.* We have indicated above the probability that the cost of borrowing by local (and state) governments could be reduced through technical assistance by the state. In addition, however, the state and local governments hold large reserves in cash and securities which, if invested to a larger extent in state and local securities, would provide a wider market for these securities.[15] In 1957, state and local

---

[15] This point was tentatively advanced by B. U. Ratchford in testimony before the Joint Economic Committee. See *Hearings . . . January, 1957, Economic Report of the President*, Washington, 1957, p. 422.

governments in the aggregate had cash and security holdings of $48 billion. Almost $20 billion of this was in cash and deposits, $17 billion in federal securities, and almost $8 billion in their own or other state and local securities.[16] An increase in the last category at the expense of the others, and particularly the first, could well be of advantage to borrowing governments as well as to those whose reserves are earning little or no income.

But more important in the area of fiscal management is the saving possible by more sensible budget practice. The widespread practice in many sections of the country of granting fiscal independence to boards of education places the power to tax and spend in the hands of groups who are advocates for a particular function. Removal of this very expensive function (education) from ordinary budget procedures may well lead to results which might better be avoided.[17] At the state level, as we have seen in an earlier chapter, the compartmentalization of budgets into special and essentially independent funds has been carried to extremes. When particular revenues are earmarked for special purposes, and fund surpluses cannot be transferred, the possibilities for efficient management of resources are rather severely limited. The appearance of special fund surplus can too easily be avoided by making relatively unnecessary expenditures.

The above paragraphs suggest several areas in which improvements in practices by state and local governments could mitigate the fiscal crisis, but it is quite unlikely that they could solve it. For most of these governments, the solution requires bold action substantially increasing revenues.

3. *New Revenues.* Taxes, charges, and miscellaneous revenues of the state governments (excluding grants from other governments and receipts from business-type enterprises and insurance systems) rose by about 86 per cent between 1950 and 1957. For local governments the rise was almost exactly the same (about 88 per cent).[18] Our earlier discussion of the property tax rather clearly indicated that for the future this neck-and-neck progression of local with state revenues is both unlikely and undesirable. The practical limits imposed upon the property tax by the inability of its base to increase uniformly with economic growth suggest that rapid increase in revenue from this source would accentuate the already serious hardship imposed upon the property owner whose income is not rising. This is not to say that property tax revenues cannot or should not increase. For additions

---

[16] *Summary of Governmental Finances in 1957*, p. 36.

[17] This is a very live issue among partisans possessing low boiling points. One might be inclined to join one side in one locality and the other side in another, depending upon many factors. But in general, the principle of budget unity is well established.

[18] *Historical Statistics on State and Local Government Finances* and *Summary of Governmental Finances in 1957*.

to the tax base, in the form of more houses, more automobiles, and more business buildings, equipment, and inventories, will swell the property tax base even if assessments and rates are not raised. But this kind of automatic expansion of the base will surely be inadequate to provide the revenue needed to cover increasing local expenditures.

It seems clearly evident, therefore, that the principal responsibility for raising revenues to cover rising state and local expenditures will rest with the state governments. Their revenue systems, based as they are upon retail sales, personal income, and corporate profits, are reasonably sensitive to economic expansion. But in addition, the rates of these major taxes can be raised with far less hardship than can those of the local governments because these tax bases are much more closely tied to income as the measure of taxable capacity. Even so, it is not to be assumed that substantial increases in state revenues can be accomplished without effort and without intelligent leadership.

A first step, if increased local as well as state expenditures are to be met primarily from increased state revenues, is to rationalize the formulae for state aid to local governments. If a state has effectively equalized or made uniform the levels at which local property is assessed, it can then compare the tax efforts of local governments in terms of their tax rates. And if, further, state grants are used to help the genuinely needy who are already putting forth a standard tax effort, no significant alteration of the grant formulae is required. The appropriate grant formula should then accomplish two objectives: (1) give special aid to those communities in which congestion forces current "housekeeping" costs per dollar of taxable property to an abnormally high figure, and (2) aid rapidly growing communities through grants for the expensive capital improvements which rapid growth entails. A locality which chooses to carry on a function at a quality above the average level would then expect to finance this quality differential out of its own resources.[19] These types of equalization grants would clearly focus state assistance where the critical problems are. Some states attempt such a program, and though it is necessary to keep it up to date, appear to be reasonably successful.

In other states the error of assuming that the intensity of fiscal crisis is inversely related to the size of the local community has led to quite irrational grant formulae. Where the principal education grants are on a per-pupil

[19] An excellent analysis of state grant-in-aid principles is found in Dorothy C. Goodwin, *Economics of a Coordinated Property Tax and State Grant System for Connecticut*, unpublished doctoral dissertation, the University of Connecticut, 1937. Chapters 3, 5–10 are especially instructive concerning the matters discussed here.

basis, declining as the number of pupils rises; where school transportation grants are made only to rural communities; and where highway grants are made on a per-mile-of-improved-roads basis, but for only the first few miles —in all these cases it is clear that the legislature is operating upon the very questionable assumption that the smaller the community the greater its fiscal problems. The local crisis is most serious, in general, for the rapidly growing locality, whether small or large. It faces rising costs per capita because of the diseconomies of congestion, and particularly because of the need for rapidly expanding capital structures. But at the same time, under the formulae described here, it faces declining per capita state grants. In order to counter this tendency, if the schedule of grant payments is raised horizontally to help the rapidly growing localities, these grants become relatively excessive for those which are not growing. This may well mean that in order to permit the hard-pressed growing towns to maintain a reasonable standard of service, the grants will allow other towns to maintain that standard without putting forth a proper local tax effort. Particular concern for the fiscal problems of small local governments is partly due to a failure to catch up to the realities of the present situation, and partly due to the fairly widespread pattern of over-representation of small rural communities in state legislatures.

When proper formulae are established, the needs for additional state aid can be more sensibly forecast. In meeting these needs, the time will inevitably arrive when the states will realize that the job cannot be done by continuing to push up the rates on minor taxes. Tax rates on motor fuels would appear to have been pressed close to a practical limit, particularly in view of recent substantial increases in federal taxes on these products. Much the same may be said about taxes on alcoholic beverages and tobacco products. The favorite commodities for special excises have been imposed upon so extensively and so intensively that there is little slack for further exploitation.

The fact is, therefore, that broad-based major tax instruments must be called upon to provide the substantially increased state revenues required for the future. And these are retail sales taxes and personal income taxes. Each has a broad enough base to provide major revenues with relatively modest rates, and the base of each is closely enough tied to the fundamental measure of economic activity (the GNP and its variants) to respond automatically to economic growth as well as to distribute burdens with reasonable equity.

In 1958 three states used neither of these major tax measures. In that year nineteen states had no general personal income tax, and twelve others assigned so minor a role to it as to derive from it less than 10 per cent of their tax revenues. Only thirty-three states used general sales and gross receipts taxes in 1958; twenty-eight of them raised more than 25 per cent of tax revenues from this source, but only thirteen raised as much as one-third.[20] The impression is easily gained that the adoption of an unused but broad-based tax is available to many of the states, while others could increase revenues by increasing the rates or broadening the base of measures already in use.

With some exceptions, the states have been slow to assign a major role to personal income taxes. It is especially interesting to note that of the fifteen states with the highest per capita personal income in 1956, only six taxed personal income directly in 1957. Of the nine of these states not employing a personal income tax, only one is ranked among the top fifteen states in the amount of state aid given to local communities for the current expenses of public education.[21] It seems fairly evident, therefore, that the high income states are rather generally missing an opportunity which is peculiarly favorable to them. One may ask why they do not capitalize on this favorable situation.

A major reason would seem to be that the high income states are particularly conscious of the heavy income tax bite of the federal government. They tend to accept the assumption that the federal government has "preempted" the field of income taxation by employing high progressive rates. This false assumption seems to imply that there are separate streams or reservoirs of income which can be reached only by instruments aimed at these reservoirs separately. The fact is, of course, that if income can justifiably be taken by any revenue measure, it can be taken directly by a personal income tax. But the widespread assumption of "pre-emption" by the federal government has an interesting additional implication. The high income states have, in general, objected to the federal "drain" implicit in a system of federal grants to the states. They have claimed—and correctly— that the federal progressive income tax takes larger amounts of revenue per capita from the high income states, while the federal grants distribute larger

[20] The figures in this paragraph are computed from various tables in *Compendium of State Government Finances in 1958*. It is not, of course, a hard and fast rule that any particular proportion of tax revenues should be derived from either of these broad tax measures. Some states may tax incomes or sales relatively heavily to avoid having to tax the other heavily. And some states, fortunately, have special resource situations which permit them to do fairly well without heavy dependence upon one or the other of these taxes (e.g., oil production taxes in Texas, property taxation in Nebraska, and corporation licenses in New Jersey).

[21] National Education Association, *Advanced Estimates of Public Elementary and Secondary Schools . . . in 1957–1958*, p. 29.

amounts per capita to the low income states. The rich states have tended—quite unsuccessfully—to check the expansion of federal grant programs in order to limit this drain. What they fail to realize is that, since state taxes are deductible from the base of the federal income tax, the best way to reduce the drain is to impose state taxes for state purposes. Especially in the high income states, where individuals fall in the high federal tax brackets, this deductibility is a very effective instrument for keeping funds within the state at the expense of the federal government. And although nearly all state and local taxes are deductible from the federal tax, a state income tax which involves lump-sum payments is more likely in fact to be deducted by the taxpayer.

Somewhat related to the presumption of federal "pre-emption" of personal income taxation is the view that the high degree of progression in the federal tax should not be intensified by a progressive state income tax, but rather should be offset by state taxes which are regressive or proportional. Quite aside from the wisdom of a particular degree of progression, it is important to observe how progressive, in fact, a state income tax can be. Here, again, we must consider deductibility of the state tax from the federal base. Repeating some of the calculations presented in Chapter 16, if we consider the 1959 New York state income tax both by itself and after deduction of the state tax from the federal base, we get the following, assuming a married couple with no children:[22]

Adjusted Gross Income	Average Rates of State Tax,[a] Ignoring Deductibility (%)	Net Burden of State Tax as % of Adjusted Gross Income after Federal Tax
$1,000	.0	.0
3,000	1.17	.3
5,000	1.84	1.24
10,000	3.08	2.64
15,000	4.42	3.54
25,000	5.97	4.76
50,000	7.48	4.90
100,000	8.24	4.64
500,000	8.65	2.80
1,000,000	8.92	3.45

[a] With personal exemption of $1,200 and deductions of 10 per cent of adjusted gross income.

The second column in the table indicates the effective rate of the state tax on various incomes if no deduction of state taxes from the federal base is considered. In this column, the tax appears to be mildly progressive, as the legislators intended it to be. Clearly, even without deductibility the state

[22] The New York and Minnesota cases following are taken from material kindly provided by Mr. Emanuel Melichar of the Federal Reserve Bank of Richmond.

tax would add rather little to the degree of progressiveness of the aggregate tax structure. But the net bite of the state income tax after deduction of this tax from the federal base is much more moderate, as shown in the third column. In fact, while the state tax taken alone is persistently (though moderately) progressive, after deduction it is more moderately progressive for a time, but actually becomes regressive for the largest incomes. This is clearly not intended by the framers of the tax.

But some states also permit deduction of the federal income tax from the base of the state tax in addition to the reverse deduction of the state tax from the federal base. This may be referred to as "mutual deductibility," and accentuates the effect shown in the third column above. For example, under the Minnesota income tax in 1959, which provides for mutual deduction, the net burden for a married couple after deduction, expressed as a percentage of residual income after federal tax, is as follows:

Adjusted Gross Income	Net Burden of State Tax after Mutual Deduction (% of Residual Income)
$1,000	.0
3,000	.80
5,000	1.70
10,000	3.16
15,000	3.80
25,000	4.15
50,000	3.59
100,000	2.68
500,000	.70
1,000,000	.63

Although there are very minor differences in the rate structures between the New York and the Minnesota taxes, it is safe to compare the second column in this table with the third column in the preceding table. In the case of the Minnesota tax the curve of net burden has a very pronounced hump, and the additional state tax on the $1,000,000 income receiver is actually less per dollar than on the $3,000 income receiver. It is important, however, to point out that while the total effect of the state income tax after deduction is one of very mild progression in the lower and middle brackets, followed by regression in the high brackets, it is the federal government whose revenues suffer primarily, and not the state's.[23] It is for this reason that the use of an income tax by a high income state serves to counteract the "drain" inherent in the federal grant system. But beyond this, the opposition to state income taxes arises largely out of the tendency to look at the raw schedule

[23] When, as in most states employing an income tax, deductibility works only one way, state revenues do not suffer at all. When deductibility is mutual, the state revenues are reduced.

of rates in state income tax laws, rather than to look at the ultimate results after deduction.

While an objection to the use of progressive state income taxes has been traditionally based upon the notion that it is inequitable to pile a progressive state income tax on to a steeply progressive federal tax, it is quite doubtful that—given deductibility—the typical state income tax distributes tax burdens very widely differently from a state sales tax. It is commonly presumed that a sales tax is regressive. This depends, of course, upon consumption habits of the public and upon the schedule of sales tax exemptions. If food is exempt, the available studies seem to indicate that, at least above the lowest incomes, the sales tax is either proportional or very mildly progressive up to the high middle incomes, after which it is regressive.[24] If food is not exempted, the sales tax is steeply regressive at the lower end of the income scale. And because services—exempt in general from sales taxes—represent major items of expenditure for high incomes, the tax becomes regressive at high income levels, whether or not food is taxed. If these conclusions with respect to the allocation of burdens under the sales tax are accepted, and if we look at the final allocations *after deductions* under the personal income tax, a strong preference for one over the other on equity grounds largely disappears. It is clear, however, that the sales tax is more burdensome upon the very small incomes than the progressive income tax, for they are or can be made exempt from the latter. And the state income tax can be made more progressive than it now is in the states, by steeper progression of rates and by elimination of deductibility.[25]

[24] There is a shameful lack of basic information on this point, which is central to the choice between sales and income taxes. Professor Due cites several rather localized studies (John F. Due, *Sales Taxation,* Urbana, University of Illinois, 1957, pp. 25–29) indicating somewhat conflicting conclusions, though having a tendency to support the above generalizations. A California study (William H. Hickman, *Distribution of the Burden of California Sales and Other Excise Taxes,* Sacramento, State Board of Equalization) seems   roughly, at least, to support the above conclusions (see especially Table 6.)

[25] The pattern of final allocations after deduction of state income taxes is as it is because of high progressive rates in the federal tax. A dollar of personal income subject to the starting 20 per cent federal rate enters the state tax return as eighty cents of income after deduction, while a dollar subject to a 75 per cent federal rate is only twenty-five cents in the state return. Thus, at the lower end of the income scale, where both federal and state rates rise rapidly, the additional state tax rises only moderately after deduction. At very high income levels, where the federal rate is very high, deduction of the federal tax from the state tax base produces very moderate amounts of state tax. It is therefore evident that the net state income tax could be made more progressive by scaling down federal rates and reducing the amount deductible from the state base at any income level, by eliminating deduction of the federal tax from the state tax base, or by making the state tax rates more steeply progressive to offset the progressively high deductions from the base.

So long as the public tends to take an unsophisticated view of the combined effect of federal and state income tax rates—failing to take deductibility into account—the possibilities for significant increase in statutory rates in state taxes are quite limited. In this unsophisticated view the combined "bite" of the two taxes is a simple sum of their marginal rates. A sum of marginal rates in excess of 100 per cent is almost unthinkable. And when the maximum marginal federal rate is 91 per cent, there is an inclination to limit the maximum state rate to 9 per cent or less.[26] When a 9 per cent maximum state rate is used, what at first glance appears to be a combined federal and state income tax of 100 per cent on ordinary income over $400,000 (for a joint return) is actually a tax of 91.81 per cent. When the federal tax of $.91 on a marginal dollar of such income is deducted from that dollar for state tax purposes, the state rate of 9 per cent is applied to the remaining $.09, and the state tax is $.0081. Thus, the combined federal and state tax on that dollar of income is $.9181. If the top state rate were 50 per cent, what appears to be a combined rate of 141 per cent on the marginal dollars of a very high income is actually 95.5 per cent.[27] Until the consequences of deductibility are understood, it seems politically unlikely that rates will be altered sufficiently to provide any significant degree of net progressivity in state income taxation.

The states have been rather slow in responding to the need for tax rate increases partly because of the fear of competitive consequences. The typical state is not a natural or integrated economic unit. The possibility of migration of industry and of population is a fact to be faced, and the states are highly conscious of this fact. This is not to say that the tax structure is a dominant factor in location; it is sufficient that the tax structure is thought to be an important influence upon location. The refusal of New Jersey and Connecticut to tax personal incomes is based partly, at least, upon the desire to attract as residents persons who earn relatively high incomes in New York City. But it is difficult to see where else these residents could have located

[26] There are several states, however, in which the maximum income tax rates exceed 9 per cent. But they exceed it only slightly. For example, the maximum New York rate is 10 per cent and that of Minnesota 11.55 per cent.

[27] Because of deduction, a top state rate of 9 per cent on the marginal dollars of high incomes subject to the federal 91 per cent rate imposes almost exactly the same additional state tax per dollar as a 1 per cent state rate imposes upon income in the lowest (20 per cent) federal bracket.

Per dollar of net income in excess of $400,000, the federal tax is 91 per cent, or $.91, and the state tax is 9 per cent of $.09, or $.0081. The net tax added by the state is therefore at the rate of 0.81 per cent of the dollar of net income. If the income falls in the first federal bracket the federal tax is 20 per cent, or $.20. A state tax at 1 per cent on the remaining $.80 is $.008; the additional state tax is therefore at the rate of 0.8 per cent of the dollar of net income.

if these states had imposed income taxes like that of New York. And it is highly unlikely that imposition of an income tax now would generate any measurable movement out of those states. Where would they go? A similar geographic and population situation is to be found in the District of Columbia area; both Maryland and Virgina employ income taxes, as does the District.

Neither of the broad-based state taxes—on sales and on personal income—directly affects the profitability of business and industry. That is, these are taxes on persons and not on business enterprises, and they therefore do not represent costs of doing business. It is sometimes claimed that the imposition of a state income tax, since it affects the personal after-tax incomes of those who determine the location of business firms, is a factor in business location. This view is hardly convincing, for the personal tax influence must be far down in the list of considerations which affect business location decisions. Availability to markets or to raw materials and power, efficiency of transportation, availability of a labor force of required quality and quantity, the provision of resources such as water for certain types of manufacturing, and a level of public services which constitute a healthy business environment, have been demonstrated to be far more influential in business location than the form of taxation applied to executives. In fact, it is quite probable that if the decision is between holding back state and local services and increasing or imposing state income (or sales) taxes, the former would be more discouraging to industry than the latter. Availability of good highways so the workers can get to work, availability of good schools, and availability of recreational facilities, hospitals, and the like are much more important in industry location decisions than the level of personal taxation by the state.[28]

The competitive consequences of a major rise in sales tax rates is potentially a slightly more serious matter than a rise in income tax rates. Since use taxes cannot be very effectively administered, except in special cases such as automobiles, a rise in sales tax rates in a given state may be disadvantageous to sellers in that state *vis-a-vis* sellers in an adjoining state with lower sales tax rates. This competitive disadvantage will apply, however, only in border areas where the inconvenience of buying and transportation costs do not offset the sales tax difference. The effect is therefore somewhat spotty. Where areas of population congestion spill over state lines, the effect

---

[28] Though studies on this point are not extensive, those that have been made agree that the level of taxation in general is a relatively unimportant datum entering into location decisions. The level of local property taxation is more important, however, than the level of personal taxation, and the increase of broad-based state personal taxation is advocated to substitute for an otherwise inevitable major increase in property tax burdens.

is more significant than in other areas.[29] But while sales tax state X, which is subject to this competitive disadvantage, may hesitate to lead out in widening the gap by raising its tax rate, state Y without a sales tax may well find it can afford to narrow the gap by imposing such a tax. A ratchet effect may be created, which permits both states to improve their revenues without serious competitive consequences for either.

4. *Federal Aid.* Up to this point we have considered solutions to the state-local fiscal "crisis" only in terms of what these governments can do for themselves. There remains the possibility that these governments might turn to the federal government for revenue assistance through grants-in-aid. This has always possessed a considerable amount of public attractiveness, particularly in the lower income states whose tax contribution to these programs would be less than the amounts of grants they would receive. But on a higher plane of rationality, such programs would be carried out at the state and local levels with funds raised through the superior federal tax system. Since state and local tax systems are on the whole regressive in character, while that of the federal government is progressive, there is much to be said for raising the funds by use of the superior federal system. The opposition to increased federal aid comes from those who would be required to contribute more heavily under the progressive federal tax system, from those who fear that the provision of funds by the federal government would involve excessive federal control in their use, and from those who feel that the federal budget is already too large and federal taxes too high. Both sides seem to agree that it is easier to get substantial funds for a new project from the federal government than from the state and local governments.

Federal aid to state and local governments has remained very consistently at the ratio of about 5 per cent of total federal *budget* expenditures during the decade of the 1950's. This represents nearly a doubling of the amount of aid, however, rising from $2.3 billion in 1950 to an estimated $4.1 billion in 1960. But even this does not tell the whole story, for while federal highway grants of $.5 billion were included in the budget expenditures in 1950, grants of $3.0 billion for this purpose are not included as budget but as trust fund expenditures. Federal grants to state and local governments have, therefore, increased very considerably in dollar value in recent years. Total aid grants to these governments, on budget and trust fund accounts, were $2.2 billion in 1950 and were estimated at $6.9 billion for 1960.[30] This is a large increase,

[29] The establishment of branches of Washington, D. C., stores across the river in Virginia is in some degree the consequence of the fact that Virginia has no sales tax while Washington has.

[30] Figures from *Budget of the United States Government . . . 1952*, and *idem.*, 1960, Special Analysis G in both cases.

but the question is, to what extent does it represent relief of state and local budgets? The answer hinges upon whether the states would have undertaken these services on their present scale in the absence of federal aid. It is instructive to note the categories in which major increases in federal grants to states and local governments have occurred during the 1950's. These are shown in Table 38.

TABLE 38

Federal Grants, by Purpose, 1950, 1960*

Purpose of Grant	1950 (Actual) ($ million)	1960 (Estimates) ($ million)
Highways	406	3,015
Public Assistance	1,123	2,018
Employment Service	208	316
School Lunches	83	228
Housing and Urban Renewal	9	220
Special School Aid	39	130
Hospital Construction	56	128
All Others	302	797
TOTAL	2,226	6,852

* *Idem.*

About 55 per cent of the total increase in grants between the two dates was for highway purposes. This represents principally the program begun in 1956 for the construction of a nation-wide system of integrated super-highways. The federal share of the cost of these highways was increased to 90 per cent. To what extent does this increase represent relief to highway budgets of the states? Probably rather little, for (1) many of the states would have moved less rapidly in construction of these highways in the absence of the crash program, and (2) the high federal share is being paid for out of stepped-up motor vehicle taxes which otherwise would have been available to the states. The national highway network will be improved sooner under the Act of 1956, but relief to state highway budgets in the long run promises to be negligible.

Another 20 per cent of the over-all increase in federal grants goes into public assistance. These grants are made for administration and for benefit payments to indigent aged persons who do not qualify for OASI benefits, to dependent children, to the blind, and to the totally disabled. If these grants had not increased, a heavier load would certainly have fallen upon the general funds of the states, for it is difficult to cut back such programs substantially. However, it is unlikely that the whole difference would have been made up by the states, for many would have tightened the qualifications for benefits and either reduced the level of benefits received or thrown a part of the burden on local relief agencies. Even so, it seems probable that in the absence of federal grant increases, state and local budgets would have been burdened by some part of the difference.

In general, the remaining purposes for which grants have increased represent those for which outlays would probably be significantly lower in the absence of federal funds.[31] The grants have been made in most cases to encourage the undertaking of new or elaborated functions by the states. The portion of total cost borne by the federal government varies. Purposes of the grants (included in the "all others" category in Table 38) also vary widely; most have to do with aspects of health and with specialized forms of education and training, though included are the management of natural resources, housing, and airport construction.

It seems fairly clear that the effect of increased federal grants to the state and local governments has not been primarily to relieve pressure on their general fund budgets. This being the case, the grants have tended to increase pressures on local budgets by encouraging the undertaking of activities which would not otherwise have been undertaken. If substantial federal assistance is to relieve beleaguered budgets, the federal grants will need to be provided for the financing of those existing state and local programs which are currently producing the major pinch. This means above all, of course, federal assistance with public educational expenses.

State-local expenditures for education increased from $7.2 billion in 1950 to $14.5 billion in 1957.[32] The same amount of increase in the following seven years would put the cost at about $22 billion in 1964, or an increase of nearly $8 billion per year. If state and local tax systems were to bear no more of this increase than would be provided by normal increase of their tax bases, federal grants of several billion dollars per year would be required. Grants of this magnitude appear quite unlikely in the near future, for several reasons.

One reason is that so long as the cold war continues in the missile age, defense will be a voracious claimant upon federal revenue resources. Not only is the feeling widespread that the defense budget has been danger-

---

[31] One exception to this is the federal aid to schools in local areas where federal activities add significantly to school population and school costs. If the grants were withdrawn, the affected communities would be required to make up nearly all of the difference. The same is probably true of the employment service grants. The unemployment compensation system would be seriously crippled by a lower level of employment service activity, and the states would probably maintain the current level.

[32] Expenditures for public elementary and secondary schools alone went from $5.8 billion to $12.2 billion in the same period. See Bureau of the Census, *Historical Statistics of State and Local Government Finances, 1902–1953*, p. 17, and *Summary of Governmental Finances in 1957*, p. 28.

ously small for a number of years, but defense expenditures are believed peculiarly to stimulate research and development which contribute significantly to a high rate of economic growth. Another reason is widespread concern that major federal contributions may erode local control and direction of local education. This fear, whether justified or not, has been an obstacle to the undertaking of federal aid to public education on a substantial scale. The fear is most acute with respect to federal aid in the payment of school personnel and other expenses related to the school curriculum and classroom activities. There is much less fear of the imposition of federal standards with respect to school buildings, school lunches, transportation, and the like. While federal aid in the performance of the latter group of functions could be very helpful in the relief of local educational budgets, these account for the smaller share of the rise in educational costs. Thus, if the federal government were to assume a large share of the cost of buildings, lunches, and transportation, there would still be substantially rising claims upon state and local budgets for the central educational activity.

In recent years, several proposals for federal aid to education have been before the Congress. These proposals have provided mainly for assistance in school building construction. But the amounts involved in such proposals have seldom exceeded $1 billion per year. And most such proposals would allot a major portion of the funds to the lower income states. While this would be extremely useful in raising average educational standards in the nation, it would do rather little in relieving the burdens on property taxpayers generally. Educational costs press upon property taxpayers in localities where schools are good and improving, as well as in localities where the quality of education is low because the property tax base is small. Furthermore, in simple quantitative terms, federal aid of $1 billion per year does not go far in absorbing educational costs which are increasing at the rate of some $2 billion each year. It seems evident, therefore, that state and local governments would be sanguine indeed if they were to hope for significant relief through federal aid to education. Almost certainly, therefore, the state-local crisis must be solved by the states and their localities if it is to be solved at all. This brings us back to the need for substantially increased state aid to local communities, financed by substantially increased revenues at the state level.

In summary, both the preferences of citizens and the requirements of economic growth point to the devotion of a rising proportion of the national income to state-local public services. This appears inevitable even though every opportunity for efficient operation is cultivated. Both the pinch of debt limits and the requirements of sensible financial policy indicate the need for an increase in tax revenues relative to the national income. This implies both more intensive and more extensive use of the broad-based taxes on income and sales at the state level, for the alternative is more intensive use of the decidedly inferior property tax. Those states which now employ only one of the two broad-based taxes will be under great pressure to adopt the other before significantly raising rates on the former. It seems probable that in time most states will use both income and sales taxes. Revenue, equity, and growth considerations suggest that if this occurs, state income taxes should become more progressive than at present. The evidence indicates that the sales tax is more regressive or less progressive at lower incomes than the income tax, while both are regressive at high incomes. In practice, the sales tax can be made less regressive (or more progressive) only by lengthening the list of exempt items, but this can be done only at the sacrifice of considerable amounts of revenue. A state income tax, however, can be made less regressive (or more progressive) through the rate structure alone, without loss of revenue. If only one of these tax instruments is used, preference for the income tax is indicated. If both are used, more progression in the income tax is required to offset the regressiveness of the sales tax.

State-Local Finance and Economic Stability

The policy of annually balanced budgets, so intensively pursued by state and local governments, is a perverse policy with respect to economic stability. When boom conditions expand the tax base and produce larger revenues, these governments find it easy to increase expenditures. Larger balanced budgets, therefore, produce an expansive effect upon an economy already inclined toward price inflation. In periods of inadequate aggregate demand as the tax base shrinks, there is a tendency to pare expenditures, and this has a contractive effect upon the economy. The statistics indicate that since 1929, and with the exception of the World War II period, combined state and local expenditures have moved rather markedly in the same direction as the GNP.[33] This tendency has been particularly marked since World War II.

The persistent rise in state and local expenditures since the war has brought the magnitude of those expenditures to the point where their adverse behavior with respect to stabilization requirements can hardly longer be ignored. Direct expenditures of state and local governments were $9.2 billion in 1940; by 1957 they had risen to $47.6 billion—5.1 times the

[33] See Mabel Newcomer, "State and Local Financing in Relation to Economic Fluctuations," *National Tax Journal*, June, 1954, p. 98.

1940 figure. State and local purchases of goods and services represented slightly over 8 per cent of the GNP in 1957. This is about three-fourths as large as the ratio of federal purchases to the GNP. The point is, therefore, that federal fiscal action is no longer the only governmental action with significant effect upon the level of economic activity. Stated in another way, perverse fiscal policy of state and local governments requires more massive corrective policy by the federal government.

While it is proper to exhort state and local governments to act in the interest of stability, their failure to do so is understandable. Almost at every turn there are obstacles to counter-cycle fiscal policy by these governments. In the first place, the persistent demands for services tend to give the allocation goal higher priority than the stabilization goal. The demands for education, highways, sanitation, and health and hospitals are so insistent as to resist downward flexibility of expenditures. Second, they—and particularly the local governments—operate under a situation of relatively inelastic credit resources. Markets for their securities are in many cases essentially local, and the governments lack monetary powers to influence these markets. This suggests that it may be quite difficult at times to finance the sort of deficit required by the stabilization objective, even if highly restrictive debt limitations permit room to maneuver. Third, by tradition if not by rational choice, state and local revenue systems are heavily weighted with taxes upon consumption, and these can show marked variation in the business cycle only when rate changes are laboriously made. Finally, most of these governments face a problem of boundaries. They do not normally represent self-contained economic units, and any actions one might take could be easily dissipated among its neighbors and produce few results at home.

In general, therefore, the fiscal actions of state and local governments are capable of doing considerable economic damage, while the obstacles to effective policy in this respect are formidable. At these levels the temptation is great to give up any hope of effective policy, and to intensify the use of federal policy to negate the perversity of state-local action. On the other hand, there are areas of possible improvement which undoubtedly should be cultivated. We shall consider these possibilities under two categories: those designed to build into the state and local fiscal structures more automatically stabilizing instruments, and those designed to facilitate the employment of discretionary policies fostering stability.

As we have noted, the automatic stabilizers are those instruments of fiscal practice built into the structure of long-run governmental policy and institutions which possess the peculiar ability to react quickly and automatically to offset undesired changes in the level of economic activity. Their particular virtue is the automatic character of their operation. They do not require legislative action or administrative decision, and therefore they can go to work without delay. It is not even necessary for the legislator or the administrator to be aware that undesired conditions are in the process of development. The instrument is appropriately linked to some key variable in the economy, and will often start to work before the statistics showing movement of the variable are available.[34]

The most promising area is that of reorganizing state and local revenue systems toward automatic flexibility. Property taxes heavily predominate in local government revenue systems, and property taxes (in the absence of rate and assessment level changes) are very inflexible. In the interest of automatic flexibility, it is therefore important that the property tax play a less important role in local fiscal affairs. It is hardly feasible for local governments to substitute other more flexible *local* taxes for the property tax, for reasons indicated earlier in this chapter. But it is feasible for state aid revenue to be substituted for additional property tax revenue. If this is done with funds raised by the state under revenue measures more automatically flexible than the property tax, progress toward the institution of automatic stabilizers will have been made.

State revenue systems are heavily weighted with taxes on consumption expenditure, using sales taxes, excises, and gross receipts taxes. Since consumption expenditure shows a lesser degree of fluctuation than total economic activity in the cycle, the base of these major state taxes is also rather inflexible, and at fixed tax rates, revenues are equally inflexible.[35] Even so, a typical state sales tax is *automatically* more flexible in revenue production than a local property tax, for the typical sales tax includes some items of fairly wide cyclical fluctuation. Therefore, substitution of state grants provided by sales taxes for local property taxes will represent some improvement in the over-all flexibility of revenue systems. But to introduce genuine flexibility of the kind and magnitude which will reflect changes in economic activity, it is necessary that the base of a major tax be the measure of busi-

[34] As examples, unemployment compensation claims necessarily rise as unemployment occurs, and statistics of claims are often available before statistics of unemployment. Likewise, income tax liability under a withholding plan falls as income falls, and often before the income decline shows in the statistics.

[35] A sales tax with extensive exemptions will show greater revenue flexibility than one with few or no exemptions. For the "necessary" items of consumption which are most likely to be granted exemption are usually those most stable in the cycle. If such items are exempt, the remaining items will be more in the "comfort" or "luxury" class, and may show rather wide fluctuation in the cycle. It is hardly conceivable, however, that a state could afford to exempt enough staple items of consumption to make the sales tax truly flexible with business fluctuation.

ness fluctuation itself. The measure of business fluctuation is changes in the GNP. The nearest feasible tax base to the GNP is personal income.[36]

The substitution of taxes producing automatically fluctuating revenue for those producing stable revenue would help greatly to incorporate automatic stabilizing instruments at the state level. The possibilities available for introducing automatic changes in expenditures in the proper direction are less promising, though they should be considered. The major possibilities along this line—recalling that we are dealing with *automatic* and not discretionary measures—would seem to lie in the area of welfare expenditures. If a permanent sliding scale of state contributions for local welfare were instituted, some progress would be made in this direction. For example, state welfare grants could be made a larger proportion of total outlays per recipient when the proportion of such recipients to local population increases.[37] On the expenditure side, however, the major possibilities for the

[36] It might appear that because personal income (in the national income accounts) is highly stable in the cycle as contrasted with the GNP, it is not a good base for an automatically flexible tax structure. This would be true if taxable income were as stable as the personal income upon which it is based. Let us take as an example the changes in the GNP and personal income as the economy went into recession from the third quarter to the fourth quarter of 1957:

Change in GNP:	—$5.5 billion
Change in personal income:	— 1.7 billion
Difference	—$3.8 billion.

So far it would appear that personal income as a tax base is too stable to reflect properly the change in the GNP. But let us look at the factors which produced relative stability in personal income while the GNP was changing much more markedly. They were:

Change in undistributed corporate profits:	—$3.4 billion
Change in government transfer payments:	+ .4 billion
Change in other components (net):	$0.0 billion.

The decline in undistributed corporate profits accounts for the major share of the decline in the GNP, but they do not enter into personal income. In percentage terms the decline in corporate profits was much greater than the decline in the GNP; since these profits are subject to (federal and state) corporate income taxes, the fall in corporate tax liability was more than proportional to the fall in the GNP and flexibility is attained with respect to this component. Government transfer payments are seen to have risen as one would expect of social security and relief payments in a recession. But though these payments rose, helping to produce stability of personal income, they were substantially free from personal income taxation, either because of specific exemption or because they constituted very small personal incomes. The two variables—corporate profits and transfer payments—accounted in this particular quarter for the whole difference in change between the GNP and personal income. It would not often happen exactly this way, but these two items would nearly always be the major stabilizing elements in personal income in a recession. And because the stabilizing elements in personal income do not enter the tax base to any significant degree, *taxable income* tends to fluctuate more nearly with the GNP than with personal income, from which the personal tax base is derived.

[37] New York follows such a plan in its general assistance grants. Cf. Newcomer, *op. cit.*, p. 107.

introduction of flexibility would seem to lie in the area of discretionary policy rather than in automatic machinery.

If instruments of automatic flexibility—of revenues and expenditures— were built into state and local finance, it is inevitable that the rule of the annually balanced budget would be violated in unstable periods. To accommodate cyclical changes in the degree of budget balance, rigid and restrictive provisions in state constitutions would need to be modified or removed. Most notable are the pay-as-you-go laws, which forbid planned deficits, and restrictive debt limits, which forbid additional borrowing to cover a deficit. But flexibility of fiscal policy does not imply persistent deficits; it implies as well that there will be prosperous periods in which surpluses will be produced. Machinery for the effective management of reserve funds would need to be more adequately developed,[38] insulating the surplus from pressures to increase expenditures or reduce taxes. That is, the concept of a budget balanced over the cycle implies that the deficits incurred in recession be offset by surpluses in boom times. But if the surpluses are dissipated in tax reductions or in expenditure increases when times are good, two undesired consequences will be realized: the budget will not be balanced over the cycle, and the tax reduction or expenditure increase will have a perverse effect in "booming the boom."

With respect to discretionary policy, by which we mean legislative or administrative policy established at the time to meet a particular situation of instability, success depends upon an understanding by officials of the nature of instability and the potential ability of fiscal policy to moderate it. This means, of course, some real modification of the goal of an annually balanced budget. Were this to take place, the scope of discretionary stabilization policy would be largely limited to the expenditure side of the budget, and particularly to capital expenditures. Under present circumstances it is unlikely that school construction is amenable to counter-cycle policy, for the need for schoolrooms can seldom wait for a recession period. But highway construction and reconstruction could be fitted into a counter-cycle schedule of public works to a greater extent than they are at present, and public construction—other than schools and highways—could also be planned with stability as an objective. This requires willingness to wait for certain improvements until an economically more propitious time, and forward planning of public works so that construction can be begun quickly when the appropriate time arrives.

The need for revenue is so great, to cover the costs of persistently ex-

---

[38] This sort of thing was done by several states during World War II, when surpluses were produced and funds accumulated for postwar use.

panding requirements, that state and local tax rates will probably be raised as rapidly as politically feasible, quite irrespective of stability requirements. This means that there is little likelihood of higher and lower rates being legislated in booms and recessions, respectively. Thus, there will probably be little room for discretionary action on the tax side of state and local fiscal policy. The discretionary flexibility will therefore occur, if it occurs at all, in the programming of public works expenditure, where there is much room for improvement over present state and local practices.

As we view the state-local fiscal situation in general, it appears that these governments can hardly be expected to engage in massive stabilizing fiscal policy in the positive sense. They are individually limited by a variety of factors which point to this conclusion. But at the same time, state-local fiscal activities in the aggregate have become so impressive in absolute magnitude, and have shown such persistent increase, that perverse fiscal policy by them can be unstabilizing in serious degree. Probably the best that can be hoped for is that state and local governments will accept the rather negative responsibility of striving to reduce the impact of perverse action. If this is done, a lesser stabilizing responsibility is imposed upon the federal government. The instruments of state (and local) action of the sort contemplated are (1) the evolution of revenue systems which are more sensitive to changes in the level of business activity in an automatic way, and (2) the more systematic planning of postponable public works in order to emphasize outlays in periods of underemployment and to de-emphasize them in boom times. Developments in these directions would work toward integrated stabilization policy.

RECOMMENDED READINGS

Haig, R. M., "The Coordination of Federal and State Tax Systems," Chapter 88 in Groves, *Viewpoints on Public Finance.*
> General treatment of progress and requirements.

Hansen, A. H., and Perloff, H. S., *State and Local Finance in the National Economy,* N.Y., Norton, 1944, Chapters 7, 8.
> Chapter 7 discusses intergovernmental cooperation, Chapter 8, federal underwriting of state and local services. Very profitable reading.

Maxwell, James A., *The Fiscal Impact of Federalism in the United States,* Cambridge, Harvard, 1947, Chapter 1.
> Historical development of the position of the federal government in fiscal affairs.

Maxwell, James A., "Intergovernmental Fiscal Devices for Economic Stabilization," in Joint Committee on the Economic Report, *Federal Tax Policy for Economic Growth and Stability (Papers Submitted by Panelists Appearing before the Subcommittee on Tax Policy),* Washington, 1955, pp. 807–17.

Myers, Eugene A., and Stout, Randall S., "The Role of the States and Local Governments in National Fiscal Policy," *National Tax Journal*, June, 1957.

The two selections above and the one below, taken together, represent a competent coverage of the essentials of the problem and the possibilities for solution.

Newcomber, Mabel, "State and Local Financing in Relation to Economic Fluctuations," *National Tax Journal*, June, 1954.

Index

AAA decision, 12
Ability to pay, 295, 342, 343, 478-81; 503-4
"Accord," Treasury-Federal Reserve, 225
Adams, H.C., 255
Adjusted gross income, 362
Adler, J.H., 470n
Administrative revenues, 248, 250-1, 255-263
Allen, E.D., 510n
Angell, J.W., 123n
Apportionment, 340
Appropriations, 18, 19
  Allotments of, 30
  Deficiency, 29-30
  General vs. specific, 26-28
  Supplementary, 29-30
Assessment, 332-8
Automatic stabilizers, 151-5; 579-81

Backward shifting, 307-12
Bank reserves, 211-17, 219
Banks, 40, 123n, 211-27
Barnes, I.R., 280
Bartelt, E.F., 47
Bauer, J., 276n
Bauder, R., 528n
Benefit principle, see Tax(es)
Bills of Credit, 209-10
Bills, Treasury, 186, 187, 192
Bird, F.L., 354
Bittermann, H.J., 56n, 82
Blough, R. 82
Blum, W.J., 298n, 300n, 303
Bonds, 186, 187, 192
Boulding, K.E., 329
Bowen, H.R., 166n, 176
Brown, H.G., 329
Brown, J.A., 402n, 408
Budget(s), Ch. 2
  Allotments, 30
  And Accounting Act, 16
  Authorizations, 25, 26
  Balance, 34-6, 59, 75-7, 173-4, 559
  Bureau of, 16, 23
  Capital, 37
  Cash, 42-46

Budget(s)—*Cont.*
  Consistency, 172-6
  Conventional, 41-2
  Deficit, 103-4
  Emergency, 35
  Executive, 15-18
  Legislation of, 18-21
  "Legislative", 19-21
  Multiple, 36-8
  Ordinary, 35, 37
  Performance, 27
  Preparation of, 17, 18
  Projections, 23-5
  Receipts and expenditures, 17, 24
  Surplus, 104-6
Budget principle, 166-8
Buehler, A.G., 55n, 416n
Burns, E.M., 528n, 542
Burnstan, A.R., 259n, 261n
Business cycle, 112-15
Business taxes, see Tax(es)
Butler v. U.S., 539

Capital gains and losses, 394-407, 428
Capital stock taxes, 506-7
Capitalization of taxes, 309
Carnegie, A., 477n
Carry-over and carry-back, 389, 515
Certificates, Treasury, 186, 187, 192
Chandler, L.V., 229
Chapman, S.J., 303
Chrystie, T.W., 480n
Clark, E., 202n
Clark, J.M., 150
Classified property tax, 346-9
Cole, G.D.H., 476n
Collection at source, 372-9
Collection of property taxes, 341
Colm, G., 14, 156, 176
Commercial revenues, 249, Ch. 12
Compensatory fiscal policy, Ch. 5, Ch. 6, Ch. 7
Community property, 367
Comptroller, 39
Confidence, 121-4
Consume, propensity to, 89
Consumption, 89-91

Contingent liabilities, 197-9
Conversion, debt, 193-4
Corporation income tax, see Tax(es)
Cost elasticity, 318n, 321-3
Cost of collection, 466-7
Cost payments, 34
Coverage of U.S. income tax, 370
Counties, 546-7
Credits against tax, 435
Criz, M., 475
Curran, K.J., 510n, 523
Current tax payments, 375-7
Customs duties, 447-8

Dalton, H., 303
Davenport, H.J., 245
Debt limitation, 73-5
Debt, public, Chs. 8, 9, 10
    Burden, Ch. 10
    Composition, 185-91
    Contingent liabilities, 197-9
    Conversion, 194-6
    Default, 202
    Dispersion, 239
    Gross, 178-82
    Interest rate, 187-90, 236-8
    Interest-bearing, 186
    Management, 202-5
    Maturities, 191-3
    Monetization, 209-29
    Net, 179-82
    Ownership, 233
    Public and special issues, 190
    Refunding, 193-4
    Retirement, 193-7
    Service, 238-9
    State and local, 199-201, 559-61
    Trends, 182-5
Deductibility, 268-71
Deductions from income, 431-4
Deferred pay, 244
Deficit and Surplus, 34-6, 44, 103-6, 129-30
Demand elasticity, 309n, 318n, 321
Depreciation, 392
Dewey, D.R., 54n, 55n, 209n, 359n
Direct tax, 307n
"Diversion", 31
Dividend credit and exclusion, 419-20
Domar, E.D., 240
Donovan, C.H., 229
Double taxation, 412, 415-23, 429
Due, J.F., 82, 475, 570n

Earned income credit, 393
Eccles, M.S., 231
Ecker-R, P.L., 382
Economic growth, 168-72

Edmonds, F.S., 496n
Education, 57-60, 549-54, 556-7
Efficiency, 22, 23, 546-9, 562-3
Eisenhower D.D., 158n, 389n
Eisenstein, L., 497
Employment taxes, see Tax(es)
Equalization, 338-40
Escheats, 259
Estate tax, 476, 478-81, 488
Excess profits tax, 510-19
Excises, 449-51, 459
Exclusions from gross income, 429-31
Exemptions, 434-5, 440, 457-8
Expenditure controls, 25, 26
Expenditures, Ch. 3
    And city size, 61
    And economic growth, 168-72
    As per cent of GNP, 51
    Cash budget, 42-46
    Compensatory, 117-21, 143-4
    Conventional budget, 41-2
    Education, 57-60, 549-54, 556-7
    Highways, 55-7, 551-2, 557-8
    Income-inducing effects, 97-9
    National income accounts, 46-7
    Per capita, 51
    Relief, 65-8
    Research, 171
    Urbanization, 60-1
    Welfare, 65-8, 78
Evasion, 428, 436

Fabricant, S., 82
Fagan, E.D., 301, 304
Fairchild, F.R., 416n, 467n
Fees, 255-6, 237-8
Fellner, W., 229
Ferger, W.F., 330
Fines, 256, 258
Fiscal policy, 2, Ch. 4, 5, 6
Forced lending, 244
Forfeitures, 258-9
Forward shifting, 307
Functional finance, 286-7

Galbraith, J.K., 166, 168
George, H., 349
Gift tax, 491, 492-5
Gifts, 248-50, 253
Goldenweiser, E.A., 229
Goode, R., 330, 426, 523
Goods, public, 161
Goodwin, D.C., 565n
Government, role of, 1
    Business enterprises, 271-7
    Functions, Ch. 3, 477-8
    Powers, 8-12
    Structure, 7, 8, 545-6
    Taxing power, 12-14

Grants-in-aid, 77-9, 248-50, 253-5, 565-6, 573-5
Greenbacks, 210
Grove, H.M., 404n, 405n, 408, 421n, 422n, 426, 513, 516
Growth, 168-72

Hagen, E.E., 156
Haig, R.M., 464, 475, 582
Hall, J.K., 475, 485n, 497, 528n, 542
Hamilton, A., 196, 234
Hansen, A.H., 47, 56n, 95, 110, 131, 156, 206, 229, 475, 582
Hargreaves, H.W., 197n, 206
Harris, S.E., 156, 528n
Harriss, C.L., 12, 492n, 498, 542
Hart, A.G., 510n
Heller, W.W., 176, 383, 403, 408, 428
Hellmuth, W.F., 446
Hendrickson, E.S., 316
Hickman, B.G., 130n
Hickman, W.H., 570n
Hicks, J.R., 387, 510n
Hicks, U.K., 330
Highways, 55-7, 551-2, 557-8
Holland, D.M., 420, 426, 437n
Hollander, J.H., 218n, 229

Income, 384-7, 400-1
Income averaging, 388-91, 428
Income creation, Ch. 4
Income redistribution, 97-103
Income tax, see Tax(es)
Incentives, 438-9
Incidence, Ch. 14, 343, 460-5, 485-6, 519-23, 528-33, 541
Indirect tax, 307n
Inflation, 175-6, 471-5
Inheritance, 477
Inheritance tax, 476, 478-81, 488
Intangible property, 344-6
Investment, 91-6

Jacoby, N.H., 281
Jensen, J.P., 354
Jese, G., 206
Jevons, W.S., 296
Joint return, 368

Kalven, H., 298n, 301n, 303
Kaplan, A.D.H., 516n
Keith, E.G., 426
Kendrick, M.S., 82
Keynes, J.M., 244n

Leland, S.E., 355
Lent, G.E., 372n, 373n, 382
Lerner, A.P., 286
Lerner, E.M., 316
Leverage coefficient, 65

Licenses, 257-8
"Locked-in" problem, 402-3
Lutz, H.L., 81n, 304

Marginal utility, 296-300
Market principle, 161-6
Maxwell, J.A., 82, 83, 263, 582
May, S., 281
Melichar, E., 568n
Menger, C., 296
Merit rating, 526
Mitchell, W.C., 210
"Model Tax System", 499-501
Money supply, 207
Monopoly, 117
Morris, G.M., 72n
Multiplier, 90, 91
Murphy, H.C., 206
Musgrave, R.A., 131, 176, 328n, 470n
Myers, E.A., 583

Newcomer, M., 577, 580n, 583
Nitti, F.S., 48
Non-cost payments, 34
Non-revenue receipts, 34
Notes, Treasury, 186, 187, 192

Oakes, E., 489n, 498
OASI, 67, 129, 153, 190
Ogg, F.A., 12n
Open market operations, 220

Parity, 473
Paul, R., 396n
Pay-as-you-go, 75-7, 581
Pechman, J.A., 432, 436, 446
Penniman, C., 383
Perloff, H.S., 475, 582
Permits, 256-8
Personal Income tax, see Tax(es)
Pigou, A.C., 263
Poll tax, 537-9
Pollack v. Farmers' Loan and Trust Co., 359
Pricing of government goods, 277-80
Progressive tax, 246, 293-5, 366
Property tax, see Tax(es)
Proportional tax, 293-302
Public debt, see Debt, public
Public finance, 1-7
    And business finance, 5-7
    Method, 5
Public works, 138-9
Pump-priming, 118
Pyramiding, 452

Ratchford, B.U., 563n
Ray, O.P., 12n
Raymond, D., 82n

Receipts, cash budget, 42-6
  Conventional budget, 41-2
  National income accounts, 46-7
Redistribution of wealth, 482-5
Regressive tax, 235, 293-5, 457, 467-8
Regulated investment companies, 419
Refunding, 193-4
Research, expenditures for, 171
Resource allocation, Ch. 7
Revenue, dedication of, 29-32
Revenue receipts, 34
Rice, L.P., 542
Riefler, W.W., 205n
Robinson, R.I., 229
Rural electrification, 268

Sales taxes, 318-24
Samuelson, P.A., 110
Savings bonds, 179, 192, 233
Seligman, E.R.A., 14, 282, 478n
Shere, L., 446
Shoup, C.S., 420n, 426, 464, 471n, 472,
  475, 523, 537n
Shultz, W.J., 14, 54n, 477n
Sigafoos, R.A., 383
Simons, H.C., 390, 408, 426
Single tax, 348-51
Sinking fund, 179-80, 196-7
Situs in death taxation, 495-7
Smead, E.L., 47
Smith, A., 81n, 172, 295
Smithies, A, 47
Socialism, 68-70
Special assessments, 259-61
Special funds, 30-33, 556
Springer v. U.S., 359n
Stabilizers, automatic, 151-55
Stagnation, 116-7, 125-6
Standard deduction, 433
Stout, R.S., 583
Strayer, P.J., 383
Studenski, P., 206, 501n, 503, 523
Sumptuary taxation, 301-2, 455n, 468
Sundelson, J.W., 36n, 47
Surrey, S.S., 408
Surplus and deficit, 34-6, 44, 102-6, 129-
  130

Tarasov, H., 470n
Tax(es)
  Ability to pay, 292-3, 295-342, 343,
    478-81, 503-4
  Allocation of, Ch. 13
  Benefit principle, 290-1, 477, 500, 502
  Business, Ch. 22
  Capitalization, 309
  Compensatory, 139-42, 144-52
  Consciousness, 469
  Corporation income, 314-6, 360, 409-
    11, 508-10

Tax(es)—Cont.
  Cost principle, 290
  Death, Ch. 21
  Direct and indirect, 307n
  Employment, 524-37
  Evasion, 428, 436
  Excess profits, 510-19
  Excise, 449-51, 453-5, 459
  Exhaustible resources, 348
  Forests, 348
  Gift, 491, 492-5
  Incidence, Ch. 14, 343, 460-5, 485-6,
    519-23, 528-33, 541
  Income, personal, 312-14, Ch. 16, 17,
    18, 19, 567-73
  Income-reducing effects, 99-109
  Loopholes, 444
  Objectives, 284-7
  Poll, 537-9
  Progressive, 293-302, 470
  Property, 317-18, Ch. 15, 554-5, 564
  Proportional, 293-5
  Regressive, 293-5, 457, 467-8, 470
  Revenue importance, 283-4
  Sales, 318-24, Ch. 20, 572-3
  Social Security, 524-37
  Turnover, 451-3
  Unearned increment, 348-51
  Use, 449
Tax rate limitation, 72-3
Taxing power, 12-14
Treasury, 38-9
Troxel, C.E., 281
Trust funds, 44, 527-9
Tucker, R.S., 470n
TVA, 70, 265

Underassessment, 338-40
Undistributed profits, 415-18
Unemployment compensation, 136-8, 526-
  528
Unjust enrichment tax, 539-42
Urbanization, 60-1
U.S. v. Butler, 12n

Veazie Bank v. Fenno, 12n
Veto power, 28, 29
Viner, J., 1n

Wagner, A., 48, 50
Wald, H.P., 475
Wallich, H.C., 110
Walras, L., 296
Wars, cost of, 54, 241-5
Welch, R.B., 507n
Wright, C. W., 210n
Wilde, F.B., 158n, 177
Whittlesey, C.R., 236n